DICTIONARY OF
GERMAN SYNONYMS

DICTIONARY OF GERMAN SYNONYMS

R. B. FARRELL

McCaughey Professor of German,
University of Sydney, Australia

SECOND EDITION

CAMBRIDGE
AT THE UNIVERSITY PRESS
1971

Published by the Syndics of the Cambridge University Press
Bentley House, 200 Euston Road, London NW1 2DB
American Branch: 32 East 57th Street, New York, N.Y.10022

© Cambridge University Press 1971

Library of Congress Catalogue Card Number: 77-134623

ISBN
hard-cover: 0 521 08018 5
paperback: 0 521 09633 2

First Edition 1953
Reprinted with corrections 1955 1961 1962 1963 1966 1968
Second edition 1971

Printed in Great Britain
at the University Printing House, Cambridge
(Brooke Crutchley, University Printer)

CONTENTS

PREFACE

This work has grown out of my experience of university teaching. As the inability of students to use words correctly impressed itself upon me more and more, I came to see that this was due in the first place to the immense difficulties inherent in the study of words, and in the second to the complete lack of adequate dictionaries, whether English–German or entirely German, and of other reference-works such as Fowler's *Modern English Usage*. Dictionaries such as Eberhard's *Synonymisches Wörterbuch*, incidentally out of print for many years, have their uses, but are insufficient for the needs of the English-speaking learner in that their explanations, naturally enough, do not take into account his special difficulties. The present work represents a new departure in taking as the starting point of each article the difficult English word or group of words and in proceeding on this basis to explain the German terms. With its help a systematic study of words and, ultimately, a more sensitive feeling for their values should be possible both at school and at university level.

Only common difficult words, and within this restricted scope rarely the names of concrete objects, have been treated, i.e. principally those English terms which in each of their senses require to be translated by a number of German terms. The fact that German lacks terms of such wide application as 'take', 'way', 'leave', 'keep', 'power' (to mention only a few of the more notorious), and must therefore use specific terms, perhaps to a greater extent than even French, is an indication of what is here attempted. The English word is taken singly or in a group. In a few cases, where the magnitude of the difficulty seemed to call for it, a further explanation has been attached in brackets to the examples. Footnotes which extend the group or refer to related terms liable to be confused have also been added in order to inculcate in the student the habit of examining words in groups. Such notes are in the form of hints designed to open up fresh avenues of investigation; they are not exhaustive explanations. In the arrangement of any group of English words the most general term is usually placed first. The meanings and shades of meaning of the English word become clear through the explanation of the German term. Only in a few cases was it thought necessary to give a special explanation of the former. Sometimes the divisions are made on the basis of the meanings of the English word or words (occasionally taken from the Oxford dictionaries), so that the same German term may appear more than once in the same article. In other cases the German words themselves form the divisions, and so explain by implication the various meanings of the English. The explanations, which differ in their degree of fullness, concentrate on normal prose usage of today, but point out usage in poetry and elevated prose diction as well as obsolete uses (e.g. with *Gemüt* and *Sinn*). They also draw attention to a few errors made by Germans (e.g. *scheinbar* for *anscheinend*). Grammatical constructions have been treated only in rare cases where their understanding is indispensable for the correct use of a word. References are given to such works as the *Shorter Oxford Dictionary*, the *Pocket Oxford Dictionary* (referred to as *S.O.D.* and *P.O.D.* respectively), to Webster's *Dictionary of Synonyms* and Fowler's *Modern English Usage*, where they seem necessary or particularly helpful.

The work is addressed primarily to students and teachers, but I venture to think that parts of it will not be without interest to lexicographers. My warmest thanks are due to the following for their generous help, not only in discussing the examples, but in criticizing the explanations: the late Dr V. Stadler (former lecturer in German in the University of Sydney), Dr K. von Stutterheim (his successor), and Mr A. Scheidt.

R. B. FARRELL

1953

PREFACE TO THE SECOND EDITION

The reception accorded the first version of this work and the requests that it be enlarged have prompted this revised and expanded version. This adheres to the same general principle of taking as the point of departure the English term which must be variously translated into German. In treating new English words, however, I have begun by giving more often than in the first version their specific meanings as defined by Webster, the *Shorter Oxford*, sometimes the *Concise Oxford* or the *Advanced Learner's Dictionary of Current English*, and it has not infrequently turned out that the specific sense of the English word is the definition of the German. By this method, it seemed to me, students would be encouraged more often than at present appears to be the case, to consult the English dictionary before choosing a German word. A good number of the examples of the German term, moreover, are simply translations of the examples of the word in question given in the English dictionaries. Not all uses of the English term, however, have been treated, particularly when these are technical, since such uses are listed in the ordinary English–German dictionaries and present no difficulty. For example, under 'standard' I have not given 'standard lamp' (*Stehlampe*). A new feature of this edition is the inclusion of terms used for objects, which was a notable gap in the first version. Revision of the first version with a view to improving some of the examples and the explanations is a further feature of the present one. Since the first version, Duden's *Vergleichendes Synonym-Wörterbuch* (1964) has appeared and sheds light on a number of difficulties. It does not, however, by any means treat all the difficulties that arise for the English-speaking student of German and so does not make the present work superfluous.

Abbreviations used are: *S.O.D.* = *Shorter Oxford*, *C.O.D.* = *Concise Oxford*, *W.* = Webster's *Third New International Dictionary of the English Language* (Springfield, Mass., 1965), *W.S.* = Webster's *Dictionary of Synonyms* (Springfield, Mass., 1951), *A.L.* = *The Advanced Learner's Dictionary of Current English* (London, O.U.P., 1961), s. = substantive, v. = verb.

I should like to express my thanks for their help in the preparation of the present version to Mrs Marie Clouston, who was my research secretary during the initial stages of the work, to Dr K. von Stutterheim, formerly a member of the staff of the University of Sydney and now living in retirement in Switzerland, with whom I discussed some of the examples, and to Professor H. L. Rogers, Professor of Early English Literature and Language in the University of Sydney, with whom I discussed the meaning of some English words.

R. B. F.

Munich 1970

ACCEPT 1. Annehmen: to accept what is offered to one, the receiver being free to accept or reject. The object may be a thing, or a belief, point of view,[1] excuse, and the like.

Er nahm das Geschenk, den Vorschlag, die Herausforderung an.
Die Bedingungen wurden von dem geschlagenen Feinde angenommen.
Er nahm den christlichen Glauben an.
Meine Entschuldigung wurde nicht angenommen.

2. Hinnehmen: to accept passively something inflicted on one.[2]
Unter den Umständen mußten wir die Niederlage, die Beleidigung, unser Schicksal, die Tatsache, hinnehmen.
Er hat es hingenommen, daß sie wegging.

3. Übernehmen, auf sich nehmen: to assume, to shoulder a responsibility, duty, task, and the like.
Er will die Verantwortung dafür nicht übernehmen, auf sich nehmen.

4. Aufnehmen: to take, to admit, to receive into a society, organization, and the like.[3] A phrase involving *in* with the accusative must follow.
Er wurde nicht in den inneren Kreis aufgenommen.

5. Akzeptieren may, but never need, be used for *annehmen* in the sense of 'accept'. It is also used for *gelten lassen* in the sense of accepting anything of a mental order (reasons, excuses, and the like) that are offered one.

The only sense in which, for lack of a German equivalent, it must be used is that of accepting a person as a friend or as a suitable member of an organization. It can be used absolutely or followed by a phrase expressing 'by whom' or 'where'. It cannot be followed by *in* with the accusative, i.e. it is not an equivalent of *aufnehmen*.

Ich habe ihn als Freund akzeptiert.
Er war im (vom) inneren Kreis akzeptiert.[4]
Wenn er Sie mal akzeptiert hat, dann kann Sie nichts in seinen Augen heruntersetzen.

6. Gelten lassen: to accept as valid (reasons, excuses, and the like).
Ich lasse diese Erklärung, diese Einwendung, nicht gelten.
Seine Erfahrungen im Ausland hat man hier gelten lassen.
Tatsachen muß man gelten lassen.

7. The past participle (accepted) used adjectivally. In the sense of 'generally recognized' *angenommen* cannot be used alone.
Im allgemeingültigen Sinne des Worts.
Entgegen der allgemeinen Meinung.
Der allgemein angenommene Brauch in internationalen Beziehungen.

ACCIDENT, DISASTER. 1. In the sense of 'mishap' **Unfall** is of lesser proportions than **Unglück.** The former involves one or at most a few, the latter many, people. Both may be fatal, the latter almost always. *Unglück* is

---

[1] *Annehmen* also means 'to adopt' a suggestion, a belief, a child; 'take on' workers, a facial expression; 'assume', 'suppose'.
[2] *Sich mit etwas abfinden*: to resign oneself to a thing (e.g. *sich mit der Lage, seinem Schicksal, einer Tatsache, a.*).
[3] See also under 'take' in the sense of 'take an attitude'.
[4] *Empfangen* (received) could be used in this sense; *als gleichberechtigte.*

not normally pluralized. It corresponds to 'disaster' and to 'accident' when this is extensive.[1]

Ihm ist mit seinem Fahrrad ein Unfall passiert.

Er ist in einem Autounfall umgekommen.

Wir sind gegen Unfälle versichert.

Hunderte von Menschen wurden in dem Eisenbahnunglück getötet (accident or disaster).

Das Unglück, das Deutschland getroffen hat, ist unermeßlich (disaster).

2. In the sense of 'chance' **Zufall** must be used.

Ich traf ihn durch Zufall.

Es ist ein Zufall, daß ich gewählt wurde.

ACCUSE, SUE **1.** Neither **beschuldigen** nor **anschuldigen** are legal terms. *Beschuldigen*[2] suggests a precise accusation, while *anschuldigen*, in accordance with one of the meanings of *an*, suggests the hurling of accusations at someone, wildly and therefore less precisely.

Man beschuldigte ihn des Mordes an seinem Bruder.

Wir können nicht umhin, Sie zu beschuldigen.

Man beschuldigte ihn ungerechterweise.

Jahrelang war er den wildesten Anschuldigungen ausgesetzt.

2. Anklagen and **verklagen** are both legal terms. *Anklagen* is used in criminal cases, *verklagen* in petty offences, accidents (e.g. manslaughter) and civil suits, therefore 'to sue'. Both may be used in elevated diction and poetry without strictly legal implication.

Sie sind des Mordes angeklagt.

Er wurde wegen Hochverrats angeklagt.

Er wurde wegen einer Schuld verklagt.

> *'Hör'an, was ich dir sag'!*
> *Dein Schätzlein ich verklag';*
> *Derweil ich dieses singen tu',*
> *Herzt er ein Lieb in guter Ruh,*
> *Ein Stündlein wohl vor Tag.'*
>
> (Mörike, *Ein Stündlein wohl vor Tag.*)

ACT, ACTION, DEED The chief distinction between 'act' and 'action' is that the former is brief, single, while the latter is extended in time and may comprise a series of acts. Again, with 'act' one thinks of the result, the whole, while with 'action' the process is designated. In the plural, 'acts' does not differ so sharply from 'actions' for the very reason that it ceases to be single. In the moral sense of 'conduct' they are practically identical. 'Deed', too, draws attention to the result and often conveys the idea of achievement (in a good sense) or of something that is outstanding by virtue of its proportions (e.g. an evil deed).

None of the terms discussed can be applied to trivial things. Thus while one can speak of *ein Akt der internationalen Höflichkeit*, the only translation

---

[1] *Unheil* is a reversal of our fortunes, well-being, caused by persons, or things thought of as persons, particularly when the action is wanton. It thus corresponds to 'trouble' thus used, rather than to 'disaster'. *Er hat viel Unheil angerichtet. Unglück* can also mean 'misfortune' and 'unhappiness'. See 'unfortunate'.

[2] *Bezichtigen* is an elevated and less usual term for *beschuldigen. Gerichtlich belangen*: to take to court. *Auf Schadenersatz klagen*: sue for damages.

for 'as an act of courtesy he placed his car at my disposal' would be: *als höfliche Geste stellte er mir seinen Wagen zur Verfügung.*

'Act' and 'action' followed by 'in' and the gerund present difficulties in translation (e.g. the action of the Government in confiscating an issue of a certain newspaper caused its fall). In this case a more specific term such as *Schritt* is required.

German has no general term for 'action' in the sense of 'doing something to deal with a matter', and consequently no general term for 'to take action'. It is, therefore, difficult to translate such phrases as: to refrain from action (in the matter), to recommend action, to clamour for action; they considered the report but decided against action. In these phrases 'action' means 'the taking of action'. In most cases of 'action' used in this sense German requires a specific term.

'Action' in the legal and military senses is not discussed in this article.

Fowler's *Modern English Usage*, which has been drawn on for this article, should be consulted under 'act', 'action'.

1. Handlung is a conscious expression of the will. It is only possible in statements which describe, judge or by implication draw attention to the motives of 'acts' or 'actions'. This reference to the motive means that the action may be a purely inner impulse which does not find external expression and that what is termed *Handlung* (and 'action' in English) may in reality be an abstention from action (contrast the other words discussed, particularly *Tat*).

Handlung translates both 'act' and 'action' when they imply this reference. It is not necessarily an action extended in time, but because of its concern with motives, it does not evoke as clearly as 'act' the impression of a single, clearly visualized exertion of power.

Examples of verbs which can govern *Handlung* are, e.g., *begehen, vornehmen,* which in themselves draw attention to motives.

Sind unsere Handlungen frei oder nicht?

Nur aus seinen Handlungen kann man auf seine Gesinnung schließen.

Seine Handlungen waren schwer zu durchblicken.

Jetzt habe ich meine Handlungsfreiheit wiedererlangt.

Uneigennützige Handlungen kommen wohl vor, aber selten.

Nach langem Zögern hat er die notwendige Handlung endlich vorgenommen.

Daß er dem Krankenhause sein Vermögen zur Verfügung stellte, war eine anständige Handlung.

Eine edle Handlung muß man anerkennen.

Wir dürfen seine Handlungen nicht kritisieren.

Er hat eine sträfliche, unzüchtige, höchst zweifelhafte, Handlung begangen.

Seine letzte Amtshandlung war die Unterzeichnung einer Steueramnestie.

'*Du wirst mir zugeben, sagte Albert, dass gewisse Handlungen lasterhaft bleiben, sie mögen geschehen, aus welchem Beweggrunde sie wollen.*' (Goethe, *Werther.*)

'*...du überspannst alles, und hast wenigstens hier gewiß Unrecht, daß du den Selbstmord, wovon jetzt die Rede ist, mit großen Handlungen vergleichst: da man es doch für nichts anderes als eine Schwäche halten kann.*' (Goethe, *Werther.*)

'*Ein gewisser Mangel an Fühlbarkeit, ein Mangel — nimm's, wie Du willst; daß sein Herz nicht sympathetisch schlägt bei — oh! — bei der Stelle eines lieben Buchs, wo mein Herz und Lottens in einem zusammen treffen; in*

*hundert anderen Vorfällen, wenn's kommt, daß unsere Empfindungen über
eine Handlung eines dritten laut werden.'* (Goethe, *Werther*.)
*'Was bleibt uns übrig als . . . das kleinste aufgefundene Blättchen nicht gering
zu achten; zumal da es so schwer ist, die eigensten, wahren Triebfedern
auch nur einer einzelnen Handlung zu entdecken, wenn sie unter Menschen
vorgeht, die nicht gemeiner Art sind.'* (Goethe, *Werther*.)

2. Tat has as its closest English equivalent 'deed' (i.e. feat, exploit, achievement). In stylistic effect it also resembles 'deed', although its flavour is not
quite so old-fashioned. It refers to the completed act or action, the result,
which is seen plastically and as a whole. Whether it is brief or lengthy,
morally good or bad, is irrelevant. Its outstanding characteristic is that it is
vivid, dramatic, refers to something of imposing proportions, and is personal
in that one thinks of the doer as an individual (contrast *Akt*). It may be used
of a crime (*nach der Tat, am Tatort, in Tateinheit mit*).

It is therefore the only rendering for 'deed', 'feat'.

It must be used to translate 'act' (sometimes 'action') in the sense of 'an
act characteristic of' (the following noun denoting the type of person).

It also means 'instant of doing' (e.g. *auf frischer Tat ertappt werden*).

When it is accompanied by a word or phrase describing its nature, one
thinks of the doer (contrast *Akt*). For this reason the description is generally
given by a preceding adjective or a noun which forms a compound with *Tat*.
A following descriptive genitive is not impossible, but is less common (again,
contrast *Akt*).

Like 'deed', *Tat* means 'act' and 'action' in antithesis to 'word', 'plan',
'thought'. The effect of this use, which is limited to literary diction, is
emotional or slightly antiquated. For a prosaic equivalent see *handeln* (both
as verb and noun). *Ausführung* can also be used in an antithesis.

Tat can be followed by a dependent infinitive which describes the act or
action only if it is qualified by an adjective. 'Act' or 'action' followed by 'in'
and the gerund requires no such adjective. Thus: *seine mutige Tat, den
Knaben aus von Haifischen verseuchten Gewässern gerettet zu haben, verdient
öffentliche Anerkennung* (his act, action, in rescuing . . .).

For *in der Tat* see under 'in fact, indeed'.

Die Rettung der Schiffbrüchigen war eine heroische Tat (act, action, deed).

Der Abschluß des Handelsvertrages war des Ministers letzte Tat.

*Die Abschaffung der Folter war eine Tat, auf die Friedrich der Große stolz
sein konnte.*

Die Ermordung dieses Gefangenen war eine grauenhafte Tat.

Er hat eine gute Tat getan.

Gleich nach der Tat wurde er verhaftet.

Es war eine verbrecherische Tat, aber eine, die die Einbildungskraft fesselt.

*Moskau behauptet, die Ermordung des Brigadiers Mallaby sei nicht die Tat
javanischer Nationalisten, sondern der Japaner.*

Das war eine barmherzige Tat, daß Sie ihm zu diesem Posten verholfen haben.

Es war eine Tat, die er bitter bereuen sollte (e.g. falsely denouncing a friend;
contrast example with *Handlung*).

*England kann es sich als eine gerechte Tat anrechnen, daß es die Anerkennung
der Souveränität der kleinen Staaten durchsetzte.*

Das Anzünden des Dorfes war eine Verzweiflungstat.

Ein Mann der Tat (in conversation one more frequently hears *aktiver* or
tatkräftiger Mann).

Nach so vielem Zögern müssen wir endlich mal zur Tat schreiten (with emotional emphasis).

Auf den Entschluß muß die Tat folgen.

Es ist nicht immer leicht, einen Gedanken in die Tat umzusetzen.

Wir verlangen Taten, nicht Worte.

'*Aber auch im gemeinen Leben ist's unerträglich, fast einem jeden bei halbweg einer freien, edlen unerwarteten Tat nachrufen zu hören: der Mensch ist trunken, der ist närrisch! Schämt euch, ihr Nüchternen! Schämt euch, ihr Weisen!*' (Goethe, *Werther*.) (The stress is on the concrete reality, seen as complete, not on the motives involved.)

'*...doch hatte er sich gesagt, es solle keine übereilte, keine rasche Tat* (i.e. suicide) *sein, er wolle mit der besten Überzeugung...diesen Schritt tun.*' (Goethe, *Werther*.)

'*Aus dem Blut auf der Lehne des Sessels konnte man schließen, er habe sitzend vor dem Schreibtische die Tat* (i.e. suicide) *vollbracht.*' (Goethe, *Werther*.)

3. **Akt** is not the equivalent of *Tat*, though in certain uses it occurs in deceptively similar phrases. One of its characteristic senses is that of something staged (hence *Akt* in a drama), often a ceremonial or symbolical act. It tends to acquire this sense when not accompanied by a descriptive phrase (e.g. a following genitive describing its nature, but not an adjective such as *erst*, *letzt*).

When it is followed by a descriptive genitive meaning 'of the nature of', it is impersonal, a judgment which assigns the act to a class denoted by the noun in the genitive case. The sentence *das ist ein Akt der Barmherzigkeit, daß Sie ihm zu diesem Posten verhelfen wollen* is sober, impersonal in tone. This characteristic means that *Akt* often refers to an act of the State or to acts of groups, masses of people, since in such cases attention is not concentrated on an individual doer. Again, unlike *Tat*, since *Akt* has nothing of the meaning of 'deed', 'achievement', it need not refer, either, to anything striking or of impressive proportions (e.g. *Gewalttat* suggests something such as the murder of an important personage, *Gewaltakt* the plundering of a store). For this reason *Akt* cannot be combined with *Greuel* (but: *Greueltat*, an atrocity).

The above example (*Akt der Barmherzigkeit*) reveals another characteristic of *Akt* which distinguishes it from *Tat*. It makes one think less of the completed whole than of the fact that something is going on, i.e. a process.

The phrase which assigns *Akt* to a class is normally a following genitive, not a preceding adjective (cf. French: *une bonne action*; but: *un acte de bonté*). It forms, however, a limited number of compound nouns (see examples below). In the sense of an act staged it may be preceded by an adjective.

Die Übergabe des Schwertes war ein feierlicher Akt.

Das Erscheinen des Generals zu diesem Zeitpunkt war ein symbolischer Akt.

Der Aufruf an das Volk war unter den Umständen ein Akt der Verzweiflung.

Das Töten der Schwerkranken wurde als Akt der Barmherzigkeit bezeichnet.

Die Rehabilitierung von Dreyfus war ein Akt der Gerechtigkeit.

Sein letzter Akt war es, die weiße Fahne zu hissen.

Die Abschaffung der Folter war einer der ersten Regierungsakte Friedrichs des Großen.

Gewaltakte, Terrorakte, wurden in jedem Teil des Landes begangen.

Die Ermordung der Gefangenen war ein Racheakt.

Es war von seiten Hitlers ein Akt des Wahnsinns, Rußland anzugreifen.

Sabotageakte kommen jetzt selten vor.

ACT

Es war ein Akt der Gerechtigkeit, daß die Souveränität der Kleinstaaten wiederhergestellt wurde.

4. Tun (noun) is used in the sense of the general conduct, actions, or doings of an individual. It is vaguer than the other terms, but always refers to serious acts or actions. It occurs in the common phrases: *sein Tun und Treiben, sein Tun und Lassen.*

Er ist für sein Tun verantwortlich (acts or actions).
Sein Tun und Treiben scheint mir höchst verdächtig (goings-on).
Von seinem Tun und Treiben an diesem Abend wissen wir garnichts.
Das Tun eines Narren ist nicht vorauszusehen.
Sein übles Tun hat ihn in Verruf gebracht.

5. Aktion denotes an elaborate operation, planned and carried out in stages. It normally refers only to such actions when undertaken by the State. It is not a legal term and cannot be applied to legal action taken by the State, unless this be police action. It comes close to the sense of 'operation'. Furthermore, it does not form fixed phrases (such as 'to take action'). In the singular it is always preceded by the definite or indefinite article, or *jede, manche,* etc.

Die Millionen von Menschen, die durch den Krieg heimatlos geworden sind, wieder anzusiedeln, ist eine riesenhafte Aktion.
Die Aktion, durch die die Inflation verhindert werden sollte, ist gescheitert.
Umfangreiche Aktionen wurden unternommen, um in allen Ländern die Erzeugung von Nahrungsmitteln zu steigern.
In seinen Aktionen zieht gewöhnlich der Staat nur den Machtfaktor in Betracht (*Handlungen* would be correct, but would draw attention away from the action itself to the motive).
Eine Säuberungsaktion wurde durchgeführt.

6. Handeln (noun): 'action' as opposed to inactivity, thought, words. It is a more prosaic and less dramatic term for *Tat* used in this sense. Since it is really the equivalent of the gerund, 'acting', it can only be used in combinations where this would be possible. Thus, it could not be used in the genitive to translate 'a man of action', but would be appropriate in rendering 'a man born for action' (*zum Handeln geboren*). It is most common as the subject of a sentence or preceded by *in, von, zu.*

In conversation *handeln* used as a verb is more common.

Jetzt ist Handeln nötig. (In conversation: *jetzt muß gehandelt werden.*)
Ihm gefällt die Betrachtung, nicht das Handeln.
Handeln ist nicht seine Stärke.
Handeln kommt unter diesen Umständen nicht in Betracht.
Von Handeln kann im Augenblick nicht die Rede sein.
Im Handeln versagt er immer.
Wenn es zum Handeln kommt, ist er immer brauchbar.

7. 'Action' in the sense of 'taking action in a matter'.
(a) **Vorgehen:** 'action taken' in the sense of a 'step or series of steps taken' to deal with a specific matter. Similarly, the verb *vorgehen* can mean 'to proceed' in a matter. It is commonly used of the taking of official action. If it means 'to proceed against' someone (police action) it must be accompanied by some intensifying adverb such as *energisch.* It cannot be used as a noun to form fixed phrases (e.g. to take action). In translating 'action' followed by 'in' and the gerund ('his action in closing the banks'), *Vorgehen* cannot take a

dependent verbal infinitive after it, but either a clause (e.g. with *als*) or *im*, *beim* with the substantival infinitive.

It should only be used in a judgment, expressed or clearly implied.

Das Vorgehen des Premierministers, als er die Banken schließen ließ, führte zum Sturz der Regierung.

Sein Vorgehen gegen die Presse ließ den Verdacht aufkommen, daß er sie gern unterdrückt hätte.

Sein Vorgehen in dieser Angelegenheit war höchst zweifelhaft.

Die drei Mächte sind entschlossen, ihr gemeinsames Vorgehen aufrechtzuerhalten.

Gegen Unbefugte wird scharf vorgegangen.

(b) **Einschreiten** (as verb): to take official action against someone, in the sense of 'intervene'. *Gegen* or an equivalent must follow. It is stronger and more circumscribed than *vorgehen*.

Die Polizei schritt gegen die Schieber ein.

(c) **Schritt**: step, *démarche*, as in English.

Wir müssen Schritte unternehmen, um diesen Machenschaften zu steuern.

Der Schritt, mit dem die Türkei ihre diplomatischen Beziehungen zu Deutschland abbrach, sollte mit Genugtuung angesehen werden.

(d) **Maßnahme**: measure. It is wider than *Schritt*. *Treffen* and *ergreifen* are used with it in the sense of 'take'.

Der Senat hat sich mit dem Bericht eingehend befaßt und daraufhin Maßnahmen getroffen, um das Lehrpersonal der medizinischen Fakultät zu vergrößern.

'Ich bin überzeugt, die Griechen werden sowohl unsere militärischen als auch unsere politischen Maßnahmen begrüßen.' (Churchill.)

(e) **Unternehmen** can be used with *etwas* or *nichts*, as the case may be, in a general way to translate 'take action', i.e. in dealing with a matter (to do something about it). It is less precise, less official than *Schritt*, *Maßnahme*, *Vorgehen*, etc. The sphere of action needs to be stated unless it is clearly implied.

Wir müssen etwas unternehmen, um ihn zur Vernunft zu bringen.

Es wird von den Frontkämpferverbänden verlangt, daß in der Wohnungsfrage etwas unternommen wird (action in... is demanded).

(f) **Ausführung** may be used in the sense of 'put into action' or 'the taking of action' in antithesis to 'word', 'thought', etc.

Das Unternehmen war vielversprechend als Planung, enttäuschend aber in der Ausführung (in action).

8. 'Act', 'action' used in reference to trivial matters.

The foregoing terms apply only to 'acts' and 'actions' of considerable proportions. They cannot be used for petty doings. The following are examples:

Es war eine Dummheit, mit so wenig Benzin so weit fahren zu wollen (an act of stupidity).

Als Beweis seines guten Willens fuhr er uns zwei Stationen entgegen (as an act of goodwill).

Er hat uns zahllose Beweise seines Wohlwollens gegeben, geliefert (shown us countless little acts of kindness).

Seine zahllosen Freundschaftsbeweise sind nicht unbemerkt geblieben.

Sein Ausreißen setzte ihn dem Verdacht aus (his action in clearing out).

ACT

Das letzte, was sie tat, bevor sie zu Bett ging, war, daß sie die Milchkanne hinaustellte (her last act).

Sie wußten erst später, wie großzügig sie gehandelt hatte (...knew of her generous act, action).

ADD[1] **1.** Mathematical calculation ('add up'). **Addieren:** to add up figures. **Zusammenrechnen:** to add up in order to arrive at an estimate. *Er rechnete die Kosten zusammen. Also Zusammenzählen.*

2. Verbs compounded with *hinzu*. The idea of addition is given by *hinzu*, while the verb (often one of the 'put' group) specifies the manner. *Hinzu* indicates addition to the end, not to the body of a thing.

(a) **Hinzufügen** and **hinzusetzen** are the commonest and are used of adding remarks (points, items, etc.) to something already said or written. The latter is also used of signs (punctuation). While *hinzufügen* suggests that the added part is integrated into the whole, *hinzusetzen* indicates a less organic addition. The former is used of important, the second of trivial matters. Neither can be said of objects in the sense of joining them together.

Der Redner fügte ein paar Bemerkungen zu dem, was er schon gesagt hatte, hinzu.

'Wir stehen vor einem schweren Entschluß', fügte der Minister hinzu.

Er fügte seinem Brief noch ein paar Zeilen hinzu.

Dem Programm wurde noch eine Nummer hinzugefügt.

Um den 'Eulenspiegel' aufzuführen, wurden dem Orchester noch ein paar Instrumente hinzugefügt.

'Ihr seid alle verrückt', setzte er hinzu.

(b) Other verbs compounded with *hinzu*.

(i) **Hinzutun** (see 'put').

Noch zwei Koffer wurden zu dem schon an sich schweren Gepäck hinzugetan.

(ii) **Hinzulegen** (see 'put') is used particularly of money.

Ich lege noch etwas hinzu, und dann können Sie das Haus kaufen.

Er legte noch einige Papiere hinzu.

(iii) **Hinzunehmen:** to include at the end as an afterthought.

Wir können ihn für das Kommittee hinzunehmen (not when forming it, but as an extra, an afterthought).

Nehmen wir diese paar Tatsachen hinzu, und der Fall wird klar.

(iv) **Hinzukommen:** to be added, of intangibles.

Zu seinen Geschäftssorgen kam noch der Tod seiner Frau hinzu.

(v) Further:

Er trug noch ein paar Steine (zu dem Haufen) hinzu.

Schreiben Sie seinen Namen hinzu (to a list).

Es wurde beschlossen, die deutschen Militärs zu den Kriegsverbrechern hinzuzuzählen.

Gießen Sie noch ein paar Tropfen hinzu.

3. Often the simple verb without *hinzu* is used, particularly if the thing to which the addition is made is stated. *Noch* is added, if necessary.

Noch 50 Mark wurden auf die Rechnung aufgeschlagen.

Tun Sie noch ein Stück Zucker in den Tee.

4. Verbs compounded with *ein*, sometimes *hinein*, express the idea of insertion into the body of a thing. Examples are:

---

[1] 'To add to' (intransitive use) must be translated by 'to increase'.

8

Sie könnten hier ein einsilbiges Wort einfügen.
Eine neue Szene ist zwischen diesen beiden eingeschoben worden.
Ich möchte noch ein Fach in den Bücherschrank einbauen, einsetzen.
Das können Sie noch hineinschreiben.

5. Examples of other specific terms are:
Dem Haus wurde ein neuer Flügel angebaut.
'Die angefügte Robinsonade...verbindet das Motiv der Weltflucht mit dem des kuriosen Erlebnishungers' (inorganically) (J. Petersen, *Die Wissenschaft von der Dichtung*).
Dem Lehrpersonal wurde ein neues Mitglied zugewiesen.
Er häufte Sieg auf Sieg, Schmähung auf Schmähung.

ADVERTISE, ADVERTISEMENT To advertise a person in the sense of inform is now obsolete.

1. In general to make widely known, to give public notice of: **Bekannt machen** (s. **Bekanntmachung**) (see 'announce'); **Bekannt geben**. **Anzeigen** (which may also mean 'to indicate' and 'to denounce') suggests in the sense under consideration an official action.
Diese namhafte Einrichtung, die in Romanliteratur allgemein bekannt gemacht wird (W.).
Er fing an, absichtlich seine Bereitschaft zu Zugeständnissen bekannt zu machen (geben).
Eine ziemlich hohe Belohnung wurde angezeigt.

2. To call public attention to, esp. by emphasizing desirable qualities so as to arouse a desire to buy or patronize (*W.*) and mostly through the organs of publicity such as newspapers, radio, T.V. **Reklame machen für, werben für, annoncieren, inserieren, anzeigen.**
Für eine Frühstücksmehlspeise Reklame machen (werben) (W.).
Sie gaben ein Vermögen aus, um für ihre Filtermundstückzigaretten Reklame zu machen (zu werben) (W.).
Die neue Inszenierung des 'Don Carlos' wurde in allen Zeitungen der Stadt annonciert (angezeigt).
(a) Substantives: **Inserat, Annonce, Anzeige, Reklame.**
Die Annoncen (Inserate, Anzeigen) beanspruchen immer einen großen Teil der Samstag-Ausgabe der Zeitung.
Das Geschäft nahm einen Aufschwung, knapp nachdem es angefangen hatte, durch das Radio Reklame zu machen (W.).
(b) **'for'** after advertise is *um*.
Wir werden Samstag um eine Sekretärin annoncieren (inserieren).

AFFECT To affect 'always presupposes a stimulus powerful enough to evoke a response or elicit a reaction' (Webster's *Dictionary of Synonyms*). It thus means 'to produce an effect' of various kinds (physical, material, emotional, intellectual) on a person or thing. The effect may or may not be a change, a modification. When 'affect' implies an unfavourable effect, German generally must make this clear by a specific verb or the addition of an adverb bearing this sense.
'Affect' is also a synonym of 'concern', which is listed by Fowler (*Modern English Usage*) as one meaning and assailed as wrong usage by Webster (see *berühren* and *betreffen*).

AFFECT

Both Fowler and Webster, who should be consulted on this word, point out the confusion between 'affect' and 'effect' (verbs) and at the same time distinguish between them. 'Effect' as a noun corresponds to both 'affect' and 'effect' (affect: have an effect on).

1. Berühren

(a) To make an impact on the mind. This impact includes feeling, but not emotion in the fuller sense (i.e. not 'to move', which is *rühren*[1]). It must be accompanied by an adverb. Two uses occur:

(i) To affect one's sensibilities, either pleasantly or unpleasantly. As the contact suggested by *berühren* is never strong,[2] it cannot be combined with such adverbs as *gräßlich, schauderhaft, tragisch.*

Ihre Stimme berührt mich angenehm, unangenehm.
Diese Landschaft hat mich wohltuend berührt.
Dieses Gedicht berührt mich wie Kitsch.

(ii) Negatively or with a virtual negative with adverbs such as *sichtlich, sonderlich, wenig*, i.e. indicating extent.

Er war von ihrer Not nicht sichtlich berührt.
Ihre Not hat ihn nicht sonderlich berührt.
'Sogar der Wechsel der Jahreszeiten berührt den Stadtbewohner wenig'
(A. Huxley, quoted in Webster's *Dictionary of Synonyms* under 'affect').

(b) To have a bearing on a matter, particularly on one's interests. An adverb is not necessary. Unless otherwise stated, the effect is unfavourable. 'Touch' is also possible in this sense.

Berührt das Ihre Chancen?
Dieser Vorfall berührt die englisch-russischen Beziehungen.
Diese Maßnahmen berühren die Großgrundbesitzer.
Der Krieg hat unsere Lebensweise nicht empfindlich berührt.

2. Betreffen

means 'to be aimed, directed at', 'to hit', in a vague way. It differs from the simple verb *treffen* in that the sense is not literal and that it does not denote one clear, forceful act.[3] It rather suggests indirect effects and the diffusion of these over a wide area, and frequently carries the implication that the object is just one of a number of things affected. The subject may be: (*a*) a law, regulation or the like, the sense being 'to concern',[4] and the question of whether the effect is favourable or otherwise being left open;

---

[1] See 'move' and 'touch' for an explanation of *rühren*.

[2] See 'touch' for an explanation of *berühren*.

[3] *Treffen* means 'to hit the mark', literally with a missile, or figuratively (see 'catch'). It suggests an act that has the swiftness of an arrow. When an evil is the subject, the object is normally a person. If it is a thing, the effect is that of personification (e.g. *der Preissturz hat mein Geschäft schwer getroffen*). With evils there are two uses. (*a*) To hit, to strike home, without further qualification. In this case the subject must be something sharp and sudden (e.g. *der Blitz, der Schlag, hat ihn getroffen*). (*b*) The severe effects are emphasized by some adverb such as *schwer, hart*. In this case the subject may be something broader (e.g. *das Unglück hat ihn schwer getroffen*). *Treffen* is also used in a number of fixed phrases in the sense of 'to fall on', 'to find the mark'. *Ihn trifft die Schuld* means no more than that a crime has been committed and the evidence points to him as the guilty party. Similarly, it carries no further implications in the phrases: *die Verantwortung, der Vorwurf, trifft mich*.

[4] *Betreffen* translates 'to concern' (see also under 'concern') when a thing is the subject (e.g. *was mich betrifft*: as far as I am concerned). It differs from *angehen* in suggesting a higher degree of concern and often a need for action. *Das geht uns alle an* (we must do something about it). Being weaker, *angehen* is generally more appropriate in negative statements (e.g. *das geht mich nichts an*). *Anlangen* and *anbelangen* are still weaker. The form *anbetreffen* is not in common use.

(b) an evil. In the latter case it is often something broad and diffuse.[1,2] Except in the sense of 'concern', *betreffen* cannot be used actively in the simple tenses.[3]

Diese Maßnahmen betreffen die Großgrundbesitzer.

Sie sind von den neuen Bestimmungen mit betroffen.

Ganz Europa ist von der Grippe, von einer Hungersnot, betroffen worden.

Nicht weniger als 5 Dörfer wurden von der Überschwemmung betroffen.

Der Preissturz hat mein Geschäft auch betroffen.

Das Unglück hat auch ihn betroffen (the disaster has affected him, i.e. amongst others; not 'has befallen him').

3. Wirken and compounds.

If 'affect' implies an unfavourable effect, *ungünstig* or some equivalent must be added.

(a) **Wirken:** to produce an effect on, a reaction from a person in the sense of engaging the powers of his mind (thoughts, feelings, and the like), or acting on parts of the body. It does not indicate any change or modification of the person or thing affected. Its use in the passive voice is not possible.

Dieses Gedicht wirkt kitschig auf mich.

Diese Landschaft wirkt sehr wohltuend.

'*Auf das Trommelfell wirken höchstens acht Oktaven aus der unendlichen Lautskala*' (Jeans, quoted in Webster's *Dictionary of Synonyms* under 'affect') (our ear-drums are affected by...).

Gewitter wirken sehr ungünstig auf Geisteskranke.

(b) **Einwirken:** to produce a change or modification.

Schopenhauer, Wagner und Nietzsche haben auf Thomas Manns Entwicklung tief eingewirkt.

Die Dürre hat auf die Ernährungslage gradezu katastrophal eingewirkt.

(c) **Sich auswirken** means that the effects spread to and embrace a large number of persons, things, etc. It is implied that the process is slow, i.e. that an interval of time elapses between the cause and effect; also that the effect is important or extensive.

Was in Europa geschieht, wirkt sich auf die ganze Welt aus.

Die Rationierung, der Krieg, hat sich auf unser ganzes Leben ausgewirkt.

4. Ändern an with *was* (as a question), *nichts* (in the negative) as object is used in the sense of making an alteration to a part, not the whole. It can only be used positively if accompanied by *viel* or an equivalent. The interrogative and negative forms are much commoner. It can be combined only with nouns denoting things (not persons or substances) capable of modification in the sense of undergoing a different development. See also under 'change'.

Das ändert nichts an meiner Einstellung Ihnen gegenüber, an der Frage, an dem Ausgang des Krieges.

---

[1] But circumscribed subjects are possible in the sense not of 'affect', but to find the correct mark. *Der Vorwurf betrifft mich* (i.e. applies to me). *Treffen* with such words (e.g. *Spott, Beschimpfung*) is much stronger.

[2] Other senses of *betreffen* are: *er war ganz betroffen* (past participle can mean 'taken aback'); *die betreffenden Minister* (the present participle can mean 'concerned', i.e. following the noun).

[3] *Das Unglück, das die Stadt betroffen hat* (but not: *traf*). *Treffen* must be used actively in the simple tenses, generally with the addition of some adverb such as *hart* or *schwer* (see p. 10, n. 3(b)). It can also be used, like *betreffen*, actively in the compound tenses and passively. *Die ganze Stadt wurde durch das Unglück hart getroffen* (or: *betroffen*).

AFFECT

Ändert das was an Ihren Chancen?
Das ändert sehr viel an unseren Plänen.

5. **In Mitleidenschaft ziehen** denotes the spreading of states, conditions, and the like from one person or thing to another. It is much used of ailments spreading from one part of the body to another, but may also be applied to other things than evils.

Das ganze Bein ist jetzt durch das Gift in Mitleidenschaft gezogen.
Was in Europa geschieht, zieht die ganze Welt in Mitleidenschaft.

6. **Angreifen,** as an equivalent of 'affect', means 'to have an injurious effect on' a thing or a person. The subject must be a thing, the object a person or a thing. The thing may be (*a*) an evil (such as a disease) which operates adversely, either temporarily or permanently, on a person or a part of the body; (*b*) anything which eats away, corrodes, makes inroads on something else.

(a) *Die Überanstrengung, die Hitze, hat sein Herz angegriffen.*
Seine Augen, Nerven, Leber, Gesundheit, sind stark angegriffen.
Der Krebs hat nun auch seine Lunge angegriffen.
Meine Erkältung hat meine Stimme angegriffen.
(b) *Feuchtigkeit greift den Stahl an.*
Die Ferien haben meine Kasse gewaltig angegriffen.

7. **Schaden** (to damage; see 'damage') and **beeinträchtigen** (to impose a disadvantage on, to encroach on, to prejudice) and similar verbs must sometimes be used when 'affect' denotes an adverse effect.

Das lange Herumstehen im kalten Wasser hat ihm nicht geschadet.
Die tropische Hitze hat den Nahrungsmitteln geschadet.
Der Hunger hat seine Widerstandskraft beeinträchtigt.

8. **Nahe gehen:** to upset emotionally, cause grief to, because of misfortune.
Der Tod seiner Frau ist ihm sehr nahe gegangen.

9. **Bewegen:** to affect strongly in an emotional sense. It is applicable when 'affect' suggests powerful emotion. See 'move'.
Sie war sehr stark bewegt.

AGAIN 1. **Wieder** in the sense of 'again'[1] denotes no more than a repetition, a recurrence, a return to the same, without there being any necessary connection between the two occasions. In referring to future intentions it is therefore unemphatic and leaves the point of time vague.[2]

Ich habe ihn wieder gewarnt.
Ich habe ihn wieder daran erinnert.
Wir müssen uns hierüber wieder unterhalten.
Der Mann ist wieder da.
Ich tue es nicht wieder.

2. **Nochmals** suggests a repetition in a chain, generally with the suggestion that the original occasion was insufficient.[3] It is most often used with reference to something written or said.

---

[1] In the sense of a recurrence *wieder* often means 'back'. *Ich komme gleich wieder.* Sometimes in the sense of retaliation, e.g. *wiedervergelten.*
[2] *Wiederum* expresses the idea of recurrence with emotional emphasis, but only to indicate that the recurrence is an adversative to something else. '*Mussolini war dabei suggeriert worden, eine internationale Konferenz zur Entspannung der Lage vorzuschlagen. Aber wiederum ließ man sich in Rom durch anderslautende Nachrichten beruhigen und glaubte, Attolico übertreibe.*' (Erich Kordt, *Wahn und Wirklichkeit.*)
[3] *Abermals* has the same meaning as *nochmals*, but is now obsolete except in elevated diction.

Ich habe ihn nochmals gewarnt.
Ich habe ihn nochmals daran erinnert.
Ich habe ihm das nochmals eingeschärft.
Nochmals: die deutsche Romantik enthielt allerlei Gefahren.
Wir müssen ihn nochmals fragen.

3. **Nochmal** suggests that the occasion is the last one. Unlike *nochmals* it does not imply a chain of repetitions. It is an abbreviation of *noch einmal*, but does not express the idea as sharply.

Ich habe ihn nochmal, noch einmal, gewarnt.
Versuchen Sie es nochmal!
Sehe ich Sie nochmal, bevor Sie reisen?

4. **Noch** alone can be used when the context makes the meaning of 'again' clear by the presence of some term such as 'before'.

Sehe ich Sie noch vor Ihrer Abreise?

AGREE, BE AGREED 1. To share a person's opinion, to be in agreement.
(a) **Übereinstimmen, die Ansicht (Meinung) teilen, der Ansicht sein.**
All these phrases mean 'to share a person's opinion', without further implications. As *übereinstimmen* is a long word, it tends to be more literary than conversational. It must be followed by *mit*.

Ich teile Ihre Ansicht, daß die Lage ernst ist.
Ich bin derselben Meinung (I agree).
Ich stimme mit Ihnen, Ihrer Auslegung, überein.
Ich stimme damit überein, daß eine größere Anstrengung nötig ist.

(b) **Einverstanden sein** means that no objections are raised. It can also be used without *mit*.

Ich bin mit Ihrer Auslegung einverstanden.
Ich bin jetzt einverstanden, daß eine größere Anstrengung nötig ist.

(c) **Einig sein** is stronger than *übereinstimmen* in suggesting such identity of view as to constitute only one mind, not two minds that are alike. The reflexive dative of the pronoun may, but need not, be added. It cannot be used absolutely.[1]

Die Sachverständigen waren (sich) über den Fall nicht einig.
Ich bin mit meinem Partner darüber einig, daß wir jetzt ausverkaufen müssen.

(d) **Recht geben,** followed by the dative, is conversational in tone. It is particularly useful to translate 'agree' used absolutely.

Ich gebe Ihnen recht. (I agree!)

2. To reach an agreement after discussion or thought, to come to the same opinion.
(a) **Einig werden** implies the precedence of the agreement by debate or discussion of some length. It is used mainly in reference to formal deliberations (e.g. of a committee).

Das Kommittee wurde darüber einig, daß gewisse Änderungen wünschenswert seien.
Sie wurden endlich handelseinig.

(b) **Sich einigen** can imply immediate or quicker agreement than *einig werden*.

Sie müssen sich mit ihm über die Bücher einigen, die zu bestellen sind.
Sie haben sich über die nötigen Schritte sehr schnell geeinigt.

---

[1] *Er ist einig mit sich selbst*: he is at harmony with himself.

AGREE

(c) **Verabreden:** to agree upon, often in the sense of an appointment. It is a loose, sometimes casual, arrangement,[1] and suggests a virtual absence of initial differences. Being casual, it is out of place between people who are conscious of their class inequality.

Sie haben die nötigen Schritte verabredet.

Sie verabredeten den Ort der Zusammenkunft.

Wir haben uns verabredet, daß wir uns um 3 Uhr treffen (more commonly: *wir haben uns auf 3 Uhr verabredet*).

(d) **Vereinbaren:** to agree upon something which contains not inconsiderable initial differences and requires effort to settle. The agreement is more binding than in the case of *verabreden*.

Sie haben die nötigen Schritte vereinbart.

Wir haben vereinbart, daß wir uns immer um 5, nicht um 3 Uhr treffen werden (the difference denoted by the change of arrangements makes the use of *verabreden* impossible).

3. To tally, to coincide, of things: **übereinstimmen**[2] (in general and of grammatical concord).

Sein Bericht stimmt nicht mit dem Ihrigen überein.

4. To consent with a view to action.

(a) **Einwilligen** is used in reference to important matters.

Er willigte darin ein, daß die Maßnahmen verschärft werden sollten.

Die Bank willigte ein, der Firma größere Kredite zu gewähren.

(b) **Einverstanden sein:** to be in agreement, satisfied. *Einverstanden!* is used like 'agreed!' to denote definite or hearty acceptance.

Ich bin einverstanden, daß Sie dieses Zimmer benutzen.

Sind Sie damit einverstanden, den Brief abzuliefern?

(c) **Bereit sein (sich erklären):** to be (declare oneself) prepared. *Sich erklären* can have a formal effect. *Bereit sein* may indicate mere unexpressed willingness as well as an explicit agreement. See 'prepare'.

Sind Sie bereit zu schweigen?

Ich war bereit, ihm unter gewissen Bedingungen zu helfen.

Haben Sie sich bereit erklärt, diese Verpflichtungen zu übernehmen?

Die Universität erklärte sich bereit, den jungen Mann zum Studium zuzulassen.

(d) **Sich verständigen:** to come with someone to an understanding, which may be implicit as well as explicit, and emotional as well as intellectual.

Sie haben sich darüber verständigt, sein Versteck nicht zu verraten.

(e) **Recht sein** is conversational in tone, and, unless the context indicates the contrary, refers to an attitude of mind, not an expressed agreement.

Ist es dir recht, daß er heute früher weggeht? (Are you agreeable...?)

5. Sich vertragen. See 'bear'.

(a) To be compatible, to get on amicably.[3]

(b) Of food.[4]

Sie vertragen sich schlecht.

Ich vertrage kein Fleisch (meat does not agree with me).

---

[1] One sense of 'arrangement' is a loose agreement. See 'arrange'.
[2] More colloquially: *stimmen zu. Das stimmt nicht zu dem, was Sie früher sagten.*
[3] Similarly: *auskommen. Sie kommen gut miteinander aus.*
[4] Similarly: *bekommen. Fleisch bekommt mir nicht.*

ALL, WHOLE   A. With singular nouns.

1. Applied to things.

All is normally used only with nouns which are collective, i.e. plural in sense. It is declined and the definite article omitted. The possessive adjective may, however, follow without declension of *all*. The effect suggests emotion, not calculation.[1] In other cases *ganz*, which implies a more calculating attitude, must be used.

Mit allem Metall der Welt kann Deutschland den Krieg nicht gewinnen.

Alles Gold in der Welt wird dir das Glück nicht geben.

Alles Fleisch, das ich hier gekauft habe, ist zart gewesen.

All mein Geld ist hin.

All mein Hab und Gut ist verloren.

In aller Welt werden Sie das nicht finden (romantic in style).

Der Bankier hat sein ganzes Geld verloren.

Die ganze Stadt ist mit Fahnen geschmückt.

Der ganze obere Teil der Mauer wurde zerstört.

Die ganze Klasse stand auf.

Das ganze Innere des Apfels war schlecht.

Ganz Deutschland leidet an Unterernährung.

2. With nouns which do not denote things *all* is used freely. Where *ganz* could also be used, it is more emotional than the latter, and it is less specific than *jeder* in cases where both are possible. It remains undeclined when followed by the definite article, the demonstrative or possessive adjective.

Alle Mühe war vergebens.

Alles Unglück kommt von seiner Unentschlossenheit (*das ganze U.* would be a more prosaic statement).

'*Denn alle Schuld rächt sich auf Erden*' (Goethe).

Ich bin die ganze Zeit hier gewesen.

Seine Aufrichtigkeit ist über allen, jeden, Zweifel erhaben.

Sie müssen alle, jede, Aufregung vermeiden.

B. With plural nouns.

'All' and 'all the' are normally translated by *alle*, i.e. with omission of the definite article. This individualizes, unlike *all die*, which has the same meaning, but is often elevated or emotional in style. *Alle die* means 'all those', and is normally followed by a relative clause. *Die* is here accented, i.e. *diejenigen*.

Alle Häuser in der Straße wurden zerstört.

Alle Vorbereitungen sind schon getroffen.

All die Dichter, die jemals gelebt haben, könnten ein solches Gefühl nicht ausdrücken.

Alle die Studenten, die mitkommen wollen, sollen sich melden.

ANGRY, ANNOYED[2]   **1.** German has no term which corresponds exactly to 'annoy' in the sense of to irritate a person, to cause him to lose his equanimity or patience, to jar his nerves. *Verdrießen*[3] comes close to this meaning and to 'vex' (though not as 'perplex'), but is now as little used as the latter

---

[1] 'Whole' also suggests calculation, but 'all' is used freely to refer to an impression. E.g.: 'all the city was decked with flags'.

[2] *Zorn* and *zornig* suggest passion and correspond most closely to 'wrath' and 'wrathful'.

[3] *Verdrießlich*: peevish (applied to a person), irritating, vexing (applied to the cause of annoyance). This term and *Verdruß bereiten* (*machen*, etc.) are used more extensively than the verb.

ANGRY

verb. *Auf die Nerven gehen*, a much used expression, can suggest annoyance as the result of a continuous, but not a momentary, irritant.

2. *Böse*, as applied to persons, is, except with *auf*, possible only where there are ties of affection, friendship and the like. It then does not denote a high degree of anger, but rather displeasure[1] which can be shown by silence or a look. It is commonly used of parents who desire to give their children a sign of their displeasure. The simple dative or *mit* with the dative may follow, the former meaning 'to have something against' a person, the latter that one is 'not on speaking terms with' a person. It is used regularly in the imperative as a request not to take a thing amiss.

Further, it is the normal term for 'angry' when applied to animals, and in this case indicates an aggressive attitude.

Ich bin ihm böse (I have something against him).
Ich bin mit ihm böse (I do not speak to him).
Ich bin auf ihn böse (I am furious with him).
Sei mir mal nicht (colloquially: *nich'*) *böse.*
Der Hund, der Stier, ist böse.

3. **Sich ärgern** has a range of application which includes both 'annoyed' and 'angry', but not the weakest use of the former nor the strongest use of the latter. It is the commonest term to indicate in everyday life irritation, annoyance, anger. **Ärgerlich,** which is less frequent, is also weaker and corresponds to the weaker uses of 'irritated', 'annoyed'. It is applied both to the person and to the cause of his irritation. In the former case it sometimes suggests a disposition to nervous irritability. Both terms indicate an impulse to inflict punishment on the cause of annoyance or anger.[2,3]

Ich habe mich über dich geärgert.
Ich habe mich furchtbar geärgert, daß er mich eine Stunde lang warten ließ.
Seine dumme Ausrede hat mich geärgert.
Ihn ärgern schon die Fliegen an der Wand.
Es macht mich manchmal ärgerlich, wenn er dauernd dreinredet.

ANNOUNCE, PROCLAIM, REPORT 1. **Bekannt machen (geben)** are the most general terms for 'announce' whether in reference to trivial or to important matters. *Geben* is more official (e.g. of the Government) than *machen* and often suggests the release of information hitherto withheld.

With a personal object *bekannt machen* can only mean to introduce. Generally *b. machen* means to advertise (see under this term). Neither expression is used of the Press in the sense of 'report'.[4,5]

Die Regierung gibt bekannt, daß sie die Möglichkeit einer Herabsetzung der Steuern prüfen werde.
Die totalen Kriegsverluste werden nicht mehr bekannt gegeben.
Der Besuch des Königs wurde bekannt gegeben.

---

[1] *Ungehalten* also suggests displeasure or disapproval, which can express itself by a rebuke.
[2] *Verärgern* suggests an attitude or at least something more than a momentary outburst. A thing or a person who eventually disappoints us or makes us lose patience owing to his conduct can be the cause of the state indicated by this word. It does not necessarily imply outward demonstration of feeling. *Seine Ausflüchte, seine Vorschläge, haben mich verärgert. Du hast ihn verärgert* (alienated his goodwill).
[3] *Reizen*: to irritate, to anger by provocation. *Reiz' den Hund nicht. Aufgebracht*: incensed. *Unwillig*: mildly indignant. *Empört*: indignant at something considered to be an outrage.
[4] *Kund tun, machen, geben* are used only in elevated diction. *Bekunden*: to express.
[5] *Bekanntmachung*: a public notice or proclamation.

Der Schulrat machte bekannt, daß die Prüfungen früher stattfinden würden.
Er machte seine Absicht bekannt, ins Ausland zu gehen.

2. Ankündigen: to announce with regard to the future, i.e. to something which is to take place. A wide public as audience is generally implied.[1]

Verschärfte Maßnahmen wurden angekündigt.
Der Besuch des Königs wurde für den März angekündigt.
Die Schriftleitung kündigte an, daß die Zeitung nach Ende des Monats nicht mehr erscheinen würde.

3. Verkünden:[2] to proclaim, to promulgate far and wide, to all and sundry, ceremoniously and with reference to matters of importance.

Der Sieg wurde überall verkündet.
Ein neues Gesetz wurde verkündet.
Das Evangelium verkünden.

4. Melden[3] denotes a general report or announcement that is brief and refers to: (*a*) announcements made by the Press; (*b*) the announcing to an authority or superior of some fact (e.g. an arrival, a theft); (*c*) the denunciation of a person. Unlike *ankündigen*, *melden* does not necessarily refer to the future. It is not used in an informal or friendly announcement.[4]

Die Zeitungen melden den Besuch des Königs.
Zwanzig Grad Kälte wurden gemeldet.
Es wird aus Berlin gemeldet, daß die Russen durchgebrochen sind.
Er meldete seinen Vorgesetzten den Fall.
Der Diener hat mich, meine Ankunft, gemeldet.
Sie müssen sich, den Diebstahl, bei der Polizei melden.
Er meldete es seinem Hauptmann (reported).

5. Berichten: to report in detail, to give an account, either officially or informally. The reference to detail excludes the sense of 'announce'.

Die Zeitungen berichten über die Gerichtsverhandlungen fast lückenlos.
Der Botschafter berichtete über die Einstellung der Regierung, bei der er beglaubigt war.
Berichten Sie uns ein bißchen von Ihrer Reise.

6. Anzeigen: to report or to announce something to authorities as a duty; to denounce, whether as a duty or wrongfully. See also under 'advertise'.

Er hat seine Verlobung angezeigt.
Er hat den Verkauf seines Hauses angezeigt.
Er hat ihn bei der Polizei angezeigt (denounced).

ANSWER, REPLY, REJOIN, RETORT Sense: to say something in return.

1. Antworten only can translate the intransitive use of 'answer' and 'reply'. When followed by *auf* in order to render the transitive use, it differs from

---

[1] *Kündigen*: to give notice that one intends to leave one's employment or one's lodgings. Also: to terminate friendship.

[2] The form *verkünden* is more common than *verkündigen*, while *ankündigen* is much more used than *ankünden*.

[3] *Anmelden*: to enter one's name on a list in order to receive attention or consideration in some matter. *Seine Ansprüche, ein Telephongespräch, anmelden. Vermelden* is used only in fixed, conventional phrases. *Mit Respekt zu vermelden.*

[4] *Sich melden* is said jocularly to a friend in order to announce one's presence; e.g. over the telephone (*ich wollte mich nur melden*). Other uses include it as a military expression: *er legte das Gewehr beiseite und meldete sich.*

ANSWER

beantworten in suggesting nothing more than that the question has elicited a response, i.e. without reference to any specific type of content. **Beantworten,** on the other hand, means 'to deal with the question' with some measure of fullness.

Er hat noch nicht auf meinen Brief geantwortet.
Er antwortete auf meine Frage nur mit 'Ja'.
Er beantwortete meinen Brief, meine Frage, sehr ausführlich.

2. **Erwidern** means primarily 'to return something given' in the same or the opposite kind (e.g. *Liebe mit Liebe, Haß, erwidern*). As a synonym of *antworten*, it suggests an opposing statement, and approaches very closely to **entgegnen** (to counter with an objection).

Auf meine Behauptung erwiderte er, daß er das Gegenteil für wahr halte.
Er entgegnete, daß mein Argument sich auf falsche Prämissen stütze.

3. **Versetzen** suggests a lively answer in conversation.

Auf meine Frage versetzte er, daß ich die Frage falsch gestellt hätte.

ANXIOUS, EAGER, ZEALOUS 1. Sense: desirous. As there are no exact German equivalents except for 'zealous', only approximations are possible, the following being the commonest.

(a) **Eifrig** means 'zealous' rather than 'eager', and should only be used when these two terms are practically interchangeable, i.e. when 'eager' suggests zeal in doing a thing. Like 'zealous', *eifrig* cannot be followed by the infinitive, which is, however, possible after *großen Eifer zeigen*.

Er ist sehr eifrig in der Schule.
Er ist ein eifriger Parteianhänger.
Er lernt sehr eifrig.
Er hat meinen Vorschlag eifrig befürwortet.
Er zeigt großen Eifer zu lernen.

(b) **Begierig:** desirous of getting possession of something which satisfies an appetite or insistent desire, for oneself, not for others. It rarely refers to the desires of the higher self,[1] although an intellectual interest may be involved. *Er ist begierig, sie kennen zu lernen* can easily suggest sexual interest. It can be followed by an infinitive.

Er ist begierig nach Ruhm.
Er ist begierig, schnell reich zu werden.
Er ist begierig zu prüfen, ob die Ähnlichkeit sie täuschen wird.
Ich bin begierig, die Geschichte zu hören.

---

[1] *Gierig* emphasizes still more strongly the desire for possession, often in an animal way, and approximates to 'avid'. It cannot be followed by the infinitive (e.g. *er trinkt gierig*). *Begierde* refers only to strongly emotional desires and is thus more restricted in application than 'desire'. *Begierde* concentrates attention on the subject, *Begier* on the desire itself. *Das erweckte in ihm die Begier nach Ruhm. Da erwachte in ihm die Begierde nach Ruhm.* On the other hand, only *Begierde* admits a plural. The same distinction applies to *Zier* and *Zierde. Gier* suggests a covetous desire of the lower order, often avidity, the state of desire. When 'desire' means no more than wish it must be translated by *Wunsch* (e.g. *sein Wunsch, ein Abkommen zu treffen*). Similarly *wünschen. Begehren* is to desire strongly, emotionally to crave (e.g. *den Tod begehren*). *Verlangen*, which can also mean 'to require', 'to ask' (see 'ask') suggests a need which is accompanied by a state of restlessness owing to its non-fulfilment. It is often followed by *nach* to express the remoteness of fulfilment. *Lust*, like English 'lust', originally meant 'desire', the meaning of pleasurable sensation being a later development. The original meaning is preserved in many phrases (e.g. *Lust haben*) and in the plural (*Lüste* = carnal desires).

(c) **Neugierig** (curious), **gespannt** (literally: tense) are used in the sense of 'to desire to make acquaintance with, to experience', something hitherto unknown. *Gespannt* suggests that the outcome is anxiously awaited.

Ich bin neugierig, ihn kennen zu lernen.

Ich bin gespannt, was daraus wird (anxious to know, to see).

Ich bin gespannt, Furtwängler dirigieren zu hören.

(d) **Möchte (gern)**, 'should, would like', must often be used in reference to simple matters. The addition of *gern* suggests a slight fear of difficulties.[1]

Ich möchte gern nach Hause kommen, bevor der Sturm losbricht.

Er möchte immer gefallen.

(e) **Es liegt einem an**...means 'to attach importance to the realization of' a thing. It does not render the implication of fear conveyed by 'anxious', and instead of suggesting the emotion of desire it presents the aim as something understood and calculated as well as wanted. It should be used only of things that have a measure of importance, and not in impulsive statements.

Es liegt mir sehr daran, ihn kennen zu lernen.

Es liegt mir daran, nach Hause zu kommen, bevor der Sturm losbricht.

(f) **Darauf brennen** should only be used when 'to burn to...' is possible in English.

Er brennt darauf, mitzuhelfen.

(g) **Bemüht sein** can mean 'to be anxious' only when the context implies that the subject is already active, endeavouring to carry out a purpose.[2] It is often combined with *eifrig*. See also under 'trouble'.

Er war bemüht, einen guten Eindruck zu machen.

Er ist eifrig bemüht, der Erste zu sein.

(h) **Bedacht sein auf** can be used in the sense of 'intent upon', 'concerned with', i.e. in reference to some absorbing purpose.

Er ist darauf bedacht, nichts falsch zu machen.

(i) **Gespannt sein** is in conversation the commonest phrase with the sense of 'to be anxious to know'.

Ich bin sehr gespannt, wie er darauf reagiert.

Ich bin gespannt, was er dazu sagen wird.

2. Sense: worried, worrying.[3] See also under 'trouble'.

Er ist besorgt um seine Gesundheit.

---

[1] The commonest meaning of *mögen* is now 'to like'. Except after the form *möchte* a following infinitive is more common in the negative than in the positive (compare English 'care'). Otherwise *gern* and an appropriate verb is used. It is commonest with noun objects which refer to (*a*) people, (*b*) food and drink, again more in the negative than the positive, although it is also found with other types of object. In the latter case, however, *gern haben* is more usual. *Gern leiden mögen* is common with a personal object (*ich mag ihn gern leiden*). Examples: *Ich möchte (nicht) ins Theater gehen. Ich mag solche Sachen nicht hören. Sie mögen sich. Ich möchte ihn ganz gern. Ich mag Kartoffeln nicht. Ich habe diese Farbenmischung gern. Ich hätte gern die letzte Nummer der 'Zeit'. Gern* with the appropriate verb is common to render 'like' followed by the gerund. *Ich gehe gern ins Theater.* See also under 'like'.

[2] *Sich bemühen*: to endeavour. It stresses the consciousness of purpose, whereas *sich mühen* emphasizes the toil itself involved in doing a thing, and means 'to toil', 'to labour'. The latter verb is less commonly followed by the infinitive. Exceptions: '... *daß ich mich ernstlich mühen mußte, von allerlei Vermutungen ergriffen, wenigstens unbefangen zu scheinen*' (E. T. A. Hoffmann, *Die Elixiere des Teufels*).

> '*Du trägst seit alten Tagen*
> *Ein seltsam Märchen mit dir um,*
> *Und mühst dich es zu sagen.*'   (Mörike, *Mein Fluß*.)

[3] *Ängstlich* means 'timid', 'fearful', in a nervous way, i.e. it stresses the fear, not the desire to see a positive result.

ANXIOUS

Sie ist eine besorgte Mutter.
Es war ein besorgniserregender Augenblick.
Sie wartete voller Besorgnis.

3. In psychological use 'anxiety' is *G. Angst.*

APPARENTLY

Scheinbar differs from **anscheinend**[1] in the same way as *Schein* from *Anschein* (see 'appearance'). The distinction between *scheinbar* and *anscheinend* is being obliterated more and more, even with careful writers.

Er hat nur scheinbar seinen Standpunkt verändert (ostensibly).
Sie haben es anscheinend sehr eilig.

APPEAR, SEEM This article deals with these verbs when followed by an adjective with or without 'to be'. As with 'to be', the insertion or omission of *zu sein* after *scheinen* is determined not by the sense but solely by the formal requirements of the phrase. *Scheinen* followed by the infinitive is extremely rare in compound tenses.

1. **Scheinen:** a subjective judgment based on feeling, approximating to the meaning of 'consider'. If the judgment is not that of the speaker but of some other person (indicated by the second or third person in the dative case), it is implied that the speaker definitely knows that the judgment is that of this other person. In cases where the speaker cannot know of the judgment as a fact (e.g. with the future tense or in combinations with modal verbs[2]) *scheinen* is not used. These cases arise with the first person (the speaker) no less than with the second and third persons. English 'I seem (appear)' with infinitive cannot be *scheinen*. Use *anscheinend*.

Die Bedingungen scheinen mir hart (zu sein) (or *Ihnen, ihm,* etc., to which could be added some such phrase as *wie ich höre* to complete the sense).
Es schien mir, Ihnen, ihm, unmöglich, daß jemand so schlecht sein könne.
Seine Handlungsweise scheint mir (Ihnen, ihr), gesinnungslos zu sein.
Es schien den die Gefangenen in Freiheit setzenden Truppen unmöglich, daß der Mensch solche Greuel begehen könnte (the addition of *zu sein* after *unmöglich* would be cumbersome).
Sie scheinen zufrieden (zu sein) (mir is implied).
Scheint Ihnen der Gedanke so lächerlich?

2. **Erscheinen**[3] implies less a judgment than an impression, often, but not necessarily, visual. With *mir, uns* it expresses the impression of the speaker(s). With the dative of the second or third person it refers to an impression received by this person, which the speaker reports not as a fact known to him, but as an impression gained by him. Since the speaker may very well have an impression about his own or other people's reactions in cases where these

---

[1] *Scheinbar*, but not *anscheinend* is used adjectivally.
[2] *Scheinen* is found in combination with modal verbs in poetic or dignified and elevated diction.

> 'Heimlich muß ich immer weinen,
> Aber freundlich kann ich scheinen
> Und sogar gesund und rot.' (Goethe, *An Mignon.*)

Thomas Mann in *Briefe an einen Schweizer* published in *Schweizer Annalen* (Nr. 9/10, 1945) writes: '*Auch steht man nicht so allein, wie es einem selbst und Außenstehenden in den trübsten Augenblicken scheinen mag.*' *Mögen* used optatively is for the same reason followed by *scheinen* not *erscheinen* (e.g. *möge es scheinen . . .*).

[3] *Erscheinen* cannot be followed by an infinitive.

cannot be definitely known, *erscheinen* can be used with the future tense and with modal verbs. When the recipient of the impression is not mentioned, the sense is that anyone or everyone receives it. Since we tend to state our own reactions as judgments, *scheinen* is more common with the first, *erscheinen* with the second and third persons.

Die Bedingungen werden (müssen) Ihnen wohl hart erscheinen.

Es erschien mir unmöglich, daß jemand so schlecht sein könne.

Seine Handlungsweise kann ihr nicht anders als gesinnungslos erscheinen.

Es erschien den Truppen, die die noch überlebenden Gefangenen befreiten, unmöglich, daß der Mensch solche Greuel begehen könnte.

Lassen Sie es so erscheinen, als ob der Vorschlag von ihm kommt.

Er kann nach Belieben heiter oder traurig erscheinen.

Erscheint Ihnen der Gedanke so lächerlich?

APPEARANCE A. Outward appearance in relation to reality. The German words also translate 'semblance'.

1. Schein:[1] outward appearance(s) as opposed to reality. It can be used only when the purpose of the statement in which it occurs is to make this opposition clear.

Der Schein trügt.

Dem Schein nach ist er zu Zugeständnissen bereit.

Er spricht mit dem Schein der Überzeugung.

Die Entscheidung hat den Schein der Billigkeit an sich (ist aber tatsächlich unbillig could be added).

Unter dem Schein der Legalität setzten sie ihre Maßnahmen durch.

Der Schein ist gegen ihn.

Sie denken nur daran, den Schein zu wahren.

2. Anschein: outward appearance(s) which seem(s) to the judge, who may, but need not, be the speaker, probably to correspond to reality, though it may not.

Allem Anschein nach ist er zu Zugeständnissen bereit.

Er spricht mit dem Anschein, als ob er selbst davon überzeugt sei.

Die Entschuldigung hat den Anschein von Billigkeit an sich (to which could be added: und ist es tatsächlich auch, an addition impossible in the example involving Schein).

Um ihre Maßnahmen durchzusetzen, hatten sie den Anschein der Legalität nötig.

Das Bild hat den Anschein der Lebenswahrheit.

Der Starrkrampf erweckt den Anschein des Todes.

B. Look, aspect, air of a person or thing.

1. Äußeres refers to the general appearance of a person, particularly face and clothes in so far as care is bestowed on them.

Sie achtet sehr auf, vernachlässigt, ihr Äußeres.

Von ihrem Äußeren halte ich nicht viel.

Ich habe ihr Äußeres überhaupt nicht in Betracht gezogen, als ich sie engagierte.

Lassen Sie sich nicht von ihrem Äußeren irreleiten.

Weiße Haare betonten noch mehr die Vornehmheit seines Äußeren.

---

[1] *Schein* is used to form many compounds (e.g. *Scheinblüte, ein Scheinheiliger*) and may be rendered into English by such adjectives as 'sham', 'mock', 'illusory'.

APPEARANCE

2. Äußere Erscheinung refers also to the general appearance, but can only be applied to a high personage or to a person of some years.[1]

Es ist nur seine äußere Erscheinung, die etwas taugt.

3. Aussehen[2] refers to the general impression of a person or thing, to the natural look, not to clothes.

Sie hat ein frisches Aussehen.

Sie hat das Aussehen eines Bauernmädchens.

Das Aussehen des Parks gereicht der Stadt zur Ehre.

C. Erscheinen must be used in the sense of 'act of appearance'.[3]

Sein Erscheinen zu diesem Zeitpunkt war ganz unerwartet.

APPLY suggests the bringing of one thing into contact with another, so that something useful or desired may result. From the literal sense of laying one thing on another it passes to that of using and then to that of asking for something.

1. (a) To place into contact (*W.*): **Auflegen, auftragen.**

Ein keimtötendes Mittel auf eine Wunde auflegen (auftragen) (W.).

Diese Salbe kann auf jede Wunde aufgelegt werden (S.O.D.).

(b) With the additional implication of spreading on: **Auflegen.**

Reiben Sie das Holz mit Sandpapier ab, bevor Sie den Lack auflegen (auftragen) (W.).

(c) To superimpose: **Legen.**

Ein Dreieck über das andere legen (W.).

2. To put to use, esp. for some practical or specific purpose (*W.*): **Anwenden** suggests exactness in the procedure of application.

Applied science: angewandte Wissenschaften.

Sein Wissen anwenden.

Verwenden may suggest a specific purpose (i.e. turning a thing in a specific direction), or simply to find some use for, in which case it is a close synonym of *gebrauchen* (see 'use').

Das ganze Geld soll zu Gunsten armer heimatloser Kinder verwendet (angewendet) werden (A.L.).

Wir können dieses Holz gut verwenden.

3. (a) Make use of something as suitable, fitting or relevant (*W.*): **Anwenden.**

Die Regel auf jede Situation anwenden (W.).

Dieses Gesetz läßt sich lediglich auf die Zukunft anwenden.

(b) The intransitive use of 'apply' in this sense, to have a valid connection with: **Gelten, gültig sein** (i.e. to be valid).

Die Regel gilt hier nicht (ist nicht gültig).

Die Beweisführung gilt für den Fall.

4. To devote or employ diligently or with close attention (*W.*).

(a) Reflexively: **sich widmen.**

Er hat sich der Aufgabe, seiner Arbeit, dem Problem mit unverminderter Energie gewidmet.

---

[1] *Erscheinung* can only be used to refer to the personality and to bearing behind externals. It is used with *sein*, not *haben*, and corresponds to apparition rather than appearance. *Sie ist eine anmutige Erscheinung.*

[2] *Ansehen* is now obsolete in this sense. '*Sie scheinen keine Schelmen, und haben doch auch nicht das Ansehen von ehrlichen Leuten*' (Goethe, *Werther*). '*Aber er hatte ein düstres, störrisches Ansehen*' (E. T. A. Hoffmann, *Die Elixiere des Teufels*).

[3] *Erscheinung* would mean apparition in the sense of 'ghost'.

(b) To make use of one's gifts or of one's mind, intellect: **Gebrauch machen von** (the verbs *gebrauchen, benutzen, verwenden*—see under use—are not possible here).

> *Er machte Gebrauch von seiner Begabung, seinem Verstand, um schnell avancieren zu können.*

The English phrase 'apply your wits, your mind, to the problem' cannot be translated by this expression but only by some such expression as *denk mal richtig drüber nach.*

5. To ask to be given something. See also under 'ask'.

(a) **Sich bewerben um etwas** always implies competition.

> *Er hat sich um eine Stelle bei der Bank beworben.*
> *Er bewirbt sich um alle möglichen Stipendien.*

(b) In the sense of an application to an official to be granted something in cases where the applicant regards himself as having a right to it. G. now normally uses **beantragen** (*einen Antragstellen* is still more formal and clearly suggests that the application is in writing). **Nachsuchen,** which does not suggest that the applicant feels he has a right is also used in the same sense as *beantragen,* but now less than formerly, except in Austria. **Ansuchen** has the same meaning, but is rare.

> *Ich fliege nach Amerika und muß ein Visum rechtzeitig beantragen.*
> *Der Student beantragte die Rückgabe seiner Unterlagen.*
> *Ich beantrage die Verschiebung des Termins.*
> *Er hat wegen Krankheit um eine vorzeitige Pensionierung nachgesucht* (*angesucht,* and of course *eine v. P. beantragt*).
> *Er hat um eine Gehaltserhöhung nachgesucht.*
> *Er hat um politisches Asyl nachgesucht.*

(c) **Ersuchen** comes closer perhaps to 'exhort' rather than to 'apply'. It suggests an order and at times a threat.

> *Die Polizei ersuchte die Autofahrer um Vorsicht und Geduld bei dem starken Ferienverkehr.*
> *Nachdem ich Ihnen 4 mal geschrieben habe, ersuche ich Sie, bis zum 20 d.M. zu zahlen.*

APPOINT, NOMINATE, ENGAGE   Sense: to declare a person as one's choice for a position or task.

'Appoint' is used in the following combinations: (1) to appoint someone; (2) to appoint someone (as) (e.g. manager); (3) to appoint someone to a position; (4) to appoint someone to do something.

1. **Ernennen** is used in two ways. (*a*) To appoint, i.e. by an individual or a body possessing power of appointment without submission to the vote of an electorate. (*b*) To nominate, when this is done by an executive officer whose prerogative it is to make a selection which has then to be submitted to confirmation by the body in which power resides. Sometimes 'appoint' is used in this sense of 'nominate', particularly in reference to nomination by an executive officer after this has received confirmation. It does not mean 'nominate' in the sense of the proposal of a candidate by a member of the electorate.[1]

Ernennen, like 'appoint', is not used of humble work. Further, it can be followed by the title of the person, but not by that of the office.

---

[1] 'Nominate' in this sense is: *vorschlagen; jdn. als Kandidaten aufstellen.*

Der Senat der Universität hat ihn zum Professor ernannt.
Er wurde zum Kriegsminister ernannt.
Sie werden hiermit zum Mitglied des Prüfungsausschusses ernannt.
Die Firma ernannte ihn zu ihrem Schiedsrichter.
Ich habe ihn zu meinem Agenten ernannt.
Der Präsident der Vereingten Staaten ernennt seine Staatssekretäre (nominates, appoints).

2. **Bestellen** implies that the appointment is made from above, e.g. by a controlling body. Further, it is most commonly used of appointment to a special task. In reference to a permanent position it is only possible if the appointment is made by an exalted personage such as a king, or in old-fashioned language. It can be followed by the title of the person, but not by that of the position.[1]

Er wurde zum Vormund, Vertreter, bestellt.
Er wurde zum Prüfungsassistenten bestellt.
Die Regierung hat ihn zum Richter, hat einen Richter, bestellt, um die Vergangenheit der Internierten zu prüfen.
Ehemalige Soldaten werden als Hilfspolizei bestellt.
Er wurde als Hilfslehrer an diese Schule bestellt (not *als Lehrer* which refers to a permanent position).
Ein Ausschuß wurde bestellt, um die Zustände im Kriegsgefangenenlager zu untersuchen.
Der König bestellte ihn zu seinem Leibarzt.
Goethe bestelle Dr. Riemer zu seinem Sekretär (old-fashioned; today the meaning would be 'asked him to go to his secretary').

3. **Anstellen** is applied to permanent work of a middle or lower order, and within this framework means 'to appoint', 'to engage'.[2]

Er wurde als Dozent, als Lehrer für Geschichte, als Sekretär, als Arbeiter, angestellt.

4. **Einsetzen** most commonly suggests a specific purpose, often when a matter is urgent or when energy is required. It is used more frequently than any other term in reference to the appointment of a committee, but is rarely applied to a permanent appointment. It may be followed by a prepositional phrase denoting the office.

Während des Krieges wurden in Deutschland politische Offiziere eingesetzt, um die Haltung der Truppen zu überwachen.

[1] A closely related meaning of *bestellen* is: to request or command a person to call on one or to go to a specified place. *Ich habe ihn für 4 Uhr bestellt*, i.e. have made an appointment for him to call on me at 4 o'clock. *Er ist nach Berlin bestellt worden*, requested or commanded to go to Berlin. This meaning is now more common than that of 'appoint to a position'. Ambiguity can arise unless the context removes it. Examples: *Als junger Mann wurde J. S. Bach zum Domorganisten bestellt. Als Domorganist wurde J. S. Bach nach Leipzig bestellt* (either appointed to, or requested to come to L.).

[2] *Anstellen* cannot be used for casual work of a humble kind (use *dingen*, to hire for remuneration), nor for any permanent exalted position or temporary work demanding outstanding gifts (e.g. to engage an artist). *Ein Angestellter*: an employee (e.g. *ein Bank-angestellter*). *Beschäftigen* corresponds to 'employ' only in the sense 'to keep busy', and, by implication, to provide enough work to absorb a specified number of hands. *Diese Fabrik beschäftigt 1000 Arbeiter*. It does not mean 'to take on' (see *anstellen*), and is not used in the passive voice in the sense of 'to be in the employ' of a specified person, firm, or the like. In this sense *angestellt sein in, bei* or the various equivalents of 'to have a position, job' (see 'position') must be used. *Er ist in einer Bank, bei Wertheim, angestellt.*

Er wurde als zeitweiliger Lehrer eingesetzt.

Er wurde ins Polizeipräsidentenant eingesetzt.

Ein Ausschuß wurde eingesetzt, um dem Minister Empfehlungen über Emigrantenfragen zu machen.

5. The following terms are commonly used in the sense of (*a*) to appoint to a position; (*b*) to appoint to the place where a position is held:
Übertragen, to transfer an office to someone; **zuweisen,** to assign.[1]

Der Lehrstuhl, das Amt, wurde ihm übertragen.

Er wurde diesem Schiff als Arzt zugewiesen.

Berufen can be used of appointment to a place in the case of an important position. See 'call'. Similarly: *einen Ruf erhalten nach; einem Ruf folgen nach.*

Er ist ins Reichsinnenministerium berufen worden.

Er hat einen Ruf nach Berlin erhalten.

APPOINTMENT, ENGAGEMENT 1. An arrangement for a meeting (*W.*); the term used according to *W.S.* when a person 'because of the exigencies of his office, his profession, or his position in life must keep a calendar and apportion his time carefully among those who wish to consult him professionally or confer with him', whereas engagement 'is the general term usable in place of any of the others'. German does not distinguish between the two terms and uses **Verabredung** except in the case of an actor, when the term is **Verpflichtung.** See also 'agreement', which the synonyms of **Verabredung** tend to mean.

Der Gouverneur empfängt nur diejenigen Leute, die vorher um eine Verabredung mit ihm angesucht haben (W.S.).

Er konnte die Verabredung nicht einhalten, mußte sie absagen.

Er hat eine Verabredung mit dem Arzt für Donnerstag um 10 Uhr.

Die Verabredung wurde für 6 Uhr getroffen.

Die Sängerin hat eine Verpflichtung für die Salzburger Festspiele.

2. Somewhat colloquially: **Angemeldet sein.** Similarly: **Bestellt werden, sich ansagen. Rendez-vous** in both languages emphasizes the place of the meeting. **Stelldichein,** like 'tryst' suggests a lover's meeting. *Bestellen* always suggests a superior to an inferior.

Ich bin bei dem Arzt für eine Untersuchung angemeldet.

Der Minister hat ihn zu sich bestellt, er ist beim Minister für vier Uhr bestellt.

Ich habe mich bei ihm für Mittwoch angesagt.

Sie haben ein Rendez-vous in Grinzing.

3. The action of nominating to, or placing in an office, the office itself (*S.O.D.*) *Ernennung:* The action of nominating or installing. **Amt, Stellung:** the office itself.

Seine Ernennung wird bald erfolgen.

Ein unbemittelter Baronet, der auf ein Amt, eine Stellung, eine Ernennung hoffte (S.O.D.).

4. Equipment, outfit, furniture, or any article thereof, now usu.pl. (*S.O.D.*). The most general German term is **Ausstattung.**

Die Ausstattung des Zimmers gefällt mir sehr.

---

[1] *Zuweisung* is often used for 'appointment', particularly to a minor administrative position. *Der Referendar erhielt eine Zuweisung nach Hildesheim.*

APPRECIATE 1. **Würdigen** suggests a due awareness, recognition or understanding of the quality, worth of, or of the reason for a thing, and a willingness to pay tribute to these.[1] It must be distinguished from **schätzen,** which merely indicates a liking, and states that a person or thing makes a personal appeal to one.[2]

Er ist ein Mann, dessen wahrer Wert nie recht gewürdigt worden ist.

Ich würdige deine Ansicht, obwohl ich nicht damit übereinstimme.

Nur wenige Menschen sind tolerant genug, die Motive ihrer Gegner zu würdigen.

Hast du es recht gewürdigt, daß er dieses Opfer für dich brachte?

Er würdigt moderne Musik nicht.

Ich würdige deine Haltung, wenn ich sie auch nicht schätze.

Er schätzt moderne Musik nicht.

Dieses Lied wird allgemein geschätzt.

Nichts schätze ich gegen Abend so sehr wie ein Glas Sherry.

Er schätzt diesen kleinen Ort, die friedliche Schönheit der Landschaft.

2. When *würdigen* and *schätzen* are used in combination with **wissen** (i.e. *zu würdigen, schätzen, wissen*), the sense is 'to have the capacity to appreciate'. German requires the insertion of *wissen* when the idea of capacity is stressed, even though in English it is expressed merely as an implication of 'appreciate'. In the positive form *zu würdigen, schätzen, wissen* frequently registers a formal or polite expression of appreciation or gives an assurance in case of doubt and the like that one is not insensitive to a thing. The negative indicates a deficiency in the subject.

Ich weiß die mir erwiesene Ehre wohl zu würdigen.

Ich weiß Ihre Schwierigkeiten zu würdigen.

Einen Besuch in der Gemäldegalerie weiß er doch nicht zu würdigen.

Ich weiß Ihre Bemühungen zu schätzen.

Er weiß die Architektur dieser Stadt nicht zu schätzen.

Viele wissen die Schönheit des eigenen Landes nicht zu schätzen.

3. The following can also be used as approximations to 'appreciate'. They have other, and more frequent, renderings into English than 'appreciate'.

(a) **Verständnis haben für** can refer to emotional as well as intellectual understanding. It suggests that agreement is more unreserved than is the case with *würdigen*. See 'understanding'.

Ich habe Verständnis für Ihre Schwierigkeiten, Ihre Situation.

Er hat kein Verständnis für Kunst.

(b) **Sinn haben für:** to have a sense, a specially developed faculty of the mind, for a thing. See 'sense'.

Er hat keinen Sinn für Musik, für historische Werte.

(c) **Ein Verhältnis haben, finden, zu etwas:** to have, to find, an inner kinship, bond of sympathy, between oneself and a thing. See 'relation'.

Er hat ein inniges Verhältnis zur Kunst des Mittelalters.

Ich finde kein Verhältnis zur modernen Musik.

APPROACH 1. Literal sense. In space or in time.

(a) **Sich nähern** expresses in general the idea of approach in space without specifying the manner. It tends to suggest approach from some distance.

---

[1] *Würdigen* has a number of other meanings. Note particularly that of 'to think worthy of', 'to condescend to give' (e.g. *ich würdigte ihn meines Vertrauens, keines Blickes*).

[2] *Schätzen* also means 'to estimate'. See article.

With reference to time it can only be applied to an activity, i.e. not pure time such as 'spring', 'midnight'. It must be followed by an object in the dative case.

Er näherte sich mir, dem Haus.
Der Zug näherte sich dem Bahnhof.
Das Schiff nähert sich dem Hafen.
Die Armee nähert sich der Stadt.
Wir nähern uns der Mitte der Oper.
Der Krieg nähert sich seinem Ende.

(b) **Näher kommen,** with the same sense as *sich nähern*, translates 'approach' used intransitively. It is also the normal prose term as applied to time.

Er, der Zug, der Frühling, Mitternacht, kommt näher.

(c) **Nahen** suggests a manner of approach in space which grips the beholder by being dignified, imposing, momentous, and the like. It suggests, moreover, that the approaching person or thing is close at hand. It is used of time in literary, mainly elevated, contexts. It occurs both transitively (governing the dative case) and intransitively. In transitive use it is normally reflexive when referring to space. Without *sich*, in reference to things, the impression of majesty is still further heightened.

Der König naht.
Er naht sich dem König, dem Thron.
Das Schiff naht (sich) langsam dem Hafen.
Der Krieg naht seinem Ende (not reflexive in reference to time).
Der Frühling, Mitternacht, naht.

2. To approach with a request or about a matter.

(a) **Angehen um:** to ask for.

Er ging mich um 1000 Mark an.

(b) **Herantreten an** suggests a ceremonious, diplomatic, or at least careful, approach.

England tritt an Rußland mit Vorschlägen heran.

3. To approach a subject of study: **(heran) gehen an.**

Voll Vertrauen ging er an seine Arbeit (heran).
Wir müssen vorsichtig an dieses Problem (heran) gehen.

4. To approach in value: **sich nähern** (material values), **heranreichen an** (immaterial values).

Der Wert dieses Besitzes nähert sich einer Million.
*Keiner der anderen romantischen Dichter reicht, was Gefühlstiefe und Form-
vollendung betrifft, an Mörike heran.*

5. To approximate to, to be practically the equivalent of: **nahe kommen.**

*Was Sie jetzt sagen, kommt einer Verneinung Ihrer früheren Behauptung
nahe.*

AREA The term still carries its implication of clearly marked bounds, but may be used with reference to a space defined in a map or chart as well as to one the limits of which are actually visible. (*W.S.*).

1. Sense: amount of surface (*A.L.*) which is often stated numerically.
G. **Fläche.**

Eine Fläche von ziemlich großem Ausmaß.
Die Fläche eines Dreiecks.

Eine Oase ist eine grüne oder fruchtbare Fläche in einer Wüste (Gegend—see under district—would also be possible).

2. Sense: a particular extent of (esp. the earth's) surface (*S.O.D.*): G. **Gebiet** (see under district). **Strecke** is closer to 'tract', which suggests extent rather than limits (*W.S.*).

Das Wüstengebiet der Vereinigten Staaten hat nur wenig Einwohner (A.L.).

Große Gebiete Australiens (Strecken in sense of tracts also possible) sind noch unbesiedelt.

Ein großes Gebiet außerhalb der Sümpfe ist unter Wasser (W.).

3. Sense: a part of the surface of the human body (*W.*). G. **Stelle** (see under place).

Wenn diese Flüssigkeit die Haut berühren sollte, wasche die Stelle sofort.

4. Sense: a section, district or zone of a town or city (*W.*). G. **Viertel** (see under district) E. 'quarter' is also used in this sense.

Das Geschäftsviertel.

Das Wohnviertel.

Das Theaterviertel.

5. Sense: an area of study, interest, or research. G. **Gebiet.**

Auf welchem Gebiet arbeiten Sie im Augenblick?

Die Vormärzzeit ist ein Gebiet, das mich geradezu fesselt.

Haben Sie ein Gebiet für die Prüfung angegeben?

ARRANGE[1] **1.** To put objects, words, thoughts or matters in a certain order, to dispose.

(a) **Ordnen:** to dispose in an orderly, often practical way, according to some principle. It does not suggest the arranging of visible things in an aesthetic pattern, but may be applied to literature and music (e.g. words, scenes, movements).[2]

Er ordnete die Bücher in seiner Bibliothek nach Schriftstellern.

Er ordnete die Papiere auf seinem Pult.

Er hat seine Angelegenheiten noch nicht geordnet.

Das Ganze ist unübersichtlich geordnet (a piece of writing).

(b) **Einrichten:** to arrange the furniture in a room, each item in relation to the whole.

Das Zimmer ist geschmackvoll eingerichtet.

(c) **Zurecht machen:**[3] to adjust small things so as to bring them into the right or desired order or pattern.

Machen Sie Ihre Haare zurecht.

Sie machte die Kissen auf dem Bett zurecht.

Er machte die Möbel im Salon für die Gesellschaft zurecht.

2. Plan details beforehand.

(a) **Veranstalten** suggests elaborate arrangements with regard to something big, often a function or ceremony.

---

[1] Arrangement. The phrase 'make arrangements' is explained in this article. *Plan* is widely used (*was sind die Pläne für heute abend?*—i.e. with regard to entertainment). *Arrangement* is mostly an arrangement of flowers and the like.

[2] *Anordnen* means 'to put, arrange', in a series; also 'to order' as a synonym of 'command'. See 'order'.

[3] Specific terms compounded with *zurecht* also translate 'arrange'; e.g. *zurechtlegen, zurechtrücken. Sie rückte die Kissen zurecht, um bequemer zu liegen.*

Die Beamten haben einen Besuch zum Flughafen veranstaltet.

Ein Ball, ein Konzert, ein Siegesfest wurde veranstaltet.

(b) **Vorkehrungen treffen** implies the doing of a considerable number of things, which may be the manipulating of objects, speaking, writing, and the like. It can suggest, further, that the measures are designed to eliminate the possibility of adverse developments.

Das Hotel hat Vorkehrungen getroffen, um 150 *Gäste aufzunehmen* (furnished rooms, ordered food, engaged and instructed staff, etc.).

Das Touristenbüro hat alle nötigen Vorkehrungen für meine Reise getroffen (booked train-tickets, rooms in hotels, etc.).

Alle Vorkehrungen sind für die Wahlen getroffen worden.

(c) **Planen** is used of both large- and small-scale organizing.[1,2]

Wir haben einen kleinen Ausflug für Sonntag geplant.

(d) **Vermitteln:** to arrange a thing by negotiations, as a mediator between people. The object is normally the result of the negotiations.

Eine Heirat, den Hausverkauf, vermitteln.

(e) **Sich (es) so einrichten, dass.** This phrase translates 'arrange' when the latter is followed by the infinitive, in the sense of 'to arrange (matters) with regard to oneself'. Used with *es* the meaning can be 'with regard to someone else'. The sense of *einrichten* is 'to manipulate' matters, important or trivial, for the realization of a purpose. In this use its object can only be *sich, es* or a word meaning 'matters' (*Dinge, Sachen,* etc.).

Können Sie sich (es) so einrichten, daß Sie spätestens um 5 Uhr hier sind?

Ich richte mich (es) so ein, daß ich den Nachmittag frei habe.

Ich habe es so eingerichtet, daß er morgen meine Arbeit übernimmt.

(f) **Anstalten treffen:** to make elaborate, often ceremonious, arrangements. A following infinitive is possible.

Er hat Anstalten getroffen, den Minister zu empfangen.

3. To come to an agreement[3] with a person.

(a) **Ausmachen** implies the working out of a practical question, an examination of it from a number of sides. It is common in conversation.

Wir haben ausgemacht, wieviel wir dafür bezahlen wollen.

Ich machte den Ort mit ihm aus, wo wir ihn treffen wollten.

Ich habe mit ihm ausgemacht, mein Auto gegen sein Motorboot einzutauschen.

Sie machten einen Plan aus, der die Finanzen wieder in Ordnung bringen würde.

(b) **Abmachen** stresses the finalizing of a definite agreement.

Es ist abgemacht, daß wir morgen fahren (settled).

Ich kaufe Ihr Auto, das ist abgemacht.

4. To arrange a musical composition: **bearbeiten, einrichten.**

ASK 1. **Bitten** must be used in the sense of 'request'[4] and implies that the

---

[1] *Arrangieren* is possible in this sense.

[2] Specific terms meaning 'to attend to (details)' are: *besorgen* (to attend to); *ins Reine bringen* (to finalize, to give final form to). *Der Sekretär hat alle Einzelheiten für die Besprechung ins Reine gebracht.*

[3] See also *verabreden* under 'agreement'.

[4] *(Sich) etwas erbitten* (often reflexive) means 'to request something' with success or with the certainty of success. *Den beiliegenden Katalog erbitte ich mir nach Durchsicht zurück.* '*Die Gabe des zweiten Gesichts sei über ihn verhängt, er ... würde sie nie von Gott erbeten*

asker is a suppliant, **verlangen** that both parties consider themselves on an equal footing. *Verlangen* has also the sense of 'require' when the subject is a thing.[1]

> *Er bat um Hilfe, eine Unterredung.*
> *An der Grenze wurde verlangt, daß wir unsere Pässe zeigen sollten.*
> *Ich bat ihn, mir seinen Paß zu zeigen.*
> *Die Schullehrer haben eine Gehaltserhöhung verlangt.*
> *Diese Arbeit verlangt eine eingehende Prüfung aller Dokumente.*

2. **Auffordern** ranges in meaning from 'call upon' to 'invite' (*er forderte sie zum Tanze auf*).

3. **Fragen** must be used in the sense of 'to ask a question'.[2] It is also used passively meaning 'to be in demand' in an economic sense.[3]

> *Er fragte was für Absichten sie hätten.*
> *Die Miele-Waschmaschine wird sehr gefragt, nicht nur in Deutschland.*

ATTITUDE 1. **Haltung:** a manner of being, feeling, thinking in the sphere of moral deportment. It is a constant, unchanging manner, as far as the matter to which it is directed is concerned. It excludes on the one hand action, and, on the other, the taking up of a purely intellectual stand or point of view. In this sense it also translates the synonymous term 'bearing'.[4] 'To take' is *einnehmen* when combined with *Haltung*.

> *Er nahm eine scharfe, herausfordernde, abweisende, passive, Haltung ein.*
> *Die realistiche Geisteshaltung.*
> *Eine Haltung von leben und leben lassen.*
> *Er hat eine höchst gesunde Haltung in Bezug auf Sexualfragen.*

2. **Verhalten** is less static than *Haltung*, but can denote a more or less passive attitude of watching and waiting. It is characteristically qualified by such words as *passiv, ruhig, geschickt, klug*, and cannot be combined with adjectives which express a high degree of activity (e.g. *aktiv, energisch*). The relationship[5] between subject and object it can imply is a reaction[6] to and adjustment to a changing situation. It is not used with verbs which imply a static attitude (e.g. *haben, einnehmen*). It indicates the expression of an attitude in one's behaviour and actions and corresponds to 'behaviour' in the context of the physical sciences.

> *Sein Verhalten in der Angelegenheit war sehr lobenswert.*
> *Sein Verhalten in religiösen Fragen ist nicht ganz eindeutig.*

haben' (R. Huch, *Weiße Nächte*). Ersuchen is strong and direct. It is often used in formal or official statements and notices. *Die Botschafter ersuchten Stalin um eine Unterredung. Es wird dringend ersucht, nicht in den Wagen zu spucken. Um etwas nachsuchen* is less strong and less direct. It cannot govern a direct object. *Die Botschafter suchten bei Stalin um eine Unterredung nach.* See also 'apply'.

[1] See also footnote to 'anxious' (p. 18, n. 1) for a further explanation of *verlangen*.

[2] *Befragen* is 'to question fully or insistently', also a large number of people (*Volksbefragung*). *Anfragen (bei jemandem)* is 'to enquire' about matters which receive only a short reply, mostly officially. *Sie könnten bei dem betreffenden Minister anfragen. Ausfragen*: to question fully, to interrogate.

[3] Compare the noun: *Nachfrage* (demand); *Angebot* (supply).

[4] *Haltung* also means 'carriage', i.e. of the body.

[5] *Verhalten* denotes a relationship of the type explained. 'Relationship', however, is *Verhältnis*, which does not mean 'attitude'. See 'relation'.

[6] *Verhalten* is also applied to a chemical reaction.

3. Einstellung[1] refers predominantly to an intellectual attitude, i.e. a fixed point of view with regard to a problem. 'Take' in this connection is translated by *einnehmen*, 'to' by *zu* or *gegenüber*.

Seine Einstellung dem Leben gegenüber.
Meine Einstellung ist, daß der Streik gerechtfertigt war.
Er nahm den Kritikern gegenüber eine höchst feindliche Einstellung ein.
Er hat eine höchst gesunde Einstellung Sexualfragen gegenüber.
Ich bin mir über meine Einstellung nicht ganz klar.

4. Stellungnahme refers only to an attitude towards big questions or important matters. It can also denote an attitude taken in an official capacity in the sense of official comment. Since it contains *nahme*, it cannot be combined with *einnehmen*.

Seine Stellungnahme in der Alkoholfrage.
Die Regierung behält sich ihre Stellungnahme vor.
Die Berichte wurden ohne Stellungnahme weitergeleitet.

5. Stellung: one's inner disposition to a person or a thing. Since it is natural, spontaneous, it is unaffected by reflection. In this sense it is followed by *zu*. The phrase *Stellung nehmen* refers to an official attitude, comment.

Seine Stellung zum Tode.
Der Minister hat schon Stellung dazu genommen.

ATTRACT 1. Anziehen is used in the following ways: (*a*) of a force of nature; (*b*) to stir pleasurable feelings of anticipation;[2] (*c*) to cause to follow as a disciple. To be attracted by a person or thing: *von jdm., etwas, angezogen sein.* To be attracted to a person or thing: *zu jdm., etwas,* **hingezogen** *sein.*

Der Magnet zieht das Eisen an.
Salz zieht Feuchtigkeit an.
Sie zieht ihn stark an.
Dieser Beruf zieht mich nicht an.
Der Kommunismus zieht viele Menschen an.
Er fühlt sich von ihr stark angezogen.
Er fühlt sich zu ihr stark hingezogen.

2. Reizen. See under 'charm'.

3. The sense of 'draw to oneself' in any way other than those treated in the above section, e.g. deliberately, is often rendered by **auf sich ziehen.** This may be used to translate 'attract attention', particularly when a deliberate effort is implied, i.e. by a person. When a thing is the subject **erregen** (see 'excite') is more common. In conversation, shorter phrases such as *aufmerksam werden*,[3] *auffallen* (to strike, to catch one's attention) are preferred.

Ich versuchte, seine Aufmerksamkeit auf mich zu ziehen.
Wir zogen feindliches Feuer auf uns.
Das Bild erregte meine Aufmerksamkeit.
Sein Gesichtsausdruck fiel mir auf, ließ mich aufmerken.
Als ich vorbeiging, wurde ich plötzlich auf seinen Gesichtsausdruck aufmerksam.

---

[1] The verbs related to *Einstellung, Stellung* and *Verhalten* are widely used. Note: *eingestellt sein* (only with *sein*); *sich stellen zu etwas* (only in reflexive use); *sich verhalten* (only in reflexive use). What is your attitude to . . .? (in a casual question) *Wie stellen Sie ich zu . . .? Was ist Ihre Einstellung . . .?* expects a more detailed answer.

[2] Synonyms are: *zusagen, reizen* (see 'charm'). *Der Posten reizt mich nicht.*

[3] To draw one's attention to: *jdn. auf etwas aufmerksam machen.*

AVOID

AVOID 1. Clearly distinguished uses of *meiden* and *vermeiden*.
(a) **Meiden** is normally used in the sense of avoiding (i) persons,[1] (ii) places, (iii) a concrete situation which has the effect of a person or place. Its meaning is: to give a wide berth to a person or place.

Ich habe ihn immer gemieden.
Er meidet seine alten Freunde.
Er meidet den Ort, wo er überfallen wurde.
Er hat den Krieg gemieden (only in the sense of the theatre of war, i.e. a place).
Ich habe die Gefahr, die mit diesem Weg verbunden ist, gemieden (I kept away from the place where the danger was).

(b) **Vermeiden** is normally used in the sense of refraining or escaping from doing a thing, the latter being represented by a noun or an infinitive phrase.

Er hat den Fehler diesmal vermieden.
Sie müssen jede Anstrengung, alle Aufregungen, vermeiden, solange Ihr Herz geschwächt ist.
Wir müssen jede Anspielung auf dieses Thema vermeiden.
Dieser Ausdruck wird besser vermieden.
Schweden hat den Krieg vermieden.
Ich vermied es, ihm meine wahre Meinung zu sagen.
Ich habe die Gefahr vermieden, zu viel zu sagen.

2. Cases in which the distinction between *meiden* and *vermeiden* is subtle. The tendency is always to use *vermeiden* in such cases, while even careful speakers prefer it in conversation, since *meiden* is apt to sound precious.

The distinction is that *meiden* stresses the intention, whereas *vermeiden* merely draws attention to the result or indicates an intention without stressing it. *Meiden* therefore suggests more vividly the state of mind of the subject. It is appropriate when emphasizing the urgent need for avoiding a thing or the scruples with which it is avoided. Its intensity sometimes approximates it to 'shun'. A dictionary would say: *dieser Ausdruck wird in guter Sprache gemieden*. When Thomas Mann in *Tristan* uses *meiden* with a verbal noun as object instead of the normal *vermeiden*, the effect is to illuminate the peculiar mind of the subject (Herr Spinell): '*Von da an mied er das Zusammentreffen mit Anton Klöterjahn so weit als tunlich.*' This use, i.e. with a verbal noun (or infinitive) as object, should be left to accomplished writers.

Vermeiden can thus be regarded as the normal term for all cases not falling under 1(a) when no particular emphasis is required. Thus: *wir haben dieses Thema vermieden*; but: *wir müssen ein so heikles Thema um jeden Preis meiden.* The use of *vermeiden* with a personal object occurs, but is slovenly. Thus: '*Ich wäre so gern einmal mit ihm grob geworden, aber man konnte nicht dazu kommen. So vermied ich ihn lieber, obwohl er mich zu suchen schien*' (Theater, Hermann Bahr).[2] In the following sentence from *Die Brüder Lautensack* by Feuchtwanger *meiden* would have been more vivid, since the author is obviously describing the intention and attitude of mind of the subject. '*Proell, nachdenklich, mühte sich, den Blick des anderen zu vermeiden, versuchte, skeptisch zu lächeln.*' Further examples are:

---

[1] In conversation *jdm. ausdem Weg gehen* is more common.
[2] Examples of *vermeiden* with a personal object do occur, particularly in older German. '*Er schien . . . sie* (= her) *absichtlich zu vermeiden.*' '*Er vermied mich mit sichtlicher Angst und Beklemmung*' (both examples from E. T. A. Hoffmann's *Die Elixiere des Teufels*). '*Ich vermied meine Freundin und begrüßte sie kaum*' (Mörike, *Lucie Gelmeroth*).

Meiden Sie unter allen Umständen dieses Thema.
Wenn Sie es machen können, vermeiden Sie dieses Thema.
Ich meide diese Verpflichtung.
Ich vermeide alle Verpflichtungen.
Meiden Sie Alkohol.
Der Arzt sagte mir, soweit ich kann, soll ich Alkohol vermeiden.
'*...und es schien, als ob er nicht nur die undelikaten Äußerungen tiefer und feierlicher Gefühle, sondern auch die Gefühle selbst fürchtete und mied.*'
(Thomas Mann, *Buddenbrooks*.)

BAD, EVIL, WICKED

The adverb 'badly' presents difficulties of translation since some of the German terms are not used adverbially in all senses corresponding to their adjectival use.

1. Schlecht: lacking positive quality, failing to conform to a standard deemed proper or desirable, without value, therefore actually, not potentially, bad (see *schlimm*). The deficiency may manifest itself in any sphere: moral, intellectual, aesthetic, material, physical, practical. The judgment made is purely objective (contrast the other terms).

It also translates 'poor' with reference to quality. The distinction between 'bad' and 'poor' used in this sense can be rendered in German only by a circumlocution (e.g. a poor, a bad, performance). Applied to food and drink it means poor in quality unless the particular food or drink excludes this meaning (*ein schlechtes Ei* = a bad, rotten egg). 'Bad' in this case can only be translated by *schlecht werden* (to be, go bad) or some specific term (e.g. *das Fleisch ist ein bißchen angegangen*).

'Bad for' in the sense of 'harmful for' can be translated by *schlecht für*.

Applied to persons it means bad in character, corrupt, depraved. It does not mean 'naughty'.

It is used in impersonal phrases with reference to health, economic circumstances, general conditions.

It can be used adverbially in all senses corresponding to its adjectival use. A special adverbial use is the sense of 'hardly', 'not very well' (e.g. *ich kann heute schlecht kommen*).

Ein schlechter Mensch (*Mann* means 'husband'), *ein schlechter Kerl, ein schlechtes Kind* (in all three examples: bad in character), *ein schlechter Lehrer* (inefficient), *ein schlechter Präsident* (lacking the qualities necessary in a president), *ein schlechtes Buch* (worthless as a piece of writing, but not corrupting), *ein schlechtes Gedicht, ein schlechter Geruch, schlechter Geschmack, eine schlechte Gewohnheit* (not necessarily injurious), *eine schlechte Zensur, ein schlechter Einfluß* (only injurious by implication, i.e. because of the attraction of *Einfluß*), *ein schlechter Ruf, schlechte Absichten, ein schlechter Scherz, ein schlechtes Ergebnis* (indicating a poor performance), *ein schlechtes Gewissen, schlechte Aussichten, schlechte Nachrichten, eine schlechte Lage, schlechte Zeiten, eine schlechte Laune, schlechte Wege, ein schlechtes Deutsch, ein schlechter Lügner* (not clever), *eine schlechte Gesichtsfarbe, schlechtes Wetter, ein schlechtes Gewitter* (only in the sense of a poor representation of a storm on the stage), *schlechtes Fleisch* (poor), *schlechter Stoff* (poor), *schlechte Qualität*.
Das Fleisch ist schlecht geworden.
Es war schlecht von Ihnen, mich hinters Licht zu führen.

Zu viel Rauchen ist schlecht für Sie.

Es ist schlecht für sie, allein zu leben.

Er spricht schlecht, er arbeitet schlecht, er hat schlecht geschlafen, er hat sie schlecht behandelt, er denkt schlecht von ihnen.

Es geht ihm gesundheitlich, geschäftlich, schlecht; es steht schlecht mit seinen Plänen; mir wurde schlecht bei dem Gedanken (I felt ill . . .).

2. Schlimm differs from *schlecht* in being less definite in its reference to the objective fact, person or thing, and in expressing subjective feeling about a fact. In its objective reference it means 'bad in effects', i.e. not that a person or thing is bad in himself or itself, lacks quality. Its indefiniteness is that it fluctuates between actually and potentially bad effects. *Eine schlechte Lage* is one that is definitely and actually bad as it is and suggests no possibility of change. *Eine schlimme Lage*, while not excluding actual badness, expresses a feeling that the situation has not yet finally crystallized and may develop, in the sense of becoming either worse or better. In its suggestion of a possible development *schlimm* approximates closely to 'serious' (e.g. *eine schlimme Verwundung*).

It is used mainly with words which either mean or imply effects.

The emotional participation of the speaker expressed by *schlimm* manifests itself in various ways, e.g. as emphasis or familiarity. When applied to nouns which can also be qualified by *schlecht*, this characteristic of *schlimm* becomes strikingly clear in that the whole phrase betrays subjective feeling. In the following examples the tone of each is different, that of the first objective, detached, that of the second revealing the emotional impression made by the object: (*a*) *Wegen seines schlechten Rufes ist er nicht gewählt worden.* (*b*) *Halten Sie sich lieber fern von ihr, sie hat ja einen ganz schlimmen Ruf. Schlecht* would be possible in the last example, though with a change of tone. *Schlimm*, however, would be out of place in the first.

Another consequence of the subjective character of *schlimm* is that it is not necessarily as objectively serious as *schlecht*, though it is more so than *arg* and *übel*, and hence does not indicate as high a degree of objective badness. *Sein Einfluß ist schlecht gewesen* is a more definite statement than *sein Einfluß ist schlimm gewesen*, which may mean no more than that his influence has led to a few follies.

It follows, furthermore, from the emotional connotation of *schlimm* that it cannot qualify nouns denoting a person unless these themselves also possess this character. Thus, while it cannot be combined with *Mensch*, it is possible to say: *du bist mir aber ein ganz schlimmes Bürschchen, ein schlimmer Patron.*

On the other hand the subjective colouring is present to a less extent when it qualifies nouns which do not admit the idea of quality, but merely point to an actual or possible result or development (*schlimme Folgen, ein schlimmes Zeichen, ein schlimmer Unfall*).

Schlimm can be applied attributively but not predicatively, to an affected part of the body in the sense of 'sore' (see also *böse*).

As an adverb *schlimm* is practically restricted to a few fixed phrases: *die Sache steht schlimm; schlimm dran sein* (*schlimm* being in both cases as much adjectival as adverbial); *er ist schlimm zugerichtet; ihm ist schlimm mitgespielt worden.*

Schlimm occurs regionally in expressions which are not standard German. Thus: *es geht mir schlimm, ich habe ihn schlimm ausgezankt, schlimm krank.*

The following examples are divided into two classes: (*a*) those in which *schlimm,* not *schlecht* must be used; (*b*) those in which the noun could also be qualified by *schlecht,* if other necessary changes of tone are also made.

(*a*) *Wir haben eine schlimme Niederlage erlitten.*

Der Schaden ist schlimm.

Er hat einen schlimmen Anfall von Rheumatismus gehabt.

Das war ein schlimmer Fehler.

Das ist ein schlimmer Biß.

Er hat einen schlimmen Verstoß gegen das Anstandsgefühl begangen.

Wir haben ein sehr schlimmes Gewitter gehabt (can suggest damage).

Seine Schmerzen sind heute ganz schlimm.

Das Schlimmste ist, daß er sich seiner Taktlosigkeit garnicht bewußt ist.

Ich befürchte das Schlimmste.

Es wird schlimm für Sie sein, wenn Sie dabei ertappt werden.

Ich habe einen schlimmen Finger.

(*b*) *Das sind ja schlimme Aussichten.*

Die Nachrichten werden immer schlimmer.

Wir haben schlimme Zeiten durchgemacht.

Er ist einer ganz schlimmen Lage.

Ich weiß nicht, was die Kerle wollen, aber sie kommen ja sicher mit schlimmen Absichten.

Ach, das ist eine schlimme Gewohnheit!

Ich habe schlimme Erfahrungen mit ihm gemacht.

3. Arg suggests that the object to which it is applied strikes the eye because its 'badness' is great in extent, amount. It conveys no precise knowledge of the objective fact, but merely this impression of extent. *Der Schaden war sehr arg* is a statement which clearly illustrates this point. At the same time *arg* expresses the emotional participation of the speaker in the fact. This is not very strong, and despite the extent of the 'badness' does not view this as seriously as *schlimm* does. It can, e.g., suggest a show of sympathy, which may or may not be sincere, or a reproach which is friendly in tone. It differs, therefore, from *schlimm* (i) by telling still less about the objective fact, (ii) by expressing weaker feeling about the fact.

While certain uses of *arg* are common throughout Germany, others are regional (particularly in southern Germany and Austria). Some of these regional uses were once more widespread, but are now old-fashioned, often biblical. In general, *arg* may be used freely when applied to evils, less so, it is true, as an adverb than an adjective (see paragraph below) and less with persons, their thoughts, feelings, and the like than with nouns denoting purely objective evils. Thus *Der Arge* (the devil), *ein arger Schelm, arge Gedanken* have an old-fashioned flavour, though *ein arger Lügner* (arrant, outrageous), *ein arger Spötter, ein arger Opiumraucher* are still said in all parts of the country. The person designated by this type of noun is an agent, the meaning of *arg* being that he indulges in the activity to an enormous extent. Examples of objective evils are: *eine arge Niederlage, ein arges Mißverständnis.*

As an adverb *arg* is still more restricted to regions and old-fashioned diction. This is exclusively so when it modifies an adjective. *Arg hungrig, arg schön,* even *arg saudumm* belong to everyday speech in the south-west. With verbs the position is so complicated that it is impossible to draw a clear line of demarcation between standard and regional use. The following explanation describes nothing more than a tendency. The most prevalent standard use of *arg* is to refer to a state or the effects of an action. In other words, it is found less where great activity or a clear act on the part of a person is suggested. Thus, it is avoided with transitive verbs in the active voice, if these denote one clear act performed by a person, since they draw attention from the result to the act and the subject. For example: *er wurde arg verwundet, beschädigt; der Schuss* (i.e. a non-personal subject) *hat ihn arg verwundet* (but not in translating 'I wounded him badly'). On the other hand the active voice is used with verbs which do not imply one clear act (e.g. *ich habe ihn arg zugerichtet*). With intransitive verbs: *er lügt sehr arg, er hat arg gelitten* (a state).

Since *arg* suggests something large, it is more used as an adverb with such verbs as *verwundent, beschädigt*, than with, e.g., *gebissen*.

In some regions *arg* is used in any combination: *der Hand hat mich arg gebissen, er singt sehr arg.*[1]

The following are examples of the use of *arg* in standard German:

Er hat arge Kopfschmerzen.
Die Schmerzen sind heute sehr arg.
Es besteht ein arger Mangel an Nahrungsmitteln.
Sie haben sehr arge Fehler gemacht.
Das war ein arges Mißverständnis.
Die Niederlage war arg.
Das ist doch zu arg (that's the limit).
Er hat mit seinen Planungsversuchen arge Verwirrung angerichtet.
Die Kälte, die Hitze, ist heute sehr arg.
Er ist ein arger Säufer (*schwer* is, however, more common).
Er wurde arg geprügelt.
Das Buch ist arg zerlesen.
Man hat ihm arg mitgespielt.
Man hat ihm arg zugerichtet.
Das hat uns arg durcheinandergebracht.
Wir haben uns arg in ihm getäuscht.
Der Sturm hat das Haus arg beschädigt.
Ich wünsche ihnen des Ärgste.

4. Übel expresses an emotional dislike; particularly with reference to what is offensive to the senses, but mostly points to no objective characteristic on the person or thing that is rejected. In a few cases it does, however, vaguely suggest unsavouriness in a criminal sense (e.g. *ein übler Patron, Geselle*). 'Nasty'[2] is often a more appropriate English equivalent than 'bad'.

Since it makes no objective statement, its range of application is almost unlimited (both adjectivally and adverbially).

Nicht übel is used like 'not bad' in the sense of 'pretty good'.

Übel corresponds to 'evil' only in the colloquial use of the latter, i.e. in the normal sense of *übel* as described above. Its range of application in an objective sense was greater in earlier German.

Ein übler Bursche, ein übles Buch, ein übler Geschmack, üble Nachrichten.
Das Ergebnis war ganz übel.
Der Film war garnicht übel.

---

[1] The following use of *arg* in Goethe's *Werthers Leiden* is old-fashioned: *das ist die Sünde, die ich ärger hasse am Menschen als alle andere.*
[2] *Garstig*, nasty, is applied only to what is offensive to the senses.

Er ist übel daran.

Mir wurde übel dabei.

Ich gönne ihm Übles.

5. Böse translates both 'wicked' and 'evil' in a moral sense. It is also used of ills that afflict one. When applied (attributively) to a sore part of the body it is stronger than *schlimm* and suggests inflammation. Of illness it means 'malignant' (cf. *bösartig*). In all uses it is highly active in its literal sense of 'doing harm', or at least 'willing harm', and in some transferred senses (e.g. menacing).

Ein böser Mensch, Charakter.

Der Böse (the devil).

Eine böse Zunge, eine böse Tat, ein böser Lügner, böse Gedanken, ein böser Einfluß, böse Absichten, ein böses Gewissen, eine böse Krankheit, böse Nachrichten, böse Tage, böse Zeiten, ein böser Finger, ein böses Auge.

6. The adverb.

Owing to the restricted adverbial use of *schlimm* and *arg* other terms must be used. Recourse must often be had to the much used word *schwer* (grievously, gravely, seriously, severely), which, however, is somewhat stronger and more precise than 'badly' (e.g. *er ist schwer operiert worden* = he has had a bad operation; *er ist schwer gestürzt* = he fell badly). Some of the terms in common use are somewhat colloquial. *Tüchtig* so used verges on the conversational. Examples: *Der Wind hat mich tüchtig zerzaust.* See footnote to 'severe' (p. 305, n. 5). Another term: *er ist in seinem Examen glatt durchgefallen.*

BANISH 1. The term is now obsolete in the earlier sense of to proclaim to be an outlaw (*S.O.D.*) (which in G. is *ächten*). In modern E. the sense of to force someone to leave a country, whether his own or any other, has an old-fashioned flavour about it, and equally so in G. **bannen**, the original term in this sense; and also the later **verbannen.** In their place **des Landes verweisen, ausweisen** and similar expressions (sometimes **ausschließen**) are now used; 'expel' in English. *Verweisen* alone means 'to show someone the door'.

Er wurde aus politischen Gründen verbannt (referring to earlier times).

Er wurde des Landes verwiesen.

Er wurde aus Russland ausgewiesen.

Ausländer müssen immer damit rechnen, ausgewiesen zu werden, wenn sie gegen die Gesetze des Gastlandes verstoßen.

2. (a) One can, however, be banished from a more restricted place than a whole country. Also one can banish someone or something from his or her former place in a system of thought. In these senses *verbannen* is again old-fashioned. **Ausschließen** is more normal.

Er wurde vom Hof ausgeschlossen (verwiesen, verbannt).

Newtons kosmische Theorie schließt Gott nicht aus dem Weltall aus (verbannt ...nicht) (W.S.).

Plato wollte die Dichtkunst aus seiner Republik bannen, weil sie ihre Opfer berauschen könne (W.S.) (exalted language).

(b) In more modern idiom: **Verbieten.**

Der Militärkommandant verbot den Journalisten die eroberte Stadt.

Ihr wurde das Betreten der Werkstatt verboten.

3. To clear away, dissipate, dispel (*W*.) particularly feelings, thoughts. **Bannen** may be used, but as in the literal sense, is either somewhat old-fashioned, or exalted in tone. It implies the exorcising of something (an evil), or the casting of a spell over someone. The following examples show more modern terms.

> *Er verscheuchte* (put away) *von dem Augenblick an alle Sorgen, alle Furcht.*
>
> *Sie müssen Furcht und Angst vermeiden* (a doctor would say to a patient).
>
> *Narkose hat viel dazu beigetragen, die Angst vor Operationen zu bannen (beseitigen).*
>
> *Er bannte (leiß...fallen, löste sich von) alle deprimierenden Gedanken.*

BE, THERE IS, ARE etc. A.

(a) Since the verb *sein* emphasizes rest, inactivity, changelessness G. often prefers some other term. This preference is seen clearly in the use of **werden,** not only to form the passive voice, but in such a sentence as: *er ist gestern fünfzig geworden,* for which E. can say 'turned fifty' but just as often says 'was fifty'. The philosophical concepts of *Das Seiende* and *Das Werdende* make the meaning of the two terms abundantly clear.

(b) But G. often prefers some more specific verb to *sein* even when it does not want to express the above opposition, in particular avoiding *ist* in final position in a subordinate clause. Instead, it makes liberal use of such verbs as **sich befinden** (distinguish from **sich finden,** which means to find oneself, to be found), **bestehen** (exist), **stehen, liegen, hängen.**

> *Ich wußte nicht, daß ein Haus sich hier befindet* (*steht*) (*ist* is of course not impossible).
>
> *Der Wagen steht an der Ecke.*
>
> *An der ganzen Straße entlang stehen Bäume.*
>
> *Die Goethe-Ausgabe steht in meinem Bücherschrank.*
>
> *Paris liegt an der Seine* (typically in the sense of to be situated).
>
> *Die Briefe lagen ungeöffnet auf dem Tisch.*
>
> *Die Handtücher hängen über der Stuhllehne.*
>
> *Wolken hingen den ganzen Tag über der Stadt.*
>
> *Es bestehen Zweifel darüber, ob es ihm damit ernst ist.*
>
> *Es besteht die Möglichkeit, daß eine Finanzkrise vor Ende des Jahres ausbricht.*

(c) The verbs *stehen* and *liegen* as substitutes for *sein* are not confined to their literal use as in the above examples. In non-literal use, however, they appear mostly in fixed phrases.

> *Es steht in der Zeitung.*
>
> *Es steht geschrieben, daß...*
>
> *Es steht zu erwarten, daß* (the probabilities are that...) (distinguish from *es ist zu erwarten,* it has to be expected).
>
> *Das liegt nicht in meiner Absicht.*
>
> *Das lag mir fern* (was far from my thoughts).

(d) Though *sein* occurs in the sense of happen, take place, come about (*wann wird es sein?*) more common are **stattfinden, vor sich gehen, geschehen** and the like.

> *Die Hochzeit fand Anfang Mai statt.*
>
> *Wann findet die kleine Feier statt?*

(e) To be about, i.e. a question of: *es handelt sich um...*

Worum handelt es sich?

Bei seinen Forschungen handelt es sich immer um Detailarbeit.

(f) **Vorhanden sein.** This is merely a weightier term for *da sein* (to be there, to be present, of things, not of persons). It can only mean available when the context gives it this meaning.

Wie viele Exemplare des Buches sind vorhanden (still there)?

Genug Vorräte für den Winter sind vorhanden (the sense of available is suggested by the context).

Alle Elemente eines politischen Dramas sind vorhanden (are present).

Eine Bereitschaft zur Zusammenarbeit ist vorhanden.

(g) **Vorliegen** means to lie before one for some action, decision or judgment to be taken. At times it comes close to: *es handelt sich um*, 'it is a case of'.

Dem Minister lag der Vertrag zur Unterzeichnung vor.

Es liegt Mord vor.

Hier liegt folgender Tatbestand vor.

Hier liegt nichts vor.

Nach vorliegenden Informationen (because of the context: available).

THERE IS, THERE ARE B.

Some of the substitutes for *sein* listed above may be used also in this combination (see particularly *bestehen*). This section, however, sets out to define the distinction between *es ist* and *es gibt*. The explanation often given that *es gibt* is used in a generalization (e.g. *es gibt Menschen, die Musik nicht gerne hören*) and *es ist* refers to the individual and requires to be followed in the predicate by a statement denoting place is not adequate. Perhaps the most helpful explanation of *es gibt* is, roughly speaking, that it means: nature produces, i.e. that a person or thing exists in a natural and inevitable way. The following example should make this clear.

Es gibt Karpfen in diesem Teich (it is their natural habitat).

Es sind Karpfen in diesem Teich (not necessarily, perhaps put there accidentally).

Again, while *es ist* is static, *es gibt* suggests activity, movement, change.

Es wird eine Rauferei geben (a brawl—otherwise *wird stattfinden*).

Es gibt Gesetze, die die Rechtssprechung in Verruf bringen.

Auf dieser Reise hat es Tage gegeben (or: *waren Tage*, according to the point of view), *an die ich mich immer erinnern werde.*

Was gibt es Neues? (what's the news? i.e. what is happening?).

Es gibt Gründe für dieses Vorgehen, über die man sich klar werden sollte (or: *es sinde Gründe...da...*).

Es gibt heute noch vieles zu tun, i.e. has to be done, one of the meanings of *sein* followed by the infinitive with *zu*.

Es gibt viele Streiks in der Stahlindustrie (violent action).

Nevertheless, one finds the verb *sein* coupled with nouns expressing action where one would normally expect *es gibt*.

Das war unsere Lebensweise, als Krieg war.

But: *In zwei Jahren gibt es Krieg, wenn solche Grenzzwischenfälle sich häufen.*

BEAR   Sense: to sustain, endure.

1. Tragen is 'to bear' in a general way anything conceived as a burden, to accept it. A strain on the feelings is not necessarily implied. The object

BEAR

generally denotes in itself a burden. *Tragen* is therefore inapplicable in a sentence such as: I cannot bear his voice. In older German it was sometimes used in the sense of *ertragen*.

Sie müssen die Verantwortung dafür tragen.
Die Transportkosten müssen von Ihnen getragen werden.
Sie trug ihr Schicksal ohne zu klagen.
Er hat den Verlust zu tragen (financially).
'*Er trug ihre Unarten mit Geduld*' (Goethe, *Das Märchen*) (only *ertragen* is possible in ordinary present-day prose).

2. Ertragen stresses the patience and perseverance with which particularly trying evils are borne. Its object need not in itself denote a burden.

Er ertrug seine Leiden, seinen Verlust, sein Schicksal, sehr tapfer.
Ich konnte seine Stimme, die Hitze, nicht länger ertragen.

3. Vertragen means 'to be able to bear', to take, a thing, because it is compatible with one's physical, mental or emotional constitution. It suggests less ability to bear a thing at any particular moment than as a general characteristic of one's make-up.[1]

Er verträgt keine Kritik.
Nicht alle Wahrheiten vertragen eine objektive Analyse.
Er verträgt keinen Spass.
Er verträgt keinen Wind auf das rechte Auge.

BEAT, THRASH **Prügeln** means in the first place 'to administer corporal punishment' with a stick or a cane, then with one's hands, fists, and the like. Reflexively, it means 'to fight', particularly of boys. **Verprügeln** draws attention to the result, i.e. the damage.

Der Vater prügelte seinen Sohn.
Er verprügelte ihn nach Strich und Faden.
Sie haben sich geprügelt.
Sie haben sich schrecklich verprügelt.

BEFORE (conjunctive) **Bevor** is the general term. **Ehe** should only be used to express emotional participation, often with a sense of urgency which suggests that the moment for action is fast passing, or as a warning.[2]

Bevor wir landeten, wurde unser Gepäck von einem Zollbeamten durchsucht.
Ehe er es verhindern konnte, war er gefangen.

BEHAVE, BEHAVIOUR, CONDUCT[3] None of the German terms has as wide a range of application as 'behave' and 'behaviour', which can be used of persons, animals, and things. In reference to persons it can, e.g., be conscious or unconscious, instinctive or volitional or the result of training. It is used of persons and animals as a psychological, of substances as a scientific term.

1. Benehmen and the verb *sich benehmen* refer to the behaviour of

---

[1] *Vertragen* often needs to be translated by other English terms. See article on 'take'. *Mein Magen verträgt keine Pfannengerichte* (fried foods do not agree with me). See 'agree'. *Sich mit jemandem vertragen*: to get on with a person.
[2] In conversation both *bevor* and *ehe* are often avoided and replaced by other suitable conjunctions, e.g. *als*, followed by *schon* in the next clause. *Als sie heraufkam, hatte sie schon sauber gemacht.*
[3] Deportment, bearing, i.e. as a result of discipline, is *Haltung*. See further under 'attitude'.

40

individuals considered as free human beings in society. In so far as a standard is implied, it is that of common human decency or of good manners in society. (*Er hat kein Benehmen* =he has no manners.) Since the reference to the individual human being is so strong, these terms are not applied to large units (e.g. a country) or to official behaviour.

Sein Benehmen ist gut, schlecht, höflich, haarsträubend.
Sein Benehmen läßt viel zu wünschen übrig.
Er hat sich mir gegenüber sehr freundlich benommen.
Der Kerl benimmt sich sehr komisch.

2. Betragen and the verb *sich betragen* refer to special codes, rules, and prescriptions in much the same way as 'conduct'. Like the latter they carry a strong implication of moral responsibility and therefore of consciousness of one's acts. They can therefore only be applied to human beings.

Der Junge hat sich in der Schule schlecht betragen.
Er betrug sich nicht wie ein Offizier.

3. Sich aufführen, accompanied by an adverb of manner, refers to the impression one makes, the figure one cuts, in doing a thing. It suggests something unusual and has a subjective connotation. It requires some more expressive adverb than *gut*.

Er hat sich blödsinnig, tadellos, aufgeführt.
Die Soldaten haben sich schlecht aufgeführt.

4. Verhalten and the verb *sich verhalten* can denote conscious or unconscious behaviour under given conditions. It is therefore used as a psychological term in reference to individuals or animals, a scientific term when applied to substances (i.e. in the sense of 'reaction'). It is also the appropriate term when the element stressed in behaviour is the taking of an attitude[1] (e.g. in relation to a country, a government).

Unter diesen Bedingungen verhält sich der Mensch ganz passiv.
Rußlands Verhalten in der Angelegenheit war unverständlich.

BELIEF 1. Both **Glaube** and 'belief' can refer to (*a*) trust in a person, in God, in a thing; (*b*) mental, and partly emotional acceptance of a thing as true; (*c*) the thing believed, i.e. the content of the action or state of belief. 'Belief' is, however, a wider term than *Glaube*. The latter implies more complete acceptance and a greater absence of evidence based on the senses and on reason that 'belief' necessarily does. This becomes particularly clear when it is followed by a *daß* clause (particularly in the expression *im Glauben, daß...*). A higher degree of credulity is implied than is always implied by 'belief'. *Glaube* thus approaches the absoluteness of faith. Like 'faith' it admits no plural.[2,3]

Mein Glaube an ihn, an Gott, an die Güte der menschlichen Natur, ist
  unerschütterlich, ist erschüttert.
Sein Glaube, daß Gott ihm helfen würde, hat ihn nie verlassen.
Sein Glaube, daß alle gegen ihn sind, ist typisch für seinen jetzigen Geistes-
  zustand.
Er handelte im Glauben, daß er mir damit helfen würde.

---

[1] For a fuller explanation of *Verhalten* see 'attitude'.
[2] *Glauben* as a verb does not exclude the examination of evidence. See article on 'think'.
[3] In the English equivalents of phrases such as *im guten Glauben, auf Treu und Glauben,* 'faith' is also used.

Das ist mein Glaube.
Er ist bereit, für seinen Glauben zu kämpfen.

2. When 'belief' is a close synonym of 'opinion', 'conviction', 'supposition', and the like, i.e. when it implies limited credence or does not exclude recourse to evidence, it must be translated by terms such as *Meinung*, *Überzeugung*, *Annahme*. Similarly, it must be rendered by *Vertrauen* in the sense of 'trust in a person' when some consideration by the mind, particularly in the form of doubts, is implied. See article on 'trust'.

Ich neige zu der Ansicht, daß die Aufgabe unsere Kräfte übersteigt.
Es ist meine Überzeugung, daß ein dritter Weltkrieg nicht unvermeidlich ist.
Seine Annahme, daß die verschärften Maßnahmen ruhig hingenommen
  würden, erweis sich als falsch.
So viel ich weiß, hat er das Angebot angenommen.

BELONG 1. Gehören (plus dative) denotes possession.
Das Buch gehört der Staatsbibliothek.
Der Hut gehört mir.
Neu-Kaledonien gehört Frankreich.

2. Angehören: to be a member of society or to be a unit in a group.
Er gehört einem Musikverein an.
Welchem Jahrhundert gehört Klopstock an?
Dieses Buch gehört meiner Bibliothek an.
Er gehört dem Jahrgang 1920 an.

3. Gehören (plus *zu*) approximates to *angehören* in the sense of 'to be a part of', but means a necessary, integral part of a whole.[1]
Der Teil (des Buches) gehört zum Ganzen.
Dieses Glas gehört zu meiner Uhr.
Die Worte gehören zu diesem Lied.
Elsaß gehört jetzt zu Frankreich.
Die baltischen Staaten gehören zur russischen Interessensphäre (also *angehören*
  in the sense of being a member).

4. Gehören (plus *in*) is used to indicate the place where a person or a thing belongs, its proper place, and, in extended use, the category in which he or it is to be classified. It may be followed in the same way by other prepositions (e.g. *auf*, *unter*, *vor*).
Dieses Buch gehört in die Staatsbibliothek.
Er gehört in diese Menschenklasse.
Er gehört ins Museum.

BEND, BOW, STOOP, INCLINE 1. Biegen: to bend an object in any direction. Intransitively, it is applied to an object that changes its direction (e.g. a road). It draws attention to the curve or angle.
Er bog den Draht, das Eisen.
Der Nagel ist gebogen.
Der Mast, der Zweig, biegt sich im Winde.
Main Arm ist so steif, daß ich ihn nicht biegen kann.
Er saß mit gebogenem Rücken da.
Die Straße biegt hier nach rechts (ab).

---

[1] *Gehören zu* is also used in the sense of 'to be one of'. *Er gehört zu den Besten in der Klasse.* It is also used in the sense of 'to be required for'. *Es gehört Mut dazu.*

2. Bücken is the general term for 'to stoop' or 'to bend down or over'. It is mostly reflexive and conveys implications such as stooping to pick something up or to pass through a low opening. The past participle is also used in the sense of 'stooped', both literally and figuratively (i.e. by age, cares, or the like).

Er bückte sich, um einen Bleistift aufzuheben, um in den Wagen einzusteigen, um vom feindlichen Feuer nicht getroffen zu werden.
Er ist vom Alter, Kummer, gebückt (bent, stooped).

3. Beugen means 'to bend downwards', generally through the effect of something weighty (literally and figuratively). Reverence or submission may be implied. It thus translates 'to bow' or 'to bend' some part of the body as an expression of an emotional attitude. Reflexively, it means 'to bow' in the sense of 'to submit' to some greater power, but not as a salutation.

Der Zweig war unter der Last der Früchte gebeugt (bent downwards; *gebogen* would merely emphasize that it was not straight, and would not necessarily suggest weight).
Er beugte das Haupt, als er die traurige Nachricht vernahm.
Er ist von Kummer tief gebeugt.
Er geht vom Alter gebeugt.
Er muß sich vor dem Schicksal beugen.

4. Verbeugen is only used reflexively and is the general term for to 'bow' as a salutation.[1]

Er verbeugte sich, als er vorgestellt wurde.

5. Neigen suggests, applied to persons, liking or favour or a sign of understanding; applied to things, a weight, which is, however, less heavy than in the case of *beugen*, i.e. 'to incline'.[2]

'Neige, neige, Du Schmerzensreiche | Dein Antlitz gnädig meiner Not.' (Goethe's *Faust*.)

Sich verneigen means 'to bow' as a salutation, but is a less general term than *sich verbeugen*, and suggests ceremony. *Sich neigen* in the sense of a salutation does not suggest a deep bow.

Sie neigte das Haupt, um ihm ihre Huld zu bezeigen.
Die Bäume neigten ihre Äste.
Er neigte sich vor dem Fremden.
Er verneigte sich auf galante Art.

BLAME,[3] **CENSURE 1.** To judge a person or thing as deserving condemnation. This sense implies that the question of who or what is responsible for an act or state of affairs is already settled, and that the only issue is whether this deserves condemnation.

(a) **Tadeln** means 'to censure', i.e. 'to pronounce an adverse judgment on' (*S.O.D.*). It can only translate 'blame' in contexts which do not imply the actual utterance of such a judgment, i.e. in those which are concerned with the question of whether one should pronounce a judgment of censure (e.g. in

---

[1] *Knicksen*: to curtsy.

[2] *Neigen* is used in general of anything that inclines or declines gradually. *Die Strasse neigt sich hier zur Stadt* (slopes).

[3] *Blamieren*, a much used term in conversation, mainly reflexive, does not mean 'to blame', but 'to put in the wrong', often in such a way that one feels small or foolish before others. *Er hat sich gewaltig blamiert. Er möchte sich nicht blamieren.* Similarly the noun: *das war eine furchtbare Blamage.*

combination with *nicht können*). In all its uses *tadeln* is sharper than 'blame'.

Ich tadelte ihn wegen seines Leichtsinns.

Ich kann ihn nicht wegen des Unfalls tadeln (the accident was caused by him, but the circumstances were not such as to justify my speaking words of censure; i.e. I cannot blame him for...).

Er ist wegen des Fiaskos nicht zu tadeln.

(b) **Jemandem einen Vorwurf machen aus.** This expression is the closest equivalent to the sense of 'blame' defined in 1. It occurs mainly in negative use. *Vorwurf* in this combination does not necessarily imply a spoken reproach.

Ich kann ihm aus dem Unfall keinen Vorwurf machen.

Ich machte ihm keinen Vorwurf aus dem, was er tat.

Ich habe mir nichts vorzuwerfen (I have nothing to blame myself for.).

(c) **Übelnehmen, verübeln, verargen.** These terms used with *nicht können* suggest a measure of understanding for what has been done.

Man kann es ihr nicht verübeln, daß sie ihn verließ.

2. To fix the responsibility for something done, to put the blame on the proper shoulders. Here it is a question of determining who or what has caused something of which one disapproves.

(a) **Verantwortlich machen für.** This phrase often tends to suggest an interest in compensation.

Ich kann ihn für den Unfall nicht verantwortlich machen (someone or something else caused it).

Sie müssen das Wetter, nicht mich dafür verantwortlich machen.

(b) **Die Schuld geben:** to assign responsibility.

Er gab mir die Schuld an dem Fiasko.

(c) **Schuld sein an:** to be to blame for. In accusing directly (i.e. in the second person) the person judged responsible this expression is often preferable to *verantwortlich machen*, since the latter emphasizes too much the position of the accuser.

Sie sind schuld an dem Unfall (you are to blame...; I blame you...).

BLIND, DAZZLE 1. **Blind machen** is generally used in the figurative sense of robbing a person of control over his emotions, thoughts, actions, but not in the senses described under *blenden* and *verblenden*. Its use in the literal sense, which is rare, and somewhat slovenly can only denote a process, i.e. not a sudden action.

Die Leidenschaft hat ihn blind gemacht.

Seine Interessen machten ihn den Tatsachen gegenüber blind.

2. **Blenden:** to dazzle through the eye, both literally and figuratively. 'Blind' used as an equivalent of 'dazzle' is similarly translated. Further, it means 'to blind deliberately' in the literal sense.

Die Sonne blendet mich

Von dem Aufwand des Festes geblendet, gab er dem Geschäftsinhaber weiteren Kredit.

Die Gestapoagenten blendeten ihre Opfer.

3. **Verblenden:** to blind or dazzle by putting into a trance-like state approaching madness. Romantic characters are often portrayed as being in the grip of such states.

Von den Gewinnaussichten verblendet, stürzte er sich in ein Geschäft, das nie und nimmer gut gehen konnte.

Verblendet folgte er seinem Schicksal bis ans Ende.

4. Erblinden is an intransitive verb which means 'to go blind'. Sentences, in which 'blind' is used transitively, are best turned by this verb or *blind werden* (see *blind machen* under **1**).

Er ist als Folge der Explosion erblindet, blind geworden.

BLOCK This article deals with 'block' only in so far as it is translated by *sperren* and *versperren*.

1. Sperren is 'to block', literally and figuratively, by official action. It is often rendered into English by 'shut'[1] or 'stop'.

Die Straße ist gesperrt (by a chain, rope, or the like).

Mein Bankkonto is gesperrt.

2. Versperren: to block the passage of a person by standing or placing an obstacle in front of him or by an obstacle placed there without human agency: also to block a view.

Ich stand vor ihm und versperrte ihm auf diese Weise den Durchgang.

Die Straße ist durch Felsblöcke versperrt.

Die Bäume versperren uns die Aussicht.

BODY Körper: 'body' as opposed to 'mind'. It therefore refers to matter and is applied as an anatomical term to the body of living beings, also to any thing considered as an entity (e.g. a planet). In further use it suggests a visible surface and shape. Therefore: *Körperpflege; körperliche Züchtigung; ein schöner, verwachsenser, Körper.* It excludes any implication of human feelings, sentiments and life in its non-physical aspects. It is **Leib** which conveys this suggestion and is conceived as the vessel of the soul. Being informed with the latter, it is used in the expression *der Leib des Herrn.* Further, in such compounds as *Leibarzt, Leibgarde, Leibstandarte,* which stress life in its human rather than its physiological aspect. *Leib,* however, is sometimes used vaguely in a physiological sense, particularly in the phrase *am ganzen Leibe* (= all over).[2] *Er zitterte, schwitzte, am ganzen Leibe.* Where, on the other hand, the reference is to something visible on the surface, *Körper* is the correct term. *Er hat rote Flecken am ganzen Körper. Er ist wund am ganzen Körper.*

A 'dead body' must be translated by *Leiche* (see 'corpse').

BOTHER, TROUBLE, CONCERN ONESELF ABOUT, LOOK AFTER, SEE TO These terms are treated only as far as they are translated by the two German words discussed in this article.

Kümmern is in present-day German used almost exclusively as a reflexive verb, and means 'to do something' for a person or about a thing. **Bekümmern** is not limited to reflexive use. When used reflexively, it implies activity like *kümmern,* but suggests more feeling and is therefore stronger. In non-reflexive use it means 'to trouble', 'to distress', 'to concern'.

Sie müssen sich ein bißchen um ihn kümmern.

---

[1] *Sperren* can also mean 'to close' or 'to shut' a building or the like, officially or unofficially and 'to lock' a person or thing in a place. To lock up, i.e. imprison: *einsperren.*

[2] Similarly in phrases not translated by 'body': *eine Wut im Leibe haben; etwas am eigenen Leibe spüren. Leib* forms numerous fixed phrases.

BOTHER

Er hat sich in rührender Weise um seinen jüngeren Bruder gekümmert.
Kümmere dich darum, daß die beiden Briefe morgen auf die Post kommen.
Sie gingen nach Hause, ohne daß sich jemand um das Boot kümmerte.
Sein Schicksal bekümmert mich.
'*Seit er in Dresden in den Gemälden der Galerie schwelgte, beneidet er jeden*
Künstler, den kein Zweifel um das Wahre, das sich nirgends findet,
bekümmere, sondern der im Glauben an die Idealwelt des Schönen lebe'
(J. Petersen on Kleist, *Aus der Goethezeit*).

BOTTOM   Sense: the lowest part of anything (inside or outside).

1. Grund; Boden (see also under 'ground' for these terms). When these
terms are not interchangeable, the distinction is generally that *Grund* is
conceived as the base on which a structure rests, *Boden* as a surface. *Grund*
also suggests depth, for which reason it also appears poetically in the meaning
of *Tal*. The bottom of the sea = *Meeresgrund* and also *Meeresboden*. The
bottom of a container (*Tasse, Fass, Glas, Kiste, Beutel*) is generally *Boden*,
although *Grund* sometimes has this sense, suggesting, as pointed out above,
depth. *Im Herzensgrunde* (at the bottom of my heart, but also *aus tiefstem
Herzen*).

2. Fuss is used, particularly with natural objects, where one does not see a
surface but only sides of this as they meet the ground.
Am Fuße eines Berges, einer Mauer, einer Pyramide, einer Leiter.

3. Unten: below, at the bottom. Used particularly with a propositional phrase.
Er stand unten an der Leiter, an der Mauer.
Er kletterte schnell nach unten (to the bottom).
Unten im Koffer.
Die Anspielung findet sich unten auf Seite fünf.
Sein Name steht unten auf der Liste (also: *am Ende...*).

BOX, BAG   See also **CASE.**
Special uses of these words, particularly in compounds, are given in the
dictionaries. The sense of 'box' treated here is, as given by *W.*, a rigid
typically rectangular receptacle often with a lid or cover, in which something
non-liquid is kept or carried. That of 'bag' (*W.*): a container, made of paper,
cloth, mesh, metal, foil, plastic or other flexible material and usually closed on
all sides except for an opening, that may be closed (as by folding, fastening,
tying or sewing) being of sizes ranging from small to very large and
being specially designed for properly holding, storing, carrying, shipping
or distributing any material or products.
The German terms all have an interesting history and at some point in this
have developed additional meanings or passed from an earlier meaning to
that treated in this article.

1. The commonest equivalents of 'box' are: **Kasten, Kiste, Schachtel,
Karton.** *Kasten* is the most general term, but in careful use is applied to a
box which shows finished workmanship while *Kiste* is roughly made and
normally of wood, as *Packkiste* = packing case. *Schachtel* is made generally
of cardboard or thin wood, but also designed to take specific objects put into
it. *Karton* corresponds to E. (and F.) 'carton'. In upper German regions
Kasten is used in the sense of *Schrank* (e.g. *Kleiderkasten*). For a well-made
small box the diminutive *Kästchen* is used.

Geldkasten (or *Kasse*), *Briefkasten*.
Schmuckkästchen.
Schicken Sie Ihre Bücher in einer großen Holzkiste ab.
Eine Schachtel Streichhölzer, eine Schachtel für Schuhe, eine Schachtel Zigaretten (more often 'packet' in E.), *eine Schachtel Pralinen.*
Die Milchflaschen kamen in einem Karton an.

2. The commonest equivalents of 'bag' are: **Koffer, Truhe, Sack, Säckel, Beutel, Tasche, Tüte.** *Koffer,* for which E. would more often use 'case', is meant for carrying clothes and the like when travelling. *Truhe* is large and corresponds more exactly to what in E. is called 'trunk'. *Beutel* suggests a pouch as in *Beuteltiere,* but is also used for anything resembling this, as *Geldbeutel* and also a bag in which items of food are carried. **Sack** is a large bag made typically of hessian. *Säckel,* again, is a purse. **Tasche,** originally wages, i.e. what was carried in a bag, came to mean the bag itself (see Trübner and Kluge). In North German it means 'pocket', for which in Upper German *Sack* is used. But in the North it can also mean a bag detached from clothes and carried in the hand or over the back, typically a mail-bag, in which the postman carries letters etc. *Tasche* also means a brief-case. In the sense of purse, *Geldtasche* has largely yielded to the French **porte-monnaie** (see Trübner). *Tasche* alone is used in certain expressions in the sense of 'purse'.

BOY[1] The German terms rarely refer to a male adult.

1. Knabe is applied to a boy up to the age of puberty. In poetry it can denote a youth (normally *Jüngling*). It is an objective, not a familiar term. It is occasionally used somewhat ironically to refer to an adult, generally by a still older man. Used otherwise it has a suggestion of the poetical.
Sie haben zwei Knaben und drei Mädchen.
Er ist kaum den Knabenjahren entwachsen.
Eine Knabenschule.
Ist der Knabe Schmidt wieder hier gewesen? (ironically).
'...*jetzt kam Tell mit seinem Knaben über den Platz gegangen*' (G. Keller, *Der Grüne Heinrich*).

2. Junge may be used up to the age of seventeen or eighteen. It is a more familiar term than *Knabe* and may also mean 'son'. In the plural (the form without '*s*') it can mean 'sons' up to the age of twenty-two or twenty-three. *Die blauen Jungs*[2] refers to sailors. In compounds it denotes a boy who performs menial tasks.
Er ist ein netter Junge.
Mein Junge, du mußt fleißiger arbeiten!
Seine beiden Jungen sind im Kriege gefallen.

BRAIN Gehirn is a more dignified expression than **Hirn** and is the usual term in the sense of 'mind'. The latter is used particularly of animals, in compounds, and with a derogatory connotation. Many idiomatic expressions formed with 'brain' are translated by other terms.

---

[1] *Bube* is a 'lad' in so far as he is inclined to mischievous tricks. In southern regions *Bub*' is often used simply for *Knabe*. *Bursche* excludes childhood, and suggests vigour and an enterprising spirit. See also under 'fellow', 'chap'.
[2] In parts of northern Germany (e.g. in the Hanseatic towns) *die Jungs* has the meaning of 'the kids'.

BRAIN

Das Gehirn des Menschen wiegt so und so viel.
Sein Gehirn arbeitete sehr schnell.
Wir haben Schafhirn gegessen.
Er ist hirnverbrannt.

BREAK A. Literal.

1. *Brechen* and its compounds are used only of solid objects.[1]

(a) **Brechen,** transitive and intransitive, is applied to clean breaks, division into parts, fractures of parts of the body.

Er hat sich das Bein, den Arm, den Hals, gebrochen.
Die Mutter brach die Schokolade in drei Stücke und gab den Kindern je eines.
Er brach das Eis (also figuratively).
Er brach das Siegel.
Der Wind hat den Ast gebrochen.
Das Brett, der Zweig, brach, als zu viele Menschen sich darauf setzten.
Der Wind war so stark, daß der Mast brach.

(b) **Zerbrechen,** transitive and intransitive, means 'to break into two or more pieces' (i.e. smash into fragments) in such a way that the object becomes useless. Similarly **zerschlagen** (only transitive).

Ich habe das Glas zerbrochen, als ich die Uhr abnahm.
Ich ließ das Bild fallen und dabei zerbrach das Glas.
Er hat die Fensterscheibe zerschlagen.

(c) **Abbrechen** should be used when the breaking off of a tip or a small part of a thing is implied.[2] The object may be the thing broken, not merely the part broken off.

Ich habe meinen Bleistift, mir den Zahn, den Schlüssel, den Rand des Tellers,
  abgebrochen.

2. *Reißen* and its compounds are applied to non-solid objects which can tear.

Reißen: (intransitive and passive with *sein*) 'have a tear', implies tension, to snap, therefore not with paper unless there is pressure from inside.

Zerreißen: (transitive and intransitive) to tear, to snap, into two or more pieces.

Das Papier, in das die Schuhe gewickelt sind, ist zerrissen.
Der Schnürriemen zerriß, riß, ist zerrissen, gerissen.
Der Film riß, zerriß, dauernd.
Das Seil ist gerissen, zerrissen.
Das Seil riß, zerriß. (The latter implies great force.)

3. Umknicken: to break anything pliable such as a plant.
Sie haben diese Pflanze umgeknickt, als Sie dagegen stießen.

4. Platzen: to burst from within.[3]
Ich habe so viel in die Tüte gesteckt, das sie geplatzt ist.
Das Wasserrohr, der Asphalt, is geplatzt.

---

[1] *Eine Blume brechen*: to pluck a flower.
[2] Other compounds of *brechen* are: *aufbrechen, erbrechen* (to break open); *sich erbrechen* (vomit); *einbrechen in* (to break, force one's way into a place); *durchbrechen* (inseparable: to penetrate a line; separable: to break a thing into two parts); *herausbrechen* (to knock a piece out; e.g. *ein Stück ist aus dem Glas herausgebrochen*); *losbrechen* (of a storm); *unterbrechen* (to interrupt; e.g. *die ununterbrochenen Ebenen Norddeutschlands*).
[3] *Platzen* is 'to explode from within', often with a detonation. *Bersten* is used mainly of large natural objects and is mostly poetical (e.g. *die geborstene Erde*).

5. Specific terms are: **aufschlagen:** to break an egg in order to fry it, etc.; **springen:** to break (of a spring), e.g. *die Feder ist gesprungen.*[1]

6. Kaputt, used mostly predicatively, means 'broken' in the vague, colloquial sense of the term, specially of machines and gadgets.

Der Federhalter, due Tür, ist kaputt.
Das Auto, Radio, Feuerzeug, ist kaputt.
Das Kind hat die Spielsachen kaputt gemacht.

B. Figurative. **Brechen** is used in the following ways:

(a) To violate one's plighted word.
Sein Versprechen, Wort, brechen.

(b) To vanquish, subdue opposition.
Jemandes Willen, Widerstand, brechen.

(c) To crush by misfortune.
Er ist ein gebrochener Mann.

(d) Of the heart.
Es hat sein Herz gebrochen.

(e) To end.
Das Schweigen, einen Zauber, brechen.

(f) To emerge (often with *hervor*).
Der Mond brach aus den Wolken hervor.

(g) To change.
Die Stimme bricht (from boyhood to adolescence).

BROAD, WIDE (literal sense)   The subtle distinctions which certain uses of the English words possess (though often obliterated in common speech) are not present in *breit* and *weit*, which are easily distinguishable from each other. See Fowler's explanation of 'broad' and 'wide' in *Modern English Usage.*

1. Breit is applied to the horizontal extent of a surface with regard to its length, whether (*a*) the exact measurement is stated, or (*b*) simply a large extent is meant. It translates in this sense both 'broad' and 'wide'. Its opposite is *schmal* (narrow).[2]

Die Gasse ist nur 5 Meter breit (broad or wide).
Eine breite Straße, einer breiter Fluß ('wide' draws attention to the limits, 'broad' concentrates attention on the surface itself and also makes an appeal to the eye).
Ein breites Gesicht, breite Schultern.

2. Weit corresponds to 'wide' in the sense of 'spacious', 'expansive', i.e. in all directions. As in the case of 'wide' one thinks of the remote limits more than of what lies between. Its opposite is *eng*, i.e. narrow in the sense of cramped, constricted on all sides, whereas *schmal* is narrow between two straight lines.[3]

Ein weiter Raum, eine weite Fläche, die weite Welt, ein weiter Abstand, eine weite Öffnung, ein weites Loch, weite Schuhe, Hosen, Ärmel, ein weit offenes Fenster.

---

[1] *Gesprungen* often means 'cracked' (of a glass, etc.).
[2] In figurative use *breit* means 'diffuse'.
[3] *Weit* also means 'far' in a relative sense (e.g. *wie weit ist die Stadt noch von hier?*). *Fern* is 'far' in an absolute sense. In a few phrases 'wide' means 'far' (e.g. *weitgefehlt*: wide of, far from, the mark).

BURN

BURN A. Brennen.

1. Intransitive.

(a) To be on fire, whether due to accident or design.

Das Haus, die Scheune, das Bettzeug, brennt.

(b) Of the means of heating and lighting.

Die Sonne, das Feuer, die Lampe, das Gas brennt.

2. Transitive.

(a) To use for fuel or to keep a lighting apparatus burning, i.e. with reference to the type, but not the quantity, of fuel used.

Wir brennen nur Holz in unserem Ofen.

Die ganze Nacht brennt sie ein Licht.

(b) To treat, to process, certain substances with fire (not to burn them up).

Kohlen, Lehm, Holz, Ziegel brennen.

(c) When an adverb or a prefix is used to indicate the result *brennen* must be used.

Das Haus wurde niedergebrannt (leergebrannt).

(d) Similarly to bring about by burning:

Ein Loch in das Brett, ein Zeichen in das Holz brennen.

B. Verbrennen.

1. To burn up, consume, destroy, incinerate.

(a) Of persons and things.

Im Mittelalter wurden Hexen verbrannt.

Die Abfälle müssen verbrannt werden.

Das Haus wurde vom Feinde verbrannt.

(b) In stating the amount, but not the type, of fuel, etc. burnt.

Wir verbrennen jede Woche 5 Säcke Holz.

2. To burn on the surface, an external agency as subject (contrast *brennen* **1** (b)).

Die Sonne, der heiße Teller, hat mich arg verbrannt.

3. To burn and injure a part of the body.

Ich habe mir den Finger verbrannt.

Ich bin gegen den Ofen gestolpert und habe mich verbrannt.

C. With reference to the spoiling of food **anbrennen** (to begin to burn, to catch fire; i.e. inceptive force) is much used, either intransitively or in the passive voice. The transitive use of 'burn' in this sense is translated by *anbrennen lassen*, or by otherwise turning the phrase so as to use *anbrennen* intransitively.

Die Suppe brennt an.

Die Suppe ist angebrannt.

Die Köchin ließ die Suppe anbrennen.

Passen Sie auf, daß die Suppe nicht anbrennt (be careful not to burn...).

BURY **1. Beerdigen** is the normal term for burying a person in the earth with proper funeral rites.

Er wurde am 15. Mai auf dem protestantischen Friedhof beerdigt.

2. Bestatten stresses the ceremonial of burial. It can be burial in any form, e.g. cremation, not necessarily consignment to the earth.

Er wurde in einem Mausoleum bestattet.

50

3. Beisetzen: to bury in a vault by the side of one's family or ancestor. Also: to bury at sea.

Er wurde in der Familiengruft beigesetzt.
Auf hoher See beigesetzt.

4. Begraben: to bury in a pit, sometimes without ceremony, and therefore of animals and objects as well as persons. With reference to objects it may mean 'to bury' under anything, often with a suggestion of disorderliness. Used figuratively it means 'to renounce'.

Er wurde bei lebendigem Leibe, lebendig, begraben.
Der Hund wurde im Garden begraben.
Ich fand das Buch unter einem Haufen alter Zeitungen begraben.
Wir haben das Kriegsbeil begraben.
Wir mußten unsere Hoffnungen begraben.

5. Vergraben is in present-day German often used in the figurative sense of hiding, withdrawing from view, often with the suggestion of immersing oneself in an occupation.

Sie vergrub ihr Gesicht in den Händen.
Nach dem Skandal mußte er sich zwei Jahre auf dem Lande vergraben.
Für 14 Tage vergrub er sich in seinem Arbeitszimmer.

6. Einscharren: to cover slightly or carelessly.

Der Hund scharrte den Knochen ein.

BUSINESS

1. Sense: buying and selling; commerce; trade (*A.L.*): **Geschäft,** in singular either an individual enterprise or a piece of business, transaction and the like. In plural, either individual enterprises or collective in the sense of various pieces of business.

Er hat ein gut gehendes Geschäft.
Er hat ein gutes Geschäft damit gemacht.
Die Geschäfte gehen flott.
Er ist ein Geschäftsmann.
Geschäftsadresse.
Sind Sie in London zum Vergnügen oder in Geschäften?

2. The place where one works and the work one does there: **Geschäft.**

Er muß jeden Samstag ins Geschäft gehen.

Often *Geschäft* means 'shop', an equivalent of *Laden*.

Er ist der Inhaber eines Obstgeschäfts.
Die Geschäfte schließen um 6 Uhr.

3. A piece of work that has to be done, not necessarily of a commercial kind, particularly an item on an agenda: **Geschäft:**

Wir haben heute die ganzen Geschäfte schnell erledigt.

4. Habitual occupation, profession, trade (*S.O.D.*). In this sense these terms are more common than business, which however does occur. **Beruf** is profession, but is also used apart from the professions, particularly in the sense of 'occupation' stated on a questionnaire asking for personal particulars. **Tätigkeit,** activity, is used particularly in questions.

Sein Beruf ist der Verkauf von Automobilen (A.L.).
Was für eine Tätigkeit übt er aus?

5. Sense: task, duty, province, what has to be done: **Pflicht** (duty), **Aufgabe** (task).

Es ist die Pflicht eines Lehrers, seinen Schülern zu helfen (A.L.).

Es ist die Aufgabe eines Soldaten, seine Heimat zu verteidigen, nicht sie zu regieren (A.L.).

6. (a) Concern, thing that interests one, that one may meddle with: **Angelegenheit,** what lies close to and so concerns one.

In welcher Angelegenheit kommen Sie? (what is your business?).

Sich handeln um (impersonal): to be a question of. **Angehen:** to concern (see 'concern'). **Sich kümmern um:** to bother about, concern oneself with, is often combined with *Angelegenheit* or *Sache.*

Um was handelt es sich?

Das geht Sie nichts an (that is none of your business).

Inwiefern geht es Sie an? (what business is it of yours?)

Kümmere dich um deine eigenen Angelegenheiten (mind your own business).

(b) Negatively, in the sense of 'right', particularly in the phrase 'to have no business to'.

Er hat kein Recht, solche Fragen zu stellen.

7. Sense: subject; matter; affair; happening; thing (often contemptuous) **Sache** (see 'thing').

Ich habe Ihren Streitereien den ganzen Nachmittag lang zugehört, die ganze Sache hängt mir schon zum Halse heraus (A.L.).

BUSY **1. Beschäftigt sein,**[1] **zu tun haben.** *Beschäftigt* is more intense and more specific than *zu tun haben* which is mostly used in reference to small matters which make it impossible for one to devote one's attention to other things. *Beschäftigt* can only be used predicatively after the verb *sein* and in reference to a person. *Vielbeschäftigt* may be used attributively before a noun standing for a person.

Ich kann Sie heute nicht sehen, ich habe zu tun.

Ich habe so viel zu tun, daß ich nicht ausgehen kann.

Der Kanzler ist mit Finanzfragen beschäftigt.

Er ist vielbeschäftigter Mann.

2. 'To keep busy' may be translated by the following phrases: *Zeit in Anspruch nehmen* (time element stressed); *zu schaffen machen* (cause trouble); *eine ziemliche Lauferei verursachen* (colloquial in the sense of 'to keep on the move').

Die vielen Sitzungen nehmen meine Zeit sehr stark in Anspruch. (In Anspruch nehmen with a personal object suggests: to take toll of.)

Die Beschaffung einer Einreiseerlaubnis nach Deutschland hat ihm viel zu schaffen gemacht.

Die Reisevorbereitungen haben mir eine ziemliche Lauferei verursacht.

3. In reference to places and periods of time specific terms must be used. *Belebt* is frequently applied to places.

Sie wohnen in einer sehr belebten Straße.

---

[1] *Geschäftig* is strictly speaking not 'busy', but suggests the fussiness of small folk. *Er hat eine außerordentlich geschäftige Art.* The verb *schaffen* (weak form) is used with indefinite pronoun objects such as *viel, nichts* in the sense of 'to get through' work. *Ich habe heute nichts, nicht sehr viel, geschafft.*

Ich habe einen gehetzten Tag hinter mir.
Am Donnerstag gibt es immer eine schreckliche Hetze (colloquial: Thursday is always a frightfully busy day).

CALCULATE, RECKON   Sense: to compute.

1. Rechnen means 'to perform a mathematical computation', and often states the result in numerical terms, this being the only possible type of object. The manner of calculation is not suggested.[1]

Er rechnet schnell.
Genau gerechnet, schulden Sie ihm 98 Mark.
Ich rechne 10 Mark für die Reisekosten.

2. Ausrechnen suggests a simple calculation on the basis of concrete material which one has before one.[2]

Ich habe noch nicht ausgerechnet, wieviel ich ihm schulde.
Ich habe mir schon ausgerechnet, wie viel ich verdienen würde, wenn ich meine Möbel verkaufe.
Ich rechne mir aus, daß wir noch 5 Kilometer gehen müssen. (On the basis of given facts, therefore, the sentence tends to express exactness of conclusion, whereas: *Ich rechne, daß wir noch*. . . expresses more a guess.)

3. Errechnen can suggest a new discovery by calculation, often by a stroke of genius. It sometimes implies that the method of arriving at the result is puzzling or mysterious. Again, it can present the result as a mere possibility.

Einstein hat errechnet, daß die Bahn des Lichts keiner graden Linie folgt.
Wie ist diese Zahl errechnet worden?
Er errechnete die Kurve der Rakete.

4. Berechnen differs from *rechnen* in having as its object the thing whose measurements or the like are to be calculated. In this it resembles *ausrechnen* and *errechnen*. It can be used in place of these, but without their special implications. It is the appropriate term whenever purpose or the adaptation of means to ends is stressed. In transferred use it is therefore applied to a person who is calculating by temperament.[3]

Ich werde den Umfang des Dreiecks berechnen.
Er berechnete die Kurve der Rakete.
Der Astronom berechnete den Abstand der Planeten voneinander.
Haben Sie auch berechnet, daß Sie neben den Anschaffungskosten noch erhebliche zusätzliche Ausgaben haben werden?
In der Kalkulationsabteilung werden die Herstellungskosten berechnet.
Er ist sehr berechnend.

CALL,[4] SUMMON, NAME   1. Rufen in all literal uses means 'to produce a sound' loudly enough for it to carry some distance. It may be used of persons or things, most frequently with the implication of conveying a

---

[1] Other senses of *rechnen* translated by 'calculate', 'reckon' and also 'count' are: (*a*) to expect, be prepared for (e.g. *wir rechnen mit einer Niederlage*); (*b*) to rely on (e.g. *ich rechne darauf, daß du bald zu uns kommst*). *Rechnen zu*: to reckon among, as one of.
[2] The past participle *ausgerechnet* is used idiomatically to denote surprise or good-humoured resignation. *Er mußte ausgerechnet Dienstag kommen* (Tuesday of all days). *Ausgerechnet er hat es gesagt* (he of all people).
[3] *Berechnen* is also used for 'reckon' in the sense of 'charge'. *Der Lieferant berechnet extra für die Transportkosten.*
[4] For the senses 'to visit', 'to stop', see the dictionaries.

message, an order or a summons.[1] These suggestions are present in all figurative uses (e.g. *die Pflicht ruft; Gott rief ihn zu sich*). 'To call to a person' can only be **zurufen.**

Wer ruft da?
Der Wächter, der Kuckuck ruft.
Die Glocke ruft zum Unterricht.
Die Mutter rief die Kinder zu sich, zum Essen.
Er rief mich ins Nebenzimmer.
Er rief um Hilfe.
Er rief nach einem Glase Bier.
Die Heimat ruft.
Er rief mir die Zeit zu.
Er rief mir zu, ich solle nicht weitergehen.

2. Berufen means (*a*) to call to an exalted position[2] (see 'appoint'); (*b*) to summon a person to a place, i.e. an order given by a superior to an inferior.

Er wurde auf den Thron, ins Außenministerium, berufen.
Der Minister berief seinen Sekretär in sein Arbeitszimmer (summoned; does not imply use of the voice).

3. Other compounds of *rufen*.[3]
(a) When 'call' is an abbreviation for 'call in', 'call to one', 'summon', for use, consultation and the like, **herbeirufen** must be used.
Er rief das Taxi, den Arzt, herbei.
(b) **Einberufen:** (1) to call, convene, a meeting;[4] (2) to call up for military service, i.e. as an administrative act, *rufen* in phrases such as *zu den Fahnen rufen* being emotional.
Der Reichstag, eine Sitzung, wurde einberufen.
Alle wehrfähigen jungen Männer wurden zum Heer einberufen.

4. In the sense of (*a*) 'to name so-and-so'; (*b*) 'to describe or characterize as' (*P.O.D.*), **nennen** is the general term. **Benennen** means 'to give a thing a distinguishing name' which establishes its character, particularly, though not exclusively, one based on a principle of classification. Thus, it can only mean 'to name for the first time', but not 'to name' in the sense of 'to mention'.[5] **Heißen,** used transitively in the sense of 'call', always implies emotional participation in the statement made, and is therefore most common in exclamations. It also means 'to be called' in reference to the name of a person or thing.

Er nennt sich einen Philosophen.
Ich nannte ihn einen Lügner (or *hieß*, with emotional emphasis).

---

[1] Thus in the sense of 'to wake' in the morning only *wecken* can be used, since raising of the voice is not implied.
[2] *Berufen*, used adjectivally, means 'inwardly qualified'. *Er war der berufene Mann für den Posten.*
[3] *Anrufen* must be used in the sense of 'to telephone'. It also means 'to call upon', 'to invoke', 'to appeal to', particularly in reference to an authority. *Aufrufen* in the sense of 'to call upon' refers to an exhortation to action and is followed by *zu*. *Er rief den Schutz des Gesetzes an. Er rief das Volk zu größeren Anstrengungen auf.*
[4] *Zusammenberufen*: to call together, either in reference to a committee or the like, or its members. *Ich werde sie im geeigneten Augenblick zusammenberufen.*
[5] To change a name can only be *umbenennen. Die Straße ist umbenannt worden.*

Das nenne ich eine Gemeinheit.
Das heiß' ich aber fest schlafen!
Er wurde nach seinem Vater genannt.
Der Botaniker wußte nicht, wie er die neue Pflanze benennen sollte.
Wenn wir den Geist der Sturm-und-Drang-Bewegung benennen wollen, so
halten wir uns am besten an Goethes Wort: 'Gefühl ist alles.'

CANCEL 'Cancel' suggests in its most concrete use its origin in Latin *cancellus* (= crossbars, lattice), i.e. to draw lines resembling lattice work across something written in order to render it null and void. In its extended uses it means to undo something, whether this be a law, an arrangement, a good deed, or the like. See also under 'undo'.

1. To mark or strike out for omission or deletion, typically with lines crossed lattice-wise over the passage in question, or by a line through the symbols involved (*W*.): **streichen, aus-, durch-streichen.** The first of these German verbs conveys the suggestion either of shortening or of omitting or of wiping out, the other two of drawing lines through a passage.

Bei der Aufführung wurde der zweite Auftritt im dritten Akt gestrichen.
Die Parricida-Szene im Wilhelm Tell wird meistens gestrichen.
Der Absatz wurde als unwichtig gestrichen.
Das habe ich gestrichen (of a debt).
Der anstößige Passus wurde gestrichen, aus-, durch-gestrichen.

2. To remove from significance or effectiveness as to destroy the force, effect, effectiveness or validity of: revoke, annul, invalidate (*W*.). See also under 'undo'.

(a) **Rückgängig machen** covers all such cases.

Die Bestellung wurde rückgängig gemacht.
Das Abonnement einer Zeitschrift rückgängig machen.
Sie haben den Vertrag, den Beschluß, das Abonnement rückgängig gemacht.

(b) When the thing cancelled is the object of the verb, **abbestellen** may be used.

Die Zeitschrift abbestellen.
Wir müssen das Hotelzimmer rechtzeitig abbestellen.
Die Waren wurden abbestellt.

3. To take away, remove, or to reduce to the point of insignificance. The act of removal may get rid of, release from something imposed, but not necessarily. **Aufheben,** i.e. to lift.

Das Verbot (embargo) *wurde aufgehoben.*
Alle ihre Vorrechte wurden vom neuen Regime aufgehoben.
Das neue Regime hat sofort die Verfassung aufgehoben.
Ihre Gelübde wurden nun aufgehoben.
Er hat den Befehl wieder aufgehoben.

4. To nullify in force or effect: counterbalance, neutralize, offset, often used with 'out' (*W*.): **aufheben,** which suggests the lifting of one side of the scales till it is in counterpoise with the other.

Seine Reizbarkeit hob seine angeborene Freundlichkeit auf.
Unsere Gewinne wurden durch andere Verlust aufgehoben.
Die Aussagen des Zeugen heben sich auf.

5. To undo, call off something arranged or planned, to drop, relinquish.

(a) **Absagen** is the most common term, but while is can mean to cancel something already done, it can also mean not to accept in the first place.

Er hat seinen Besuch abgesagt.

Ich muß leider wegen Inanspruchnahme durch Arbeit absagen (not accept).

Die Reise wurde abgesagt.

Die Theatervorstellung wurde wegen der Krankheit der Hauptdarstellerin abgesagt.

(b) If the cancelling is done in writing **abschreiben** may be used (*ich habe ihm abgeschrieben*), by telephone **abtelephonieren** (*zwei der Gäste haben abtelephoniert*).

6. Stornieren is a technical term, meaning to make, declare, a thing invalid either by drawing lines across it (as a postage stamp) or in any other way.

Die Briefmarken wurden storniert.

Der Scheck muß storniert werden.

7. Some close synonyms.

(a) **Widerrufen** is to revoke something which one has solemnly proclaimed: to recant.

Er widerrief seine frühere Behauptung, die Lüge, den Befehl.

(b) **Zurücknehmen**, like English to take back, withdraw, is less solemn and refers rather to small things in personal relationships; to take back words, statements, which one later regrets.

Ich nehme meine unüberlegten Worte, Beschuldigungen, zurück.

CARE (s.) 1. Sense: burdened state of mind arising from fear, doubt, or concern about anything (*S.O.D.*).

Kummer is the state of mind caused by the adversities that have befallen one, **Sorge** is more properly the anxiety, worry arising out of apprehensions concerning the future and refers as much to the external cause as the inner state.

Aufreibende Sorgen.

Niedergedrückt durch Krankheit, Trauer und Sorgen.

Der Kummer hat ihn vorzeitig alt gemacht.

Er hat keine Sorgen.

2. Sense: serious mental attention: concern; caution (*S.O.D.*). For the phrase 'to take care' see under 'careful'.

Sorgfalt: the attention one bestows on something one is doing, the pains one takes in doing a thing. See also *sorgfältig* under 'careful'.

Die eifrige Sorgfalt eines edlen Menschen (*S.O.D.*).

Er schreibt seine Berichte immer mit großer Sorgfalt.

3. Charge, oversight with a view to protection, preservation (*S.O.D.*). **Obhut** is generally used with the prepositions *in* and *unter*, although it also occurs with *über* and in other combinations.

Sie steht unter ihres Onkels Obhut.

Sie wurde in die Obhut ihres Onkels gegeben.

Er übernahm (hatte) die Obhut für (über) seine Nichte.

Pflege suggests tending, particularly of the sick.

In diesem Spital werden wir Ihrem Kind die beste Pflege angedeihen lassen.

Die Pflege des Gartens ist seine Sache.

Aufsicht: supervision, responsibility.

Die Bibliothek untersteht der Aufsicht von Herrn Schmidt.

4. Fürsorge means less 'care' in the sense of 3 than 'welfare' organized by the State or some other body.

Eine Fürsorgeorganisation.

CARE, CAREFUL, CAUTIOUS   A. The words treated in this section cannot be used to translate 'take care' and 'be careful' followed by an infinitive or a 'that' clause.

1. Sorgfältig: painstaking in doing a thing in order to do it well. It lacks the negative sense of 'cautious' which 'careful' also has. Since it refers to the doing of a thing, it occurs chiefly as an adverb, or as an adjective applied to a thing done, a piece of work. It is not common with nouns which denote persons, being attached in this case mainly to those which denote workers of some kind (often ending in *er*), and to the word *Mensch*. *Sorgfältig* cannot be used to translate 'to be careful with '.

Ein sorgfältiger Mensch, Arbeiter, Lehrer.
Er ist nicht sehr sorgfältig bei der Wahl seiner Worte.
Das ist eine sorgfältige Übersetzung, Abschrift.
Sie müssen die Sache einer sorgfältigen Prüfung unterziehen.
Der Plan ist sehr sorgfältig ausgedacht.
Er hat es sehr sorgfältig nachgezeichnet.
Er schreibt sehr sorgfältig.
Er kleidet sich sehr sorgfältig.

2. Sorgsam: solicitous, i.e. in reference to a state of mind, and particularly a permanent attitude which prompts action.

Eine sorgsame Mutter.

3. With nouns (but not verbs) which refer to the arts and imply an aesthetic effect *sorgfältig* is not used. The idea must be expressed variously in German.

Ein um Präzision im Ausdruck bemühter (ein auf. . . bedachter) Schriftsteller.
Ein gepflegter Stil.

4. Vorsichtig: cautious; i.e. careful in its negative sense of refraining from doing certain things because one foresees the danger with which they are attended.

Ein vorsichtiger Mensch.
Er ist immer vorsichtig in seinen Meinungsäußerungen.
Seien Sie vorsichtig, Sie können leicht rutschen.
Seien Sie vorsichtig mit dem Gewehr.
Das war eine vorsichtige Antwort.
Er ging sehr vorsichtig zu Werke.

5. Behutsam means 'cautious', but refers exclusively to action, never to the thought behind it. It cannot therefore be applied adjectively to persons.

Er trat behutsam ins Zimmer.

B. To be careful, to take care; followed by an infinitive or clause.

1. Aufpassen is the most general term and is appropriate in all but elevated or very serious contexts.

Ich passe immer auf, den Termin nicht zu versäumen.
Sie paßt immer auf, daß es genug im Hause zu essen gibt.
Sie müssen aufpassen, daß Sie mich rechtzeitig benachrichtigen.
Er paßt nicht immer auf, was für eine Wirkung seine Worte haben.
Ich passe immer auf, das, was er sagt, aufzuschreiben.

2. Achten auf suggests a higher degree of attention than *aufpassen*, but is by no means strong. It is used particularly in the imperative to impress instructions on a person.

Achten Sie darauf, daß die Kinder gute Manieren haben.

Achten Sie darauf, daß Sie das Paket heute noch abschicken.

Ich achte darauf, mich regelmäßig bei der Polizei zu meldon.

3. Acht geben auf is stronger than *achten*, and implies a warning, i.e. watch, lest something untoward should happen.

Sie müssen acht geben, daß man Sie nicht übervorteilt.

Geben Sie acht darauf, daß die Kinder sich nicht anstecken.

Er gibt acht darauf, daß er nicht in schlechte Gesellschaft gerät.

4. Sich in acht nehmen is used when the following infinitive or clause contains a negative (i.e. to take care not to. . .). *Nicht* is more correctly omitted, but sometimes inserted. It suggests a warning of a danger.

Nehmen Sie sich in acht, daß Sie ihm nichts Wichtiges mitteilen.

Nimm dich in acht vor ihm. (The phrase need not be split.)

5. Other expressions which can be used in this sense are: *sich hüten* (to beware; with omission of the negative before the following infinitive); *dafür sorgen* (to make arrangements, provision); *zusehen* (to see to it that. . .); *Sorge tragen* (emphatic, final, apt to be biblical in tone).

Ich werde mich schön hüten, mich da sehen zu lassen (I'll take good care not to. . .).

Er sorgt immer dafür, daß Wein im Hause ist.

Sehen Sie nur zu, daß Sie die Gelegenheit nicht versäumen.

Sie müssen dafür Sorge tragen, daß er den Eid leistet.

C. The words treated in **B** and also *vorsichtig* may be followed freely by prepositional phrases.

Seien Sie vorsichtig mit den Gläsern, Sie können sie leicht zerbrechen.

Geben Sie acht auf Ihre Gesundheit, Temperatur, Verdauung.

Nehmen Sie sich mit Ihrer Gesundheit in acht.

Nehmen Sie sich vor dem Hund in acht.

CASE See also 'box'. Compared with 'box', a case is generally made with care and looks attractive, for which reason *Kasten*, *Kästchen* and *Tasche*, all treated under 'box', are often appropriate equivalents of case (e.g. *Schau kasten*, a display case, *Notentasche*, a music case). On the other hand, 'case' sometimes denotes a roughly made box, e.g. packing case (German *Packkiste*).

Schrank is properly a cupboard, but the compound *Bücherschrank* denotes what E. understands by a 'bookcase'.

Etui (French word) is used for a cigarette case (*Zigarettenetui*).

Überzug is pliable and can be pulled over something else, e.g. *Polsterüberzug* (pillow-case).

Futteral is elongated like a scabbard or sheath.

Necessaire (French word) is used in the compound *Reisenecessaire*, which contains the essential items of toilet that one has to take with one when travelling.

CASUAL There is no exact German equivalent of this term in any of its senses, so that the terms that have to be used in German are more or less close synonyms of it.

1. In the sense of accidental, chance: **Zufällig**, applied to happenings.
Es war ein zufälliges Zusammentreffen.
Eine zufällige Entdeckung.

2. Sense: occurring, encountered, acting or performed without regularity or at random. German: *Gelegentlich*, i.e. occasional. Also: *Gelegenheit* in compounds.
Gelegentliche Freundlichkeiten (casual kindness).
Übermüdete Feuerwehrmänner bekamen gelegentlich Suppe und schliefen zeitweilig auf dem Boden (W.).

3. **Beiläufig** is applied to something said.
Eine beiläufige Bemerkung, Antwort.
Er sagte beiläufig.
Er machte einen beiläufigen Vorschlag.

4. **Flüchtig**, fleeting, suggests failure to pay sufficient attention to what one is doing. This sense occurs in the term *Flüchtigkeitsfehler*, a slip. It can therefore also mean 'superficial'.
Ein flüchtiger Blick.
Die Arbeit war flüchtig geschrieben.
Er las den Brief flüchtig.

5. (a) The greatest difficulty in finding a suitable German equivalent occurs when 'casual' is applied directly to a person, either as a predicative or an attributive adjective. For the former, the closest thing in German is: **alles auf die leichte Schulter nehmen.**
Er nimmt alles (es, die Sache etc.) auf die leichte Schulter.
(b) **Leichthin**: lightly.
Er nimmt seine Freundschaften ziemlich leichthin.
(c) **Es nicht so genau nehmen**: not to be precise about a thing.
Er nimmt es nicht so (sehr) genau mit seinem Hilfeangebot.

6. **Ungezwungen** without pressure from without. It must be distinguished from **zwanglos**, free and easy in manner, i.e. in oneself.
Er bezog sich auf liebe Freunde, indem er ihre Vornamen in zwangloser und vertrauter Weise nannte (W.).
Eine schwierige Leistung mit zwangloser Meisterschaft ausgeführt (W.).
Ein zwangloser Abend (informal).
In zwangloser Reihenfolge (in casual order, of a publication).
But: *Sie haben sich ungezwungen für Deutschland entschieden.*

7. Other terms: **Gleichgültig** (indifferent), **nonchalant** (as in English), **planlos, Stegreif** (in compounds meaning 'improvised'), **salopp** (untidy, without precision, particularly in dress), **unbedeutend** (of little weight, particularly of matters discussed); **Unbekümmert** (not worrying about things, applied directly to a person), **leichtsinnig** (frivolous; taking things lightly), **leichtfertig** (irresponsible), **unbesonnen** (heedless, thoughtless). None of these is a very close synonym of 'casual' and the list could be extended.
Er versuchte gleichgültig, nonchalant, dreinzuschauen (W.).
Ein planloses Verfahren.
Eine Stegreifmethode.
Er war salopp gekleidet.
Gegenstände, die leicht, schlicht und unbedeutend sind (W.).
Er sah unbekümmert aus, als er sich die Berichte anhörte.

Es war eine leichtsinnige, leichtfertige Antwort.
Er ist ein unbesonnener Mensch.

CATCH 'Catch' has both the active sense of 'pursue and seize' and the passive of 'receive' or 'be subjected to' something.

1. Fangen: to get into one's power, either by a trap,[1] which may be a net and the like, or by laying hold of a thing by the hand, the mouth, etc. These images are present in all figurative uses.

Unsere Katze ist zu alt, um noch Mäuse zu fangen.
Wir haben viele Fische mit dem Netz, aber keine mit der Angelschnur gefangen.
Viertausend Mann wurden vom Feind gefangen genommen.
Der Hund fing das ihm zugeworfene Fleisch mit dem Maul.
Er hat den Ball gefangen.
Dieser Verbrecher hat sich in seinen eigenen Schlingen gefangen.

2. Auffangen: to intercept a thing in the air, mostly something falling from above, in order to prevent it falling further or hitting something else.

Er stürzte die Treppe herunter, und im letzten Augenblick habe ich ihn aufgefangen.
Er fing den Koffer auf, als dieser aus dem Gepäcknetz fiel.
Ich fing das Buch auf, das er mir zuwarf.
Er stellte eine Tonne in den Garten, um den Regen aufzufangen.

3. Erwischen: to catch in the nick of time, i.e. someone or something that is about to elude one. This element is always stressed.

Die Polizei hat den Verbrecher am Bahnhof erwischt.
Ich habe den Briefträger gerade noch erwischt, als ich von zuhause wegging.

4. For 'catch' in the sense of 'seize and retain one's grip on' a thing (e.g. I caught him by the scruff of the neck) see 'seize'.

5. Einholen: to catch up, overtake.

Können Sie das andere Auto noch einholen?

6. Erreichen: to reach in time (of means of transport), when it is a question of whether one will arrive in time.[2]

Ich habe den Zug nicht erreicht.

7. Überraschen: to surprise, descend upon, envelop, of an evil. (See footnote to 'wonder', p. 384, n.2.)

Sie wurden vom Regen, von der Flut, von einem Luftangriff überrascht.

8. Ertappen: to come unawares upon a person who is in the act of doing something, in the sense of 'catch out', 'detect'. The construction used is: *dabei, wie. . .* (*auf* also with noun).[3]

Er hat ihn auf frischer Tat ertappt.
Ich habe ihn dabei ertappt, wie er das Geld nahm.

9. To become entangled, stuck. The commonest German terms are **hängen bleiben** (*in, an, auf etwas*), the literal sense of 'hanging' being preserved,

---

[1] *Fangen* also translates 'to trap'.

[2] When the intention of catching a certain train (boat, etc.) is emphasized, but not the question of whether one will be in time for it or not, *fahren mit* must be used. *Ich möchte mit dem 6 Uhr Zug fahren.*

[3] *Betreffen bei* is used in the same sense, but is less common.

and **stecken bleiben** (*in etwas*), i.e. to get stuck.[1] English says either 'her dress caught in the barbed wire' (i.e. intransitively) or 'she caught her dress in the barbed wire', with practically identical meaning. In German only the intransitive form is possible, and where it is a question of a person, a part of him or of his clothing, the person is made the subject of the sentence, the part caught being expressed by a phrase with *mit*. To make the part the subject would suggest that the part is separated from the whole person.

Sie blieb mit ihrem Kleid am Stacheldraht, an einem Nagel, hängen.
Er stürzte vom Dach, blieb jedoch in den Ästen eines Baumes hängen.
Das Auto blieb im Schlamm stecken.
Das Boot blieb auf dem Grund stecken.
Ich bin mit der Hand in der Flasche stecken geblieben.[2]
Die Gräte blieb ihm im Hals stecken.

10. Zu spüren bekommen: to be subjected to, to suffer with reference to something violent. See 'feel'.

Das Schiff bekam die ganze Wut des Sturms zu spüren.
Du wirst seinen Zorn zu spüren bekommen.

11. Treffen: to hit. For *treffen* see also **13**.

Die Kanonenkugel traf das Flugzeug in der Mitte.
Er traf ihn auf die Schläfe.

12. Sich holen is said of a contagious sickness (see 'get').

Er hat sich die Masern geholt.

13. Treffen: to catch atmosphere, tone and the like, in reference to art.

In diesem Gedicht hat er den echt lyrischen Ton getroffen.
Shakespeare hat die Atmosphäre einer Sommernacht wunderbar getroffen.
Die Ähnlichkeit ist sehr gut getroffen.

14. Einfangen is only correctly used in reference to art in the sense of catching a number of scattered, elusive impressions and unifying them.[3]

Er hat alles eingefangen, was in der Luft lag, und es dann im Gedicht in wunderbarer Weise wiedergegeben.

15. Heraushören: to be receptive to a tone and the like, in reference to art, i.e. from the point of view of the listener, beholder, not of the creator.

Sie haben den Ton der impressionistischen Lyrik ganz richtig herausgehört.

16. Verstehen: to catch the meaning of something said. It also translates 'hear' used to state that one has not caught a remark. In this sense *hören* is not used alone, but coupled with some adverb such as *richtig*.

Ich habe Ihre Bemerkung nicht ganz verstanden (nicht richtig gehört).

17. Verfangen is used in several ways.

(a) Intransitively in the sense of 'prove effective', 'catch on', 'interest'.

Diese Tricks verfangen nicht mehr bei uns.
Ihre Tränen verfangen nicht mehr bei ihm.

(b) Reflexively in the sense of being caught in an enclosed space, of wind and the like (French: *s'engouffrer*).

Der Wind hat sich im Schornstein verfangen.

---

[1] Where the idea of remaining is not stressed, these expressions are inapplicable (e.g. *er ist zwischen zwei Züge geraten*).

[2] None of these expressions are appropriate in the first person, present indicative, to tell others that one is caught. In this case verbs with *fest* are common. *Meine Hand ist zwischen zwei Stühlen festgeklemmt.*

[3] *Einfangen* also means 'to corner and catch' an animal, bird, etc.

18. Einschnappen: of locks, bolts, etc. Another sense of *eingeschnappt*: sullenly resentful.

Er ist furchtbar eingeschnappt, daß er übergangen wurde.

19. Catch and make one's own, in reference to someone else's habits, style, mannerisms, etc. This sense can often be rendered by verbs with the prefix *ab* (*ablernen, abgucken, abhören, ablauschen*).

Er hat diesen Ton abgelauscht (caught from).

CAUSE (s) , REASON, OCCASION (s)

1. Cause, as defined by *W.* is: a person, thing, fact or condition that brings about an effect or that produces or calls forth a resultant action or state. In German this is **Ursache**. *W.S.* says that 'Reason is interchangeable with cause only as meaning specifically a traceable or explainable cause; it always implies therefore, as cause does not necessarily, that the effect is known or has actually been brought about.'

The interchange of **Ursache** and **Grund** appears also in German in this way, but the limits of the interchange are strict. In this sense it is often preceded by *gut*.

Sie versuchen die Ursache des Unfalls festzustellen.

Fahrlässigkeit ist oft die Ursache von Bränden.

Ursache und Wirkung.

Die Ursache der Explosion bleibt unbekannt.

Die Ursache ihrer Migräne ist noch zu untersuchen.

Was war die Ursache (better than *Grund*) *für den Ausbruch dieser Epidemie?*

Es gab einen guten Grund (*eine Ursache*) *für Mark Twains Pessimismus, einen Grund für seine Verdrießlichkeit. . .*

Seine Verbitterung war die Folge eines Erlahmens seiner Schaffenskraft, einer gehemmten Persönlichkeit. . . (W.S.).

Seine Gründe angeben (to show cause).

2. In ordinary speech, when cause implies responsibility or guilt, it is more usual in German to say **verantwortlich, schuld sein an** than *Ursache*.

Er ist für meinen Mißerfolg, Untergang, verantwortlich. (*an meinem M., U., schuld*).

3. (a) In the sense of 'a principle or movement supported militantly or zealously: a belief advocated or upheld' (*W.*). German uses **Sache** which originally meant a law-suit.

Unsere Sache ist eine gerechte.

Die Sache der Aufständischen.

Er diente der Sache der Wahrheit mit weniger Ergebenheit als der Sache der Partei (*W.*).

(b) If the cause in this sense is not stated, German uses **gute Sache**.

Er ist bereit, für die gute Sache zu sterben.

Der guten Sache hat er alles geopfert.

4. According to *W.S.* 'Occasion applies to any person, place, or event which provides a situation that, either directly or indirectly, serves to set in motion causes already existing or to translate them into acts: German **Anlaß**.

Die Ursache eines Krieges ist oft eine tief eingewurzelte Feindschaft zwischen zwei Völkern, während der Anlaß für den Krieg manchmal ein unbedeutender Vorfall sein kann.

CEILING   In the sense of the lining or inside overhead covering of a room (*A.L.*) the term most generally used is **Decke** (which can also mean a covering of various kinds, e.g. *Bettdecke, Tischdecke*). In Austria the French word is used, i.e. **Plafond**.

CHANGE, EXCHANGE, ALTER, TRANSFORM   Only *umändern* and *wandeln* and its compounds can normally be followed by *in* (to change into, turn into).

1. **Ändern** is the most general term. It must be used in the sense of 'to change a part' of a whole, 'to make a small change', i.e. 'to alter', and is frequently used in the sense of 'to change a whole', 'to make radical changes'. It is the most usual term in reference to a deliberate or a sudden change, but can also, chiefly in reflexive use, be applied to unconscious changes of nature, particularly in so far as they are sudden (see *verändern*). It is used of external acts, inner movements of feeling and thought, changes of external nature.

Ändern Sie dieses Wort in Ihrem Aufsatz.
Die Tatsache ist nicht mehr zu ändern.
Sie hat ihr Kleid geändert (either made alterations to details or changed it as a whole).
Sie haben ihre Pläne, die Gesetze, ihre Meinungen geändert.
Er hat sich in letzter Zeit geändert (in his conscious self, i.e. his views, conduct, rather than in physical appearance).
Der Volkscharakter hat sich geändert.
Das Wetter hat sich geändert.

2. **Verändern** is mostly used to denote the result of an unconscious process of change in human or external nature. In this sense it occurs mainly as a reflexive or in the passive voice. Used otherwise, it mostly means 'to change' more or less involuntarily something about one's person. It is also, though less frequently, used in reference to the changing of things external to the self, particularly something broad, e.g. the appearance of a whole town. *Sich ändern* = change character or attitude; *sich verändern*: in appearance.

Er sieht verändert aus.
Als ich nach 20 Jahren zurückkehrte, fand ich die Stadt vollkommen verändert.
Der Nationalcharakter hat sich in den letzten 100 Jahren langsam verändert.
Nach dem Kreig haben sich die Machtverhältnisse in Europa stark verändert.
Er verändert den Ton, die Stellung, den Gesichtsausdruck.
Sie haben ihre Wohnung von Grund auf verändert.
Umstände verändern die Sache.
'...*den Fluß der Zeit, welcher vieles....fortwährend verändert*' (Th. Mann, *Dr. Faustus*).

3. **Abändern:** to change the inner structure of a thing, particularly with reference to the text of a document (not isolated words), and to a system.

Wir müssen die Bestimmungen abändern.
Das Prüfungssystem ist abgeändert worden.
Der Plan muß abgeändert werden.

4. **Umändern:** to rearrange the parts so that something new is formed. It may be followed by *in*.

Er hat das Haus in eine kleine Fabrik umgeändert.

5. Wechseln: to give, substitute one thing for another of the same kind, whether tangible or intangible, and for the same purpose, often discarding the old. It can translate 'exchange' in a few cases. It is used particularly of money and means 'to substitute' the same value in smaller coins, but not, in correct use, in another currency.

Ich habe mein Geld gewechselt.
Ich muß meine Kleider wechseln.
Er wechselte die Pferde.
Er wechselte sein Zimmer.
Er wechselte seine Pläne.
Er wechselte seine Ansichten.
Er wechselte den Text des Liedes.
Er wechselte seine Diät.
Sie wechselten Blicke.
Sie wechselten Plätze, Ringe, Briefe.

6. Tauschen: to exchange one thing for another, which need not be of the same kind or for the same purpose. It therefore translates 'barter' in a commercial sense. While *wechseln* involves two things but not necessarily two persons, *tauschen* emphasizes the latter and the equality of the exchange. It is used where intimate feelings are implied. The sense of discarding the old is excluded. It is impossible, therefore, with a word such as *Ansichten*.

Sie tauschten Münzen.
Er tauschte ein Pferd gegen drei Schweine.
Sie tauschten die Pferde.
Ich muß meine Kleider tauschen.
Sie tauschten ihre Rollen.
Sie tauschten Plätze (exchanged, whereas *wechselten* could mean simply that they went to other seats, not necessarily an interchange).
Sie tauschten Ringe, Blicke, Küsse (*wechseln* impossible with *Küsse*).

7. Austauschen emphasizes the equality of the exchange, a mutual give and take. It is therefore the correct term in reference to free association such as social or diplomatic intercourse. The object may be persons, things or ideas.

Die beiden Länder haben ihre Minderheiten ausgetauscht.
Die Universitäten tauschen Professoren aus.
Sie tauschen Briefmarken aus (more on a friendly than on a strictly commercial basis).
Sie saßen stundenlang da und tauschten Erfahrungen, Ansichten aus.

8. Auswechseln means (*a*) in technical things, to take out an old and put in a new part; (*b*) to change people from one sphere to another. It is not a dignified term, and so cannot be used in reference to ideas.

Der Fahrer wechselte den Reifen aus.
Die Gefangenen wurden ausgewechselt.

9. Umtauschen: to return goods one has bought to the seller and receive others of the same kind, the original purchase not being what is desired; and more generally, to exchange a thing for another thing one wants more.

Ich muß das Buch, die Schuhe, mein Geld, umtauschen.
Ich habe mein altes Radio gegen ein neues umgetauscht.

10. Eintauschen: to trade in one thing for another, which can but need not be of the same kind. (*Der Bauer hat seine Pferde gegen einen Traktor einge-tauscht.*) **Einwechseln:** to change money of one currency for that of another. (*Belgische Franken in englische Pfunde einwechseln.*)

11. Wandeln,[1] mostly reflexive, denotes an inner change of nature, a trans-formation (compare *verändern*). It can be followed by *in*. In itself it does not indicate the extent of the change.

In den letzten 10 Jahren hat sich sehr viel gewandelt.

Seine Anschauungen haben sich gewandelt.

Seine Liebe hat sich in Haß gewandelt.

12. Verwandeln[2] indicates a complete and, generally, a quick change (not necessarily a change of nature). It can therefore suggest magic, or, in reference to the real world, that the result is unrecognizable. It can be followed by *in*.

Der Krieg hat die Landschaft in eine Wüste verwandelt.

Ich erkenne ihn nicht mehr, er ist wie verwandelt.

Sie wurde in eine Hexe verwandelt.

Seine schauspielerische Begabung ist so groß, daß er sich in fast jeden Menschentyp verwandeln kann.

13. Umwandeln:[3] to transform one thing into another. It is used only of things of considerable size, and almost exclusively of deliberate actions (i.e. not of changes of nature). It is followed by *in*.

Ich habe den Blumengarten in einen Gemüsegarten umgewandelt.

Das Haus wurde in eine kleine Fabrik umgewandelt (stresses the complete-ness of the change, while *umändern* suggests a rearrangement of parts).

CHARM, APPEAL   1. In the sense of a spell which radiates from a person and produces a harmonious and soothing effect, the only German equivalent is **Scharm.** When a thing produces charm of this kind, **Zauber** may be used. **Reiz** suggests a strong stimulation of the senses, accompanied not by a feeling of harmony, but by desire. It corresponds more closely to 'appeal',[4] and to 'attraction'.

Er, sie, hat Scharm.

Die Musik, die Landschaft, übt einen sanften Zauber auf mich aus.

Sie hat einen unwiderstehlichen Reiz für ihn.

2. The verb *reizen* means 'to appeal to', 'to attract' or 'to tempt' by rousing desire, rather than 'to charm'.[5] To charm painful feelings: *lindern*

---

[1] The noun *Wandel* refers to change as a general phenomenon of life. (*Uberall sieht man Wandel. In den letzten Jahren ist ein grundlegender Wandel im politischen Leben der Völker eingetreten.*)

[2] *Vertauschen* and *verwechseln* mean 'to mistake for', 'to confuse' one thing with another. *Vertauschen* is actually 'to take the wrong' thing (e.g. *sie haben ihre Hüte vertauscht*), *verwechseln* 'to confuse mentally' (e.g. *ich habe die beiden Brüder verwechselt; ich verwechselte die beiden Geldsorten*).

[3] To change, turn one thing into another in reference to small things: *machen aus* (e.g. *aus den Fleischresten machte ich eine Pastete*). 'Turn into', with reference to big things, also must be translated in the same way as 'change into'.

[4] *Anmut* and *anmutig* refer to 'grace' of form or manner, particularly in reference to movement. Thus *ein anmutiges Gedicht* suggests its formal qualities as harmonious move-ment. *Ein anmutiges Bild* is one which reveals this quality in its lines.

[5] *Reizen* also means 'to provoke', 'to irritate' (see 'angry'), particularly with a personal subject. *Sie reizt ihn ständig.*

(=assuage). In other uses of 'charm', synonyms must be used: e.g.
bezaubern (=enchant).[1]

Ihre Figur reizt ihn sehr.
Der Posten reizt mich.
Die Schönheit der Landschaft, die ihn umgab, linderte seinen Kummer.
Die Landschaft hat mich bezaubert.

3. The adjective 'charming' can be rendered by *scharmant* in the sense defined in section 1. *Reizend* is, however, used more widely and loosely than
Reiz, and does not suggest desire as strongly as the latter. It does not exclude
the feeling of harmony, though it does not emphasize it. It is mostly applied
to small, graceful things.

Sie ist reizend, eine reizende Frau.
Das Buch, die Musik, die Landschaft, ist reizend.

CHEEK Wange differs from **Backe** (sometimes *der Backen*) in two ways.
(1) It refers only to the part of the face immediately beneath the eyes and
extending downwards as far as the nose reaches. Further, it denotes only
the visible external side of the flesh. *Backe* extends to the ears and downwards
to the jaw (*Kinnbacken* =jaw) besides referring to the inside of the mouth.
(2) *Backe* is the term in ordinary use, *Wange* being a more elevated and
poetical term, though both are applied to young children. In technology,
e.g. the cheek of a vice, *Backe* is always used.

Er hat rote Backen, blühende Wangen.
Ich gab ihm einen Backenstreich.
Er hat dem Mädchen die Wangen gestreichelt.
Er hat dem Kinde die Wangen (die Backen) gestreichelt.
Der alte Herr hat rote Bäckchen.

CHOICE, SELECTION Wahl is the act of choosing, also 'selection' in this
sense, while **Auswahl** refers to the things or persons chosen.

Die Wahl eines Berufs ist manchmal schwer.
Eine Auswahl der besten lyrischen Gedichte.

CHOOSE, SELECT[2] **1. Wählen** stresses the decision involved in the act
of choosing. With a personal object it can only mean 'to elect'. It also means
'to dial' when telephoning.

Ich habe gewählt.
Wählen Sie!
Iche habe dieses Sofa, dieses Haus gewählt.
Wir haben dieses Muster gewählt.
Der neue Kanzler ist gewählt worden.

2. Auswählen: to choose from a considerable number of persons or things.
This reference to number must always be clearly implied. With things there
is a suggestion that the thing or things selected are taken into the hand or
separated from the others for examination. From this it follows that *auswählen* is generally applicable only with such things as can be carried by
hand (e.g. a chair, but not a sofa or a house). With persons the implication

---

[1] *Zaubern* means 'to practise magic, work charms'. *Bezaubern* is 'to enchant' in the sense
of 'charm, delight', but not so as to rob of all will-power. *Verzaubern* denotes an absolute
state, to cast over a person a spell which robs him of his consciousness of everything else.
It suggests a trance. The distinction between *behexen* and *verhexen* is similar, i.e. to bewitch.
[2] *Kiesen* and *küren* are now used only in verse or very elevated diction.

is that of a careful selection. Intransitive use is, in the light of this explanation, not possible.

Ich habe diese Bücher für die Bibliothek ausgewählt.

Wählen Sie sich eins aus!

Der Präsident hat seine Minister sorgsam ausgewählt.

Hundert Mann wurden für den Angriff ausgewählt.

Ich habe ein schönes Pferd ausgewählt.[1,2]

3. Sich aussuchen is used more familiarly without reference to the type of object and without implying a decision which requires discrimination.

Haben Sie sich schon ausgesucht, was Sie essen wollen?

Er hat sich ein paar Leute für die Arbeit ausgesucht.

4. Choose, followed by the infinitive.

(a) If the personal, at times arbitrary, element in 'choose' is strong (to follow one's fancy, to do as one pleases), **belieben** (personal or impersonal) may be used as a polite formula, ironically or to indicate an inclination not based on serious reasons.

Nehmen Sie, was Ihnen beliebt.

Ach, Sie belieben zu kommen.

Wenn es Ihnen beliebt, heute zu Hause zu bleiben, so tun Sie das ruhig.

(b) When the act of choosing is preceded by serious consideration **vorziehen** may sometimes be used.[3]

Er zog es vor, von seinem Amte zurückzutreten, als (rather than) *nachzugeben.*

CLAIM When followed by an infinitive or a clause 'claim' can be rendered by **in Anspruch nehmen** only in the sense of 'to assert' something good about oneself. **Für sich** is generally added. In the sense of 'to assert' something about someone else or about a misadventure that has befallen oneself **behaupten** must be used.

Rußland nimmt als einziges europäisches Land für sich in Anspruch, dieses Jahr eine gute Ernte gehabt zu haben; aufrichtig für den Frieden arbeiten zu wollen.

Rußland behauptet, daß Amerika und England einen neuen Krieg vorbereiten.

Er behauptet, sein Leben sei gefährdet.

CLEAR 1. **Klar** in general means clear to the mind. It is also used of things which are transparent, e.g. *klare Luft*, and by transference applied to *Sicht*, *klare Sicht* = good visibility.

Er sah es klar (intellectually).

Drücke dich klar aus.

Die Zusammenhänge sind mir völlig klar.

Er denkt klar.

Er sagte es ganz klar.

Ich bin mir darüber klar (im klaren), daß das Verfahren falsch war.

Die Auskunft ist nicht klar.

---

[1] The prefix *er*, added to any of the words discussed (and to *lesen*), suggest the value of what is chosen (e.g. *erlesene Pracht*). They are used mainly in the past participle as adjectives.

[2] When *aus* is prefixed to *er*, the sense is 'chosen out of many'. These verbs, too, are mainly used in the past participle (e.g. *das auserwählte Volk*).

[3] *Gewählt* as an adjective means 'choice' and is applied to the use of language (e.g. *ein gewähltes Deutsch*).

CLEAR

Er behält einen klaren Kopf.
Der Himmel ist heute sehr klar.

2. Deutlich. (a) Of things, means clear to the senses, the eye or the ear. It has something of the meaning of English 'distinct', i.e. not confused or merged with other things, not blurred.

Er sah die Berge deutlich (not *klar*).
Das Schloß hebt sich deutlich (not *klar*) *von den anderen Gebäuden ab.*
Sprich deutlich (i.e. make distinct sounds).

(b) In certain cases it suggests clarity to the mind, i.e. in the sense of unambiguous, of something emerging into clarity from obscurity or standing out from other things.

Seine Absichten wurden deutlich (not *klar*).

CLEVER, SKILFUL, SHREWD[1]

1. Geschickt, the most general term, refers to dexterity in doing things, particularly with the hands or in handling people. In the latter case a clever manœuvre, a capacity for making quick adjustments, slipping out of difficulties, is suggested. In neither application is it a term of superlative praise. It does not refer to intellectual ability or brilliance. *Etwas ungeschickt machen*: to bungle.

Er ist geschickt mit seinen Händen.
Er ist geschickt im Zeichnen.
Er ist ein geschickter Arzt, Handwerker.
Der Arzt hat die Operation geschickt ausgeführt.
Das war ein geschicktes Manöver.
Er hat die Verhandlungen sehr geschickt geführt.

2. Gewandt implies a talent which manifests itself in a form that is neat, elegant and the like. It suggests an impression of artistic skill, particularly in movement. It is a term of higher praise than *geschickt*.

Er ist ein gewandter Redner, Diplomat, Tänzer.
Das war eine gewandte Abwehr.

3. Klug suggests clear- and far-sightedness, wisdom, and prudence in action. It is a quality which a diplomat must possess, but may also be ascribed to a child or a dog in the sense of not acting blindly or wildly. It does not refer to pure intellect, but contains something of 'shrewd' (i.e. quick and clear-sighted enough to guess) and 'astute' (wideawake).[2]

Er ist ein kluger Diplomat, Vater.
Er hat klug und besonnen gehandelt.
Es war nicht sehr klug von dir, ihm so viel zu sagen.
Das war eine kluge Antwort.

4. Gescheit approaches the meaning of *klug*, but in fine discrimination implies rather shrewdness, a capacity not to allow oneself to be deceived, than skill in action; common sense, solidity of judgment, rather than brilliance. It is a much used term in conversation, and often has a colloquial ring.

---

[1] The terms discussed in this article must also be used on occasion to translate 'adroit', 'dexterous', 'smart' and the like. None of the English corresponds closely to any of the German terms. *Fix* and *patent* are used colloquially for 'quick', 'bright', 'smart', 'slick', and the like (e.g. *ein fixer Junge, eine fixe Antwort*). *Patent* is applied only to persons (*ein patenter Kerl*).

[2] 'Shrewd' and 'astute' lead to the group 'crafty', 'sly', etc., which imply secretiveness. *Schlau* refers particularly to cunning in the execution of designs; *listig* draws attention to the secrecy with which a thing is done; *hinterlistig* suggests mendacity and trickery.

Er ist ein gescheiter Kerl, er täuscht sich nie.
Er hat einen gescheiten Bericht über die Lage geschrieben.
Er hat sehr gescheit gehandelt, geantwortet.

5. **Geistreich** refers to brilliance of mind which expresses itself in clever, often witty, sayings or remarks. See footnote to 'mind' (p. 215, n. 3).
Eine geistreiche Komödie, Bemerkung.

6. In the sense of 'talented' none of the above terms can translate 'clever', particularly in the phrase 'to be clever at. . .'. **Begabt**, gifted, is the most general term. The following examples include other approximations.
Er ist für Mathematik, Sprachen, sehr begabt (clever at).
Er hat eine rasche Auffassungsgabe für Sprachen.
Er ist ein begabter, aufgeweckter, (more colloquially) *heller Junge.*

7. In post-war years German has adopted 'clever' as a *Modewort*.

CLIMB 1. **Klettern** means to climb vertically (upwards or downwards) and suggests difficulty. *(Er)steigen* is simply 'to go up'.
Er kletterte den Baum hinauf, auf den Baum (den Baum hinauf suggesting slower progress than *auf den Baum).*
Er kletterte über den Zaun.
Er ist die Leiter heruntergeklettert.

2. **Erklimmen** means 'to scale' great heights.
Sie haben den Gipfel erklommen.

3. **Sich ranken:** to climb along, of plants.
Die Rosen ranken sich am Spalier entlang.

COAT The most general term for 'coat' as part of a male suit is **Jacke**, although in some regions *Rock, Kittel* and other terms are used. **Rock**, which was originally a garment worn over a shirt by men and women alike, now generally appears in compounds (e.g. *Leibrock, Gehrock, Schottenrock*) and is normally a longer garment than the coat of a suit, sometimes the whole attire (as in *Schottenrock*, kilts). Likewise, the modern term for overcoat is **Mantel** (*Überrock* being old-fashioned).

In the sense of 'something resembling a coat in covering' (W.), the German term varies according to the covering and the thing covered (e.g. *Anstrich*: coat or coating of paint; *eine dichte Decke von Dunkelheit verhüllte die Prärie* (*W.*); *die Sonnenbräune*: a coat of tan).

COMFORTABLE, COSY 1. **Bequem** is applied to things and persons. It means 'comfortable' of such things into or on to which the body or part of it fits comfortably. Contact between the thing and the body is implied. It can thus be used of a motor-car, but not of a house.[1]

It is not applied to persons except adverbially in combination with such verbs, as *liegen, sitzen*, which clearly imply the type of object which provides

---

[1] *Bequem* also translates 'convenient', 'handy' when applied to objects as close synonyms of 'comfortable', i.e. well adapted to the posture or movements of the body or part of it, easy to handle (e.g. *Der Apparat ist sehr bequem zu handhaben. Dieser Koffer ist sehr bequem zu tragen*). In an extended sense it is applied in the expression *bequem liegen* to places in the sense of 'to be conveniently situated, easy to reach'. *Der Ort, das Hotel, liegt sehr bequem.* Also: *eine bequeme Verbindung.* In the above senses *bequem* may be followed by the infinitive. *Es ist sehr bequem, einen solchen Apparat zu besitzen, hier zu wohnen. Unbequem* is much used in the sense of giving bother.

the comfort. 'I am, feel, comfortable' in this sense must therefore be translated by *ich liege, sitze, bequem*, as the case may be. After *sein* with a personal subject *bequem* is impossible in this sense.[1] To make oneself comfortable = *es sich bequem machen*.

It is applied to uncritical mental activity which takes a rosy view of things. Applied directly to a person it means 'easy-going'.

Bequem translates the adverb 'comfortably' in the sense of 'without effort'.

Diese Schuhe, dieser Anzug, dieser Lehnstuhl, der Wagen ist sehr bequem.

Ich liege, sitze, hier sehr bequem.

Machen Sie es sich da bequem.

Eine bequeme Ansicht.

Wir können den Bahnhof bequem in einer halben Stunde erreichen.

Das Haus ist, liegt, bequem.

2. Behaglich is applied in the first place to feelings which are compounded of the sensation of mental and physical relaxation and ease and of sensuous well-being (e.g. *ein behagliches Gefühl, ich fühle mich behaglich*). It is then used of such an atmosphere (clearly shown in the impersonal phrase: *es ist behaglich in. . .*). People who habitually feel in this way and show it in their actions are termed *behaglich*. Finally, it is applied to a few objects of the external world that prompt such sensations and have such an atmosphere about them (e.g. a small room rather than a big house).[2]

Er fühlt sich behaglich: he is, feels, comfortable.

Ein behaglicher Zustand.

Ich fühle mich hier sehr behaglich.

Er führt ein sehr behagliches Leben.

Ich fühle mich sehr behaglich in diesem kleinen Zimmer.

Mein Zimmer ist klein, aber ganz behaglich.

An einem Winterabend sitzt man sehr behaglich am Ofen.

3. Gemütlich is applied to feelings not so much of ease and harmony with the world, but rather of friendly intimacy, with a touch of sentiment and at times of imagination. It is a much used term and carries a large number of implications, which cannot all be rendered by any single English word. When applied to things and places it remains untranslatable, but approximates more to 'cosy' than 'comfortable'.[3]

Ein gemütliches Zimmer.

Ein gemütlicher Abend (carries human implications beyond 'cosy').

4. Angenehm, pleasant, must often be used for lack of a more precise term. It is wide enough to imply physical comfort, though much more vaguely than 'comfortable' does.

Das Hotel war ganz angenehm.

Das war eine angenehm Reise.

5. Komfortabel is only a commercial term used in advertising houses (*ein komfortables Haus*). A similar phrase is *mit allem Komfort der Neuzeit*.

---

[1] Applied to a person *bequem* does not mean 'comfortable', i.e. easy to get on with, but 'easy-going', i.e. averse to effort (e.g. *ein bequemer Mensch*). In some uses 'comfortable' and 'easy-going' are close synonyms (e.g. *ein bequemes Leben*).

[2] *Unbehaglich* has a wider range of application (e.g. *ein unbehagliches Haus*).

[3] *Ungemütlich werden* is applied to things with which *gemütlich* is not possible. *Das Wetter ist recht ungemütlich geworden.*

6. Gut is used (*a*) of financial circumstances; (*b*) of physical condition in relation to sickness.

Er lebt in guten Verhältnissen.
Er ist gut situiert.
Nach dieser Medizin fühle ich mich viel besser.
Der Patient hat eine gute Nacht gehabt.

7. Other approximately equivalent terms sometimes used are: **glatt** (in the sense of being able to do a thing with a comfortable margin to spare); **leicht** (easy).

Er hat das Examen glatt bestanden.
Sechs Personen gehen glatt in diesen Wagen hinein.
Dieser Wagen kann leicht sechs Personen fassen.

COMMON, GENERAL 1. Gemein[1] meant, originally, 'opposed to particular', i.e. common to many, but admitting exceptions. In this sense it is no longer freely used. Numerous fixed expressions, in which it occurs, have, however, survived in common use. These refer mostly to public life, State institutions and the like. It is also commonly applied to words which in themselves denote an evil (e.g. *ein gemeiner Verbrecher*). Its freest use is to denote lack of quality, refinement, but it is in this sense stronger than 'common', approximating more closely to 'vile', 'mean of spirit'.[2]

Fixed phrases are given in dictionaries (e.g. *das gemeine Wohl, Recht*). A sentence such as '*die Lüge ist gemein* (prevalent) *bei ungezogenen Leuten*' (Sanders-Wülfing, *Handwörterbuch der deutschen Sprache*) is no longer normal German. Similarly '*das gemeine Volk*', and '*der gemeine Mann*, have been discarded in favour of '*das einfache Volk*', '*der einfache Mann*', '*ein gemeiner Soldat*' (a private). The form *gemeinhin*, not *gemein, is used* adverbially (e.g. *es wird gemeinhin angenommen. . .*).

2. Allgemein means in the first place 'universal, admitting no exception'. It has, however, come to mean also 'common to most, if not all'. In the emphatic predicative position it only has the former sense. Even in attributive use it should only be used when 'general' could be substituted for 'common', i.e. when the exceptions are negligible, not in the sense of 'widespread'. It is used freely as an adverb.

Das ist die allgemeine Meinung, die allgemeine Erfahrung.
Es ist allgemeines Gerede.
Es ist allgemein bekannt (common knowledge).
Es wird allgemein angenommen, daß der König bald abdanken wird.

3. In the sense of 'prevalent, widespread', but not 'general, almost universal', terms such as the following must be used: **gebräuchlich** (=customary), **üblich** (=usual), **häufig, weit verbreitet, alltäglich**. See footnotes to 'habit' (p. 150, n. 1).

Es ist eine gebräuchliche Redensart.
Seine Klagen werden allzu häufig.
Solche Leute sind so häufig wie Blaubeeren.
Diese Ansicht ist weit verbreitet.
Es ist eine alltägliche Erfahrung.

[1] Only *gemein* amongst the German words forms fixed phrases.
[2] Examples: *eine gemeine Gesinnung*; *gemeine Redensarten*; *eine gemeine Sorte Zigaretten*; *ein gemeiner Kerl*; *das war gemein von Ihnen.*

COMMON

4. Gemeinsam: shared by two or more, joint, concerted. This term does not express frequency, but the idea of community. Often = joint.

Der gemeinsame Feind.
Unser gemeinsamer Besitz.
Wir haben gemeinsame Interessen.
Es ist ihr gemeinsamer Garten.
Wir müssen gemeinsame Schritte unternehmen.
Sie verfolgen ein gemeinsames Ziel.

5. Gewöhnlich and **ordinär** must be used in the sense of 'lacking quality' and 'vulgar'[1] respectively. *Ordinär* is stronger than 'ordinary',[2] which approximates more closely to *gewöhnlich. Gemein* is stronger than either term.

Sie ist sehr gewöhnlich, ordinär, in ihrer Sprache.
Es ist eine ganz gewöhnliche Sorte Wein.

COMMUNITY 1. Gemeinschaft is used only of feelings which cause people to have a sense of belonging together or of the ethical ideas associated with the term community.

Er hat ein starkes Gemeinschaftsgefühl.
Er wurde aus der Gemeinschaft ausgestoßen (expelled from the company of human beings rather than from a specific place).
Der Gemeinschaft der Gläubigen angehören.
Eine Völkergemeinschaft.

2. Gemeinde is an organized unit of a populated area, either in a governmental administrative sense (municipality) or in an ecclesiastical sense (parish of a given confession).

Im Gemeinderat wurde über die Verbreiterung gewisser Straßen heftig diskutiert.
Die Gemeinde hat die Kosten für die Renovierung der Kirche getragen.

3. Öffentlichkeit must be used when 'public' is meant, **Volk** (see 'people') when the nation as a whole is implied.

Der Vorschlag erregte großes Aufsehen in der Öffentlichkeit, im Volk, unter den Leuten.
Die Öffentlichkeit, das Volk, wird solche Maßnahmen nie gutheißen.

COMPLAIN Sich beschweren: to make a statement about an offence done to one to the relevant authority. **Sich beklagen:** to give vent to one's feelings of having been wronged, of annoyance, grievance and the like in words spoken to a third party. **Klagen:**[3] to give expression to a grievance, to talk of a bodily ailment, an untoward fate that has overtaken one, but without necessarily implying a reproach to anyone.[4] The complaint may be expressed in wails and lamentations. In certain expressions it means to sue (*auf Schadenersatz klagen*).

Ich habe mich bei der Polizei beschwert.
Er rief den Kellner zu sich und beschwerte sich über das schlechte Essen.
Er hat sich über Sie beschwert.

---

[1] *Vulgär* is very little used.
[2] *Alltäglich* also means 'ordinary' 'undistinguished', but does not mean 'vulgar'. *Ein ganz alltäglicher Mensch.*
[3] *Auf etwas* (e.g. *Schadenersatz*) *klagen*: to sue for damages. See 'accuse'.
[4] With a direct object of the thing accompanying dative of the person *klagen* suggests the 'pouring out' of one's sorrow to a listener (*jdm. sein Leid klagen*).

Er beschwerte sich über den Arzt, daß er nicht kam.
Er hat sich über Sie beklagt.
Der Schüler beklagte sich über die Strafe, die ihm auferlegt wurde.
Er beklagte sich über die schlechte Ernährung.
Er klagt über Kopfschmerzen, die schlechte Ernährung.

COMPLETE,[1] PERFECT, ENTIRE The distinctions between *vollkommen*, *vollständig* and *völlig* are less perceptible in their adverbial than in their adjectival use. This means that while in some contexts it is possible to use two or more as adverbs without radically changing the sense, only one is possible as an adjective. In the sentence given by Duden: *du kannst mit der völligen Wiederherstellung deiner Gesundheit rechnen*, it would be incorrect to use *vollkommen*. Both terms, however, are possible as adverbs. *Deine Gesundheit ist völlig* (or *vollkommen*) *wieder hergestellt.*

In adjectival use the meaning of *vollkommen* and *vollständig* is much more clearly defined in the predicative position, which possesses greater objectivity than the attributive use. *Völlig* is not used predicatively.

1. **Vollkommen** denotes quality and thus corresponds to 'perfect',[2] which tends to be its only meaning in the predicative position, except in cases where 'complete' and 'perfect' are practically interchangeable. In the attributive position the sense of 'perfect' is commonest with nouns which denote objects.

Both in the sense of 'complete' and 'perfect', *vollkommen* indicates an absolute state which the speaker regards as final and which he looks upon with detachment. In other words, it is objective in the attitude it expresses and static in its reference to the objective fact (contrast *völlig*). It concentrates, furthermore, attention on the whole, not on the parts and their individuality (contrast *vollständig*).

Duden in his introduction to the *Stilwörterbuch* censures the widespread use of *vollkommen* where the idea of value is absent, and gives as an example of this undesirable practice: *Das ist vollkommen unnötig.* This use is, however, felt to be less objectionable than the English 'perfect' in the sense of 'complete'.

Er ist ein vollkommener Narr.
Das ist vollkommener Unsinn.
Sein Glück ist vollkommen (perfect or complete; *vollständig* and *völlig* impossible).
Seine vollkommene Unschuld ist klar erwiesen (*vollständig* and *völlig* impossible).
Sie haben im Rahmen der Gesetze vollkommene Freiheit, zu tun, was Sie wollen.
Es war eine vollkommene Niederlage für den Feind.
Seine vollkommene Gleichgültigkeit seinen Verpflichtungen gegenüber ist bekannt.
Ihre vollkommene Unkenntnis der Lage ist bedauerlich.
Es besteht vollkommene Eintracht zwischen uns.
Der Krieg endete mit der vollkommenen Vernichtung des Feindes.

[1] Study together with 'quite' (see article).
[2] *Vollendet* (=consummate) is a close synonym. *Perfekt* is not used in the full sense of 'perfect', but is applied with some exaggeration to skills, achievements (e.g. *eine Sprache perfekt sprechen*). *Tadellos* is much used in conversation as a term of praise (e.g. *er hat die Rolle tadellos gespielt*).

Sie brauchen vollkommene Ruhe.
Die Aufführung war ein vollkommener Erfolg (not *völlig*; but *ein völliger Mißerfolg*).
Eine Minute nach dem Alarm lag die Stadt vollkommen im Dunkeln.
Die Stadt ist vollkommen zerstört.
Sie haben mich vollkommen mißverstanden.
Es ist vollkommen unmöglich, ihm zu helfen.
Das Rätsel ist vollkommen gelöst (not *völlig*).
Sein Vorgehen war vollkommen berechtigt.
Der Plan hat vollkommen versagt.

2. **Vollständig:**[1] having all the parts, items, etc. necessary for a thing to fulfil its purpose. The whole thus formed need not be organic, it may be, e.g., of a merely numerical kind. When not combined with a noun (or adverbially with a verb) which denotes an object, it means 'complete in every respect, aspect'. In concentrating attention on the parts it differs from *vollkommen*, which suggests the whole as something more than the sum of its parts. It cannot be applied to a person.

As the sense of 'complete in all parts' is clearest in the predicative position, it should be avoided in this use with expressions which denote the absence of a thing. Thus while it is correct to say: *ihre vollständige Unkenntnis der Lage ist mir bekannt,* it is not possible, not even ironically, to use *vollständig* to translate 'their ignorance of the situation is complete'.

Die Liste der Namen ist noch nicht vollständig.
Ein vollständiges Gebiß.
Die Niederlage des Feindes ist vollständig.
Es besteht vollständige Eintracht zwischen uns.
Der Krieg endete mit der vollständigen Vernichtung des Feindes.
Das ist ein vollständiges Abrücken von Ihrem früheren Standpunkt.
Sie brauchen vollständige Ruhe.
Die Stadt ist vollständig zerstört.
Sie haben mich vollständig mißverstanden.
Das Rätsel ist vollständig gelöst.
Sein Vorgehen war vollständig berechtigt.
Der Plan hat vollständig versagt.
Das Haus wurde vollständig durchsucht.

3. **Völlig** expresses a subjective, often emotional, interest on the part of the speaker and therefore lacks the convincing sense of finality conveyed by *volkommen*. This subjectivity makes it more dynamic than *vollkommen* and *vollständig*. Although the objective fact may be felt more strongly, this is, of course, not more complete in an objective sense.

Used adjectivally, *völlig* cannot be applied to concrete objects, and can qualify a noun denoting a person only if this noun is really equivalent to an adjective, i.e. indicates a quality capable of provoking a subjective interest. Predicative use is not possible.

Er ist ein völliger, Narr, ein völliges Kind.
Ihre Antwort zeigt nichts als eine völlige Unkenntnis der Lage.
Es besteht völlige Eintracht zwischen uns.
Das ist ja ein völliges Abrücken von Ihrem früheren Standpunkt. (The subjective interest is expressed also by *ja*.)

[1] See also *vervollständigen* under 'finish, complete'.

Die Stadt ist völlig zerstört.
Sie haben mich ja völlig mißverstanden.
Es ist völlig unmöglich, ihm zu helfen.
Er ist völlig verschwunden.
Das ist mir völlig gleichgültig.
Er trat auf den völlig menschenleeren Platz.
Sie haben das Feuerzeug nun völlig kaputt gemacht (colloquial).
Ich kann Ihre Schwierigkeiten völlig nachfühlen.
Wir tappen völlig im Dunkeln.
Er ist ein völlig unbrauchbarer Mensch.

4. **Vollends** denotes the final stages of completion and suggests a contrast with preceding stages. It is only used adverbially.

Jetzt ist es aber vollends dunkel (it was dark before, but not completely).
Eine zweite Welle genügte, um das Boot vollends zum Kentern zu bringen.

5. **Gänzlich** is an emphatic word and thus has an emotional connotation. 'Utter' and 'entire' are often closer approximations than 'complete'. As an adjective (it is not used predicatively) it can be combined only with abstract or verbal nouns.

Die gänzliche Harmlosigkeit des Mannes sollte doch klar sein.
Das gänzliche Ausbleiben der gewöhnlichen Stürme war eine angenehme
Überraschung.
Er ist gänzlich ohne Schuld.
Ich verlasse mich gänzlich auf Sie.
Er ist gänzlich zu Grunde gerichtet.
Seine Worte wurden gänzlich verdreht.
Es ist gänzlich überflüssig, zu dem schon Gesagten noch mehr hinzuzufügen.
Die Symptome sind gänzlich verschwunden.

6. 'Complete' used in the sense of 'completed' must be translated by *fertig*, *vollendet* or the other terms discussed under 'finish, complete' (see article).

Mein Bericht ist noch nicht fertig.
Das ist ein unvollendeter Satz.

CONCERN (v.) 1. Sense: to be the business, interest, of someone, affect. (a) In the phrase 'as far as (I) am concerned' (as for me), German uses *was mich angeht, was mich betrifft, was mich anbelangt*. The longer form *anbetrifft* has now more or less passed out of use. For *betreffen* see 'affect'. The concern expressed by *betreffen* is stronger than that expressed by *angehen*.
(b) Apart from such fixed phrases, both *betreffen* and *angehen* are used in this sense of concerned.

Das geht Sie nichts an.
Solche Dinge, die die Ehre Schottlands betreffen, angehen (S.O.D.).
Das Problem der Rassenunruhen geht uns alle an (betrifft uns alle) (W.).
Streitigkeiten zwischen einem Ehemann und seiner Frau gehen die ganze
Familie an (betreffen...).
(c) For the sense of affect adversely see under 'affect'.

2. Sense: To be a care, trouble or distress to (*W.*). This sense is frequent in the past participle 'concerned'. German: **Besorgen, Sorgen machen, kümmern, bekümmern** (see under 'bother'), **beunruhigen** (to alarm).

Die Verschlechterung seines Gesundheitszustandes besorgt mich sehr (macht
mir große Sorgen, beunruhigt mich) (W.).

CONCERN

Sie hat einen besorgten Ausdruck.
Sie macht eine besorgte Miene.
Es bekümmert mich zu hören, daß die zeit vergeht und nichts geschieht.

3. Sense: to engage, occupy, interest: (*sich*) *beschäftigen* (*mit*).
Er beschäftigt sich mit nichtssagenden Kleinigkeiten.

4. For the sense of 'involve', see 'involve'.

5. Sense of 'solicitous' in the past participle 'concerned'. German: *Es liegt* (*mir*) *an* + dative, *es ist mir gelegen an* + dative, *es kommt* (*mir*) *darauf an* (particularly with negative).

Es lag uns sehr daran (*war uns sehr daran gelegen*), *die Erwartungen eines kleinen Kindes nicht zu enttäuschen* (*W.*).

Es kommt uns nicht darauf an, zu entscheiden, welche von den verschiedenen Schulen der Sozialtheorien die richtige ist (*W.*).

CONFESS, ADMIT, CONCEDE[1] All these terms imply varying degrees of reluctance. 'Confess' normally suggests an admission of wrong-doing, either in a religious sense, i.e. to a priest and the like, or to others. It is also used as a polite way of registering dislike (e.g. I confess, I don't care for it much). 'Admit'[2] suggests an absence of wholeheartedness, and is often followed by 'but', irrespective of the truth. 'Concede' expresses a recognition of one's opponent's point of view despite reluctance.

1. Beichten: to confess in a religious sense, the only German term used in this way.
Er hat dem Priester alles gebeichtet.

2. Zugeben is the most general term, and suggests no more than that one refrains from disputing a point of view, i.e. it does not necessarily imply acceptance. 'Admit' is the closest English equivalent.
Geben Sie mal zu, daß die Aufgabe kompliziert ist.
Zugegeben, daß er es ehrlich meint. . . (admitting).

3. Gestehen and its compounds imply a recognition of the truth or justice of a statement and the like, and therefore approximate closely to 'confess'. *Gestehen* means 'to confess' or 'reveal' a fault, a misdemeanour, crime. Like 'confess', it can also be used as a polite expression of dislike. It suggests in general an emotional state of mind, reluctance, hesitancy. As object, a clause is more frequently found than a noun.
Er hat gestanden (a fixed phrase).
Ich gestehe meine Schuld.
Er gestand, daß er die Frau ermordet hatte.
Ich gestehe, daß ich mir keine Mühe gegeben habe.
Ich gestehe, daß ich keine Freude daran finde.

4. Eingestehen is more common with a noun object in the sense of 'to confess' a fault, crime. It must be accompanied in normal use by the reflexive dative when followed by a *daß* clause. It implies a fuller recognition of the truth than *gestehen*.

[1] 'Grant' is also used in the sense of 'to admit the truth or justice of' a statement, and implies greater readiness to recognize this than the other terms. For its use in the sense of 'accede to' a request see separate article.
[2] 'Admit' is also used in the sense of 'to let into' a place ((*her*)*einlassen*) and 'to accept into' an institution and the like (e.g. *zum Universitätsstudium zugelassen werden*).

Er hat seine Schuld eingestanden.
Endlich mußte er sich eingestehen, daß er sich zu viel zugemutet hatte.

5. Zugestehen implies a qualified recognition of an opponent's point of view, and therefore means 'to concede'.

Sie gestehen mir zu, daß das zuviel verlangt wäre.

6. Bekennen differs from the other terms in suggesting a full, unreserved, and spontaneous confession. It has no close English equivalent. (*Sich bekennen zu etwas*: make a profession of faith in a thing.)

Ich bekenne offen meine Schuld.
Ich bekenne, daß ich Wein gerne trinke.
Er bekannte, daß er seine Gedichte erst in Prosa geschrieben hatte.

CONSIDER 1. Sich überlegen is the most general term in the sense of 'apply the mind to, give thought to', a matter. While the thinking is carried on with a view to arriving at a judgment, whether purely intellectual or with reference to action, this judgment is stressed less than the thinking itself. Since the meaning is 'to think about',[1] it is, for example, inappropriate when 'consider' means to consider the granting of a request, an application, and the like. The activity of thinking is suggested only in a general way, without reference to the close examination of details. The addition of the reflexive dative suggests more careful, its omission more superficial, thought, but both forms are often used indiscriminately, the omission, however, only being possible when the object is a clause, i.e. not a noun, or when it is used absolutely.

Ich werde mir die Frage, den Plan, Ihren Vorschlag, überlegen.
Er überlegte einen Augenblick, bevor er antwortete.
Ich überlege mir, wo ich meine Ferien verbringen könnte.
Er überlegte (sich), ob er das Angebot annehmen sollte.
Ein wohlüberlegter Plan.

2. Erwägen, to weigh, suggests a close examination of all details, factors, with regard to their relative importance. It is used particularly with reference to requests. When the weighing of point against point is stressed, **abwägen** is the preferred term. See 'weigh'.

Ich habe alle Möglichkeiten erwogen.
Sie müssen die Kosten erwägen, bevor Sie sich entscheiden.
Die Regierung erwägt gewisse Maßnahmen, um den Handel mit Südamerika zu beleben.
Der Senat erwägt Ihr Gesuch.
Er hat das Für und das Wider gegeneinander abgewogen.

3. In Erwägung ziehen suggests that the consideration is given more hesitantly or reluctantly than is the case with *erwägen*. Similarly, if used in making a request, it implies that the latter is put forward more humbly.

Ich werde Ihren Vorschlag in Erwägung ziehen.
Würden Sie folgendes in Erwägung ziehen?

4. Bedenken: to think a thing all over (i.e. the force of *be-*), in the sense of 'to realize its consequences, results', 'to bear these in mind'. Because of this reference to consequences it conveys a suggestion of hesitation, of stopping to think.[2] The noun *Bedenken* means 'misgiving'.

---

[1] To reflect, ponder, i.e. protracted thinking, is *nachdenken*. See 'think'.
[2] *Sich besinnen* is 'to stop to think' in the sense of 'to try to remember'. The success of this effort, i.e. to remember, is expressed by *sich entsinnen, sich erinnern*. The latter is the

Sie müssen die Wirkung, die Folgen, eines solchen Schrittes bedenken.
Ich hatte die Schwierigkeiten nicht bedacht, als ich den Vorschlag machte.
Bedenken Sie, was ich ihnen gesagt habe.
Wemm man bedenkt, daß er fast keine Schulung gehabt hat, muß man seine
  Leistung bewundern.

5. Prüfen: to examine, scrutinize, as the action of an authoritative body.[1]
Die Regierung prüft die Ernährungslage.
Der Senat prüft Ihr Gesuch.

6. Betrachten (a) only translates 'consider' in reference to thought[2] when
it is accompanied by some phrase which denotes the angle, point of view,
from which a matter is seen.
Er betrachtet das Problem von diesem Standpunkt aus, unter diesem Gesicht-
  spunkt, von allen Seiten, in einem falschen Licht.
(b) Followed by *als* it also means 'to regard as', 'to take to be'. It differs
from **halten für** in suggesting finality and conviction, while the latter states
an opinion in a more argumentative way, and so is a closer equivalent of
'consider'.
Wir können die Verhandlungen als abgeschlossen betrachten.
Ich betrachte ihn als einen Freund.
Betrachten Sie sich als entlassen (not *halten*, since there can be no question
  of opinion).
Ich halte den Preis für zu hoch.
Ich halte ihn für unzuverlässig.

7. In the sense of 'to be of the opinion', when this phrase is followed by a
'that' clause, 'consider' can only be translated by **der Meinung, Ansicht,
sein,** and the like. '*Dafür halten, daß. . .*' is rare.
Ich bin der Ansicht, daß Sie zuviel verlangen.

8. In the sense of 'to examine' a person or thing with a view to acceptance
or rejection or suitability the following phrases are used: **in Betracht ziehen;
in Betracht, Frage, kommen.**
Ich würde ihn nie für den Posten in Betracht ziehen (consider as suitable).
Eine Gehaltserhöhung kommt nicht in Betracht.
Würde Donnerstag eventuell für Sie in Frage kommen? (would you consider. . .as suitable, acceptable?)

9. Berücksichtigen: to take into account, to pay due attention to a thing as
a determining factor. It does not mean 'to be sympathetic', and cannot
therefore be interchanged with *Rücksicht nehmen.*
Sie müssen diese beiden Momente berücksichtigen, bevor Sie sich entscheiden.
Er hat den Einfluß des Klimas nicht genügend berücksichtigt.
Haben Sie das Risiko, das damit verbunden ist, berücksichtigt?

more general term in the sense 'to recall', while *sich entsinnen* suggests more forcibly the
re-awakening to consciousness of something forgotten. 'Remember' in the imperative in
the sense of bearing in mind, not forgetting, is sometimes translated by *bedenken Sie*,
particularly in reference to a warning about consequences, but in general by *vergessen Sie
nicht!*
  [1] *Sich befassen mit* is a close synonym.
  [2] *Betrachten* also means 'to contemplate', 'to gaze at' a thing in such a way as to be
absorbed in it in mind and spirit. *Besehen, besichtigen* (view, inspect) suggest merely that
the intellect is brought to bear on a thing in order to discover some external characteristic
of it.

10. Rücksicht nehmen auf: to show sympathetic consideration, to be considerate towards.[1]

Er nimmt keine Rücksicht auf andere.

Auf seine Wünsche hat man keine Rücksicht genommen.

CONSOLIDATE Frequently, the German words here discussed are better rendered into English by terms other than 'consolidate'.

Befestigen[2] is 'to consolidate' a place in the sense of fortifying it against military attack. It also means 'to consolidate' such intangibles as fame, power, in an external way. When followed by 'in' it can mean 'to confirm' someone in a habit of mind.[3] **Festigen** is 'to consolidate, fortify inwardly', particularly with reference to an attitude of mind. The inner strength and coherence of the person or thing is emphasized more than the means by which this is accomplished.

In reflexive use both can mean 'to become stabilized', of prices and the like. If there is any distinction, it is that *sich festigen* suggests greater permanence because its reference is inward.

Die Stadt, die neuen Gebiete, wurden schnell befestigt.

Diese Maßnahmen haben die Macht des Regimes befestigt.

Eine kluge Politik hat die Stellung der Kirche befestigt.

Er hat seinen Ruhm durch neue Leistungen befestigt.

Dieses Erlebnis hat ihn in seinem Glauben gefestigt.

Die Preise haben sich befestigt (gefestigt).

Er hat eine gefestigte Lebensauffassung.

Innerlich gefestigt, rief er das Volk zum Protest gegen das Vorgehen der Regierung auf.

Das Verhalten vieler Ausländer hat in nicht geringem Maße dazu beigetragen, den Nationalsozialismus in Deutschland zu festigen.

Jeder Kompromiß konnte die Herrschaft der Gewalt und des Unrechts in Deutschland nur festigen.

CONSTANT, PERMANENT, PERSISTENT[4] **1. Ständig:** continuing, without end, whether applied to a thing or to activities or facts connected with a person. If the noun to which it refers is a person, the noun denotes the activity of the person (e.g. *ein ständiger Begleiter*). *Ständig* thus translates 'permanent' as well as 'constant'. It differs from **beständig** in that the latter denotes not merely continuance, but also an attitude of mind which does not relax its efforts or vigilance. This holds good, too, when the accompanying noun denotes not persons, but the actions of persons. Applied to things, it implies that these have the capacity to vary, but do not, i.e. are persistent. *Ständig* draws attention not to an inner quality or attitude, but to the mere fact of continued existence. It comes from *stehen* and means 'standing', 'continuing', while *beständig* comes from *bestehen* used in the sense of 'persist'. *Ständig* is not emphatic and cannot be used predicatively. It concentrates attention on the action or fact, *beständig* on the person.

Eine ständige Adresse.

Eine ständige Drohung.

---

[1] *Du bist dem alten Herrn auf den Fuß getreten, das war eine Rücksichtslosigkeit* (a lack of consideration).

[2] *Befestigen* also means 'to fasten' one thing on to another.

[3] See also 'strengthen'.

[4] See also *dauernd* and *andauernd* as footnote to 'last' (p. 181, n. 2).

Die Zeitungen melden ständige Durchbrüche zum Rhein hin.
Eine ständige Zufuhr von Waffen.
Ein ständiges Mitglied.
Er ist ständig hier.
Die Beurteilung der Lage bedarf der ständigen Korrektur.
Ein beständiger Mensch.
Ein beständiger Liebhaber.
Beständige Schmerzen.
Ein beständiger Wind.
Ihre beständigen Nörgeleien gehen mir auf die Nerven (persistent, whereas *ständig* would be more objective and less of a reproach).
Die Helden fast aller romantischen Bücher sind beständig auf Reisen (ständig would tend to make them real people).

2. Both **stet** and **stetig** mean 'unvarying' and therefore 'uninterrupted', particularly with regard to intensity, whereas *ständig* and *beständig* merely denote continued existence and do not exclude fluctuations, pauses, even if they do not necessarily imply them. *Stetig* is the normal prose term and is used both adjectivally and adverbially, *stet* occurring only in poetry and elevated prose and only as an adjective. *Stets,* the adverbial form derived from it is, however, used in ordinary prose. It means 'invariably',

> *Ein stetiges (stetes) Herz; sein steter, stetiger, Herrscherwille; ein stetiges Fieber; ein stetiger Regen; stetiges Wachstum.*

3. Hartnäckig: stubborn, not yielding or abating.
Ich habe hartnäckige Kopfschmerzen (a persistent headache).

CONTINUE   A. Transitive.

1. Fortsetzen is used, with a noun object, only in the sense of continuing an action or an activity.[1]
Nach dem Kriege setzte er seine Studien fort.
Wir können das Gespräch nun ungestört fortsetzen.
Er setzte seinen Weg durch den Wald fort.

2. Weiterführen: to extend an object or a line.
Die Straße ist um 100 Kilometer weitergeführt worden.
Der Bau ist seit letztem Winter nicht weitergeführt worden.

B. Intransitive.

1. Followed by the infinitive or the gerund.
(a) **Fortfahren** is used only of a continuous activity, whether resumption after a pause is implied or not. It is not applied to the repetition of an activity from time to time.
Nach einer kurzen Pause fuhr er zu schreiben, zu essen, fort.
Nach der Unterbrechung fuhr er zu sprechen fort.
(b) In the sense of 'to repeat an action from time to time' **weiter** should be used with an appropriate verb. It includes also the meaning of *fortfahren.*
Er drängte weiter auf Änderungen.
Er bekämpft den Plan weiter.
Sein Zustand bleibt weiter kritisch.

---

[1] *Weitermachen* is much used in conversation, like 'to go on', mostly intransitively, but also transitively with neuter pronoun objects such as *es, das,* and with nouns which mean 'work, activity'. *Wir können nicht weitermachen. Machen Sie Ihre Arbeit weiter.*

2. In other intransitive uses more specific terms must be used. The commonest are equivalents of 'to last' (see article) and **weitergehen,** 'to go on', of a line or an activity.

Sein Glück kann nicht dauern.
Der Regen hielt drie Tage an.
Der Weg geht noch einige Kilometer weiter.
Der Kreig muß weitergehen.

CONTROL (v. and s.) Control originally meant to check one thing by another, especially one register or account by a duplicate register or account. This sense is now comparatively rare except in science (thus a controlled experiment is one that is checked or verified by counter or parallel experiments) but the idea of keeping within the bounds of what is correct, essential or proper, or the like, still prevails, with the result that the term usually implies a regulation or a restraining by getting or keeping the upper hand (*W.S.*).

1. Kontrollieren (Fr. *contrôler*) is mainly limited to this sense of checking or verifying (i.e. *überprüfen*). When it means to restrain, to prevent from getting out of hand, the implication is that administrative measures are taken to bring this about and it is thus a close synonym of *regulieren*. It does not imply subduing by the exercise of will-power or strength. The noun *Kontrolle*, on the other hand, tends, like the English term, to extend its meaning. Similarly *unkontrollierbar.*

Die Fahrkarten werden an der Sperre kontrolliert.
Alle Verdächtigen werden kontrolliert.
Das Experiment wird in jedem Stadium kontrolliert.
Der Verkehr wird jetzt ganz rationell kontrolliert.
Es wurde keinerlei Versuch gemacht, durch Staatsautorität die Produktion und den Absatz des Reichtums (Kapitals) zu kontrollieren.
Preiskontrolle, Lohnkontrolle.
Eine Kontrollvorrichtung, Kontrollstation.
Unter väterlicher Kontrolle.
Die Polizei verlor die Kontrolle über die Demonstrierenden.
Die rebellierenden Studenten wurden endlich unter Kontrolle gebracht.
Der Waldbrand konnte nach fünf Stunden unter Kontrolle gebracht werden.
Die Kinder waren einfach unkontrollierbar.

2. The aspect of supervision is expressed by **beaufsichtigen** and **überwachen.** The suggestion here is the will to forestall any attempt of a person or thing to act contrary to the will of the subject.

Die Kinder wurden die ganze Zeit beaufsichtigt.
Unter Aufsicht der Polizei.
Die Ausgaben überwachen.

3. Repress, gain mastery of what has got out of order or is threatening to do so: German uses here a variety of expressions. **Beherrschen** (dominate), **Herr werden über** (or with genitive), **(be)zähmen** are amongst the commonest.

Er konnte sich, seine Stimme, seine Bewegungen nicht beherrschen.
Er wurde bald Herr der Situation.
Man muß seine Leidenschaften bezähmen, zügeln.
Er hat die Herrschaft über den Wagen verloren (lost control of).

CONTROL

Die Sängerin hatte eine vollkommene Beherrschung ihres Stimmregisters.

Die Studenten sind außer und Band (out of control).

Es gelang ihnen mit großen Anstrengungen, der Überschwemmung Einhalt zu gebieten (die Ü. einzudämmen).

Wer das Meer und den Himmel beherrscht, gewinnt Kriege (dominates).

Er kann sich nicht kontrollieren (is a modernism, no doubt due to Anglo-American influence).

CONVENTIONAL, UNCONVENTIONAL 1. In the sense of lacking in originality, individuality, imagination, **koventionell** exists, but is much less used than the English term. Often **reaktionär** is used instead. The noun **Konvention,** however, is more common, and in appropriate phrases can render the sense of the English word. Frequently, adjectives which are more or less close synonyms of 'conventional' are used.

Er ist sehr konventionell, reaktionär in seinen Ansichten, seinem Geschmack, seiner Kleidung.

Konventionelle Moral.

Ein konventionelles, konventionsbeherrschtes Benehmen.

Das was wesenhaft, beseelt, ausdrucksvoll ist, von dem Abgenutzten, Abgedroschenen, Abgeleiteten unterscheiden (W.).

Er trug die konventionelle, die übliche, die von der Konvention geheiligte weiße Krawatte.

Er ist ein phantasieloser Mensch.

Sein Denken bewegt sich in ausgefahrenen Gleisen.

2. In the sense of 'traditional' *traditionell* or one of its derivatives should be used.

Es wird traditionsgemäß angenommen, daß die Hortiten eine sagenhafte Rasse von Höhlenbewohnern waren (it has been conventional to regard the H. as...) (*W.*).

3. In the sense of commonly encountered, observed or performed: commonplace, ordinary, usual (*W.*) the adjectives used in the examples under 1 are more common than *konventionell.*

Halbtote Durchschnittsmenschen..., die sich kaum bewußt sind, daß sie wirklich leben, außer daß sie einer gewöhnlichen, (üblichen, banalen) Beschäftigung nachgehen (W.).

Wir haben im Geschäft nur die üblichen Muster.

4. 'Unconventional' in the sense of disregarding or not according to convention, out of the ordinary: **unkonventionell** exists in German, but is used still less than *konventionell.* Other adjectives and expressions are more common, e.g. **original** (*originell* means not influenced by others), **ungeniert** (not inhibited by restraints), **ausgefallen** (out of the ordinary), **frei von jeder Konvention, salopp** (see under casual), **zwanglos** (free and easy; see under casual). **Genial** has come down from the *Sturm-und-Drang* age, in which unconventional behaviour tended to be equated with genius.

Er ist ein Original (French: *c'est un original*).

Er ist sehr ungeniert in dem, was er tut.

Er ist frei von jeder Konvention.

Es ist eine originale Zeichnung.

Er sagt dauernd ausgefallene Dinge.

Er trägt saloppe Kleider.

Diese Familie ist ganz unkonventionell.
In diesem Haushalt geht es genial zu (not a harsh judgment).
Ihren Haushalt führen sie ganz genial.

COOK, BOIL, SEETHE 'Cook' means 'to apply heat to a substance so as to remove it from the state of rawness'. 'Boil' means 'to heat liquid to the point where it is converted into gas'.

1. Kochen generally means 'to boil' liquids. It is applied transitively and intransitively, to the cooking of food only in reference to the preparation of the whole meal, but never to any particular item of food unless these are cooked by boiling (e.g. *Erbsen*). For 'cook' in reference to particular items of food German can only use specific terms which indicate the method of preparation.

2. Sieden can mean 'to bring a liquid to a point of heat where it leaps or spouts up', i.e. to seethe. In addition it is sometimes applied to describe the state and movement of water just before the boiling point, i.e. it is used to denote a subjective impression rather than an objective condition. Expressions in which it is applied to the boiling of food exist, but are rarely used (e.g. *gesottene Eier, gesottenes Huhn*).

Sie hat das Essen schon gekocht.
Sie kocht ausgezeichnet.
Zum Abendessen haben wir gekochtes Huhn.
Kochst du die Kartoffeln oder brätst du sie?
Siedend heißes Öl.

COPY (s. and v.) **1.** One of a series of especially mechanical reproductions of the same original text, engraving or photograph: an individual example of a series of identical impressions (as of type, a printing plate) (*W.*): **Exemplar** (the only sense in which this term corresponds to copy).

Ein Buch, von dem fünfhundert Exemplare gedruckt wurden (W.).
Ich habe mein Exemplar von den 'Buddenbrooks' antiquarisch gekauft.

2. An imitation, transcript or reproduction of an original work (as of a letter, an engraving, a painting, a statue, a piece of furniture, a dress) (*W.*).
(a) **Kopie** may be used for a copy of all these types of original work.

Man sollte nie eine Kopie eines Bildes kaufen, sondern immer nur das Original.
Er gab mir die Kopie eines Briefes, die er gemacht hatte.

(b) **Abschrift** is used of anything handwritten or typed.

Er ließ sich eine Abschrift des Testaments geben.

(c) **Druck** really corresponds to 'print' (*Der Aufsatz ist noch nicht im Druck erschienen*) and by extension comes close to 'edition' (*erster Druck* 1707 *bei*...), particularly in reference to early printing.

Einer der frühen Drucke der Gutenberg-Bibel.

(d) **Abdruck** can be used of printed material in language or in relation to the visual arts, but *abdrucken* is a technical term in bookprinting (see Trübner).

Das ist ein Abdruck der Laokoon-Gruppe.

(e) **Durchschlag** is used only in the sense of a carbon copy.

Machen Sie bitte zwei Durchschläge dieses Briefes (also: *kopieren*).

(f) **Abschreiben** as well as its sense of reproduce has the specific one of copying or cheating at an examination or in a written exercise.

Er hat das Dokument sorgfältig abgeschrieben (kopiert).
Er hat die Hälfte bei seinem Nachbarn abgeschrieben.

(g) **Abzug** is used of a copy of something run off by a duplicating machine.
Ich brauche fünfzig Abzüge dieses Gedichts.

(h) **Reproduktion** corresponds to English 'reproduction' in reference to a work of art.

3. In the sense of 'imitate' German uses a number of verbs beginning with the prefix *nach*, of which **nachahmen** is the most general. More specific terms are: **nachäffen** (derogatory, i.e. to ape), **nachbilden, nachmachen, nachsprechen.**

Der Bildhauer bildet den Kopf genau nach.
Versuchen Sie, mir nachzusprechen (make the sounds as I do).
Der Komponist ahmt an dieser Stelle einen anderen nach.

CORNER   Ecke is the general term. **Winkel** means primarily 'angle'. In the sense of 'corner' it refers only to one that is remote or secluded.

Er stellte seinen Regenschirm in die Ecke.
Er bog plötzlich um die Ecke.
Ich habe Sie in jeder Ecke gesucht.
Sie wohnen in einem verborgenen Winkel des Waldes.

CORPSE   Leiche is the ordinary, **Leichnam** a more dignified, term. **Leiche** must also be used to translate 'dead body'.[1]

Die Leiche wurde verbrannt, war verstümmelt.
Der Leichnam wurde feierlich aufgebahrt.

COSTLY, EXPENSIVE, PRECIOUS, DEAR   Kostspielig is 'costly or 'expensive' in the sense of costing more than one estimates the thing to be worth. It is applied, like 'costly', mainly to what is elaborate, particularly activities. **Kostbar**[2] implies great expense, but denotes primarily that which has great value, especially when it is gorgeous, sumptuous. It corresponds to 'costly' only when this primary meaning is present. 'Precious' is its most common equivalent. **Preziös** means 'precious' only in the sense of 'artificial'. **Teuer** corresponds exactly to 'dear' in reference to the cost of an object.[3] *Teuerung*: a general rise in prices.

Das Reisen ist ein kostspieliges Vergnügen.
Es war ein kostspieliges Unternehmen.
Sie besitzt allerlei kostbare Edelsteine.
Er hat viel kostbare Zeit verschwendet.
Seine Ausdrucksweise ist manchmal preziös.
Ich kann mir den Wagen nicht leisten, er ist zu teuer.
Alle Lebensmittel sind viel teurer als vor dem Kriege.

COST(S), EXPENSE(S)   Kosten denotes in general what a thing costs, whether in money, time, energy, or the like. It may be followed by the

---

[1] Both terms once had the meaning of 'body' in general. *Leichnam* has survived in this sense in a few fixed phrases.

[2] Do not confuse with *köstlich* which has the general sense of 'lovely' as a term of praise and in reference to food means 'delicious'. *Der Hering war köstlich.*

[3] In the sense of 'held in affection', *teuer* is used only to show an awareness of what the person so addressed means to one (e.g. *ein teurer Freund*). Otherwise 'dear' must be rendered by the more general term *lieb*.

genitive of the noun, representing the thing purchased, the activity carried out. **Unkosten**, which cannot be followed by the genitive in this sense, means 'expenses' for which one feels one has no positive return, e.g. as involved in the removal or alleviation of an evil (e.g. in an accident), needless expense. As a commercial term it differs in no appreciable way from *Kosten*. **Ausgabe(n)** refers to expense(s) which yield(s) a positive return. **Spesen** is exclusively a commercial term which does not differ in meaning from *Kosten* and *Unkosten* used in this sense.

Er berechnete die Kosten, und fand, daß sie zu hoch waren.

Ich kann die Kosten des Umbaus nicht bestreiten.

Es tut mir leid, Ihrer Bitte um Hilfe nicht stattgeben zu können, aber ich habe in letzter Zeit allerlei Unkosten gehabt.

Durch den Autounfall sind mir ziemliche Unkosten entstanden.

Stürzen Sie sich nicht meinetwegen in Unkosten.

Wir müssen unsere Ausgaben stark einschränken.

Die beiden Firmen haben die Spesen geteilt.

COURSE (in the course of) **1. Im Lauf** implies that something is done or happens once, at one point during the course of an activity. It need not be the result of what precedes. Only in this sense does *Lauf* mean 'course'. **Verlauf,** on the other hand, refers to the whole action and is consequently freely used (*der Verlauf der Verhandlungen*), often being translated into English by some other word (e.g. *nach Verlauf vieler Jahre*, 'lapse').[1] *Im Verlauf* is applied to something that takes place or emerges as a result of what has preceded, or is thought of in connection with the action as a whole.

Im Laufe der Operation fuhr dem Arzt der Gedanke durch den Kopf, daß die Zahl der Lungenkranken im Steigen sei.

Im Verlauf der Operation hat sich der Zustand des Patienten erheblich verschlechtert.

Im Laufe des Gesprächs erwähnte er, daß seine Frau krank sei.

Im Verlauf des Gesprächs stellte sich heraus, daß er ein paar Unwahrheiten gesagt hatte.

2. Ablauf refers to the way a thing runs its course.

Die Verhandlungen hatten einen reibungslosen Ablauf.

COVER 1. Bedecken is the ordinary prosaic term. It suggests no interest or emotional participation on the part of the speaker, but concentrates attention on the action. The force of the prefix *be* is that the covering is 'all over'.

Der Schnee bedeckt die Berge.

Der Himmel ist mit Wolken bedeckt.

2. Decken conveys secondary associations. In the active, though rarely in the passive, voice it suggests in elevated or poetical diction to 'cover here and there'. It can also suggest the performing of an action in stages. Further, it means 'to protect', literally and figuratively.[2]

Der Schnee deckt die Berge (here and there).

'Die Treppen deckten sie zuletzt auch schwarz, ich sah es wohl' (Goethe, *Egmont*).

---

[1] *Ablauf*: the lapse or course of a fixed period in relation to a pre-determined end. Thus *im Ablauf des Gesprächs* means 'while the conversation is moving to a known end or goal'.

[2] Note further: *die beiden Begriffe decken sich durchaus* (coincide completely).

COVER

Das Dach wird mit Schiefern gedeckt.
Unsere Stellungen sind vor der Bombardierung gedeckt.
In diesem Unternehmen bin ich genügend gedeckt (financially).

3. Zudecken: to cover up, on all sides. It can suggest emotional participation.
Sie deckten den Sarg mit Blumen zu.

4. Verdecken: to cover in such a way as to make invisible.
Wolken verdeckten die Sonne.

CROSS 1. Kreuzen: to place one thing crosswise over another, e.g. parts of the body, streets, lines (i.e. which intersect). Extended senses are: the mutual passing of objects without actually touching (e.g. trains, letters); to thwart plans, etc. (more commonly *durchkreuzen*); to clash, of interests.

2. Überqueren is little used.[1] It suggests an elaborate operation (e.g. the mountains, ocean). In most cases German uses the equivalents of 'to go across'.

> '*Gegen Mitte März bricht die Stellung der Wehrmacht...so jäh zusammen, daß...die Alliierten ungefähr gleichzeitig mit dem Rheinübergang Montgomerys und Bradleys den Strom bei Oppenheim fast spielend überqueren.*'
> (From a German newspaper, Surprise is indicated, because the crossing would in most cases be difficult.)

3. To go across, when the points of departure and arrival are outside the limits of the space crossed. See 'go'.
Ich ging über die Straße.[2]
Hannibal zog über die Alpen.
Der Zug fuhr über die Brücke.
Wir flogen über den Kanal.
Wolken ziehen über die Sonne (pass across).

4. To cross a space when the points of departure and arrival are within its limits.
Er ging auf die andere Serte des Zimmers (he crossed the room).

5. Überschreiten: to cross a line or anything conceived as a line.
Die Grenze überschreiten.
Das Überschreiten der Gleise ist verboten.
Die Alliierten haben den Rhein auf breiter Front überschritten.

6. Example of a more specific term:
Die Brücke führt über den Fluß.

CUPBOARD, CHEST German **Schrank** is the most general term, whether as a container of food or clothes or anything else. It frequently appears in compounds.
Speiseschrank, Kleiderschrank, Bücherschrank (in English more often bookcase), *Gesdschrank.*

German **Kasten** (see box) is used in this sense in South German, particularly Austrian.

German **Spind,** originally belonging to the North East, reached the Rhineland as far south as Trier. As a military term it is used of such objects

---

[1] *Durchqueren:* to traverse (e.g. *die Wüste*).
[2] *Quer* should only be added in the sense of 'obliquely'.

in barracks, and in most parts of the country is understood exclusively as such.

German **Anrichte** may not be an enclosed cupboard but simply a shelf or board or set of these on which cups, saucers, plates and the like are kept.

CURSE, SWEAR **Fluchen** generally means 'to curse' or 'to swear' in the sense of 'to use profane oaths'. In this sense it is used absolutely or followed by *auf* (to swear at a person). Followed by the dative it occurs in elevated language in the sense of 'to utter an invocation of destruction or punishment' on a person or thing. **Verfluchen** is only used in the latter sense, and may indicate either momentary annoyance or a solemn imprecation. **Verwünschen** also has this sense, but is less strong. It suggests: to wish a person ill. **Schwören** has as its only meaning: to swear a solemn oath.

Er flucht unaufhörlich (swears).
Er hat schrecklich auf mich geflucht (swore at).
In seinem unendlichen Schmerz fluchte er den Göttern (cursed).
Der Vater verfluchte seinen Sohn.
Er wurde wegen seiner Willkür von seinen Untertanen verflucht.
Er verwünschte sein Schicksal.
Er schwor, sein Leben für die gute Sache einzusetzen.

CUT Sense: literal, to part something with pressure of an edge (*P.O.D.*).

1. **Schneiden** is 'to cut' by any instrument or means which does not require great force on the part of the person performing the act. It is therefore not applied to the cutting down of trees or the cutting of firewood.[1]
Er hat das Brot, das Fleisch, das Tuch, das Gras, das Korn, das Glas, geschmitten.
Er hat sich die Haare, die Nägel, in den Finger, geschmitten.

2. **Aufschneiden:** to cut open. It should be used when 'open' is implied.
Schneiden Sie die Seiten des Buches auf.
Die Leiche wurde aufgeschmitten.

3. **Durchschneiden:** to intersect.
Die Landschaft ist von Kanälen durchschnitten.

4. Both **hauen** and **spalten** imply the expenditure of force. The former approximates to 'hew', 'chop', and suggests the hewing out or away of pieces from an object by repeated blows. The latter approximates to 'split', and suggests that the instrument goes clean through the object and severs it.
Wir müssen ein Loch in das Eis hauen.
Er spaltet Holz, um ein Feuer zu machen (e.g. large blocks into smaller pieces).[2]

5. **Hacken:** where energy is required and repeated blows are implied.
Er hackt Holz für den Winter.

DAMAGE **1. Beschädigen:** to cause actual physical damage.
Das Haus ist vom dem Sturm schwer beschädigt worden.

---

[1] *Beschneiden* is 'to trim', 'to lop'; also 'to circumcise'. Figuratively: to curtail. *Verschneiden* is 'to cut wrongly'; also 'to fortify' wine. *Zerschneiden* is 'to sever', particularly of things that should remain whole. Examples: *der Arzt zerschnitt den Nerv; das Band zwischen ihnen wurde zerschnitten.*
[2] *Fällen* is 'to cut down' trees, 'to fell'.

DAMAGE

Kriegsbeschädigte (cripples and the like).
Die Feuchtigkeit hat das Klavier beschädigt.
Der Regen hat das Obst beschädigt.

2. **Schaden:** to damage in any way, externally or internally, physically or morally, directly or indirectly. The harm is more potential than actual. The sense is therefore 'to be bad for' in a vague, indefinite way.

Zu viel Regen schadet dem Hause.
Das Trinken wird Ihrer Gesundheit schaden.
Der Preissturz hat meinem Geschäft sehr geschadet.
Das Eingreifen der Regierung schadet nur dem Kulturleben eines Landes.
Zuviel Regen schadet dem Obst.
Es schadet seinem Ruf.

3. **Schädigen** means 'to cause loss to' a person, in two ways. (*a*) By far the commonest use, in reference to property or money. (*b*) A rarer use: to damage the inner principle or vitality of a person or thing, generally in a psychological or spiritual sense.

Kriegsgeschädigte, Bombengeschädigte (those who have suffered loss or destruction of property through war or bombs).
Der Preissturz hat mein Geschäft geschädigt.
Durch diese Transaktion bin ich geschädigt worden.
Er hat mich geschädigt.
Meinungsverschiedenheiten schädigen ihre Freundschaft nicht.
Die systematische Philosophie hat nach Nietzsches Ansicht das Leben schwer geschädigt.

DARE 1. **Wagen:** to venture, to have the audacity, spontaneously, from within oneself.[1]

Er wagte nicht, zu widersprechen.

2. **Dürfen** is used negatively and interrogatively when 'dare' denotes a prohibition from without. It is often accompanied by a statement of the consequences which would result from an ignoring of the prohibition. The third person singular of 'dare' is in this sense 'dare (i.e. not 'dares').

Er darf das nicht tun, es würde sicher seine Aussichten verderben ('dare' or 'must not').

DATA See also under 'date' and 'evidence'. The singular 'datum' is much rarer. Sense: something that is given either from being experimentally encountered or from being admitted or assumed for specific purposes: a fact or principle granted or presented: something upon which an inference or argument is based or from which an intellectual system of any sort is constructed (*W.*). German: **Daten** or **Gegebenheiten.**

Man kann keine weitere Bewertung wagen, bis nicht mehr Daten vorhanden sind (*W.*).
Aus diesen Daten, Gegebenheiten, kann man folgern, daß...(W.).

DATE 1. German **Datum** is more restricted in use than English 'date', being used when the exact day of the month if not the year is mentioned.

Welches Datum haben wir heute? (also possible: *den wievielten haben wir heute?* Also: *was ist das heutige Datum, was ist heute für ein Tag?*).

---

[1] In this sense *wagen* also means 'risk'.

Sein Geburtsdatum war der 20. März 1925.
Der Brief ist mit keinem Datum versehen.

2. When the exact date is not mentioned, German uses **Zeit** and **Zeitpunkt Tag**; also **wann** etc.

Aus welcher Zeit stammen diese Ruinen? (What is the date of...?)
Haben sie einen Tag für die Neueröffnung des Museums bestimmt?
Der Zeitpunkt seiner Abreise wurde immer wider verschoben.
Zu dem Zeitpunkt, an dem (als) er benachrichtigt, entlassen wurde (S.O.D.).
Zu dieser Zeit (damals) gab es noch kein elektrisches Licht (A.L.) (at that date...).

3. **Termin:** The latest date by which a thing must be done. Also an appointment to see someone.

Sie haben den Termin für die Einreichung des Antrags schon überschritten.
Bitte genau auf den Termin achten!
Lassen Sie sich einen Termin vom Arzt geben.

4. **Jahreszahlen** is used for the learning of dates in history.

Als ich in die Schule ging, bestand das Fach Geschichte aus Jahreszahlen.

DECEIVE, CHEAT, DELUDE 1. **Trügen** can have only a thing as subject and therefore cannot indicate deliberate deception. The thing deceives because of its nature, i.e. because it is such that human beings are prone to error when confronted by it. *Trügen* is normally intransitive (but Kleist uses it transitively in *Die Verlobung in St. Domingo*: '*Wenn mich nicht alles trügt*').

Der Schein, das Gedächtnis trügt.
Wenn nicht alle Anzeichen trügen...(see 'sign').
Derartige Gesichter trügen.

2. **Betrügen** always implies deception or disappointment in an expectation or conviction, whether in material things or otherwise. It does not mean simply 'to tell a lie'. It is frequently followed by an expression denoting what one has lost (with *um*), and is often best translated by 'cheat (of)'.[1] Furthermore it need not be deliberate, and the deception can be in act as well as in word.

Er wurde um seine Erbschaft betrogen.
Er hat mich in der Frage des Gehalts betrogen.
Seine Versprechen haben mich betrogen.

3. **Täuschen:** to cause to mistake the false for the real, to involve in a delusion, illusion,[2] hallucination. It frequently, but not necessarily, suggests an optical delusion (*vortäuschen*). The subject, i.e. what causes the delusion, can be the same as that of *trügen*, but, unlike the latter, *täuschen* may be used transitively. The deception can be deliberate or otherwise.

Mein Gedächtnis hat mich getäuscht.
Er hat mich mit seinen Schilderungen vollkommen getäuscht.
Ich hielt ihn für einen Schauspieler, aber ich habe mich vielleicht getäuscht.
Ich habe mich in ihm getäuscht.
Ich tat es nicht, um Sie zu täuschen (very close to *irreführen*).

---

[1] In this sense *betrügen* also translates 'swindle'. *Schwindeln* means 'to tell tall stories'. 'To cheat' in the sense of using dishonest means (e.g. at an examination), but not robbing a person of anything, is in popular language *mogeln, schummeln.*
[2] See Fowler's *Modern English Usage* for the distinction between 'delusion' and 'illusion'.

4. Belügen must be used when 'deceive' means 'deliberately to tell a lie', without further implication.[1]

Warum hast du mich belogen?

DECIDE, RESOLVE, DETERMINE   1. Sich entschließen, entschlossen sein (to be resolved, determined) imply strong determination, will-power. The original meaning of *entschließen* was 'unlock', i.e. unlock one's mind, clarify, make definite one's thoughts.

Nach langem Zögern entschloß ich mich, seinem Rat zu folgen.
Er ist entschlossen, alles zu riskieren.
Er kann sich nicht entschließen.

2. Beschließen is used in two ways: (*a*) when no particular exercise of will-power is implied, i.e. as the ordinary term for 'decide'; (*b*) when it is a question of decisions or resolutions which are passed by virtue of authority. The passive is possible only with a non-personal subject. Reflexive use is not possible.

Ich habe beschlossen, meine Ferien am Meer zu verbringen.
Ich beschloß, mich nicht von seinen Einwänden beeinflussen zu lassen.
Der Senat hat beschlossen, daß die Prüfung früher stattfinden soll.
Es ist beschlossen worden, die Steuern herabzusetzen.

3. Entscheiden: to settle a question intellectually, to choose between various possibilities. It may be used reflexively in this sense. *Sich entscheiden für*: to decide on.

Die Frage, ob wir diesen Sommer verreisen, ist noch nicht entschieden.
Der Streit ist entschieden worden.
Wir haben uns schließlich entschieden, ins Theater zu gehen (as against some other possibility).
Ich habe mich für diesen Mantel entschieden.

4. Bestimmen is used with a non-personal subject and a personal object in the sense of inducing a person to a course of action. It also translates 'determine' when the object is a thing.

Die Aussichten auf eine bessere Stellung haben ihn bestimmt, nach London zu fahren.
Die Größe des Hauses hat die Zahl der Gäste bestimmt.
Haben Sie den Treffpunkt schon bestimmt?

DEMAND (noun)   **1. Forderung:** a demand made by a person.

Er stellte viele Forderungen an mich.
Ich habe alle seine Forderungen erfüllt.

2. Anforderung: a demand made by a thing. See also under 'standard'.

Die Vollendung der Sixtinischen Kapelle stellte große Anforderungen an die Arbeitskraft Michelangelos.
Die Anforderungen der Lage sind erfüllt worden.
Er ist den Anforderungen nicht gewachsen.

3. Economic terms: **Bedarf, Nachfrage.** In an economic context 'supply' is *Angebot*.

Den Bedarf decken, eine starke Nachfrage nach gewissen Waren.

---

[1] *Anlügen* means 'to lie to a person on a vast scale'. For a similar use of *an* see *anschuldigen* under 'accuse'.

DEMAND[1] (verb)   **1. Fordern** is used with a personal subject or with things which stand for persons, and is the general term for to demand peremptorily.

Sie fordern zu viel von mir.
Die Generale forderten mehr Truppen.
Die Schlacht forderte viele Opfer.

2. Erfordern is used with a non-personal subject.
Die Lage erfordert harte Maßnahmen.

3. Anfordern, with a personal subject, is only used in the sense of 'to demand by virtue of powers vested in one' and then only in an administrative capacity. It is common in contexts referring to the number of men or the amount of material required for specific work. In other contexts it suggests insistence after the original response has not been met.

Er fordete 17 Leute an, um diese Arbeit auszuführen.
Er hat meinen Pass angefordert.

DENY   A. Sense: declare untrue or non-existent, disavow or repudiate.

1. Leugnen means 'to declare' a statement (mostly in the form of an accusation) 'to be untrue' or, less often, a thing 'to be non-existent'. It refers to matters which can be accepted as facts (e.g. doings or happenings) and religious beliefs, only to opinions when used negatively. Thus, it is possible in the sentence 'I don't deny that it is a good poem', but is less common in the positive form of this statement. In this sense it is perhaps more frequent with a following *daß* clause than with a noun object.

Leugnen is connected etymologically with *lügen*, and refusal to admit a fact is its commonest sense. The etymology suggests why *leugnen* is used with reference to religious matters (i.e. the denial of God's existence was once regarded as a lie), and with reference to opinions in the negative (i.e. one cannot deny or tell a lie about something obvious).

Der Angeklagte leugnet.
Er leugnete, daß er den Mord begangen hätte. Er leugnete den Diebstahl.
Er leugnet das Dasein Gottes.
Er leugnet das Vorhandensein einer Gefahr, die Absicht einer Beleidigung.
Die Regierung leugnet ihre Verantwortlichkeit (denies theoretically, not in any specific case, the existence of its responsibility).
Ich will garnicht leugnen, daß es ein gutes Bild ist.

2. Bestreiten, to dispute, contest, argue, is used in statements which must be taken as matters of opinion and which refer to any matter which is disputed. It is obligatory when 'deny' is used positively, optional when used negatively (see *leugnen*).

Ich bestreite (nicht), daß es ein gutes Bild ist.
Ich bestreite, daß Goethe das meinte.

3. Verneinen only means 'deny' in the sense of a categorical contradiction of the validity of an affirmation or of the value of a thing. It governs a noun object, but not a clause. In other cases it corresponds to 'say no', 'negate', etc.

Ich verneinte seine Behauptung, diese Anschauung, die Gültigkeit dieser Theorie.
Er verneint all bestehenden Werte.

[1] See also *verlangen* under 'ask'.

DENY

Die Weltschmerzler verneinen überhaupt den Sinn des Daseins.
'Ich bin der Geist der stets verneint' (says no—Goethe's *Faust*).

4. Ableugnen: to deny emphatically an assertion, mostly something imputed to oneself, an accusation.[1] It is normally used with a noun object which denotes the specific accusation (i.e. where *leugnen* is impossible) and with a following *daß* clause. In the latter case it differs from *leugnen* in being more emphatic and referring to more important matters.[2]

Der Angeklagte leugnete die Tat, den ihm zur Last gelegten Diebstahl, den Mord, ab.

Er leugnete die Schuld, die Verantwortung, ab.

Der Minister leugnete energisch ab, daß solche Maßnahmen ins Auge gefaßt worden seien.

5. Dementieren: to deny officially a report, a rumour.

Der Bericht ist von der Regierung schon zweimal dementiert worden.

6. Verleugnen: as a rendering of 'deny', to be able to make a personal trait appear to others different from what it is, or as non-existent. It is mostly used with *nicht können*. The object must be a noun, not a clause. *Er ließ sich verleugnen*: had someone say for him that he was not at home.

Er kann seine Nationalität, niedrige Herkunft, nicht verleugnen.

'Es (=das Blatt) war von Larkens, wie er augenblicklich sah, wie selbst die angenommene Handschrift kaum verleugnen wollte' (Mörike, *Maler Nolten*).

7. Absprechen is followed by a double object, dative and accusative, and means 'to deny' that a person possesses a quality. It is often translated by other terms than 'deny'.

Kunstsinn kann man ihm nicht absprechen.

B. Sense: to withhold something from a person. **Versagen.**[3]

Ich versagte ihm meine Unterstützung.

Er muß sich den Luxus nun versagen.

DESTROY, ANNIHILATE[4] **Zerstören** implies the violent wrenching asunder of the parts of an object, not necessarily its complete disappearance without trace. When only the latter is meant, **vernichten** must be used. It is also the appropriate term when utter annihilation (i.e. without surviving traces) involving violence is suggested. In figurative use *vernichten* is stronger than *zerstören*. **Zunichte machen** is used figuratively in the sense of 'to annul', 'to rob of existence'. It is less emphatic than *vernichten*. See also under 'undo'.

'To destroy' not wanted animals can be translated by *vernichten* if it is done on a large scale and by officials, as at a zoo. In reference to private animals *erschießen* (see article on 'shoot') or some other specific term must be used.

---

[1] With the words *Anschuldigung, Beschuldigung, zurückweisen* is used, with words which denote the specific charge *ableugnen*.

[2] *In Abrede stellen* is a close synonym of *ableugnen*.

[3] See also 'fail'.

[4] *Vertilgen* is 'to obliterate', 'to destroy all trace of' a thing, generally by devouring it, literally or figuratively. *Die Spinne vertilgt eine Menge Ungeziefer. Ungeziefer vertilgte die Obsternte. Tilgen* is 'to wipe out', 'to annul' in technical senses. *Eine Schuld tilgen. Austilgen*: to wipe out by a process, to extirpate, particularly large sections of people. *Die russische Revolution hat das Bürgertum systematisch ausgetilgt.*

Die Stadt wurde durch die wiederholten Bombardierungen fast gänzlich zerstört.

Der Hagel hat die Ernte zerstört.

Sie müssen alle belastenden Dokumente vernichten (not *zerstören*).

Hitler wollte Polen vernichten.

Sie zerstören den guten Eindruck, den ich von Ihnen bekommen habe (*vernichten* would be too emphatic).

Das hat meine Hoffnungen zerstört (more emphatic: *vernichtet*).

Der Krieg hat meine Pläne zunichte gemacht.

Die Tiere müssen vernichtet werden, da sie nicht mehr gefüttert werden können.

Wir müssen das Pferd erschießen.

DIFFERENT 1. **Verschieden** is used when two or more persons or things are described as having different attributes which distinguish them from each other. The adjective *verschieden* is, according to the sense, attached to the persons or things on the one hand, or to the attribute on the other.

Die Brüder sind verschieden.

Die zwei Stühle sind nur in der Farbe verschieden.

Wir sind verschiedener Ansicht.

Verschiedene Leute haben verschiedene Interessen.

Sie faßten die Arbeit verschieden an.

Er ist sehr verschieden von seinem Bruder.

2. Ander (*anders* in predicative and adverbial use).

(a) A different person or thing from that mentioned before.

(b) A person or thing is different, has changed from what he or it was before. *Ander* does not distinguish from each other the persons or things of whom a change is predicated.

Die Brüder sind jetzt anders.

Wir sind jetzt anderer Ansicht geworden.

Andere Leute haben andere Interessen.

Sie faßten die Arbeit anders an.

3. Unterschiedlich: varied.

Die Wirkung war unterschiedlich.

DIFFICULT 1. **Schwierig** denotes an objective quality in the person, thing, action, to which it is applied, and means 'complicated', 'intricate', 'involved'. In the case of a person it has the sense of inwardly complicated in such a way as to be difficult to have dealings with. In all cases the complication distinctly implies a process with all its stages and details. It is the normal rendering of 'difficult' when the latter qualifies nouns or pronouns.

2. Schwer refers in the first place to the effect on the subject, and means 'arduous' for him, whether it is or is not so for others. The object is apprehended in a general way as difficult, but without reference to details or the relationship between its parts. It thus approximates more closely to 'hard' than to 'difficult'. It is a widely used term, its fundamental meaning being 'grievous', 'hard to bear'. Accordingly, it is not the normal word for 'difficult' as applied to nouns and pronouns. With nouns which in themselves denote an ordeal and the like it can only mean 'grievous', 'severe', etc. and therefore must not be used in the sense of 'difficult' (*eine schwere Prüfung* = a severe ordeal; *eine schwierige Prüfung* = a difficult examination).

DIFFICULT

With nouns which in themselves do not suggest the sense of 'grievous' both terms may be used, the distinction being approximately the same as between 'hard' and 'difficult', *schwer*, however, being less colloquial than 'hard' (*ein schwieriges, schweres Examen*).

Schwer cannot be applied to a person in the sense of 'difficult' (*ein schwerer Junge* = a criminal).

3. 'Difficult' followed by the infinitive ('it is difficult to see'; 'he is difficult to catch') requires special attention. Since in this construction the meaning is generally that the difficulty lies with the subject and is not a quality of the object, *schwer* is the normal term and can always be used, even in those cases where *schwierig* would be more discriminating. *Schwierig* does not often occur in this combination. It may be used, provided an involved process, extended in time (e.g. manœuvres, a technical process, an action requiring constant readaptation) is indicated. The examples show that in cases where a verb alone does not convey this sense, the substitution of a phrase can do so.

(a) *Ein schweres Problem.*
Ein schwerer Vortrag (the speaker thinks of his trouble in following, but not of any objective characteristic of the lecture).
Es ist eine schwere Aufgabe, den Schutt der zerstörten Stadt wegzuschaffen.
Ein schwerer Krieg.

(b) *Ein schwieriger Mensch.*
Ein schwieriger Dichter.
Ein schwieriges Gelände zum Kämpfen.
Ein schwieriges Problem.
Ein schwieriger Vortrag.
Es ist eine schwierige Aufgabe, den Schutt der zerstörten Stadt wegzubringen.
Ein schwieriger Feldzug.
Eine schwierige Stelle.

(c) *Es ist schwer, ihn zu befriedigen.*
Er ist schwer zu befriedigen.
Es ist schwer, den Umzug unter solchen Umständen zu veranstalten.
Das Kind ist ein schwieriger Fall und daher schwer zu behandeln.
Die Einwendung ist schwer zu verstehen.
Es ist schwer, mit ihr zu leben.
Es ist schwer, diese beiden Wörter zu unterscheiden.
Es fällt mir schwer, das zu glauben.

(d) *Es war höchst schwierig, diesen Feldzug zu planen und auszuführen.*
Es war schwierig, bei derartigen Einschränkungen immer die richtigen Grenzen zu beobachten.
Es ist schwierig, das Geschäft wieder in Gang zu bringen.
Es ist schwierig, eine Lebensgemeinschaft mit ihr aufrechtzuerhalten (not: *zu leben*).
Es ist schwierig, zwischen diesen beiden Wörtern einen Unterschied zu machen.
Es ist schwierig, den Vortrag zu verstehen.
'*...viel schwieriger schien es mir, die Geldangelegenheit zu lösen*' (Ricarda Huch, *Fra Celeste*).
'*Deshalb war ihm eine Last Goldes nicht so begehrenswert wie ein menschlicher Körper für eine Untersuchung, wie denn in der Tat ein solcher schwieriger zu erhalten war, da man es in der Christenwelt für sündlich hielt, das zur Auferstehung und Verwandlung bestimmte Kleid der unsterblichen Seele zu zerstören*' (Ricarda Huch, *Der Arme Heinrich*).

DISAPPEAR **Verschwinden** is the general term and means 'to become invisible'. **Schwinden** means 'to dwindle away and cease to exist'. It emphasizes the process, not sudden extinction. *Verschwinden* sometimes implies cessation of existence, and stresses the result, not the process. **Entschwinden** is not used in everyday prose, and is often followed by phrases such as *dem Auge, den Blicken*. It means 'to disappear', not 'to cease to exist', and stresses the stages in which a person or thing disappears from sight.

Die Kerze ist verschwunden.
Die Kerze schwindet.
Er verschwand unter der Oberfläche.
Er verschwand um die Ecke.
Mein Vermögen verschwindet (either: someone is taking it away, or: it is being used up; *schwindet* being also possible in the latter sense, with emphasis on the process).
Der Winter verschwand (there was no trace of it left; also *schwand* and, in elevated style, *entschwand*).
Die Vorräte verschwinden dauernd.
Die Vorräte schwinden.
Mein Mut, meine Hoffnung, schwindet (*verschwindet* not possible).
Er entschwand dem Auge, den Blicken.

DISCOVER, FIND OUT 1. **Entdecken** is to discover by chance or at least without the idea of purpose being emphasized even if the discovery is the result of research. (*Aufdecken* means 'to uncover'.)

Er hat ein Heilmittel, wenn auch kein hundertprozentig zuverlässiges, gegen Blutkrebs entdeckt.
Er entdeckte, daß keiner der Insaßen des umgekippten Wagens einen Führerschein bei sich hatte.
Ich habe entdeckt, daß gewisse Obstsorten, die Säure enthalten, meiner Gesundheit abträglich sind.

2. **Ausfindig machen** implies a clear and deliberate attempt and effort to discover something.

Sie müssen ausfindig machen, wer ihm die Erlaubnis dazu erteilte.
Er hat versucht, ausfindig zu machen, wer den ersten Schuß abfeuerte.

3. **Ermitteln:** to discover as a result of investigation, particularly of police or detective work.

Der Detektiv hat ermittelt, wer zwischen 10 und 11 Uhr in der Gegend gewesen war.

4. **Herausbekommen** is a colloquialism in the sense of find out.

Ich habe endlich mal herausbekommen, was er wollte.

5. **Hinter etwas kommen** is also a colloquialism, which includes something of the meaning of 'see through' as well as 'find out'.

Ich bin hinter seine Schliche gekommen.

6. See also under 'investigate'.

DISTRICT 1. **Bezirk** is today an administrative division of a town or country area and has therefore to do with government. It appears often but not exclusively in compounds. In Vienna it is customary to refer to an area as a *Bezirk*. **Verwaltungsbezirk, Polizeibezirk, Postzustellbezirk,**

DISTRICT

Bezirksrat, Bezirksgericht. Revier is used in the same sense as *Bezirk*, but less extensively. **Polizeirevier, Jagdrevier.**

In diesem Revier gibt es viel Wild.

2. Sense: A tract of country of vaguely defined limits (*S.O.D.*). German: **Gebiet, Gegend.** *Gebiet*, which is connected with the verb *gebieten*, developed the meaning of a district over which government extends and then finally an area of any kind with recognizable characteristics. *Gegend* comes closer to English countryside.

Ein landwirtschaftliches Gebiet.

Ein Ackerbaugebiet.

Eine romantische Gegend.

Ein gebirgiges Gebiet (or *eine g. Gegend*).

Ein unfruchtbares Gebiet.

Am Ende des zweiten Weltkrieges hat Rußland viele fremde Gebiete annektiert.

Eine öde Gegend.

3. **Viertel** is an area of a town, quarter in the loose sense of part. It has nothing to do with government and it mostly appears in compounds.

Regierungsviertel (not the area over which government extends, but the district where government-buildings are to be found).

Armenviertel.

Elendsviertel (slums).

Theaterviertel (but *Theatergegend* is also found).

Villenviertel.

Das von Italienern bewohnte Viertel.

DIVE In the intransitive sense, **tauchen** means 'to dive' from the surface of the water in which one is already immersed.[1,2]

Springen is 'to dive' from a height, often as a feat of skill. Only the context can show whether 'dive' or 'jump' is meant.

Er tauchte so tief, daß er nicht mehr sichtbar war.

Er springt gut.

Er sprang vom Deck ins Wasser (dived or jumped).

DO A. Sense: perform, execute, carry out, bring about, effect, cause, accomplish.

Tun, machen[3]

1. With an indefinite pronoun as object.

Tun refers to acts that are viewed as serious or important or thought of with precision, *machen* to those that are regarded as trivial or unimportant

---

[1] In transitive use *tauchen* means 'to plunge' or 'to dip'. *Tunken* also means 'to dip', in reference to light objects.

[2] The direction of *tauchen* can be changed by the prefix (e.g. *umhertauchen, auftauchen,* particularly of submarines).

[3] Some close approximations to this sense are: (*a*) *Anfangen* (followed by *mit*, and taking *nichts, wenig, etwas, nicht viel* and the like as object): achieve something with, get somewhere with, find some use for. *In Italien konnte ich mit meinen paar Brocken Italienisch nichts* (*wenig*) *anfangen. Was kann man mit solchen Studenten anfangen? Können Sie mit diesen Fleischresten irgendwas anfangen?* (*machen aus* = make out of). (*b*) *Anstellen* suggests half-humorously what one ought not to do (to be up to). *Was haben Sie bloß angestellt?* (*c*) *Schaffen* (weak): get through work, get done. As object: *viel, wenig,* etc. It is widely used in south Germany. *Heute habe ich recht wenig geschafft.*

or thought of only vaguely. In tone *machen* is lighter, more familiar than *tun*.[1]

This distinction means that in general *tun* is used to express the idea of being busy, *machen* that of spending one's leisure, filling in time. *Tun* refers to important, *machen* to humbler work. The border-line is vague. Only *tun* can ask what right a person has to be in a stated place (*was tut er hier?*).

With an adverb of appraisal (e.g. well, badly, brilliantly) only *machen* can be used.

The following sentences contain examples in which both *tun* and *machen* are possible, with the distinction explained above, examples in which *tun* alone is correct, examples of *machen* with an adverb of appraisal.[2,3]

(a) *Was tut er im Büro* (what is his work or what right has he to be in the office)?

Was macht er im Büro (what is his work or what does he happen to be doing there at the moment)?

Was tun Sie da (presses for a serious answer)?

Was machen Sie da (lightly)?

Was tun Sie heute abend (expects a precise answer or implies a more serious pursuit)?

Was machen Sie heute abend (how are you spending..., amusing yourself)?

Was tun Sie mit Ihrer Freizeit (what serious use do you find for...)?

Was machen Sie mit Ihrer Freizeit?

Was kann man tun, um die Schmerzen etwas zu betäuben (expects a full explanation)?

Was kann man machen, um die Schmerzen etwas zu betäuben (expects a quick or simple remedy)?

Wer hat das getan?

Wer hat das gemacht?

Wie tust du das nur?

Wie macht man das (e.g. cracking one's fingers)?

Sowas tut man doch nicht!

Sowas macht man doch nicht (said lightly, e.g. of an old woman who tries to look young).

Sonntag taten wir nichts als zu Haus faulenzen (we ought to have done something more useful).

Sonntag machten wir nichts als zu Hause faulenzen (we spent our leisure in this way).

Was haben Sie mit Ihrem Bein getan (a more serious injury)?

Was haben Sie mit Ihrem Bein gemacht (e.g. a scratch)?

Ich habe etwas Dummes gemacht (*getan* is possible but is more appropriate with a serious adjective such as *töricht*).

(b) *Ich habe morgen (viel) zu tun* (busy).

Im Augenblick tut er nichts, er könnte Ihnen helfen.

Dieser Student hat das ganze Jahr nichts getan.

Tu' doch mal was, sitz' doch nicht da, wenn alles schief geht.

Das englische Volk fragt sich, was es getan hat, um solche Vorwürfe zu verdienen.

---

[1] The same type of distinction exists between *aufmachen* and *auftun* (see 'open').

[2] If *tun* is combined with such adverbs they acquire a moral connotation (e.g. *das war schlecht von dir getan*).

[3] 'To do well' followed by the infinitive: *gut daran tun* (e.g. *Sie täten gut daran, es zu gestehen*).

Kulturell hat der Adel in Deutschland wenig getan.
Das Kind tut nichts als schreien.
Er tat alles, was ihm befohlen wurde.
Ich will nichts mit einem derartigen Vorschlag zu tun haben.

(c) *Das haben Sie gut (schlect, richtig, falsch, verkehrt, glänzend, besser als er) gemacht.*

2. With a noun object.

(a) In this combination *machen* is familiar and conversational in tone in the sense that a more precise term would in most cases be used in serious writing (e.g. *einen Aufsatz schreiben, ein Examen bestehen* (pass), *den Dr. phil. erlangen, die Klassik behandeln, studieren*). Its use is practically limited to the following senses and types of nouns:

(i) To perform, to carry out, with *Sache* (not *Ding*) preceded by an adjective or with a noun which is an equivalent.

Sie haben dumme Sachen gemacht (or: *Dummheiten gemacht*).
Sie haben tolle Streiche gemacht.

(ii) To produce, fabricate a thing, particularly an academic exercise. With other types of writing (e.g. a leading article, correspondence) the use of *machen* is slovenly.

Haben Sie Ihre Arbeit (e.g. an essay), *Ihren Aufsatz, die Übersetzung, Ihre Aufgabe* (home-work) *gemacht?*
Machen Sie sechs Durchschläge ('do' or 'make').

(iii) To sit for, study for, pass an examination.

Er hat in letzter Zeit sein Examen gemacht ('sat for' or 'passed').
Er macht den Dr. phil., seinen B.A. ('is working for' or 'sitting for').

(iv) With the noun *Arbeit* when stating the nature of one's job.

Er macht die Gartenarbeit für X.

(v) In the sense of 'teach, lecture on', 'study' (from the point of view of the student) a subject or a branch of a subject. It should not be used with a proper name (*er behandelt, studiert Goethe*), and sounds slovenly with the name of a faculty (*er treibt Medizin, Jura*).

Ich mache die Klassik, er die Romantik ('lecture on' or 'study').
Er macht dieses Jahr Latein mit dem Jungens (teaches).
Wir machen Deutsch mit ihm (study).
In diesem Semester machen wir Lyrik, Metrik.
Im vorigen Jahr hat er Strafprozeß gemacht.

(b) *Tun* is used with most other types of nouns.

Seine Pflicht, schreckliche Dinge, Wunder, Schaden tun.
Er hat gute, wichtige, Arbeit getan.

It is used, too, with neuter substantival adjectives.

Sein Bestes, Möglichstes; Gutes, Böses, tun.

B. Sense: operate on, deal with, prepare, put in order.

1. In this sense *machen* is only used in a few well-defined senses, mostly 'to clean', 'to tidy up' a room (*sie hat das Zimmer, die Küche, die Bibliothek schon gemacht*). Also: *die Haare machen, den Weg* (but not: *die Gasse*) *machen* (do up), *Reparaturen machen*. Most other uses of *machen* with the thing operated on as object sound slovenly.

2. In other cases *besorgen, erledigen* (attend to) or a specific term should be used.

Er besorgt die Korrespondenz im Büro (*macht* sounds slovenly).

Sie hat das Aufwaschen, die Wäsche, schon besorgt.
Haben Sie meine Schuhe besohlt?
Sie sind der Nächste an der Reihe (I'll do you next, e.g. said by the hair-dresser).
Sie schnippelt Bohnen.

C. To cause harm and the like. Accompanied by an indefinite neuter pronoun (e.g. *nichts, was*) and the dative case. **Tun** is obligatory in direct statements (e.g. *ich habe dir nichts getan*) and is usual in direct questions (*was haben Sie ihm getan?*). **Antun** must be used in indirect statements and questions (*ich erzählte ihnen, was er mir angetan hatte; wer weiß, was er mir noch alles antun wird?*), and is possible in a direct question (*was haben Sie ihm angetan?*).

D. In cases where a verb substitute is needed, this must be *tun*.
Wer wäre bereit, ihm die Nachricht beizubringen? Ich habe es schon getan.
Sie sang besser, als je vorher.

E. Other senses.

1. Fare: *gehen, machen* (in the form: *was macht...?*).
Es geht dem Patienten besser.
Was macht das Bein, die Arbeit?

2. To serve the purpose, to be permissible, to suit: *gehen*. Sometimes *tun*.
Dieses Wort geht nicht.
Geht das?
Es geht nicht, daß er mit solchen Forderungen kommt.
Das tut's (not: *tut es*) (will achieve what is wanted).

3. To study: *studieren, treiben.*[1]
Er studiert Medizin, treibt Sprachen.

4. To be able to manage, to be good at: *fertig werden mit.*
Mit Latein werde ich nicht fertig.

5. To cover a distance: *zurücklegen.*
Wir haben heute 400 Kilometer zurückgelegt.

6. To be travelling at a certain speed: *fahren.*
Das Auto fuhr mit 80 Kilometer Geschwindigkeit.

7. To be able to achieve a speed: *schaffen, leisten.*
Dieses Auto kann 150 Kilometer die Stunde schaffen (leisten).

8. To serve time: *absitzen, abdienen*, both as a part of the time.
Er hat seine Strafe im Gefängnis abgesessen (seine Zeit bei der Infanterie abgedient).

9. To play a role: *spielen.*
Er hat den Hamlet gut gespielt.

10. To achieve: *ausrichten* (stronger than *tun*).
Versuchen Sie, was freundliche Worte bei ihm ausrichten können.

---

[1] *Betreiben* is also used in the sense of 'to carry on' a thing (e.g. *ein Geschäft betreiben*), including studies. In reference to the latter it is an intensive, and is often accompanied by an adverbial phrase to make this clear. *Er betreibt Medizin, seine Studien, mit Eifer.* 'Keine (Fassung) konnte der Selbstkritik des Dichters, der die Kunst schließlich mit einer beinahe wissenschaftlichen Grübelei betrieb, voll genügen' (J. Petersen, *Die Wissenschaft von der Dichtung*). Again, *betreiben* can mean: to endeavour to bring a thing off successfully (e.g. *eine Heirat betreiben*).

11. To have finished with: *fertig sein mit.*
Ich bin mit der Zeitung fertig.

12. To bestow, cause to have, affect favourably or unfavourably: *tun.*
Die Medizin hat mir gut getan.
Er hat mir Unrecht getan.

13. As a rebuke: **genügen.** *Das genügt* (that will do).

DOUBT **1.** With a noun object.
Bezweifeln presupposes an argument or statement to the contrary. It therefore comes as an objection. **Zweifeln** (followed by *an* with the dative) does not imply any such preceding assertion.

Ich bezweifle seinen guten Willen.   *Ich bezweifle seine Ehrlichkeit.*
Ich zweifle an seinem guten Willen.   *Ich zweifle an seiner Ehrlichkeit.*

2. Followed by a clause.
The distinction explained above means that *bezweifeln* is followed by a *daß* clause, *zweifeln* by an *ob* clause or a clause introduced by an interrogative pronoun (*was*). It also means that *zweifeln* is usual when there is a negative and a *daß* clause follows. *Bezweifeln* with a negative and a direct noun or pronoun object follows.

Ich zweifle, ob er rechtzeitig ankommt.
Ich bezweifle, daß er rechtzeitig ankommt.
Ich zweifle nicht, daß er es schaffen wird.
Ich bezweifle es nicht.

DRESS, CLOTHE, INVEST[1] **1.** **Sich anziehen** is the normal prose term. **Sich ankleiden** is more dignified, though it is often used in the same way as *sich anziehen*. The same implication is conveyed by *anziehen* when it is used without *sich*, i.e. in reference to individual items of clothing in the sense of 'put on'.[2] The more elevated term in this meaning is *anlegen* (e.g. *Geschmeide*). *Ankleiden* is not used in this way. **Sich kleiden** can only refer to the way one dresses (e.g. *gut, auffällig*).

Ich mußte mich schnell anziehen.   *Er kleidet sich elegant, schlecht.*
Sie kleidete sich für den Ball an.   *Er ist immer sorgfältig gekleidet.*

2. **Bekleiden** is, in its literal sense, 'to clothe' as a contrast to the unclothed state, therefore often 'to provide the essentials of clothing'. It is then extended to mean: to cover any object as with clothes (e.g. to drape). Another sense is: to invest with the insignia of office; and in figurative extension of this: (*a*) to invest with the office itself; (*b*) to occupy the office.

*Es ist eine ungeheure Aufgabe, die Bevölkerung Asiens auch nut notdürftig zu
    bekleiden und zu ernähren.*
Es ist nicht erlaubt, hier unbekleidet herumzugehen.
Der Bischof wurde mit Ring und Stab bekleidet.
Er wurde mit einem hohen Amt bekleidet.

---

[1] *Verkleiden* means 'to disguise', but normally only where the disguise is effected by clothing in the literal sense (e.g. *er verkleidete sich als Mönch*) or in the sense of 'to choose words which hide one's real meaning' (e.g. *er verkleidete seine wahren Absichten in schön klingenden Worten*). But: *er machte seine Schrift unkenntlich.*

[2] *Anziehen* in the sense of 'put on' can only be applied to articles of clothing that are 'pulled on'. Otherwise: *aufsetzen* (a hat); *umbinden* (a tie).

3. **Einkleiden** is 'to clothe as befits one's office', therefore 'to put into the uniform of this office'. Figuratively, it refers to the clothing of thoughts in suitable words.

Er wurde als Mönch eingekleidet.

Es gelingt ihm immer, solche Bemerkungen in freundliche Worte einzukleiden.

DRINK 1. **Getränk** is the general term for any kind of beverage, whether taken for pleasure or to slake thirst, and whether intoxicating or not.

Tee ist ein angenehmes Getränk.

Allerlei Getränke standen auf dem Tisch.

2. **Trank** is a more special term for beverage. On the one hand it can be an elevated term, on the other it can denote a drink prepared for a special purpose, particularly a concoction, in which case it often expresses a subjective attitude to the beverage in question. In the second application it occurs frequently in compounds.

Das ist göttlicher Trank.

Versuch' mal meinen Trank (concoction).

Ein Fruchttrank, ein Liebestrank.

3. **Trunk** means (a) a draught, a gulp. It translates 'to take a drink' of a beverage, only in a few fixed phrases. (See also 4.) (b) In a few fixed phrases, mostly only in literary use, it means excessive drinking of intoxicating liquors. (See also 5.)

(a) *Das war ein erfrischender Trunk* (in literary language).

  Er hat einen Trunk Wein getan.

(b) *Er ist dem Trunk ergeben.*

4. In the sense of 'draught', in such phrases as 'to take, ask for, give, a drink', without mention of the beverage, German uses **etwas zu trinken.** The omission of *etwas* is possible only in exalted, e.g. biblical style.

Er verlangte etwas zu trinken.

Er gab dem Kind etwas zu trinken.

5. In the sense of the excessive drinking of intoxicating liquors **Alkohol** is generally used. **Trinken** is possible where 'drinking' could be used in English.

Die Alkoholfrage wurde lebhaft debattiert.

Der Alkohol hat viele Ehen zerstört.

Er hat sich dem Alkohol, dem Trunk, ergeben.

DRUNK **Betrunken** is the literal term, i.e. intoxicated through indulgence in alcohol. **Trunken** is mostly figurative, i.e. intoxicated in mind, spirit, and is used only in exalted language. Only in elevated style can it be used in the literal sense. 'Drunken', i.e. a permanent characteristic, cannot be translated by these terms without their modification.[1,2]

Er kam betrunken nach Hause.

Man sieht ihn kaum, ohne daß er betrunken ist.

  '*Wo bist du? Trunken dämmert die Seele mir*

    Von aller deiner Wonne....' (Hölderlin, *Dem Sonnengott.*)

---

[1] *Trunkenbold*: drunkard.

[2] *Berauscht* is used literally and figuratively. In the literal sense it does not necessarily assign the case of drunkenness to alcohol. Drugs and the like may be the cause. *Besoffen*, a somewhat vulgar term, suggests the consumption of vast quantities of alcohol. *Saufen*, normally applied to animals, suggests immoderate drinking when used of human beings. *Er säuft wie ein Loch.*

EDUCATE

EDUCATE Erziehen[1] refers to the process, **bilden**[2] to the result of the process of educating.

Er wurde in dieser Schule erzogen.
Er wurde schlecht erzogen.
Er ist ein gebildeter Mensch.

EMBITTER i.e. a lasting state, is **Verbittern.**
It should not be confused with **erbittern,** to incense, to provoke, to make fierce, i.e. a temporary state.

Der Mißerfolg seines Buches hat ihn, ihm das Leben, verbittert.
Die Demütigung hat ihn erbittert.
Es wurde erbittert gekämpft.

EMOTION *W.S.* says of 'emotion' that it is the preferred term (i.e. preferred to feeling, affection, sentiment, passion, with which terms the article compares it) in modern psychology because it suggests the physical as well as the mental reaction, and usually carries in non-technical use a stronger implication of excitement or agitation than feeling.

German has no special term except in the technical-psychological sense where it is **Affekt,** also used in non-technical language, but by no means as extensively as English 'emotion'. There is also the Fremdwort **Emotion,** which however, despite recent advances, has not yet established itself securely in the language. It is often used of emotions directed to a cause or a belief (e.g. *politische Emotionen*). In non-technical contexts German uses terms which express the particular type or quality of emotional excitement. **Gefühl, Empfindung** (for these two see under 'feel'), **Gemütsbewegung** (a state of emotional excitement), **Rührung** (the state of being touched and implying tenderness), **Erregung, Aufregung** (for the last two see under 'excitement'), **Regung** (a stirring).

Wie kann ich meine Gefühle angesichts dieser Katastrophe beschreiben?
Er empfand eine plötzliche Wut, konnte aber diese Gemütsbewegung unter-
drücken.
Er versuchte seine Gemütsbewegung nicht zu zeigen.
Er hörte das Bekenntnis mit immer sich steigernder Erregung an.
Der Appetit auf Gefühlserregungen und Abenteuer (W.S.).
Ein Gefühl der Kraft, durch starke innere Erregung hervorgerufen (W.S.).

---

[1] *Aufziehen* refers to the care bestowed on the physical growth of persons, animals, plants, and means 'to bring up', 'to rear', 'to raise'. *Großziehen* is a general term (used mostly in the passive voice) for the bringing up of children. *Ein unerzogenes Kind* = a naughty, ill-bred, child. *Ziehen* is used transitively in the related sense of 'to grow' plants, vegetables, etc. (e.g. *er zieht Tomaten*). *Anbauen* is used of cereals. *Wachsen* can only be used intransitively. 'To grow up' = *aufwachsen, heranwachsen,* the latter denoting only the process, and therefore is not used in the past participle (e.g. *heranwachsende Kinder*). *Groß werden* is used in compound tenses in the sense of 'grow up' (e.g. *sie sind auf dem Lande groß geworden*).
[2] The same distinction applies to the nouns *Erziehung, Bildung* (e.g. *er hat eine schlechte Erziehung gehabt, er hat keine Bildung*), though at times the distinction tends to disappear (e.g. *Erziehungs-, Bildungsanstalten*). *Bildung* now means exclusively 'education'. In the classical and romantic periods it meant 'culture', which is now expressed by *Kultur. Kultur* also means 'civilization', *Zivilisation* referring mainly to mechanical inventions as the result of industrial progress. The two stand in sharp contrast to each other, unlike the English and the French terms. Some of the implications of civilization cannot therefore be expressed succinctly in German. *Gesittung* = civilized behaviour. Often 'Schulen' must be used for 'education' (*Staatsunterstützung für Schulen*).

Er besitzt die Mittel, religiöse Regungen, Gefühle zu erwecken (*Regung* needs an adjective stating the kind of stirring).
Politische Emotionen werden leicht aufgepeitscht.

EMOTIONAL 1. German has no general term except **emotionell,** which however, unlike the English term, is not widely used. The specific terms are for the most part related to the nouns discussed under 'emotion', *erregt* in particular being common. It applies to emotion of the moment, not to a permanent characteristic of a person. *Erregt* means emotional in the sense of 'upset'.

Er ist stark emotionell und wird oft vom Pathos seiner eigenen Worte bis zu Tränen gerührt (*W.*).
Er hat eine emotionelle Natur.
Das ist ein rein emotionelles Urteil.
Das ist mir zu emotionell.
Erregte Worte, die in der Hitze des Gefechts ausgesprochen wurden.
Bei der Auseinandersetzung ging es sehr erregt zu.
Er war sehr erregt, als er die Nachricht erhielt.
Er war sehr bewegt, als ihm der Orden verliehen wurde.

2. **Leicht erregbar, leicht erregt:** when 'emotion' is used predicatively or one wishes to avoid *emotionell*.

Er ist leicht erregbar (easily upset).

3. In the sense of motivated chiefly by the emotions as opposed to the intellect (*W.*) and applied to the actions of people, but not to people directly: **gefühlsmässig, gefühlsbetont, gefühlsbeladen.**

Eine gefühlsmäßige Handlung (*eine gefühlsbetonte H.*).
Ein gefühlsmäßiges Urteil (*gefühlsbetont*).
Er reagiert auf alles gefühlsmäßig.
Das sind gefühlsbeladene Worte (also: *erregte, aufgeregte*).

4. **Affektvoll** and phrases involving **Affekt** (see under 'emotion').

Er hat einen affektvollen Stil.
Er schreibt immer sehr affektvoll.
Er läßt, sich nicht von Affekten beeinflussen.

ENJOY 1. **Genießen**

Unlike 'enjoy', *genießen* cannot be used in generalizations as a synonym of 'like' (e.g. I enjoy good conversation), but only in reference to a particular occasion (e.g. I enjoyed the music). Nor can it be used as a synonym of 'have' (e.g. we are enjoying the first holiday in five years; last week we enjoyed a spell of good weather). In the latter sense only *haben* is possible in German.

When the object of *genießen* is a noun denoting food or drink, its meaning is not 'enjoy' (see 'taste', *schmecken*), but 'partake of', 'consume'. This use is, however, apt to sound affected.

Genießen translates 'enjoy' in the following senses:
(a) To possess something that is of benefit to one, to have the use of, to have as one's lot.[1,2]

Er genießt die Achtung seiner Mitbürger.

---

[1] *Genießen* is etymologically connected with *nutzen* (compare *Nutznießer*).
[2] *Sich einer Sache erfreuen*, to rejoice in the possession of a thing, is a close synonym.

Er genießt keinen guten Ruf.
Er hat einen gründlichen Unterricht genossen.
Er genießt dieselben Rechte wie wir.
Er genießt die Zinsen des Vermögens seiner Frau.

(b) With things that have the power to absorb one emotionally, sensuously or spiritually *genießen* means 'to enjoy intensely' by surrendering oneself to this power. Such things include: (i) states of being, feelings and words that indirectly stand for these (e.g. *Gegenwart*); (ii) words that denote sight and sound, i.e. sense-perceptions, and the objects of these if they suggest vastness, the illimitable (e.g. *Landschaft*); (iii) a few activities which possess this power of absorption, mostly artistic performances.

> *Das Leben, das Landleben, den Aufenthalt* (i.e. being somewhere), *die Freude des Wiedersehens, das Glück, das Alleinsein, seine Jugend, die Ruhe nach der Arbeit, den Humor einer Situation, den Anblick* (e.g. *einer Statue, des Meeres*), *die Natur, den Sonnenaufgang, das Licht, die Luft, die Musik, das Rauschen* (*der Wellen*), *die Schönheit* (*des Waldes*), *die Klarheit eines Stils, die Aufführung eines Theaterstücks, das Spiel* (of music).

> '*Trägheit fesselte den Geist, indes die Sinne die ungeheure und betäubende Unterhaltung der Meeresstille genossen*' (Thomas Mann, *Der Tod in Venedig*). (*Genießen* could not be used with *Unterhaltung* in its ordinary sense.)

(c) It is used with other words if it is emphasized either (i) by emphasis in the spoken word; (ii) by the addition of some adverb such as *wirklich* or *sehr*; (iii) by being used in certain constructions that have this force (e.g. the imperative, the purpose infinitive with *um...zu*, a contrast).

Ich habe den Spaziergang wirklich genossen.
Wir haben den Vortrag, den Film, das Konzert, sehr genossen.
Wir genießen den Feiertag in vollen Zügen.
Genießen Sie Ihre Ferien, den Ausflug!
Genießen Sie das schöne Wetter, solange es anhält.
Wir gingen aus, um das schöne Wetter zu genießen.
Heute ist es das erste Mal, daß wir die Fahrt genossen haben.
Gestern haben wir den Ritt genossen, aber heute nicht.
Er fand den Vortrag schlecht, ich aber habe ihn genossen.

(d) With reference to smoking.

Ein Pfeifchen, eine Zigarre, eine Zigarette genießen.

2. To enjoy oneself: **sich amüsieren.**
Instead of this verb, however, the verbs treated in the next section are more commonly used.

Ich habe mich auf der Reise gut, köstlich, amüsiert.

3. When *genießen* is not possible, 'enjoy' must be rendered by terms such as: schmecken (food and drink); gefallen (often stronger than 'please'); *einem Freude, Vergnügen, Spaß, machen, bereiten; Freude, Vergnügen, Spaß haben, finden an; ein (Hoch)genuß sein, schön sein.*[1]

---

[1] *Sich freuen an* suggests the enjoyment of something before one's senses. *Er freute sich an den Klängen der Musik, am Anblick des Bildes, an meiner Verlegenheit, an dem Grün der Wiese. Freuen* is mostly used reflexively or with the impersonal *es* as subject, and means that joy is given by the presence or existence of a thing. For distinctions between it and *erfreuen* see Paul and Euling, *Deutsches Wörterbuch*. To the explanations given in that work can be added that when the subject is a thing (e.g. *Nachricht*) the distinction is generally

Der Wein hat mir geschmeckt.
Das Konzert hat mir gut gefallen, Freude gemacht; war ein Genuß.
Ich habe viel Freude an seinem Besuch gehabt.
Wie hat Ihnen Ihr Aufenthalt auf dem Lande gefallen?
Ich kann an einem Gespräch, das immer wieder abschweift, keine Freude finden.

ENTER Literal sense.

'Enter' is often interchanged with 'go into'. In discriminating use it suggests with a personal subject something special about the circumstances of entry, e.g. the state or attitude of mind of the person who enters, the effect on others present. With a thing as subject, it suggests a passage through a medium, sometimes a resisting medium.

The use of the German terms is determined in particular by the following factors: (*a*) whether the space entered is enclosed or not; (*b*) whether an official (i.e. permission to enter) or a human term is required.

1. Gehen (*fahren, reiten, fließen,* etc., see 'go') must be used when 'enter' does not suggest anything special about the circumstances of 'entry', i.e. when it is interchangeable with 'go'.

Hinein is added to these verbs only (*a*) if it is desired to give a vivid picture of the space entered or to express violent motion; (*b*) to render the intransitive use of 'enter' (to go inside). In (*a*) the prefix really suggests a stage after entry. Thus: *wir fuhren in die Hauptstraße* (turned into it); *wir fuhren in die Hauptstraße hinein* (a picture of the whole street). Further: *wir fuhren in den Hafen* (the normal statement); *wir fuhren in den Hafen hinein* (a picture of a stretch of water with its shores); '*Ich ging also in das alte Haus hinein und holte meine Geige*' (Eichendorff, *Aus dem Leben eines Taugenichts*) (a picture of the *Taugenichts* in the house); *wir fuhren blindlings in die Menge hinein* (violent movement).

Er ging ins Zimmer und legte sich hin.
Er ging durch eine Seitentür ins Theater (hinein).
Der Strom fließt hier in das Meer.
Er fuhr in meinem Wagen hinein (crashed into).

2. Treten and its compounds. These primarily mean 'to step', and should only be used when this meaning is present, i.e. to put one's foot across the threshold. *Treten* and *eintreten* as renderings of 'enter' can be applied only to to entry into an enclosed space.

(a) **Treten**, used in the sense of 'enter', always suggests a circumscribed space, mostly a room, but sometimes merely a part of a larger area. It conveys an impression of the manner of entry, e.g. by a description of the effect on others. It must always be followed by *in*, i.e. it cannot be used absolutely.

Er trat in das Zimmer, und alle verstummten sofort.
Als er in die Versammlung trat, horchten alle auf.
In andächtiger Stimmung traten wir in die Kapelle.
Er trat behutsam ins Wasser.

(b) **Eintreten** is used in three ways. (*a*) In the sense of 'step into' it implies a contrast with the space outside. (*b*) In the sense of 'enter' it refers almost exclusively to a room, and suggests a more intimate relation with the person in the room than *treten*. (*c*) It can be used absolutely.

that *freuen* expresses a simple impulsive feeling, whereas *erfreuen* suggests detachment (e.g. *die Nachricht hat mich gefreut, erfreut*). *Sich freuen über* means 'to rejoice at' a fact, *sich freuen auf* refers to the future and means 'to look forward' to a thing with pleasure.

Wir traten in das Gebäude ein, um uns vor dem Regen zu schützen (stepped into).

Vom Garten aus tritt man gleich in sein Arbeitszimmer ein (steps into).

Mein alter Freund Karl trat ganz unerwartet in mein Arbeitszimmer ein und wollte mich zu einem Spaziergang abholen (entered).

Er trat ein.

(c) **Hineintreten** suggests a certain hesitation at the threshold.

Er zögerte eine Weile vor der Tür und trat dann hinein.

(d) **Betreten** is used in two ways. (*a*) It suggests on the part of the person who enters a strong emotional attitude or an awareness that the entry is or has proved to be a fateful step. 'To set foot in', is the closest English equivalent. (*b*) As an official term it refers to the right or permission to enter.[1] In neither case is it applied solely to a confined or enclosed space.

Ich werde sein Haus nie wieder betreten.

Voll Ehrfurcht betrat er das Heiligtum.

Als er deutschen Boden betrat, hatte er keine Ahnung, daß er ihn nie wieder verlassen würde.

Bevor man eine Moschee betritt, muß man die Schuhe ausziehen.

Sie haben keinen Haftbefehl, der Sie berechtigt, dieses Haus zu betreten.

3. Hinein-, hereinkommen are used in the sense of 'to enter' a large area, e.g. a country, a town, a harbour, i.e. to get into.

Hereinkommen is used, though not as a formal, official term, in reference to permission to enter. It suggests in a general way the steps necessary to enter, e.g. the obtaining of permission, but less clearly the specific act of attempting to enter. The latter is expressed by *hineinkommen*. Neither of these words can be used when the place of entry is mentioned (e.g. I entered Germany at Basel).

Es ist schwer, in die Schweiz hereinzukommen (generally, and in particular: to get permission).

Es ist schwer, in die Schweiz hineinzukommen (difficulties at the frontier itself).

Sobald Sie nach Holland hereinkommen, fühlen Sie sich in einer anderen Welt.

4. Words compounded with **ein.**

Einziehen is used of a body of people which enters an area, e.g. an army, a procession. See article on 'move'. **Einsteigen:** to climb into a thing, particularly into a vehicle as a passenger. **Einreise** and the verb **einreisen** are official terms which refer to permission to enter a country.[2,3]

Das Heer zog in die Stadt ein.

Als Sieger zog er in Wien ein.

Er stieg in den Zug ein.

Der Dieb stieg durch das Fenster ein.

Die Einreiseerlaubnis für Deutschland wurde ihm nicht bewilligt.

Er ist am 13ten März nach Deutschland eingereist.

Seine Einreise nach Deutschland erfolgte am 3ten September.

---

[1] The English equivalent is often 'to walk on'. *Das Betreten des Rasens ist verboten.*

[2] *Ausreise* is the official term for 'exit' from a country.

[3] Further verbs compounded with *ein* are: *einrücken* (see 'move'); *einmünden*, to empty into, of water, streets and the like; *einbrechen*, to burgle, to irrupt into. *Einfahren* and *einlaufen* mean 'to arrive'.

5. Both **dringen** and **eindringen** are used with a person or a thing as subject. They correspond more closely to 'penetrate' than to 'enter', but in the absence of a more exact term must be used to translate the latter. With a non-personal subject, both can refer, amongst other things, to the entry of objects into the human body and to the entry of gases, liquids and the like into a confined space. The distinction between the two terms is that *eindringen* suggests greater difficulty in entry than *dringen*, often a burrowing action.

Der rostige Nagel drang in seinen Schenkel ein.

Das Gift drang in den Blutstrom.

Der Blutklumpen drang in sein Herz ein.

Der Rauch drang ins Zimmer (the addition of *ein* would suggest clouds of smoke billowing at the door or window).

Der Rauch drang in meine Nase.

Die Sonne dringt kaum in das Dickicht (*ein*).

Der Regen dringt in meine Schuhe.

Der Feind dringt in die Festung (the addition of *ein* would clearly denote difficulty).

ESCAPE A. Of living beings.

1. Verbs compounded with *ent*. Of these *entkommen* is the most general, while the others suggest the particular manner of escape. With the exception of *entgehen* all mean 'to escape from' the power of a person or thing into which one has fallen or is about to fall. When the escape is made from a place, this can be a building, a restricted area such as a town, but can be neither an area as large as a country nor a thing which grips or entangles the body (e.g. a trap, a net, chains, a small bag). *Entkommen* suggests that one escapes from something which has held one in its grip, not that one avoids a thing by not being near it.

(a) **Entkommen**

Er entkam aus dem Konzentrationslager.

Er ist seinen Wächtern entkommen.

Er ist nach den Bergen entkommen.

Er ist der Gefahr entkommen.

Er entkam aus dem brennenden Gebäude.

(b) The others compounded with *ent* suggest the manner of escape. This reference is, however, often more figurative than literal. Therefore these verbs are not normally used when the concrete situation with reference to its details (e.g. the thing from which the escape is made) is visually evoked. They would, for instance, be inappropriate to call attention to an escape which is being effected before one's eyes. Thus while it is possible to say: *er ist aus dem Gefängnis, dem Zug, entsprungen* (an event in the past), this verb would be unsuitable to translate 'escape' in the sentence: look, he's escaping from the train. Since an escape from small objects emphasizes the concrete and realistic character of the situation, these verbs should not be used in such cases (e.g. to render: the cat escaped from the sack). *Ent* generally suggests that the act is viewed from a certain distance. Hence its tendency towards figurative application.[1]

---

[1] *Ent* stresses separation as a result more forcibly than the action of separating (e.g. *er entnahm es der Schublade* is less concrete than *er nahm es aus der Schublade*). This characteristic makes these verbs elevated in tone or, if misapplied, precious (e.g. *er ist dem Zug entstiegen*).

(i) **Entspringen:** to escape by jumping (*aus einem Zug*) or by a sudden coup (*aus dem Gefängnis*). In all cases actual captivity is implied.[1]

(ii) **Entschlüpfen** is used in the figurative sense of slipping through one's fingers, i.e. nimbly and adroitly. It approximates to 'elude', i.e. to escape capture by a hair's breadth. It is used particularly of animals.

Der Verbrecher, der Hase, die Schlange, ist uns entschlüpft.

(iii) **Entweichen:** to escape silently, stealthily.

Der Gefangene ist entwichen.

(iv) **Entwischen** suggests that the escape is effected by seizing the right moment, so that one cheats one's would-be capturer.[2] It thus approximates to *entschlüpfen* and 'elude', but has a somewhat colloquial flavour.

Der Täter ist im letzten Augenblick entwischt.

(v) **Entfliehen,** which is much used, means 'to escape by flight', and suggests distance.

Nachdem er seinen Wächter niedergeschlagen hatte, konnte er entfliehen.

(vi) **Entrinnen** is an elevated term and used figuratively, particularly with the noun *Gefahr*.

(vii) **Entgehen:** to escape being caught or involved in a situation, generally by a wide margin.[3]

Er ist dem Schiffbruch entgangen (by not travelling on the wrecked ship).

Er ist dem Tode, der Gefahr, der Entdeckung, entgangen.

2. To escape from something which holds the body, e.g. a trap, net, chains. **Sich befreien** can be used when a struggle with the trap, etc. is implied. Otherwise specific terms such as *springen, kriechen* must be employed.

Die Ratte befreite sich aus der Falle.

Er hat sich aus dem Netz, seinen Ketten, befreit.

Die Katze sprang aus dem Sack.

3. Simple verbs (*schlüpfen, springen*, etc.) should be used where the action is stressed as much as or more than the result, and where the context makes it clear that the purpose of the action is escape.

Der Fisch ist durch das Netz geschlüpft.

Sieh mal, der Gefangene springt aus dem Zug.

4. Sich retten is used particularly in reference to shipwreck. It can be followed by a prepositional phrase denoting separation or destination.

Er hat sich aus dem Schiffbruch, ans Ufer, gerettet.

5. Fliehen, to flee, does not denote the success of the action of flight (contrast *entfliehen*) unless accompanied by a phrase which makes this clear. It is used particularly of escape from a wide area (e.g. a country). **Flüchten** differs from it in that it means 'to seek refuge' and thus stresses the goal rather than the attempt to get away from the pursuer. It can, however, be accompanied by a phrase meaning 'from', whereas *sich flüchten* only suggests the goal and is followed by *in* or an equivalent.

Er ist aus Deutschland geflohen.

Er ist in die Schweiz geflüchtet.

Er hat sich in das Haus geflüchtet.

---

[1] *Ausbrechen* is often used of escaping from prison (e.g. *ein ausgebrochener Häftling*).

[2] The time-factor is also uppermost in *erwischen* (see 'catch').

[3] There exist a number of other verbs compounded with *ent*, not treated here (e.g. *entlaufen, entfliegen*). *Der Hund ist entlaufen. Unser Vogel ist uns entflogen.*

6. Davonkommen: to escape, get off, with less injury than might be expected.

Er ist mit dem Schrecken, mit einem gebrochenen Arm, davongekommen.

B. Of gases, liquids, things.

1. Entweichen is the normal term in reference to gas.[1]

Das Gas entweicht aus dem Ofen.

2. Ausströmen, ausfließen (in smaller quantities), **rinnen** (trickle) are used of escaping liquids.

Das Benzin fließt aus; das Gas strömt aus.

3. In reference to things the appropriate specific term must be used.

Das Mehl rinnt aus dem Sack.

C. Figurative use. The subject is a thing.

1. Entgehen: to escape the mind, observation, appreciation.[2]

Der Sinn Ihrer Bemerkung ist mir entgangen (I missed).
Die Schönheit der Landschaft entging ihm nicht.

2. Entschlüpfen is used of remarks that one makes inadvertently.

Die Bemerkung entschlüpfte ihm.

3. Entfallen: to escape the memory.

Sine Name ist mir entfallen.

ESTIMATE[3] **Schätzen:**[4] to estimate roughly.[5] **Einschätzen:** to estimate exactly. 'To estimate at' followed by a numeral can only be *schätzen auf* (with the accusative) or **abschätzen auf,** which is used to estimate distances and prices of articles and is more exact than *schätzen.* It cannot be followed by a personal object.

Wie hoch schätzen Sie den Verlust?
Wie hoch schätzen Sie den Verlust ein?
Ich schätze, die Brücke ist 3 Kilometer entfernt.
Ich habe ihn immer so eingeschätzt.
Er hat sich genau so betragen, wie ich ihn eingeschätzt habe.
Ich habe die Entfernung bis auf 1 Kilometer, die Möbel auf 750 D.M., abgeschätzt.

EVALUATE Werten is often used in contexts which are concerned with basic principles. **Bewerten** suggests an evaluation carried out according to standards of measurement already established. Its purpose may be purely practical. In reference to numbers it implies exactness, unlike the synonymous term *schätzen* (see article on 'estimate'). Both verbs are used transitively and intransitively. In transitive use *werten* means to assess, without any reference to value.

Wie haben Sie den Aufsatz bewertetz (what numerical mark did you award?)
Er wertet nach strengen Gesichtspunkten.
Verschiedene Generationen werten Kunstwerke anders.
Dieses Bild ist höher zu werten als jenes.

---

[1] More popularly: *herauskommen.*
[2] *Sich eine Gelegenheit entgehen lassen:* to let an opportunity slip.
[3] Study together with 'evaluate'.
[4] See also 'appreciate'. With a personal object it can only mean 'appreciate' or 'esteem'.
[5] *Schätzungsweise:* at a rough estimate, guess.

EVALUATE

'*Völlig falsch ist es, dies zugleich eiskalte und brennende Werk als ein dich- terisches Weltbild, als Ausdruck einer Lebensanschauung zu werten*' (Gundolf, *Heinrich von Kleist*).

Ein ehrlicher Materialist ist höher zu werten als ein wurzelloser Idealist.

Das Kommittee hat die Bilder schon bewertet (judged their merit, fixed a price, and the like).

Der deutsche Generalstab hat die Macht der englischen Luftwaffe bei Dünkirchen falsch bewertet.

Wie bewerten Sie die Geschäftskapazität dieses Unternehmens?

Die zum Verkauf stehenden Autos müssen heute offiziell bewertet werden.

Die Rede wurde von Bonn als eine Verhandlungsbereitschaft von seiten Polens gewertet.

EVEN (adverb) **Sogar** and **selbst** are often interchangeable. Where, however, emphasis is required, as in a climax or a contrast, *sogar* should be used.[1] When 'even' modifies a verb, *selbst* is impossible in this sense, since it would mean 'self'.

With *nicht* (**ein**)**mal** is usual, except in emphatic contexts, in which case *sogar* is preferable. *Nicht* retains its ordinary position in the sentence; it does not precede *sogar*.

Auch nur is used in phrases or clauses depending on a negative, e.g. after *ohne* (=without so much as what is stated, let alone more). *Sogar* is also possible in this combination where great emphasis is desired.

Sogar, selbst, seine Freunde haben sic von ihm abgewandt.

Sogar, selbst, mit Geld ist hier nichts zu machen.

Ich mag den Mann nicht, und sogar sein Name ist mir verhaßt (*selbst* would be too weak).

Selbst im Frieden können Sie das nicht kaufen (unemphatic).

Sie sagen, der Mann ist nicht ganz ehrlich, er ist sogar ein ausgesprochener Betrüger (*selbst* would be impossible).

Wegen seiner Verspätung wurde er sogar entlassen (*sogar* modifies the verb, *selbst* is therefore impossible).

Nicht einmal Brot war zu haben.

Das Dorf war derartig ausgeplündert, daß sogar Brot nicht mehr aufzutreiben war (*sogar* preferable to *nicht einmal* because of the emphasis).

Er blieb eine Woche in der Stadt, ohne uns auch nur anzurufen.

Ich hätte nicht gemeint, daß er sich des Abends auch nur erinnerte.

EVENT, INCIDENT 1. **Ereignis** is the most general term. It is connected with *Auge*, and means that which becomes visible, real ('*Das Unzulängliche, Hier wird's Ereignis*', Goethe, *Faust II*). Since it conveys the idea of 'become visible', it can only refer to definite, specific events, not to vague or obscure happenings.

Die Ereignisse haben uns recht gegeben.

Diese Konferenz ist ein wichtiges Ereignis.

Das ist schon ein wirkliches Ereignis.

Die Ereignisse der letzten Woche waren gradezu katastrophal.

Die Reihenfolge der Ereignisse ist wichtig.

2. **Begebenheit** is something out of the ordinary, whether some dramatic manifestations of Nature, something in the human world that strikes us by its

---

[1] In this sense it approximates closely to 'indeed', 'in fact'. See under these terms.

dimensions, or something in the realm of fantasy. It has a strong subjective colouring.

Erzählen Sie uns eine Begebenheit aus dem 14. Jahrhundert!
'Was ist eine Novelle anders als eine sich ereignete, unerhörte Begebenheit?'
  (Goethe to Eckermann, 1827).

3. Vorgang refers to something changing, evolving, a process. The plural is used of a vague, undefined series of happenings. It thus contrasts with the specific term *Ereignis*.

Die Vorgänge in Europa sind nicht ermutigend.
Die Vorgänge jenes Tages bleiben mir ein Geheimnis.

4. Vorfall: a sudden happening, often unpleasant. It corresponds to 'incident' in all senses except that treated under **5.**

Dieser Vorfall hat die ganze Situation geändert.

5. Zwischenfall: an incident in a diplomatic sense, i.e. fraught with dangerous possibilities.

Der Zwischenfall an der deutschen Grenze.

6. Geschehnis is the most abstract term for 'happening'. Its use is confined to the written word.

Vorgänge sind eine Reihe von Geschehnissen.

EVENTUALLY 1. **Schließlich** means after a long time.

Schließlich haben wir uns geeinigt.
Schließlich sah er ein, daß er einen Fehler begangen hatte.

It should be distinguished from **letzten Endes** which means that while a thing may not be very good, it is best to accept it without further argument.

Wir mußten letzten Endes den Vertrag unterzeichnen.

2. For German *eventuell* see under 'possible'.

EVIDENCE 1. An outward sign: indication, token (*W*.). **Zeichen, Anzeichen** (see 'sign'), **Spur, Beweis(e).**

Gib uns ein Zeichen, Anzeichen, einen Beweis deiner guten Absicht.
Das Land zeigt Spuren, Anzeichen von ungenügender Kapitalanlage.
Man konnte keine Spuren, Zeichen seiner Anwesenheit in dem Hause finden.

2. Something that furnishes or tends to furnish proof, proof, testimony (*W*.). Often German uses **Beweis** (i.e. proof) in the sense of a piece of evidence, **Beweise,** plural, in the collective sense of evidence. **Beweisstück** is also used in the sense of a piece of evidence, **Beweismaterial** in the collective sense. Use is not limited to legal contexts.

Das kann nicht als Beweis angesehen werden.
Ich habe ihm das ganze Beweismaterial vorgelegt.
Das Beweismaterial geht ins Uferlose.
Als Beweismaterial vorgelegte Papiere (in, as evidence).

3. Testimony.
(a) **Aussage.** See also 'statement'. Used particularly in a legal context.

Die Zeugenaussagen ließen keinen Zweifel an seiner Schuld.
Laut der Aussagen vieler Menschen, die diese Gemälde gesehen haben, ist ihre
  Bildersprache einer Art, die einen packt und nicht wieder losläßt (W.).
Laut aller Aussagen, die uns zur Verfügung stehen (W.).

(b) **Zeugnis:** particularly in the term *Leumundszeugnis* (evidence of character) and in the phrase *Zeugnis ablegen.*

Er legte Zeugnis für die (von den) guten Absichten seines Vorgesetzten ab.

(c) **Beleg:** a written piece of evidence, documentary evidence; often used in philological contexts.

Haben Sie irgendwelche Belege für den Gebrauch dieser Konstruktion bei Schiller gefunden?

4. The state of being evident, conspicuous (*W.*), mostly in the phrase 'to be in evidence'. **Da, anwesend, sichtbar sein, zu sehen sein.**

Bei der Diskussion war er nicht zu sehen.

EXCITE 1. Aufregen refers to excitement which is visible, i.e. manifested externally, in act or gesture, and is therefore the common equivalent of 'excite'.

Regen Sie sich nicht so auf.

Er war so aufgeregt, daß er kaum sprechen konnte.

Das Schließen der Banken hat die Bevölkerung sehr aufgeregt.

Das Kind regt sich zu sehr auf, wenn es ins Kino geht.

2. Erregen has no precise equivalent in English. Its meaning is to excite inwardly, to throw into an emotional state, particularly in reference to anger, indignation, and the like. It is sometimes better rendered into English by 'stir', 'work up'.[1] When a feeling or state of mind is the object it is the normal translation of 'excite', i.e. in the sense of 'cause'. It is always used to render the electrical sense (cf. *Erregerkreis* = exciter circuit).

Er war furchtbar erregt, als er die Nachricht hörte.

Er sprach mit erregter Stimme (aufgeregt is impossible).

Zuviel Alkohol erregt das Gehirn.

Er hat meinen Haß, Neid erregt.

Hunger, Durst erregen.[2]

Das Ereignis hat mein Interesse, meine Neugierde erregt.

'*Der Geselligkeitsdunst hat sich verstärkt—dieser trockensüßliche, verdickte, erregende, an Ingredienzien reiche Festbrodem...*' (Thomas Mann, *Unordnung und Frühes Leid*).

3. Anregen means 'to stimulate'. It must be used to render 'excite' when the latter is followed by 'to' plus a noun or an infinitive.[3]

Seine Rede hat die Bevölkerung zur Tat angeregt (excited...to action).

EXCUSE (v. and s.), PARDON, APOLOGIZE 1. Entschuldigen (Entschuldigung) is the most general term. *Sich entschuldigen*: to apologize in the modern sense of this term. Excuse me: *entschuldigen Sie*, when one has bothered or is about to bother a person in a trivial matter.

2. Verzeihen (Verzeihung) in careful use implies a greater offence, but is often used (particularly the noun) indiscriminately with *entschuldigen. Ach Verzeihung*, when e.g. one has spilt something over a person's clothes. **Pardon**, which was once common, has become much less so.

Die Vergehen meines Neffen können nur durch seine Jugend verziehen werden (*S.O.D.*).

---

[1] *Erregung* comes very close to 'emotion'. See under this term.
[2] But *den Appetit anregen*, *Appetit* being too weak to use with *erregen*.
[3] In older German *aufregen* was sometimes used in the sense of *anregen*.

3. Gestatten means to allow (see under 'grant') and is used when in advance one asks to be excused for what one is about to do. In this context it is a polite formula.

Gestatten Sie bitte (e.g. when making one's way past people to one's seat in a theatre).

4. Vorwand, i.e. 'pretext', should be used when in English 'pretext' is a more appropriate term than 'excuse'.

Er suchte einen Vorwand, ihn zu entlassen.

5. Ausrede is talking one's way out of a situation by specious arguments. **Ausflucht** (more common in plural) suggests evasions and subterfuges.

Ich weiß nicht, warum er zu solchen Ausflüchten greifen mußte.

Das ist eine faule Ausrede (lame e.).

6. Abbitten suggests genuine and humble repentance and comes closer perhaps to English beg forgiveness.

Wir haben Ihnen sehr viel abzubitten.

EXPERIENCE A. Verb.

1. Erleben: to pass through an experience without necessarily more than witnessing it.[1] It can thus be ambiguous.

Er hat die Schrecken des Krieges erlebt.

Die Firma erlebt einen neuen Aufschwung.

Ich habe Wutausbrüche von ihm erlebt (not necessarily directed against oneself).

Tu's, sonst wirst du was erleben.

2. Erfahren: to receive, be subjected to a thing,[2] often but not invariably unpleasant, i.e. in the sense of 'befall'. It never means merely 'to witness'.

Sie haben eine schwere Enttäuschung erfahren.

B. noun.

1. Erlebnis: something that is lived inwardly and intensely. Its permanent effects, if any, are changes in the inner, emotional life. It can be used absolutely in the sense of an intense imaginative or spiritual experience. Thus used it is stronger than 'experience' which tends to be more external.

Das Erlebnis der Wüste ist unvergeßlich.

Von seinen Kriegserlebnissen wollte er nichts erzählen.

Für Rilke war die Reise nach Rußland das erste, große Erlebnis seines Lebens.

Das Konzert war wirklich ein Erlebnis.

2. Erfahrung refers to external happenings and to the wisdom, practical knowledge, general rules drawn from them.

Ich weiß es aus Erfahrung.

Auf Grund meiner Erfahrung habe ich den Vorschlag abgelehnt.

Ich habe schlechte Erfahrungen mit ihm gemacht.[3]

EXPRESS 1. Ausdrücken is only used when the manner or form is stated or clearly implied or intensity is suggested.

[1] Similarly: *ich habe es erlebt, daß er zwanzig Stunden hintereinander geschlafen hat* (I have known him to sleep...). A related sense is: to live to see. *Er wird seinen 80. Geburtstag sicher noch erleben.*

[2] *Erfahren* can also mean 'to be subjected to' a process, a treatment. *Eine Zubereitung erfahren.*

[3] *Die Erfahrung machen* combines the ideas of having the experience and making the discovery.

Drücken Sie sich etwas deutlicher aus.
Er drückt sich schlecht aus.
Wie soll man diesen Gedanken ausdrücken?
Dieses Gedicht drückt Körners Begeisterung für den Freiheitsgedanken aus.
Ich habe ganz offen mein Mißfallen ausgedrückt.
Darf ich Ihnen mein Beileid ausdrücken.
Ich habe ihm meinen aufrichtigen Dank ausgedrückt.
Er drückte seinen Zweifel in nicht mißzuverstehender Weise aus.
Seine ganze Haltung, sein Gesicht, drückt Freude aus.

2. **Äußern** and **aussprechen** (the latter of something important) mean 'to make the content of a thing known'.[1] It is also used of emotions and the like in so far as they manifest themselves in action, not only in language.

Äußern Sie sich etwas deutlicher (tell me what you really mean, i.e. in content).
Er äußerte den Wunsch, hier bleiben zu dürfen.
Er äußerte seine Zweifel darüber, ob der Bericht in jeder Einzelheit stimme.
Er sprach die Überzeugung, die Meinung, aus, daß der Krieg noch lange dauern würde.
Wer kann umhin, die Treue der Neger zu bewundern, auch wenn sie sich in so furchtbarer Weise äußert?

3. **Zum Ausdruk bringen** is fuller, more plastic with regard to manner and is used of something vaster in content.

In grandioser Weise hat Michelangelo den Geist der Renaissance zum Ausdruck gebracht.
Das Volk brachte seine Entrüstung über die Politik seiner Führer energisch zum Ausdruck.

EXTENT, DEGREE, MEASURE, SCALE 1. **Maß** corresponds closely to 'measure', and can translate 'extent' and 'degree' only when these are close synonyms of 'measure'. In a measure = *in einem Maß*. 'Great' as an adjective qualifying 'measure' must be translated by *hoch*. In all uses *Maß*, like 'measure', suggests definite limits. *Gewissermaßen* = in some measure.[2]

Sie haben in hohem Maße recht.
Er hat das volle Maß seiner Macht noch nicht erreicht.
Das Maß seiner Sünden ist voll.

2. **Grad** corresponds closely to 'degree'. To a degree = *in einem Grade*, up to = *bis zu*. 'Great' as an adjective qualifying 'degree' is translated by *hoch*.
Das ist mir im höchsten Grade verhaßt.
Die Skandinavier sind in hohem Grade zivilisiert.

3. **Ausmaß** suggests absence of limits, and corresponds to 'extent', 'scale', 'magnitude' thus used, particularly in reference to intangibles. To an extent = *in einem Ausmaß*.

Das Ausmaß seines Größenwahns ist gradezu unheimlich.
Das Ausmaß seiner Verschwendungssucht steht in gar keinen Verhältnis zu seinem Einkommen.
Das Ausmaß seiner Verbrechen ist noch nicht bekannt.
Das Ausmaß des Schadens ist unübersehbar.
Solche Verbrechen kommen jetzt in geringerem Ausmaß vor.

---

[1] In fixed phrases other words are found; e.g. *ich möchte Ihnen für Ihre Unterstützung unseren Dank sagen.*
[2] For *einigermassen* see footnote to 'mind' (p. 215, n. 8).

4. Umfang means primarily 'circumference', which suggests the idea of limits in the sense of 'extent'.

Der Umfang des Schadens ist gering.

Der Umfang unseres Handels mit Südamerika is befriedigend.

'*Hier ruht zunächst, von dem Ausmaß und Umfang seines Wesens abgesehen, Stefan Georges geschichtlicher Sinn: er allein beherrscht heute die neue Ebene die Nietzsche zuerst wieder sah, die Ebene des ewigen Menschen, nicht die der modernen Menschheit*' (F. Gundolf, *George*).

5. Ausdehnung is 'extent' in one dimension, i.e. in reference to something stretched out. See article on 'spread'.

Die Ausdehnung der Stadt hat mich überrascht.

6. 'To an extent' presents difficulties in translation. When the above terms are inapplicable, use may often be made of *Teil* and of such formations as *großenteils* (largely), *größtenteils* (for the most part).

Ein großer Teil des Heeres wurde vernichtet (to a large extent).

Es ist großenteils seine Schuld.

EXTINGUISH (something burning) **Löschen** is the ordinary term in reference to any fire except a small one. **Auslöschen:** to put out a flame or embers which are burning a small object, to snuff out a candle. 'Put out' is therefore translated by both verbs.[1]

Die Feuerwehr löschte den Brand.

Er löschte die Kerze aus.

FACT 1. In the original sense of fact, namely 'a thing done, deed' (*W.*) as in the phrase accessory after the fact, German uses **Tat** (see under 'action').

2. In the modern sense **Tatsache,** introduced into German in the eighteenth century as an equivalent of English 'matter of fact' is the general term corresponding to nearly all uses of 'fact'. **Faktum** is used in exactly the same sense, but confined more to intellectual and academic writing.

Vor Tatsachen soll man die Augen nicht verschließen.

Tatsache bleibt, daß alle unsere Bemühungen scheiterten.

Sich an die Tatsachen halten.

3. Where 'fact' appears in a context which contradicts or casts doubt on its meaning German uses **Angabe** (see under 'statement'), **Unterlage** (see under 'evidence'), **Daten** (see under 'data') and the like.

Seine Angaben (Unterlagen, Daten) sind fragwürdig (his facts are open to question—*W.*).

Wenn die Sache wahr ist (if the facts be true).

4. Sachlage: facts of the case; for **Sachverhalt** and **Tatbestand** see Duden. It remains to add that the latter is always a legal term, while the former may but need not be so.

Der Sachverhalt, den ein Autor ersinnt, ist nicht immer zuverläßig (S.O.D.).

Die Geschworenen entscheiden bloß den Sachverhalt (issues of fact).

5. I know it for a fact: *ich weiß es gang sicher.*

---

[1] Both verbs are used figuratively. *Löschen* refers more to the action, *auslöschen* stresses complete cessation of existence. The former is used sometimes as a legal and commercial, the latter only as a human term. *Die Eintragung wird gelöscht; eine Schuld löschen; den Durst löschen* (slake, quench); *jeden Verdacht löschen. Das löscht seine Schuld nicht aus; diese Tatsache ist wie ausgelöscht.*

IN FACT, INDEED The distinction between these two terms is that the former states clearly what was before unclear, doubtful or merely implicit, while the latter lends subjective emphasis, which may be hearty agreement or indignation or a number of other emotional colourings, to the statement.

When 'in fact' occurs in a *Steigerung* it is represented in German by **sogar** (see under 'even') or (**ja**) **sogar**, otherwise it is generally **tatsächlich,** which can only cover 'indeed' when this term is interchangeable with 'in fact'. When 'indeed' is used absolutely to indicate agreement its equivalent in German is **jawohl** or **allerdings** or **freilich.** (The last two terms express an agreement which can be a concession, i.e. 'certainly'.) When 'indeed' is said with more fervour it is represented in German by **in der Tat. Und zwar** means 'what is more', 'and in truth'.

> *Ich habe ihn in den letzten Jahren tatsächlich nicht mehr gesehen* (it may not have been clear before, now I am stating it as a fact).
>
> *Er ist tatsächlich ein begabter Musiker* (there was doubt in some minds about this before).
>
> *Nein, er kann nicht ausgehen, er ist tatsächlich sehr krank.*
>
> *Er ist sehr reich, (ja) sogar ein Millionär.*
>
> *Hören Sie Bach gern? Jawohl* (indeed, or yes indeed, or indeed I do).
>
> *Hat Ihnen Salzburg gefallen? Allerdings.*
>
> *Er ist in der Tat ein ausgezeichneter Schauspieler.*
>
> *Er ist ein Dieb, und zwar ein vorbestrafter.*

FAIL   A. To prove unequal to the demands made on a person or thing with reference to a specific occasion or situation.

1. Versagen implies the disappointment of expectations and emphasizes the inner weakness or defect which causes the failure rather than the collapse of an undertaking during its execution.

> *Meine Kräfte haben versagt.*
>
> *Die Stimme versagte ihr.*
>
> *Der Plan zur Regelung des Verkehrs hat versagt.*
>
> *Das Gewehr, die Maschine, hat völlig versagt* (i.e. *den Dienst versagt*).
>
> *Das Licht versagte* (electric light, lamp, etc., not daylight).
>
> *Diese Maschine wird sicher versagen.*
>
> *Er versagte in seinem Beruf.*
>
> *Der Lehrer hat versagt.*

2. Scheitern: to crash completely in the execution or in action, whether owing to internal weakness or not.

> *Der feindliche Angriff ist gescheitert.*
>
> *Das Unternehmen wird aus Mangel an Vorbereitung scheitern.*
>
> *Der Plan zur Regelung des Verkehrs ist gescheitert* (suggests, unlike *versagen*, an external cause).
>
> *Alle unsere Hoffnungen sind gescheitert.*

3. Fehlschlagen: to go awry, to miscarry, at some point or with reference to some detail. The failure need not be absolute, but may be retrieved. It can be coupled with the same nouns as *scheitern*. A further example:

> *Der Versuch ist fehlgeschlagen.*

4. Durchfallen: to fail in an examination.

> *Der Kandidat ist in allen Prüfungen durchgefallen.*

B. Not to come, not to eventuate, of something expected.

Ausbleiben can often be used,[1] particularly with reference to the phenomena of nature. Sometimes 'fail to come' or some such equivalent is a more appropriate translation.

Die Weizenernte ist ausgeblieben.[2]
Der Wind, der Regen, der Sturm, ist ausgeblieben.
Die unheilvollen Folgen dieser Handlungsweise werden nicht ausbleiben.
Ihm blieb der Atem aus.

C. To become weaker or less, with reference to things. German has no general term to render this use as the following examples show.

Seine Geisteskräfte nehmen ab (his mind is failing).
Sein Gedächtnis wird schwach.
Seine Augen werden schlecht.
Seine Gesundheit läßt sehr nach.
Die Vorräte werden knapp.
Der Brunnen ist versiegt.

D. 'Fail' followed by the infinitive.[3]

1. When failure in conscious effort or purpose is implied, **nicht gelingen**[4] is the most common rendering.

Es ist mir nicht gelungen, ihn zu überzeugen.
Den Truppen gelang es nicht, die feindlichen Stellungen einzunehmen.
Es gelang mir nicht, die Zigarette selbst zu drehen.

2. With phrases denoting mental perceptions conscious effort may or may not be implied. For the latter case, which is merely equivalent to a strong negative, German lacks a general term. Somewhat colloquially the emphatic *gar* may be added to the negative. *Entgehen* (to escape[5] one's notice) can indicate conscious effort or its absence. With sense perceptions *übersehen* (fail to see) and *überhören* (fail to hear) are often appropriate terms to denote absence of effort. Frequently an emphatic phrase is the only solution.

Ich sehe gar nicht ein, warum das verlangt wird (I fail to see).
Der Witz entging mir.
Es entging mir, daß er nicht da war.
Ich übersah die Zeitungsnotiz.
Ich überhörte seine Bemerkung.
Seine Handlungsweise ist mir vollkommen unbegreiflich.

3. 'Fail' can also indicate that something expected or desired of the subject, who may even be unaware of it, does not eventuate. The subject may be a thing as well as a person. German lacks a term for this use. Examples: I failed to react to his threats, I failed to feel impressed, they failed to get my letter, the letter failed to arrive. This sense cannot be translated into German, unless somewhat colloquially by *garnicht*, as with **2**.

[1] Also in the phrase *es kann nicht ausbleiben, daß* (*die Regierung gestürzt wird*), i.e. the Government cannot fail to fall. See 'fail' followed by the infinitive.
[2] Or *ist ausgefallen* (of something which otherwise recurs regularly).
[3] See also footnote 1.
[4] *Mißlingen* means 'fail' with reference to something attempted. It is not normally followed by the infinitive, and is more common without than with an accompanying dative. Example: *der Versuch mißlang (ihm)*.
[5] See 'escape'.

4. Vernachlässigen (to neglect) and **unterlassen** (to omit, to abstain) are often close approximations to 'fail'. *Unterlassen* implies conscious abstention, but says nothing about the reasons for this, nor the type of action from which one abstains. **Ermangeln:** not to do a thing which is expected of us and which is often, but not exclusively, conceived as an obligation. It is confined to negative use, and occurs mainly in the future tense. Conversational use is apt to sound servile or precious.[1]

Er hat es vernachlässigt, mich zu verständigen.

Er hat es unterlassen, uns diese Woche zu besuchen.

Ich werde nicht ermangeln, mich nach seinem Befinden zu erkundigen; alle in seinem Brief enthaltenen Fragen zu beantworten.

'...*zu seinem Erstaunen blieb darauf Olympia bei jedem Tanze sitzen, und er ermangelte nicht, immer wieder sie aufzuziehen*' (E. T. A. Hoffmann, *Der Sandmann*).

5. The following verbs, which primarily mean 'to miss' (see article on 'miss') may sometimes be used to translate 'fail': **versäumen, verfehlen, verpassen.** All three may be followed by the infinitive, which is, however, less common with *verpassen*. To translate 'fail' with the infinitive, it is sometimes not only possible but preferable to use these verbs in the sense of 'miss' with a noun object.

Er hat es versäumt, seine Schulden zu bezahlen.

Er versäumte es nicht, mich zu benachrichtigen.

Er verfehlte den richtigen Weg (or: *den richtigen Weg einzuschlagen*).

Die Kugel verfehlte ihn.

Ich werde nicht verfehlen, ihm alles mitzuteilen.

Die Uhr verfehlte zu schlagen (in this as in the following example *nicht* would be more usual).

Die Bombe explodierte nicht (or: *versagte*).

Die Medizin verfehlte ihre Wirkung.

Ich verpaßte es, ihm mein Beileid zu sagen.

Der Bote verpaßte mich (failed to reach me, i.e. missed me).

6. 'Cannot fail' with the infinitive as a synonym of 'cannot help' must be variously translated. Common renderings are: *müssen, nicht anders können als, unfehlbar, nicht* strengthened by an appropriate adverb.[2]

Er muß, kann nicht anders als, dem Plan zustimmen.

Er wird sich dem Einfluß seines Vaters einfach nicht entziehen können.

Er wird unfehlbar eine Dummheit machen.

FAIRLY, PRETTY, RATHER All these terms mean 'to a certain extent', i.e. not completely, not absolutely. The distinction between 'fairly' and 'pretty', not always observed, is that 'pretty' indicates 'to a greater extent' than 'fairly' does and therefore makes the adjective or past participle it modifies appear in a much more positive light. It is clearly audible in such phrases as 'pretty good', 'fairly good'. 'Fairly' therefore expresses a greater qualification.

In general, German uses **recht** like 'pretty', **ziemlich** like 'fairly', but this distinction applies more clearly when the adjective modified has a

---

[1] See 'lack'.

[2] *Nicht umhin können* is now apt to sound out of place, unless used in eloquent or emotional diction.

positive than when it has a pejorative sense. Thus, while *ziemlich gut* can only mean 'fairly good', *ziemlich schlecht* can come close to 'pretty bad'.

1. *Es geht ihm ziemlich gut* (*recht gut* is closer to good unmodified).
   Es ist ziemlich spät (*es ist recht spät* means still later).
   Dieser Wein ist ziemlich gut (fairly—said by a connoisseur—much more of a qualification than *ein recht guter Wein*).
   Wir hatten recht kaltes Wetter (colder than *ziemlich kaltes Wetter*).
   Das Haus ist ziemlich baufällig (hardly to be distinguished from *recht baufällig*).
   Er wirkt recht lächerlich in dieser Rolle.
   Der Profit wurde ziemlich gleichmäßig verteilt.

2. **So ziemlich,** on the other hand, means 'pretty much', i.e. almost.
   Ich bin so ziemlich erledigt.
   Er ließ die Dinge so ziemlich wie sie waren.
   Das stimmt so ziemlich, nicht wahr?

3. There is, however, a use of 'fairly' in the sense of 'thoroughly'.
   Wir saßen richtig in der Klemme (*A.L.*).
   Ordentlich, tüchtig (colloquial), *ganz schön* can also mean 'thoroughly'.
   Es ist ganz schön, tüchtig, kalt ('extremely').

4. 'Rather' has as one of its meanings 'to some extent', 'somewhat' (*A.L.*): **etwas, ziemlich.**
   Eine etwas (ziemlich) ungewöhnliche Geste.
   Wir waren am Ende des langen Aufstiegs etwas ermüdet (*A.L.*).
The use of 'rather' as understatement (I found it rather good; it is really rather wonderful) has no equivalent in German.

5. **Lieber** indicates a preference, i.e. sooner, preferably.
   Was möchtest du lieber trinken, Tee oder Kaffee? (*A.L.*).
   Ich würde lieber sterben als soetwas mitmachen.

6. **Eher:** with better reason or ground, more properly or justly. An objective judgment is expressed.
   Deswegen verdiene ich eher die Todesstrafe als er (*S.O.D.*).
   Er ist eher zu bemitleiden als zu rügen.
   Er ist eher kühl als kalt.
   Es war eher töricht als verbrecherisch.
   Es ist eher Starrsinn als Mut, wenn er nicht aufgibt.
   With the suppression of the *als* phrase, *eher* can mean 'more likely'.
   Das ist eher der Fall.
   Ja, eher.

7. **Vielmehr:** more truly or correctly; more properly speaking (*S.O.D.*). Often used to introduce what is exact after saying something inexact.
   Ihre Eingebung, vielmehr ihr Idol (*W.*).
   Es geht ihm nicht besser, vielmehr schlechter.
   In cases where either *vielmehr* or *eher* could be used the distinction still holds good.
   Er ist nicht despotisch, sondern vielmehr (eher) egoistisch.

8. 'Rather' appears also as an interjection to express some decided affirmation (*W.*): **gewiss, freilich, allerdings** and more colloquially, **na und ob.**
   Gefällt Ihnen die junge Dame? Allerdings, na und ob.

FALL

FALL 1. Sense: literal, to come to the ground, of persons.

Fallen indicates nothing more than downward movement, either from a height or from a level with the ground. In the sense of 'to crash violently and to sustain injuries' **stürzen** must be used.[1] *Fallen* does not exclude abrasions, particularly in cases of tripping and slipping, but does not necessarily imply them.

> *Er fiel von der Leiter, aus dem Fenster* (leaves open the question of injuries).
> *Ich bin beim Tennis gefallen.*
> *Er glitt aus und fiel auf den Rücken.*
> *Ich bin da scheußlich hingefallen* (*hin* = lengthwise).
> *Er stürzte von der Leiter, aus dem Fenster* (crashed violently).
> *Ich bin mit meinem Motorrad gestürzt* (*fallen* would be out of place with *Motorrad*).

2. Sense: to pass, lapse, into a subjective[2] state.[3]

This sense is generally rendered by **verfallen**. When followed by *in*, the implication is that the state expresses itself actively. A following dative without preposition gives the meaning of 'to fall a victim to a state'.

> *Es liegt in der menschlichen Natur, immer wieder in die alten Fehler, den alten Fehlern, zu verfallen.*
> *Er ist in Wahnsinn, in seine alten Gewohnheiten, verfallen* (suggests activity).
> *Er ist seinen alten Wutanfällen, seinen alten Gewohnheiten, verfallen* (these things have a hold of him).

3. Sense: to divide into parts.

This sense is rendered by **zerfallen**[4] and **sich gliedern**.

> *Der Aufsatz, die Stadt, zerfällt, gliedert sich, in drei Teile.*

FALSIFY, FORGE, ADULTERATE **Fälschen** means (1) to put something spurious in place of the genuine article, i.e. to forge (e.g. a document, a signature); (2) to falsify, corrupt, adulterate a thing by mixing something else with it, e.g. a text, wine). **Verfälschen** has only the second meaning of *fälschen*. If there is any distinction between the two terms used in this sense, it is that *verfälschen* denotes more the result, *fälschen* the action. But this distinction is not rigidly observed.[5]

> *Das Geld ist gefälscht* (counterfeit).
> *Der Text, der Wein, ist gefälscht, verfälscht.*
> *Er hat die Tatsachen gefälscht, verfälscht.*

FARM Sense: a tract of land held (originally on lease) for purpose of cultivation (*S.O.D.*). It may be used for growing crops, vegetables, fruit, etc. or for raising animals. The commonest German term is **Bauernhof**, which includes the buildings as well as the cultivated land, **Gut**, more

---

[1] *Abstürzen* is often used in the sense of 'to crash from a height', particularly when the destination is not given. It is the regular term in reference to an aeroplane crash. *Das Flugzeug ist abgestürzt.*

[2] For a state or condition which is not subjective *fallen* is used. *In Ungnade fallen.*

[3] 'To get into a state, condition', is *geraten. Er gerät sehr leicht in Wut.*

[4] Both *verfallen* and *zerfallen* are used in the sense of 'to decay'. The latter indicates complete disintegration of the parts of a thing, and can therefore only be used of a dead, not a living, body. *Verfallen* means 'to fall, waste away', i.e. to a point approaching disintegration, but short of the latter. *Das Haus, die Leiche, zerfiel. Das Haus, der Mensch verfällt. Ein verfallenes Gesicht.*

[5] *Ein gedokterter, ungedokterter, Wein.*

specifically and clearly **Landgut,** is bigger (in German conditions particularly the estates of the aristocrats in East Prussia).

Viehwirtschaft is for cattle. Farm-house: **Bauernhaus** or **Gehöft** (collective of *Hof*). Dairy-farm: **Molkerei** (*Meierei* is old-fashioned). Chicken-farm: **Geflügelhof** (in Anglo-Saxon countries: *Hühnerfarm*).

FARMER 1. Bauer (originally an inhabitant of a house, now only with something of this sense in *Vogelbauer* = cage) is a peasant and as such non-existent in Anglo-Saxon countries. In present-day German use it refers to someone who owns a small tract of land which he cultivates for the purpose in question.

2. A farmer on a bigger scale and equipped with more scientific knowledge is: **Landwirt.** The terms **Gutsbesitzer** and **Gutsherr** emphasize ownership of the land.

3. A dairy-farmer: *Molkereibseitzer.*
    Er lebt von der, besitzt eine, Milchwirtschaft.

4. Landarbeiter: a person who works on a farm but does not own it.

5. Farmer as a German word refers to non-European countries.

FARMING, AGRICULTURE The former emphasizes the production of crops or animals for the market (*W.S.*) In German **Ackerbau** is the strict though little used equivalent, though the more comprehensive term and modern **Landwirtschaft,** agriculture, which includes not only 'the production and harvesting of crops, the care and breeding of livestock' but also other 'pursuits such as horticulture, forestry, dairying, sugar-making, bee-keeping' (*W.S.*), is generally the preferred term.
    Hier in diesem Gebiet gibt es nur Ackerbau (i.e. no cattle etc.).
    Die Landwirtschaft hat die E.W.G. vor schwierige Probleme gestellt.

FATE[1] Schicksal denotes both the power which predetermines events and these events themselves. **Geschick** refers only to the latter. **Verhängnis,** that which is decreed, inflicted, is always used in an unfavourable sense, i.e. an untoward fate.[2] The first two terms may be used in the plural.
    Das Schicksal hat es gut mit ihm gemeint.
    Er hat ein furchtbares Schicksal erlitten.
    Er bejammert sein widriges Geschick.
    Es war sein Verhängnis, daß er in seinen eindrucksfähigen Jahren in üble Gesellschaft geriet.

FEAR (verb) **1. Fürchten** is 'to feel real fear, dread of' someone or something, but is also used as a polite formula. **Befürchten** does not express the emotion of fear, but means 'to be convinced that something that one dislikes or is contrary to what one wants will take place.' It is therefore the only appropriate term to translate 'it is to be feared that...', 'it is feared that...', since these impersonal phrases do not strongly suggest the emotion of fear. *Fürchten* does not in itself imply expectation that a thing will take place. *Befürchten* cannot because of its meaning take a personal object.

---

[1] *Los* corresponds exactly to 'lot'.
[2] The phrase *einem zum Verhängnis werden* means 'to prove fatal to someone'. *Sein Erfolg wurde ihm zum Verhängnis.*

Ich fürchte ihn, seine Wutausbrüche.
Er wird (or: *ist*) *überall gefürchtet.*
Ich fürchte für seine Sicherheit.
Ich fürchte, daß es zum Schlimmsten kommen wird.
Ich fürchte, Sie sind falsch verbunden (polite).
Ich fürchte seinen Besuch.
Ich befürchte das Schlimmste (since the meaning is 'I am convinced the worst will happen', *fürchten* is impossible).
Es wird in London befürchtet, daß bald ein Krieg ausbricht.
Ich befürchte seinen Besuch.
Ich befürchte das Gegenteil von dem, was Sie behaupten.

2. Sich fürchten vor jemandem (etwas) is an emotionally stronger expression and suggests the concrete presence of danger.

Ich fürchte mich vor ihm, vor seinen Wutausbrüchen, vor seinem Besuch (one visualizes the situation).

3. Angst haben is used colloquially in the sense of *fürchten*. It is, however, weaker and suggests an uneasy feeling. In psychological use *Angst* corresponds to 'anxiety'.

Ich habe Angst vor ihm, seinem Wutausbrüchen, seinem Besuch.
Ich habe Angst, daß es zum Schlimmsten kommt.

FEED 1. Nähren can only translate 'feed' in the sense of 'nourish', i.e. out of the substance of the feeder. It can also be used figuratively in this way.

Die Mutter nährt ihr Kind (at the breast).
Die Kinder sehen gut genährt aus.
Das wird seinen Rachedurst nur nähren.
Den Geist des Widerstands nähren.

2. Ernähren: to support, to provide for. It often implies the organization and distribution of food.

Der Vater ernährt seine Kinder, eine zahlreiche Familie.
Wir mußten ein ganzes Heer von Arbeitslosen ernähren.
Die Vorräte, die noch übrigbleiben, werden wohl kaum reichen, um auch nur die Ausgebombten zu ernähren.
Dieses Gut kann so viele Menschen nicht ernähren.

3. Zu essen geben, das (sein, ihr) Essen geben, zu essen (das Essen) bekommen. These expressions must be used when the number of meals or the time of feeding is referred to.

Die Mutter gibt den Kindern um 6 Uhr zu essen.
Der Gefangenen wird nur einmal täglich zu essen gegeben.
Unter den Umständen bekamen die Truppen erst um Mitternacht ihr Essen (zu essen).

4. Speisen: to dine (intransitive only). Its use is often a sign of false refinement. Correct use: *Majestät haben gespeist.* It is the normal term in technology (e.g. *mit Strom speisen*).

5. Beköstigen, verpflegen (see 'food'). *Die Pensionsmutter muß* 30 *Gäste beköstigen* (cater for). *In disem Hotel wird man gut verpflegt.* **Verköstigen** implies large numbers.

6. Füttern: to feed animals. *Dick füttern:* feed, fatten up. Also: *Mästen.*

7. Abfüttern: to feed masses of people in a rough-and-ready way.

Horden von Flüchtlingen wurden abgefüttert.

Eine Schule abfüttern.

FEEL 1. Fühlen is the most general term in the meaning: to be aware of a thing through no special sense,[1] but generally several at once and sometimes including that of touch. It must be distinguished from **empfinden**. *Fühlen* refers simply to the strength or weakness of the feeling, *empfinden* to one's capacity to react to or to be aware of stimuli, therefore to one's sensitiveness[2] and powers of subtle discrimination, particularly (*a*) with regard to pain; (*b*) aesthetic experience. At times 'to be sensitive to' is a more suitable English equivalent than 'to feel'.[3]

Iche fühlte etwas unter meinem Fuß.

Ich habe keine Schmerzen gefühlt.

Er fühlte die Kälte sehr.

Er fühlte ein starkes Bedürfnis nach Ausspannung.

Ich fühlte die Macht seiner Argumente.

Seine Worte ließen mich fühlen, wie töricht ich gehandelt hatte.

Ich fühle, daß ich genug gesagt habe.[4]

Ich empfinde die Kälte sehr.

Sie empfindet sein weiteres Fortbleiben als schmerzlich.

Ich empfand seine Worte als wohltuend.

Ich empfinde Verehrung für ihn.

Ich empfinde diese Farbenmischung als eine Störung der Harmonie.

2. When 'feel' means 'to exercise deliberately one's sense of touch' the following verbs are used: **fühlen, befühlen, nachfühlen, tasten, betasten, abtasten**. *Fühlen* and its compounds mean 'to touch' a thing in order to ascertain something through it, but not to test its quality. *Fühlen*, which can also refer to awareness which comes from accidental contact (see first example under **1**) means 'to touch in one spot', *befühlen* 'to touch in many, all over', while *nachfühlen* may imply one or many places, and means to check, to investigate, but in this sense always takes a clause (generally *ob*) as its object.[5] *Tasten* and its compounds suggest still more definitely the use of the sense of touch, a fingering of objects. *Tasten* is generally intransitive and mostly means 'to search' for a thing by using one's sense of touch. It often suggests 'groping'. *Betasten* is 'to touch' a thing in a number of places, often in order to test its quality. *Abtasten* is 'to touch up and down', mostly in the meaning of 'to search thoroughly all over'.

Der Arzt fühlte seinen Puls (one spot).

Der Arzt befühlte seine Lunge (here and there).

Er fühlte nach, ob noch etwas Tabak in seiner Tasche wäre.

[1] In earlier German *fühlen* meant only 'to be aware through the sense of touch'.

[2] *Empfindlich* means 'sensitive' to pain, also 'touchy', and further 'sore'. See footnote to 'severe' (p. 307, n. 3). See also under 'sensitive'.

[3] Close synonyms of *fühlen* in the sense of 'to notice a thing as an effect' are *spüren* and *verspüren*. *Spüren* is the general term and suggests merely ordinary intensity (e.g. *Hunger, Schmerzen, spüren*). *Verspüren* is an intensive and means to feel something that is strong or insistent (e.g. *Hunger, Schmerz, Übelkeit, verspüren*).

[4] The sense is 'to be emotionally aware'. *Fühlen* cannot be used in the sense of 'to hold a conviction' when it is desired to express this tentatively (e.g. I feel we ought to do something to help him).

[5] Except in the sense of 'sympathize'. *Das kann ich Ihnen nachfühlen.*

Er tastete im Dunkel nach seinem Hut.
Er betastete das Tuch (to test its quality).
Er betastete den Hund (e.g. to see whether it had ticks on it).
Der Detektiv tastete ihn ab.

3. **Sich fühlen** with a following adjective or past participle has the sense of 'to be consciously'. It can only be used with a person, i.e. unlike 'feel' (e.g. 'my feet feel sore') not with a specific part of the body, as subject. Furthermore: (*a*) it can only be followed by such adjectives as can also be combined with the verb *sein* used personally, i.e. not to translate 'I feel hot' and the like (*mir ist heiß*); (*b*) it is not normally used with adjectives expressing anger, indignation, curiosity.[1]

It is also used with *wie* and a following noun in the sense of 'to feel that one resembles' something.[2]

Ich fühle mich glücklich, traurig, krank, müde, schwach, betrogen, befangen.
Ich fühle mich wie ein geschorenes Schaf.

4. **Sich anfühlen** with an adverb of manner and a thing as subject is used to denote the kind of tactile sensation communicated by a thing. This must not be confused with non-tactile sensations as, e.g., with parts of the body (e.g. my brow feels hot, feverish).

Das Tuch fühlt sich hart, weich, an.

FELLOW, CHAP 1. 'Chap' is defined by *W.* as 'man, boy, fellow'. For its meaning as boy see under 'boy'. As one of the meanings of 'fellow' (the original sense was one associated with another, comrade, *C.O.D.*), *S.O.D.* gives man, male person, and calls this familiar. 'Chap' normally sounds more friendly when used to refer to the male sex. German: **Kerl, Bursche,** but the distinctions are not quite the same as between the English terms.

Kerl spreading from the low German area (with plural 'Kerls') to the south (plural 'Kerle') (cognate with Anglo-Saxon *ceorl*, English *churl*) originally meant simply 'man', but is now colloquial and may even refer to a female (e.g. *sie ist ein netter Kerl*). It suggests strength, activity and extroversion. It is generally accompanied by an adjective, but when not, it is always pejorative and may be pejorative when coupled with an adjective.

Er ist ein famoser, ekelhafter, Kerl.
Der Kerl hat mir allerhand weismachen wollen.
Dem Kerl traue ich nicht.

Bursche, a male in his late teens, again can suggest strength and also size (strapping) (for history of the term see Trübner). It is more often than not used positively, but can also be used pejoratively. It need not be but generally is qualified by an adjective. Its use in compounds is common and here it corresponds rather to the special use of English boy (*ein Offiziersbursche, ein Laufbursche*).

Zwei junge Burschen saßen da und spielten Karten.
Ein kräftiger, stämmiger, tüchtiger, übler, Bursche.
Nimm dich vor dem Burschen in acht, er kann unangenehm werden.

---

[1] For 'to feel sure' see 'sure'.

[2] In this sense *vorkommen* with the reflexive dative is more common. It suggests rather 'to have a certain impression of oneself' than real feeling. *Ich komme mir wie ein geschorenes Schaf vor.*

2 (a) 'Fellow' in sense of one associated with another as a sharer, partner, companion, comrade, associate (*W.*): **Kamerad, Genosse** (*Waffenkameraden, Tischgenosse, Schulkamerad*).
(b) When coupled with another noun and meaning comrade and belonging to the same class, the German equivalent is *mit* as the first part of a compound.

Unsere Mitmenschen (fellow human being), *Mitbürger* (fellow citizens).

3. 'Fellow' in sense of a member of a learned society or an incorporated member of a collegiate foundation or a member of the corporation or governing body in one of certain colleges or universities (*W.*). German can only say **Mitglied**.

Ein Mitglied der amerikanischen chirurgischen Vereinigung, der Akademie der Wissenschaften.

FEW **1.** With animate beings and objects the inflected form **wenige,** which individualizes, must be used, except in statements about the existence of a species. In the latter case the uninflected form **wenig** is normal.

Auf dieser Insel gab es nur wenige Menschen, Tiere.
Auf dieser Insel gab es nur wenig Menschen, Tiere.
In dieser Gegend habe ich wenige Eingeborene gesehen.
Es gibt heute nur noch wenig Eingeborene in Australien.
'Ein von wenig Menschen besuchtes Tal' (Kleist, *Das Erdbeben in Chili*).

2. With nouns which do not denote animate beings or objects **wenig** is the usual form. **Wenige** individualizes and expects an enumeration.[1]

Er sind wenig Fehler in dem Aufsatz.
Sie haben nur wenige Fehler gemacht (with a following enumeration).
Es hat mir wenig Schwierigkeiten gemacht.
Der Junge hat mir wenig Sorgen gemacht.

FIELD, MEADOW, PADDOCK 'Field' is, like German **Feld**, a piece of ground marked off for growing things, i.e. for agricultural purposes. In modern use 'meadow' is any piece of grass land (formerly a piece of land permanently covered with grass mown for use as hay, *S.O.D.*). German **Wiese** has this modern meaning, e.g. *Bergwiesen*. **Matte** is always on a mountain and occurs mostly in Alpine regions.

Die Wiese vor unserem Hause.

When low-lying, moist grass land along a water-course is meant, German **Au** is the specific term, though *Wiese* may also be used. 'Paddock' in English usage denotes a plot of pasture land adjoining a stable (*S.O.D.*), in Australian usage an often extensive area (as of grassland) usually fenced in and often used as pasture. For this German has no specific term, it being necessary to use **Weideland** or **Feld**, and in the more extended Australian sense, *Wiese* where this is meant.

FIGHT 'Fight' is used intransitively, transitively, with a cognate accusative. The third use involves mostly fixed phrases, the German equivalents of which are given in dictionaries.

---

[1] The distinction between the two forms *wenig* and *wenige* also applies to *viel*, *viele* (many), but is less strictly observed. *In diesem Teich gibt's viel(e) Fische. Es hat viel(e) Schwierigkeiten bereitet. Er bewilligte es, ohne viel(e) Worte zu machen.*

FIGHT

1. **Kämpfen** implies great effort. It is applied (*a*) to participation in battle, both by the individual and the group (e.g. a nation); (*b*) to boxing; (*c*) to the action of struggling against anything that threatens to overwhelm us or defeat our purposes, both physically and morally. This latter meaning includes fighting for a cause. (*d*) It may be followed by *Kampf* as a cognate accusative. (*e*) In the animal world it is applied to stags. (Otherwise terms such as *aufeinander losgehen, sich herumbeißen* are used of animals. *Es gab eine Beißerei zwischen den Hunden.*)

> *Er hat in drei Kriegen gekämpft.*
> *Hitler irrte sich in seiner Annahme, daß England nicht kämpfen würde.*
> *Die Boxer kämpften wie besessen.*
> *Ich kämpfe seit Tagen gegen einen Schnupfen.*
> *Wir kämpfen gegen unerhörte Schwierigkeiten.*
> *Er kämpfte hartnäckig gegen den Vorschlag.*
> *Er kämpft für die Wahrheit, seinen Glauben.*
> *Wir haben einen harten Kampf gekämpft.*

2. **Ankämpfen** emphasizes the action of fighting against that which threatens to overwhelm us or which is greater than we. It is used of a struggle against institutions, ideas, the elements of nature, and, unlike *kämpfen*, against feelings, but not against persons. It is always followed by *gegen*.

> *Er kämpfte gegen die Lehren der Kirche, gegen diesen Unsinn, an.*
> *Es hat keinen Zweck, gegen einen solchen Standpunkt anzukämpfen.*
> *Auf unserer Bergtour hatten wir uns verirrt und mußten 3 Stunden gegen ein schweres Schneegestöber ankämpfen.*
> *Er kämpfte gegen sein Müdigkeit, seine melancholischen Anwandlungen, an.*

3. **Bekämpfen:** to combat something one wants to kill. It suggests an effective use of the means of combat, but less the exertion of the struggle itself. Hence 'to combat' and 'to oppose' are often close equivalents. It governs the same type of object as *ankämpfen*. A personal object (in the sense of 'oppose') is rare.

> *Wir müssen diesen Vorschlag, diese Maßnahmen, diese Ideen, bekämpfen.*
> *Wir bekämpfen das Feuer mit aller Macht.*
> *Ich bekämpfe meine Müdigkeit mit Mengen schwarzen Kaffees.*

4. **Fechten,**[1] strictly used, means only 'to fence'. In colloquial speech, particularly university students' slang, it can, however, be applied to the participation by a country in warfare. In his book *Von anderen Deutschland* von Hassel uses it continually in this sense.

5. To come to fisticuffs.
None of the above terms can be used in this sense. The commonest are:
(a) **Sich schlagen**, which is very strong and implies a high degree of animosity.[2]

> *Die zwei Männer schlugen sich zehn Minuten lang vor dem Gerichtshof* (the addition of *herum* makes it less serious).

(b) **Such hauen**[3] (a brief scrap); (c) **sich in den Haaren liegen** (to quarrel either with physical violence or a dispute); (d) **sich balgen**, more playful, to scuffle.

---

[1] *Verfechten* is 'to fight for' in the sense of 'to champion' an idea or cause.
[2] Compare the noun *Schlägerei. Im Wirtshaus entwickelte sich eine Schlägerei.*
[3] *Verhauen* in the sense of 'to give a hiding' cannot be reflexive. In the latter use it means 'to make a blunder'.

Die beiden Jungens haben sich gehauen, liegen sich dauernd in den Haaren, balgen sich.

6. To scramble in order to seize a thing, i.e. of a number of people, a crowd.

(a) **Sich reißen um:** to try to snatch, tear, a thing from each other's hand.
Sie reißen sich um die Zeitungen, die Lebensmittelpakete.

(b) **Sich drängen und schubsen:** to push, to elbow and the like, in order to get a seat or a desired position.
Sie drängten und schubsten sich, um die besten Plätze zu bekommen.

7. To quarrel[1] over the possession of a thing, by argument or physical violence.

(a) **Streiten**[2] can imply physical violence, but more often suggests a dispute with words. It may be for the possession of a thing or to establish truth.

(b) **Sich in den Haaren liegen, haben** (see above) is a more colloquial expression, in reference to both physical violence and a dispute with words.
Die beiden Kinder stritten sich um das Buch.
Sie stritten sich um die väterliche Erbschaft.

FILL 1. Füllen: (*a*) to fill in the literal sense; (*b*) to fill a period of time; (*c*) to fill with emotions, thoughts, when the seat of these is mentioned. It is uncommon in the passive voice, except in the literal sense (coupled with *werden*, not *sein*).
Er füllte das Faß mit Wasser.
Das Faß wurde mit Wasser gefüllt.
Dieses Zeug füllt das ganze Haus.
Der Theaterdirektor füllte das Theater mit Inhabern von Freikarten.
Er hat ganze Hefte mit Zeichnungen gefüllt.
Das Theater war vollkommen gefüllt.
Ein abendfüllendes Stück (a technical term).
Ihre Augen füllten sich mit Tränen.
Warum füllen Sie sich den Kopf mit solchen Gedanken?
Sein Herz füllte sich mit Dankbarkeit.
Der Anblick solcher Schönheit füllt unser Herz mit Ehrfurcht.

2. Erfüllen:[3] (*a*) to fill a person, his doings, utterances (as distinct from the localized seat of these) with strong[4] emotion, his thoughts with meaning; (*b*) to fill a large space with sound, light, smoke, and the like.[5]
Die Nachricht erfüllte mich mit Abscheu.
Er war von Wut erfüllt (with =*von* after the passive voice).
Das waren haßerfüllte Ausbrüche.
Der Anblick solcher Schönheit erfüllt uns mit Ehrfurcht.
Bei Versen muß jede Silbe sinnerfüllt sein.
Das Zimmer war von Sonne erfüllt.
Die Luft war von wilden Schmerzensschreien erfüllt.

---

[1] *Zanken* means 'to quarrel' when accusations and abuse are hurled to and fro.
[2] For *bestreiten* see 'deny'.
[3] Another meaning is 'fulfil'.
[4] If the emotion is not intense other verbs are preferred (*die Nachricht erweckte Freude in uns*).
[5] Goethe in *Faust* uses *erfüllen* in the literal sense:

> '*Hier ist ein Saft, der eilig trunken macht.*
> *Mit brauder Flut erfüllt er Deine Höhle*' (i.e. of a beaker).

FILL

3. Voll is commonly used for 'filled' instead of *gefüllt sein*. See 'full'.
Der Wartesaal war voll von Passagieren.
Die Stadt war voll von amerikanischen Soldaten.
Sein Leben war voller Vorfälle derartiger Natur.
Die Zeitungen waren gradezu voll von solchen Anschuldigungen.

4. Anfüllen: to fill up, to the brim. It is occasionally used figuratively in the passive voice.
Füllen Sie die Gläser an.
Sein Kopf ist mit solchen Gedanken angefüllt.

5. Ausfüllen: The literal sense is to make one thing fit exactly into another. The figurative use preserves this image. It also translates 'fill in' (e.g. a form).
Er füllt den ganzen Stuhl aus.
Meine Zeit ist mit allen meinen Beschäftigungen sowieso schon ausgefüllt.
Er füllt seine Stellung wunderbar aus.
Wir haben nicht genug Rekruten, um die Reihen auszufüllen.

6. Überfüllen is used mostly with the verb *sein* in the sense of 'crowded'.
Die Straßen waren mit Soldaten überfüllt.

7. Besetzen: in reference to appointment to a position.
Alle Posten sind schon besetzt.

FIND In phrases of the type 'I find it difficult, painful, gratifying, cold', **finden** can only be used to express a judgment. Its meaning is 'to consider'. When 'find' suggests an experience, impersonal phrases formed with **sein, fallen** and the like, or **empfinden** (see 'feel') when emotional experience is implied, must be used. **Befinden** suggests an expert judgment.
Ich finde das Gedicht sehr schön.
Ich finde die Prüfung schwierig.
Die Prüfung fiel mir sehr schwer.
Es fällt mir schwer, ihn zu überzeugen.
Ich fand es kalt.
Es war mir kalt.
Es ist mir peinlich, ihn auf solche Sachen aufmerksam machen zu müssen.
Ich empfand den Sonnenschein als wohltuend.
Sie empfindet es als sehr schmerzlich, daß er noch länger wegbleiben soll.
Der Plan wurde für gut befunden.

FINISH,[1] END, COMPLETE[2] 'Finish' may be followed by a noun object or by a gerund. In some cases the former implies the latter (e.g. he finished his meal, finished eating his meal). Sometimes the omission of the gerund produces ambiguity (e.g. he finished the book, i.e. reading or writing).

1. Fertig means 'ready'[3] for something by virtue of having done the necessary work required. It thus comes to mean: having done (with) (active), being done (passive). In these senses it is used in the following combinations: (a) **Fertig machen** suggests the making or production of an object. If the noun it governs denotes an activity, the results of this activity must be visible

---

[1] For 'finish' see Webster's *Dictionary of Synonyms*. The sense of 'kill' is not discussed in this article.
[2] See also the adjective 'complete'.
[3] *Bereit* means 'ready' in the sense of 'prepared, willing'. *Fertig* meant originally 'ready for a journey'. It cannot be followed by an infinitive. Other senses are (a) dexterous, (b) done for (in the sense of *erledigt*).

as a thing, i.e. it cannot govern a noun which expresses merely an activity (e.g. to finish a game). It is normally used only of simple, everyday things.

Ein Kleid, das Essen (preparing, not eating), *einen Aufsatz, seine Arbeit, fertig machen.*

(b) **Fertig sein**[1] **(mit)** means 'to have finished, to have done', in the sense of finishing an activity, finishing the making of a thing, 'not to need any longer', 'to have consumed'. Without *mit* it can also mean 'to be finished' in the passive as well as the active sense.

Ich bin fertig (have, am, finished; am ready).
Das Haus, die Arbeit, ist nun fertig.
Sind Sie mit Ihrem Koffer fertig (packing or using it)?
Sind Sie mit Ihrer Toilette fertig?
Er ist mit dem Buch fertig (writing or reading it).
Er ist mit dem Gemälde noch nicht fertig (painting or using it).
Er war schon vor zwei Jahren mit der Schule fertig.
Er war mit dem Abschreiben des Briefes nicht fertig.
Sind Sie mit dem Rasieren schon fertig?

(c) *Fertig* can be combined adverbially with a small number of specific verbs, but not with every verb. Either the point of time when the action is finished is stated or inferable, or the completion of the thing which is being made is stressed, i.e. this is not left unfinished. The following is not a complete list.

Der Koch hat den Kuchen fertig gebacken (someone else started it).
Er hat den Roman, Brief, fertig geschrieben.
Nach vielen Schwierigkeiten (or: *endlich*) *haben sie das Haus fertig gebaut.*
In dieser Woche werden wir das Haus fertig gebaut haben.
Er hat den Tisch soeben fertig gezimmert.
Er hat sich fertig angezogen.
Er hat das Buch fertig gelesen.
Er hat sich nicht fertig rasiert.

(d) *Fertig sein* and *fertig werden* are not used in the imperative.

2. Zu Ende is used with a number of verbs in the sense of carrying the activity to a conclusive finish, covering all the ground, i.e. not ceasing before the end. It can only be used where (in English) 'to an end' or 'at an end' expresses the sense.

Den Krieg zu Ende kämpfen.
Das Lied zu Ende singen.
Die Zeitung zu Ende lesen.
Er hat die Verhandlungen erfolgreich zu Ende geführt.
Das Konzert ist jetzt zu Ende.

3. Compound verbs.
(a) Of the prefixes which express the sense of finishing *aus* is the most common. It can be combined with some verbs that denote an activity.

Ich habe die Zeitung noch nicht ausgelesen.
Lassen Sie mich ausreden.
Er trank seinen Wein aus und ging zu Bett.
Schlafen Sie sich ordentlich aus.

(b) Examples of other compounds (with the meaning of 'consume') are:
Essen Sie die Bratkartoffeln auf.
Wir haben unsere Vorräte schon längst verbraucht.

---

[1] *Fertig werden* (*mit*) means 'to get a thing finished', 'to manage', 'to cope'.

4. Alle (used predicatively and therefore undeclined) means 'finished' in the sense of 'all gone'.

Der Wein, das Fleisch, ist alle.

5. Beenden, beendigen

Like 'end' these verbs mean 'to add (or to perform) the last part', and refer more often to an activity (e.g. to end a game) than to the production of a thing (e.g. to end a book). With the latter they are practically restricted to writing, speeches, and the like, where the sense of a development is strong. Both the English and the German terms convey a heightened sense of finality of action as compared with 'finish'. None of them is applied to trivial activities (e.g. washing-up).

Beenden suggests less forcibly than 'end' the sense of 'putting an end, a stop to', i.e. before the natural end except in the sense of 'to terminate officially'.

Beendigen is a more recent formation than *beenden*, and is often used colloquially instead of the latter. In colloquial speech only *beendigen* supplies the imperative mood. In discriminating use it is often accompanied by a statement as to what the last stage of the action is, e.g. a statement introduced by *mit* or some equivalent. But it can also be used without any such phrase in the emphatic sense of 'to put an end to'.

'Egmont' wurde in Frankfurt begonnen und erst in Italien beendet.

Er hat seine Studien, seine Grammatik, seinen Ferienaufenthalt, den Abend mit einem Spaziergang, beendet.

Der Krieg wurde nur nach schweren Anstrengungen und Verlusten beendet.

Er wird die Besichtigung des Lagers bis 12 Uhr beendet haben.

Er hat seine Rede mit einem Appell an das ganze Land beendet, beendigt.

Er beendigte seine Reise mit einem kurzen Aufenthalt an der See.

Beendigen Sie Ihren Aufsatz mit einer Zusammenfassung der Hauptpunkte.

Wir müssen diesen unhaltbaren Zustand beendigen.

6. Ein Ende machen (bereiten):[1] to put an end, a stop, to something undesirable (see also 'stop'). It suggests forceful intervention rather than an official act of the kind implied by 'terminate'.

Wir müssen seinem Treiben, dem Unsinn, ein Ende machen (bereiten).

Er machte seinem Leben ein Ende (beenden is impossible in the sense of suicide).

7 Vollenden corresponds to 'complete' in the sense of finishing a thing, an activity in such a way that one thinks of the whole and its effect, not merely the addition of the final section (see *beenden*). It is only applied to things or activities in so far as their completion adds to their quality, suggests perfection or maturity of what is produced, or the value and thoroughness of what has been done. *Vollendet* is used adjectivally in the sense of 'perfect', 'consummate'.

Er hat den Aufsatz vollendet.

Der Maler hat sein Bild vollendet.

Er hat seine Schulbildung vollendet.

Er hat seine Aufgabe glänzend vollendet.

Er hat trotz allem seine Reise vollendet.

Er hat sein dreißigstes Jahr vollendet.

Ein vollendetes Kunstwerk.

---

[1] More colloquially: *Schluß machen (mit)*.

8. Vervollständigen means 'to add a part or parts' necessary to form a whole, the nature of which is numerical, inorganic. Unlike *vollenden* it does not imply inner value, but a mere accumulation of parts.

Haben Sie Ihre Briefmarkensammlung vervollständigt?

Er ist bemüht, sein Verständnis der Theorie zu vervollständigen.

Um mein Bild vom amerikanischen Leben zu vervollständigen, muß ich noch ein Jahr im Lande bleiben.

9. Ergänzen: to add a missing part or parts necessary to form an inner unity, particularly with reference to meaning. It suggests more strongly than *vervollständigen* that the idea of a given whole is present to the mind.[1]

Einen Satz, einen Gedanken, den Sinn ergänzen, eine Briefmarkensammlung, ergänzen.

10. Voll machen is used figuratively in the sense of intensifying or multiplying emotional experiences.

Sein Unglück, seine Leiden, seine Freude, voll machen.

11. The sense of 'do', i.e. without particular merit or distinction, 'fulfil requirements', must be variously translated. Examples are:

Er hat alle Anforderungen erfüllt.

Er hat alle Fächer absolviert.

FIRE   1. Feuer means (*a*) the element fire; (*b*) the state of combustion; (*c*) burning fuel in a grate and the like. It can be used in the sense of a 'conflagration, destructive burning', only when this sense is interchangeable with those listed. In a sentence such as *Waren im Werte von 100000 D.M. sind vom Feuer zerstört worden* the meaning is 'by fire' as opposed, e.g., to flood. *Feuer* does not admit of a plural.

Das Feuer reinigt.

In dem Zimmer brennt ein Feuer (im Kamin).

Wir hatten ein Feuer, ein kleines Feuer, in der Fabrik.

2. Brand means 'destructive burning'. **Feuersbrunst** is always on a large scale, e.g. a whole street.

In der Fabrik ist ein Brand ausgebrochen.

Der Brand wurde auf seinen Herd beschränkt.

3. Brennen is the commonest term in the sense of 'there is a fire', 'to be on fire'. It is used with the thing or the impersonal *es* as subject.

Es brennt in der Scheune.

In der letzten Zeit hat es in der Stadt oft gebrannt.

Das Haus brennt.

FIRST, AT FIRST   1. Zuerst means (*a*) in the beginning, in the first stages, i.e. at first; (*b*) for the first time; (*c*) before anyone, anything else in a sequence, whether this refers to time, rank, or the like, the order being external and therefore indicating no inner dependence of the second on the first such as a condition. This meaning can be translated also by the more emphatic **als erst-er, -e, -es** (compare *zuletzt* and *als letzt-er, -e, -es*).[2]

---

[1] A related sense is 'to restore a missing part' (e.g. *ein Standbild ergänzen*). It can also mean simply 'to supplement' (e.g. *sein Einkommen ergänzen*).

[2] 'To go first', i.e. to lead the way, is *vorangehen*. In stepping aside to allow someone else to go ahead, *vorgehen* is usual, particularly in the imperative. *Gehen Sie vor !*

Zuerst habe ich das anders beurteilt, aber jetzt sehe ich ein, daß Sie recht haben.
Ich möchte Sie auf das aufmerksam machen, was ich zuerst sagte.
Wann haben Sie ihn zuerst gesehen?
Als er zuerst in den Krieg zog, hatte er keine klare Vorstellung, was Krieg bedeutet.
Er kam zuerst, als erster, an.
Wer spielt zuerst?
Tun Sie das zuerst, als erstes.
Gehen Sie zuerst zum Arzt und dann zu Ihrem Rechtsanwalt (a mere time-table, without inner necessity in the order).

2. **Erst** never means 'at first'. As an equivalent of 'first',[1] it can only mean 'first' in a sequence. In this sense it must be used if the second action is dependent on the first. It may, however, be used, like *zuerst*, when there is no such dependence, provided a second action is reported (mostly with the imperative mood).

Sehen Sie erst mal den Arzt, und dann können wir entscheiden, ob die Arbeit Sie überanstrengen würde oder nicht (*zuerst* impossible).
Erst iß mal deine Suppe auf, dann kannst du die Erdbeeren haben (*zuerst* impossible because the order given in the first clause is a condition of the fulfilment of the promise given in the second).
Setzen Sie sich erst mal hin, dann bringe ich Ihnen eine Tasse Tee (or *zuerst* because the order is casual, not an absolute condition).

3. **Zunächst** means 'first', 'first of all', 'in the first place'. It indicates concentration on a given matter and suggests that what follows is or seems to be of less importance. A close German equivalent is *in erster Linie*.

Tun wir zunächst mal dies, wir können immer noch sehen, ob wir Zeit für das andere haben.
Er behauptet, zunächst Weltbürger und erst in zweiter Linie Deutscher zu sein.
Das Angebot sah zunächst sehr verlockend aus.

FIX (v.t.) Whether as a synonym of 'set', 'settle', 'establish' or of 'fasten', 'attach', this verb suggests more stability and permanence in position, condition, character and the like than the others (see *W.S.*), a making firm or fast, so that the thing thus fixed will not deviate or fall from this position. As a synonym of 'adjust', 'regulate', of 'repair', 'mend', it is a colloquialism originating in America.

Particularly in the literal, but also in some extended uses, German often uses verbs formed from *fest* (= firm).

1. Sense: make fast or firm (*A.L.*).
(a) literal: **befestigen** (see under 'consolidate'), **fest machen**.
Er befestigte, machte...fest, das Regal an der Wand, einen Pfosten in dem Boden.
Die Klinge der altmodischen Sense wird oft locker, wenn sie nicht besonders gut befestigt, festgemacht ist (*W.*).
Sie werden ein silbernes und rotes Abzeichen an die Fahrzeuge festmachen, befestigen können (*anmachen*, i.e. attach, also possible).
(b) In figurative use it occurs in this sense mainly in such phrases as to fix

---

[1] For another meaning of *erst* see 'only'.

responsibility, the blame, on a person, and to fix something in one's mind, memory.

Sie haben seine Schuld festgestellt (see under 'state') (fixed the blame on him).

Er hat sich unzählige Tatsachen, Jahreszahlen eingeprägt (impressed on his mind).

2. (a) Sense: arrange, decide, settle. German **festsetzen, bestimmen** (determine). The latter draws attention more to the mental act of determination, the former to the firmness of what is decided.

Ein Zeitpunkt muß bald für die Sitzung festgesetzt, bestimmt werden.

Preise, Mieten sind festgesetzt worden.

Die Zahl der zuzulassenden Studenten festsetzen.

Greene und andere haben den Dramenstil bestimmt, den Shakespeare weiter entwickelte.

(b) **Festlegen** as compared with *festsetzen* stresses the binding nature of what is done, committal (*sich auf etwas festlegen*: commit oneself to something). If used with the date of a meeting it suggests that this is unalterable. But it is mainly used with something basic (often corresponding to 'lay down' in English).

Er hat die Richtlinien seiner Politik festgelegt.

Der Wechselkurs der DM. muß noch festgelegt werden.

Es ist in der Verfassung festgelegt.

Der Tag der Sitzung wurde endgültig festgelegt.

(c) The past participle 'fixed' used adjectivally in this sense is in German normally the pure adjective *fest*.

Feste Preise, Zeiten.

Feste Ansichten, Prinzipien haben.

3. Sense: to direct steadily on, to rivet: German **richten** (direct), **heften** (rivet), **fixieren** (one of the commonest uses of this verb), **konzentrieren** (the mind).

Er richtete, heftete die Augen auf sie.

Er fixierte sie mit den Augen (not: *er f. die A. auf sie*).

Er richtete seine Gedanken auf das Ziel.

Er konzentrierte sich auf seine Arbeit.

4. Sense: to put in order, put right, mend: German **richten** (i.e. put right), **in Ordnung bringen.**

Er hat die Uhr, den Wagen, eine beschädigte Maschine gerichtet.

Er hat den Klempner gerufen, um den Abfluß zu richten.

Diese Arznei hat ihn wieder ganz in Ordnung gebracht.

5. The colloquialisms to fix food and drink can only be rendered into German by the appropriate specific term.

Sie hat ihm einen Salat angerichtet.

Soll ich Ihnen einen Whisky einschenken?

FLAT Flach is a more objective term than **platt,** which can suggest an impression of flatness, particularly that of being pressed flat. Thus: *ein Boxer hat oft eine platte Nase; platt auf dem Boden liegen* (pressed against the ground). *Er mußte flach liegen*, merely suggests a horizontal position. Both terms are applied in the literal sense to the same objects, but *platt* is more vivid because of its subjective connotation (e.g. *platt wie ein Pfannkuchen*, a fixed phrase). In figurative use *flach* means 'shallow' (i.e. *oberflächlich*), which meaning it also has in literal application (e.g. *die Ruhr ist flach*). In figurative use *platt* indicates lifelessness.

FLOAT (intransitive) 1. **Treiben** means 'to drift', and is used of inanimate objects. It implies (*a*) motion over, not rest on, the surface of water or through the air; (*b*) involuntary, and sometimes aimless, action. If a decision to drift or (in this sense) to float is meant, as in the case of a person, **sich treiben lassen** must be used.
Das Schiff trieb weit von der Küste ab, auf Felsenriffe.
Wolken treiben am Himmel.
Wir können uns (vom Winde) treiben lassen.
Er ließ sich den Strom hinunter treiben.

2. **Schwimmen** is used of objects and substances in contrast to 'sink', i.e. to indicate that they are capable of remaining on the surface of liquid.[1]
Ein schwimmender Palast.
Allerlei Schutt, Öl, schwimmt auf der Oberfläche des Wassers.

3. In reference to water sports German can only say *auf dem Rücken liegen* to express the idea of floating without movement.
Er liegt (regungslos) auf dem Rücken.

4. **Schweben** means in its literal sense 'to float' through or 'hover' in the air.
Der Ballon schwebt hoch über der Erde.
Töne schwebten durch die Luft, den Raum.

FLOOR 1. Sense: the lower surface of a room: **Fußboden**.
Er saß auf dem Fußboden.

2. In compounds this often becomes simply *Boden* (see also under 'ground' and 'bottom'), e.g. floor cloth or floor covering: *Bodenbelag, Tanzboden*.

3. Sense: the bottom, the lowest ground surface: **Grund** (see also under 'ground' and 'bottom'). *Der Meeresgrund, der Höhlengrund.* But *Boden* occurs also: *Talboden* as well as *Talgrund*.

4. Sense: A number of rooms etc. on the same level in a building: German **Stock, Stockwerk, Etage** (feminine in German). Ground floor: *Erdgeschoss.*
Er wohnt im zweiten Stock, auf der zweiten Etage.

FOLLOW, PURSUE, ENSUE 1. **Folgen**, like 'follow', is the most comprehensive term. Its use in the passive voice is mostly limited in literary German to the past participle without the auxiliary verb (e.g.: *von seinem Assistenten gefolgt, trat er ins Zimmer*). It occurs in the following senses:
(a) To go, come after, to move in the same direction.
Der Detektiv folgte dem Dieb.
(b) To keep to a direction, road, etc.
Folgen Sie dieser Straße bis zur Ecke.
(c) To come after in a sequence or series, whether in time, in rank, or as effect after cause. With reference to time or to cause of effect *auf* with the accusative (cf. English 'on') or the dative without preposition may be used.

[1] In reference to a ship *flott sein, werden* is used to indicate that it is seaworthy (e.g. *Das Schiff ist wieder flott*). Similarly: *flott machen.*

Ein Unglück folgte dem, auf den, Beschluß.
Georg der Fünfte folgte auf Eduard den Siebenten.
Auf die Verlängerung der Arbeitszeit folgten Streiks.
(d) To take as a leader, to accept as an authority.
Die Massen folgten blind dem Führer.
Ich folge dem Kritiker Gundolf in seiner Deutung Kleists.
(e) To act in accordance with, to obey (conjugated with *haben* in the sense of 'obey').
Ich folgte seinem Rat, der Regel, diesen Richtlinien.
Er hat in dieser Angelegenheit seinem Vater nur gefolgt (a rare use).
(f) To pursue a line of conduct, work.
Er folgt Kursen an der technischen Hochschule.
Die Regierung folgt der Politik der Gewerkschaften.
(g) To watch the progress or course of a thing, literally and figuratively.
Ich folgte dem Flugzeug mit den Augen, bis es verschwand.
Er folgt aufmerksam der politischen Entwicklung.
Er folgt mit Interesse den neuesten literarischen Veröffentlichungen.
(h) To understand.
Ich folge Ihnen ganz gut.
Ich kann seinen Gedankengängen nicht folgen.
Er kann genug Deutsch, um den Vorlesungen zu folgen.
(i) To emerge as a conclusion.
Aus Ihrer Behauptung folgt, daß Sie diese Ansicht nie geteilt haben.

2. Verfolgen

The prefix *ver* has here an intensive force and gives the meaning of 'pursue', 'prosecute'[1] in all senses of these terms. It must be used to translate 'follow' when intensified mental activity is implied, i.e. in the sense of tracing, tracking down, or of attending alertly and critically, not merely in understanding the words of others (contrast **1** (h)).

Um sein Buch zu schreiben, mußte er die ganze Entwicklung der Klassik verfolgen.
Es ist reizvoll zu verfolgen, wie allmählich der Spieß umgedreht wird.
Er verfolgte die Vorgänge mit Interesse.
Die Regierung verfolgt eine kühne Politik.
Er verfolgt seine Studien mit Eifer.
Die Abstimmung hat bewiesen, mit wie kritischem Blick das Volk die Arbeiten seiner Gesetzgeber verfolgt.

3. Nachfolgen: to follow or succeed a person in office and to follow in death.
Er ist seinem Vater als Chef der Firma nachgefolgt.
Er ist seiner Frau bald nachgefolgt.

4. Befolgen has only one meaning: to act in accordance with (see *folgen* (e)). Unlike *folgen* it does not mean 'to obey' a person.
Er hat die Vorschriften des Arztes genau befolgt.

5. Erfolgen: to follow as the effect of a cause, particularly as the result of the fulfilment of a condition. The subject cannot be a person.
Seine Zulassung erfolgte sofort.
Seine Entlassung ist wider alles Erwarten nicht erfolgt.

---

[1] *Verfolgen* also means 'to persecute'.

FOLLOW

6. Nachkommen is used in reference to arrangements for one person to go ahead and for another to follow later. In colloquial language, it, not *folgen*, is the normal term in this sense.

Gehen Sie vor, ich komme nach.

FOOD (with notes on 'nourishment', 'nutrition', 'fare', 'meal', 'provisions'). **1. Nahrung** translates 'food' only with reference to its capacity to maintain life, to promote growth and energy, i.e. when 'food' is a synonym of 'nourishment', which is itself translated by *Nahrung*. It is also used figuratively in the same way.

Seit drei Tagen hat er keine Nahrung zu sich genommen (only in the sense that he is too ill to eat or drink, not because no food is available; see *essen* for the latter).

Die Nahrung, die er bekommt, genügt nicht.

Der Nahrungswert von Kartoffeln.

Das ist nur Nahrung für seinen Verdacht.

Wir gehen ohne Nahrung, ohne Heizung und ohne warme Kleidung dem Winter entgegen.

2. Lebensmittel ('provisions') and **Nahrungsmittel** (both plural) are sometimes, but not always, interchangeable. The distinction is that *Nahrungsmittel* is vaguer, more general, and refers more to the raw material of food and to its growing, while *Lebensmittel* suggests food in relation to its purchase. It is the appropriate term when food is thought of as tinned.[1] Thus one can only speak of a *Lebensmittelgeschäft*. *Nahrungsmitteleinfuhr* suggests meat, wheat, potatoes, and the like; *Lebensmitteleinfuhr*, butter, bacon, tinned food (though no hard and fast dividing line can be drawn). Again *Lebensmittelkontrolle* is the accepted term because the distribution and purchasing of food is meant. When the type of food is not specified the choice of term depends on whether the context suggests the purchase of food or its properties.[2]

The plural 'foods' is translated by *Nahrungsmittel* when the variety produced is indicated.[3]

Die Mutter besorgt die Lebensmittel für das Wochenende.

Unsere Lebensmittel reichen kaum für eine Woche (or: *Nahrungsmittel*).

Die Lebensmittel sind in dem Korb.

In diesem Sack sind nur Nahrungsmittel.

Deutschland muß seine Nahrungsmittelproduktion steigern (or: *Lebensmittel-*).

Halten Sie die Nahrungsmittel kühl in dem Schrank (better than *Lebensmittel*).

Diese Nahrungsmittel werden in Java erzeugt.

3. Essen (both as noun and verb) must be used in the sense of 'meal'.[4] It includes everything that comprises a meal. It is used freely with reference to the type or quality of food that is or should be eaten.

Seit drei Tagen hat er nichts gegessen.

Das Essen steht schon auf dem Tisch.

---

[1] To translate 'tinned food' the kind must be specified. *Fleisch- und Gemüsekonserven.*

[2] A food-producing land = *ein Rohstofferzeuger.*

[3] The ugly term *Nahrungssorten* is also used.

[4] *Essen* is the commonest word for 'meal'. *Mahl* is an elevated term. *Mahlzeit* is used in reference to the number of meals taken or the hour when they are taken.

Wir haben das Essen auf unseren Ausflug mitgebracht.
An kalten Tagen muß man etwas Warmes essen.
Wie war das Essen in London?
Das Essen in diesem Hotel ist schlecht.
Man ißt sehr gut in diesem Restaurant.

4. Speise may be prepared or unprepared, and often approximates to 'dish' (*Gericht*). It is used for 'food' as opposed to 'drink' (*Speise und Trank*), and is sometimes an abbreviation for *Mehlspeise*. The use of *Speise* sometimes savours of a genteelism (e.g. *diese Speise ist zu scharf für mich*).

Diese Speise ist angegangen, ungenießbar.
Speiseschrank, Speisekammer.

5. Kost approximates to 'fare', i.e. a type of food, particularly in reference to its effect on health. It is always simple in character and therefore used only in connection with small hotels, restaurants, and boarding-houses. It refers only to food and drink, i.e. it excludes board.

In dieser Pension gibt man uns nahrhafte Kost.
Vegetarische Kost (Rohkost) esse ich gern.

6. Verpflegung refers exclusively to food and drink, i.e. not board. It is restricted in its reference to one's permanent place of residence, which may be either a cheap or an expensive hotel.

In diesem Hotel ist die Verpflegung gut.

7. Ernährung (see 'feed'): 'feeding' in the sense of 'providing for'. It must be used for 'food' when by the latter its administration, organization, distribution is referred to.

Die Ernährungslage ist befriedigend.
Der Reichsernährungsminister.
Das Reichsernährungsamt.

FOOL **1. Tor** and **Narr.** A man may be a *Tor* because he is inexperienced (compare the conception of *der reine Tor* in *Parzival*), or because he has made mistakes, applied the wrong means in pursuing some serious purpose. Such a person does not necessarily lack intelligence. If, on the other hand, his doings and sayings are so devoid of intelligence as to appear clownish or grotesque, he is a *Narr*.

Tor is now exclusively, and *Narr* (except in southern Germany) mostly, a literary term. Used in conversation *Narr* is very strong.

> '*Da steh' ich nun, ich armer Tor,*
> *Und bin so klug als wie zuvor.*'   (Goethe, *Faust I.*)

Du bist doch ein Narr, dich so zu benehmen.

2. 'Fool' as a familiar term must be translated by adjectives meaning foolish, mad, crazy, etc.

Sei doch nicht so verrückt.
Ich war sehr dumm, mein Geld so anzulegen.

FOOTPATH In the sense of a path for foot-passengers (*S.O.D.*) at the side of a street German used the French **Trottoir,** but in the middle of the nineteenth century invented German compounds **Bürgersteig** and **Geh-steig.** (*Steig* was originally a path that led over heights as its connection with *steigen* suggests, but very early lost this exclusive sense of heights;

Steg, another form of the word, originally meant the same thing, but now also means a narrow bridge as well as—like *Steig*—any path whether over hilly country or on the flat).

FORMAL 1. **Formal**: having to do with shape.
Die formalen Eigenschaften eines Gedichts.
Formal betrachtet ist der Roman verworren.

2. **Formell**: conforming to the rules of behaviour, strictly correct.
Ein formeller Besuch.
Die Atmosphäre war so formell, daß der Empfang fast zu einem Fiasko wurde.
Er ist immer sehr formell, wenn er redet.

3. **Förmlich** used to mean 'in proper form', i.e. *formell*. Today it has acquired a pejorative sense, i.e. 'stiff' in manner.
Er wurde sehr förmlich empfangen.

FOUND Sense: to call into existence an institution, school of thought, etc.

1. In this sense German uses **gründen** and **begründen**. The distinction is that *gründen* suggests one clear act, therefore an official ceremony or act, or at most a few of the stages involved in founding an institution.[1] *Begründen*, which is less common, is wider in its implications and is not limited to any official act or to particular stages. It suggests both the idea from which the foundation sprang and also consolidation. Through the latter reference it approaches the sense of 'establish', when this is used as a synonymous term. When reference is solely to ideas, *gründen* is impossible.

Despite the implication of consolidation conveyed by *begründen*, it is possible to say *fest gegründet*.

To found on, i.e. base, ground on = *gründen auf*[2] (followed by the accusative case).

2. When 'found' means 'endow', i.e. provide funds, it must be translated by **stiften**.[3] *Stiftung* means a foundation in this sense.
Er hat verschiedene Schulen, Vereine, Firmen, Zeitungen, gegründet (or: *begründet*).
Bismarck hat das zweite Reich gegründet (or: *fest begründet*).
Er hat einen Geheimkult begründet (*gegründet* could suggest a ceremony).
Friedrich Schlegel begründete die romantische Welt- und Kunstanschauung.
Er hat verschiedene Stipendien, einen Lehrstuhl, gestiftet.

FREEZE 1. **Frieren** is used of persons and of Nature. Applied to persons it means, whether used impersonally or with a personal subject, and whether in reference to the whole body or only a part, no more than 'to be very cold'. Of things it means 'to turn to ice' (i.e. of liquids) or 'to be covered with ice'.[4] Used of persons, a personal subject is in present-day German more usual than the impersonal form.

---

[1] See 'found' in Webster's *Dictionary of Synonyms*.
[2] *Gründen auf* is also used in reference to ideas in the sense of 'to base on'. *Begründen*, applied to ideas, points of view, means 'to substantiate, to give reasons for'.
[3] In its wider sense *stiften* means 'to bring about' something intended to be permanent (e.g. *Frieden, eine Versöhnung*). It is used also in reference to what is bad, i.e. to instigate (cf. *anstiften*).
[4] *Tiefgefroren*: quick-frozen, of fruit, fish. *Gefrierfleisch*: frozen meat.

Ich friere; habe (furchtbar, arg) gefroren.
Meine Hände frieren.
Es friert mich (an den Händen).
Das Wasser, der Fluß, ist gefroren.
Das Fensterglas ist gefroren.

2. Zufrieren: to freeze all over, of large areas of water, such as a lake.[1]
Der See, der Fluß, ist zugefroren.

3. Erfrieren has intensive force, and means, applied in the active voice to persons, 'to freeze to death'. In the passive with *sein* it means, used either of the whole person or a part of the body, 'to be numbed and rigid with cold'.
Noch so ein Winter, und wir erfrieren alle.
Er war ganz erfroren.
Mein kleiner Finger ist erfroren.

4. Einfrieren is used of things which are either ice-bound themselves or filled with ice. It is also applied figuratively to the freezing of money.
Das Schiff im Hafen, die Wasserleitung, ist eingefroren.
Die Regierung hat alle Kredite eingefroren.

FRIENDLY[2] **1. Freundlich:** kindly, affable, displaying friendly feelings, showing these by smiling, etc.
Er ist ein freundlicher Typ.
In diesem Dorfe wohnen freundliche Leute.
Der Wirt war sehr freundlich zu uns.
Wir wurden im Ausland sehr freundlich behandelt.

2. Freundschaftlich must be used in the sense of 'bearing the relation of friendship, as a friend'.
Es bestehen freundschaftliche Beziehungen zwischen den beiden.
Er hat sich mir gegenüber sehr freundschaftlich verhalten.

3. Befreundet mit: friendly with.
Ich bin mit ihm befreundet.

FRIGHTEN, CAUSE ANXIETY, WORRY The following verbs are derivatives of *Angst* (from *eng*),[3] correspond to 'frighten' only in the sense of 'to put into a state of anxiety', i.e. not in that of 'to give a sudden fright', which is *erschrecken, einen Schreck geben.* The accepted term for Freud's use of *Angst* as opposed to *Furcht* is 'anxiety'.[4] The German terms approximate closely to 'worry', but refer to the psychological state rather than to thoughts associated with it. When 'worry' implies the latter it is translated by *sich*

---

[1] *Gerinnen*, to coagulate, is used freely in Holstein of the sea in the sense of starting to freeze.

[2] Friend. *Freund* is only an intimate friend. When 'friend' means casual friend, it must be translated by *Bekannte(r)*. *Freund* and *Freundin*, applied to the opposite sex, mean 'sweetheart'. To avoid this sense 'friend' must be rendered by *guter Freund, gute Freundin* (e.g. *Frau X ist eine gute Freundin von ihm*). Note further: *ich bin gut Freund mit dem Bäcker* (I am good friends with...).

[3] See also article on 'to fear'.

[4] *Bange* and *Bangigkeit* express a lesser degree of anxiety than *Angst*, and correspond roughly to 'apprehensive', 'uneasy'.

FRIGHTEN

Sorgen machen,[1] or, when it implies little more than 'thinking about', *sich Gedanken machen*.[2]

1. **Ängstigen** emphasizes the state rather than the capacity of the agent to cause the state. It therefore often suggests unfounded anxiety or unawareness of the cause. It is most common in reflexive use.

Er ängstigte mich mit seinen erdichteten Geschichten.
Ein böser Traum hat mich geängstigt (example from Duden, the anxiety arising from the unconscious).
Du brauchst dich meinethalben nicht zu ängstigen.
Sie ängstigte sich sehr um die Gesundheit ihres Kindes.

2. **Beängstigen** suggests the capacity of the agent to produce the state of anxiety. For this reason it is used freely in the present participle as an adjective, but rarely as a reflexive verb.

Seine erdichteten Geschichten haben mich beängstigt.
Sein ungewisses Schicksal beängstigt mich.
Seine Drohungen beängstigen mich nicht.
Er hat beängstigende Geschichten erzählt.
Seine Worte sind beängstigend.

3. **Verängstigen** draws attention to the result as one of complete anxiety, and can for this reason only be used in the past participle, either as this appears in the perfect tenses or as an adjective.

Seine Geschichten haben uns ganz verängstigt.
Das Benehmen des Vaters hat die Kinder vollkommen verängstigt.

FRUSTRATE, FRUSTRATION *W.S.* says of this term that it means 'to render vain or ineffectual all efforts, however feeble or however vigorous, to fulfill one's intention or desire'. There is no exact German equivalent unless it be *frustrieren*, which is admittedly being used more and more. Synonyms of 'frustrate' and sometimes circumlocutions are the only possible German approximations.

1. Sense: bring to nothing; prevent (a person) from doing something (*A.L.*). German: **vereiteln** (to make vain, i.e. to thwart), **durchkreuzen** (to prevent a thing by using counter-measures), **zunichte machen** (to bring to nought). The object of such verbs is generally a plan or an intention.

Meine Pläne, Absichten wurden vereitelt, durchkreuzt, zunichte gemacht.

2. Sense: to bring about 'a deep chronic sense or condition of insecurity, discouragement and dissatisfaction arising from thwarted desires, inner conflicts or other unresolved problems' (*W.*). None of the verbs under 1 suggests this inner condition, and the phrases which could suggest it do not at the same time render the idea of thwarting. The following are examples of phrases that at times may come within striking distance of the sense. In general German can suggest the condition or the cause, but not both together.

Sie leidet unter Enttäuschungen.
Als seriöses Nachschlagewerk enttäuscht es unsere Erwartungen.

---

[1] *Sorge* means a definite, often rational 'care' or 'worry', and may refer to the agent as well as the feeling.
[2] See also *sich (be)kümmern* under 'bother'.

Der Admiral endete sein Leben unbefriedigt (*W.*), *in dem Gefühl, versagt zu haben.*

Er ist ein Versager.

Er fühlte sich in seiner Entschlußfähigkeit eingeschränkt durch eine blinde Mauer von Mißtrauen und bürokratischer Trägheit.

Ich habe heute viel Ärger gehabt (a frustrating day).

Heute ging mir alles schief (a frustrating day).

Eine Persönlichkeit, auf deren Entfaltung der praktische Sinn der Amerikaner lähmend wirkte.

FULL (adjective)[1]   Full of.

(*a*) *Voll* followed by *von* is the most objective term, and emphasizes the absence of everything else except that with which a given thing is said to be filled. If it is used otherwise than in the literal sense, it indicates a super-abundance. (*b*) Followed by a noun in apposition, *voll* merely denotes a large number or quantity. (*c*) The form *voller* suggests a subjective impression or emotional participation.

Das Beet war voll von Unkraut.

Das Beet war voll Unkraut.

Das Beet war voller Unkraut.

Das Zimmer ist voll Ungeziefer. (*Voll von* is not possible, because it would mean literally 'full', with nothing else there.)

Das Zimmer ist voller Ungeziefer.

Der Zug ist voll von Flüchtlingen.

Der Zug ist voller Flüchtlinge.

Die Kiste ist voll von Büchern.

Sein Herz war voll von Liebe.

Sein Herz war voller Liebe.

Die Eltern waren voller Liebe für ihre Kinder.

FUNNY[2]   The term is applied to someone or something which raises laughter in the sense of pure fun or because of an element of queerness or incomprehensibility. One aspect alone or both can be present. The German term **komisch** rarely suggests pure fun, at least not in a naïve, innocent way. Its most characteristic feature is a twist, a touch even of the ironical or grotesque. A regular meaning is: not understood and not expected (also: 'funny' or 'strange': it's funny that he did not keep the appointment). For lack of a closer equivalent *komisch* must, however, be used in most senses of 'funny', except where exclusively pure fun is meant. In such cases *lustig* (see 'merry', 'gay') is often used (e.g. *er unterhielt uns mit lustigen Kunststücken*).

Er erzählt dauernd komische Geschichten.

Er sah urkomisch aus.

Er sieht immer die komische Seite der Dinge.

Er ist immer sehr komisch (queer, or funny with a twist of irony and the like).

---

[1] *Voll* is used adverbially practically only in the senses of (*a*) without reservation (e.g. *ich weiss das voll zu würdigen*); (*b*) in full (e.g. *er hat es voll bezahlt*). Otherwise the German terms for 'quite' or 'complete' (see articles) or 'in detail' (*ausführlich*) must be used. Example: *ich bin restlos, völlig, davon überzeugt.*

[2] Study together with 'strange'.

GATHER

GATHER, COLLECT, ASSEMBLE 1. **Sammeln** is the normal term for gathering or collecting things in the sense of bringing them together in the same place, particularly in reference to the action of a collector of interesting objects (e.g. pictures, stamps, butterflies) and to appeals for charitable purposes, but also more generally (e.g. *die gesammelten Werke eines Dichters*).

Used with a personal object it differs slightly according to whether it is reflexive or not. Reflexively it means: (*a*) in the literal sense, to come along to a place casually, a few at a time without any set purpose; (*b*) figuratively, to rally round someone.[1] With a non-reflexive object it means: to gather what lies apart in order to build the parts into a solid whole. It must be carefully distinguished from *versammeln*.

Ich sammle Material für ein Buch.
Er sammelt Münzen.
Er sammelt Äußerungen über die sozialistischen Maßnahmen der Regierung.
Es wird für ein Waisenheim gesammelt.
Eine Menschenmenge sammelte sich am Ort des Unfalls.
Die Ausgebombten sammelten sich auf dem Marktplatz.
Er hat viele tüchtige Menschen um sich gesammelt.
Der Feldherr sammelte die Reste seiner Armee um sich.

2. **Versammeln** is used only with a personal object. As a reflexive verb it emphasizes the idea of purpose, i.e. it does not suggest casual appearance as *sammeln* does. In non-reflexive use it means: to summon, to call together for a purpose.

Die Teilnehmer am Umzug versammelten sich auf dem Marktplatz.
Der Minister versammelte seine Berater zu einer Besprechung.
Der Alte versammelte seine Freunde um sich, um seinen achtzigsten Geburtstag zu feiern.

3. **Einsammeln** particularly stresses the length or the extent of the process.
Ich sammle meine Außenstände ein, um mein Geschäft zu verkaufen.

4. **Ansammeln** means 'to accumulate', when a heap is actually present, and can refer to a crowd of people. 'Tartar has accumulated, collected, on my teeth' (i.e. just a coating) would, however, be: *Zahnstein hat sich... angesetzt.*[2]

Ihre Briefe haben sich hier angesammelt.
An der Unfallstelle sammelten sich viele Menschen an.

5. Some other senses of 'collect', 'gather'.

(a) 'To collect', in the sense of 'to go and get' one or more things already in the same place, can only be rendered by **abholen**.
Vergessen Sie nicht, Ihre Pakete bei mir abzuholen!

(b) 'To gather together (a few things) quickly' is generally translated by verbs compounded with *zusammen*. *Er packte seine Sachen zusammen und reiste ab.* *Sammeln* implies a process extended in time and in space. *Aufsammeln* does not, however, necessarily suggest length of time, but means 'to pick up' things scattered over an area. *Auflesen*: to pick up what lies close to one. 'To gather' in the sense of 'to pick', but not 'to seek far and wide': *pflücken*.

---

[1] *Sich sammeln* also has the special sense of 'to collect one's thoughts, to pull oneself together emotionally'.

[2] Figuratively, 'accumulate' is often translated by *häufen* and its compounds. *Die Beispiele, die Schulden, häufen sich.*

GET (sense: receive, come by, go and get, obtain).[1] **1. Bekommen:** to come by a thing passively. Since it mostly suggests inactivity on the part of the subject, it cannot be used in the imperative or in the sense of getting a thing for someone else, which would imply effort. If activity is expressed, it is either of an inner, unconscious kind, or movement conveyed by some prefix such as *ab*, or mental activity (*herausbekommen*).

Ich habe das Buch bekommen.
Wir haben gestern Schnee bekommen.
Er hat drei Wochen Ferien bekommen.
Er bekam Hunger.
Können Sie überseeische Funkstationen mit Ihrem Apparat bekommen?
Die Erde hat große Risse bekommen.
Der Baum bekommt jetzt neue Blätter.
Mit den Jahren bekommt er mehr Weisheit.
Ich kann den Deckel nicht abbekommen (get off).
Haben Sie die Antwort schon herausbekommen?

2. Kriegen is often a colloquial equivalent of *bekommen*. Apart from this popular use it suggests activity, effort, vigour.

Ich habe diesen Tisch billig gekriegt (suggests bargaining).
Ich muß den 8 Uhr Zug kriegen.
Ich werde dich schon kriegen.
Können Sie überseeische Funkstationen mit Ihrem Apparat kriegen?
Er kriegte einen Messerstich in den Rücken (*bekam* would be colourless).
Haben Sie die Antwort schon herausgekriegt?

3. Verschaffen:[2] to procure for oneself or for others. It suggests the trouble one takes, the ways and means one adopts, often tactics or manœuvres, to make it possible to come by a thing. It does not mean 'to fetch', and should not be used where the operation is so simple as to require no effort or contrivance. The object need not be a thing that can be moved, but may be something intangible (contrast *beschaffen*).

Verschaffen Sie mir bitte das Buch (not 'fetch', but adopt the necessary measures to obtain it).
Könnten Sie mir eine Stellung in diesem Geschäft verschaffen (e.g. by negotiations, influence)?
Ich habe ihm ein Zimmer in einem entlegenen Teil der Stadt verschafft (by my enquiries I put him on to the track of a room).
Ich werde Ihnen schon die Erlaubnis verschaffen.
Seine Tüchtigkeit verschaffte ihm Zutritt zum Direktor.

4. Anschaffen: to purchase. It stresses possession and is used mostly of big or important objects or of things in bulk.

Wir haben uns einen Wagen, neue Geräte, neue Vorräte, angeschafft.

5. Beschaffen: to obtain a thing, particularly a concrete object, and also to bring it to where it is required. The latter idea is prominent and is expressed by the prefix *be*. Unlike *verschaffen* it does not imply tactics.

Ich werde mich bemühen, die Bücher neu oder antiquarisch zu beschaffen.
Er hat uns das Material, die Instrumente beschafft.
Sie besprachen, wie sie ein neues Boot beschaffen könnten.

---

[1] For 'get' used causatively see 'make'. See also 'go' for its use as a synonym of the latter.
[2] For *schaffen* as a rendering of 'get' in the sense of 'move' see the latter verb.

6. Besorgen suggests the buying of and paying for things[1] for other people. (Compare *sorgen für* under 'provide'.) Though very common, it is not well used in reference to single articles which cost only a few pence (e.g. a newspaper), or with words which do not denote things (e.g. a doctor, permission). It is, however, used indiscriminately for both *verschaffen* and *beschaffen* (see above).

Die Hausfrau hat die Lebensmittel für Sonntag besorgt.

Ich habe ihm ein Zimmer in einem entlegenen Teil der Stadt besorgt.

Besorgen Sie mir bitte die Theaterkarten, wenn Sie in der Stadt sind.

Ich werde Ihnen eine Zeitung, die Erlaubnis, besorgen.

7. Holen must be used to translate 'get' in the sense of 'fetch', 'go for'. It also means 'to catch' an infectious illness.

Holen Sie bitte die Stühle aus dem Nebenzimmer.

Er hat sich eine Erkältung geholt.

8. Gewinnen:[2] to obtain products from the earth or substances from other substances by chemical process.

Gold, Salz wird in diesen Bergen gewonnen.

Petroleum aus Kohle gewinnen.

9. Hernehmen is used in a question with *wo* in the sense of 'look for', 'find'.

Wo soll ich das Geld hernehmen?

GIVE The following are the commonest senses of 'give' in which *geben*, which in literal use means simply 'hand over', is not used.[3]

1. Schenken: to make a personal gift to someone.[4]

Er hat mir zu Weihnachten ein Buch geschenkt.

Was soll ich ihr zu Weihnachten schenken?

2. Bereiten or **machen:** to cause a continued state of being or of mind to a person.[5]

Es hat mir Vergnügen, Kummer, bereitet, gemacht.

3. Hingeben (reflexive) or **widmen:** to devote oneself to a task. *Hingeben* is also used reflexively in the sense of 'to give oneself up' to pleasurable states of mind.

Er hat sich der Aufgabe hingegeben, gewidmet.

Er gibt sich Illusionen, süßen Träumen, hin.

4. Hergeben: to lend oneself, to stoop, to a course of action.

Dazu gebe ich mich, meinen Namen, nicht her.

---

[1] *Besorgungen machen*: to go shopping. *Besorgen*, apart from its meaning of 'to fear', also means 'to attend to' duties (e.g. *die Küche besorgen*).

[2] *Gewinnen* has a wider range of application than the English 'win'. It often translates 'gain', 'obtain'. The latter is also rendered by *verschaffen, erlangen. Erlangen* is now becoming old-fashioned except as an official, chiefly legal term (e.g. *eine Scheidung, einen Aufschub, Gebiete bei einer Friedenskonferenz, den Doktorgrad, erlangen*). *Erreichen* is 'to reach' something desired, strived after, and implies effort on the part of the subject. It translates 'achieve', 'attain'.

[3] For *geben* used in other senses than 'give' see e.g. 'put'.

[4] *Geben* is used in the sense of 'to give to charity' or 'to make bequests'.

[5] *Geben* is used in reference to a sharp, momentary reaction (e.g. *einen Schreck, Schock, geben*).

GLAD, JOYFUL A. To be glad.

1. Es freut mich (**dich,** etc.) is a polite, conventional expression, and is therefore weak.

Es freut mich, Sie zu sehen, kennen zu lernen.
Es freut mich, daß ich es ihm gesagt habe.

2. Sich freuen expresses a genuine feeling of joy, and is therefore more intimate.

Ich freue mich aber wirklich, Sie zu sehen.
Wir haben keinen Grund, uns zu freuen.

3. Froh: relieved that something important has not been missed or that something unpleasant has been avoided.

Ich bin froh, daß ich Sie zu Hause treffe.
Ich war froh, nicht länger bleiben zu müssen.
Seien Sie froh, daß Sie rechtzeitig weggekommen sind.

B. In other combinations.

1. Froh suggests here, too, the absence of any cause for depressing feelings. It is used particularly, but not exclusively, in biblical and elevated style.

Ein froher Mensch (inwardly).[1]
Eine frohe Botschaft, Nachricht (e.g. the birth of Christ).
Ein frohes Ereignis.
Die Musik Bachs stimmt einen froh (suggests a catharsis).

2. Freudig: causing joy. It therefore corresponds more closely to 'joyful', 'joyous' than to 'glad'. It is mostly applied to actions, to persons only in so far as they imply activity.[2] It suggests strong joy, but not the religious implication of *froh*.

Eine freudige Botschaft, Nachricht.
Ein freudiges Ereignis (e.g. the birth of a child).
Er ging freudig in den Tod.
Die Nachricht hat mich freudig gestimmt.

GO (literal sense) **1.** To go on foot, to walk:[3] **gehen.**
Ich gehe, ich fahre nicht.
Ich gehe jetzt nach Hause.

2. Kommen must be used instead of *gehen* to translate 'go' when the place of arrival is not, or only weakly, vaguely, conceived as a goal purposefully pursued, i.e. when arrival is conceived as accidental or incidental. English 'get'[4] even more frequently than 'go' in this sense and sometimes the perfect tense of 'to be' followed by the preposition 'to' (e.g. have you ever been to Munich?).

Wie weit sind Sie nach Norden gekommen?

---

[1] *Fröhlich*: showing joy outwardly, merry. See 'merry'.
[2] *Ein freudiger Arbeiter*: one who finds cause for joy in his work.
[3] *Zu Fuß* may be added to *gehen* for clarity or emphasis (e.g. *sind Sie zu Fuß gegangen?*), but *gehen* itself means 'walk' as a contrast to transport. *Laufen* in North Germany means 'to walk much' and can imply haste (e.g. *ich laufe sehr gerne, ich bin den ganzen Tag gelaufen*). See 'run'. *Wandeln* is 'to walk without effort'. It is used in elevated and biblical style, and in the phrase *im Schlafe wandeln*.
[4] *Geraten*, like 'get', expresses still more strongly the accidental result of an action or movement, sometimes in an unfavourable sense (e.g. *er ist in die falsche Straße geraten*). It also means 'to get into a state, condition' (e.g. *in Wut geraten*).

Sind Sie schon mal nach München gekommen?
Auf meiner Reise bin ich nicht nach Wien gekommen.
Ich bin sehr spät ins Bett gekommen.
Er kommt sehr viel herum (geht would mean 'walks').
Er ist sehr viel in Deutschland herumgekommen.

3. To go in a vehicle.

Fahren must be used when the means of transport, the time of departure or the actual journey is prominent in one's mind. See also footnote to 'leave' (p. 184, n. 2). **Gehen** concentrates attention on what one intends to do on reaching one's destination (e.g. a holiday, to see someone, to do business, to settle permanently.)[1, 2]

Ich muß morgen nach Melbourne fahren.
Ich muß morgen in die Stadt gehen.
Wollen Sie jetzt nach Sydney fahren?
Gehen Sie heute abend in die Stadt?
Ich fahre jetzt zur Universität.
Wir fuhren bei Basel über die Grenze.
Als wir von Griechenland nach der Türkei fuhren, erlebten wir ein Gewitter.
Ich fahre morgen zu meinem Vetter in Hamburg.
Wie lange fahren Sie nach Hause?
Ich muß morgen zur Universität gehen, um Bücher zu holen.
Ich gehe zu meinem Vetter in Hamburg.
Er ist ins Ausland gegangen.
Er ging nach Wien, um Kunstgeschichte zu studieren.

4. The means of transport as subject.

With phrases indicating destination or time of departure *gehen* may be used except with *Autobus* and *Strassenbahn* in phrases of destination. *Fahren* is always possible.

Wann geht der Zug?
Das Schiff geht nach Indien.
Dieses Flugzeug geht nach Rom.
Die Straßenbahn, der Autobus, fährt nach Chelsea.

5. **Reiten, fliegen,** etc. must be used when these methods of movement are indicated.

GRANT,[3] ALLOW[4] The object of 'grant' can be either the thing requested or the term 'request' itself (or a synonym).

1. **Bewilligen** is the most general term in the sense of 'to grant' the thing requested or the term 'request'. It means: to give approval,[5] particularly as an official or administrative act, to accept or pass a motion.

Seine Einreise in die U.S.A. ist bewilligt worden.

---

[1] *Reisen*: to travel.
[2] *Gehen* may be used of a passenger on a ship, unless the means of transport is emphasized. *Mit welchem Schiff gehen Sie nach England?* (casually). *Mit diesem Schiff bin ich nicht nach England gefahren* (more emphatic).
[3] See also 'admit' and related synonyms dealt with in the same article. Further: *genehmigen*, to sanction; *erhören*, to grant, hear, a prayer.
[4] *Erlauben* is 'to allow' only as a synonym of 'to permit', not, e.g , to grant a sum of money.
[5] 'To approve' is *billigen* and *gutheißen. Billigen* suggests unqualified approval, *gutheißen* a subjective attitude which may imply reservations. See *heißen* under 'call'.

Für die Ausstattung des Saals ist eine beträchtliche Geldsumme bewilligt worden.

Sein Gesuch ist nicht bewilligt worden.

2. Gewähren implies a gracious act by a superior or by a person in a position of vantage.[1]

Der König gewährte ihm eine Unterredung.

Sein Gesuch, seine Bitte, wurde ihm gewährt.

3. Gestatten is simply 'not to prevent', particularly in reference to what is allowed by officialdom. It can suggest, particularly in the imperative, a polite request to allow the speaker to trouble the addressee. It translates 'allow' rather than 'grant'.

Das Betreten des Rasens ist nicht gestattet.

Allerlei Freiheiten wurden uns gestattet.

Gestatten Sie bitte! (e.g. when pushing past others to take a seat in the theatre or a vehicle).

4. Verstatten suggests that permission is given after deliberation and then without qualification. It is an uncommon word.

Der Vater verstattete seinem Sohn allerlei Vergnügungen.

5. Vergönnen is an elevated term and suggests that one is singled out as a special favour, particularly by fate.[2]

Das Schicksal hat es uns nicht vergönnt, uns wiederzusehen.

6. Einräumen suggests a concession. What is granted is therefore partial, qualified.

Unter einer Diktatur wird der Presse so gut wie keine Freiheit eingeräumt.

Sogar besiegten Völkern müssen gewisse Rechte eingeräumt werden.

GREET **1. Grüßen:** to hail, to salute with words or gestures, to say good-day to a person in passing;[3] also figuratively with a subject such as the phenomena of nature.

Er grüßte mich freundlich, als ich ihn an der Ecke traf.

Die Sonne grüßte uns.

2. Begrüßen: to greet someone expected, to welcome, to receive (the act of a host).[4]

Die Dame begrüßte ihre Gäste.

GROUND, LAND   Boden, Erdboden, Grund und Boden, Grundstück, Land, Anlage(n), Gelände, Platz.

1. In the sense of 'soil', 'earth': **Boden, Erde.**

2. The surface of the earth (*W.*): **Boden, Erdboden.** Like English 'ground', *Boden* in certain contexts may mean 'floor' (*auf dem Boden* = on the floor)

Er lag, saß, auf der Erde.

Der Apfel fiel auf den Boden.

Er fiel zu Boden.

---

[1] The subject may also be a thing. *Dieser Kurs gewährt manche Vorteile.*

[2] *Gönnen* means 'not to begrudge', 'to be glad' that something has befallen a person, both in a favourable and an unfavourable sense. The latter may at times be translated by 'to serve a person right'. *Ich gönne ihm sein Schicksal* (which may be good or bad).

[3] *Jemand grüßen lassen:* to send regards.

[4] Also 'to welcome' in figurative use. *Ich würde etwas mehr Rücksicht begrüßen.*

Ein Zweig etwa sechzig Fuß über dem Boden (W.).
Er war froh, wieder festen Boden unter den Füßen zu fühlen.
Er kniete auf dem Boden neben dem Sofa und beugte sich über sie (W.).
Das ist guter, schlechter, Boden (quality thought of).

3. **Boden** is also used in an agricultural context when ownership or the quality of the soil is thought of. But one speaks of *Grundherr*, i.e. 'landlord'.
Der Boden in diesem Tal gehört nur ganz wenigen Familien.
Das ist guter Boden.

4. (a) English 'land' on which a building in a town is erected: **Grundstück** in an urban context.
Ein Grundstücksmakler.
Der Wert des Grundstücks ist in den letzten Jahren sehr gestiegen.
(b) In the country: **ein Stück Land.**

5. English 'land' which is owned: **Grund und Boden.**
Er besitzt viel Grund und Boden.
Sein Besitz besteht fast ausschließlich aus Grund und Boden.

6. Land round a building in so far as it is shaped, laid out, in some way: **Anlage(n)**, normally plural.
Sie gingen in den Schloßanlagen spazieren.
Die Park-Gartenanlagen.
Die weiten Anlagen der neuen Universität.

7. An area appropriate to or used for a particular purpose: **Platz.**
Der Paradeplatz, der Camping(Lager)platz.

GROW, GROWTH   A. Grow
(a) In the literal sense the intransitive use of the verb corresponds to German **wachsen.**
Er ist sehr schnell gewachsen.
In einem solchen Boden wächst so gut wie gar nichts.
(b) **Aufwachsen:** to grow up of people, emphasizes the result, while **heranwachsen**, also of people, draws attention to the process.
Er ist jetzt aufgewachsen und muß entsprechend behandelt werden.
Die heranwachsende Generation.
(c) **Anwachsen auf** with accusative: is used in the sense of to increase numerically to a certain point.
Die Zahl der Deserteure ist auf 500 angewachsen.
(d) For the transitive use of 'grow' the German equivalent is: **ziehen** in a small way, **anbauen** or **kultivieren** on a large scale.
Er zieht Gurken, Rosen, Apfelsinen in seinem Garten.
Hier wird Weizen angebaut.
(e) **Kultivieren** implies effort.
Wir haben eine Weizenart kultiviert, die Hitze gerade aushält.

B. Growth
(a) **Wachstum:** the process of growth.
Das Wachstum unserer Industrien hat Schwierigkeiten hervorgerufen.
Die Wachstumsrate der Wirtschaft ist sehr befriedigend.
(b) **Gewächs:** something grown, and like 'growth' can be used in a medical sense.

In diesem Lande finden sich viele sonderbare Gewächse.
Der Arzt hat ein krebsartiges Gewächs festgestellt.
(c) **Wuchs** means 'figure' rather than 'growth' (e.g. *von schönem Wuchs*) with people and also trees.
(d) **Zuwachs**: in the sense of increase, particularly of population.
Der Zuwachs der Bevölkerung Indiens ist im Verhältnis zu seinen Lebens-mittelmöglichkeiten beunruhigend.
Zuwachsrate (rate of growth).

GUARD 1. **Posten** is a sentry, whether armed or not; normally placed outside a building or an enclosed area.[1]
Bei Regen tritt der Posten ins Schilderhäuschen.
Der Posten schoß auf eine verdächtige Figur, die sich in seiner Nähe bewegte.
Das Konzentrationslager wurde von zahlreichen Posten bewacht.
Die Diebe haben einen Posten ausgestellt.

2. **Wache** generally refers to a body of men, but can also be applied to one man in so far as he is considered as a representative, not as an individual. In the latter sense it is preceded by the definite, but never the indefinite, article.[2] The compound term **Wachtposten** is also used in reference to one man.
Die Leibwache des Führers.
Die Wache mußte verstärkt werden.
Die Wachen sind pünktlich abgelöst worden.
Die Wache am Kasernentor wollte das Auto nicht passieren lassen (one man as a representative or a body of men).
Der Wachtposten wurde ermordet.
Ich hatte eine Auseinandersetzung mit dem Wachtposten.

3. **Wächter** generally refers to a man who keeps watch or guard inside a building. It refers particularly to a (night) watchman or a warder, jailor.
Der Wächter machte die Runde durch das Bankgebäude.
Der Zuchthäusler wurde von seinen Wächtern erschossen.

4. **Wärter** is an attendant or a caretaker rather than a guard, i.e. one whose sole duty is to keep watch. It implies, however, that certain things are entrusted to him for safe keeping.
Er ist Wärter in einer Irrenanstalt.
Der Bahnwärter.[3]

5. **Garde** is only used, collectively, to denote the guard of an exalted personage and particularly in connection with a ceremonious occasion. It is the military term for names of traditional regiments. **Gardist** is a member of such a guard.
Eine Ehrengarde wurde für den französischen Ministerpräsidenten bestellt.

GUN According to *A.L.* a general name for any kind of fire-arm, except a pistol or a revolver (though in U.S.A. these are also, in colloquial use, called guns). Further: gun is the word used of big modern weapons instead of the

---

[1] *Streikposten*: picket.
[2] *Wache* also means: vigil (*die Nachtwache, Wache halten*); an official station (*Polizei-wache*). The alternative form *Wacht* is generally confined to elevated diction, except in compounds (*die Wacht am Rhein; der Wachtmeister*). The verb *wachen* means 'to be watchful, on the alert'.
[3] The fare-collector on a vehicle is *Schaffner*.

older word cannon, just as rifle is now used for the obsolete musket. German has no general term such as gun and uses the specific term. However, if it does not wish to be specific it uses *Waffe, Schußwaffe, Feuerwaffe,* i.e. fire-arm (e.g. *der Einbrecher machte von der Schußwaffe Gebrauch; werfen Sie die Waffe weg* = drop your gun). **Gewehr** is a rifle, **Revolver** and **Pistole** as in English, *Maschinengewehr,* however, is the normal term for machine gun, **Flinte** (*Schrot* as ammunition) is used by a hunter. **Büchse** (*Kugel* as ammunition) (see also under 'tin') is now confined to light manual weapons. **Geschütz:** big guns, cannon.

GUTTER 1. Sense: a narrow metal channel or trough fixed to the edge of a roof to carry away rain water (*A.L.*). German: **Dachrinne,** or **Traufrinne.** (*Rinne* is a depression anywhere which allows water to flow away; in some regions it is also used in the sense of kitchen sink, i.e. for *Rinnstein*).
2. Sense: a channel along the edge of a street (between the street itself and the footpath or pavement) to carry away rain (*A.L.*) or any other water. German: **Gosse, Straßenrinne, Straßengraben.**

HABIT, CUSTOM[1] 1. Gewohnheit is that which by repetition has become second nature. It corresponds exactly to 'habit', and is accordingly applied in the first place to the activities of individuals, not of groups. **Angewohnheit** is only a habit that has become so ingrained that one cannot resist it. While *Gewohnheit* can express this sense, it does not stress it.

> *Er hat die Gewohnheit, morgens um 5 Uhr aufzustehen.*
> *Er kann diese schlechte Gewohnheit nicht mehr ablegen.*
> *Das Lügen ist bei ihm zur Gewohnheit geworden.*
> *Rauchen ist eine üble Angewohnheit.*

2. Sitte, custom, is the most general term for anything that is habitually practised by a group and has grown spontaneously. It is applied particularly to the customs of such groups as a country, a class, a family. It may be morally good or bad. In the plural it corresponds in this sense also to 'ways'.[2]

> *Die Sitten und Gebräuche eines Volkes.*
> *In Deutschland ist es Sitte, den Hut abzunehmen, wenn zwei Herren sich grüßen.*
> *Es ist in Deutschland eine alte Sitte, daß der Heilige Abend zu Hause gefeiert wird.*

---

[1] The adjectives *gewöhnlich, gebräuchlich, üblich* are distinguished as follows. *Gewöhnlich,* the most general term, means 'done' or 'happening' in most cases. It corresponds most closely to 'ordinary' (also in the sense of 'vulgar'; see 'common') and 'usual'. It is used freely both as an adjective and an adverb, but is uncommon in the predicative position except in the sense of vulgar. Examples: *das ist der gewöhnliche Preis; wir essen gewöhnlich zu Hause. Gebräuchlich,* which is only used as an adjective, simply means 'in use', particularly of words, idioms, and the like. Example: *diese Redensart ist nicht mehr gebräuchlich.* It implies: used on certain occasions, in certain places. *Üblich,* on the other hand, means 'practised at all times' (*üben* = practise). *Dann kamen die üblichen Entschuldigungen. Es ist üblich, vorher anzurufen, wenn man einen Besuch machen will. Üblich* is free from all suggestion of vulgarity. It is used only as an adjective.
[2] In the singular *Sitte* can also mean 'decorum, propriety', either as correct or polished behaviour (e.g. *die Sitte verlangt es; ein Verstoß gegen die Sitte*). In the plural *Sitten* can also mean (*a*) 'manners' in the sense of customary ways, (*b*) the 'morals' of an individual. See also footnote to 'educate' (p. 102, n. 2).

3. **Gebrauch** mostly means 'use'.[1] In the meaning of 'custom' it is rare, particularly in the singular, in which it occurs mainly in fixed phrases. It refers to a way of doing things that has been agreed upon by a number of people.

Die Diplomatie hat Gebräuche, an denen sie festhält.

Dies sind hier die Gebräuche.

4. **Brauch** is used in reference to time-honoured and ceremonious occasions.

Es ist ein alter Brauch, daß am Weihnachtstag Truthahn gegessen wird.

5. 'Custom' when applied to an individual, particularly in the phrase 'it is my (his, etc.) custom to...', cannot be rendered by any of the above terms. **Pflegen** or a synonymous verb should be used. It is applied only to an activity which is careful, controlled, not to what is wild, unrestrained. Thus it cannot be used to translate the synonym 'would' in the following sentence: They would push and scramble to get a seat. The same implication is associated with the other meaning of *pflegen*, 'to look after, to nurse, to tend, to bestow care on'. *Ein gepflegter Garten*: trim, well looked after.

Er pflegt, an seinem Geburtstage seine Freunde um sich zu sammeln.

Ich pflege nicht, solche Angebote anzunehmen.

HALL 1. Sense: the residence of a territorial proprietor, a baronial squire's hall (Ox.): German **Herrenhaus** or, if attached to farming lands, **Gutshaus**.

2. Sense: the largest room in the palace of a king or in the castle of a lord, bishop or other great person, used for receptions, banquets, merrymaking, etc. (*A.L.*): **Saal** (see under room), **Halle, Festhalle**. Today the word hall is used of the largest room in a palace or big house, chiefly for dining, as a banquet hall (*A.L.*); **Fest-Speisesaal**. **Halle** has normally a vaulted ceiling.

3. Sense: a large usually imposing building used for public purposes (W.), mostly in compounds. **Rathaus** (town hall), **Stadthalle, Justizpalast**.

4. Sense: a building where university students live, a hall of residence. German **Kollegium**.

5. Sense: a large room for assembly usually equipped with seats (as for lectures or concerts), auditorium (*W.*). German **Hörsaal** (lecture room); **Konzertsaal** or **Konzerthalle, Zuschauerraum**.

6. Sense: the entrance room of a residence or other building (*W.*): German **Diele, Hausflur, Vestibül**.

7. Sense: passageway in a house leading from one part to another and off which doors open: German **Korridor, Gang** (see under passage).

8. **Halle** can be either a building itself or a large room in a building. It was originally used in the sense of entrance hall, vestibule.

HANG (to put to death) 1. **Hängen** or **henken**: the normal literary terms.[2]

Der Mörder wurde gehängt (gehenkt).

[1] Compare: *im Gebrauch sein*, to be in use, to be customary. *Gebrauch* approximates closely to 'usage', either as an established way of behaviour that serves as a guide, or in reference to the correct meaning of words.

[2] *Durch den Strang hinrichten* is common in legal language.

2. **Aufhängen** is a popular term for *hängen*, *henken* or *erhängen* (cf. 'string up').

Ich hoffe, daß die ganze Bande aufgehängt wird.

3. **Erhängen** is in careful use only reflexive.

Er hat sich erhängt.

HEAD In the literal sense **Kopf** (cognate with middle L. *coppa*) is the ordinary term. **Haupt** (L. *caput*) is more dignified, and is normally restricted to human beings[1] (but also: *das Löwenhaupt*). L. *coppa* denotes a drinking vessel and *Kopf* suggests shape or form in both literal and figurative senses. In the latter it is applied only to the top of an object which has a form of this kind. *Haupt* in figurative use refers to what is most important, particularly to the chief of an organization.

Er hat einen runden, schönen, Kopf.
Ich musterte ihn vom Kopf bis zu den Füßen.
Er neigte das Haupt vor dem König.
Die gekrönten Häupter Europas.
Der Kopf eines Nagels.
Das Haupt der Familie.

HEAR (of, from) **Hören von** means 'to hear of, about', unless it is followed by a statement giving information (mostly a *daß* clause), in which case it can mean 'to hear from'. In the sense of 'to receive letters, a message', or the like, from a person, when this is not followed by the content of the letter or message, phrases such as **Nachricht bekommen von** should be used.

Haben Sie von ihm gehört? (of).
Ich hörte von ihm, daß wir Ihren Besuch bald erwarten können (from).
Haben Sie in letzter Zeit Nachricht von ihm bekommen?
Hat er in letzter Zeit von sich hören lassen?

HEART In compounds *Herz-* is a physiological term, *Herzens-* is regarded as the seat of the emotions.

Er hat einen Herzfehler.　　　　*Er zeigte wirkliche Herzensgüte.*

HEARTY **Herzlich** means 'heartfelt', i.e. it stresses inner feeling, without, however, excluding reference to its outward expression. **Herzhaft** refers primarily to the outward manifestation of heartiness conceived as zest, robust enjoyment. It is not, however, applied adjectivally to a person.

Er dankte mir, grüßte mich, herzlich.　　*Er lachte herzhaft.*
Er lachte herzlich.　　　　　　　　　　*Er griff herzhaft zu.*

HEAT **Heizen** is used transitively and intransitively of heating a hollow space, particularly a room. **Einheizen** is applied in its literal sense only to the latter, *ein* having intensive force. **Erhitzen** means in its literal application 'to heat to a given degree', figuratively it refers to feelings. 'To heat' food or water for ordinary domestic purposes is **heiß machen**.

Wir müssen das Zimmer, den Ofen, heizen.
Ich habe tüchtig eingeheizt.
Ich habe das Wasser auf 80 Grad erhitzt.
Bei einer Diskussion erhitzt er sich immer.
Bitte, machen Sie etwas Wasser heiß.

---

[1] Hence *enthaupten*, to execute, behead, is a more elevated term than the usual *hinrichten*.

HIDE 1. Verstecken suggests the putting away of a thing in order to out-wit the seeker, i.e. a purely practical purpose. As with *stecken* one thinks of the object to be hidden as being put *into* something else, although this is not necessarily the case. The action itself is emphasized. While what is hidden is generally a concrete object, it may also in the past participle, i.e. as an adjective, be applied to something intangible (e.g. *Absichten*).

Sie versteckte den Schlüssel.
Er mußte sich vor der Polizei versteckt halten.

Die Kunstschätze des Landes wurden kurz vor dem Einmarsch des Feindes so weit wie möglich versteckt.
Die Sonne versteckte sich hinter den Wolken. (But *verstecken* could not trans-late literally 'the clouds hid the sun', since *verstecken*, used actively, so strongly suggests the action of putting away by a person.)
Er hegte versteckte Absichten. (Since *verstecken* used actively has the literal sense, it cannot be used to translate: he hid his intentions.)

2. Verbergen refers to the hiding of anything about one's person or any-thing connected with one's inner self. The action it suggests is frequently that of putting one thing over another in order to protect it (*bergen* means 'to bring to safety'). It is used also of things hidden by nature, not by man.

Er verbarg das Papier in seiner Manschette.
Er versuchte, seine linke Hand zu verbergen, weil ein Finger fehlte.
Sie verbarg ihr Gesicht.
Ein Tuch verbarg sein Gesicht.
Er verbarg sich vor dem Überfall.
Wir müssen die Flüchtlinge verbergen.
Er verbarg sich vor dem Gesetz.
Die Mauer verbirgt das Haus vor unserem Blick.[1]
In dieser Gegend sind viele Naturschätze in der Erde verborgen.
Ich habe einige verborgene Zigaretten (saved up).
Die Wolken verbargen die Sonne.
Ich konnte meine Freude kaum verbergen.
Du sollst mir Deine Gedanken, Absichten, nicht verbergen.
Sie verbarg das Geheimnis im Innersten ihres Herzens.

3. Verhehlen suggests dissimulation and often an accusation. It is not used of concrete objects.

Verhehle mir nichts!
Sie haben mir die Wahrheit verhehlt.
Er verhehlte ihr, daß er schon zweimal verheiratet gewesen war.
Er kann beim besten Willen den Nazi nicht verhehlen (the Nazi in him).

HOLIDAY(S), LEAVE A single day's holiday is **Feiertag** in so far as this is a day set aside to commemorate someone or something (in Germany most of such days are religious holidays). Otherwise for a single day: **frei haben** (*morgen haben wir frei*, i.e. just freedom from work). **Ferien** are holidays that one spends in relaxation, recuperation, mostly away from home (*dieses Jahr verbringen wir unsere Ferien am Meer; wir fahren nächste Woche in die Ferien;*

---

[1] But: *die Mauer versperrt die Aussicht* (see article on 'block'). The above verbs are impossible, because German has no term which corresponds exactly to 'view' in the sentence: the wall hides the view. See article on 'view'.

die Schulferien sind in den deutschen Bundesländern wegen des Verkehrschaos, das sonst eintreten könnte, gestaffelt). **Urlaub** is leave of any kind from one's normal occupation (*wir haben jährlich vier Wochen Urlaub, er hatte Krankenurlaub*). The distinction between *Ferien* and *Urlaub* is rigidly observed in Switzerland, but in Germany itself there is a strong tendency to use *Urlaub* also in the sense of *Ferien* (*dieses Jahr verbringen wir unseren Urlaub am Meer*).

HOWEVER, NEVERTHELESS, YET, ALL THE SAME 1. **Jedoch** is only used as a qualification of a preceding absolute statement, and corresponds to this sense of 'however'.

> *Er ist schwer verwundet, es besteht jedoch keine Gefahr, daß er stirbt.*
> *Er hat triftige Gründe vorgebracht, hat mich jedoch nicht überzeugt.*
> *Es gab unzählige Gegner des Nazi-Regimes, jedoch war nur eine Handvoll organisiert.*

2. **Dennoch** indicates a contrast between the result and what the preceding clause leads one to expect. It does not express a qualification, but is a direct and emphatic adversative, often following a concessive clause. The meaning is really 'even then', i.e. *dann noch*.

> *Alle Voraussetzungen für den Erfolg des Unternehmens waren da, und dennoch ist es mißlungen.*
> *Wenn er mir auch 1000 Mark anbieten würde, gebe ich mich dennoch nicht dazu her.*

3. **Doch** is also an adversative and indicates a contrast between the result and what the preceding clause leads one to expect, but is much less emphatic than *dennoch*.[1] If it stands at the beginning of the clause it normally requires the inversion of subject and verb. There are, however, cases, particularly in literature, of non-inversion. The closest English equivalent is 'yet', sometimes 'after all' (here often preceded by *schließlich*).

> *Er meldete sich freiwillig für den Dienst im Ausland, doch ließ seine Begeisterung rasch nach.*
> *Er ist reich, doch keineswegs zufrieden.*
> *Sie haben noch nicht Ihre früheren Schulden zurückgezahlt und bitten doch um eine weitere Anleihe.*

4. **Trotzdem** (i.e. despite that) and the more literary **dessenungeachtet** (i.e. notwithstanding) imply that the preceding statement, the truth of which is indisputable, is to be left out of account.

> *Er hat mich mehrere Male im Stich gelassen, aber ich werde mich heute trotzdem auf ihn verlassen.*

5. **Immerhin**, like *trotzdem*, implies that the preceding statement, which is indisputable, can be left out of account. It often has a strong emotive value and stresses a redeeming feature in an apparently hopeless situation. The closest English equivalent is 'all the same'.

> *Das Stück ist ungünstig beurteilt worden, aber ich möchte es mir immerhin ansehen.*

---

[1] *Doch* frequently, particularly in the body of a clause, denotes an opposition to something felt and not expressed in a preceding clause. Its shades of meaning are numerous. It can, e.g., express uncertainty that seeks confirmation in a question (e.g. *du hast es ihm doch nicht gesagt*, i.e. I hope), an unfulfilled wish (e.g. *wenn ich es doch nur wüßte*).

6. Allerdings and **Freilich** approach some uses of 'however', though more closely 'certainly', 'it is true' when these denote a concession in the form of a qualification. When they express a concession not in the form of a qualification they are often followed by 'aber'.

Er ist ein reicher Mann, allerdings nicht so reich wie sein Vater.
Er hat es mir allerdings schon gesagt, aber nicht deutlich genug.

HURRY, HASTEN The distinction between 'hurry' and 'hasten' is that the first is prompted primarily by an external, the second by an inner cause (e.g. an emotion). The German *hasten* resembles the English 'hasten' in this point, but is confined to a few special uses. *Hastig* too indicates a lack of inner composure, whereas *eilig* indicates external needs.

This article deals with the translation of the intransitive uses of the English terms and then offers a few suggestions about the transitive uses.

A. Eilen denotes primarily a change of position, i.e. hurrying or hastening from one place to another.[1] In reflexive use it is now limited to the imperative, with the sense of *sich beeilen*. **Sich beeilen:** to do something speedily or to make haste to do something. In the imperative it is more common than *sich eilen*.

Er eilte nach Hause, ihr zu Hilfe.
Er beeilte sich, es zu leugnen.
Beeilen Sie sich (or less commonly: *eilen Sie sich*).
Sie müssen sich mit dem Abendessen beeilen.

B. Transitive uses.
(a) **Übereilen:** to do a thing before the time is ripe or too quickly. **Überstürzen:** also, to precipitate or to do a thing so quickly that it becomes confused (particularly with regard to speech). These verbs are used reflexively and in the past participle when 'hurry' and 'hasten' denote excess. Apart from the reflexive use, the object cannot be a person.

Übereilen Sie sich nicht mit der Arbeit.
Der Entschluß, die Arbeit, hätte nicht übereilt werden sollen.
Seine Reden sind immer überstürzt.

(b) Frequently a specific term must be used (often *eilig* with an appropriate verb). The following is not an exhaustive list.

Sorgen haben seinen Tod beschleunigt.
Dränge mich nicht so!
Truppen wurden eilig an die Front geworfen.
Er hat sein Frühstück hinuntergestürzt.

IDEA, CONCEPT, CONCEPTION[2] 1. Idee has all meanings of 'idea', from its philosophic use to that of 'notion', whether vague or clear, 'belief', 'fancy', 'plan'. It is, however, often preferable to use a native German term such as *Vorstellung*.[3]

Die platonischen Ideen.

---

[1] *Eilen* with a thing or the impersonal *es* as subject means 'to be urgent'. *Die Sache eilt nicht. Es eilt nicht mit der Sache.*
[2] See also 'view'.
[3] Further: *ich hatte keine Ahnung* (inkling), *daß Sie hier waren; er hat manchmal gute Einfälle* (only in sense of 'brain-waves'); *der Gedanke, meine Ferien dort zu verbringen, ist mir nie vorher eingefallen* (*Gedanke* refers to something more normal, obvious, *Idee* can be sudden, ingenious; see also 'thought').

Die Gottesidee.
Eingeborene Ideen.
Das entspricht nicht meiner Idee der königlichen Würde.
Das ist eine vernünftige Idee.
Er ist auf die Idee verfallen, daß wir ihn loswerden wollen.
Er ist voller Ideen.
Meine Idee war, ein Zimmer hier anbauen zu lassen.
Die Idee der Pflicht (contrast example with *Vorstellung*).

2. **Vorstellung** is a mental picture of a thing. It draws attention less to the thing in its objective aspects than to the state of mind of the subject, particularly with regard to the intensity, vividness, clarity, persistence or otherwise of the image. Hence: *er leidet an Zwangsvorstellungen*, fixed ideas (or *an fixen Ideen*). It should not be used when this subjective element is absent. Hence: *seine* (but not *die*) *Vorstellung der Pflicht.*

Er hat klare, verworrene, Vorstellungen.
Die Vorstellung, daß er eine unheilbare Krankheit habe, beherrscht ihn ganz und gar.
Stefan George hat seiner Zeit strengere Vorstellungen der Dichtkunst entgegengehalten als die, welche in der zweiten Hälfte des 19ten Jahrhunderts gang und gäbe waren.

3. **Begriff** means both 'concept', i.e. the typical or generic idea of a thing divested of all its accidental features, and 'conception', particularly in the sense of 'ability to conceive, to represent to the mind'.[1]

Der Gottesbegriff.
Der Begriff des Staates.
Klare, feste, Begriffe.
Das ist ein überwundener Begriff.
Nach seinen Begriffen von dem, was schicklich ist.
Ich kann mir keinen rechten Begriff von den dort herrschenden Verhältnissen machen.

ILLUMINATE   In literal application **beleuchten** is a purely objective term, while **erleuchten** refers to an impression. In figurative use *beleuchten* is 'to throw light on' a thing, *erleuchten* denotes the illumination or inspiration of the mind.

Gut beleuchtete Straßen.
Die hell erleuchtete Stadt wurde plötzlich sichtbar.
Die Scheinwerfer beleuchteten den Hafen.
Das Schloß war hell erleuchtet.
'Den andern Abend nach seiner Rückkehr waren Krespels Fenster ungewöhnlich erleuchtet...' (Hoffmann, *Rat Krespel*).
Wir gingen in den festlich erleuchteten Saal.
Er beleuchtete seine These mit einer Fülle von Beispielen.
Er ist ein erleuchteter Geist.

---

[1] *Konzeption* means 'conception' only in the sense of the actual process of conceiving, bringing to birth, a product of the mind such as a work of art (e.g. *die Konzeption des 'Faust' war schon früh in großen Zügen fertig; bei der Konzeption dieses Gedichts*). In post-war years its meaning has been extended to cover that of the English term. *Konzept* does not mean 'concept'. It is used only in a few fixed phrases meaning 'train of thought' (e.g. *Sie bringen mich aus dem Konzept, Sie verderben mir das Konzept*). In Goethe's day it meant a 'rough draft' of a letter. *Empfängnis* is the physiological term for 'conception'.

IMAGINE[1] **1. Sich vorstellen:** to make a conscious effort to picture a thing to oneself, whether real or unreal.

Stellen Sie sich vor, Sie wären ein reicher Mann.
Ich kann mir den Ort ganz schön vorstellen.

2. Sich einbilden denotes an involuntary act, and often an illusion. As it is involuntary it is rare in the imperative.

Das haben Sie sich nur eingebildet.
Er bildet sich ein, er sei ein Genie.
Bilde dir nicht ein, daß du ein Genie bist.

IMMEDIATELY **1. Sofort** is more emphatic than **gleich**, which can mean in a minute. When, however, a waiter in a restaurant says *kommt sofort* of the customer's order, the term is not to be taken too literally. *Sofort* suggests normally 'without losing any time'.

Wir müssen sofort telephonieren.
Er braust sofort auf, wenn man ihm widerspricht.
Ich bin gleich wieder da (I'll be back in a minute, a second).
Sie haben gleich Anschluß (of connecting trains).
Ich bin gleich fertig (ready in a minute).

2. Alsbald ranges in meaning from 'immediately' to 'in due course', and because of this ambiguity almost provoked an incident when used by the National Socialist government in a note to London in the mid thirties.

Wir erwarten, daß Sie uns alsbald die Berichte zur Verfügung stellen.

3. Unmittelbar means following straightway on something else, but it is not peremptory and therefore not used in imperatives. It is normally followed by a preposition.

Die Verleihung der Preise folgte unmittelbar auf das Festessen.

IMPLY **1.** Sense: to convey or communicate not by direct forthright statement but by allusion or reference likely to lead to natural inference: suggest or hint at (*W.*). Cases considered here occur when the subject of the sentence is personal. German: **zu verstehen geben, damit sagen wollen** (in interpreting what someone has said); **andeuten** (hint).

Er gab zu verstehen, daß er nicht mehr kandidieren würde.
Er deutete an, daß sie zu weit gegangen waren.
Damit willst du sagen, daß du nicht mehr mitmachst.
Ich habe nicht damit sagen wollen, daß Sie sich keine Mühe gegeben haben.

2. Sense: to indicate or call for recognition of, as existent, present, or related, not by express statement but by logical inference or association or necessary consequence. German: **schließen lassen auf** (to allow an inference to be drawn about), **besagen,** (see 'mean'), **implizieren** (Gelehrtendeutsch), **bedeuten** (often used although the sense is 'to mean' rather than 'to imply'). In reference to the implications of a word: **mit enthalten sein in, mitschwingen in.**

Rauch läßt auf Feuer schließen.

---

[1] *Einbildungskraft, Vorstellungskraft*: the faculty of imagination. These terms are used chiefly in analyses of the nature of this faculty. Otherwise *Phantasie* is the usual equivalent of 'imagination' (e.g. *er hat eine rege Phantasie; ein mit Phantasie begabter Mensch*). *Einbildung* is the specific content of any act of the imagination, often 'imaginitis' (e.g. *das ist doch nur Einbildung !*).

Die ausweichende Antwort des Mädchens und ihre brennenden Wangen ließen darauf schließen, daß ihr Verehrer sich anders besonnen haben mußte (W.).

Notlage und Krise lassen auf Konflikte schließen (W.).

Schon die Daten implizieren (lassen schließen auf) ein Umdenken des Stoffes.

Das Wort besagt einen totalen Abstand.

Das bedeutet einen Widerspruch, einen Bruch in unseren Beziehungen.

Das bedeutet, daß du ablehnst.

In dem Wort ist das Moment der freien Willensentscheidung mit enthalten.

In diesem Ausdruck schwingt die ganze Subjektivität der Romantik mit.

IMPROVE[1] **1. Bessern:** to bring about a limited, but unspecified, degree of improvement with regard to (*a*) health; (*b*) behaviour, conceived in a wide sense including both moral and intellectual aspects; (*c*) social conditions. It occurs mainly in the reflexive form. With a personal object in non-reflexive use, which in present-day German is less common than formerly, it refers to morals, not to health, and comes to mean 'to reform to a certain degree, but not completely'. Non-personal objects are generally words referring to the moral side of man (e.g. *Charakter, Betragen*) or *Zustand, Lage* or equivalents.[2] A process, not a brief act, is suggested, which explains the prevalence of the reflexive use.

Bessern an, followed by the dative, denotes, however, a series of brief acts, and means 'to effect improvements in' an object by alterations, by removing errors or other imperfections. It is applied particularly to writing.

Sein Gesundheitszustand hat sich erheblich gebessert.[3]

Er hat sich politisch nicht gebessert.

Er hat sich in der Schule nicht gebessert.

Die sozialen Verhältnisse haben sich in der letzten Zeit kaum gebessert.

Der Weltverbesserer sagt: Ich habe die Lage der Arbeiterschaft gebessert.

Gewisse Maßnahmen, die in letzter Zeit ergriffen worden sind, haben den Gesundheitszustand des Volkes gebessert.

Früher starben viele Frauen am Kindbettfieber, die Einführung antiseptischer Mittel durch Lord Lister hat diesen Zustand gebessert.

> *'Bilde mir nicht ein, ich könnte was lehren,*
> *Die Menschen zu bessern und zu bekehren.'* (*Faust I*, ll. 372–3.)

'Euphemie ist religiös schon aus Temperament, vielleicht gelingt es ihrer besonderen Rednergabe, tief in ihr Herz zu dringen, sie zu erschüttern und zu bessern, daß sie den Verrat am Freunde,...unterläßt.' (E. T. A. Hoffmann, *Die Elixiere des Teufels.*)

'Ich finde mich erst wieder, als die Mutter meinen Anzug, soviel es ihr möglich war, besserte und ordnete.' (E. T. A. Hoffmann, *Die Elixiere des Teufels.* Not possible in present-day German.)

2. Verbessern: to bring a thing closer to the ideal type by raising it to a standard which is objectively recognized as a step towards the ideal and which, in some cases, is capable of being tested by measurement. It is therefore applied particularly to things which can be improved as types, often in accordance with specifications and by a technical process. As objective

---

[1] *Ausbessern*: to mend (shoes, streets, etc.).

[2] *Die Gehälter bessern* is somewhat colloquial, as is also *er wurde aufgebessert* (= he was raised, i.e. in salary).

[3] Compare the use of the corresponding noun in the expression *gute Besserung.*

recognition tends to be accorded to public or large-scale institutions, inventions and enterprises which are in the hands of experts more than to small private objects and activities with which one 'muddles through', *verbessern* is more often applied to the former than the latter. It thus corresponds to 'improve' as a close synonym of 'to improve on', which it also translates.[1] Since it should only be used when the reference to an objective standard is clear, the nature of the improvement must in some cases be indicated, e.g. by mention of the process. Thus while the sentence 'the park has been improved' cannot be translated by *verbessern*, the addition of a phrase such as 'by building a playing area for children' or 'by the addition of fountains' makes its use possible. The addition brings the park more into conformity with the ideal of a park. With reference to the economic circumstances or the social standing of an individual, the meaning is 'to raise (them) to a standard recognized as satisfactory'.

The changes necessary to bring a thing closer to the ideal type can imply 'correction' of errors, and 'to correct' is a meaning of *verbessern*, particularly with reference to errors in writing. The object may be the piece of writing itself (short rather than long pieces), the error, or the person who makes the error. With writing therefore *verbessern* means 'to correct', i.e. to eliminate errors, not 'to improve' in the sense of removing other types of imperfection.[2]

Reflexive use with a personal subject is limited to the following meanings: (*a*) to correct a slip of the tongue, i.e. to correct oneself; (*b*) to seek a better job, i.e. to better oneself.

In all cases a deliberate act, not an unconscious process, is implied.

Die öffentlichen Anlagen wurden durch einen Spielplatz für Kinder verbessert.

Um den allgemeinen Gesundheitszustand zu verbessern, wurde dem Wasser Jod entzogen.

Der Geschmack des Weins wurde durch gewisse Zusätze verbessert.

Die Befestigungswerke, die Museen, müssen verbessert werden.

In den letzten Jahren sind die Unterrichtsmethoden fast überall verbessert worden (improved or improved on).[3]

'*Ehe wir mit der Aufklärung vorschreiten, d.h. ehe wir die Wälder umhauen, den Strom schiffbar machen, Kartoffeln anbauen, die Dorfschulen verbessern,...ist es nötig, alle Leute von gefährlichen Gesinnungen, die keiner Vernunft Gehör geben und das Volk durch lauter Albernheiten verführen, aus dem Staate zu verbannen*' (E. T. A. Hoffmann, *Klein Zaches*).

Dieser Mann hat die Rechtsprechung des Landes verbessert.

Er hat seinen eigenen Rekord, eine Spitzenleistung, verbessert.

Er war in der Lage, seine gesellschaftliche Stellung zu verbessern.

Er hat sich verbessert (corrected or bettered himself).

3. In other cases, which are numerous, German uses more specific terms. Common amongst these are *steigern* (see 'increase'), *heben* (see 'raise'), *verstärken* (see 'strengthen'), *veredeln, verfeinern, vertiefen, erweitern, fördern*. With an object such as 'things', 'the state of affairs', *besser machen* may be used. *Meliorieren* means to improve the value of land property.[4]

---

[1] 'To improve' mostly implies changes in the same object, but is also used in the sense of 'to improve on', which implies another object that is compared with the first. Example: to improve (on) a record.

[2] *Verbessern* also means 'to amend', and 'to emend'.

[3] Also 'to reform', with reference to an institution.

[4] Note also *ameliorieren* (=ameliorate).

Die Leistungsfähigkeit der Arbeiter steigern.
Das Niveau der Volksgesundheit heben (with *Zustand, bessern* and *verbessern*
could be used).
Sie müssen Ihre Kenntnisse des Deutschen zu vertiefen, erweitern, versuchen.
Ein Aufenthalt in den Bergen wird Ihrer Gesundheit zugute kommen.
Das wird Ihre Chancen kaum fördern.
Das wird die Sache nicht besser machen.

INCIDENTAL   *W.S.* says of this word that it 'may or may not imply
chance; it often suggests a real, and it may be, a designed relationship, but
one which is secondary and non-essential'.

1. If the above is correct, it follows that **zufällig** (accidental) will only sometimes be the German equivalent of our term. Thus an incidental discovery
may be *eine zufällige Entdeckung* only if it is accidental.

2. Beiläufig (see also under 'casual') from the meaning of 'running along
beside' has developed the meaning of 'subsidiary', which in German can
also be **nebensächlich.**
Eine beiläufige Entdeckung (by-product).
Nebensächliche Spesen.

3. German compounds with **neben** or **bei** will often come close to the mean-
ing of the term.
Nebenausgaben (*or nebensächlich*).
*Die irische Frage ist nur ein Beiprodukt des größeren schwerwiegenden
Problems* (*W.S.*).
*Arbeiterprobleme, die Nebenprodukte (Beiprodukte) der raschen Ausdehnung
der Fabriken waren* (*W.S.*).

4. Incidental music, i.e. to a film and the like: **Begleitmusik.**

5. Followed by 'to'. German can mostly only use **gehören** (see under
belong), **verbunden mit** (connected with, see also under 'join'); **eigen** with
the dative (peculiar to).
*Die Beschwerden, die mit der Erschließung eines noch unerforschten Landes
verbunden sind* (*A.L.*).
Krankheiten, die zu dem vorgeschrittenen Alter gehören (or: *dem v. A. eigen
sind*) (*W.S.*).

6. The adverb incidentally used as an interjection or digression in the sense
of in passing, parenthetically. German **nebenbei gesagt** (bemerkt) or
übrigens. (*Im übrigen* means 'for the rest').
*Eine weitere führende Industrie hat, nebenbei bemerkt, ihr Geschäft in den
letzten fünf Jahren vervierfacht* (*W.*).
Übrigens war er gestern hier.

7. In the sense of 'by chance' or 'as a matter of minor import' the adverb
is simply **nebenbei.**
In dieser Diskussion werden ernste Fragen nebenbei angeschnitten.

INCLUDE   There is in German no term corresponding widely to 'include'.

1. Mit einbegreifen is used in reference to the inclusion of an item in a
price. It is generally used passively. In general it suggests a list of items, one
or more of which are said to be included in the total price.

Bedienung ist mit einbegriffen (in the stated price of a meal).

Sie brauchen nicht noch mehr zu zahlen, die Besichtigung der Bilder ist mit einbegriffen.

Das Stück Land ist mit einbegriffen (in the total price).

2. **(Mit)einschließen,** also generally passively, is used in the same sense as *mit einbegreifen,* but less commonly.

Die Heizung ist mit eingeschlossen (in the rent).

Die Möbel sind mit eingeschlossen (in the price of a house).

Er hält jede Maßnahme, die eine Kritik an seiner Haltung einschließt, für ungerechtfertigt.

3. **Dabei sein** may be used in the sense of 'to be included' when the word *Preis, Miete* or the like is not mentioned.

Bedienung ist dabei.

Heizung ist dabei.

4. In other cases *mit* with an appropriate verb, often but not always passive, is frequently used. **Mitenthalten sein** is common.

Ich habe ihn noch mit eingeladen (included him among my guests).

In dem Buch ist ein Bericht über Studentenunruhen mit enthalten.

Werden Sie solche Vorfälle in Ihre Memoiren mit aufnehmen?

Haben Sie in Ihr George-Buch die Frage seiner Beeinflussung durch Dante mit einbezogen? (or: *mit erwähnt, behandelt*).

5. Some other possibilities:

Das Verbot erstreckte sich auf viele prominente Leute.

In der Prüfung wurde auch eine Frage über Grillparzer gestellt.

Bei den Ordensverleihungen wurde er übergangen (he was not included in the decorations).

INCREASE **1.** **Mehren** is only used reflexively and in reference to the numerical increase of things. Though the Bible has '*Seid fruchtbar und mehret euch*', it is in present use rarely applied in ordinary prose to the increase of population.

Die Beschwerden, seine Sorgen, mehren sich.

Die Fehler in dieser Arbeit mehren sich ganz bedenklich.

Die Anzeichen einer Krise, die Anfragen, mehren sich.

2. **Vermehren:** to increase in number. With other objects, particularly feelings, it is now common only in elevated or poetic diction, except occasionally in the past participle. In reflexive use it commonly refers to an increase in population. Other reflexive uses in reference to number should not be imitated. It cannot be followed by a prepositional phrase meaning 'to a level'.

Die Eingeborenen vermehren sich schnell.

Er hat die Zahl der Polizisten, der Beispiele, vermehrt.

'*Selbst ihre Unruhe schien ihre Zärtlichkeit zu vermehren*' (Goethe, *Wilhelm Meisters Lehrjahre*; no longer normal usage).

3. **Steigern** and **erhöhen** both mean 'to increase in intensity to a higher level'. *Steigern* is 'to increase to a maximum or to an unlimited extent'. *Erhöhen* is weaker and denotes a definite level.[1] 'To' is translated by *bis zu* after *steigern*, and by *auf* after *erhöhen*.

---

[1] See also *erhöhen* under 'raise'.

INCREASE

Die Preise erhöhen.
Die Preise steigern.
Ich habe meine Ansprüche, meine Anforderungen, erhöht (not *gesteigert*).
Der Wert des Grundstücks wurde durch diese Maßnahme erhöht (not *gesteigert*).
Die Rationen wurden erhöht (not *gesteigert*).
Er hat seine Technik bis zur vollkommenen Beherrschung des Instruments gesteigert.
Der Beifall steigerte sich bis zu Begeisterung.

4. Examples of more specific terms are: *einen Verdacht verstärken* (see 'strengthen'); *eine Strafe verschärfen* (to make more severe; see footnote to 'severe', p. 306, n. 4).

5. Zunehmen, only in intransitive use, 'to increase in numbers or intensity'[1].
Die Zahl der Einwohner nimmt rasch zu.
Das Gewitter nimmt an Heftigkeit zu.

INHABITANT   1. Einwohner suggests the idea of a community, and approximates to 'citizen'. It must therefore be used in reference to the number of inhabitants of a place; also with a following genitive which denotes a community settlement (e.g. *Stadt, Stadtviertel, Ort, Dorf*).
London ist eine Stadt von 8 Millionen Einwohnern.
Die Einwohner dieses Dorfes haben bei den Wahlen fast alle sozialdemokratisch gewählt.

2. Bewohner is applied to people who are thought of as happening to be in a place, to have their dwellings there. It must be used with a following genitive which denotes a house or a street, and also with a land or region when the people there are thought of merely as inhabiting these.
Die Bewohner dieses Hauses, dieses Schloßes, sind augenblicklich verreist.
Fast alle Bewohner dieser Straße sind Ausländer.
Die Bewohner dieser nördlichen Gegenden sind zu einem schweren Leben verurteilt.

3. Bevölkerung, population, should be used in reference to the human characteristics, customs, and attitudes of a group of people settled in a place.
Die Bevölkerung dieses Dorfes ist degeneriert.
Die Bevölkerung des Spreewaldes hat ihre alte Sprache erhalten.
Die Bevölkerung dieses Ortes war feindlich eingestellt (a border-line case for *Einwohner*).

INHERIT   Erben is the general term, both literally and figuratively. It stresses the possession of a thing which has, so to speak, been handed to one. **Ererben** refers to what is handed down, often through generations, and of which the possessor may be unaware, particularly in reference to a cultural inheritance. It is common only in the past participle and has adjectival force, corresponding to 'hereditary'. The process of passing from generation to generation, rather than the act of reception, is emphasized. Goethe uses it verbally in this sense. '*Was du erbt von deinen Vätern hast, erwirb es, um es zu besitzen.*' The second part of this quotation is based on the implications of *ererbt*, i.e. that what is handed down is not thought of in close association

---

[1] *Zunehmen* is used also in the sense of 'put on weight'. *Er hat stark zugenommen.*

with the receiver, as a conscious part of him. *Erben* used adjectivally in the past participle is more active.[1]

Er hat ein beträchtliches Vermögen, den Jähzorn seines Vaters, geerbt.
Eine geerbte Krankheit.
Eine ererbte Krankheit, Sünde.
Sein Jähzorn ist ererbt.
Das ererbte Traditionsgefühl der Hansastädte.

INHERITANCE, LEGACY, BEQUEST, ESTATE **Erbschaft** may or may not be bequeathed by deed of will. **Vermächtnis** always implies in the literal sense a deed of will, often to someone who is not the natural heir, and thus corresponds most closely to 'legacy', sometimes to 'bequest' (*vermachen* = bequeath). Figuratively, it denotes something expressly addressed to someone (e.g. words of advice). **Hinterlassenschaft** is simply what is left behind, i.e. the testator's estate.[2] *Erbschaft* is the normal term for 'inheritance' in reference to property, but is also used figuratively in an unfavourable sense, i.e. as something that is a handicap, or as a disorderly state of affairs that has to be straightened out. **Erbe**[3] is used in reference to both material and spiritual goods, but more often to the latter. Applied to material goods, it suggests moral or sentimental ideas associated with inheritance, while *Erbschaft* is purely objective.

Er hat zugunsten seines Bruders auf seine Erbschaft verzichtet.
Er trug ein Leben lang an der Erbschaft seines Vaters.
Die Männer, die die Nazi-Erbschaft angetreten haben, stehen vor kaum zu bewältigenden Problemen.
Goethes Vermächtnis an das deutsche ist von diesem nicht immer geschätzt worden.
Seine Hinterlassenschaft war nicht beträchtlich.
Das Kulturerbe der Deutschen ist vom Nationalsozialismus mißverstanden worden.

INTERESTED IN **Sich interessieren für** refers to an intellectual or emotional interest. Without qualification it is not strong, merely indicating the direction or object of an interest. **Interessiert sein an** denotes (*a*) a more intense and active interest of an intellectual or emotional kind; (*b*) a commercial interest. The same distinction holds good for these prepositions when they follow the noun *Interesse*.

Er interessiert sich für Kunst, Blumenzucht, die Frau.
Er ist an Kunst, Blumenzucht, der Frau, interessiert.
Er ist an dem Unternehmen interessiert.

INTERPRET **Deuten** should only be used in reference to lofty or important matters. **Auslegen** is applied to humbler or everyday matters. **Interpretieren** is used in both ways. **Dolmetschen** now means only 'to translate orally' from a foreign language for two or more people who are ignorant of one of the languages concerned.

---

[1] *Vererben*: to bequeath, to transmit (a quality, disease, or the like). *Beerben*: to be someone's heir.
[2] *Nachlaß*: (1) the posthumous works of a writer; (2) the 'effects' of an unknown dead person (e.g. a deceased soldier). Nowadays also used for *Hinterlassenschaft*.
[3] *Der Erbe*: the heir.

INTERPRET

Er hat Goethes 'Faust' neu gedeutet, interpretiert.
Wie legen Sie seine Absage, diese Stelle, aus?
Er hat die Rede falsch interpretiert, ausgelegt.
Wie würden Sie seinen Besuch interpretieren?
Er hat für die beiden Staatsmänner gedolmetscht.

INTRODUCE 1. **Vorstellen** refers only to the act of presenting one person to another.[1]
Darf ich Sie vorstellen?
Ich bin ihm noch nicht vorgestellt worden.

2. **Einführen** means (*a*) to bring about an association between people, but without reference to formal presentation. It is followed by a preposition such as *in* or *bei*. (*b*) To introduce a person to something abstract, e.g. a world of thought. (*c*) To establish a thing as a practice.
Er führte mich bei Schmidts, in diese Gesellschaft ein.
Er, dieses Buch, führte mich in die romantische Gedankenwelt ein.
Er hat eine neue Mode, Sitte, Russisch in den Schulplan, eingeführt.

3. **Einleiten** is 'to take the preliminary or first steps', particularly in reference to something written or spoken.[2]
Er leitete das Buch mit einer propagandistischen Vorrede ein.
Er leitete das Thema mit einigen Anekdoten ein.
Das Schuljahr wurde von dem Direktor mit einer feierlichen Ansprache eingeleitet.

4. **Bekannt machen** can mean (*a*) to present one person to another, but is less formal than *vorstellen*; (*b*) to introduce a person to a thing.
Darf ich Sie bekannt machen?
Ich habe ihn schon mit unseren Weinen bekannt gemacht.

5. **Einbringen:** to submit a bill to Parliament for approval.
Ein neuer Antrag, eine Gesetzesvorlage, wurde heute eingebracht.

INVESTIGATE   See also under 'discover'.

1. **Untersuchen** is the most general term and is applicable to investigations of any kind.
Er untersucht die Beschaffenheit der Zelle.
Die Polizei untersucht drei Mordfälle, die einen ähnlichen Charakter aufweisen.
Ein Ausschuß untersucht, ob eine Gehaltserhöhung gerechtfertigt sei.

---

[1] *Vorstellen* also means 'to represent' in reference to art. It differs from *darstellen* which also means 'to represent', in that it means no more than 'to convey the idea of' a thing (*Vorstellung* = idea), while *darstellen* suggests the evocation of a thing with a wealth of sensuous detail. *Das Bild stellt einen Hafen vor*, i.e. is meant to convey the idea of a harbour, though the resemblance may not be striking. *Das Bild stellt einen Hafen dar*, i.e. in its sensuous reality. *Darstellung* has as one of its meanings 'performance', 'impersonation', in reference to theatrical art. *Vorstellung* in the sense of a theatrical performance and the like means 'session' (e.g. *seine Darstellung von Hamlet, die 5 Uhr-Vorstellung*).

[2] The introduction to a book in the sense of a preliminary chapter is *Einleitung*. *Einführung* is the introduction to a subject and may consist of an entire book (e.g. *eine Einführung in die griechische Sprache*). The distinction between *führen* and *leiten* is as follows. *Führen* implies the absolute subordination of those led, *leiten* means 'to give general directions' how an activity is to be carried out, hence 'to direct, to guide'. *Lenken* means 'to guide every step, every change of direction', 'to steer'.

2. Erforschen is used exclusively of scientific and scholarly research.

Er hat das Problem der Beeinflussung Kleists durch das Gedankengut der französischen Revolution erforscht.

3. Nachforschen is used of ordinary, non-scientific and non-scholarly investigation, particularly of police-work and means to attempt to bring to light what has been hidden.

Die Polizei hat die Angelegenheit der Passfälschung nachgeforscht.

Der Steuerbeamte hat nachgeforscht, ob er in seiner Steuererklärung nichts verschwiegen hat.

INVOLVE This is a much over-worked word, particularly when used simply for 'necessitate' or 'include'. Correctly used, it should imply entanglement, difficulty in freeing oneself from this, or embarrassment.

1. As a synonym of 'implicate' it need not, unlike the latter, impute disgrace to the circumstances or situation or cast a reflection on a person's reputation or imply definite proof of association with the crime (see *W.S.*). In German **verwickeln** is the most common term, but these are others, particularly when it is a case of more or less fixed phrases.

Bevor der Krieg zu Ende ist, werden alle Nationen Europas in ihn verwickelt sein (W.S.).

Er war in eine unangenehme Sache verwickelt gewesen, die es ihm schwer machte, in die Stadt zurückzukehren (W.S.).

Der Fall eines Richters, der durch die Forderungen seines hohen Amtes in einen tiefen Konflikt zwischen seiner öffentlichen Pflicht und seinem persönlichen Interesse der Freundschaft verwickelt (stronger: *verstrickt*) *war.*

Er steckt tief in Schulden.

2. Sense of 'necessitate', 'entail', 'imply' (see 'imply'). Here common German terms are **voraussetzen** (i.e. presuppose), **mit sich bringen, zur Folge haben.**

Der Plan setzte einen Aufwand von vielen Millionen Dollar voraus.

Ein Auftrag, der viele Gefahren mit sich bringt, zur Folge hat.

3. The sense of 'contain', 'include' (see 'include') is closely related to **2.** In addition to 'mit sich bringen' German also uses **enthalten, umfassen, einschließen, mit einbegreifen.**

Die tragische Oper muß eine überzeugende Behandlung eines elementaren Konflikts umfassen (einschließen, enthalten) (W.).

Der Arbeitsplan einer Gemeinde, der sportliche, kulturelle und wirtschaftliche Kennzeichen umfasst (mit einbegreift).

4. To occupy (oneself) absorbingly: especially commit (oneself) emotionally—usually with 'in' or 'with' (*W.*). German **sich identifizieren mit, aufgehen in** (with dative), **sich einlassen mit jdm** (*in etwas*).

Er geht in seiner Arbeit auf.

Sie hatte nie die geringste Absicht, sich mit ihm einzulassen.

5. To have an effect on: concern directly, affect (*W.*). German, such terms as **betreffen** (concern, affect—see 'affect'), **in Anspruch nehmen** (to claim).

Biologische Prozesse wie das Atmen und die Verdauung nehmen den ganzen Körper in Anspruch (W.).

Arbeitseinstellungen betrafen mehr als 100.000 Arbeiter (W.).

6 'Involved' as adjective in sense of 'intricate': **kompliziert.**
Er schreibt sehr komplizierte Sätze.

ITEM There is no exact German term for 'item' except *Posten,* which, however, only corresponds to some of its uses; mostly approximations are used, which have English equivalents that are synonymous of 'item'.

1. Posten is an item on a list, particularly an item of expenditure. (An itemized account: *eine aufgeschlüsselte Rechnung.*) It refers particularly to wares in trade.
Alle Posten müssen angegeben werden.
Es fehlen ein paar Posten in Ihrem Verzeichnis der Waren.
Er erwähnte einen weiteren Posten des Einkommens.

2. An item on a program: **Nummer** (see also under 'number').
Die erste Nummer auf dem Programm des Konzerts.
Er sah diese Nummer, die blendend getanzt wurde (W.).

3. An item, i.e. piece, of news is simply: *eine Nachricht.*
Die Zeitungen haben heute morgen eine interessante Nachricht gebracht.
Eine Nachricht nach der anderen erreichte ihn, jede schrecklicher, als die vorhergehende.

4. Sense: something singled out from a specified or implied category of things of the same kind (*W.*). German **Artikel.**
Ein wichtiger Artikel des internationalen Handels.
Verschiedene Kleidungsartikel.
Große Mengen von Postartikeln.

5. Sense: something produced by manufacturing or manual labour in some other way: commodity (*W.*): German **Artikel, Gegenstand.**
Ein gut verkäuflicher Artikel, Gegenstand (W.).
Nur einige Artikel werden en gros verkauft.

6. Sense: an object of attention or concern or interest to a specified degree (*W.*). German: **Sache** or in the sense of detail: **Einzelheit.**
Eine sehr bedeutende Einzelheit (W.).
Der Garten ist eine wichtige Sache beim Kauf eines Hauses (Posten would suggest an item of expenditure).

7. A point under discussion or consideration, topic, subject, matter. **Punkt:** an item on an agenda. Otherwise **Sache.**
Es gibt zu viele Punkte auf der Tagesordnung.
Es gibt noch eine Sache, über die ich sprechen möchte.

8. A piece of writing (as an article, story, poem) usually short in length that forms a contributory part of a large work (as an anthology, reference book, periodical) (*W.*). German **Artikel** or **Gedicht, Kurzgeschichte** etc. if that is what is meant.
Er steuerte einen interessanten Artikel zu einer Gedenkschrift bei.

JOIN A. Of persons, to come into contact, association, etc.
1. German has no special term for 'join' with reference to social entertainment and the like.
Gehen wir zu den Damen hinüber.
Wir treffen uns in London (I'll join you...).[1]

---

[1] See 'meet'.

Ich treffe Sie zum Frühstück.

Setzen Sie sich zu uns (when seated).

Trinken Sie ein Glas Bier mit uns (see **A. 6**).

2. Beitreten: to join a club or a school as a teacher. In suggesting free association it differs from **eintreten**,[1] which implies more rigid compliance with a code of rules (particularly with reference to business and military organizations).

Er trat dem Verein bei.

Er trat der Schule als Hilfslehrer bei.

Er trat in den Verein ein.

Er trat in die Firma, ins Heer, in die Luftwaffe, ein.

3. Sich anschließen: to join a person or a group of persons with the purpose of doing something or going somewhere; also to associate oneself with the expression of a point of view (i.e. join in).

Schließen Sie sich der Reihe an (or: *an die Reihe;* the queue).

Er hat sich der Expedition angeschlossen.

Sie schlossen sich den Rebellen an.

Darf ich mich Ihnen anschließen? (e.g. on a walk, in some action).

Ich möchte mich dem Protest, Ihnen bei Ihrem P., anschließen.

4. Stoßen zu is used of joining a person after encountering difficulties (e.g. traversing difficult country).

Als wir ankamen, stieß eine Abteilung Kavallerie zu uns.

Er stieß zu uns auf den anderen Seite des Gebirges.

5. Zusteigen: to board a conveyance at a stopping place and so join people already there.

Er ist in Wannsee zugestiegen.

6. 'To join in' an activity can sometimes be translated by verbs with the prefix *mit*, particularly *mitmachen* (which has the extended sense of to be a party to a thing).

Wir müssen mitmachen.

Er macht den Ausflug, jeden Unsinn, mit.

Singen Sie mit.

Er lachte mit.

B. To put things together. The commonest terms are:

1. Fügen (*an...*, *zusammen...*): to make fit exactly, to dovetail, in order to make two things one.[2]

Er fügte die beiden Bretter aneinander, zusammen.

Versuchen Sie, die zerbrochenen Teile wieder zusammenzufügen.

2. Verbinden in some uses corresponds closely to 'connect', i.e. by some intermediary link, so that the two things retain their identity.[3]

---

[1] See 'enter'.   [2] See also 'add'.

[3] The main figurative uses of *verbinden* are: (*a*) to combine qualities (e.g. *Strenge mit einem Gerechtigkeitsgefühl v.*); (*b*) to combine substances chemically; (*c*) to associate in an emotional bond or as allies (e.g. *sie sind freundschaftlich miteinander verbunden*); (*d*) to associate mentally one thing with another (e.g. *ich verbinde keinen bösen Zweck mit seiner Bemerkung*); (*e*) of things, in passive with *sein* and followed by *mit*: to be associated with, involved in, bound up with (e.g. *mit Ihrem Vorschlag sind gewisse Vorteile, Gefahren, verbunden*); (*f*) followed by *zu* in the sense of to bind to an obligation; a rare use and weaker than *verpflichten*.

Binden is also used figuratively in the sense of 'to bind, tie down' someone to a thing,

JOIN

Die Zwei Häuser sind durch einen Gang verbunden.
Die wichtigen Städte sind durch erstklassige Autostraßen verbunden.
Der Hals verbindet Kopf und Körper.

3. **Vereinigen:** to 'unite' various units so that they function as one, but not necessarily in the sense of physical contiguity[1]. **Wiedervereinigung:** re-unification of parts of a country which has been divided.

Die britische und französische Flotte wurden im zweiten Weltkrieg unter einer Führung vereinigt.

4. **Zusammenlegen:** to unite in a whole things already joined, i.e. to remove the artificial dividing line.

Er legte die beiden Felder, Grundstücke, zusammen.

5. Examples of specific terms (formed with *zusammen*) are:

Sie nähte die Fetzen zusammen und machte ein Kleid daraus.
Die Wagen wurden zusammengekoppelt (or: *gekuppelt*).
Er hat die Seile zusammengeknotet.

C. Of things, to be, come, together.

Grenzen an (to border on), **stoßen an** (to adjoin) may be used of land and buildings lying side by side, **fließen** (or *münden in*) with reference to rivers.

Bei Basel grenzt Deutschland an die Schweiz.
Die Wiese grenzt, stößt, an dieser Stelle einen halben Kilometer lang an die Straße.

JUDGE   Sense: to form or to pronounce an opinion.[2]

1. **Urteilen** suggests an expert or at least highly qualified judge, and therefore a thorough study of the matter judged. Both the matter examined and the formulation of the judgment are mostly weighty. Modification by an adverb which denotes the opposite of an intensive study is, however, possible in order to indicate that the judgment is contrary to what should be (e.g. *er urteilt oberflächlich*). It is followed by *über* to render the transitive use of 'judge'.

Goethe urteilte sehr hart über die Romantiker.
Er urteilt sehr ruhig, sehr klar.
Nach seinem Erfolg zu urteilen, muß er ein tüchtiger Mann sein (the reference to the judge is less audible in this expression).
Wie urteilt er über die Lage?

with the implication of restricting his free movement. 'To' here is normally *an* (e.g. *an einen Eid binden, an eine Aufgabe binden*).

Verknüpfen indicates a closer connection than *verbinden*. When applied to thought, it therefore denotes a logical connection, not a casual association (e.g. *logisch verknüpfte Gedanken*).

'Connect' and 'combine' are often translated by compounds with *zusammen*. *Zusammentun* and *zusammenstellen* suggest the gathering together of various things into a heap. *Zusammensetzen* suggests the fitting together of parts so that they function as a whole while retaining their separate identity (e.g. to connect parts of machinery, to combine classes of a school, units of an army).

[1] Distinguish *vereinigen* from *einigen*, which means 'to unite' in the sense of 'unify', i.e. 'to make a true whole of the parts, to integrate', not merely 'to bring separate things together' (e.g. *ein geeinigtes Volk*). See also 'agree'.

[2] To judge in a court of law: *richten*. Followed by an adjective and an infinitive in the sense of 'deem', 'consider', it must be translated by equivalents of the latter. See article.

168

2. Beurteilen differs from *urteilen* in that it does not draw attention to the qualifications of the judge. The opinion may be that of the man on the street. Neither weightiness in formulation of the judgment nor in the matter judged is necessarily implied. On the other hand, attention is concentrated on the judgment, i.e. not on the judge as with *urteilen*. This is particularly noticeable in questions beginning with *wie*. Intransitive use is possible when it is accompanied by an adverb of manner. 'To criticize' is a common rendering and clearly shows the reference to the merits or defects of a thing.

Goethe beurteilte die Romantiker sehr hart.

Er beurteilt alles sehr ruhig, sehr klar.

Wie beurteilt er die Lage?

Er hat die Aufführung günstig beurteilt.

JUST **1.** (a) The most common meaning is 'exactly', and when this sense is clearly and emphatically required German uses **genau**.

Er hat genau das verlangt.

Er kam genau zur verabredeten Zeit.

Er ist genau so groß wie sein Vater.

(b) **Eben** and **gerade** are close synonyms of *genau*. As an adjective *eben* means 'even' as applied to a surface, on the same level as other objects in the same plane (and in M.H.G. and early N.H.G. 'appropriate'). *Gerade* as an adjective originally meant 'quick', 'dexterous', 'long' and passed through the meaning of 'slim' to that of 'straight', i.e. the opposite of 'crooked' (see H. Paul, revised by W. Betz).

The two are often used indiscriminately in the sense under discussion. The distinction, when made, is that *eben* presents a thing as clear, obvious, expected, and so often comes close to the meaning of 'in fact', 'the fact is that...'. while *gerade* can suggest the unexpected, the dramatic and so is more emphatic. The sense of chance, coincidence, which it also has, is related to that of the unexpected. The distinction between the two terms is seen clearly in comparisons, *eben* being the normal and *gerade* the emphatic term.

Ich werde eben (gerade) das tun, was Sie von mir verlangen.

Da kommt er eben (gerade would heighten the sense of coincidence or of the unexpected).

Wir waren eben (gerade) beim Frühstück, als wir einen Schuß hörten.

Das ist gerade richtig, das Richtige (eben would suggest that there were doubts but that it turned out to be right).

(Ja) eben (just so!).

Das ist gerade nicht der Fall (emphatic, while *eben* would suggest that there is no intention of doing anything about it).

Er wohnt mir gerade gegenüber (straight, right, opposite; *eben* not possible here).

Er ist ebenso begabt wie sein Bruder (gerade so is more emphatic).

Sie müssen es eben hinnehmen (accept it as a fact).

2. Sense: with little to spare. Here 'just' is sometimes preceded by 'only'. German uses **gerade noch**, which puts the situation positively, i.e. that there is still a little, even if not much, to spare. Also **knapp**, which stresses more the negative, i.e. barely, hardly, certainly no more than. (*Knapp* also, as a synonym of *eng* means 'tight' of clothes and the like, in which the meaning of nothing to spare is clearly visible; further: in short supply, of goods.) It is used frequently, but by no means exclusively, with **expressions of time**.

Man kann sagen, daß er gerade noch lebt.
Das Buch geht gerade noch (knapp) in die Tasche.
Wir haben den Zug gerade noch erreicht.
Ich habe es gerade noch geschafft.
Er war vor knapp einer Stunde da.
Vor knapp 30 Jahren ist der zweite Weltkrieg ausgebrochen.
Die Aufführung dauerte knapp 4 Stunden (no more than).
Er wohnt knapp ein Kilometer von hier (no more than).
Er hatte knapp Platz zum Stehen (barely).

3. Sense: 'no more than', 'only'. A sense related to **2** but without suggestion of a margin. German: **nur, bloß.**

Bloß ein paar Zeilen, um Sie ins Bild zu setzen.
Er hat es nur zum Spaß gesagt (or: *eben nur, eben* meaning 'the fact is that...').

4. In a temporal sense.
(a) Right now, at this very moment: **gerade jetzt.**

Tun Sie es gerade jetzt.

(b) Sense: recently, a minute ago etc. Often in English 'just now'. **Gerade, eben, soeben. Eben erst** implies that the action was not earlier as may have been thought.

Er ist gerade (eben, soeben) angekommen.
Der Präsident hat den Botschafter erst eben empfangen.
Sie haben eben erst geheiratet und schon ist das erste Kind da.

5. With an imperative or an implied imperative. **Mal** softens the peremptory nature of the imperative. **Doch** persuades in the face of opposition real or felt. **Nur** (or *bloß*) presents the order as urgent.

(Einen) Augenblick mal, bitte! (just a second!).
Schauen Sie mal hin.
Kommen Sie mal her.
Setzen Sie sich doch (or together: *doch mal*) *einen Augenblick.*
Hören Sie ihm doch mal zu.
Gehen Sie nur (just be off).
Kommen Sie nur nicht spät.

6. With an expression of intention (often the future tense) the effect is to make this sound more modest or casual. German uses **mal.**

Ich will mal fragen, ob die helfen können.
Ich möchte erst mal den Brief zu Ende lesen, bevor ich ein Urteil über den Vorschlag abgebe.

7. Absolutely, indicating that the statement or word (often an adjective) is to be understood as an extreme. English often uses in this sense 'positively', 'simply' as well as 'just'. German: **geradezu** or **einfach** (i.e. simply) (the latter is common with a negative).

Die Forderung ist geradezu grotesk.
Die Aufführung war geradezu genial.
Ich halte es einfach nicht länger aus.
Es ist einfach unmöglich.

8. Slang use with the effect of an intensive. German: **na und ob.**
Did he swear? Didn't he just!
Hat er geflucht? Na und ob!

KEEP, MAINTAIN, PRESERVE 1. Retain in one's possession, custody or control: **behalten** (literally or figuratively).

Sie können das Buch behalten.

Er hat seinen einfachen religiösen Glauben behalten.

Ich kann ihn nicht länger in meinem Büro behalten.

Sir wird das Kind für einen Monat im Hause behalten.

Behalten Sie Platz.

Er kann so viele Regeln nicht im Kopf behalten.

2. Preserve from decay, deterioration, destruction, maintain alive (for this sense when followed by an adverb or adverbial phrase of manner see next section).

Erhalten can, but need not, suggest active measures to ensure preservation, but, as it points to the result, use in the reflexion and in the passive is more common. It is used mainly with persons and things subject to decay, deterioration, destruction, but also with inner possessions. **Wahren** suggests watching over, guarding, an attitude of preparedness to take action if necessary. It is a more elevated term than *bewahren*. **Bewahren** is less active, meaning no more than 'not to lose'. Only *bewahren*, however, can be followed by *vor* in the sense of 'preserve from', even when activity is implied. Both *wahren* and *bewahren* convey the idea of preserving something regarded as precious, particularly inner possessions or concrete objects regarded as such.

Gott erhalte den König!

Die meisten Gebäude sind im diesem Stadtviertel erhalten geblieben.

Nur eine einzige Handschrift des Werkes ist uns erhalten geblieben.

Sie müssen versuchen, sein Interesse zu erhalten.

Trotz allen Mißgeschicks hat er sich seinen Humor erhalten.

Erhalten Sie sich Ihren Humor, was immer kommen mag.

Erhalte mir deine Freundschaft (actively).

Diese Sitten haben sich jahrhundertelang erhalten.

Völker Europas, wahret eure heiligsten Güter! (but: *bewahret...vor dem Verfall*).

Sie wahrt ihre Tugend.

In einer schwierigen Situation hat er seine Würde, seine Ehre, den Anstand, gewahrt.

Wahren Sie dieses Geheimnis.

Er hat seine Passivität bewahrt.

Er hat seinen Humor bewahrt (simply: not lost it).

Er hat sein Gleichgewicht bewahrt.

Er hat seine Fassung, Haltung, bewahrt.

Bewahre mir deine Freundschaft (don't forget me).

Bewahren Sie dieses Geheimnis (don't talk).

Unsere Vernunft bewahrt uns vor dem Irrtum.

Sein Rat bewahrte uns davor, uns lächerlich zu machen.

3. With an adverb or adverbial phrase indicating condition.

Erhalten should only be used in the sense of keeping alive, preserving from decay and the like. It draws attention to the result. Otherwise **halten**[1] must be used in the sense of 'to keep in a state, at a level' (but see section **4**). *Erhalten*, however, is sometimes found where good usage requires *halten* (e.g. *seine Leistungen auf einem hohen Niveau erhalten*, instead of the more

---

[1] See under 'last' for a closely related meaning.

correct *halten*). *Erhalten* is also used with the phrase *in einem...Zustand*, whereas only *halten* is possible with the simple adverb (e.g. *frisch halten* but *in frischem Zustand erhalten*). **Bewahren** suggests an absence of effort, nature often being the cause which keeps a person or thing in the given condition. Preserved fruit: *eingekochtes Obst*.

Halten replaces *erhalten* in the imperative and in rapid questions in the meaning of the latter.

Wir müssen ihn am Leben erhalten.

Das Haus ist gut erhalten (preserved from decay).

Die Blumen wurden frisch erhalten (but: *Halten Sie mir die Blumen frisch, in frischem Zustand*).

Österreichs Grenzen müssen unversehrt erhalten werden.

Ich habe die Erinnerung an dich ungetrübt erhalten.

Er hat die Tradition seiner Familie unverfälscht erhalten (or *gehalten*, a border-line case).

Sie hat ihre Figur, ihr Aussehen, gut, jugendlich, erhalten.

Die Straßen dieser Stadt werden in gehörigem Stand erhalten (or: *gehalten*). (*Instandhaltung:* maintenance of streets etc.)

Das Haus ist gut gehalten (clean, tidy).

Sie hielt ihm sein Essen warm.

Die Regierung hat das Volk in völliger Unwissenheit gehalten.

Der Eisschrank hält das Fleisch frisch (but: *erhält in frischem Zustand*).

Er hat seine Ausgaben niedrig gehalten.

Halten Sie sich den Mittwoch frei.

Der Bericht hat uns in Spannung gehalten.

Er hat sein Gewissen, seine Seele, rein gehalten (*bewahrt*) (less correctly: *erhalten*).

Sie hat ihre jugendliche Figur, ihr jugendliches Aussehen, gut bewahrt.

4. Keep (up), maintain (in synonymous use). An extension of section 3.

To keep up or to maintain at a certain standard, level: **aufrechterhalten**. In this combination the simple verb *halten* is uncommon.

Das Niveau (standard), *die Moral* (morale), *das Interesse* (or *erhalten* alone, i.e. to keep alive), *die Ordnung, die Disziplin, die Blockade, die Beziehungen, den Frieden, ein mörderisches Feuer, stundenlang aufrechterhalten.*

When 'keep (up)', 'maintain' suggest no more than 'carrying on', 'having', 'keeping going', without particular effort, **unterhalten** must be used (to maintain, support a family: see 11). It is also applied in this sense to the maintenance, the keeping in order of streets, parks, and the like.

Ein Gespräch, einen Briefwechsel, Beziehungen (little more than 'have'), *ein Feuer* (merely keep from going out) *unterhalten; gut unterhaltene Straßen.*

5. To keep in, not to remove from, a place or position.

(a) When 'keep' implies effort, however slight, **halten** is used. In this sense it also translates 'hold'[1] with which it is practically interchangeable.

Er hielt seine Hände in den Taschen.

Halten Sie die Hände hoch.

Halten Sie den Finger auf diese Stelle.

Er hielt den Fuß gegen die Tür.

---

[1] The figurative uses of 'hold' rarely correspond to those of *halten*. The compound *abhalten* means 'to hold' a function (e.g. *eine Versammlung, eine Parade, eine Prüfung*). Often *haben* must be used (e.g. *Ansichten*).

Er hielt die Gefangenen in einem kleinen Saal.
Ich rate Ihnen, sich ihn vom Leibe zu halten.
Die Rebellen wurden durch Maschinengewehrfeuer ferngehalten.

(b) When it is necessary to distinguish between 'keep' and 'hold', the former must be translated by **behalten** (e.g. with clothing and in figurative senses).

Er behielt den Hut auf dem Kopf (hield = held).
Behalten Sie Ihren Mantel an.
Das werde ich im Auge behalten.

(c) When no activity is implied **lassen** (really short for: *sein, bleiben lassen;* see 'leave') must be used.

Wir ließen das Verdunklungspapier während des ganzen Krieges auf den Fenstern.
Ich werde Ihren Namen auf der Liste lassen (or: stehen lassen).
Sie müssen die Tür offen lassen (halten = hold).
Wir können es uns nicht leisten, den Jungen noch länger in der Schule zu lassen.
Wir lassen nachts die Fenster immer auf.

6. To keep a thing in a place where it is normally stored or housed: **halten**. This sense should be carefully distinguished from that of 'have available', a sense which mentions the place incidentally (see **7**).

Wir halten die Teller in diesem Schrank.
Ich halte mein Geld immer im Schreibtisch.
Wir halten den Hund nachts in der Waschküche (or: sperren).

7. To keep something for use or pleasure sometimes with incidental mention of the place.

(a) When expense is implied, **sich** (*etwas*) **halten** is used, mostly with servants, animals, vehicles.

Wir können uns nur einen Diener halten.
Er hält sich einen Hund, zwei Pferde und einen Wagen.

(b) When little or no activity is implied, only **haben** is possible. *Immer* or an equivalent is generally added.

Ich habe immer Geld im Hause.
Ich habe immer ein Wörterbuch auf meinem Schreibtisch.
Um nicht von Einbrechern überrascht zu werden, habe ich immer einen Revolver in meiner Nähe.
Wir haben ständig ein Thermometer auf der offenen Veranda.

8. To keep safe, with mention of the place.

Both **bewahren** and **verwahren** refer to things considered as valuables and mean 'to keep (them) in a safe place'. They are thus distinguished from *halten*, which suggests neither valuables nor the safety of the place. *Verwahren* is the stronger of the two and can imply 'under lock and key', for which reason it cannot be used with a person or an animal. It is most common in the past participle after *sein* and with some adverb such as *gut*.

Wo bewahren Sie Ihre Geldscheine, Ihr Geld, Ihre silbernen Teller (but: wo halten Sie Ihr Kleingeld, Ihre Teller)?
Ihre Wertpapier, Juwelen, sind in meinem Schrank gut verwahrt.

9. To keep a thing which is to be called for later: **aufbewahren**.

This need not refer to valuables. It suggests a relatively short period.

KEEP

Note the phrase: (*Gepäck*) *in Aufbewahrung geben* (at luggage rooms on railway stations and the like). A safe place is implied, even if not stated.

Ich kann Ihre Wertsachen für Sie aufbewahren, während Sie verreist sind.
Wollen Sie mir diese Bücher eine Zeitlang aufbewahren?
Bewahren Sie uns etwas warmes Essen (im Ofen) auf.

10. To keep, to reserve for later use, save up (i.e. not to use, throw away): **aufheben.** (For another meaning see under 'cancel'.)

This meaning is also expressed by *aufbewahren* (see last section), the distinction being that with *aufbewahren* the idea of place is important, while *aufheben* stresses that of not using or losing at the moment, and does not imply that the place, if mentioned, is of consequence.

Die Mutter versprach, dem Kind etwas Kuchen aufzuheben.
Heben Sie mir meine Ringe auf.
Sie hat ihm sein Essen (im Eisschrank) aufgehoben.
Den zweiten Band dieses Romans hebe ich mir für später auf (since place is not implied, *aufbewahren* would sound unnatural).
Ich hebe mir meinen Urlaub für nächstes Jahr auf.

11. Maintain, support, provide for (with the necessities of life).

Unterhalten: to support the person one is normally expected to support, without undue strain. It is a close synonym of *ennähren.* **Erhalten:** to support as an additional burden.

Er muß eine zahlreiche Familie unterhalten.
Er unterhält seine Familie in einer gradezu luxuriösen Weise.
Er hat drei Kinder seines Bruders, eine kranke Schwester zu erhalten.

12. To keep a person, oneself in a commodity. Use must be made of the various verbs meaning 'to provide' (see under this term).

Der Junge sorgt für seine eigenen Kleider.

13. To abide by laws, rules, agreements.

Halten: to keep, in general. **Einhalten:** to keep, with regard to details. With a general term such as *Vertrag, halten* is used. If details are implied by some word such as *Einzelheiten, genau, strikt, einhalten* is necessary. In some case either term is possible according to the point of view.

Er hat den Vertrag, sein Wort, seinen Eid, die Gesetze, die Gebote gehalten.
Er hat jede Bestimmung des Vertrages, alle Paragraphen der Gesetze einge-halten.
Er hat alle Vorschriften genau eingehalten.
Er hat zwei Drittel seines Versprechens gehalten (or: *eingehalten*).

14. To keep a line of goods: **führen** (e.g. *Kämme, die Frankfurter Zeitung*).

15. To keep accounts, a diary, etc.: **führen** (e.g. *ein Tagebuch*).

16. To keep, run, a business, shop: **betreiben** suggests activity (cf. 'run'), otherwise **haben** (e.g. *er betreibt zwei blühende Lebensmittelgeschäfte*).

17. To detain: **halten,** which is normally followed by an adverb of place. If emphasis is desired: **festhalten** or **aufhalten** (hold up, delay). (To keep in at school, i.e. detention: *nachsitzen lassen*.)

Die Mutter hat ihn zu Hause gehalten.
Die Gefangenen sind Monate lang in Ketten gehalten worden.
Ich will Sie nicht länger aufhalten.
Er ist durch Geschäfte hier festgehalten worden.

Nichts kann mich länger in England festhalten.
Ich habe Sie zu lange (fest)gehalten (aufgehalten).

KILL A. Literal.

1. Töten.

(a) With a personal subject and object *töten* is much less used than 'kill'. It mostly suggests savagery, even butchery, but not what is legally known as murder. With a personal object it is rarely used in the first person. It occurs in the following ways:

(i) In elevated language and with reference to the gods and the like.

'*Du sollst nicht töten*' (biblical).
Die Götter töteten ihren Liebling.

(ii) With reference to accidents in which many are killed; particularly with scuffles, collisions, blows and the like.

Er wurde bei einem Straßenkrawall getötet.
In meiner Wut packte ich ihn an der Gurgel, und fand zu meinem Entsetzen, daß ich ihn getötet hatte.
Bei dem Eisenbahnunglück sind 40 Menschen getötet worden.

(iii) Deliberately, with reference to a threat which may be legal (e.g. in self-protection). In this sense it is mostly intransitive and used as an infinitive of purpose.

Ich schieße mit der Absicht zu töten.

(iv) Deliberately, with reference to mercy killings.

Er tötene seine Frau, um sie von ihren entsetzlichen Leiden zu befreien.

(b) To kill a person by one's behaviour and the like.

Er hat seine Frau durch seine Herzlosigkeit getötet.

(c) With a thing or a feeling, habit, etc., as subject.

Das Trinken, das Gift, der Kummer, ein Schlag des Propellers, hat ihn getötet.

2. Other renderings. These occur with a personal subject and object.

(a) **Ermorden** must be used with any act officially classified as murder (see 'murder').

(b) **Umbringen** is used of acts of violence which may or may not be murder. It is not a legal term for 'murder'. It denotes intention and is only used of persons.

Er hat seine Frau in einer eifersüchtigen Anwandlung umgebracht.
Sie haben ihre Gefangenen umgebracht.
Der Vater brachte seine Tochter um, weil er sie nicht entehrt sehen wollte.
Er brachte sich um, als ihm klar wurde, daß er gefoltert werden würde.

(c) **Totschlagen** suggests violence of feeling and of act, normally a blow from a heavy instrument. At times, e.g. in poetry, violence in general is suggested, not necessarily a heavy instrument.

Er hat ihn mit einem Hammer totgeschlagen.
Ich lasse mich totschlagen, bevor ich so was unterzeichne.
'*Schlagt ihn tot! das Weltgericht*
Fragt euch nach den Gründen nicht.' (Kleist, *Die Hermannsschlacht*).

(d) **Umkommen:** to be killed in an accident, in which a person and a thing, often a means of conveyance, are involved.

Er ist in einem Eisenbahnunglück umgekommen.

(e) **Fallen** must be used, even in conversation, in the sense of 'to be killed on the field of battle'.

Drei von seinen Söhnen sind in Afrika gefallen.

(f) **Den Tod finden** is used in official statements and in 'journalese' in the sense of 'to be killed accidentally'. Compare 'to meet one's death'.

Bei einem Autozusammenstoß fand er den Tod.

(g) Often it is preferable to use specific terms such as: *erschießen; erdolchen; zu Tode prügeln, quetschen.*

B. Figurative.

Töten is used in the sense of killing anything which has vitality (e.g. feelings), also in a number of idioms (but less widely than 'kill').

Das hat alle Hoffnung, mein Interesse, das Stück, getötet.

Er tötet die Zeit mit Gartenarbeit.

KIND, SPECIES, SORT, TYPE[1] 1. **Art[2]** primarily means 'species', i.e. a subdivision of a 'genus',[3] and translates 'kind', when the latter is a close synonym of 'species'. Like 'kind', though not to the same extent, it has been extended to denote mere similarity, being applied to inanimate objects and to actions, states and the like as well as to living structures. The plural *Arten* rarely has the looser sense. In the singular note particularly the following loose uses: *eine Art von* (i.e. something like); *so eine Art von; aller Art* (genitive; i.e. of all kinds); *in dieser Art.*

Difficulties in the plural, 'kinds'. *Pflanzen aller Art*: all manner of plants, plants of every kind. *Pflanzen aller Arten*: of all species. *Alle Arten von Pflanzen waren in seiner Sammlung vertreten*: all species.... *Allerlei[4] Pflanzen waren*...all kinds, sorts of ....

Difficulties in the singular. The loose uses of 'kind' are rendered by the following terms (amongst others): *solch, so ein, derartig, so etwas, was für ein.* E.g. this kind of rain, wind.

'*Die Entstehung der Arten*' (the origin of species).

Welche Art Baum ist das? (what species...?).

Was für ein Baum ist das? (what kind, sort...?).

Menschen aller Art.

Menschen aller Arten (white, negroes, etc.).

Diese Art Vogel ist mir unbekannt.

Diese Art Männer haben Deutschland ins Unglück gebracht.

Diese Art Bücher lese ich sehr gerne.

Ich mag diese Art Kuchen, Menschen, nicht.

Das ist eine Art Kuchen.

Er fühlte eine besondere Art Besorgnis.

Sie hat eine Art Kranz geflochten.

'*Es gibt sehr verschiedene Arten Einsamkeit*' (F. Gundolf, *Heinrich von Kleist*).

Das Bild ist vollkommen in seiner Art.

Einen solchen Regen haben die Bauern gern (that's the kind of rain...).

Ein solcher Wind macht einen verrückt (that, this kind of wind...).

---

[1] *Schlag* is used as a vigorous term for 'kind', 'stamp' (e.g. *Menschenschlag*), and particularly in the genitive case (e.g. *Leute seines Schlages*).

[2] See also 'way'.

[3] *Gattung* = genus.

[4] *Allerhand* means 'many and varied' and stresses subjectively the idea of number.

Und Sie wollen sich so einen langweiligen Menschen anhören!
Ich habe so eine Idee, daß....
So einer ist er! (that's the kind, sort, of person he is!).
So etwas kann ich nicht ausstehen.
Etwas derartiges meine ich!
Allerlei Kunst- und Kitschgegenstände standen auf dem Kaminsims.

2. Sorte is limited to two uses. (*a*) It is applied to things, particularly food, in so far as they are bought and sold. (*b*) It is a term of contempt applied particularly to persons.

Sie verkaufen die besten Obstsorten.
Diese Sorte Bücher sollte man nicht lesen.
Diese Sorte Menschen liegt mir gar nicht.
Das ist eine furchtbare Menschensorte.

3. Typ, Typus (plural of both: *Typen*).

The distinction between these two forms, both of which mean 'type', is that the former is looser and more familiar, the latter more scientific. *Typ* is, however, frequently used in reference to a particular model of a thing.

Er ist ein preußischer Typ.
'*Guter Typ des Wirtschaftskapitäns seiner Generation*' (reference to Bosch in U. von Hassel's *Vom Anderen Deutschland*).
'*Der Typus des dämonischen Müssers*' (reference to Kleist in F. Gundolf's work on that poet).
'*Der dritte Typus ist ja der Typus dieser Gotik, der erste der Typus des klassisch-antiken Menschen, des Lateiners*' (O. Walzel, *Gehalt und Gestalt im dichterischen Kunstwerk*).
Das ist ein ganz verschiedener Strukturtypus.
Ein neuer Wagentyp (model).

KIND, KINDLY 1. Gütig means 'kindly' (i.e. in inner disposition) rather than 'kind' (i.e. in act) and refers to the manner of oldish people and to young women who have something motherly about them. It can also be applied to the powers that influence human life, e.g. fate. As a polite, almost over-deferential, formula, it occurs in the phrase: *Seien Sie so gütig...*, and as a superlative adverb in requests (e.g. *wollen Sie gütigst...?*).

Ein gütiger alter Herr.
'*Was soll der gütige Blick, mit dem sie mich oft...ansieht*' (Goethe, *Werthers Leiden*, applied to Lotte).
Ein gütiges Schicksal.

2. When 'kind' is followed by 'to' or 'towards', or by the infinitive (e.g. be so kind as to...) it is translated by **gut, freundlich, liebenswürdig**. The last two are also used in polite formulas.

Er ist sehr gut zu seiner Mutter.
Bitte seien Sie so freundlich, dieses Paket für mich auf die Post zu tragen.
Ich danke Ihnen für Ihre freundlich Einladung, Ihre freundlichen Worte.
Wollen Sie so liebenswürdig sein und mir das Buch leihen?
Das war sehr liebenswürdig von Ihnen.

3. When 'kind' is not followed by 'to' or 'towards' or used in a polite phrase, it is generally best rendered by **gutherzig**. As the meaning of *liebenswürdig* has been watered down by its use in conventional expressions, it mostly lacks the full sense of 'kind'.

Ein gutherziger Mensch.
Er ist sehr gutherzig.

KNOW[1] **1. Kennen:** to be acquainted, familiar, with a person or thing. Direct experience and retention in the memory of the distinguishing marks of the person or thing are implied. **Wissen:** to be aware (of), to have information (of), as a fact. While *wissen* does not exclude experience, it must be used whenever knowledge is conceived of as fact, therefore before a following *daß* clause and the like (e.g. *ich weiß aus Erfahrung, daß...*).

Wissen is in ordinary prose followed by a noun in the accusative case only when this refers to something intangible (e.g. *Ich weiß ein Mittel, wie...*), but not to a person or an object.[2] In reference to the latter, 'to know' in the sense of 'to know of' must be *wissen von*.

Neither *kennen* nor *wissen* is used in the passive voice. In this construction **bekannt** has the meanings of both *kennen* and *wissen*.[3] It can also mean 'well-known' without the addition of *wohl*.

Ich kenne den Mann, den Ort, die Musik.
Ich kenne das Gedicht auswendig.
Ich kenne seine Launen, seine Ansichten.
Er kennt keine Grenzen.
Er kennt die Geschichte des 17. Jahrhunderts sehr gut.
Ich weiß nicht, worauf Sie hinaus wollen.
Das weiß ich ganz genau.
Ich weiß ein gutes Mittel gegen Rheumatismus.
Ich weiß von einem Hotel, wo man Sie bestimmt unterbringen kann.
Der Mann ist mir schon lange bekannt.
Er ist ein bekannter Schriftsteller.
Es ist bekannt, daß die beiden sich nicht vertragen.

2. 'To know how to' is translated by *wissen, wie...sollen*, when knowledge of a method is implied. *Wissen* followed by *zu* and the infinitive refers rather to an innate capacity and often approximates to 'can'.[4]

Ich weiß nicht, wie man mit ihm fertig werden soll.
Er weiß zu schweigen, wenn es nötig ist.
Er weiß sich nicht zu beherrschen.

3. For **erkennen** used in the sense of 'know' see 'recognize'.

4. 'To know' an academic subject of study is **können,** in so far as the use of it is implied, particularly for examination purposes. It is most common in reference to a language, since in this case use is generally meant. In the sense of 'to be familiar with' *kennen*, however, is used.

Er kann Deutsch, nicht viel Deutsch.
Er kann nicht viel Geschichte.
Er kennt die deutsche Sprache gründlich.

---

[1] See also 'knowledge'.

[2] It is sometimes used without a noun object somewhat poetically or in reference to something remote or mysterious. *Ich weiß einen schönen Platz, Ort, wo...; ich weiß ein Haus im Walde.*

[3] *Bewußt* is also used with an impersonal subject and the dative of the person in the sense of 'to be aware', and particularly to emphasize that one is not unaware of a fact. *Es ist mir ja bewußt, daß er solche Absichten hegt.* With a personal subject and the dative of the person *bewußt* means 'to be conscious' of a thing. *Er ist sich seiner Schuld bewußt.*

[4] See also 'appreciate'.

5. When 'know' is followed by the accusative and the infinitive in the sense of 'to come at some time within one's experience that...', it must be translated by **erleben, daß**... (see 'experience').

Ich habe es niemals erlebt, daß er zu viel verlangt hätte (I have never known him to...).

6 Sich auskennen in: to know one's way about, both in a place and in a field of study. **Bescheid wissen:**[1] to know all about a matter and to know one's way about in a place.

Er kennt sich in der Stadt, in der Geschichte Spaniens, aus.
Ich weiß Bescheid über seine Pläne.
Ich weiß Bescheid in der Stadt.

KNOWLEDGE 1. Kenntnis (singular) is used in the sense of 'cognizance, awareness', of a specific fact. It occurs mainly in set phrases.

Ich spreche mit voller Kenntnis von dem, was geschehen ist.

2. Kenntnisse (plural) suggests detailed knowledge (i.e. pieces, items of knowledge) of (*a*) any specified matter, whether of ordinary matters or in a branch of learning; (*b*) unspecified general knowledge. It must be used in the sense of (*a*) to translate 'knowledge' followed by a genetive.

Seine Kenntnisse der russischen Sprache reichen nicht sehr weit.
Seine Kenntnisse des Dramas zeigen viele Lücken auf.
Er hat ungeheure Kenntnisse.

3. Wissen means 'general knowledge or awareness', but unlike *Kenntnisse* does not strongly suggest items of knowledge. It can be interchanged with *Kenntnisse* when not followed by a phrase denoting a specific matter or field of knowledge. When such a specific matter or field is stated, *Wissen* cannot be followed by the genitive. *In* and such phrases as *auf dem Gebeit* are common. When followed by *von* and *um* intimate or secret knowledge is implied. *Wissen* must be used in general statements about the nature and purpose of knowledge.

Er hat ein ungeheures Wissen.
Sein Wissen auf dem Gebiet des Dramas hat viele Lücken.
Sein Wissen von dem Mord.
Sein Wissen um Gott.
Wissen ist Macht.
Wissen ist ein mächtiges Werkzeug.

4. Erkenntnis: philosophical, scientific knowledge, i.e. of the real nature of things.

Die Erkenntnistheorie (epistemology).
Diese Betrachtungsweise besitzt keinen Erkenntniswert.
Auf diesem Wege wird er kaum zur Erkenntnis des Wesens der Kunst gelangen.

LACK[2] **1. Fehlen** denotes the complete absence of a thing. In the sense of 'lack' its subject can only be impersonal.[3] When the thing lacking is put

---

[1] *Bescheid*, which is mostly used in fixed phrases, means 'information' (e.g. *ich sagte ihm Bescheid*), or 'official notification' (e.g. *ich erhielt Bescheid von dem Auswärtigen Amt*).
[2] In a few phrases *entbehren* followed by the genitive means 'to lack' something considered necessary. *Das Gerücht entbehrt jeder Grundlage. Lie entbehrt jeden Reizes.* With the accusative case and a personal subject the sense is 'to do without', 'to dispense with', often with the idea of suffering privations. See also 'spare'.
[3] *Du fehlst mir* = I miss you (see 'miss'). *Er fehlt* = he is absent.

in the nominative case, the lack is thought of in relation to a specific purpose.[1]
Thus *mir fehlt Geld* is practically equivalent to *das nötige Geld* and expresses
this specific reference. If, however, the thing occurs in the dative case preceded by *an*, the lack is conceived as more general, i.e. with no implication
of a specific purpose. In practice, the two are often interchanged.

Ihm fehlt die nötige Erfahrung, eine solche Anstalt zu leiten.
Es fehlt ihm noch an Erfahrung.
Es fehlt ihm der Mut dazu.
Es fehlt ihm an Mut.
Es fehlt ihm die Kraft, sich weiter zu schleppen (*an Kraft* also possible, but
less correct).

> *'Den Köchen tut kein Mangel wehe;*
> *Wildschweine, Hirsche, Hasen, Rehe,...*
> *Sie gehen noch so ziemlich ein,*
> *Jedoch am Ende fehlt's an Wein.'*   (*Faust II*, ll. 4856 ff.)

2. Mangeln expresses not complete absence, but a deficiency, whether in
quantity or quality. In present-day German the thing is put in the dative
case preceded by *an*, its occurrence in the nominative is obsolete or confined
to poetry and archaic style.[2]

Es mangelt mir an Geld.
Es mangelt ihm an Takt.

3. Ermangeln denotes, like *mangeln*, a deficiency, but implies more strongly
that a serious view is taken of it.[3] It is hardly used in conversation or everyday
prose. It is followed by the genitive of the thing lacking.[4]

Seine Worte ermangelten der Überzeugungskraft.

LAST   1. Dauern suggests primarily that the duration of a thing or an
action is due to its nature. In reference to the durability of things[5] it is used
in the following ways.

(a) Of things that 'endure' because of their spiritual qualities, although they
may be subject to physical destruction.

Die Werte der Kunst werden ewig dauern.
Ihre Freundschaft hat nicht lange gedauert.

(b) Of things that are subject to decay, particularly those conceived as
having life, or in reference to the 'season' of flowers and fruits.

Die Blumen haben nicht lange gedauert.
Die Apfelsinen haben dieses Jahr bis in den Sommer hinein gedauert.

(c) Of things that withstand the ravages of time in so far as long periods are
meant.

Eine gute Lederhose dauert ein Leben lang.
Moderne Häuser dauern nicht wie die aus früheren Zeiten.

---

[1] With this construction the meaning can also be 'to miss' in the sense of 'to notice the
absence of a thing'. *Mir fehlen 2 Pfund* (I had them before).

[2] Examples: (i) '*Der Herr ist mein Hirt, mir wird nichts mangeln*' (Luther, Psalm xxiii. 1).
(ii)   '*Wenn sie den Stein der Weisen hätten,*
                        Der Weise mangelte dem Stein.'   (*Faust II*, ll. 5063–4.)

[3] Its most characteristic use is therefore to express a determination not to be found
wanting with regard to an obligation, i.e. when followed by an infinitive in the sense of
'fail' (see 'fail').

[4] *Mangeln* with the genitive is obsolete. '*Sie sind allzumal Sünder und mangeln des
Ruhmes.*' (Luther, Romans iii. 23.)

[5] *Dauerhaft*: lasting, enduring.

(d) In reference to the consumption of commodities *dauern* should only be used when the dwindling of supplies or of a heap is implied, i.e. not with single objects (e.g. a pair of shoes).

Die Kohlen, die Lebensmittelvorräte, müssen einen ganzen Monat dauern.

(e) Applied to activities, *dauern* can imply that these, because of their character, take, require a certain time.[1]

Der Vortrag dauerte zwei Stunden.

Der Ausbildungskursus dauert ein Jahr.

Die Probezeit hat 6 Monate gedauert.

(f) It can refer to a period of time the limits of which have been fixed.

Wir lange dauert Ihr Urlaub?

(g) Finally, it is used of the mere passing of time, in the sense of 'go on', without the activity requiring the stated time. This is the only meaning of the less common **währen**.

Der Lärm dauerte, währte bis Tagesanbruch.

Die Mahlzeit dauerte, währte, zwei Stunden.

2. Andauern suggests persistence or duration despite difficulties or despite what is expected. The subject may be an activity, a condition, either of man or of Nature, but it cannot be a person. Emotional emphasis, whether pleasurable or otherwise, is expressed.[2] **Anhalten,** which is a close synonym, is purely objective. See also 'continue'.

Der Streik, die Unruhe, das Fieber, der Regen, der Frost, dauert, hält, noch an.

Unsere Freundschaft hat ein Leben lang angedauert (said, e.g. in a funeral speech, and therefore not replaceable by *anhalten*).

In vielen Ländern Europas haben alte Volkstrachten angedauert.

Für Sonntag wird anhaltender Regen gemeldet.

3. Halten is used of things in reference to their use as wear and tear, particularly in the sense of 'hold' when resistance to strain on joins, seams and the like is implied. In reference to things which are subject to decay, **sich halten** should be used, although the reflexive pronoun is sometimes dropped. See also 'keep'.

Die Schuhe, die Möbel, die Reifen, haben nicht lange gehalten.

Dieser Stoff, dieser Anzug, dieses Segeltuch, hat gut gehalten.

Der Anzug wird jahrelang halten müssen.

Dieser Stoff, dieser Anzug, dieses Segeltuch, hat gut gehalten.

Wie lange halten sich diese Blumen?

Bei warmem Wetter hält (sich) die Butter nicht lange.

4. Vorhalten is used of things which imply the using up of a reservoir. These may be (*a*) things which are conceived as having strength, intensity, particularly effects; (*b*) commodities which are thought of as supplies, not as single objects. This use is closely synonymous with that of *dauern* as explained in **1**(d).

---

[1] With a non-personal subject *dauern* regularly translates 'take' used in this sense. *Die Wiederherstellung der Kirche wird Jahre dauern. Es dauerte lange, bevor er sich zu der Tat entschließen konnte.* See 'take'.

[2] The present participles of both *dauern* and *andauern* are used adjectivally and adverbially. *Dauernd* means 'continuous, permanent, constant' (e.g. *ein dauernder Wohnsitz, dauernde Liebe*) and also 'continual, frequent' (e.g. *er reist dauernd zwischen Wien und Berlin*). *Andauernd* adds to both these meanings that of persistence, often in an unwelcome form (e.g. *er ist andauernd hier; er redet andauernd von sich selbst*). It has therefore an emotional connotation.

Das Betäubungsmittel hat nur eine Stunde vorgehalten.
Wie lange kann seine Kraft noch vorhalten?
Meine Ermahnungen haben nicht lange vorgehalten.
Die Vorräte werden noch eine Weile vorhalten.
Wird das Holz für den Winter vorhalten?
Das Geld hielt nicht lange vor.

5. Reichen refers to the consumption of commodities in the sense of 'to be sufficient' for a given purpose. It carries no implication of time or resistance to decay or disintegration, and approximates more closely to 'suffice' or 'do' than to 'last'.

Der Wein wird für den ganzen Abend, für so viele Menschen, kaum reichen.
Das Fleisch muß für zwei Tage reichen.
Das Holz muß für den Winter reichen.

6. Auskommen mit, to manage, to make do, with, can be used when the capacity of the person to make a thing last is stressed.

Werden Sie für das ganze Jahr mit zwei Hemden auskommen? (Can you make them last?)

LAST, AT LAST, FINALLY, IN THE END[1] **1. Endlich** means (*a*) after a long time, particularly of expectation or hesitation, corresponding to 'at last', 'at length', and (*b*) after a long time and followed by nothing further, corresponding to 'at last', 'finally', 'in the end'. It does not mean 'finally', in the sense of 'decisively', 'irrevocably' unless the lapse of a long time is implied.

Er hat endlich von sich hören lassen (at last, at length).
Sie haben uns allerhand Scherereien gemacht, bis wir endlich mit ihnen fertig wurden.

2. Zuletzt, used only as an adverb, means (*a*) as the last of a series without any inner connection between the units (compare *zuerst*). It is a close synonym of the more emphatic **als letzter, letzte, letztes.** (*b*) On the last occasion before the present. Both these meanings correspond to 'last'. (*c*) 'Finally', 'in the end'. It differs from the second meaning of *endlich* in drawing attention to the number of things that have preceded rather than to the length of time that has elapsed.[2]

Er sprach, kam, zuletzt, als letzter.
Tun Sie das zuletzt, als letztes.
Wann haben wir uns zuletzt gesehen?
Zuletzt mußten wir unabhängig handeln.

3. Schließlich corresponds to 'finally', 'in the end', and draws attention more to the various stages of what precedes than to the length of time that has elapsed. It differs from the third meaning of *zuletzt*, with which it is

[1] The synonymous term *eventual* (i.e. bound to follow from causes already operating, or which is bound to follow if certain causes operate) can only be translated (approximately) by *endlich, schließlich*, or if the result is strongly hypothetical, by *etwaig. Eventuell*, mostly used as an adverb, means only 'possibly'. *Endlich* as a rendering of 'final' in the sense of *endgültig* is antiquated. Similarly 'ultimate', which stresses all that has preceded, must be translated by *endlich* and *schließlich*.

[2] *Zu guter Letzt* denotes a conclusion which is satisfying because of either its friendliness or its reasonableness. *Zu guter Letzt tranken wir alle noch einmal auf sein Wohl. Zu guter Letzt hat er seinen Fehler doch zugegeben.*

closely synonymous, in presenting the final point and the preceding stages as parts of a whole. Because it suggests a whole, *schließlich* often implies a calculation or an inference.[1]

Schließlich haben wir uns doch geeinigt.
Schließlich möchte ich noch sagen....
Er wird schließlich doch recht behalten.

4. Am Ende merely denotes what the end is, often despite what reason suggests, i.e. 'in the end'. Similarly **zum Schluss** means 'in conclusion'.

Am Ende wird er wohl doch noch recht behalten.
Zum Schluß möchte ich sagen...(does not necessarily imply a summing-up of what precedes).

5. Zum letzten Mal must be used for 'finally' in warnings and the like when reference is less to what precedes than to the future, i.e. not again.

Ich warne Sie zum letzten Mal.

6. Endgültig means 'finally' in the sense of 'decisively', 'irrevocably', i.e. more in reference to the future than to the past.

Er hat endgültig mit ihm gebrochen.

LAZY, SLUGGISH Faul[2] corresponds closely to 'lazy', i.e. averse to effort, **träge** to 'sluggish', i.e. slow in moving.

Der Lehrer sagte zu dem Jungen: 'Du bist faul!'
Er ist von Natur aus träge.
Träge Darmtätigkeit.

LEARN 1. Lernen can refer to both process and result, but stresses the former more than the latter. It therefore sometimes means 'to study'.[3] When the result is emphasized as complete mastery of the material **erlernen** must be used. The latter is never followed by the infinitive.

Er lernt Deutsch, Mathematik.
Er hat die Verse auswendig gelernt.
Sie lernt singen, Klavier spielen.
Sie müssen lernen, wie man sich in diplomatischen Kreisen benimmt.
Er hat viele Tricks von ihm gelernt.
Wer eine Fremdsprache erlernen will, muß nicht nur in dem fremden Land leben, sondern die Sprache bewußt analysieren.

2. Neither of the above terms can be used in the sense of 'to receive information'. *Hören, erfahren,* and the like must be used (see 'hear').

Ich habe gehört, daß Sie bald verreisen.
Ich habe es von ihm erfahren.

AT LEAST Wenigstens indicates a lower limit which one is prepared to accept, even though it is far from the ideal. It has a subjective colouring. **Mindestens** refers, on the other hand, to an objectively established indispensable minimum. The estimate it expresses is therefore exact, mostly,

---

[1] In this sense it mostly corresponds to 'after all', 'in the last resort', 'in the last analysis'. *Wir haben uns schließlich nichts vorzuwerfen. Letzten Endes* is a close synonym.

[2] *Faul* also means 'rotten', i.e. decayed, and 'foul' in reference to the smell, taste, and the like caused by decaying matter.

[3] *Studieren* is only applied to university students (e.g. *er studiert Germanistik*). Of schoolboys and girls *lernen* must be used in the sense of 'study' (e.g. *er lernt sehr fleißig*).

though not exclusively, in numerical form.[1] **Zumindest** is an intensive of *mindestens*, i.e. in no case less, rather more; English: at the very least.

Geben Sie mir wenigstens 3 Pfund für die Reise (I am prepared to accept as little as this).

Ich brauche mindestens 3 Pfund für die Reise (I could not do it with less).

Er hat wenigstens drei Monate daran gearbeitet.

Er hat mindestens drei Monate daran gearbeitet.

Laden Sie ihn doch wenigstens einmal ein!

Sie müssen ihn mindestens einmal einladen.

Hitler mußte mindestens Frankreich besiegen, bevor er Rußland angreifen konnte.

Man muß zumindest sechs Semester studiert haben, bevor man das Examen machen darf.

LEAVE[2] **A.** To depart from a person, place, activity, the person or thing that departs and the separation of subject and object being emphasized.

Verlassen translates 'leave' in this sense, whether the departure is temporary or permanent, whether it means simply 'to go away' or carries the implications of 'abandon',[3] 'desert'.

Ich verließ ihn an der Ecke.

Ich verließ das Haus um 8 Uhr.

Er hat das Land verlassen.

Er verließ den Klub sehr früh.

Er hat die Schule schon verlassen.

Warum hat er seinen Posten, Ihren Dienst, verlassen?

Sein Verstand, die Besinnung, hat ihn verlassen.

B. To allow, to cause to remain, in a place or condition, or to put into a new condition, the person or thing left and the condition being emphasized rather than the departure of the subject. The activity of 'put' and the inactivity of 'allow' or 'cause to remain' must be clearly distinguished. 'Leave' followed by an infinitive or a present participle, or gerund requires special attention, since each of these constructions admits of various meanings and must be variously translated. 'Leave' followed by 'with' also has numerous senses, all of which must be differently rendered into German. Of the German verbs treated in this article only *zurücklassen* and *sitzenlassen* can be followed by *mit*.

1. Lassen: to allow to remain in a place or condition, i.e. inactively, *sein* or *bleiben* being understood (i.e. to let be, remain). It must be followed by a complement (which may be a prefix; see compounds). If a place is implied but not mentioned with 'leave', *lassen* is impossible (see *zurücklassen*). The idea of departure is not expressed prominently. The act of leaving can be deliberate or accidental.

Ich ließ den Brief auf dem Tisch.

Ich muß meine Tasche in der Bahn gelassen haben.

---

[1] *Minder* and *mindest*, used adjectivally, are close synonyms of *geringer* and *geringst*, from *gering*, 'slight in value, importance'.

[2] 'Leave' is etymologically connected with *bleiben* (O.H.G. *be-lîban*) and means fundamentally 'to let remain'. The primary sense of *lassen*, on the other hand, is 'to let'. When it means 'leave' some following infinitive such as *sein* or *bleiben* is understood. See also under 'keep'.

[3] But: *sie ließ alles stehen und liegen, um ihm zu folgen* (left everything, i.e. gave up).

Ich ließ ihn an der Ecke stehen.
Sie ließ das Kind im Kinderwagen und besorgte die Hausarbeit.
Können wir das Kind bei Ihnen lassen?
Ich ließ mein Gepäck im Wartesaal.
Er ließ die Tür offen.
Lassen Sie mich in Ruhe.
Das Konzert ließ mich kalt, gleichgültig.
Diese Erklärung hat mich ganz verwirrt, konfus, unbefriedigt, gelassen.
Das hat meine Sehnsucht ungestillt gelassen.
Alles beim Alten lassen (leave things as they are).
Er ließ die Stadt hinter sich.

2. Liegen-, stehen-, sitzen- (etc.), lassen.[1]

These expressions translate 'to leave lying, standing', sitting, etc. in the literal sense. They are also preferred at times as a translation of the literal sense of 'leave'. *Stehen lassen* refers particularly to things that cannot be carried by hand. Sometimes they have special meanings (e.g. *sitzen lassen*: jilt, leave stranded).

Ich ließ meinen Wagen an der Ecke stehen.
Er ließ das Fleisch stehen (at table).
Er ließ sein Kapital stehen.
Er ließ mich auf der Bank sitzen.
Er ließ sie mit den Kindern sitzen (deserted her and left her to care for the children).
Ich ließ ihn mit der Korrekturarbeit sitzen (left him to do it and went away).

3. Zurücklassen

is used in a number of ways. In each case it is clearly implied that the subject departs, moves away.

(a) Used literally, with a place as object, *hinter sich* (*mir*, etc.) must be added (though *zurück* may be omitted; see *lassen*). The phrase also has the figurative sense of 'outstrip'.

Wir ließen die Stadt hinter uns zurück und strebten den Bergen zu.
Er ist so begabt, daß er alle anderen Studenten weit hinter sich zurückgelassen hat.

(b) To leave in a place, which is stated or implied. *Zurücklassen* must be used when the place is not stated, but implied, or when English adds 'behind'. When the place is mentioned, it is also the correct term to express a deliberate leaving, i.e. for some purpose. It also stresses the distance between subject and object. With words such as *Nachricht, Anweisungen*, it suggests a material object, i.e. that these are written on paper. With a non-personal subject, the action is, of course, not deliberate.

Sie liessen ihn tot zurück (they left him dead; *zurück* being necessary, since a place is implied but not stated).
Er hat sein Gepäck am Bahnhof zurückgelassen.
Er hat seine Uhr als Pfand zurückgelassen.
Ich ließ einen Zettel für ihn zurück.
Ich werde Ihnen Anweisungen zurücklassen (on paper, see *hinterlassen*).
Das Obst ließ große Flecken auf der Jacke zurück.

(c) 'To leave' with and without a following 'with'. Sense: to leave in a condition. *Zurücklassen* is used if (i) the cause, i.e. the subject, moves on; (ii) the condition is inactive (e.g. a feeling, not an act of willing).

[1] Compare further: *es dabei bewenden lassen, es auf sich beruhen lassen* (leave it at that).

Die Feuersbrunst ließ die Fabrik in Trümmern zurück.
Ein Sturm fuhr über das Land und ließ die Gärten in chaotischem Zustand zurück.
Er ließ sie als unbemittelte Witwe zurück.
Der Krieg ließ die Besiegten mit einem blinden Haß gegen die Sieger zurück.
Er ließ sie mit dem Gefühl zurück, daß ihr übel mitgespielt worden war.
Er ließ mich mit dem Eindruck zurück, daß es ihm nicht ernst war.
Das Schauspiel ließ uns mit dem Gefühl zurück, daß es nicht genug eingeübt worden war.

(d) Neither *lassen* nor *zurücklassen* is possible in the sense of 'put' into a condition when (i) the subject does not move on; (ii) the object by his activity has brought about his condition; (iii) the condition is active (e.g. an act of willing). German uses an active verb, often *machen*.

Die vier Treppen haben mich ermüdet.
Der Ausbruch des Vulkans machte die Stadt zu einer Ruine.
Der Krieg ließ in vielen Menschen den Entschluß reifen, eine neue Ordnung zu schaffen.
Der erste Teil der Oper machte mir wenig Appetit auf den Rest.

4. Hinterlassen: (*a*) to leave behind after death what belongs to one, either material possessions (i.e. bequeath) or a family; (*b*) to leave intangible things (e.g. *Eindruck, Spur, Nachricht, Anweisungen*). Since what is left must be intangible, *Nachricht* and *Anweisungen* refer to spoken, not to written messages. (Contrast *zurücklassen*.)

Er hinterließ seinem Sohn sein ganzes Vermögen.
Er hinterließ eine Frau und zwei Kinder.
Er hinterließ einen starken Eindruck auf mich.
Er hat mir Anweisungen hinterlassen.

5. Überlassen: (*a*) 'To commit, refer to another person or agent instead of oneself' (*S.O.D.*). In this sense it is followed by an accusative and a dative, and may be followed by an infinitive (i.e. to hand over a thing to a person to do, for it to be done). (*b*) To abandon a person, a thing, to another person, another thing. A dative and an accusative must follow.

In the imperative *überlassen* tends to refer to important matters, while for trivial things *lassen* is widely used.[1]

Ich überlasse Ihnen die Korrektur dieser Bogen.
Ich überlasse es Ihnen, uns das nötige Material zu verschaffen.
Ich überlasse es ihm, den Brief zu schreiben.
Er wurde seinem Schicksal überlassen.
Überlassen Sie mir das (e.g. paying heavy costs).
Lassen Sie mir das (e.g. washing up).

6. Belassen: to leave in a place or condition. It must be followed by *in*. The distinction between it and *lassen* is that it stresses the intention of the subject, while *lassen* may imply an intention or not.

Er beließ uns in dem Wahn, daß wir das Schlimmste schon hinter uns hätten.
Er wurde im Amt belassen.

7. Übriglassen: to leave, yield as a remainder after deduction (leave over). *Übrigbleiben* is often used as a substitute for the passive.

---

[1] The same distinction exists between *lassen* and *überlassen* in the sense of 'let have'. *Er ließ mir das Buch für ein paar Tage. Er überließ mir seine Notizen über Kant.*

Der Tod des ältesten Sohnes läßt nur noch ein Kind übrig.
Es bleibt sehr wenig von meinem Gehalt übrig, wenn so viel für Steuern abgezogen wird.

8. Loslassen may be used negatively with reference to a thought or feeling in the sense of 'not to let go'. (Also: to let go a thing, *Geländer, einen Ball*.)

Das Gefühl ließ ihn nicht los, daß man ihm sein Verhalten übelgenommen hätte.

9. 'Leave' in the sense of 'go away' or 'abandon' followed by the accusative and the infinitive. Here English gives equal prominence to the action of going away, abandoning, and the action which the object is left to perform. This sense must be distinguished from that of 'let remain' (*lassen*) and 'hand over' (*überlassen*). (She left the clothes on the line to dry = *Sie ließ die Kleider auf der Wäscheleine zum Trocknen*; I left him (= it to him) to write the letter = *Ich überließ es ihm, den Brief zu schreiben*.) Since German has no standardized way of expressing this meaning, only a few hints can be given.

(a) When the context allows 'let' to be substituted for 'leave' *lassen* may be used, but does not render the idea of going away.

Sie ließen ihn verhungern (left him to starve).

(b) *Sie überließen ihn dem Hungertod* (left him to starve).

(c) *Sitzen laßen*. The use of this expression is limited by the type of adverbial phrase possible with *sitzen*.

Ich ließ ihn damit sitzen (I left him to get it done unaided, i.e. I dissociated myself from him so that, if he did it, he would have to do it alone).

Er ließ sie mit den Kindern sitzen.

Er ließ sie mit den Kindern fast ohne Geld sitzen.

10. 'Leave' followed by the gerund. German cannot express by one verb the two ideas of going away and causing sometimes contained in 'leave'.

Die Flieger ließen die Stadt in Flammen (left the town burning).

Sie ließ das Gas brennen (left burning, or let burn).

Ich verließ ihn, als er dabei war, das Haus zu streichen (I left him painting).

C. Intransitive use of 'leave'.

1. By transport.

(a) **(Ab)fahren** is only used when thinking of the time of departure of the means of transport. The use or omission of *ab* fluctuates. It can, however, only be dropped if the context makes it clear that departure is meant. In general, its use is more common when the means of conveyance is the subject, and is then obligatory in the perfect tenses. With persons it is less common.

Der Zug ist schon abgefahren.

Der Zug fährt gleich ab (*ab* usual, but could be omitted).

Wann fährt (see 'go') *der Zug?* (*ab* could be added, but is less usual).

Ich fahre morgen um 9 Uhr (*ab* possible, but unusual).

Wann fahren Sie? (*ab* not used).

(b) **(Ab)reisen** concentrates attention on the fact that a journey is being made and emphasizes the leaving of a place, whether this be a town, country, hotel, or the like. In the perfect tenses *ab* must be used. Otherwise, the use of *ab* suggests that departure is imminent, its omission that it is more remote.

Er ist schon abgereist.

Wann reisen Sie (ab)?

LEAVE

2. When walking is implied, **gehen** (see 'go') is used with the addition of *weg* if the context does not in itself make clear the idea of departure. Instead of the perfect tenses **weg sein** is usual.

Wir müssen jetzt gehen.

Er ging früher als ich (weg).

Er ist schon längst weg.

LEND, BORROW 1. (a) **Leihen** is the act of lending, not the state of being lent. In the passive it is therefore used with *werden* (i.e. the action of handing over), but not with *sein*. It must be followed by the dative of the person in order to indicate the particular act.

Ich habe ihm ein Buch geliehen.

Können Sie mir 100 Mark leihen?

Das Auto wurde uns geliehen.

(b) *Leihen* also has regularly the meaning of 'borrow', with or without the reflexive dative. To avoid ambiguity the latter can be added. Except in reference to money *leihen* is more common than *borgen* in the sense of 'borrow'

Ich habe seinen Wagen geliehen (to translate 'I have *lent* his car', German must add to whom, if *leihen* is to be used).

Ich leihe Bücher grundsätzlich nicht (contrast example with *verleihen*).

2. Verleihen.

(a) In the literal sense *verleihen* expresses (i) a generalization, often as a principle; (ii) in the passive voice (with *sein*) a state. It is followed by *an* and the accusative in order to denote the receiver. The dative is impossible in this sense.

Ich verleihe Bücher grundsätzlich nicht.

Bücher soll man nicht an fremde Leute verleihen.

Das Buch ist verliehen.

(b) *Verleihen* has also the figurative sense of 'lend': bestow, impart a quality to something. In this use it is followed by the dative.[1]

Das verleiht seinem Verhalten eine gewisse Würde.

3. Ausleihen: to lend or (with reflexive dative) to borrow, in reference to libraries and the commercial hiring and lending out of objects (not money).

Dieses Buch ist ausgeliehen.

Wir haben uns einen Wagen ausgeliehen.

4. Borgen: to borrow and, less frequently, to lend, money or other things that are consumed by use. It is not in careful use applied to objects which in themselves are valuable, and, suggesting a casual arrangement, is therefore inappropriate in elevated contexts.[2]

Ich habe 10 Mark geborgt (and in Austria: *ausgeborgt*).

Können Sie mir 10 Mark borgen?

5. Entlehnen and **entleihen** are dignified terms, which only mean 'borrow'. The former is used particularly of ideas, and does not suggest the obligation to repay.

Milton hat viele Ausdrücke und Bilder aus der Dichtung der klassischen Altertums entlehnt.

Ich habe viele wertvolle Bücher von ihm entliehen.

[1] *Verleihen* also means 'to bestow', 'to confer' orders, decorations, academic degrees, and the like.

[2] *Pumpen* is a slang term for *borgen*.

LIKE (v.) 1. Mögen is used of both things and persons. *Ich möchte*: 'I should like' followed by infinitive. This is today its most common meaning, but see also under 'may'.

Ich mochte ihn sehr.
Mein Töchterchen mag Kuchen.
Ich mag nicht, daß man mir schmeichelt.

2. Gern haben and *gern* with other appropriate verbs are the commonest equivalents. (*Lieb haben* is stronger and is practically the equivalent of *lieben*.)

Ich habe ihn gern.
Ich habe dieses Bild sehr gern.
Ich esse Austern gern (I like oysters).
Ich schwimme nicht gern.

3. Etwas, viel, nichts, wenig übrig haben für ... is used colloquially in this sense.

Ich habe viel für ihn übrig.
Für solche Methoden habe ich nicht viel übrig.

4. Gefallen: to please. May be used for 'like' when this is interchangeable with 'enjoy' (see under this term).

Wie hat Ihnen das Konzert gefallen? (how did you like, enjoy...)?

LIMIT, RESTRICT[1] 1. Einschränken: to reduce, curtail, retrench, i.e. to make a thing less than it was before. It can only be used when the following factors are present. (*a*) The reduction is brought about by a deliberate act of intervention (i.e. by a person or his actions, e.g. a decree). This being so, its use in the passive voice requires *werden*, not *sein*. (*b*) Its noun object mostly refers to material goods, but may also be such things as power, authority, concrete freedoms. (*c*) It can only be followed by *auf* when the noun governed by *auf* refers to material goods (i.e. not power, etc.). (*d*) Used reflexively it can only indicate material goods (*sich einschränken* = tighten the belt). (*e*) It is always emphatic and so it is used characteristically with adverbs such as *stark, wesentlich, noch weiter*. When its object is not material goods, it is generally accompanied by some such phrase.[2]

Wir können unseren Gasverbrauch nicht weiter einschränken.
Die Kontinentalsperre schränkte den deutschen Handel ein.
Als das geschah, haben wir unseren Milchverbrauch auf 5 Liter wöchentlich eingeschränkt.
Der Betrieb schränkte seine Produktion auf 1000 Lokomotiven ein.
Wir müssen unsere Mahlzeiten auf täglich 2 einschränken.
Infolge meines Augenleidens mußte ich meine Lektüre stark einschränken.
Der Krieg hat die Zahl[3] der verfügbaren Ärzte wesentlich eingeschränkt.

---

[1] *Begrenzen* means no more than 'to draw boundaries' (e.g. *die Mauer begrenzt unsere Aussicht*). The past participle *begrenzt* can be used in a derogatory way with reference to the mind. Unlimited possibilities = *unbegrenzte Möglichkeiten*.

[2] *Einschränken* was formerly used more extensively. The following examples are from Goethe's *Werther*: '*Der alte M. ist ein geiziger rangiger Filz, der seine Frau im Leben was rechts geplagt und eingeschränkt hat....*' '*Und dann, so eingeschränkt* (i.e. from without) *er ist, hält er doch immer im Herzen das süße Gefühl der Freiheit, und daß er diesen Kerker verlassen kann, wann er will.*' '*Der Fürst fühlt in der Kunst, und würde noch stärker fühlen, wenn er nicht durch das garstige wissenschaftliche Wesen und durch die gewöhnliche Terminologie eingeschränkt wäre.*' The explanation of *beschränken* is sufficient to show that it could not be used in these cases either.

[3] *Herabsetzen, kürzen* are mostly used when *Zahl* is the object. See 'reduce' and 'shorten'.

Die neue Verfassung schränkt die Macht des Königs noch weiter ein (or:
derartig ein, daß er nur noch Ratschläge erteilen darf).
*Während des Krieges wurde die Bewegungsfreiheit feindlicher Ausländer
eingeschränkt.*
Wir genießen noch das uneingeschränkte Vertrauen des Königs (emphatic).
Ich habe, sage ich Ihnen, uneingeschränkte Vollmacht (emphatic).

2. **Beschränken** has the definite meaning of 'not to allow a thing to exceed
a certain limit'. It can, however, also mean 'to reduce', but rather by implication, without emphasis and without necessarily suggesting a deliberate
act of intervention. The latter is implied if the passive voice formed with
werden is used, *sein* indicating a continuing state. It is used freely with
non-material things in the sense of 'reduce'. It may be followed by *auf*,
whatever the type of noun governed by the latter (i.e. not only a noun
denoting material goods as in the case of *einschränken*). The use of *auf* often
makes *beschränken* necessary, even if without it *einschränken* would be possible (e.g. *die Pressefreiheit wurde stark eingeschränkt*; but: *die Pressefreiheit
wurde auf ein Minimum beschränkt*).

Sich beschränken, used absolutely, has a moral signification. *Beschränkt*,
applied to persons, means 'limited intellectually', almost 'stupid'.

Wir haben unseren Gasverbrauch beschränkt.
*Die Kontinentalsperre beschränkte den deutschen Handel auf das Fest-
land.*
Wir haben unseren Milchverbrauch auf 5 Liter wöchentlich beschränkt.
Wir mussen unsere Mahlzeiten auf täglich zwei beschränken.
Früher habe ich Wein getrunken, jetzt beschränke ich mich auf Wasser.
Infolge meines Augenleidens mußte ich meine Lektüre beschränken.
Ich mußte meine Unterstützung auf 20 Mark monatlich beschränken.
Früher bin ich 3 Kilometer gegangen, jetzt beschränke ich mich auf zwei
(*einschränken* impossible).
*Infolge dieses Ereignisses haben wir unseren Aufenthalt auf eine Woche
beschränkt* (*einschränken* impossible).
*Die schwierigen Verhältnisse veranlaßten mich, die Zahl der wöchentlichen
Artikel auf zwei zu beschränken* (*einschränken* impossible).
*Die neue Verfassung beschränkt die Macht des Königs auf Erteilung von
Ratschlägen* (*einschränken* impossible because of the *auf* phrase).
*Während des Krieges wurde die Bewengungsfreiheit feindlicher Ausländer auf
die Vorstädte beschränkt* (see comment on previous example).
Unsere Freiheit ist beschränkt (*einschränken* impossible).
Die Macht des Parlaments its durch das neue Gesetz beschränkt (or: *wird
eingeschränkt*).
Sie können Ihre Pflicht nicht so beschränken (*einschränken* impossible).
Sie müssen sich auf das Notwendigste beschränken (*einschränken* impos-
sible).
Ich schenke ihm unbeschränktes Vertrauen.
Ich habe unbeschränkte Vollmacht.

LISTEN 1. Hören is used in generalizations and intransitively in the
imperative, either as a remonstrance or as a request for attention.

Ich höre Radio, klassische Musik, gern.
Hören Sie mal!

2. Zuhören: (*a*) to listen passively, without taking part, transitively and intransitively; (*b*) to surrender oneself to sound as a sensuous, spiritual experience.[1]

Ich war bei der Sitzung und hörte zu.

Ich hörte (ihm) zu, während er mir seine Pläne auseinandersetzte.

Ich hörte der Debatte zu.

Ich hörte dem Rauschen des Wassers zu.

Mit geschlossenen Augen hörte ich der Musik zu.

3. Anhören: (*a*) to give a fair hearing (only transitively); (*b*) with the reflexive dative the sense is 'to want to hear', 'to go to hear', particularly as pleasure, entertainment.

Hören Sie mich an!

Ich hörte seinen Rat an, aber fand ihn nicht klug.

Ich danke Ihnen dafür, daß Sie mich so freundlich angehört haben.

4. Hören auf: to listen actively and intently, often with a view to action, and therefore sometimes with the implication of responding to a suggestion, order, and the like.

Er wollte nicht auf meinen Rat hören.

Hören Sie auf meine Worte.

Er hört nie auf das, was ich sage.

Ich höre gespannt auf die Klänge der Violine.

LITERAL(LY) **1. Wörtlich** means (*a*) following the letter, text, or exact or original words (*C.O.D.*); (*b*) taking words in their usual or primary sense and applying the ordinary rules of grammar, without mysticism or allegory or metaphor (*C.O.D.*). **Wortwörtlich** may also be used in these senses, and may imply an excess of this virtue. *Wortgetreu* comes very close to *wörtlich*, like English 'faithful' to 'literal'.

Im wörtlichen Sinne.

Eine wörtliche Übersetzung (wortgetreue).

Eine wörtliche Auslegung der Bibel.

Er versteht alles wortwörtlich.

2. Buchstäblich asserts that a statement is entirely accurate, not exaggerated (even though it may be grossly exaggerated). It is therefore emphatic.

Die Kinder verhungerten buchstäblich.

Er wurde buchstäblich in Stücke geschnitten.

3. Applied directly to a person or his mind: **phantasielos** (lacking in imagination); **nüchtern** (sober, matter-of-fact, prosaic).

Er ist ein ganz phantasieloser, nüchterner Mensch.

LIVE **Wohnen** means 'to dwell', 'to be domiciled'. It is used (*a*) in giving one's address; (*b*) in reference to larger areas, e.g. a country, when the ties of home or occupation are emphasized; (*c*) when the circumstances of occupying a house are stressed. **Leben** (*a*) means 'to be alive', i.e. not dead; (*b*) refers to the way one spends one's life.

Während meines Urlaubs werde ich im Hotel Bristol wohnen.

Er wohnt in London.

Sie wohnen zu viert.

---

[1] *Lauschen* to listen intently, with all one's senses alert, to drink in sounds. It is much used in poetical language.

LIVE

Sie leben augenblicklich in Frankreich, aber sie wohnen eigentlich in Italien.
Viele Ausländer leben augenblicklich in Deutschland als Mitglieder der
Besatzungsarmeen (not *wohnen*, which would suggest the idea of 'home').
Er lebt noch.
Er lebt zurückgezogen.
Er lebt nur der Kunst.

LIVELY **Lebendig:** full of life, vital, i.e. more than simply 'not dead'.
In this intensive sense it also corresponds to 'living' (e.g. *ein lebendiger*
Glaube). While *lebendig* refers more to inner vitality, though not excluding
its external manifestations, **lebhaft** denotes a heightening of the external
manifestation in such a way as to strike one forcibly. Both words often need
to be translated by some term other than 'lively'.
Eine lebendige Phantasie.
Eine lebhafte Phantasie.
Ein lebendiges Kind.
Ein lebhaftes Kind.
Eine lebendige, lebhafte, Beschreibung.
Lebhafte Farben.
Ich bedaure lebhaft.
Ein sehr lebendiger Stil.
Ein sehr lebhafte Art.

LOCK **1. Schließen** means (*a*) both 'to close'[1] and 'to lock' a house,
room, door, etc. but should not be used when the idea of locking with a key
or bolt is stressed. It is, however, regularly used in reference to the locking
of windows. (*b*) It is also used in the sense of locking something to be
guarded in a place or a container. (*c*) It can be used intransitively.[2]
Schließen Sie das Fenster.
Er schloß das Geld in den Kasten (ein).
Dieser Schlüssel, diese Dose, diese Tür, schließt nicht.

2. The following compounds of *schließen* stress the idea of locking.
(a) **Zuschließen** suggests the turning of a key, the shooting of a bolt, and
the like, and is used more of single objects than larger complexes such as a
room, a house.
Ich habe die Tür schon zugeschlossen.
(b) **Abschließen** means 'to lock up' (i.e. something consisting of a number
of parts).[3]

---

[1] To use *schließen* for *zumachen* is as much a genteelism as 'close' for 'shut'. *Zumachen*
and 'shut' emphasize the action, *schließen* and 'close' the permanent state, official action,
the closing of gaps. In South Germany *sperren* and *absperren* for 'to lock' are very common.
[2] *Schließen*, also means 'to lock' in the sense of 'to join by interlacing parts', 'to clasp'
(e.g. *jemand in seine Arme schließen*); also figuratively (e.g. *in sein Herz schließen*).
[3] *Schließen, abschließen, beschließen* also mean 'to end', 'to close', 'to conclude'. Like
'close' *schließen* suggests little more than the opposite of 'open' (e.g. *er schloß seinen*
Vortrag mit der Bemerkung...). *Abschließen* suggests greater finality, often a formal ending,
and corresponds closely to 'conclude' (e.g. *ich habe meine Untersuchungen, die Verhandlungen,*
abgeschlossen). *Beschließen* means 'to mark the end' by some special feature and is frequently
followed by a *mit* phrase or some equivalent (e.g. *sie beschlossen die Versammlung mit der*
Nationalhymne; *wir beschlossen den Tag mit einem Konzert*; *er beschloß seine Rede mit einem*
weiteren Appell; *hiermit ist die Vortragsreihe abgeschlossen*). Both *schließen* and *abschließen*
are also used in the sense of concluding, bringing about an agreement, *schließen* meaning
little more than 'make', *abschließen* 'to finalize' (e.g. *einen Vertrag schließen, abschließen*).

Schließen Sie hier ab! (intransitive in the sense of 'lock every door or opening').

Ich habe den Wagen abgeschlossen (all doors and windows).

(c) **Verschließen** is an intensive and is used (*a*) of an enclosed space (a room, house, safe). In this use it is more common in the passive with *sein* (i.e. to indicate a state) than in the active. In the latter mood *gut* or an equivalent is often added. (*b*) With doors and windows it is emphatic, i.e. not the normal term. (*c*) The object may also be a thing guarded in the locked room, safe, etc.

Ich habe den Schrank, das Geld, gut verschlossen.

Ich fand das Zimmer verschlossen.

Die Tür ist verschlossen.

Sue müssen alle Türen und Fenster unbedingt verschließen, bevor Sie ausgehen.

LONGER (NO), NO MORE In reference to duration of time, the distinction between **nicht länger** and **nicht mehr** differs somewhat from that between the English expressions. *Nicht mehr* simply denotes a cessation and is the general term. *Nicht länger* suggests (*a*) an emotional attitude towards the fact of cessation, or (*b*), particularly when followed by *als*, at least a heightened awareness of the limits of the period in question. It is therefore more emphatic than *nicht mehr*. In reference to the frequency with which an action or state is repeated, German only uses *nicht mehr*.

Ich bin sein Freund nicht mehr, nicht länger.

Ich kann es nicht länger aushalten (*nicht mehr* would be weak in such an emotional context, but not impossible).

Er arbeitet nicht mehr, nicht länger, als 2 Stunden pro Tag.

Er war nicht mehr, nicht länger, als 3 Jahre weg.

Er kommt nicht mehr hierher (*nicht länger* impossible because frequency is meant).

LOOK AT[1] **1. Ansehen** is used when only the eye, i.e. not the mind, is engaged. It suggests that the object is at close quarters and is looked at steadily, i.e. for more than the duration of a glance. Combination with an adverb such as *lange* clearly reveals these implications. These also make its use in the imperative unusual, i.e. except when a certain intensity is to be conveyed (e.g. *sehen Sie das nur mal an*, where *nur* suggests intensity). In the interrogative form *ansehen* is also rare.

Ich sah ihn an, aber erkannte ihn nicht.

Sie hat ihn nicht mehr angesehen.

Er sah ihn schief, argwöhnisch, mit Verachtung, an.

Es hingen wunderbare Bilder im Zimmer, aber er sah sie nicht mal an.

Ich sah ihn forschend an.

Das Haus ist schön anzusehen, aber nicht sehr fest gebaut.

2. Sich etwas ansehen implies an enquiry by the mind into the object

---

[1] *Schauen*, when strictly used, stresses the intensity of the action, not the result. Only *sehen*, therefore, can be used in the following: *ich sah sofort, worauf er hinaus wollte*. To denote the action *schauen* is used in southern Germany and Austria without any implication of intensity, where standard German requires *sehen*. In northern Germany *gucken* or *kucken* is used colloquially in reference to the action.

looked at, an effort to form an idea about it. Only adverbs which suggest such an examination can be combined with it.[1]

Ich habe mir den Aufsatz angesehen und finde ihn gut.

Sehen Sie sich das Kleid genau an.

Ich muß mir das Auto ansehen, bevor ich es kaufe.

3. Sehen with a direct object or with a preposition must be used to translate 'look at', when *ansehen* and *sich etwas ansehen* as explained above are inapplicable. The direct object is usual with the imperative, the choice of preposition is determined by the implications conveyed by the verb.

Sehen Sie mal das Flugzeug da (an cannot be added).

Wonach sehen Sie? (What are you looking at?)

Ich sah auf meine Uhr und stellte fest, daß ich schon seit einer Stunde wartete.

LOOSE A. Some literal senses.

1. Locker is the more general term. It can refer (*a*) to objects which are not firmly fixed into or on to each other, but should be; (*b*) to objects which are not taut, i.e. slack; (*c*) to objects the parts of which do not cohere, i.e. are not compact. The verb *lockern* can mean to relax regulations, restrictions and the like.

(a) *Ein lockerer Zahn.*

Die Backsteine sind locker geworden.

Das Tischbein ist locker.

(b) *Ein lockeres Seil.*

(c) *Lockere Erde.*

2. Lose is applied to objects (which may be of the same kind) which lie separately, often close to each other, but not bound or tied together at all, or at least not tightly. A contrast is often implied to the tying together of things in a bundle or parcel.

Ich habe nur lose Blätter.

Die Backsteine lagen lose aufeinander.

Die Waren sind nur lose zusammengepackt.

3. Los as a translation of 'loose' is only applied to persons, animals or things that have broken away from chains and the like. It is confined to predicative use.

Der Hund, die Mine, ist los.

B. Some figurative senses.

Both *locker* and *lose* are used figuratively in reference to (*a*) morals, (*b*) the connection between thoughts. *Lose* is stronger, and conveys more forcibly the sensuous impression. Sometimes, particularly when applied attributively to persons, they form fixed expressions, and cannot then be interchanged.

Die Gedanken sind nur locker, lose, aneinandergereiht.

Locker, lose, Sitten.

Ein loses Mädchen.

Ein lockerere, loser, Vogel.

LOW (a) **Niedrig:** not high, not rising far beyond a surface. It is therefore applied to objects which have no height in themselves. **Tief** (often *tiefgelegen*)

---

[1] *Sich ansehen* is also used in reference to entertainment, e.g. the drama, the film. *Ich muß mir diesen Film ansehen.*

is applied to that which lies below a line, real or imaginary. **Nieder** is used adjectivally for *niedrig* in South German.

> *Ein niedriges Gebäude, eine niedrige Mauer, eine niedrige Brücke, eine niedrige Stirn, eine niedrige Hügelkette, ein niedriger Preis, eine niedrige Temperatur, niedere Rassen.*
> *Der Tiefstand des Wassers* (but also: *niedriger Wasserstand*).
> *Der Mond steht tief am Horizont.*
> *Ein tief ausgeschnittenes Kleid.*
> *Bäume, die an tiefen und schattigen Plätzen wachsen (S.O.D.).*
> *Er leidet an niedrigem Blutdruck.*
> *Ihre Kultur steht auf einem tiefen Niveau.*
> *Er ist tief gesunken.*
> *Er verbeugte sich tief vor der Königin.*

(b) One says **Tiefland** for 'lowlands' (opp. *Hochland*: highlands), but nevertheless **Niederlande** for the Netherlands (Holland). Also from the earlier *Niederdeutschland* has survived *Niederdeutsch* (low German; opp. *Oberdeutsch*, whereas *Hoch* refers to the standard language).

(c) **Unter** is used adjectivally as a comparative (lower) when a point in a scale is thought of and means at or near the bottom. But: *niedrig geboren* (of low birth).

> *Die unteren Klassen* (in society).
> *Die unteren Stufen der Gesellschaftsleiter.*

(d) In the figurative sense of 'abject', 'mean', *niedrig* occurs but more common are **niederträchtig, gemein** (see 'common').

> *Er bediente sich niedriger Listen* (low cunning).
> *Der Betrug an seinen Eltern war eine niederträchtige Tat.*

(e) Coarse, vulgar (see under 'rough'): **gemein, vulgär, ordinär.**

> *Er geht gemeinen Vergnügungen nach.*
> *Er hat einen gemeinen Geschmack.*
> *Er ist ein sehr ordinärer Mensch.*

(f) Of sound. *Tief* corresponds to English deep; *leise* (see 'soft') means 'not loud'.

> *Sie sprach mit leiser Stimme.*

(g) Of an opinion: *schlecht* (see 'bad').

> *Er denkt schlecht über sie.*

MAKE   I. Sense treated: to bring (a material thing) into being by forming, shaping, or altering material (whether animate or inanimate): to fashion, to manufacture.

While it is possible to use **machen** in this sense just like English 'make' and it is so used freely in everyday speech or in order to be deliberately vague about the method of production, German prefers, particularly in writing, a more specific term.

1. (a) **Machen** does not draw attention to the process but simply to the result.

> *Er hat diese Kiste aus altem Mahagoni gemacht.*
> *Der Schneider hat mir einem neuen Anzug gemacht.*
> *Sie macht immer ihre eigenen Hüte (fabriziert).*
> *Ich haben den Stuhl selbst gemacht (gezimmert).*
> *Sein Vater will einen Arzt aus ihm machen.*

(b) It is also used of things that are not solid objects.

Er hat ein Verzeichnis der Bücher, der Fehler gemacht.

Aus einem viel behandelten Motiv ist es ihm gelungen, ein schönes Gedicht zu machen (schreiben better).

2. **Anfertigen** suggests care taken in the process of making, sometimes too that a model is used. **Verfertigen**, now little used, stresses the mechanical nature of the making. The simple verb **fertigen** is used only of hand-made things and is rare.

Er hat eine Schachtel, einen Stuhl, ein Gemälde angefertigt.

Er verfertigt Gedichte dutzendweise (i.e. churns out).

3. **Herstellen** may suggest by hand or production in a factory. It tends to be used of small things and not large ones, and not of mass production.

Fünfmarkstücke werden aus Silber hergestellt.

Diese Firma stellt Waschmaschinen, Kühlschränke her.

Er stellt schöne Tische aus ainfachem Material her.

4. For mass production **produzieren** is the appropriate term.

Diese Firma produziert jetzt 100 000 Autos im Jahr.

5. In the building industry **bauen** is the preferred term.

Während des Krieges konnten nicht genug Schiffe gebaut werden.

Diese Straße wurde erst kürzlich gebaut.

6. With food and drink **machen** is used in some cases, particularly where the material and the result more than the method of preparation are thought of. Where the preparation is emphasized: **zubereiten** (see 'prepare'). More specific terms are: **backen, mischen** (in the sense of prepare, mix drinks).

Brot wird aus Weizen gemacht (hergestellt also possible).

Bier wird aus Malz und Hopfen gemacht.

Soll ich den Tee, Kaffee machen?

Ist das ein selbstgebackener Kuchen? (home-made).

Er mischt gerade die Getränke.

7. In the sense of put in order, tidy, *machen* is used in some contexts. It also corresponds to English 'do' (see 'do') in such contexts.

Sie hat die Betten schon gemacht (made, done).

8. In the context of literature and art, *machen* easily sounds derogatory, for which reason a specific term is mostly preferable.

Er schreibt, verfaßt Gedichte.

Der Garten, der Park ist von ihm angelegt worden (laid out, planned).

Das Gipsmodell ist von meiner Schwester gebildet worden.

9. In the sense of 'constitute' there are no well defined terms in German.

Was du sagst, gibt, hat seinen Sinn (makes sense).

10. Of the work of the divinity **(er)schaffen** (create) must be used.

Gott (er)schuf Himmel und Erde, den Menschen.

11. With a few nouns **treffen** is used where English uses make: *Wahl, Entscheidung.* (It also corresponds to English 'take' with certain nouns, e.g. *Maßnahmen treffen,* though with this noun *ergreifen* is also used in the same sense.)

MAKE, GET, LET, HAVE,[1] **CAUSE**[2] **II.** Used causatively. In some cases English makes a clear distinction between 'make', 'get' and 'let' (e.g. despite his protests I made him rewrite his report; after much effort I got him to rewrite his report; I let him rewrite his report, even though it meant a delay). In other cases the distinction between these terms is so slight that they are practically interchangeable (e.g. I'll make the firm pay all expenses; I'll get the firm to pay all expenses; I'll let the firm pay all expenses). Often two, if not three, are interchangeable (e.g. he made, let, me feel my inferiority; he made, let, his eyes roll; I can't make (get...to) the engine start).

The following examples illustrate 'let' used in the sense of 'cause', and reveal the transition in meaning from 'not to prevent' to 'to make' and 'to have'.

I let him see he was not wanted.

Let me know as soon as possible (French: *faire savoir*).

Let the prisoner come, be brought, before me (the regular use of 'let' in the 3rd person imperative).

'Get' and 'have' can be followed by the infinitive, the present or past participle. 'Make' can be followed by the past participle[3] as well as the infinitive.

In the causative sense 'make', 'get' and 'let' can be used in the passive voice. *Lassen* can be used passively only in the meaning of 'let', *machen* only actively. The other German verbs treated are capable of passive use.

'Cause' should in this construction be translated by *verursachen*, which can be followed by a *daß* clause, but not by the infinitive. When the idea of causation is not emphasized and no infinitive follows, other terms (e.g. *bewirken*) are more usual.

A. Lassen translates 'make' in the senses explained below and also 'get', 'have' and 'let' when they are practically interchangeable with 'make'. It corresponds most closely to English 'have' used in this way.

1. *Lassen* cannot emphasize the idea of insistence or force which is sometimes expressed by 'make'. Nor can it suggest any activity of the will (in the form of resistance) or deliberation on the part of the person on whom pressure is brought to bear.

It can, however, be used in a context denoting insistence or even force, if it stands in an unemphatic part of the sentence. 'The strong current made them turn back' = *die starke Strömung machte sie umkehren*. But: *es war die starke Strömung, die sie umkehren ließ* (*machte* is, of course, possible). Here the fact of turning back is already known, the point of the sentence being to draw attention to the cause.[4]

The style in which *lassen* is used is that of report, of plain objective statement. It does not indicate any emotional participation on the part of the speaker (contrast *machen*).

[1] For 'have' in the sense of 'suffer' there is no general term in German. You'll have the roof falling down if you don't do something about it = *das Dach wird Ihnen zusammenstürzen, wenn Sie untätig zusehen.*

[2] 'Leave', 'keep', 'set', 'send' are also used causatively (e.g. to send somebody flying). They must be rendered by the German verbs explained in this article or by some specific verb (e.g. to set moving = *in Bewegung setzen*).

[3] The past participle is translated variously, generally by an adjective: *sich verhaßt* (hated), *fühlbar* (felt, of a thing), *beliebt* (liked), *bekannt* (known), *verständlich* (understood) *machen*. Note also: *ich werde mich schon fürchten machen* (feared; but more commonly: *ich werde mir schon Respekt verschaffen*).

[4] For the importance of emphasis see also 'prevent'.

2. The constructions used with *lassen*.

The infinitive depending on *lassen* can only be passive in a few fixed phrases where *lassen* means 'let' (e.g. *ich ließ es mir gesagt sein*). Otherwise the dependent infinitive must (except in old-fashioned diction) be active in form, even though it be passive in sense (e.g. *ich ließ das alte Haus abreißen* = had...pulled down).

The origin of this construction is probably to be found in the desire to leave vague the agent of the action expressed by the infinitive (i.e. I had someone pull down the old house). The feeling of such an omission must have been lost by the time it became possible to insert *von* or *durch* to denote the agent.

When the object of the infinitive depending on 'make', 'get', 'have' is a pronoun referring to the subject of these verbs, the *von* or *durch* construction is usually used in German, i.e. the object of the dependent infinitive in English becomes in German the reflexive pronoun[1] and the object of 'make', etc., is turned by the *von* or *durch* phrase. The same construction is possible in English after 'get', 'have', though followed by the past participle, not the infinitive (e.g. he had, got, himself carried over the river by the natives).

Ich ließ mir den Vorfall von ihnen schildern (I had, got, them to...).

Lassen Sie sich von Ihrem Vorgesetzten die nötigen Anweisungen geben.

The two constructions exist in German. The distinction, which is often ignored, is that the less usual form (i.e. *ich ließ ihn mir den Vorfall schildern*) tends to mean 'let'. It suggests that the subject lets the object have his way. The more usual form is, on the other hand, more energetic and implies that the subject acts in his own interest, i.e. it tends to mean 'get'. *Lassen* may be stressed in the sense of 'let'.

Laß dir noch mal von ihm die Geschichte erzählen.

Laß ihn dir doch mal die Geschichte erzählen.

While these constructions are possible with the first and second person pronoun, only the *von* or *durch* form can be used with the third person if the subject of 'make', 'let', etc. and the object of the dependent infinitive refer to the same person.

Ich ließ sie mich tragen ('let').

Er ließ sich von ihnen tragen ('let', 'made', 'got').

A reflexive infinitive depending on *lassen* is mostly avoided and is impossible if it would involve the repetition of the same pronoun (i.e. in the first and second persons). The object of the infinitive must then be dropped or another verb used. For example: it made me wonder = *es ließ mich wundern* (or *staunen*).

3. *Lassen* can best be understood by considering it in the following combinations:

(a) Both subject and object are persons; the dependent infinitive denoting a conscious act.

In this case *lassen* translates 'make' in the sense of 'order'. The order may amount to little more than a request or even a suggestion, it may be given by virtue of authority accepted as a matter of course. On the other hand, it may be accompanied by a threat of force, even with a gun in the

---

[1] *Sich lassen* is widely used: in the sense of 'to be able' followed by the passive infinitive, in which it often acquires idiomatic force (e.g. *der Vorschlag läßt sich hören, der Film läßt sich sehen*, is worth listening to, seeing; *er läßt mit sich reden* = is a reasonable man).

hand. In all circumstances the giver of the order expects this to be complied with unquestionably.

If a phrase indicating opposition and implying the need for insistence or the application (as distinct from the threat) of force (see *zwingen*, p. 202 (**D**)) is added, *lassen* is no longer possible. Frequently, expressions formed with 'can' and 'must' convey the idea of insistence (I can't make him wear a hat, if he doesn't want to).

When 'have' implies an order it, too, is translated by *lassen*.

Ambiguity in this use of *lassen* can arise, since the meaning can be 'let' as well as 'make'.[1]

Ich ließ ihn Platz nehmen (made, got, let).

Ich ließ ihn die Zeitung holen (made, got).

Laß sie um die Zugeständnisse bitten ('make' and 'let' interchangeable).

Ehe er den Studenten erlaubte, den Umzug abzuhalten, ließ der Rektor sie versphrechen, daß sie sich ordentlich verhalten würden.[2]

Sein Vater ließ ihn Latein studieren (made, got, let).

Die Mutter ließ ihre Tochter Klavier lernen, obschon diese wenig Begabung däfur hatte.

Er ließ mich für das Telephon zahlen.

Der Offizier ließ die Kompanie stramm stehen.

Der Offizier ließ seine Leute in den sicheren Tod marschieren.

Die Gestapo ließ ihn zwei Stunden lang auf einem Bein stehen.

Laß ihn doch für ein paar Minuten den Mund halten.

Abends läßt die Mutter die Kinder abwaschen.

Durch Vorhalten der Pistole ließ er ihn sein Geld aushändigen.

Der Lehrer ließ das Kind in der Ecke stehen.

Der Lehrer läßt die Schüler fleißig arbeiten.

Er hat nicht das Recht, uns das Haus räumen zu lassen.

Ich bin entschlossen, sie für ihren Unterhalt arbeiten zu lassen ('let' and 'make' interchangeable).

Ich drohte, ihn das Schuljahr wiederholen zu lassen.

Er ließ uns stundenlang warten ('make', 'let', 'leave', 'keep' interchangeable).

Er läßt den Hund durch den Reifen springen.

(b) The subject is a person, the object his creation. Here 'make' and 'let' are interchangeable.

Im 'Werther' läßt Goethe den Helden sterben.

In diesem Stücke läßt der Dichter Szene auf Szene ahne Einteilung in Akte folgen.

(c) The subject is animate or inanimate, the object animate, the infinitive denotes something between a voluntary and an involuntary act, one carried out under the stress of some emotion and not after reflection, or as a result of a free decision.[3] Here, again, 'get' and 'make' will sometimes be interchangeable.

---

[1] To avoid ambiguity *zulassen* can be used (e.g. *die Mutter ließ es zu, daß ihre Tochter Klavier lernte*).

[2] *Versprechen* combined with *lassen* is somewhat solemn. In trivial matters use would be made of *müssen* (e.g. *ich mußte ihm versprechen, ihm das Buch in 8 Tagen zurückzugeben* = he made me promise). Similarly with many other words.

[3] *Lassen* is rare with reflex action denoted by a single verb, but it occurs in phrases such as: *die Hitze ließ ihn in Schweiß ausbrechen* (or: *machte schwitzen*).

MAKE

Lassen is at times used in the sense of 'make' when the action denoted by the infinitive is the result of a decision rather than prompted by emotion (see *veranlassen*, p. 201 (**C**)). The cause is, however, always a compelling one.

Der Hunger ließ ihn stehlen.

Die plötzliche Hitze ließ mich vom Ofen zurückspringen.

Die Hitze ließ mich schlaflos im Bett hin und her wälzen.

Seine Willkür ließ mich Widerspruch erheben.

Der Anblick des Flugzeugs ließ sie alle fliehen.

Was ließ Sie damit herausplatzen?

Die Entdeckung von einigen roten Flecken am Körper ließ ihn sofort zum Arzt laufen.

Die Angst vor Einbrechern ließ sie die ganze Nacht aufsitzen.

Diese Erwägung ließ die Behörden gegen X. einschreiten.

Das Außermenschliche in Kleist ließ Goethe die 'Penthesilea' völlig ablehnen.

Das schlechte Gewissen ließ ihn nicht zur Ruhe kommen.

(d) The subject is animate or inanimate, the object a person, the dependent infinitive denotes an involuntary mental or emotional reaction.[1]

Lassen is only possible when the infinitive denotes an involuntary reaction or a passive state of being (but not with thought as an active, willing process).[2] When 'let' and 'make' are interchangeable, both may be translated by *lassen*.

Since *lassen* is weak, it should not be used in a statement made under the impression of an emotion, e.g. in the present tense (e.g. the incident makes me wonder...).

Der Wein ließ ihn seine Sorgen vergessen.

Seine Tüchtigkeit läßt (=lets) *mich hoffen, daß ihm irgendein einflußreicher Posten übertragen wird.*

Seine Kritik ließ mich fühlen (or: *durch seine Kritik ließ er*), *daß ich zum Versemachen ganz unbegabt bin.*

Sein Treiben läßt mich den Verdacht schöpfen (*den Verdacht in mir aufkommen*), *daß er dunkle Pläne hegt.*

Seine Worte ließen mich fürchten, daß es um meine Aussichten nicht zum besten bestellt sei.

Seine Schilderung ließ den Wunsch in mir aufkommen (made me want), *das Land selbst zu sehen.*[3]

Laß (=let) *ihn glauben, daß es dir ernst mit dem Vorschlag ist.*[4]

Ihre Freundlichkeit läßt (=lets) *mich manche Kränkung vergessen.*

Sein Fieberzustand ließ ihn sich allerhand Dinge einbilden.

Seine Arbeitsweise ließ mich staunen, daß ihm eine so wichtige Arbeit anvertraut worden war.

(e) Both subject and object are things or forces that belong to the world of nature. The subject may also be God. *Lassen* is used regularly in this combination, unless exceptional force is indicated or unless the action resembles a reflex action of persons (see *machen*, p. 201 (**B**)).

Der anhaltende Regen ließ den Fluß über seine Ufer trenten.

---

[1] To make feel. *Ich ließ ihn meinen Ärger fühlen.* But when 'to make feel' is followed by a predicative adjective *lassen* cannot be used. His treachery made me feel sick=*bei seinem Verrat wurde mir übel.* His success made me feel happy = . . . *machte mich glücklich, beglückte mich* ('feel' in this expression is often redundant).

[2] Expressions such as 'to make see' (with the mind), 'to make understand', which imply effort, are translated variously. *Ich machte ihm klar* (*verständlich*) (*brachte ihm bei*), *daß er sich geirrt hatte.*   [3] 'To make want' is often translated by *reizen.*

[4] 'To make believe' in the sense of 'deceive' is often *vormachen.*

Der Wind hat den Schornstein herunterpurzeln lassen.
Der starke Seegang ließ das Boot umkippen.
Die Hitze ließ die Blätter welken.
Die Mauer ließ die Kugeln zurückprallen.
Gott ließ sein Herz erweichen.

(f) The subject is a person, the object a thing.

Lassen can only be used in the sense of 'make' or 'get' if these are interchangeable with 'let'. For other renderings of 'make', 'get' in this combination see *bringen* (p. 202 (**E**)).

Er läßt die Augen rollen.
Er läßt die Geige singen.
Er ließ seine Stimme ertönen.
Durch Andrehen einer Schraube ließ er das Wasser nach allen Seiten spritzen.
Sie müssen es so aussehen lassen, als ob Sie alles schon wüßten.
Lassen Sie die Rosen das Spalier hinaufklettern.

B. Machen, used in this sense, is now antiquated except in reflex actions, certain mental reactions, and short, vigorous exclamations, and even here in more or less fixed phrases, which are survivals of an earlier, more extensive use. Apart from this, it is a stylistic device and makes for vividness in the hands of an accomplished writer.

Die Kälte machte mich zittern (reflex action).
Er machte mich lachen.[1]
Er machte sie erröten.
Sie machen mich zweifeln, ob Sie es ehrlich meinen (involuntary mental reaction).
Ich kann ihm nicht glauben machen, daß es mir ernst mit dem Vorschlag ist.
Den mach' ich schon gehorchen (a short, vigorous phrase).
'*...als noch Ihr Vater neben Ihnen stand und seine Geige jene Töne singen ließ, die Sie weinen machten*' (Thomas Mann, *Tristan*).
'*...weil es auf Erden mein unausweichlicher Beruf ist, die Dinge bei Namen zu nennen, sie reden zu machen*' (Thomas Mann, *Tristan*).
'*Vielleicht war es das Erbteil seines Vaters in ihm...das ihn dort unten leiden machte und manchmal eine schwache, sehnsüchtige Erinnerung in ihm sich regen ließ an eine Lust der Seele, die einstmals sein eigen gewesen war*' (Thomas Mann, *Tonio Kröger*).

C. Veranlassen implies reflection before the performing of the action expressed by the infinitive. A decision, which presupposes a measure of free will, is taken. This term thus corresponds to both 'make' and 'get' thus used.

Was hat sie veranlaßt, das zu sagen (ließ würde suggest impulse)?
Seine Willkür veranlaßte mich zum Protest.
Sie veranlaßte ihren Mann, zu Bett zu gehen und seine Arbeit auf den nächsten Tag zu verschieben (got).
Diese Überlegung veranlaßt mich, nach Paris zu fahren.
Die Hitze veranlaßte uns, die Jacke auszuziehen.
Durch freundliche Überredung veranlaßte sie ihn, das Geheimnis preiszugeben.
Ehe sie die neue Vorlage unterstützten, veranlaßten sie die Regierung, der Verfassung eine Klausel hinzuzufügen, welche die Redefreiheit gewährleisten sollte.

---

[1] Also: *er brachte mich zum Lachen* (as a report, without emotional colouring); *ich mußte aber lachen* (conversational with emotional participation).

D. Zwingen must be used when the application of force is implied. When 'made' is in the passive voice, it is often the only possibility.

Ich kann Sie nicht zwingen, die Poesie zu lieben.

Wir zwangen den Feind zum Rückzug.

Durch die Folter zwangen sie ihn, seine Mitarbeiter zu verraten.

Die Deutschen wurden gezwungen, bis zum letzten zu kämpfen.

E. Bringen is used in a number of combinations, with differing shades of meaning, to express the idea of difficulty and effort in bringing about an effect. It translates 'make' and 'get'. Both subject and object may be either animate or inanimate. It occurs in the following combinations:

1. With *zum* and the substantival infinitive.

The substantival infinitive denotes an action which comes dramatically as a climax or represents a final development. When the object is a person, this noun often, but not necessarily, suggests a reflex action or an uncontrollable action (e.g. an outburst of emotion). A typical example would be: *der Witz brachte mich zum Lachen.* On the other hand *Lächeln* would here be impossible, as it would be an anticlimax. Such a weak term could only be used in a phrase of the type: *seine Witze brachten mich nicht einmal zum Lächeln*; i.e. in a phrase which indicates that the cause did not produce a lesser, let alone the desired, effect.

When the object is a thing, the substantival infinitive may have the character of a climax (e.g. *zum Kochen bringen*), or simply indicate perfect functioning (e.g. *zum Rotieren bringen*), or the cessation of movement (e.g. *zum Stehen bringen*).

The substantival infinitive may be compounded of various parts of speech (e.g. *zum Reißausnehmen bringen*), and it may be followed by a genitive (see examples under **2**).

Mit meinen Sticheleien brachte ich ihn zum Weinen, Rasen, Schreien, Verzweifeln.

Der Minister brachte den König zum Unterschreiben des Todesurteils.

Ich brachte ihn endliche zum Reden.

Ich werde versuchen, ihn endlich zum Schweigen zu bringen.

Ich kann das Rad nicht zum Rotieren bringen.

Können Sie das Auto nicht zum Laufen bringen? (*lassen* = let).

Durch die richtige Behandlungsweise brachte er die Rosen schnell zum Blühen.

Durch Nachlagen vieler Zweige brachte er das Feuer bald zum Brennen.

Nur mit großer Mühe brachten wir das Feuer zum Erlöschen.

2. With an infinitive or a *daß* clause preceded by *dazu, dahin, so weit.*

The infinitive is possible only in the case of a verb which implies a free decision (normally a verb of external action, not of emotion).

The *daß* clause, on the other hand, merely indicates a result and may be substituted for the infinitive as well as used in all other cases.

The distinctions between *dazu, dahin* and *so weit* are, if made, as follows. *Dazu* is used when no special effort is suggested and the result may be looked upon as an ordinary, normal action. It cannot be stressed. *Dahin* presents the result as the accomplishment of a goal, which may be followed by further action, without this, however, being the concern of the speaker. The result may be an attitude of mind in which a person is favourably or unfavourably disposed towards a thing. *So weit*, which is not normally followed by the infinitive, can imply that a stage that is not conclusive has been reached.

Again, it can imply that the result is something unusual, difficult, unexpected or extreme.

(a) Examples of the infinitive.

Ich habe ihn dazu gebracht, ja zu unserem Plan zu sagen.

'*Er (Hitler) werde als größter Feldherr in die Geschichte eingehen und bei einer Offensive den Feind dahin bringen, grade an die Stelle zu marschieren, wo er ihn haben wolle*' (U. von Hassel, *Vom Anderen Deutschland*).

Ich habe ihn dahin gebracht, in Ruhe darüber nachzudenken.

(b) Examples of a *daß* clause.

In the examples of the preceding section a *daß* clause could be substituted for the infinitive. A *daß* clause must, however, be used in the case of an involuntary action or an emotion. *Sie brachte ihn so weit, daß er bei seinem Nachbarn einbrach* could mean that he performed this act under the stress of emotion. The infinitive would clearly indicate a decision.

Er hat sie so weit gebracht, daß sie ihn haßt.

Er hat ihn so weit gebracht, daß er sie Schönheit der Bachschen Musik empfindet.

Sie brachte ihn so weit, daß er sich aus dem Fenster stürzte.

3. Other expressions formed with *bringen*. In these *bringen* governs not a person or a thing, but a *daß* clause anticipated by *es*.

Es dahin (soweit) bringen, daß...; es fertig bringen (kriegen), daß...; es zustande (zuwege) bringen, daß....

Ich will es schon dahin bringen, daß sie mich fürchten (make them fear me).

Ich kriege es nicht fertig, daß der Pfahl aufrecht steht (I can't get the post to stand up straight).

Er hat es zustande gebracht, daß die Arbeiter in seiner Fabrik nicht mehr streiken.

F. Examples of other renderings which involve a *daß* clause. These can often be used when the object of 'make' or 'get' is a thing. They are frequent in familiar style.

Sehen Sie mal zu, daß der Pfahl aufrecht steht.

Sie müssen dafür sorgen, daß die beiden Bretter sich berühren.

Können Sie es nicht so machen, daß die zwei Wege sich kreuzen? (make the two paths cross).

MAN 1. **Mann:** a member of the male sex. It is only used in this sense, i.e. in contrast to woman. The form *Mann* may, however, stand as plural, when preceded by a numeral, in reference to the numerical strength of a team, squad, army, or the like. *Mann* also means 'husband'.

Er ist ein kluger Mann.

Der Mann had vielseitige Interessen.

Die Männer sind spät gekommen.

Ich brauche 1000 Mann, um das Manöver durchzuführen.

(a) The plural is the same in form as the singular when a body of men is meant.

Hundert Mann waren bereit, einzugreifen.

2. **Mensch:**[1] human being, the human race.

---

[1] See also 'people'. *Mensch* must also be used to translate 'individual' and 'person' when these are synonymous terms. The German *Person* denotes: (i) human beings as contrasted with things; (ii) persons of rank (i.e. personage); (iii) females, mostly of the lower orders and often in a disparaging sense; (iv) the characters of a play.

Der Mensch ist sterblich.
Der Mensch braucht Beschäftigung.
Kein Mensch weiß das.

3. In the sense of 'servant', 'worker', 'soldier', 'sailor', and the like whether singular or plural, German can only use the specific term.
Die Arbeiter verließen die Fabrik um 4 Uhr (the men).

MARK (v.) **1.** Put a mark upon something.
(a) Against or under words in a text in order to emphasize their importance: **anstreichen** (against), **unterstreichen** (underline).
Ich habe die einschlägige Stelle angestrichen, unterstrichen.
(b) Put a sign in a book to indicate how far one has read: **Ein Zeichen machen** (*setzen*).
Als er das Buch beiseite legte, machte er ein Zeichen an dem Punkt, wo er zu lesen aufgehört hatte.
(c) Put a mark on something to indicate something about it, e.g. the price or manufacturer of an article. The mark may be an object, e.g. a monument, which indicates where something took place. **Bezeichnen**, often followed by a phrase with *mit*. **Markieren**, a *Fremdwort* with the same meaning as *bezeichnen* but more technical: to put a stamp on. *Mit rinem Zettel versehen* (see 'provide').
Jeder Artikel ist mit dem Preis bezeichnet.
Der Mantel ist mit dem Namen der Firma markiert.
Die Gefahrenstellen waren nicht deutlich markiert.
Der Koffer ist mit einem Zettel versehen, auf dem sein Name steht.
Die Stelle, wo das Unglück stattfand, ist mit einem Kreuz bezeichnet.
(d) In the sense of to sign-post: **beschildern**.
Die Straße, Abzweigung ist klar beschildert.
(e) In the sense of to draw lines on something: **einzeichnen**.
Er zeichnete die Reiseroute auf der Karte ein.
(f) To be a distinguishing mark or feature of, to characterize (*S.O.D.*), often in passive voice: **kennzeichnen, charakterisieren, im Zeichen stehen von**.
Desillusionierung und eine hektische Vergnügungssucht kennzeichneten die zwanziger Jahre unseres Jahrhunderts.
Die zwanziger Jahre standen im Zeichen der Desillusionierung und einer hektischen Vergnügungssucht.

MARK (s.) **1.** Anything that spoils or destroys a surface; a spot, stain, smear, scar, scratch, line, etc. (*A.L.*): **Fleck**.
Wer hat diese schmutzigen Flecken auf meinem neuen Heft verursacht? (*A.L.*)
2. A physical peculiarity; something on the body by which a person or animal may be recognized (*A.L.*): (a) **Mal** if the person is born with it or it is or becomes permanent.
Sie hat ein Mal auf der Haut.
Ein Muttermal: birth mark.
Er hat ein Brandmal auf dem Bein.
(b) **Narbe**: the mark left by a wound, an incision.
Die Operation hat Narben auf seinem Rücken gelassen.
(c) **Fleck** may disappear.
Sein Gesicht hatte blaue Flecken, die auf Schläge hindeuteten.

3. An end in view: goal, object (*W.*).
(a) In the specific sense of target, something towards which a missile is directed, a thing aimed at (*W.*): **Zielscheibe**, which can also be used figuratively.

> *Die Zielscheibe genau in der Mitte treffen* (or: *ins Schwarze treffen*, hit the bull's eye).
> *Viele sind die Zielscheibe seines Spottes, seiner Witze gewesen.*

(b) The point desired to be made: the question under discussion (*W.*), mostly in the phrases 'beside the mark', 'wide of the mark' (near the mark), German uses such phrases as: **nicht am Platze sein, fehlgetroffen, danebengelungen** (see 'miss'), **am Ziel vorbeischießen**.

> *Seine Vermutungen, seine Vorwürfe waren nicht weit fehlgetroffen.*
> *Seine Erklärungen schossen am Ziel vorbei.*

(c) A standard or acceptable level of performance, quality or condition: norm (*W.*), mostly in the phrase 'up to the mark'. **Auf der Höhe sein**: of physical death.

> *Ich fühle mich heute nicht ganz auf der Höhe.*
> *Den Anforderungen genügen, entsprechen*: to come up to demands (see 'demand').
> *Seine Arbeit genügt allen Anforderungen.*

4. In the general sense of *sign*.
(a) Something that gives evidence of something else: sign, indication, token (*W.*): **Zeichen** (see 'sign'), **Kennzeichen** (i.e. a sign by which one knows, recognizes something).

> *Als ein Zeichen, Kennzeichen ihres Gesinnungswechsels* (*W.*).
> *Ein sicheres Zeichen, Kennzeichen der gesellschaftlichen Stellung dieser Familie* (*W.*).
> *Ein Zeichen von Intelligenz* (*A.L.*).

(b) A characteristic or distinguishing sign or quality (*W.*): **Kennzeichen, Merkmal, Charakteristikum**.

> *Demut sollte ein Kennzeichen* (*Merkmal* etc.) *jedes Christen sein.*

(c) A character, device, label, brand, seal, or other sign put on an article especially to show the maker or owner, to certify quality or for identification: trademark (*W.*): **Schutzmarke**.
(d) A written or printed symbol (*W.*). Punctuation mark: **Interpunktion, Zeichensetzung**.
(e) Postmark: **Poststempel**.
(f) A symbol used by a teacher to represent his estimate of a student's work or conduct (*W.*): **Note, Zensur** (the total mark); **Punkt(e)** when it is a question of awarding or deducting single marks in numerical terms.

> *Für seinen Aufsatz hat er eine gute Note, Zensur bekommen.*
> *Er verlor viele Punkte wegen seiner unklaren Ausdrucksweise.*
> *In Geographie hat er 95% als Note, Zensur bekommen.*
> *Der Lehrer hat wegen der schlechten Handschrift 10 Punkte abgezogen.*

5. Attention, notice (*W.*).
(a) Rather old-fashioned in the combination 'of mark', i.e. worthy of note, distinguished, but common in the phrase 'to make one's mark'.

> *Nichts Bemerkenswertes geschah, während Sie fort waren.*
> *Er kann sehr leicht ein Mann von Bedeutung werden.*
> *Er machte sich einen Namen auf verschiedenen Gebieten.*

MARK

(b) A lasting or strong impression: an enduring effect (*W.*), again particularly in the phrase 'to make one's mark'. A strong favourable impression. No exact German equivalent.

Er leistete Vorzügliches auf dem Gebiet der Entwicklungsgeschichte (W.).

Bestrebt, mit meinem ersten Buch Eindruck zu machen (W.).

Als Laufbursche machte ich einen so guten Eindruck, daß sie mich zum zweiten Buchhalter beförderten.

MARRY 1. **Heiraten** refers to the act by which the two parties marry each other. It cannot be used in the passive voice.

Er hat sie geheiratet.

Sie hat ihn geheiratet.

Er hat geheiratet.

Sie haben geheiratet.

2. **Verheiraten** draws attention to the state of matrimony, not the act of marrying. It is used passively, reflexively, and, in the sense of 'to give in marriage', actively.

Er ist verheiratet.

Sie haben sich verheiratet.

Sie hat sich mit einem alten Bekannten verheiratet.

Der Vater hat seine Tochter mit seinem Geschäftspartner verheiratet.

3. **(Sich) vermählen** is a dignified term for *verheiraten*, and is applied to important personages. It is also used figuratively.

Hoheit haben sich vermählt.

4. **Trauen** is used of the official who performs the marriage ceremony.

Der Geistliche hat das Paar getraut.

MATTER (v.)   Sense: to be of importance, concern.

1. The idiomatic phrases 'it doesn't matter' (i.e. negative); what does it matter? does it matter? (i.e. interrogative): German **machen, tun, schaden** (i.e. to do damage), **ausmachen** (impersonal subject and, if required, dative of person) (to make a difference). Of these *machen* is the most general and suggests that the thing is taken lightly, *tun* has the same meaning but is less general, *schaden* means 'no harm done'. *Ausmachen* may be modified by such adverbs as *viel, wenig*. It is more common in the question form than the other verbs.

A. *Ich habe das Buch nicht mitgebracht.* B. *Es macht (tut) nichts.*

A. *Ich habe den Kotflügel des Wagens ein bißchen gekratzt.* B. *Es schadet nichts.*

Es macht weiter nichts (addition of *weiter* common), *ob er kommt oder geht.*

Was würde es schaden, wenn die Monarchie abgeschafft werden sollte?

Was macht es aus, wenn wir eine Stunde früher oder später ankommen?

Macht es dir was aus, wenn ich das Buch etwas länger behalte?

Es macht nichts (aus), wenn es regnet, wir gehen sowieso hin.

Wenn Sie es nicht so fest versprochen hätten, würde es wenig ausmachen.

Es macht mir weiter nichts aus, ob die Wahlen dieses Jahr stattfinden oder später.

2. When the subject in English is not impersonal, German still uses *ausmachen*, but also a number of other expressions: **ankommen auf** (with

impersonal *es* as subject and the person in the dative case); **wichtig** (important) *sein*, **bedeuten** (mean). *Ankommen auf* is also used as an equivalent of the English 'to attach importance to', 'to set store by'.

Ein Tag mehr oder weniger macht nichts aus.
Auf einen Tag mehr oder weniger kommt es nicht an.
Auf dein Wohlergehen kommt es mir sehr an.
Es kommt mir darauf, an, daß er dke Anweisungen genau liest.
Alles andere bedeutet wenig für mich (*ist wenig wichtig*).

MAY, MIGHT   A. The meanings of 'may' and 'can'.

'May' is related to the noun 'might' (=power), as *mögen* is with *Macht*. The original meaning of both 'may' and *mögen* was 'to have power', i.e. to have ability, to be able. 'Can' and *können* also denote ability in persons,[1] capacity in things. In addition, they express possibility.[2] 'Can' expresses it not in the sense of uncertainty whether a thing will be, happen, etc., but of capability of being, happening, etc. under certain circumstances. The *S.O.D.* defines this meaning (II. 3) as follows: 'Expressing possibility: *can you*...? = is it possible for you...?' It gives the examples: 'And can you blame them' (Stubbes); 'Thy way thou canst not miss' (Milton). The connection between these two senses of possibility, 'capability of being' and 'uncertainty of being', is close. In other words, it is a short step from the type of possibility expressed by 'can' to that expressed by 'may' (i.e. uncertainty). This becomes particularly clear in questions (e.g. can it be that...?, may it be that...?). It will be seen later that *können* expresses both types of possibility.

'May' can denote both power or ability and possibility in the sense of uncertainty, one sense predominating sometimes to the exclusion of the other. Thus, 'may' sometimes means 'may be able', as in the sentence: you may win a prize, if you work hard. In the following example, 'the University may, if it thinks fit, dispense students from examinations', the sense is 'has the power, though it may not exercise it'. Such a use clearly contains also the germs of the idea of permission. The sense is seen more clearly in the following: 'this passage may be interpreted in two ways'. The meaning is: I regard these two interpretations as possible, but I state this as my own opinion, i.e. subjectively, not as an objective fact. The latter would be expressed by 'can'. Again 'may', used in purpose clauses or depending on a verb such as 'hope', combines the ideas of ability and possibility (e.g. work that you may succeed; I hope our association may endure).

The various senses of 'may' in present-day use all express the idea of possibility (uncertainty) with or without some other idea. The *P.O.D.* classifies them as follows: possibility, permission, request, reproach, aim, wish.

'Possibility' may be apprehended more objectively or more subjectively. The use of 'may' in concessive clauses is an instance of the latter.

Both *mögen* and *können* originally had the same meanings as 'may' and 'can' respectively. In the course of development the German words, while retaining some meanings of the English words, have lost others. These losses have been offset by the growth of new meanings (e.g. *mögen* in the sense of 'like'). (See under 'like'.)

---

[1] 'Can' like *können* formerly meant also 'know' (*Ich kann Deutsch*). Both are related to *kennen*. Compare also English 'ken', 'uncouth'.

[2] 'Possibility' comes from Latin *posse*, to be able.

MAY

B. Mögen meant in the Middle High German period 'to be able'. This meaning is now extinct[1] as a primary sense, and, as a secondary sense, has survived in fewer uses than is the case with 'may'. In reference to possibility as a primary meaning and when combined with other ideas (e.g. request), it is also less widely used than 'may'. On the other hand, it has acquired the sense of 'like'.[2]

1. Possibility as the primary meaning. Here *mögen* has to a varying extent a subjective colouring. It can indicate an inclination to regard the possibility as a probability (in English 'well' is often added to 'may' in this sense, in German *wohl, ja,* or *schon* may, but need not be added to *mögen*). From the idea of probability it is a short step to that of concession (expressed by *mögen*), i.e. an admission that a thing is a fact, or at least highly probable, though without bearing on something else. In this sense *mögen* is practically confined to literature, conversational use[3] being extremely rare. Even in writing it is often apt to sound precious. Examples that require no further explanation are:

Das mag schon sein (that may well be).

Gewisse Kreise in Deutschland mögen wegen der Spannung zwischen Rußland und den Westmächten auf mildere Friedensbedingungen rechnen.

Ich bin gespannt, was das wohl sein mag.

Ich war mir nicht klar darüber, was das sein mochte.

Was er auch immer tun mag, ich weiß, daß es mit den besten Absichten geschieht.

(a) A limitation to the use of *mögen* in the above sense is that apart from subordinate clauses in strictly concessive form *mögen* can be used freely in the positive and the negative interrogative, but not at all in the negative indicative, and only in certain circumstances in the interrogative. In the latter it occurs only in conjunction with an interrogative pronoun or adverb (e.g. *wer, was, wie, wann*), and imparts to the phrase a kind of poetic wonder. The English 'may' is used 'to render a question less abrupt or pointed' (*S.O.D.* II. 6). For 'may' in questions see also *können* (below, **C**); for its use with a negative, see **D**.

Was mag das wohl sein?

Mag es nicht auch sein, daß er es schon weiß?

(b) The translation of the compound tenses (may have been, might have been) presents special difficulties. The forms *mag gewesen sein, mochte sein* and *mochte gewesen sein* must be distinguished. *Mag gewesen sein* records a judgment or impression made at the moment of speaking, i.e. from the point of view of the present. *Mochte sein* records a judgment or impression already made, and implies that the action or state expressed by the infinitive was contemporaneous with this judgment. It is therefore used in connected historical narrative. *Mochte gewesen sein* records a judgment or impression made in the past about an action or state anterior to the making of the judgment.

Mochte sein translates 'may have been', i.e. the distinction between the

---

[1] It is preserved in *vermögen*, which generally refers to inner ability, particularly of an emotional, ethical character; less to external skills, and not to external circumstances.

[2] The connection between the idea of possibility and that of liking is seen in a sentence such as: I suggest you might see this play. In the sense of 'like' *mögen* may take a direct object or be followed by an infinitive. See also footnote to 'anxious' (p. 18, n. 1).

[3] Examples, which are all border-line cases, are: *das mag sein, er mag wollen oder nicht.*

English terms does not correspond to that between the German. As an equivalent of 'might' *mochte* can only refer to what is contemporaneous, i.e. not to the future (for 'might' in the latter sense see *können*, below, **C**).

In this combination *mochte* never becomes *möchte*, which can refer to the future, even in indirect speech.

Es mögen insgesamt 30 Personen dagewesen sein.

Er berichtete, es mochten insgesamt 30 Personen da sein.

Er berichtete, es mochten insgesamt 30 Personen dagewesen sein.

Ich ging spazieren und sah einen Mann, der bessere Zeiten gesehen haben mag.

Ich ging spazieren und sah einen Mann, der bessere Zeiten gesehen haben mochte.

Er schrieb, er habe einen Mann getroffen, der in seiner Jugend bessere Zeiten gesehen haben mochte (not *möchte* despite indirect speech).

2. *Mögen* is used in literature, but not in conversation, in subordinate clauses after verbs which express emotional states of mind, e.g. verbs of wishing, fearing, hoping. Also in purpose clauses and in indirect question (expressing wonder in the latter case). Except in indirect question this use serves as a periphrastic subjunctive (*S.O.D.* II. 7, *a*). After verbs of wishing, fearing, and in purpose clauses the subjunctive of *mögen* is usual (mostly *möchte*).

Ich wünschte, er möchte kommen.

Ich fürchte, es möchte schon zu spät sein.

Ich hoffe, daß die Verbindung zwischen uns noch weiterhin bestehen mag.

Ich nahm das Angebot an, damit es nicht aussehen möchte, daß es mir gleichgültig war.

3. In principal clauses *mögen* is used in the present subjunctive[1] as an equivalent of *mag* to express a wish.

Möge Gott dich erhalten!

4. *Mögen* is used in conversation as well as in literature in indirect command, request. This use is general in German, whereas 'may' in English is confined to a few verbs such as 'request'.[2]

Ich sagte ihm, er möchte doch nicht annehmen, daß ich den Plan unbedingt ablehnen würde.

Ich schlug vor, er möchte das im Auge behalten.

C. Können expresses possibility in an objective way. It is, however, also used in conversation and in ordinary prose where *mögen* would be used in literature, except in clauses which are strictly concessive in form. In the concessive sense *wohl, ja, schon* may be added. It is used similarly after verbs of fearing, hoping and in purpose clauses, though not to express a wish, an indirect command, or an indirect question. It must be used when 'may' combines the senses of ability and possibility (see the examples under **A**).

Since *können* also means 'to be able' ambiguity is possible, particularly in the present tense *kann*. In conversation this ambiguity can be eliminated by the inflection of the voice. In writing the ambiguity remains. See **D** for renderings which avoid it. As 'might' and 'could' are often practically inter-

---

[1] *Möchte* in this sense is rendered into English by 'would'. *Möchte er doch bald kommen!*

[2] *Mögen* in the present indicative and present subjunctive also expresses a command which is expressed in English by 'let'. *Er mag, möge, nur sagen.* The indicative makes the command shorter.

changeable, unlike 'may' and 'can', *könnte* can mostly be used to translate both terms.

With a negative, *können* can only mean 'to be able'. In the positive inter-rogative, and negative interrogative it can mean both 'may' and 'can'.

Vielleicht is often added in a question and with the conditional tenses: *könnte (sein), hätte (sein) können.*

Können is used to translate 'might' when it denotes a reproach. It is unusual in conjunction with another modal verb (e.g. he may have to leave).

Es kann heute regnen.

Er kann heute kommen (may or can).

Das kann wahr sein.

Das kann vorkommen (may or can).

Das kann wohl, ja, schon, sein.

Er kann das gesagt haben.

Kann er das gesagt haben?

Glauben Sie, daß wir noch Erfolg haben können?

Es können insgesamt 30 Personen dagewesen sein.

Ich weiß nicht, wie er sich zu dem Vorschlag stellt, er könnte ihn zu radikal finden.

Ich fürchte, Sie können sich zuviel zugemutet haben.

Kann das vielleicht die Ursache des Fiaskos sein?

Er hätte vielleicht den Preis gewinnen können, wenn er gearbeitet hätte.

Sie hätten es mir doch sagen können! (a reproach).

Sie könnten mich vielleicht verständigen, wenn das Buch ankommt (a request).

D. Other renderings of 'may' in the sense of 'possibility'. To avoid the ambiguity admitted by *können* and to render 'may' accompanied by a negative, resort may be had to such phrases as *vielleicht, es kann sein, daß. . . .* These are used as commonly as *können.*

Vielleicht kommt er heute.

Vielleicht regnet es heute nicht mehr.

Er hätte es vielleicht getan, wenn sie ihn gebeten hätten.

Es kann sein, daß wir zu hart gewesen sind.

E. Permission.

Dürfen expresses permission, both with regard to the asking for and the granting of it, and whether the request is justified or not. It refers to import-ant matters without taking the granting of the permission as a matter of course. **Können** expresses the idea more familiarly, and is used particularly when asking permission to do something for someone else. Though 'can' is sometimes used in the same way, it is still accepted by many authorities as good English only when accompanied by a negative. *Dürfen* with a negative (but not the negative interrogative) indicates a strong denial of permission, which is expressed in English by 'must not'.[1, 2]

Darf ich auf Ihre Hilfe rechnen?

Sie dürfen gehen.

Sie dürfen annehmen, daß Ihnen keine Schwierigkeiten in den Weg gelegt werden.

---

[1] *Nicht müssen* corresponds to 'need not', 'not to have to', or 'must not' when this is no stronger than 'need not'.

[2] *Mögen* only expresses permission in the sense that the person who grants it places no obstacle in the way because he is indifferent to what happens. English expresses this by 'let. . .' (for all I care).

Kann ich dieses Buch borgen?
Kann ich Ihnen dabei behilflich sein?
Sie können das Buch mitnehmen.
Der Stuhl kann hier bleiben.

MEAN[1] **1. Meinen:** to intend, to indicate or to convey a certain sense, or to intend a remark to have a particular reference. In the sense of 'to be disposed' (e.g. to mean ill) it can like 'mean' be used only in a few fixed expressions. In all uses except those in the passive voice, the subject must be a person, the object may be a person or a thing.[2]

Was meinen Sie?
Ich meine, daß unsere Aussichten schlecht sind.
Er meint Sie.
Sind Sie gemeint?
Das Gesetz ist mit diesem Hinweis gemeint.
Er meint es gut (mit Ihnen).

2. Bedeuten. Applied to things[3] this term means 'to have a certain signification, import', 'to portend'. With a personal subject the meaning is 'to be of importance' to another person. See also under next section.[4]

Was bedeutet dieses Wort?
Der Name bedeutet mir nichts.
Diese Hilfe bedeutet mir sehr viel.
Es bedeutet wenig, daß er mir so viel versprochen hat.
Diese Wolken können Regen bedeuten.
Eine solche Politik bedeutet Krieg.
Er bedeutet sehr viel für mich.

3. Heißen implies a categorical assertion that such and such is the meaning of something previously referred to. It is final, while *bedeuten* leaves room for doubt, for other interpretations. It can only be followed by a clause, i.e. not a noun.

Die Regierung hat das Benzin rationert. Das heißt, wir können Sonntags nicht mehr ausfahren.

4. Besagen is 'to make clear' something that is unclear or not definite. It is more tentative than *heißen*. In reference to a preceding word or statement it comes close to 'imply'.[5] Its subject can be personal only in combination with a modal verb such as *wollen* (see example below). When it does not refer to any specific preceding word or words, it can mean 'to tell', 'to reveal' something that was not known or apparent before.[6]

Die Rationierung des Benzins besagt, daß der Handel mit Amerika ins Stocken geraten ist.

---

[1] The sense of 'intend' is not treated in this article.

[2] Followed by the infinitive and in certain cases a *daß* clause, *meinen* means not 'intend' but 'to be of the opinion' that a thing, denoted by the infinitive, is possible. *Ich meinte, dir damit zu helfen. Vater meint, wir sollten jetzt gehen.*

[3] With a personal subject and followed by a dative denoting a person, the sense is 'to intimate to a person' that he must do a certain thing. *Ich bedeutete ihm, daß er auf seinen Plan verzichten müsse.*

[4] For *Bedeutung* see 'sense'.

[5] German has no general term for 'imply'. In reference to the implications of a word considered as a term in a dictionary the following phrases are common: *in dem Wort ist (mit) enthalten, daß . . .*; or more colloquially: *in dem Wort steckt (noch), daß. . . .*

[6] Example: *ein Blick in den Raum besagt alles.*

Willst du damit besagen, daß ich das Geld gestohlen habe? (*Besagen* suggests more strongly than *sagen* that the accusation was expressed indirectly.)
Es ist ein Name, der mir nichts besagt.[1]

MEET A. Of persons: to come into each other's presence or company (without secondary associations such as 'receive', 'get to know').

1. Begegnen is, strictly speaking, used of people coming from opposite directions, and indicates a chance encounter (i.e. to run across). It frequently suggests that the persons are known only casually to each other, or that the encounter is unwelcome to one or more of the persons. Generally subject and object can be interchanged without any perceptible difference in meaning. Similarly *Begegnung*: a chance encounter.

Ich bin ihm nie begegnet.
Ich bin ihm heute auf der Brücke begegnet (or: *er ist mir...begegnet*).
Der ist mir verschiedentlich in London begegnet.
Die D-Züge von und nach Berlin begegnen sich in Hannover.
Er ist der letzte Mensch, dem ich begegnen will.

2. Treffen[2] can denote a chance or an arranged meeting. While not excluding casual acquaintance, it more often suggests closer relations and the spending of a certain time in each other's company.

In arranging meetings *sich treffen* is more common than *Sie*, etc. as object (e.g. *wir treffen uns vor dem Rathaus* = I'll meet you...). *Uns* conveys no implication of intimacy.

To emphasize that a meeting is arranged, often for an important discussion, and is not accidental, *sich treffen mit jdm.* is sometimes used. It is unnecessary to use it with reference to the future.

Wir haben uns heute auf der Brücke getroffen.
Ich habe ihn ganz zufällig in der Bahn getroffen.
Wir treffen uns heute abend.
Ich habe mich mit ihm im Wirtshaus getroffen.

3. Zusammentreffen[3] is used (*a*) to emphasize the place at which a number of people coming from opposite directions meet; (*b*) of a meeting which has results (often momentous).

Die Ausflügler trafen auf dem Marktplatz zusammen.
Immer wenn wir zusammentrafen, heckten wir irgendwelchen Unsinn aus.
Als Churchill mit Roosevelt im Atlantischen Ozean zusammentraf, ahnte die Welt kaum, wie folgenschwer ihre Besprechungen sein sollten.

4. Entgegengehen: to go to meet, in the sense of 'to go forward a few steps to meet' someone approaching. Similarly *entgegenkommen, -eilen*, etc.
Er ging seinen Gästen entgegen.

B. Of persons with secondary associations. Some common uses are:

1. Zusammentreten, of deliberative bodies.
Das Parlament, das Kommittee, tritt heute zusammen.

---

[1] *Es ist ein Name, der mir nichts sagt*: which conveys nothing to me.
[2] *Treffen* also means to 'hit the target' (see 'strike' and footnote to 'affect', p. 10, n. 1). *Treffen auf* means to 'come, hap upon'. *Antreffen*: to find a person in a place or condition. An adverbial phrase of place or condition often follows.
[3] *Zusammentreffen* can also mean a 'clash'. Compare *Treffen*, as a noun, which can mean an 'engagement' in the sense of combat (as well as a meeting of a large number of people).

2. Empfangen: to receive, sometimes for the purpose of discussion.
Der Außenminister empfing den neuen Botschafter am Bahnhof.
Der Premierminister empfängt heute die Gewerkschaftsführer.

3. Abholen (to go, call, for a person); **erwarten** (to await a person): to meet a person on his arrival and take him to some destination.
Er holte meinen Bruder am Bahnhof ab (erwartete...).

4. Kennen lernen: to get to know, to make the acquaintance of.
Möchten Sie den neuen Konsul kennen lernen?
Er lernte seine Frau in Paris kennen.[1]

C. Of things.

1. Of vehicles.
Verschiedene internationale Züge begegnen sich in Basel (coming from
   different directions).
Ein Autobus wartet auf den 10 Uhr Zug.

2. Of geographical features. See 'touch', 'join'.
Die Linien berühren sich in diesem Punkt.
Die beiden Grundstücke stoßen hier aneinander.
Bei Koblenz fließt die Mosel in den Rhein.

D. Figurative. Some common renderings are:

1. Begegnen
(a) To counter. *Einwänden begegnen.*
(b) To comply with a wish. *Er ist immer bestrebt, meinen Wünschen zu begegnen.*
(c) To return one kind of treatment for another. *Feindschaft mit Freundschaft begegnen.*
(d) To come upon examples of a thing. *Beispiele dieses Wortes begegnen uns bei Goethe* (occur, i.e. the thing as subject).
(e) To meet the gaze. *Eine grauenhafte Szene begegnete unserem Blick.*[2]

2. Entgegenkommen: to arrive at a compromise with a person.
Ich werde mein Bestes tun, Ihnen in dieser Sache entgegenzukommen.

3. 'To satisfy demands, needs' and the like, is translated by **erfüllen** (fulfil), **nachkommen** (comply with), **entsprechen** (comply with).[3] Other, less frequent renderings are given by the dictionaries.
Er hat meinen Forderungen, Wünschen, nicht entsprochen (hat sie nicht erfüllt, ist ihnen nicht nachgekommen).

4. 'To meet (with)' in the sense of 'to receive', 'to experience', a certain treatment or fate must be variously translated. Sometimes *finden*, *erfahren* (see 'experience'), *erleiden* (see 'suffer') are used.
Das Stück fand eine gute Aufnahme.
Er hat viel Freundlichkeit von dir erfahren.
Er hat schwere Verluste erlitten.

MERRY, GAY, CHEERFUL, SPRIGHTLY 'Merry' suggests uninhibited enjoyment, festivity, fun, animal spirits; 'gay' a carefree state of

---

[1] 'To meet one's spouse for the first time' can also be translated by *treffen*.
[2] But: *das Ohr treffen.*
[3] These verbs, like the English equivalents given, are wider in application than this meaning of 'meet'.

mind overflowing with good humour, laughter, and the like; 'cheerful' a disposition to look on the bright side of things and not to yield easily to depression (e.g. the English have a cheerful temperament). The German terms are not close equivalents.[1]

1. Lustig is a wide term and suggests an uninhibited outward expression of high spirits, divorced from all reflection. It can be applied to loud merriment, practical jokes, the romping of children, and the like. See also article on 'funny'.

Er hat viele lustige Geschichten erzählt.
Es war ein sehr lustiger Abend.
Die Kinder sind heute abend sehr lustig.
Ein lustiges Feuer brennt im Kamin.

2. Fröhlich suggests laughter and good spirits as these are manifested in talk, singing, dancing, in association with festivity. Unlike *lustig* it excludes wild, unrestrained actions, but not reflection. See also footnote to article on 'glad' (p. 145, n. 1).

Das war ein fröhlicher Tanz.
Ich wünsch Ihnen ein fröhliches Weihnachtsfest.
Er ist wieder der alte, fröhliche Mensch, den alle liebten.

3. Heiter is applied to a state of mind which manifests itself inwardly more than outwardly and which is unclouded, serene. It can be applied to the higher activities of the mind, e.g. art (e.g. *die Heiterkeit der klassischen Kunst*), and also to its state in relation to everyday tasks and events. In the first case 'serene', 'bright'[2] must often be used in English for lack of closer equivalents. In the latter case it approximates to 'cheerful'. Common to both *heiter* and 'cheerful' are harmony and balance. The German term tends, however, to say more than the English. *Ein heiterer Abend* could mean 'exhilarating to the mind'.

Er hat ein heiteres Wesen.
Der Engländer bleibt sogar in Kriegszeiten heiter.
Er hat ein heiteres Zimmer (heiter can refer to the appearance of things,
  e.g. *ein heiterer Himmel*, serene).

4. Munter suggests animation which expresses itself in movement, particularly in play. Its closest equivalent in English is perhaps 'sprightly' (in German often *lebhaft*) (see article on 'lively'). It often implies too much activity to be translated by 'cheerful'.

Das muntere Spiel der Kinder (suggests running, jumping about).
Sie hat muntere Augen (mobile).

MIND[3] **1.** When the verb makes the reference to the mind clear, it is sufficient to translate 'mind' by the person to whom it is attributed.

Die Propaganda verwirrt die Menschen (confuses people's minds).

---

[1] *Freudig* (see article on 'glad') sometimes approximates to 'cheerful', e.g. *eine freudige Nachricht*, i.e. causing joy, but suggests more positive joy than the English term. *Ein freudiger Spender.*

[2] The normal prose term for 'bright' in reference to light is *hell. Licht* as an adjective in this sense is a more elevated word.

[3] '...in all cases, despite a difference in stress on certain qualities, it denotes a complex of powers of which man is conscious and which includes the perceiving, the remembering, the thinking, and less often, the feeling and willing powers or functions' (Webster's *Dictionary of Synonyms*).

Beruhigen Sie sich (set your mind at rest).
Er ist auf andere Dinge bedacht (his mind is taken up with other things).

2. Geist corresponds to 'spirit' more frequently than to 'mind'. As an equivalent of the latter when this refers to the thinking faculty, *Geist* is generally a lofty term and inclines more to abstract than to concrete use. It is thus to be found more often with the definite article than with the possessive adjective, which, however, is possible.

Der Geist ist der kostbarste Besitz des Menschen.
Der deutsche Geist.
Sein Geist war auf höhere Dinge gerichtet.
Das Allumfassende seines Geistes.

Though the most characteristic use of *Geist* is to suggest loftiness and range of content, it may be qualified by adjectives which denote the opposite.

Ein beschränkter Geist.

Since in the meaning of 'spirit' it can denote life, vitality,[1] particularly the subtle, invisible essence of a thing, it can also, as an equivalent of 'mind', be qualified by adjectives which express vitality and be used in contexts which by implication attribute this characteristic to the mind.[2, 3]

Ein reger, lebhafter, Geist.
'*Der Pfarrer war die Güte selbst, er wußte meinen lebhaften Geist zu fesseln...*' (E. T. A. Hoffman, *Die Elixiere des Teufels*).
'*Du weißt, mein lieber Rufin, daß ich nichts in der Welt so fürchte und scheue, als die brennenden Sonnenstrahlen des Tages, welche die Kräfte meines Körpers aufzehren und meinen Geist dermaßen abspannen und ermatten, daß...*' (E. T. A. Hoffman, *Klein Zaches*).

Geist is used much less with *haben* than 'mind' with 'have'.[4] The following examples are fairly common.

Er hat einen regen, lebhaften, zersetzenden, Geist.

3. Geistig (intellectual,[5] spiritual) can often be used in phrases which describe the characteristics or power of an individual's mind.[6]

Er ist seinem Bruder geistig überlegen (has a better mind than...).

4. Verstand is the 'faculty of understanding',[7] 'reason',[8] and may be used

---

[1] Examples: *den Geist aufgeben, die erschlafften Geister erfrischen.*

[2] In this sentence *Geisteskräfte* or *geistige Kräfte* is sometimes used for 'mind'. Example: *seine geistigen Kräfte haben nachgelassen.*

[3] An extension of this characteristic leads to wit, which meaning *Geist* has in a few expressions (e.g. *Geist haben*). Compare French *esprit*, *spirituel*, Dutch *geestig*. Similarly *geistreich* suggests a brilliance, cleverness of mind that is akin to wit.

[4] *Geist* is used freely with the verb *sein*, but the reference is less to the thinking faculty than to the person in general. Thus *er ist ein edler, lebhafter, Geist* suggests the nature of the person's actions more than his thoughts.

[5] Since *geistig* combines the meanings of intellectual and spiritual, it is a wider term than either and has no exact equivalent in English.

[6] *Geistig*, used adjectivally, can be coupled with a thing, but not a person, except in the case of *Mensch* (e.g. *der geistige Mensch*). Examples: *eine geistige Kunst, geistige Interessen.*

[7] See 'understanding'.

[8] Kant's distinction between *Verstand* (the faculty of clear and logical thinking on sensuous material) and *Vernunft* (the faculty of perceiving the relationships in non-sensuous material and of integrating them into a whole) is not observed in the everyday use of these terms. *Verstand* is more widely used and translates 'mind', 'understanding', 'reason', 'sense' (often expanded to *gesunder Menschenverstand*, i.e. common sense). It suggests the operation of the mind on specific material more forcibly than *Vernunft*, which refers more exclusively to a state of mind, i.e. reasonableness, sensibleness, and is mostly, though

to translate 'mind' when the reference contained in the latter is to logic and clarity of thought. Unlike *Geist* which is mostly directed to elevated spheres, it can operate on any kind of material: it can be combined freely with *haben* and with any adjective that can be associated with the term intellect.

Its additional meaning of 'common sense',[1] 'practical sense', has given rise to a number of fixed expressions which, mostly negative, denote the absence of this quality. They may be translated by 'mind' or 'wits'.

Er hat einen klaren, scharfen, durchdringenden, Verstand.
Er hat seinen Verstand an den verschiedenartigsten Problemen ausgebildet.
Sie haben Ihren Verstand gar nicht gebraucht.
Der Verstand stand ihm still.
Er ist nicht recht bei Verstand.

5. **Kopf** is used in much the same way as 'head', though perhaps more extensively so, in the sense of 'mind'. Like *Verstand*, it refers to capacity for clear, logical thought, and, preceded by an appropriate adjective, is used with both *haben* and *sein*.

Like 'head', it is also used, mostly in fixed expressions, as the place where thoughts reside, without reference to the activity or the quality of the mind. Compare *Sinn*.

Er ist ein hervorragender, schlauer, gescheiter, Kopf.
Man braucht die besten Köpfe, um so schwierige Probleme zu bewältigen.
Ich kann so viele Tatsachen nicht im Kopf behalten.
Der Gedanke ging, schoß, fuhr, mir durch den Kopf.
Er hat es sich in den Kopf gesetzt, daß man sich über ihn lustig mache.
Schlagen Sie nich den Gedanken aus dem Kopf.
Sein Kopf steckt voller dunkler Pläne.

6. **Gedanken** should be used to refer to the content of the mind at any given moment.

Seine Gedanken sind verwirrt.
Richten Sie Ihre Gedanken auf diese wichtige Angelegenheit.
Seine Gedanken kehren immer zu demselben Punkt zurück.
Seine Gedanken schweifen ab.
Ihre Gedanken sind nicht be der Arbeit.
Ich war anderswo mit meinen Gedanken, als Sie mich anredeten.

7. **Sinn** is the faculty which makes consciousness of external and internal impressions possible. It refers to any of the special organs of sense[2] through

not entirely, restricted to fixed phrases. *Vernunft* is, however, the appropriate term for 'reason' conceived as an attribute that ennobles man. Compare *Faust I* (ll. 283–6):

> *'Ein wenig besser würd' er leben,*
> *Hätt'st du ihm nicht den Schein des Himmelslichts gegeben;*
> *Er nennt's Vernunft und braucht's allein,*
> *Nur tierischer als jedes Tier zu sein.'*

The adjective *vernünftig* translates 'sensible' and sometimes 'reasonable'. In many cases, however, the latter cannot be rendered by *vernünftig*, particularly as an adverb (e.g. *er weiß einigermaßen Bescheid*). 'Reasonable' differs from 'sensible' in emphasizing the exercise of a sense of measure. For example: Please return the book in a reasonable time (*in absehbarer Zeit*). While *vernünftig* refers to an attitude or state of mind, *verständig* draws more attention to the object on which the mind operates, and means 'displaying intelligence' (logic or commonsense) in dealing with this object. *Sachverständig* = expert.

[1] See footnote p. 215, n. 8.
[2] See 'sense'.

which these impressions pass, and to consciousness in general. In the latter case it is often associated with one of the faculties of thinking, feeling or willing. In earlier German[1] it was used in this way more freely than at the present day, when it is mostly confined to fixed expressions. As a translation of 'mind' it occurs in the following senses.

(a) Consciousness of the most general kind. Compare *Kopf*.

Der Idee kam mir in den Sinn.

Der Gedanke fuhr mir durch den Sinn.

Ich werde Ihre Wünsche im Sinne behalten.

Schlagen Sie sich den Plan aus dem Sinn.

Die Sinne vergingen ihm (his mind became a blank, i.e. in the sense of a mental black-out).

'*Ein Märchen aus alten Zeiten | Das kommt mir nicht aus dem Sinn*' (Heine, *Die Lorelei*).

(b) Wits, sanity. Compare *Verstand*.

Bei Sinnen sein (in one's right mind).

Von Sinnen sein (out of one's mind).

Seine fünf Sinne beisammen haben.

(c) Opinion, intention.

Anderen Sinnes werden (change one's mind, either opinion or intention).

Wir waren eines Sinnes (of one mind).

8. Gemüt is the seat of certain types of feelings, particularly those which embrace the world and its objects with warmth and affection.[2,3] It excludes sexual emotion and, though it may be deeply moved, violent feelings. The sanity, stability, equilibrium, excitement of the mind may, however, be implied. It is, further, sometimes conceived as the source of poetry, par-

---

[1] The following examples, which would not now be used in ordinary prose are taken from the works of E. T. A. Hoffmann. From *Meister Martin*: (i) '*Ich bin ein Küfer worden ...aber einer andern, wohl schönern Kunst war mein ganzer Sinn zugewandt von Kindheit auf*' (mind in the sense of 'desire' and 'will'). (ii) '*Wessen Sinn jemals ein böser Traum verwirrte, daß er glaubte in tiefer Nacht zu liegen...*' (wits, reason). From *Die Elixiere des Teufels*: (i) '*Ach wie ein fernes herrliches Land, wo die Freude wohnt und die ungetrübte Heiterkeit des kindlichen unbefangenen Sinns, liegt die Heimat weit, weit hinter mir...*' (disposition). (ii) '*Aber finstre Gestalten steigen auf, und...versperren...die Aussicht und befangen meinen Sinn mit den Drangsalen der Gegenwart...*' (thoughts and feelings). From *Der Sandmann*: (i) '*Haben wir festen, durch das heitre Leben gestärkten Sinn genug, um fremdes feindliches Einwirken als solches stets zu erkennen...*' (will and intellect). (ii) '*Sage du mir, Sigmund, wie deinem sonst alles Schöne klar auffassenden Blick, deinem regen Sinn Olimpias himmlischer Liebreiz entgehen konnte?*' (sensibility). (iii) '*Es wäre daraus zu schließen, daß Clara das ruhige häusliche Glück noch fand, das ihrem heitern lebenslustigen Sinn zusagte...*' (disposition). From Kleist's *Robert Guiskard* (ll. 511–12):

> '*Ja, in des Sinns entsetzlicher Verwirrung*
> *Die ihn zuletzt befällt...*'

From Friedrich Schlegel: '*Künstler ist ein jeder, dem es Ziel und Mitte des Daseins ist, seinen Sinn zu bilden*' (*Athenäum*, 20). Gundolf's use of the term in the following passage from his *Heinrich von Kleist* is only possible in elevated diction of this kind. '*Der Kurfürst... kämpft gelassenen Sinns in sich das aus was der Prinz im Tatenfeuer und in Todesqual auszukämpfen hat.*' The following use from Mörike's *Maler Nolten* is obsolete: '*...sie selbst gab sich eigentlich mehr aus Gutmütigkeit zu alledem her, als daß sie ungeteilten Sinnes dabei gewesen wäre.*'

[2] *Ein hartes Gemüt* as well as *ein weiches Gemüt*. Compare the use of *Geist* which attributes to it characteristics which are the opposite of its essential nature.

[3] The expression *das deutsche Gemüt* cannot be paralleled by the use of an adjective which denotes another nationality.

---

ticularly of the romantic order.[1] English lacks an equivalent term and resorts to approximations such as 'soul', 'heart', 'disposition'. If 'mind' is used, the reference must be to its emotional side, to feelings of the type described above.

The plural is used in the sense of 'people's minds'.

'*Und ganz von selbst umkreiste sein Gemüt — besessen von Wunschbildern äußerster Jugendschönheit, Manneswildheit und Götterhuld — den homerischen Achill, das unausweichliche Ideal solcher Träume*' (Friedrich Gundolf, *Heinrich von Kleist*).

'*...und gleich, als ob der eine plötzliche Eindruck, der sich seinem Gemüt eingeprägt hatte, alle früheren daraus verdrängt hätte, weinte er vor Lust, daß er sich des lieblichen Lebens voller bunter Erscheinungen, noch erfreute*' (Kleist, *Das Erdbeben in Chili*).

'*Die Oper stimmt durch die Macht der Musik und durch eine freiere harmonische Reizung der Sinnlichkeit das Gemüt zu einer schöneren Empfänglichkeit*' (Schiller in a letter to Goethe).

Um die Gemüter zu beruhigen, sagte er, daß die Gefahr nicht ernst sei.

Die Propaganda hat die Gemüter entflammt.

Er ist gemütskrank.

Er hat seine Gemütsruhe verloren.

9. **Seele** is used in a few fixed expressions which suggest worry or stress of soul, where English would use 'mind'.

Sine Untreue lastet, liegt, ihm auf der Seele.

10. Examples of other terms that must sometimes be used are:

Er hat eine sprunghafte Denkart.

Er denkt sehr schnell.

Er hat eine rasche Auffassungsgabe.

MISS 1. (a) **Vermissen:**[2] to notice or to regret the absence of a person or a thing.[3]

---

[1] Compare Novalis: (i) '*Poesie ist Darstellung des Gemüts, der inneren Welt in ihrer Gesamtheit.*' (ii) '*Es ist höchst begreiflich warum am Ende alles Poesie wird. Wird nicht die Welt am Ende Gemüt?*' It would be inappropriate, however, to ascribe *Gemüt* to a poet such as Stefan George. See Gundolf's judgment in his *George*, p. 25 : '*Seinem stetig tiefen Herzen, weiten Geist und mächtigen Willen...mangeln alle die deutschen Lieblingseigenschaften, die eben jener Zwiespalt erst zeitigt: das "Gemüt", das wohlige oder schmerzlich-dumpfe Überwölken des Zwiespalts....*' But Gundolf, in his essay on Mörike (*Romantiker, Neue Folge*), writes: '*Eichendorff, der beschwingte Sänger von Wald und Wandern, Genius nur, wo dieses Erscheinen und eins ein ward mit sienem Gemüte....*' The writings of the romantics abound in the description and evocation of feelings, and the term *Gemüt* occurs again and again. Examples from E. T. A. Hoffmann are: (i) '*...aber den Gläubigen, der ohne zu grübeln sein ganzes Gemüt darauf richtet, erfüllt bald eine überirdische Begeisterung, die ihm das Reich der Seligkeit erschließt, das er hienieden nur geahnt...*' (*Die Elixiere des Teufels*). '*...du mögest mit recht heitrem, unbefangenem Gemüt es dir gefallen lassen, die seltsamen Gestaltungen zu betrachten, ja dich mit ihnen zu befreunden, die der Dichter der Eingebung des spukhaften Geistes, Phantasus geheißen, verdankt...*' (*Der Sandmann*). The word is used to-day more in critical than in narrative prose. Goethe felt called upon to protest against its excessive use by the romantics, since, according to him, it had come to denote nothing but indulgence with weakness. The following is an example of Goethe's use of the term in *Werther*: '*Das klare Wetter konnte wenig auf sein trübes Gemüt wirken, ein dumpfer Druck lag auf seiner Seele, die traurigen Bilder hatten sich bei ihm festgesetzt, und sein Gemüt kannte keine Bewegung als von einem schmerzlichen Gedanken zum andern.*'

[2] *Missen* means 'to do without'.

[3] *Fehlen* can also have this meaning. *Du fehlst mir sehr.* See 'lack'.

Ich vermißte mein Gepäck, als ich wieder in das Coupé zurückging.
Ich vermisse jetzt Ihren Gruß, wenn ich im Büro ankomme.
Ich habe Sie in der letzten Zeit sehr vermißt.
Er wurde beim Appell vermißt.
Die Vermißten (missing, i.e. a casualty list).

(b) **Verschollen:** (or a person) missing for a long time without a trace.

2. Versäumen:[1] to let something that is regarded by oneself or by others as valuable or necessary pass by without either (*a*) taking, using, being present at it, or (*b*) doing it. The cause may be remissness, in which case it implies blame more strongly than *verpassen* and *verfehlen*, or adverse circumstances. Like *verpassen*, but unlike *verfehlen* it can suggest tardiness, i.e. being too late to take or do a thing.[2] It must have a person as subject, a thing as object, and one cannot therefore mean to miss, i.e. fail to meet, a person.

> *Er hat den Zug, die Gelegenheit, den richtigen Augenblick, der Vortrag, seine*
> *Pflicht, versäumt.*
> *Sie haben nichts versäumt* (nothing worth while.).

3. Verpassen is said more lightly than *versäumen* and therefore implies a less serious situation and less blame. The cause is inattentiveness[3] or a piece of bad luck (e.g. absence, tardiness) at the crucial moment. Like *versäumen* it implies the missing of something wanted or worth while, but, unlike it, does not mean to neglect the doing of something considered as a duty. Its object may be a person as well as a thing (in the sense of 'to fail to meet a person'), while the subject can sometimes—loosely used—be a thing (particularly something sent to a person such as a letter). It is never a dignified term.

> *Er hat den Zug, die Gelegenheit, den richtigen Augenblick, den Vortrag,*
> *den Anschluß, verpaßt.*
> *Ich kam zu spät und verpaßte ihn* (him).
> *Der Brief hat mich verpaßt.*

4. Verfehlen: to miss by reason of a mistake made. The object may be not only a thing, but also a person or a place, in which case the meaning is 'to miss by going to the wrong place', or it may be anything else that is conceived as a goal, the implication being that failure to reach it is due to error. The error rather than the value of the goal is stressed.

> *Wir haben uns, den Weg, verfehlt.*
> *Er hat seinen Beruf verfehlt.*
> *Die Rede hat ihren Zweck, ihre Wirkung verfehlt.*

5. A number of verbs (see dictionaries) may be compounded with the prefix *vorbei* and followed by the preposition *an* in the sense of going past the goal, not hitting it.[4]

> *Er schoß an der Scheibe vorbei.*
> *Sie reden an der Sache vorbei* (you are missing the point, i.e. talking
> irrelevantly).

---

[1] *Verabsäumen* is a commercial term.
[2] *Säumen* means 'to delay' and may be followed by the infinitive.
[3] *Passen auf* means 'to watch for', *aufpassen* is 'to pay attention'.
[4] Colloquialisms compounded with *vorbei* and *daneben* and meaning 'to miss' are: *vorbei (daneben) gelingen, vorbei (daneben) greifen, vorbei (daneben) hauen. Er hat arg danebengehauen.*

6. Very often German requires a specific verb used negatively or a verb meaning 'to fail'.[1] At times the English is ambiguous (e.g. 'to miss the ball' can mean: not to hit, not to catch). If 'miss' is followed by the gerund of the verb, the ambiguity is removed. Of the verbs treated in this article only *versäumen*, *verpassen*, *verfehlen* cannot be used with the infinitive. Examples of specific verbs are:

Er hat die fünfte Seite übersprungen, ausgelassen.

In seiner Beschreibung des Vorfalls hat er die richtige Stimmung nicht getroffen.

7. 'Just to miss' with the gerund (i.e. by a narrow margin) may in the past tense be translated by *wenig fehlte*. This expression occurs only in literature, and even here is inclined to be archaic.

Wenig fehlte, so wäre er gewählt worden.

MISTAKE, ERROR[2] **Fehler** is a definite imperfection in a thing which ought not to be there. In this sense it translates both 'mistake' and 'error'.[3] **Irrtum** corresponds to 'mistake' only in the sense of 'misunderstanding', 'misconception', 'mistaken judgment', i.e. which is confined to the mind, not embodied in something done or made.[4, 5]

Die Übersetzung hat zu viele Fehler.

Sie machen beim Sprechen zu viele grobe Fehler.

Diese Annahme war ein Irrtum meinerseits.

MIX, MINGLE, BLEND **1. Mischen** generally means 'to mix' elements in such a way that they are indistinguishable in the product. It thus corresponds to 'mix' rather than to 'mingle', and is applied characteristically to liquids, colours, and substances which can merge by the addition of liquid.

It is, however, also applied to substances such as ingredients of food dishes (e.g. a salad) which do not lose their identity though they are meant to form a harmonious whole. With reference to the act of mixing such ingredients, *zusammenmischen* is common.[6]

It is applied to feelings, though less frequently than *vermischen*.

In the sense of mixing with people, it is used of mixing with a crowd and of mixing or mingling races, but not of association with individuals in society.

The past participle occurs in a number of fixed expressions (see dictionaries).

Wein und (or: *mit*) *Wasser mischen.*

Mischen Sie die Farben gut.

Ich habe den Salat ordentlich gemischt.

Er hat sich unter die Menge gemischt.

Die beiden Völker haben sich gemischt.

---

[1] See 'fail'.

[2] 'Error' expresses a more severe criticism than 'mistake'.

[3] *Fehler* is also a positive fault or flaw in a person or a thing with regard to right and wrong. *Mangel* is a deficiency, an absence of something, but also a visible flaw, blemish, in an aesthetic sense.

[4] *Versehen* is a petty mistake, an oversight, a slip due to inadvertence. *Aus Versehen* = by mistake. *Mißgriff* and *Fehlgriff* are mistakes in doing a thing as the result of an error in judgment.

[5] 'To make a mistake, to be mistaken', in the sense of 'to be the victim of a delusion'. is generally *sich täuschen*. See 'deceive'.

[6] With cocktails: *mixen*.

2. Vermischen.

Ver suggests completeness in the result, often shown by the addition of some adverb such as *gut* or *stark*. Sometimes a deliberate, careful process is suggested, sometimes the sense is pejorative (e.g. to confuse ideas). It is applied to liquids, to metals, to feelings, to the mixing of races, to the confusing of ideas. The past participle used adjectivally means 'miscellaneous'.

Wasser und Öl vermischen (or: *mischen*) *sich nicht* (given by Duden).

Vermischen Sie diese Farben gut.

'*Das Märchen des Frühlings…vermischte sich mit dem Zauber der heiligen Legende von Jesus*' (Hauptmann, *Der Narr in Christo*).

'*Wie im deutschen Geistesleben überhaupt die Empfindsamkeit zwei ganz verschiedene Ströme hatte, die sich indessen bald vermischten und vereinigten, nämlich das beseelte Christentum und die humanisierte Natur…*' (Gundolf, *Goethe*).

'*…so war der Schmerz in jeder Menschenbrust mit so vieler süßer Lust vermischt, daß…*' (Kleist, *Das Erdbeben in Chili*).

Diese Völker sind stark vermischt.

Sie haben diese beiden Begriffe ganz und gar vermischt.

3. Mengen generally means 'to combine' things so that they remain distinguishable in the result, and is therefore mostly applied to solid substances, or at least to one substance which is kneaded with liquid. In poetry it is sometimes applied solely to liquids. It also means 'to confuse', 'to mix up'; and further (in the reflexive) 'to mix' among a crowd (but in the latter sense is less common than *mischen*).

Vermengen has intensive force, is often used with *stark*, etc. and is applied to the mixing of solid substances and to the confusing of ideas. Neither verb is used as commonly as *mischen* and *vermischen*.

Sie mengte die verschiedenen Ingredienzien in einem Topf.

Er hat die beiden Begriffe vermengt.

4. In the sense of 'associate with': **verkehren.**

Er verkehrt in guter Gesellschaft.

5. In the sense of 'to be involved' (i.e. mixed up in, with): **verwickelt sein.**

Er ist in die Angelegenheit verwickelt.

MOUNTAIN, HILL 1. Mountain is higher than hill and normally has steeper sides. In strict use **Berg** and **Hügel** stand in the same relation to each other as the two English terms, but in every-day speech *Berg* is also used of only a slight rise in the ground, e.g. a slight rise in the level of a street. *Hügel*, however, is a more accurate term and so would be used in geographical descriptions for a low rise. Further: *Berg*, like *Hügel* refers to one distinct rise, not to hilly country in general. For the latter **Gebirge** must be used.

Die Spitze des Berges.

Sie kletterten mühsam den Berg hinauf.

Gehen Sie den Berg hinauf und an der zweiten Verkehrsampel sehen Sie das Postamt vor sich (e.g. of a street in a town).

Nur im Gebirge finden Sie solche Blumen.

Ein Bergsteiger.

In der Schweiz werden Soldaten hauptsächlich als Gebirgstruppen ausgebildet.

MOUNTAIN

2. Further: **Bühel** is Upper German for *Hügel* and appears mostly in place names, e.g. *Kitzbühl*. **Anhöhe** is a rise (*das Schloß steht auf einer Anhöhe*).

MOVE[1]   **A.** To be, to set in motion as opposed to a state of rest.

1. Sich bewegen.

The character of the movement suggested by *bewegen* is that it is round about, to and fro, i.e. it does not indicate primarily a change of position towards a destination, whether this be remote or close at hand. This characteristic can imply sustained motion, but does not exclude a single movement. Applied to a person it denotes only physical movement of the limbs without secondary associations (contrast *rühren*). From this fundamental meaning arises that of taking physical exercises, which may be confined to the movement of the limbs without change of position or include such exercises as marching, running about. To give *bewegen* the sense of 'move' care should be taken that the context excludes that of 'exercise'. (Note also *sich Bewegung machen*, to take exercise.) *Bewegung* means 'motion' rather than movement.

In its application to persons, whether reflexive or with a part of the body as object it therefore means (i) positively: to move the body or a part of it about; (ii) negatively: not to move so much as a muscle. When the object is a person other than the subject, *bewegen* is mostly combined with *von der Stelle* (see **B**).

> *Ich kann mich nicht bewegen* (I am paralysed or bound, and in the idiomatic sense of *gauche* in society).
> *Ich kann den Arm jetzt wieder bewegen.*
> *Seine Lippen bewegten sich kaum.*

Bewegen Sie sich nicht (move your limbs to show that they are capable of movement, contrast *rühren*).

Bewigen Sie nicht (don't move even a muscle, e.g. when being photographed).

2. *Bewegen* can be accompanied by a phrase denoting direction (to or from), destination, provided the manner of the movement is stated or clearly implied. It is never the equivalent of 'go' when the manner of going is not specified (contrast **A, 6**). *Bewegen* rarely suggests a straight line, but rather 'hither and thither'. In reference to means of transport it can be applied only to boats (i.e. not with trains, cars; see section **A, 6**).

> *Das Schiff bewegte sich langsam aus dem Hafen.*
> *Langsam bewegte sie sich von mir fort.*
> *Nur mit Schwierigkeit konnte er sich von der Stelle fortbewegen, die unter feindlichem Feuer lag.*
> *Tanzend, mit leichten Schritten, bewegte sie sich von der Bühne weg.*
> *Sie bot ein liebliches Bild, wie sie sich zwischen den Blumen bewegte.*

---

[1] 'To move emotionally' is *bewegen* when the emotion is strong (*der Tod ihrer Mutter hat sie sehr bewegt*; *der Entschluß, die Nachricht, die Aufführung hat mich bewegt*; *ich war gradezu bewegt*). *Bewegen* cannot, however, be used in this sense in the present participle (use *ergreifend, erregend*). For the gentler emotions (e.g. tenderness, melancholy) *rühren* is used. In other figurative uses *bewegen* suggests turbulence (e.g. *ein bewegtes Meer, bewegte Zeiten*). To move to a decision, i.e. 'to induce' is *bewegen* conjugated as a strong verb.

'To move' in the sense of 'to force (someone) to abandon a position, an attitude', 'to yield', can only be translated by *bewegen* in the combinations *zu bewegen sein, sich bewegen lassen. Er war durch Drohungen nicht zu bewegen. Er ließ sich durch Drohungen nicht bewegen* (I, they, etc., could not move him by threats).

*In voller Natürlichkeit (ganz ungezwungen) bewegte sich die Königin unter
ihren Gästen.*

Die Menge der Streikenden bewegte sich unruhig auf den Straßen hin und her.

Der Trauerzug bewegte sich zum Friedhof.

Die Herde bewegte sich in der Richtung auf den Fluß.

3. A special application of this fundamental sense of *bewegen* is 'to make go,
run' (i.e. to keep in motion) of machinery, a boat.[1] The subject can only be
the force that provides the impetus, not a person.

Die Elektrizität bewegt die Maschine.

Der Wind bewegt das Boot.

Die Uhr wird durch eine Feder bewegt.

4. *Sich bewegen* is used in the figurative sense of 'live, have one's being'
in a certain sphere. Distinguish from the sense of 'move' explained in **A, 2**
and in the last example of **A, 6**.

Er bewegt sich viel in musikalischen (politischen) Kreisen.

5. Rühren can suggest not only physical movement of the body, but also
any activity that may accompany it, and furthermore a change of place.
This is its meaning when applied to persons, whether used reflexively
or with a part of the body as object, whereas *bewegen* is primarily limited
to physical movement of the limbs without a change of place. In the positive
the sense is predominantly 'to bestir oneself' (*rührt euch!* = 'bestir yourselves'
or 'stand at ease'; *er will keinen Finger rühren* = he won't lift a finger, do a
tap of work). The negative means 'not to change one's position and at the
same time to remain inactive'.

Rühren (with or without *von der Stelle*) is not used transitively with a
personal object other than the reflexive pronoun in the sense of 'move'.

Der Dieb sagte: 'Rühren Sie sich nicht, oder ich schieße.'

Ich konnte kein Glied rühren.

When the object is not a person or a part of the body, but something
in the world of nature, *rühren* in the sense of 'move' suggests greater
freedom than *regen*, which is only used reflexively (stir, i.e. the beginning
of a movement), but less than *bewegen*.

Der Wind rührt die Blätter.

Es rührt sich kein Lüftchen (*bewegt* is impossible; *rührt* is here almost
identical with *regt*).

6. To set in movement, to move about, without reference to the manner of
movement.

In this case 'move' must be translated by the various German equivalents
of 'go' (see article on 'go'). It occurs mainly in two types: (i) with reference
to the means of locomotion; (ii) in the sense of 'to go, to walk about' amongst
people.

Das Auto fährt sehr schnell.

Das Auto läuft schon.

Der Zug fährt (geht) jetzt.

Der König geht viel unter die Armen.

B. To move away, out of the way, the new position being unimportant
and not mentioned. Specific terms (for some of them see **C**) are mainly used,
the commonest being:

---

[1] In this sense *bewegen* means 'to keep a thing moving'. *In Bewegung setzen* (or stressing
the change from absolute rest: *versetzen*) is 'to set moving'.

MOVE

1. To get out of the way, of persons.
(a) Positive: *zur Seite treten, rücken, Platz machen, weitergehen* (move on), *verschwinden*.
> *Bitte, Platz machen.*
> *Er trat beiseite, um mich vorbeigehen zu lassen.*

(b) Negative.
> *Rühre dich nicht* (don't change your position).
> *Bleiben Sie da* (*sitzen*, etc.).

2. To move a thing out of the way.
(a) *Nehmen Sie Ihren Arm, den Stuhl, weg.*
(b) To move a little: *zur Seite* (*weg*) *schieben, rücken* (see **C**).
> *Rücken Sie den Schrank von der Wand weg.*
> *Schieben Sie den Tisch zur Seite.*

3. To budge, to make budge: (*sich*) (*von der Stelle*) *bewegen, rühren, rücken, kommen*.
> *Drei Krankenschwestern waren nötig, um ihn von der Stelle zu bewegen.*
> *Das Auto, rührt* (*bewegt*) *sich nicht* (*von der Stelle*).
> *Wir versuchten, den Stein fortzurollen, aber er rührte, bewegte, sich nicht.*

C. To change position, posture, place, abode, the destination being mentioned or clearly implied.

The most general terms are the German equivalents of 'take' and 'put', which must be used when the more specific terms are inapplicable. The verbs compounded with *ver* denote a change of position (transfer), those with *um* either a change or interchange, rearrangement, generally in a confined space, e.g. a room, *ver* suggesting a wider area.

(a) Verbs meaning 'take' and 'put' (see articles on these words). All these verbs, with the exception of *bringen*, suggest that the object moved is either in one's hands, arms, or near by, and that it is moved only a short distance. The destination must be stated, unless some adverb such as *weg* (see **B**) is added.
> *Ich legte die Pakete auf den Stuhl* (or *tat*).
> *Ich tat meinen Regenschirm in die Ecke.*
> *Tragen Sie den Kohlenkasten auf die andere Seite des Kamins.*
> *Wir brachten unsere Möbel in die neue Wohnung.*

(b) **Verlegen** (transfer) often suggests the moving of things which consist of a number of units (e.g. complex masses), also the transfer of one's official abode or the seat of one's activities. The destination need not be stated. *Verlegen* can also mean to mislay (*einen Brief v.*).
> *Die Geschäftsführung hat ihre Verwaltungsräume in ein anderes Stadtviertel verlegt.*
> *Die Betriebsverwaltung ist in andere Räume verlegt worden.*
> *Die Hälfte der fünften Armee ist an eine andere Front verlegt worden.*
> *Das Lager ist verlegt worden.*
> *Die Ostgrenze Deutschlands ist faktisch an die Oder verlegt worden.*
> *Die Universität wurde während des Krieges nach einer Kleinstadt verlegt.*

(c) **Versetzen** frequently refers to the transferring of a person from one place to another where he will carry on the same work or occupation and to the promotion of school children. It can also denote the transposing of things in a pattern and the moving of things to another fixed position (e.g. plants). The destination need not be stated. *Versetzen* can also mean to pawn (*einen Ring v.*).

Der Gesandte, der Lehrer, wurde nach Berlin versetzt.

Die Bäume müssen versetzt werden, bevor sie höher wachsen.

Der Grenzstein ist versetzt worden.

(d) **Verpflanzen:** to move plants and the like, to uproot people and settle them elsewhere. The destination need not be mentioned.

Wir müssen die Lilien an einen kühlen Ort verpflanzen.

Unzählige Menschen wurden während des Krieges (nach fremden Ländern) verpflanzt.

(e) **Verrücken:** (i) to move a thing elsewhere by stages (see *rücken*), particularly things which have to be moved in parts. It points to the result, i.e. the new position, while *rücken* denotes the action of moving. (ii) Since the new position can be desired or otherwise, *verrücken* can also mean 'displace', 'disarrange'. The past participle should be used warily because of its frequent use in the sense of 'crazy'. The destination need not be mentioned.

Da wir ein neues Stück Land gekauft haben, müssen wir den Zaun etwas verrücken.

Verrücken Sie nichts.

(f) **Verschieben:** to move masses of people, complex or heavy things.

Juden sind während des Krieges massenhaft nach Polen verschoben worden.

Wir haben den Schrank, das Sofa, ein bißchen verschoben.

Die Grenze ist 100 Kilometer nach Westen verschoben worden.

(g) **Verstellen:** to move objects that are thought of as standing. *Sich verstellen*: to dissimulate.

Einen Zaun, die Kulissen verstellen.

Sie haben überall die Möbel verstellt (e.g. in the house, i.e. over a wider area than *umstellen*).

Sie haben das Schilderhaus verstellt.

(h) **Sich verlagern:** to shift to another place, often of activities (*Die Unruhen haben sich nach Berlin verlagert*).

(i) Verbs compounded with *um* mostly denote a rearrangement, an interchange of position in some pattern which can be surveyed, whereas those with *ver* suggest no arrangement.

Wir sollten die Möbel in diesem Zimmer umstellen.

Die Bilder wurden im Museum umgehängt.

Die Klasse wurde in ein anderes Zimmer umquartiert.

(j) **Rücken** (transitive and intransitive): to move gradually or in short stages (*der Ruck*=jerk). It is used characteristically of furniture, which must be moved in this way, or of things set in some order (e.g. words). In intransitive use it generally suggests movement to a fixed position within some formation or scheme (e.g. in a row), a sudden step in some direction or the marching of troops (i.e. as a stage of a march). It must be followed by a phrase denoting destination, or *weg, fort.*

Er rückte seinen Stuhl an den Tisch heran.

Rücken Sie den Schrank in die Ecke.

Rücken Sie bitte eins weiter (move along one).

Rücken Sie hier (in diese Reihe) ein.

Er rückte an die Wand, einen Schritt zur Seite.

Die Truppen rücken in die Stadt.

Der Uhrzeiger rückte vorwärts.

Rücken Sie diesen Ausdruck an den Anfang des Satzes (*stellen* would not clearly indicate a change of position).

(k) **Ziehen** in intransitive use suggests a long line (from the idea of drawing denoted by its literal transitive sense). Unlike *bewegen* it can imply speed and conveys the idea of passing on, even wandering, without interruption, to some distant destination. It is used widely with persons or natural phenomena. It also means 'to move one's place of abode', the compounds *ein-*, *aus-*, *unziehen* (used intransitively) being the normal terms for moving oneself and one's goods from one dwelling to another. The term suggests a long line.

Das Heer zog über den Fluß in, durch, die Stadt.

Die Burschen zogen an dem Wirtshaus vorbei.

Die Schafe zogen über das Feld.

Die Vögel ziehen im Winter nach wärmeren Ländern.

Die Wolken ziehen über den Himmel.

Der Nebel zieht nach Westen.

Die französische Regierung zog nach Bordeaux, als die Deutschen in Paris einbrachen.

Sie sind in eine ganz neue Wohnung eingezogen.

(l) **Schaffen** (when conjugated as a weak verb) can mean 'to cause something to be done or to be made available'. The sense of 'move' is an extension of this causative use and comes closest to 'get', thus applied. The overcoming of some difficulty, sometimes by quick or rough means, or the remedying of a situation, the averting of a danger is often implied. The act of moving itself may involve difficulty. It is frequently combined with *zur Stelle* and *aus dem Wege.*

Schaffen Sie das brennende Holz weg.

Wir müssen die Urkunden an irgend einen sicheren Ort schaffen.

Wir haben unsere Möbel noch nicht in die neue Wohnung geschafft.

Wollen Sie bitte mein Gepäck in das nächste Abteil schaffen?

Schaffen Sie den Schlauch ins Gartenhaus.

(m) **Schieben** can translate 'move' in the sense of 'push' or 'shove'. It is also the correct term (not colloquial like 'push' or 'shove') for moving masses of people about.

Wir müssen das Klavier in das Wohnzimmer hinüberschieben.

Während des Krieges wurden Millionen von Menschen umhergeschoben.

Diese Truppen werden morgen näher an die Front geschoben.

MUCH, VERY MUCH **Sehr** refers to intensity, **viel** to quantity, frequency.

Meine sehr geliebte Mutter (I love her deeply).

Meine vielgeliebte Mutter (many people love her).

Er hat sich sehr getäuscht (a serious mistake).

Er hat sich viel getäuscht (often).

Das wird sehr bewundert.

Das wird viel bewundert.

MURDER 1. **Ermorden** is the normal equivalent of 'murder' used transitively and in its literal sense.

Er hat ihn ermordet.

2. Morden is used in several ways: (*a*) Intransitively in the literal sense. (*b*) Sometimes in the literal sense with a direct object such as *niemand*, this being practically equivalent to the intransitive use with *nicht*, and in the sense of murdering on a large scale. (*c*) Poetically for *ermorden*. (*d*) In the sense of 'to murder a person indirectly' by one's behaviour towards him, not by direct action. (*e*) Figuratively.

Sie plündern und morden überall.

'*Wir haben niemand gemordet*' (Martin Niemöller, *Deutsche Blätter*).

Frauen und Kinder sind gemordet worden (on a vast scale).

'*Nicht Ihr habt ihn gemordet! Andre taten's*' (Kennedy to Maria; Schiller, *Maria Stuart*).

Du mordest mich noch mit der Geschichte (more commonly: *du bringst mich noch um...*).

Er hat sie durch sein Verhalten gemordet.

Mordet die Unschuld nicht (poetic, figurative diction).

3. Totschlag: manslaughter.

NARROW 1. Schmal in its literal sense means 'of small width in proportion to length'.

Ein schmaler Weg, ein schmales Tal.

2. Eng means both literally and figuratively 'confined', i.e. without particular reference to any dimension, though the object so described may be of small width.[1]

Der Weg ist hier sehr eng.

Ein enges Tal.

Im engeren Sinne des Wortes.

3. Knapp means 'with little margin'.

Eine knappe Mehrheit.

Mit knapper Not entkommen.

4. In the sense of 'illiberal', *engherzig, engstirnig, beschränkt, begrenzt* (see 'limit') must be used.

Ein engherziger, beschränkter, Mann.

NATIVE 1. Belonging to one by nature, conferred by birth, born with one, not acquired, inherent, inborn (*W.*).

(a) Inborn, innate: **angeboren**.

Eine angeborene Schlauheit und die Fähigkeit, die richtige Entscheidung zu treffen (W.).

Ehrgeiz und angeborene Eignung, Begabung (W.).

(b) Belonging to or associated with a particular place (as a region or country) by birth.

(i) **Einheimisch**, also **heimisch**, which however has contracted in meaning and is now used less and less in this sense. The first term covers most uses of 'native' in this sense except those under (ii)–(vi).

Einheimische Weine, Tiere, Vögel, Trachten (native to a certain region).

Der Tabak ist in Amerika heimisch.

(ii) When native land or country is meant German uses **Vaterland** or **Heimat** (adj.: **heimatlich**). Both suggest love for this, the former adding

[1] In the sense of 'confined', 'cramping' or 'cramped', *eng* also translates 'tight' (e.g. *die Schuhe sind mir zu eng*), 'close' (e.g. *er schreibt sehr eng*), 'poky' (e.g. *ein enges Zimmer*).

political sentiments of patriotism. *Heimat* can also have the narrower sense of region from which one comes, i.e. not necessarily the whole country.

In seinem Vaterland Schweden ist er als einflußreicher Dramatiker berühmt.

Das Salzkammergut ist seine Heimat.

Er kehrte in seine Heimat zurück.

Ich freue mich, wieder auf heimatlichem Boden zu stehen.

(iii) In phrases denoting that one is a native of a town German says e.g. *er ist geborener Wiener, Prager*, etc., but not if this is an accident of birth and one left soon after. In the latter case: *er ist in Wien, Prag geboren.*

(iv) The present-day use of **heimisch** is rare and suggests the feeling of being at home in a place, whereas *einheimisch* merely denotes the fact of one's birth there. A sentence such as the following is not impossible, though somewhat forced:

Er ist in Österreich einheimisch, fühlt sich aber in Amerika heimisch (normally: *zu Hause*).

(v) Native tongue can only be: **Muttersprache.**

(vi) *Eingeboren* as a substantive is applied only to primitive peoples.

Die Eingeborenen Afrikas und Australiens.

The use of 'native' to denote simply not belonging to one's own country and particularly non-European, if not coinciding with the meaning of *eingeboren*, can only be *einheimisch.*

Einheimische Frauen (e.g. non-American) *müssen den linken Ausgang benutzen.*

2. In the sense of bestowed by nature, not acquired: **angeboren** (or: **natürlich**).

Ihre angeborene Grazie gewann ihr alle Herzen.

Seine angeborene Geschicklichkeit.

Angeborene Rechte.

3. According to nature, natural, normal (*W.*) is a sense no longer common. When it occurs, only **natürlich** is a German equivalent.

Sie halten Frankreich und England für die natürlichen Führer Europas.

4. Left or remaining in a natural state: being without embellishment or artificial change: simple, unadorned, unaffected (*W.*): **natürlich, urwüchsig.**

Unsere Gefühle waren noch natürlich und echt, unverfälscht durch Pedanterie (*W.*).

Urwüchsiger Humor.

NATURE 1. Natur is ascribed (*a*) to what is animate (e.g. human beings, animals, vegetation) and to things in so far as they are thought of in relation to what is animate (i.e. unlike the English 'nature', not in relation to their purely physical structure or properties). The term denotes qualities, characteristics, character and is applied to persons in the sense of the character they possess. (*b*) It is used to refer to the phenomena of the material world as a whole and to the physical power which produces this world (i.e. nature). (*c*) It denotes what is unspoilt in contrast to the artificial products of civilization (e.g. in the state of nature; back to Nature!).

Es widerspricht der menschlichen Natur.

Er ist eine robuste, gesunde, faustische, Natur.

Er ist von Natur aus grausam.

Die Liebe ist von Natur aus eifersüchtig.

Es liegt in der Natur der Dinge, daß der Mensch ewig unbefriedigt ist.

Es lag in der Natur des römischen Reiches, daß es früher oder später zusammenbrechen mußte.

Er liebt die Natur.

Die Natur ist lieblich in diesem Tal.

Der unerschöpfliche Schoß der Natur.

Naturvölker (i.e. not *Kulturvölker*).

Zurück zur Natur!

2. In the sense **1** (*a*) *Natur* must be distinguished from **Wesen**. The latter means 'being',[1] 'essence' (from Latin *esse*, to be) and refers to the inner, particularly spiritual, principle of things.[2] Thus: *das Wesen der Planwirtschaft*; *das Wesen der Einbildungskraft*. *Natur*, on the other hand, refers more to the character of a thing as it manifests itself externally, as it functions.

Es liegt im Wesen der westlichen Kultur, daß sie die Freiheit des Menschen achtet.

Es liegt in der Natur der westlichen Kultur, daß sie eine Beschneidung der menschlichen Freiheit nicht dulden kann.

Es liegt in der Natur des Krieges, Länder zu zerstören, die Menschen grausam zu machen.

Das Wesen des Krieges hat niemand bis jetzt verstanden.

3. In reference to an analysis of the physical structure or elements of a thing only **Beschaffenheit** (i.e. the way a thing is created, made) can be used.

Die Beschaffenheit des Bodens, des Klimas, des menschlichen Gehirns.

4. In the sense of 'kind' *Natur* can only be used when it itself is in the genitive case and accompanied by an adjective, otherwise **Art**[3] must be used.

Dinge so grauenhafter Natur haben sich ereignet, daß wir sie uns kaum vorstellen können.

Nach der Art des Verbrechens zu urteilen, muß es ein Irrsinniger begangen haben.

NECESSARY **1. Nötig:** necessary in a subjective sense, for some personal purpose, which may even be an arbitrary one.

Ihre Hilfe ist gar nicht nötig, ich kann nämlich das Fenster selbst aufmachen.

Es ist nötig, den Treffpunkt klar zu bestimmen, wenn Sie ihn nicht verfehlen wollen.

2. Notwendig.

(a) Necessary in the nature of things.

Es ist notwendig, daß der Mensch sich dauernd wandelt (otherwise he would not be man).

(b) Necessary in an objective sense, though not in the nature of things. In this sense it is often used indiscriminately with *nötig*, but is stronger than the latter.

Dieses Gesetz ist unbedingt notwendig in solchen Zeiten.

NEED, NECESSITY **1. Not:** 'need' in the sense of 'distress, want'. It means 'need for something to be done' only in the expression *not tun*. This

---

[1] *Wesen* also means 'being' in the sense of 'person'. *Ein armseliges Wesen. Alle Wesen* can mean 'all creation, all created things'.

[2] It can, however, refer also to the way a person expresses, conducts, himself. *Sein Wesen ist mir unangenehm. Sein unberechenbares Wesen.*

[3] See 'kind'.

can be followed by a *daß* clause, but not by a genitive or prepositional phrase.

Sie haben ihm in seiner Not beigestanden.

Sie hat große Not gelitten.

Vorsicht tut hier not (elevated diction).

2. Notwendigkeit means (*a*) the power, both material and moral, which acts as compulsion; (*b*) imperative need. It thus corresponds to 'necessity', never to 'need'. It is used in the same formal combinations as 'necessity', not as 'need', e.g. a following genitive denotes the thing necessary, not the person on whom the necessity is imposed.

Die Macht der Notwendigkeit.

Die Notwendigkeit seines Todes.

Es besteht immer noch die Notwendigkeit, eine sichere Grundlage für den Frieden zu finden.

Der sibirische Winter macht warme Kleidung zur absoluten Notwendigkeit.

Es besteht gar keine Notwendigkeit für Sie, heute in die Stadt zu gehen.

Die Notwendigkeit dieser Maßnahmen sieht er jetzt ein.

Er betrachtet es als eine Notwendigkeit, Lebensmittel nach Asien zu schicken.

3. Bedürfnis is a subjectively felt want, desire, whether physical, emotional, or intellectual, for something, not an objective necessity. It is followed characteristically by *nach* (=for).

Er hat ein starkes Bedürfnis nach Ruhe.

Ich verstehe sein Bedürfnis nach solcher Lektüre nicht.

Seine Bedürfnisse sind unersättlich.

4. Bedarf (without plural): need or needs for material things, particularly in the economic sense of 'demand'. See also under 'demand'.

Unser Bedarf ist nicht gedeckt.

Der Bedarf an Lebensmitteln ist sehr stark.

Bürobedarf.

5. It will be seen that apart from the terms explained under 1, 2, 4, German has no word for 'need'. This means that many uses of 'need', particularly in fixed expressions such as 'to be in need of', 'to have need of', 'there is (no) need of (to)' must be translated by such phrases as *nötig haben; nötig, notwendig sein; brauchen; benötigen; müssen.* The phrase 'in need of' can sometimes be rendered by a compound, the second part being *bedürftig* (e.g. *reparaturbedürftig, ruhebedürftig*). If a sentence such as 'the need for teachers to read widely' is rendered by *die Notwendigkeit für Lehrer, gut belesen zu sein,* 'necessity' rather than 'need' has been translated.

NOTE (s.) **1.** A tone of definite pitch (*W.*): **Note.**

2. In the sense of a key (now the usual term in English) of a pianoforte or an organ: **Taste.**

3. The musical call or song of a bird (a): **Gesang.**

Sein Gesang war vollkommen in seiner flüssigen Klarheit.

4. A tone of voice expressive of some mood, attitude, or emotion.

Ihre Stimme klang gereizt (carried a note of irritation) (*W.*).

Sie sprach in einem Ton verzweifelten Flehens.

5. A characteristic feature, theme or quality: element, motif (*W.*). German uses such terms as **Charakter, Merkmal** (see below), **Grundton.**

Das sind die Hauptmerkmale, der Hauptcharakter, des mittelalterlichen Lebens (W.).

Der Grundton seiner Satire (W.).

6. Mood, tone, tenor (*W.*).
Ich hatte nicht die Absicht, in diesem Ton zu enden.

7. A concrete object that sets the tone or constitutes an identifying or characteristic feature (*W.*): **Merkmal.** See 'mark'.
Unermeßliche Grundbesitze, deren einziges modernes Merkmal hie und da ein Ölbohrturm ist (W.).

8. A brief writing intended to assist the memory or to serve as a basis for a fuller statement, memorandum, minute (*W.*): **Notiz.** More exactly 'memorandum' = **Denkschrift.**
Ich habe eine Notiz auf einen Zettel geschrieben.

9. A condensed record of a speech, lecture, lesson or discussion made at the time of listening (*W.*). Mostly plural: **Notizen.** To take down what is said: **mitschreiben.**
Er macht ausgiebige Notizen in allen seinen Vorlesungen (W.).
Er hat fleissig mitgeschrieben.

10. Observation, heed (*W.*). In the phrase: to take note of: **achten auf.**

11. Vermerk (see also *vermerken* under 'record') as an official note often in the nature of a stamp made on a document. A bureacratic word.
Der Vermerk auf der Urkunde läßt deren Ausstellungsdatum ganz klar erkennen.

12. *Achten Sie genau auf das, was er über sein Treffen mit dem Kanzler sagt* (take careful note of). Negatively, 'to take no note of' is less common than 'to take no notice of' (*keine Notiz nehmen von*).

13. A comment or explanation (*W.*), e.g. to a text: **Anmerkung. Glosse,** like English gloss, is limited to ancient texts.
Die Anmerkungen, die in dieser Ausgabe des 'Faust' enthalten sind, werden Sie sehr nützlich finden.

14. A letter from one government to another (*W.*): **Note.**
Ein Notenaustausch zwischen Deutschland und Frankreich.

15. A short informal letter (*W.*): **Zettel, ein paar Zeilen.**
Ich habe ihm einen Zettel hingelegt, ein paar Zeilen geschrieben.

16. Paper money: **Note, Schein.**
Eine 50 Mark Banknote, Geldschein.

NOTE (v.) **1. Feststellen** can mean to note in the sense of take cognizance of and at the same time to state, say. In this sense the more learned term *konstatieren* is an equivalent. *Feststellen,* however, can also mean 'to ascertain', 'to establish' a fact. See also under 'state'.
Ich habe keine Meinung sondern habe lediglich festgestellt, was vorgefallen ist.

2. To make a mental note of a thing: **sich etwas merken** or **sich etwas notieren.**
Das werde ich mir merken, falls ich danach gefragt werde.

NOTICE

NOTICE (s.) **1.** The original meaning of information, intimation, warning, announcement is now rare except in such expressions as to give notice, without notice (for these see below). In German the appropriate synonym must be used. See in particular 'announce'.

Die Preisänderung erfolgte ohne weitere Warnung.

Das kann als Hinweis dienen, daß wir zu einem so schwerwiegenden Schritt nicht bereit sind.

Von etwas Kenntnis haben.

Bis auf weiteres (till further notice).

2. A warning announcement or intimation given a specified time before the event to take place (*W.*), mostly in fixed phrases (e.g. at...notice). German has no specific and in fact no exact term for this sense, so that only a paraphrase can approximate to the sense of the English. Phrases involving **Frist** are common, and use may be made of *baldigst, unverzüglich*.

Er mußte es in kürzester Frist tun (at short notice) (see under 'time').

Das Gebäude mußte innerhalb ganz kurzer Zeit geräumt werden.

Er mußte kurzfristig handeln (*unverzüglich*).

Wir mußten bereit sein, mehr oder weniger sofort zu gehen.

Laß' es mich zehn Minuten vorher wissen (*W.*). Allow me ten minutes notice.

Gib' mir zehn Minuten Zeit.

3. Notification by one of the parties to an agreement or relation of intention of terminating it at a specified time (*W.*), i.e. in the phrase 'to give notice'. **Kündigen.**

Es ist das Recht der Mieter, jederzeit kündigen zu können (*W.*).

Er hat ganz unerwartet gekündigt (given notice of intention to quit a job as well as moving out of lodgings, a house).

4. Kündigen can also mean to give advance notice of dismissal from a job.

Dem Dienstmädchen wurde gekündigt (or colloquially: *das D. macht ihre vierzehn Tage*).

5. A communication of intelligence or of a claim or demand often required by statute or contract and prescribing the manner or form of giving it (*W.*): **Kündigung,** i.e. the same sense as the corresponding verb under **4.**

Eine Kündigung der gemieteten Wohnung (a notice to quit).

6. A written or printed announcement or bulletin (*W.*). Here German uses terms which are really synonyms of notice. See 'advertisement' (particularly **Anzeige,** which suggests that something is being made public knowledge and is not just a private communication; **Bekanntmachung,** which suggests an official proclamation of some importance).

Eine Anzeige in die Zeitung setzen (*W.*) (put a notice in the newspaper).

Eine Heirats- Todesanzeige.

Er schlug Auskunft über die Vorlesungsstunden an das schwarze Brett (put a notice concerning...on).

Plakat is a poster.

Riesige Plakate überall riefen die Bevölkerung zur Ruhe auf.

7. A critical account or commentary on a book, a play, or the like: **Besprechung, Rezension, Kritik.**

Ich habe die ganzen Buchbesprechungen gelesen.

8. Attention, heed, observation (*W.*) mostly in fixed phrases (e.g. to attract attention). German uses synonyms such as **Aufmerksamkeit, beachten, zur Kenntnis bringen.**

> *Durch seinen ersten Roman lenkte er die Aufmerksamkeit auf sich* (*Durch...*
> *fiel er auf*).
> *Der Vorfall wurde der Polizei zur Kenntnis gebracht.*
> *Er nahm keine Notiz davon* (took no notice of) (see also 'note').

NOTICE (v.)[1] **1. Merken** suggests alertness of the senses, that the mental realization comes immediately through these, i.e. without reflection. It is therefore the only term that can be applied to animals. Negatively, it implies that one is not sufficiently alert to notice what is obvious.[2]

Since it so strongly suggests the activity of the senses, a word denoting a smell can be the object. On the other hand, the object cannot be a person.

In general, only *merken* is possible when 'notice' is followed by 'from'.[3]

> *Heute nacht waren Einbrecher bei uns im Haus, und wir haben nichts*
> *gemerkt.*
> *Obgleich der Mann eine Stunde bei mir war, habe ich nicht gemerkt, daß er*
> *ein Snob ist.*
> *Ich trat ins Zimmer und merkte sofort, daß die Möbel umgestellt waren.*
> *Er merkte nicht, daß er seinen Geldbeutel hatte fallen lassen.*
> *Haben Sie gemerkt, daß er schielt?*
> *Ich merkte an seinem Gesichtsausdruck, daß er einen Schreck gekriegt hatte.*
> *Haben Sie gemerkt, daß er hinkt?*
> *'Überall merkt man die zufallsfeindliche Gesinnung, deren dichtester*
> *Ausdruck "Die Wahlverwandtschaften" sind'* (Gundolf, *Goethe*).
> > *'Engel nicht, Menschen nicht,*
> > *Und die findigen Tiere merken es schon,*
> > *daß wir nicht sehr verläßlich zu Haus sind*
> > *in der gedeuteten Welt.'*   (Rilke, *Duineser Elegie I.*)
> *Ich merkte einen üblen Geruch.*

2. Bemerken[4] is less vivid and sensuous than *merken*. It implies mental activity, however brief, after the sense perception, and an inference from the sense material, the meaning of which is not immediately obvious. The observation is therefore more subtle than with *merken*.

A personal object may follow, but only to indicate that something special, noteworthy, attaches to the presence of a person in a certain place.[5] A smell cannot be the object.

> *Bemerken* cannot be used in the imperative.
> *Ich habe nicht bemerkt, daß er ein Snob ist.*
> *Ich glaubte zu bemerken, daß die Möbel umgestellt waren.*

---

[1] *Auffallen,* to strike, to attract attention, is widely used as a close synonym of 'notice', and approximates more to *merken* than to *bemerken. Ist Ihnen etwas Sonderbares an ihm aufgefallen?*

[2] *Sich etwas merken* means 'to note a thing', i.e. to record it in one's memory.

[3] But compare the following from Goethe's *Werthers Leiden*: '*Was mich am meisten betrübte, war, daß ich an seinen Gesichtszügen zu bemerken schien, es sei mehr Eigensinn und übler Humor als Eingeschränktheit des Verstandes, der ihn sich mitzuteilen hinderte.*' If *merken* were used, *schien* would contradict the force and directness of the impression it should convey.

[4] *Bemerken* also means 'to remark', i.e. to say something.

[5] Otherwise *sehen* should be used.

Ich habe oft bemerkt, daß Vorträge in diesem Saal gehalten werden.
Haben Sie seinen Gesichtsausdruck bemerkt?
Haben Sie bemerkt, daß er hinkt?
Unter den Anwesenden bemerkten wir den Präsidenten.
Zufällig habe ich ihn im Theater gemerkt (but: *ich habe ihn im Theater gesehen*).

3. Spüren: to feel bodily sensations, atmospheres, to detect a smell. See 'feel'.

Ich habe einen üblen Geruch gespürt.
Ich spüre Schmerzen im linken Arm.
Ich spürte sofort die Feindlichkeit der Atmosphäre, als ich in den Raum trat.
Ich habe die starke Spannung gespürt.

NOW (in temporal sense) **1. Jetzt** means 'at this moment', without reference to any other unless it be as contrast. It can, however, refer to the immediate past and the immediate future in so far as these are felt to be present. It is emphatic.

It can be preceded by prepositions, e.g. *bis jetzt, von jetzt an.*
Jetzt ist der Augenblick gekommen, wo wir uns verabschieden müssen.
Soll ich es jetzt oder später tun?
Jetzt müssen Sie aber gehen.
Er war eben jetzt hier (just now, i.e. the immediate past).
Er wird jetzt gleich kommen (the immediate future).

2. Nun expresses a relation of the present to what precedes and views the present as the result of a development. It is therefore less emphatic than *jetzt*, and tends to combine the idea of 'so', 'accordingly' with its time sense. At times it is no more than a vague connecting link (e.g. *es gibt nun verschiedene Gründe dafür*). See also under 'well'.

It can be preceded by prepositions, though not by *bis* (e.g. *von nun an*).
Er ist nun endlich gekommen.
Siehst du nun ein, wie schwierig die Aufgabe ist?
Es wird nun allmählich Zeit, daß wir gehen.
Wir können uns nun etwas Ruhe gönnen (combines the idea 'that being so' with the temporal sense).

3. Nunmehr is used in the sense of 'now' decisively, without possibility of return to the previous state of affairs. *Nun* can be substituted, but without expressing the idea as definitely.

Nach all dem bleibt uns nunmehr keine andere Wahl.
Die Gefahr ist nunmehr vorüber.

NUMBER 1. Zahl means a 'definite or fairly definite number'. It must be used when the number is stated, and may be used when preceded by the definite article and followed by the genitive.

Wir waren drei an der Zahl.
Die Zahl der Teilnehmer ist sehr beschränkt.

2. Anzahl means an 'indefinite number'. It must be used when preceded by the indefinite article and followed by the genitive, and may be used when preceded by the definite article and followed by the genitive.

Eine, die, große Anzahl von Büchern.

3. Nummer: a number in a series.

Die Nummer des Hauses, des Regiments.

Welche Nummer haben Sie gewählt?

OBJECT, OBJECTION, PROTEST 1. A stated, formulated objection.
(a) **Einwand** is a general objection to a matter as a whole, **Einwendung**
to a specific point. The distinction is often ignored. Combined with *machen*
and *erheben* (*Einwendung* generally only with *machen*) they translate 'to
object'. They are rarely used in the first person, present tense (i.e. they do
not translate 'I object').

Er erhob Einwände gegen den Plan.

Was für Einwendungen hat er gegen den Plan gemacht?

Das sind keine stichhaltigen Einwendungen.

Es ist bei ihm zur Gewohnheit geworden, Einwände zu erheben.

(b) **Einspruch** is a stated, formal objection or protest made during discussion. It is generally combined with *erheben*. It translates 'I object' in
this formal sense.

Ich erhebe Einspruch gegen den Vorschlag, gegen seine Ernennung.

(c) **Einwenden:** to object in the sense of (a). It is followed by a *daß* clause,
or by an indefinite pronoun (e.g. *vieles, nichts*). It is rare in the first person
present tense.

Ich wandte (dagegen) ein, daß er die nötigen Schritte noch nicht getan habe.

(d) **Sich etwas verbitten:** to object in a subjective way, to resent something
felt to be offensive. It translates 'I object'.

Ich verbitte mir eine solche Bemerkung.

(e) **Sich verwahren** denotes an objective objection. It translates 'I object',
'I protest'.

Ich verwahre mich gegen Ihr Benehmen.

2. An unstated objection which approximates to a mere feeling.

(a) **Was, etwas, vieles, nichts, (einzuwenden) haben gegen....**
These expressions are used in this weaker sense of 'object', i.e. 'to
mind'. The addition of *einzuwenden* suggests a more serious context and
more reasoned objections.

Was haben Sie dagegen, gegen ihn? (what's your objection to...?)

Haben Sie etwas dagegen, daß ich das Fenster aufmache?

Ich habe nichts dagegen, daß er hier übernachtet.

Ich habe nichts dagegen einzuwenden, daß Sie das Geld so anlegen.

Es ist nichts dagegen einzuwenden (there is no objection to it).

(b) **Gegen sein:** to be opposed, averse, to. It is common as a translation
of 'object' in conjunction with 'why'.

Warum sind Sie gegen den Verkauf des Autos?

3. When 'objection' denotes an emotional reaction rather than a reasoned
argument, German uses terms such as *Abneigung* (dislike, aversion).

Ich habe eine eingewurzelte Abneigung gegen diesen Baustil.

4. Followed by the gerund, the implied subject being the same as that of
the object (e.g. I object to doing it). This use can only be translated by a
paraphrase, as the following suggestions show.

Ich bin nicht gesonnen, ich weigere mich, mir das noch länger anzuhören
    (I object to listening...).

Ich lasse mich doch nicht so behandeln (I object to being treated like that).

OCCUR

OCCUR **Vorkommen** can only be applied to things or acts which are conceived as instances or cases of a species,[1] i.e. not simply as an equivalent of 'happen'. For the latter see 'event'.

Solche Fehler kommen häufig vor.
So etwas ist hier nie vorgekommen.
Das darf nicht wieder vorkommen.

OFFER **1.** With a noun object.

(a) **Anbieten** carries the implication of handing a thing over to a person as a conscious act, sometimes with the idea of pressing it on the person. The object may also be a noun denoting an action that one intends to perform for the person in question. The subject is a person or something which stands for a person. The intended receiver must be mentioned (in the dative case).

Sie bot mir eine Tasse Tee an.
Ich bot ihm meine Hilfe an.
Die Universität Berlin bietet ausländischen Studenten größere Vorteile als Jena an (the suggestion is that Berlin takes active steps to attract such students).

(b) **Bieten** in its commonest use suggests not a conscious act of offering, but that what is offered is simply available. A frequent synonym is 'present'. The subject here is generally not a person. When the subject is a person, the object is generally a part of the body (e.g. *Arm, Hand*).[2]

Der Hügel bietet einen weiten Blick über die Stadt.
Die Universität Berlin bietet ausländischen Studenten größere Vorteile als Jena (the advantages are there, without any suggestion that the university authorities take steps to bring them before the notice of such students).
Er bot ihr seinen Arm.

2. With a following infinitive.

Anbieten refers to ordinary acts or to contracts. **Sich erbieten**: to volunteer in bigger matters.

Ich habe ihm angeboten, den Brief für ihn zu übersetzen.
Er hat uns angeboten, unseren Wagen für 2000 Mark zu kaufen.
Sie hat sich erboten, die Diphtheriekranken zu pflegen.

ONLY (adverb) The uses treated refer to time, number, or quantity.

Erst[3] in reference to numbers or quantity implies that more are to come. **Nur** means 'not more' or 'not other than' that indicated, and makes no reference to anything outside this. Applied to a point of time *erst* means 'not before', *nur*, 'on that occasion only'.

Der Junge ist erst 10 Jahre alt, erwarte nicht zu viel von ihm.
Von einem Jungen, der nur 10 Jahre alt ist, kann man nicht zu viel erwarten.
Erst drei Schiffe haben den Hafen verlassen.
Nur drei Schiffe haben den Hafen verlassen.
Ich bin erst am 22. September nach Berlin gefahren.
Ich bin nur am 22. September nach Berlin gefahren.

---

[1] The addition of *mir* means: as far as my experience goes. *So etwas ist mir nie vorgekommen*: I have never known, heard of, such a thing. It can also give *vorkommen* the meaning of 'seem'.

[2] *Bieten* is also 'to bid' at an auction.   [3] See also 'first'.

OPEN (v.)[1] **1. Aufmachen** is the general prose term which translates 'open' in its literal sense.[2] In particular, it is applied to small things, and without any suggestion beyond the action of opening itself. It is also the familiar term for opening a small business.

Das Fenster, die Tür, die Kiste, die Schublade, den Brief, den Mund, die Augen, aufmachen.

Er hat ein kleines Geschäft in der Nähe aufgemacht.

2. Auftun is used only in more elevated diction. It implies the opening of something inward through externals, and so is not normally applied to inanimate objects. It thus easily passes over into figurative use.[3]

Die Augen, die Lippen, auftun.

'Gleichwie in Wollust und kaltem Entsetzen waren die Münder weit aufgetan' (Gerhart Hauptmann, *Der Narr in Christo*).

Die Blumen tun sich am Morgen auf.

Das Erlebnis hat ihm Herz und Sinne aufgetan.

3. Öffnen is mostly a literary term though common in Austria in every-day speech. It is, however, still the preferred term in reference to the opening of something big, particularly when associated with the idea of some ensuing activity. Applied to small things it is affected or old-fashioned. It is the normal term for 'to be open' in reference to a public building.

Er öffnete feierlich das Testament.

Die Türen der Halle werden um 8 Uhr geöffnet.

Die Bank ist von 10 bis 3 Uhr geöffnet.

4. Eröffnen: (*a*) to start an activity, proceedings; (*b*) to establish a business or an institution of some size.

Die Sitzung wurde um 3 Uhr eröffnet.

Feindseligkeiten wurden plötzlich eröffnet.

Er hat ein neues Konto in dieser Bank eröffnet.

Er wird bald ein großes Warenhaus eröffnen.

5. Aufschlagen is used mainly in fixed phrases (e.g. *ein Buch, die Augen*, the latter only in elevated diction).

OPINION, VIEW, CONCEPTION **1. Meinung** stresses the personal element and the possibility of error in the conclusion reached about a matter. It is held sincerely and seriously, without thought of display. It cannot, however, unlike 'opinion', be applied to an expert judgment.

It can, on the other hand, be used, like 'opinion', in phrases meaning 'to esteem' (*eine hohe, schlechte, Meinung von jemand haben*), i.e. when a judgment of value about a person or his abilities and the like is implied, but not where a mere estimate of probabilities is meant (e.g. in the sentence: what's your opinion of his chances?).

Ist das Ihre Meinung?

Ich bin der Meinung, daß keine Gefahr besteht.

Nach meiner Meinung müssen wir abwarten.

---

[1] *Aufschließen*: unlock (*die Tür, sein Herz*). *Erschließen*: open up, in the sense of 'explore' (*das Innere Australiens*); make available for use (*einen neuen Markt*).

[2] To open a bottle: *entkorken*.

[3] Similarly *zumachen* is the general term for 'shut'. *Schließen* like *öffnen* is applied to bigger things. The past participle *geschlossen* is mostly used in the sense of 'firmly', 'permanently closed', also in the sense of 'self-contained' (*ein geschlossenes Kunstwerk*).

OPINION

Ich bin ganz und gar Ihrer Meinung.
Er äußerte vorsichtig seine Meinung.
Er hat seine Meinung geändert.
Ich habe keine große Meinung von ihm, von seinem Talent.

2. Gutachten is an expert opinion of any kind, given professionally and used in a formal context. While it can be used in this way of a medical opinion, a term such as *Urteil* would be preferred in reference to the every-day relationship between doctor and patient.

Nach dem Gutachten eines Sachverständigen ist mein Auto 20 000 Mark wert.
Der Arzt gab ein Gutachten über die Gesundheit des Angeklagten ab.
Ich habe einige Gutachten über den Fall eingezogen.
Das Urteil des Arztes über die Möglichkeit einer völligen Wiederherstellung meiner Gesundheit ist günstig.

3. Beurteilen (see article on 'judge') refers to an estimate of probability and in this sense translates phrases such as: what is your opinion of...? See also *Urteil* in the previous section.[1]

Wie beurteilen Sie meine Chancen?
Ich beurteile sie günstig.

4. Erachten is only used in a few fixed phrases (*meines Erachtens, nach meinem Erachten*) and is apt to sound pretentious since it claims a thorough scrutiny of the grounds for an opinion.

5. Ansicht corresponds to only one meaning of 'view' as a synonym of 'opinion'. It cannot be used like the English term to denote a theory of a matter (e.g. Schiller's view of art). It suggests rather an attitude to, a judgment about, a thing, often in relation to something extraneous to it, than an understanding, a conception, of the matter itself. It is often super-ficial, particularly in the plural. The title of E. T. A. Hoffmann's novel *Die Lebensansichten des Kater Murr* is ironical. The singular *Ansicht* refers to a specific question, not a whole field of knowledge for which the plural must be used.

'To take a view' cannot be translated literally. 'Hold' with 'view' is *haben.*

Was ist Ihre Ansicht über das Buch?
Meiner Ansicht nach kann der Plan nicht gelingen.
Die Ansicht der Kirche über Ehescheidung.
Der Mann hat merkwürdige Ansichten.
Er teilte mir seine Ansichten über die Demokratie mit.
Ich will keine Ansichten, sondern Begründungen hören.

6. Anschauung means 'view' in the sense of a 'conception' and can include a theory. This meaning is connected with other uses of the term: (i) contemplation in the sense of seeing into the inside of things; (ii) 'intui-tion' as a philosophical term (e.g. Fichte's '*intellektuelle Anschauung*'); (iii) experience of the concrete, the visible, mainly in fixed phrases (e.g. *Anschauungsunterricht; seine Sprache kommt aus der Anschauung*). In the sense of 'view' it suggests origin in the inner life, the workings of intuition on experience, although it does not exclude a certain amount of analytical thought. In strict use it is applied to the great spheres of knowledge and

---

[1] See also *halten* under 'think'.

experience (e.g. life, art, love, and the like), but is also used loosely and popularly in much the same way as *Ansicht*.

Eine Lebensanschauung, Weltanschauung.

Schillers Kunstanschauung.

Ich teile diese Anschauung nicht.

Er hat komische Anschauungen.

Sag' mir mal ein bißchen deine Anschauungen darüber.

7. Auffassung approximates more closely to 'conception' than to 'view'. It denotes a personal way of conceiving, understanding, a matter,[1] particularly important spheres of knowledge, i.e. it is a way of understanding, taking the matter itself, not an attitude to it.[2]

Schillers Auffassung der Kunst.

Die Staatsauffassung der deutschen Romantik unterschied sich stark von derjenigen der westlichen Demokratie.

ORDER   Sense of 'command', 'instruct', 'bid'.

In this sense the verb of motion (e.g. go, come) may be omitted after 'order' if a phrase expressing destination follows (e.g. he was ordered to the front, to Paris, back). Of the German verbs treated in this article only *beordern, ausweisen* and *verweisen* dispense with the verb of motion.

1. Befehlen should only be used when 'order' is practically interchangeable with 'command', to which it more closely approximates. It suggests the formal exercise of authority by virtue of an exalted position (e.g. a king, general, government, but not a parent or schoolteacher), and is only appropriate in reference to matters dealt with officially and solemnly by high personages. Its object may be the person commanded or the action to be performed.[3,4]

Der General befahl dem Heer, die Waffen zu strecken.

Die Regierung befahl, die Stadt zu räumen.

Der Richter befahl, den Gefangenen abzuführen.

Die Regierung befahl eine allgemeine Säuberungsaktion.

2. German has no exact term to translate 'order' used peremptorily and suggesting opposition or at least doubt as to whether compliance will follow. **Auffordern,** to call upon a person to do a thing, sometimes approximates to this sense. In addressing the person ordered, **verlangen** (followed by a *daß* clause) may be used (see 'ask' and footnote to 'anxious', p. 18, n. 1).

Er forderte den Dieb auf, stehen zu bleiben.

Die Festung wurde zur Übergabe aufgefordert.

Ich verlange, daß Sie das Zimmer aufräumen.

3. To instruct, direct, bid.[5,6]

---

[1] See *auffassen* under 'take'.

[2] See also *Begriff* under 'idea'.

[3] *Befehlen* is also used as a polite or deferential term, mostly in fixed expressions. See dictionaries.

[4] *Gebieten* is used in the sense of 'command', 'enjoin' in lofty contexts. It suggests that refusal is impossible.

[5] *Lassen* (see 'make') may also be used in this sense. In the past tense it means that the order was obeyed. *Der Lehrer ließ das Kind in der Ecke stehen. Laß die Pferde satteln.*

[6] *Heißen,* to bid, suggests that the order is given orally. It can be more familiar than 'bid'.

ORDER

(a) **Anordnen** is used of the orders given by persons possessed of official authority and tends to refer to actions carried out by a number of people. The object can only be the action performed, expressed by a clause, an infinitive or a noun, i.e. it cannot be the persons required to act. It approaches the meaning of 'decree' (*verfügen, bestimmen*).

> *Die Regierung ordnete an, daß die Streikenden zur Arbeit zurückkehren sollten.*
> *Der Gewerkschaftsführer ordnete einen Streik an.*

(b) **Anweisen** corresponds exactly to 'instruct', and must be used to translate 'order' when the two are close equivalents.

> *Sie werden hiermit angewiesen, sich alle 14 Tage bei der Polizei zu melden.*

(c) **Beordern**: to order a person to proceed to a place in an official capacity. The verb of motion is omitted.

> *Der Gesandte wurde nach Hause, an den Hof des Königs, beordert.*

(d) **Auferlegen,** to impose, is used as a legal term in the sense of 'to order to pay'.

> *Ihm wird auferlegt, die Kosten zu zahlen.*

4. Sense of 'prescribe' (medically).

(a) **Vorschreiben** suggests the prescription (often in writing) of the details of a course of action.

> *Der Arzt schrieb ihm eine neue Diät vor.*

(b) **Verordnen**: to prescribe in general, without reference to detail.

> *Der Arzt verordnete einen Luftwechsel.*

5. Sense of 'to direct (a thing) to be furnished or supplied' (*S.O.D.* II, 3): **bestellen**. For *abbestellen* see under 'cancel'.

> *Haben Sie schon bestellt?* (a waiter to guests).
> *Er hat einen neuen Anzug bestellt.*
> *Ich habe den Wagen für 8 Uhr bestellt.*

OTHER **Ander** can be used to translate 'another' only in the sense of 'different' from the one mentioned or implied. See article on 'different'. In the sense of 'additional' to the first, but not different from it, **noch ein, weiter,** or **zweit** must be used. The idea of difference conveyed by *ander* may be no more than 'better', i.e. not necessarily different in kind, e.g. *geben Sie mir ein anderes Streichholz,* which could imply: better than the first, which broke, or which would not strike. The other terms suggest the idea of addition, which may imply retention of the first. *Geben Sie mir ein weiteres Streichholz,* which could mean: I need two. *Weiter* carries this implication more clearly than the other terms.[1]

> *Geben Sie mir noch ein Stück Brot.*
> *Ich habe noch eine Frage an Sie.*
> *Er machte eine weitere Bedingung.*
> *Ich möchte das kein zweites Mal erleben.*

PAINFUL 1. **Schmerzhaft** refers only to physical pain.

> *Die Wunde ist sehr schmerzhaft.*
> '*Es schwoll darin von schmerzhaft entzückter Sehnsucht nach...*' (G. Hauptmann, *Der Narr in Christo*).

---

[1] *Noch* is also used to translate 'more' preceded by a numeral or by 'some', 'a few', in the sense of additional. *Geben Sie mir noch etwas Wein, noch drei Pfund. Es kommen noch einige Leute.*

2. Schmerzlich refers to mental anguish springing from the sense of loss.

Er hat einen schmerzlichen Verlust erlitten.

Ich habe mich zu der schmerzlichen Erkenntnis durchgerungen, daß das Leben einen Kompromiß mit unseren Idealen erfordert.

Die Nachricht hat mich schmerzlich berührt.

Er wurde von dem Vorfall schmerzlich betroffen.

'"Mir ist das All, ich bin mir selbst verloren"—ein schmerzliches Bekenntnis bei jedem Menschen, ein erschütterndes bei einem dessen All und dessen Selbst Goethe war' (Gundolf, *Goethe*).

3. Peinlich is applied (*a*) to that which embarrasses one or wounds, grates on one's sensibilities or aesthetic feeling; (*b*) in the sense of over-exact, punctilious, which it also translates.[1]

Es war eine peinliche Begegnung, ein peinlicher Augenblick.

Es ist mir peinlich, das sagen zu müssen.

Es ist höchst peinlich, so etwas mitansehen zu müssen.

Wir können es nur als eine peinliche Pflicht betrachten.

Es herrschte eine peinliche Stimmung.

Seine Stimme wirkt peinlich.

Ich fühle mich von der Angelegenheit peinlich betroffen.

Er spricht sogar von alltäglichen Sachen mit peinlicher Präzision.

Sein Deutsch ist geradezu peinlich.

4. Mühselig, mühsam, beschwerlich: laborious, arduous, onerous, with reference to work, effort, and to ways (literally, and figuratively in the sense of 'courses of action'). *Beschwerlich*: attended with physical discomfort, hardship, difficulty.

Es war ein ganz kleiner Staat, der mühselig bestrebt war, sich gegen ungünstige Umstände durchzusetzen.

Er kroch mühsam aus den Trümmern hervor.

Das Gehen fällt ihm beschwerlich.

PALE, PALLID **Blaß** indicates an absence of colour greater than what is regarded as normal and approaching white. It corresponds to 'pale'. **Bleich** is stronger and means 'pallid'. *Erbleichen*: to blanch.

Er war blaß vor Angst.

Das ist ein blasses Blau.

Ihr Gesicht ist bleich.

Er war bleich vor Schrecken.

PAPER 1. Material on which one writes, prints or with which one wraps parcels and the like: **Papier.**

Briefpapier, Luftpostpapier, Packpapier.

2. General sense of documents which are valuable as a source of information or serve to establish identity or attest permission to go somewhere, mostly plural: *Papiere* appears regularly in a number of compounds (*Schiffspapiere, Amtspapiere, Wertpapiere, Wagen-* or *Autopapiere*). There is a tendency today, furthermore, to use *Papiere* in the English sense even when it does not form part of a compound.

---

[1] *Penibel* (French: *pénible*) is used in the sense of *peinlich*, particularly in the sense of 'over-punctilious', 'fastidious'. It is more commonly applied to a person than *peinlich* (e.g. *er ist sehr penibel*).

PAPER

Wir haben diese Papiere unserem Anwalt übergeben.
Haben Sie Ihre Papiere mit?

There are, however, other German terms which are commonly used.

3. Personalausweis(e): personal papers which establish one's identity, one's record and the like.

(a) **Ausweis** is a 'pass', most commonly one which entitles the bearer to pass frontiers, to enter places, in certain cases to be granted concessions.

> *Personalausweise sind mitzubringen, wenn die Aufenthaltserlaubnis beantragt wird.*

(b) **Unterlagen** go beyond establishing identity and attest qualifications and the like and are officially required, e.g. when an application for something is being dealt with.

> *Alle Unterlagen müssen da sein, wenn das Interview mit dem Kandidaten stattfindet.*

(c) See also under 'evidence' for terms meaning document.

4. An exposition of or treatise on a subject involving careful research and read before a body with some expert knowledge of it such as a learned society: **Referat.**

> *Sein Referat über die Probleme von Goethes 'Clavigo' wurde mit Beifall aufgenommen.*

5. A literary composition, especially of brief, occasional or fragmentary nature, usually in plural (*W*.): **Schrift(en).**

> *Seine gesammelten Schriften.*

6. Examination question paper. There is no specific term for this in German, which can only speak of **schriftliche Prüfung, Klausurarbeit, Fragen** or **Examensfragen.**

> *Die schriftliche Prüfung in Latein war schwierig.*
> *Die Prüfungsaufgaben* (examination paper).

PASSAGE 1. Sense: the act or action of passing: movement or transference from one place or point to another or through or across a space or element: transit (*W*.). German often compounds with **durch** or **über**, the verbal substantive part being determined by the type of movement.

> *Der Durchgang durch ihren Grund (das Durchgehen ihres Grundes) war Fremden verboten.*
> *Die Durchfahrt durch die Mündung war gefährlich.*
> *Die schwarzen Enten waren auf dem Durchflug (Durchzug) von nördlichen in südliche Gegenden.*
> *Der unbestimmte Übergang der Jahreszeiten* (but the passage of time, flux, der Fluß, der Verlauf der Zeit).
> *Der Übergang von der Barbarei zur Kultur* (i.e. transition).

2. Sense: a specific act of travelling or passing from one place to another: a journey especially by sea or air between two points (*W*.).

> *Die Überfahrt von New York nach Southampton war schnell* (crossing).
> *Die Hinreise war ohne jeden Zwischenfall* (outward passage).

3. A privilege of conveyance as a passenger: accommodation: German **Karte** (ticket).

> *Es gelang mir, eine Karte für den nächsten Flug zu bekommen.*
> *Wir haben unsere Schiffskarten gelöst* (booked our passage).

4. A means of passing: a road, path, channel, or course through or by which something passes: a way of exit or entrance: pass.

(a) **Gang** is a corridor or hall in a building (**Diele:** entrance hall to a house, also called **Flur**, see under 'hall'). German also uses **Korridor**.

Die Gänge in diesem Haus waren eng und dunkel.

Er verirrte sich in den langen Gängen des Hotels.

(b) **Durchgang:** a narrow lane in a built-up area.

Die meisten Straßen waren nur Gassen, Durchgänge zwischen Häusern und Gruppen von Gebäuden.

5. Something that has taken place between two persons mutually: a mutual act or transaction (as a negotiation, a quarrel or lovemaking) (*W.*).

Waffengang (passage of arms), *Wortgefecht*.

6. A usually brief portion of a written work or speech that is quoted or referred to by itself as relevant to a point under discussion or is noteworthy for content or style (*W.*).

(a) **Stelle** could be ambiguous since in the context of a written work it can mean either place or point, i.e. something very restricted, or something longer, but it is the commonest term for passage (see under 'place').

Eine der besten Stellen des Romans.

(b) **Passage** is used exactly as the English term. It is a passage in an official document, but hardly in literature.

Er hat eine lange Passage aus dem Bericht vorgelesen.

(c) **Passus** (pl. *Passi*) tends to mean a passage that is extended. It is less common than the other terms.

Er verrät seine Ungenauigkeit in vielen Passi (Stellen) des Berichts.

7. Passage is also used for passage in the sense of an arcade in a town leading from one street to another, and at the sides of which there may be shops. It is covered over, often by glass.

Wenn Sie diese Passage benutzen, werden Sie schnell hinkommen.

PATTERN There is no exact equivalent in German for any of the uses of this term, and, where they exist, German uses terms which correspond to close synonyms of 'pattern' in English (e.g. *Vorbild, Muster, Schablone, Modell*). Otherwise German resorts to a variety of paraphrases.

1. Excellent or normative example worthy of imitation: **Vorbild.**

Die Arbeiterpartei hat in diesem Fall ein praktisches Vorbild für eine schöpferische Opposition (W.).

2. Something designed as a model for making things, outline, plan (*W.*).

Schneidermodell, Schnittmuster: dressmaker's pattern.

3. A specimen offered as a sample of the whole: **Muster.**

Muster ohne Wert.

4. The design in an object in so far as this is not pure art: **Muster, Modell.**

Das geometrische Muster eines Teppichs (W.).

Maschinen, die alle nach einem Muster, Modell gebaut sind.

Modell suggests more clearly than *Muster* the copying from an original finished object, *Muster* the design.

5. In art, whether literature, the visual arts, or music: **Plan, Struktur, Anlage.**

PATTERN

Man fühlt sofort den Plan (or: *Grundplan*) *aus diesem Bilde heraus.*

Alle Kunst muß eine Struktur aufweisen.

Das Buch als Ganzes gesehen besteht aus einer wertvollen und sinnreichen, jedoch sehr integrierten Struktur (*W*.).

6. Constantly recurring features in actions or behaviour. No one German term for this.

Diese Reihe von Morden zeigt gemeinsame Merkmale auf.

Das Profil einer Persönlichkeit (personality pattern).

PAY Zahlen denotes simply the operation of handing over money or any other form of payment. **Bezahlen** adds to this the idea of discharging an obligation. When the object is what is paid, i.e. the money, or the account, etc., both verbs are used, but with the distinction indicated. When the object is a person, *bezahlen* must be used with a direct object, or *zahlen* with the dative of the person and with mention of what is paid or paid for. In the figurative sense (e.g. to pay for one's folly) only *bezahlen* is possible.

'To pay for' may be translated by *bezahlen* with the thing acquired as direct object, or *für* may be added; also: *zahlen für*.

Ich habe das Geld, die 100 Mark, schon gezahlt.

Zahlen, bitte, Herr Ober!

Wollen Sie bitte mittels Scheck zahlen.

Sie müssen endlich mal das Geld bezahlen, das Sie ihm schulden.

Ich habe alle meine Rechnungen bezahlt.

Du kannst für den Wein, ich werde für das Essen zahlen.

Du mußt den Wein jetzt bezahlen, du hast den Mann schon lange genug warten lassen.

Ich werde Sie gleich bezahlen.

Ich habe ihm drei Mark dafür gezahlt.

Er hat seine Dummheiten teuer bezahlen müssen.

Wir haben den Wagen noch nicht bezahlt (or: *für den Wagen*).

PEOPLE 1. Menschen: human beings. It is used when the general characteristics of human beings as such are thought of; often, therefore, in opposition to other animate beings or to things.

Wieviele Menschen wohnen in London?

Sie müssen die Menschen verstehen, ehe Sie ein Urteil über sie fällen können.

Leider vergessen die Menschen sehr schnell.

Was für Menschen haben Sie dort gefunden?

Es geschah zu einer Zeit, wo die Menschen normalerweise im Bett sind.

Seine Menschenkenntnis geht nicht sehr weit.

2. Leute: any odd group or class of people that one thinks of in connection with some specific matter, but not in reference to their general characteristics as human beings. It is not a dignified term and can often be disparaging.[1]

Die Leute is sometimes used colloquially for *die Menschen.* It can also mean 'men' in the sense of 'workers' or 'followers'.[2]

Die Leute drüben machen sehr viel Lärm.

Die Leute im Finanzamt sind dagegen.

Es waren fünf Leute im Zimmer.

---

[1] Applied to servants it is free from disparaging suggestions.

[2] Example: *wir haben 3 Leute im Garten.*

Kleider machen Leute.
Was für Leute haben Sie dort getroffen?
Reiche, arme, kluge Leute.
Die Leute wollen das nicht glauben (colloquial for *die Menschen*).
Die Partei hat ihre Leute überall.

3. Volk.

(a) 'People' in the sense of a 'community' bound together by common customs, sentiments, language.

Das deutsche Volk.
Die Völker der Erde.

(b) 'People' in the sense of the 'common people' as distinct from their leaders.

Das Volk muß politisch erzogen werden.

PERFORMANCE **1. Leistung**: an achievement which has required effort.

Seine Leistung bei dem Hochsprung übertraf alle anderen.
Seine Leistung bei den Verhandlungen weist ihn als einen geschickten Taktiker aus.

2. Ausübung (see under 'practise') must be followed by a genitive.

Ausübung der Pflicht (or: *Pflichterfüllung*).

3. Darstellung: in a theatrical context means the performance of a play in the sense of the impersonation of a role.

Seine Darstellung des Mephisto war hervorragend.

4. Aufführung is the performance of a play as a whole, acting, staging and the like.

Die Aufführung von Goethes 'Tasso' wurde günstig kommentiert.

5. Vorstellung in the context of the theatre and the like is performance in the sense of 'session'.

Es gibt täglich drei Vorstellungen.
Ich gehe zu der 8-Uhr Vorstellung.

PLACE **1. Ort** is the most general term. It can therefore indicate in the most general way existence in space (e.g. *Ort und Zeit angeben*; *er hat keinen Ortssinn*). Only in this sense can it denote a building, e.g. in definitions (e.g. *eine Bibliothek ist ein Ort, wo Bücher gelesen oder ausgeliehen werden*). It can also refer to (*a*) an inhabited locality (e.g. town, village); (*b*) a more circumscribed area, e.g. the scene of some happening, but vaguely, never an exact point (therefore never a place, spot, on the body); (*c*) the place where a thing belongs, in which use it denotes position more exactly; (*d*) figuratively: the proper place.

Wir müssen den Ort ausfindig machen, wo er sich versteckt hat.
Berlin ist sein Geburtsort.
Die Einwohner dieses Ortes sind alle sehr arm.
Sie wohnen in einem sehr schönen Ort.
An diesem Ort habe ich ihn zuerst getroffen.
Das ist ein geheiligter Ort.
Stellen Sie Ihr Fahrrad, das Buch, an den richtigen Ort zurück.
Hier ist nicht der Ort, solche Bemerkungen zu machen.

2. Stelle[1] denotes a more exact point, and so approximates to 'spot'.[2] It can therefore refer to a point in an area, on the body, in a book, speech and the like,[3] place where a thing belongs, ordinal position. It also corresponds to 'place' used in the sense of 'stead' (e.g. in place of you, in your place). It never denotes a building.

Hier ist die Stelle, wo er ermordet wurde.
Ich sah ihn an der Stelle, wo der Pfad abbiegt.
Das ist eine empfindliche Stelle an meinem Arm.
An dieser Stelle spricht der Dichter von seiner Jugend.
Bringen Sie das Buch an die richtige Stelle zurück.
Ich würde das an zweiter Stelle erwähnen.
An Ihrer Stelle würde ich das nicht tun.

3. Platz denotes (*a*) primarily a place made for the carrying on of some activity, and is frequently translated by 'square', 'ground' as well as 'place' (e.g. *Marktplatz* = market place, *Spielplatz* = playing ground). See also under 'ground'. (*b*) It then means 'place' in the sense of 'room, accommodation' for sitting, standing, or the like;[4] (*c*) further, the place where a thing belongs, and (*d*) figuratively: the proper place; (*e*) finally, the position obtained in competitive activities.

Ist da Platz für mich? (see also under 'room').
Hier ist noch Platz für den Schrank.
Der Platz an der Sonne (figuratively).
Stellen Sie das Fahrrad an den richtigen Platz zurück.
Hier ist nicht der Platz, solche Bemerkungen zu machen.
Die Bemerkung war nicht am Platz (an idiom, 'in place').
Er gewann den dritten Platz bei dem Preisausschreiben.

4. Stätte, which was originally the plural of *Statt* but subsequently became a singular, is an elevated term and often suggests a place that endures and possesses spiritual associations. It can denote a building.

Eine heilige, geweihte, Stätte, eine Kultstätte.

POOL, PUDDLE, POND 1. Pool: a small body of standing or still water (*S.O.D.*). 'Pond' is generally but not invariably artificially made and contains fish. Accordingly, **Weiher**, in popular use a South German word, otherwise poetic, and **Teich** (in North Germany) approximate more to 'pond' than 'pool'. **Lache** (sometimes **Lacke**) is a shallow collection of any liquid (*S.O.D.*) and so corresponds to both 'pool' and 'puddle', e.g. *eine Blutlache.* **Pfütze** is a 'puddle', often dirty, left on the street or elsewhere after rain. **Tümpel**, often a dirty or stagnant pool, but sometimes a deep spot in flowing water, too big generally to be a puddle. **Pfuhl** is always pejorative and denotes a dirty pool which may vary in size; also figurative as cesspool. **Becken** is artificial, typically part of a fountain, i.e. basin, but may also be a swimming bath, which is generally **Schwimmbassin**, though

---

[1] See also 'position'.
[2] *Der Fleck* is 'spot' both in the sense of 'highly circumscribed area' and 'stain'. *Der Flecken* is 'spot' in the sense of 'blemish'. *Der Flecken auf seiner Ehre.*
[3] *Stelle* can also mean 'passage' in a book, speech, musical composition, and the like. See under 'passage'.
[4] *Platz* further means 'seat' in so far as its occupation or the intention, right, and the like, to occupy it, and not the object itself, is meant. *Seinen Platz verlassen, einen Platz belegen.*

in commercial advertisements for domestic swimming pools one also finds the English term *Pool*.

POPULAR 1. **Beliebt** means 'liked'. In the attributive position, it can qualify only nouns which indicate a middle-brow level of entertainment unless it is accompanied by an intensifying adverb such as *sehr* or *allgemein*.

Franz Lehar ist ein beliebter Komponist.

Er ist ein beliebter Artist, Clown.

In meiner Jugend war Whist ein beliebtes Kartenspiel.

Das ist ein beliebter Schlager, ein beliebtes Lied.

Er ist ein allgemein, sehr, beliebter Redner, Prediger, General (allgemein or *sehr* must be added).

Er ist bei jedem beliebt (liked by everyone).

2. **Populär** is used in various ways: (*a*) in the sense of 'non-expert', mostly in fixed phrases; (*b*) popular because of a certain heartiness, often in a slightly derogatory sense; (*c*) accepted, mostly negative.

Die Populärphilosophen (e.g. Nicolai).

Ein populärwissenschaftliches Werk.

Populärwissenschaftliche Aufsätze.

Göring war in weiten Kreisen des Volkes sehr populär (because of his hearty and clownish manner). *Beliebt* would suggest stronger liking.

Gewisse amerikanische Ausdrücke sind sehr populär unter der jüngeren Generation.

Ich meine nicht den populären Sinn des Wortes Romantik.

Der Krieg war wenig populär in Italien (not *beliebt*).

Das ist keine populäre Maßnahme (not *beliebt*).

3. **Volkstümlich:** partaking of the characteristics of the *Volk*; appealing through such characteristics; used by the *Volk*. Unlike *populär*, which can suggest superficiality, it is always used in a good sense and denotes the simplicity, vigour, and freshness of the *Volk*.

Volk is used in a few fixed compounds (e.g. *Volksausgabe*).

Ein volkstümlicher Redner, Prediger, Schriftsteller, Ausdruck.

4. For many uses of 'popular' German has no well-defined term, particularly in reference to political life. 'Popular government' could be paraphrased as *Regierung durch das Volk*. (*Regierung des Volkes* is a leftist government.) Popular election = *allgemeine Wahl*. The popular cry for victims: *der Schrei der Menge, der Massen, nach Opfern*. With reference to the popularization of knowledge: *allgemeinverständlich (allgemeinverständliche Vorträge*). A popular fallacy: *ein allgemeiner, weitverbreiteter Irrglaube*.

POSITION,[1] **SITUATION I.** (in space) 'Position' suggests an occupied place, and can mean 'position in relation to something else' in terms of strict measurement or more vaguely the 'position relative to other things', or again, still more vaguely, the 'whereabouts' of a thing. 'Situation' suggests relation to the surrounding district or countryside, often in reference to its picturesqueness.

---

[1] The *Fremdwort 'Position'* in reference to space is used in the same way as English 'position', and its use is growing. See also footnote (p. 250, n. 2) to 'position' and 'situation' in the sense of external circumstances.

POSITION

The German nouns are strictly limited in their range of application, and are never identical with 'place' (*Ort, Stelle, Platz*). When those listed are inappropriate, verbs must be used.

1. Lage denotes the position of an object in a district or landscape, and therefore corresponds most closely to 'situation'. It is applied only to objects which are more or less broad-based, i.e. which appear to lie. Thus it can refer to a building, even if tall, but not to a tree, to heavy machinery but not to furniture. It also translates 'position' as a relation expressed in exact measurement or in general directions. The position is in each case fixed. Hence expressions such as: *aus der gehörigen Lage bringen*.

It is applied to persons only in so far as 'lying' is meant, and then only in reference to comfort and the like.

Das Haus, der Garten, hat eine schöne Lage.

Durch seine Lage war Leningrad einem Angriff vom Westen her ausgesetzt.

Durch seine Lage ist der Busch scharfen Winden ausgesetzt.

Den Fliegern wurde die Lage des Bahnhofs genau erklärt.

Er hat die Maschine aus der gehörigen Lage gebracht.

Der Kranke hat eine unbequeme Lage im Bett (more commonly: *liegt unbequem*).

2. (a) **Stellung** refers not to where, but to how a thing is placed, either in relation to surrounding persons or things or in the relation of its parts to each other.[1] In the first case the angle at which one object points to another is implied. No other kind of relationship is expressed. Thus it cannot translate 'his position on the stage gave him a good view of the artist', because there is no question here of angle, but of proximity. In a sentence such as 'he chose a position from which he could see everything clearly', *Stellung* would be possible if a crouching, squatting, leaning position, or the like, is meant, but not if position refers, for example, to a hill, i.e. merely a place.

(b) *Stellung* can refer to the position or order of words in a sentence (though *Wortfolge* is the ordinary term for word-order).

(c) As a military term *Stellung* refers to an entrenched or in mobile warfare a heavily fortified position.

Er blieb eine Stunde lang in liegender, knieender, gekrümmter, Stellung.

In vorgebeugter Stellung kann ich besser sehen.

Der Hund hob das rechte Bein und verharrte eine Minute lang in dieser Stellung.

Wenn Sie das Klavier in dieser Stellung belassen, werden Sie die Tür nicht öffnen können. (Although such a sentence is possible, *an dieser Stelle*, i.e. place, would be more usual.)

Alle feindlichen Stellungen wurden erobert.

Die Stellung dieses Wortes macht den ganzen Satz unklar.

3. Stand is regarded as a fixed position at any moment of something that moves. It is little used,[2] being applied only in a few cases with which the verb *stehen* is regularly associated. It implies measurement. As a hunting

---

[1] *Haltung* as applied to the body means 'carriage, attitude', in so far as it expresses an inner state. See article on 'attitude'.

[2] The idea of a fixed point is always present, no matter what the English translation is. Sometimes it corresponds to 'level', 'mark'. *Der Stand des Wassers, des Getreides.* See also article on 'state', 'condition'.

term it denotes not only position, but also a 'stand' in the sense of an 'object'.[1]

Der Stand der Sonne (considered as a fixed point at any given moment).
Der Stand des Beobachters.
Der gegenwärtige Stand der nuklearen Forschung.

4. **Stelle** and other terms which mean 'place' (see article) can be used when 'position' does not stress the idea of relationship, i.e. when 'place', 'spot' would be more appropriate in English.

Setzen Sie den Strauch an eine andere Stelle.
Ich suchte mir eine schattige Stelle aus, wo ich ungestört lesen konnte.
Wer diese Stelle für den Brunnen wählte, hat nicht viel Kunstsinn an den Tag gelegt.
Von meinem Platz auf dem Podium konnte ich den Redner gut beobachten.

5. The verbs *liegen, gelegen sein* (to be situated), *sein, stehen, stellen,* and others are often used, when the above nouns are inapplicable.

Die Stadt liegt sehr schön.
Ich kann Ihnen nicht sagen, wo die dritte Armee sich im Augenblick befindet.
So wie das Klavier steht, stört es die Harmonie des Zimmers.

POSITION, SITUATION II. 'Position' is vague in its reference to external circumstances, but suggests the interest of the person in dealing with them. It forms a number of fixed phrases. Examples: That's the position! The position is that... The (beer, food) position is... The position with (your application) is... What is the position with...? 'Situation' does not in itself suggest action on the part of the person, and in this sense it is more objective than 'position'. It can refer (*a*) to a wide set of external circumstances (e.g. the political, military, situation) or (*b*) to a moment characterized by the interplay of human personality, emotion, the dramatic (e.g. I found myself in a ludicrous situation).

German has no term of German origin for 'position' thus used.[2]

1. **Lage** corresponds to 'situation' in its reference to a set of circumstances, i.e. meaning 2(*a*). It suggests that these have come about gradually, that they hold the person, and does not stress human intervention in order to change them, i.e. the person tends to be thought of as a victim. 'Plight' is sometimes an English equivalent. 'Position' must be translated by *Lage* when it is practically interchangeable with 'situation' (e.g. the food position, situation: *die Lebensmittellage, die Ernährungslage*). *Lage* is in general combined only with a few fundamental commodities (e.g. *Brennstofflage, Brotlage,* not with *Butter, Wein,* though, exceptionally, with *Zigaretten*). *Lage* cannot be used to translate the other fixed expressions formed with 'position'.

[1] Further: *Standort* in military contexts (e.g. in reference to aircraft, the position of a ship in convoy) corresponds to 'location'. It is also used as a gardening term for the position of shrubs and the like.

[2] *Position* is used as a *Fremdwort* in many of the senses of the English term, except in fixed phrases, particularly as 'job'; 'place from which one can survey a scene'; 'point of view'; and more generally in the sense treated in this article. Examples: (*a*) *Wir hatten eine gute Position und konnten von da aus die ganze Rennbahn überblicken.* (*b*) 'Freilich hat Goethe dadurch auch seine Position aus Höflichkeit selbst geschwächt...' (Gundolf on Kleist, referring to Goethe's criticism of Kleist). (*c*) 'Das ist ja die günstige Position dieser hohen Funktionäre der braunen Revolution, daß sie abstreiten oder behaupten können, was ihnen für ihre Unschuldslegende paßt, weil die Belastungszeugen beseitigt sind' (H. B. Gisevius, *Bis Zum Bitteren Ende,* vol. 2).

2. Situation corresponds to the English 'situation' only in the second sense as described above. It is applied typically to a situation which arises suddenly, is of short duration, and in which the interest is in the human element, not the external circumstances as such.

(a) *Die militärische Lage ist sehr ernst.*
   Die politische Lage kann sich grundlegend ändern.
   Die Ernährungslage hat sich verschlechtert.
   Ich bin in einer wenig beneidenswerten Lage, ich soll die beiden wieder versöhnen (position or situation).
   Die Lage ist für einen weiteren Appell an seine Freigebigkeit sehr ungünstig.
   In Ihrer Lage würde ich die Wahlergebnisse abwarten.

(b) *Eine tragische Situation* (e.g. in a drama, novel).
   Ich befand mich in einer peinlichen, lächerlichen, Situation (*sich befinden* goes well with *Situation* because it expresses the mental and emotional reaction of the person).
   In dieser Situation kann ich nichts tun.

3. Some translations of 'position' used to form fixed expressions.

(a) The most general are: *wie steht, ist, es mit...?* (what is the position with...?); *es ist so mit...* (the position with...is...).[1]
   Wie steht (ist) es mit dem Ausflug? Findet er statt?
   Wie steht es denn mit der Gehaltserhöhung? (What stage of the negotiations has been reached? what are the chances?)
   Es ist so, daß wir Ihnen die versprochene Reise nicht mehr bezahlen können.
   Es ist also so! (So that's the position!) *Die Rationen müssen wieder gekürzt werden.*

(b) *Es verhält sich mit..., wie verhält es sich mit...?* are used to give or ask for details or clarification of something obscure or not understood.
   Wie verhält es sich nun eigentlich mit dem Mann?
   Wie verhält es sich mit Ihrer Reise, Ihren Ferienplänen?

(c) *Es ist...bestellt mit..., wie ist es mit...bestellt?* are used typically with *gut* or *schlecht* of persons and their interests rather than of external circumstances. With the latter they are apt to sound precious.
   Wie ist es mit deinen Zigaretten bestellt?
   Wie ist es mit seiner Professur bestellt?
   Es ist schlecht um ihn, mit ihm, bestellt.

POSITION, SITUATION, JOB   III. Stellung is the most general term and suggests the person[2] in relation to the position more than the nature of the position itself. **Stelle**, on the other hand, emphasizes the nature of the position, which is thought of as having real existence, even if vacant. For this reason it is often extended, particularly in compounds, to mean 'office', 'board', and the like. If there is no indication to the contrary, it tends, however, to denote a humble job. *Stellenangebot*, as the heading of an advertisement column, refers to jobs of this kind. **Posten** is an already created position into which a person moves. It strongly suggests either his suitability for the position or the material advantages it brings, or the opposite

---

[1] *Die Sache ist die, daß...* means: the point is that....
[2] Since *Stellung* concentrates attention on the person, it is also used of social rank, standing in any group, professional or otherwise. *Seine Stellung in der Gesellschaft verbietet ihm, unvorsichtige Äußerungen zu machen.* 'Position' thus used should be distinguished from the sense of external circumstances (see article on 'position', 'situation' in this sense).

of these. It is most common in reference to administration or business, but is not applied to the professions or labourers' jobs. **Arbeit** and the verb *arbeiten* are often used for a labourer's job, particularly in reference to the seeking or finding of it. **Platz**, which is little used, is a small job, generally in the commercial world. **Anstellung** corresponds rather to 'appointment' than to any of the above terms (see article on 'appoint').

Er hat eine hohe Stellung im Heer, in der Verwaltung, im Geschäft.
Er ist auf der Suche nach einer neuen Stellung.
Er nahm die erste freigewordene Stellung an.
Er eignet sich nicht für diese Stelle.
Diese Stelle ist freigeworden.
Er bewirbt sich um diese Stelle.
Er eignet sich in hohem Grade zum Posten des Vize-Kanzlers.
Er hat einen Posten in einer Bank gefunden.
Er sucht Arbeit in einer Fabrik (job).
Seine Arbeit behagt ihm nicht.
Er arbeitet in einer Mehlfabrik (has a job).
Er hat jetzt einen Platz in einem Exportgeschäft.
Seine Anstellung erfolgte sofort.

POSSIBLY 1. Möglicherweise[1] is used in the sense of *vielleicht*, but is more strongly concessive, and at the same time implies a nicer weighing up of possibilities than the latter.[2]

Möglicherweise haben wir zuviel verlangt.

2. In the sense of 'in accordance with what is possible' (*P.O.D.*) **nur** (colloquially **bloß**) is used,[3] except when 'possibly' is accompanied by 'not'. In this case German uses *unmöglich*.

Er braucht den besten Arzt, den man nur finden kann (in a relative clause following a superlative).
Wie können Sie so was nur (bloß) sagen? (see also *auch nur* under 'even').

POST, STAKE, PILLAR, COLUMN, POLE, STICK 1. (a) Post as 'a strong piece of wood, metal or stone, usually long, placed upright to support or mark something' (*A.L.*) is generally German **Pfosten**.

Bettpfosten, Türpfosten, Telegraphenpfosten.
(b) A sign post: **Wegweiser**; sign-posted (of a road): **beschildert** (*Schild* = sign).
(c) Lamp post: **Laternenpfahl** (see under 'stake').

2. Stake, 'a strong stick or post, sharpened at one end and driven into the ground' (*A.L.*), mostly as a support for something or to hold something, e.g. a plant, in place: German **Pfahl**.

---

[1] The adverbial form compounded with *weise* must be used when the adverb modifies the whole clause, not one word. *Er hat vernünftigerweise nicht zu viel angestrebt. Er hat mir seltsamerweise nichts davon gesagt.*

[2] *Eventuell*, though sometimes translated by 'possibly', has a more special meaning than the latter. While 'possibly' simply denotes a concession that a thing may be as indicated as the alternative to its not being so, *eventuell* means that a thing may be as indicated in the event of certain circumstances operating. It is most commonly used to indicate a second possibility, in the sense of 'or', and 'in a certain contingency'. *Ich fahre Montag, eventuell Dienstag. Er wird eine Gehaltserhöhung von 20, eventuell 25 R.M. pro Woche, bekommen.* It refers to the future.

[3] A close synonym is *irgend* (at all), which is used in this way in *wenn* clauses. *Wenn ich irgend kann.* Often it is combined with *nur*.

Holzpfahl, Grenzpfahl, Marterpfahl (to which martyrs condemned to be
burnt to death were tied, but more often one speaks of *Scheiterhaufen*),
Rebenpfahl.

3. Pillar (which helps to support a roof or the like): German **Pfeiler**, mostly
of stone. **Brückenpfeiler.**

4. Column: German **Säule** (an older plural of *Saul*, now a singular). In
literal use it is always fashioned artistically. *Die Säulen des Palastes.* Figuratively, it is used in the same way as 'column'.
Feuersäule, Wassersäule.

5. Pole (cognate with German *Pfahl*): German **Stange**. (The German term
also has various figurative uses, e.g. *eine Stange Geld*, a lot).

6. (a) Stick: German **Stock**, both corresponding in most cases. But *Stock*
also translates 'baton' of a musical conductor.
Spazierstock, Prügelstock (cane).
(b) **Stab** corresponds rather to staff, and to wand (*Zauberstab*).
(c) **Stecken** can be the equivalent of *Stock* and *Stab*, even a stick to help one
walk, but it is also characteristically a stick with which to prod animals (e.g.
a herd of cattle) on. It is roughly made, often a branch of a tree: a *Wan-
derstecken*, unlike *Wanderstab*, would not be on sale in a shop.

POWER, STRENGTH, FORCE   A.   Sense: ability to exert effort; person
or thing possessing such ability.

1. **Macht,** when held by persons, suggests a position of power by means of
which we are enabled to exert influence, control over people and things. In
reference to political power it implies this weight of influence, whether legal
or illegal, not the specific organs of power (see **Gewalt**). Attributed to things,
it likewise suggests power to influence. Further, a person, a country, and,
with personification, a thing, a natural or supernatural force may be termed
as **Macht.** Used in the plural, it only has this latter application.

It will be seen that compared with 'power' its range of meaning is limited,
and that it corresponds more exactly to the cognate term 'might', which,
however, tends to be used exclusively in elevated diction or in reference to
the supernatural.
Er besitzt fast unbeschränkte Macht.
Er hat Macht über ihn gewonnen.
Er mißbraucht seine Macht.
Die absolute Macht verdirbt den, der sie besitzt.
Ich bin in seine Macht geraten.
Er hat sich in eine Machtstellung hineinmanövriert.
Eine revolutionäre Partei hat die Macht an sich gerissen.
Das steht, liegt, nicht in meiner Macht.
Die Macht der Liebe, des Hasses, der Musik, der Gewohnheit.
Er ist eine Macht im Lande.
Machtpolitik ist untrennbar von dem Begriff 'Großmacht'.
Wissen, Geld, ist Macht.
Die Mächte der Hölle.

2. **Gewalt** is power to force people to do one's will. It suggests more
definitely than *Macht* the actual application of power, force, the overcoming
of resistance, and therefore corresponds closely to both 'power' and 'force'

used in this sense. With the implication of overwhelming[1] power it can also be attributed to things (e.g. *die Gewalt der Musik, des Sturmes*). A close synonym is 'violence', which it sometimes, but by no means invariably, translates.[2]

Ich bin in seine Gewalt geraten.
Er hat mich in seiner Gewalt.
Sie müssen Gewalt anwenden.
Er hat es mit Gewalt durchgesetzt.
Die Gegensätze wurden durch Waffengewalt entschieden.
Er schrie mit aller Gewalt.
Die Gewalt des Windes war unbeschreiblich.
Die Gewalt seiner Sprache ist geradezu hinreißend.

3. **Kraft** is the energy, physical or moral, in persons or things which produces an effect. In this sense of 'energy, vigour, vitality', it translates 'power' (e.g. *elektrische Kraft, seine geistigen Kräfte*), 'strength' (e.g. *das geht über meine Kraft*), 'force' as a close synonym of 'strength' and in the sense of 'efficacy, cogency' (e.g. *die Kraft eines Arguments*) and 'validity' (only in fixed phrases; e.g. *das Gesetz ist in Kraft getreten*).

With reference to bodily strength, the plural *Kräfte* is used when the waxing or waning of the energy of the mind and body as a whole is meant (e.g. *seine Kräfte nehmen rasch ab*, of a dying person). As an equivalent of 'strength' distinguish from *Stärke* (see **A, 4**).

For *Kraft* in the sense of 'faculty of the mind' see section **B, 3**.[3]

Pferdekraft, Dampfkraft.
Die Kräfte der Natur der Menschheit dienstbar machen.
Ich werde alles tun, was in meiner Kraft liegt.
Die Kraft des Widerstandes ist gebrochen.
Es steckt eine unheimliche Kraft in seiner Sprache.
Ihre Stimme hat keine Kraft.
Die Suppe hat keine Kraft (more commonly: *ist nicht kräftig genug*).
Er ist wieder zu Kräften gekommen (has regained his strength).
Das Gesetz bleibt noch weiter in Kraft.

4. **Stärke** is not strength in the sense of 'energy' (see *Kraft*), but strength which can be more or less measured. It can be applied to the human body and to things.[4]

Die Stärke seines Arms, der feindlichen Armee, der Festung, des Biers, des Fiebers, seiner Stellung.

5. **Wucht:** weight,[5] weightiness, which is forcibly felt, either literally or as an impression on the mind. As a rendering of 'force' it refers to an impact.

Er fiel mit voller Wucht auf das Pflaster.
Die Wucht seiner Argumente.

---

[1] *Überwältigen*, to overwhelm, contains the same root.

[2] Mostly in fixed phrases, e.g. *Gewalt antun*. 'Violence' is generally *Gewaltsamkeit, Gewalttätigkeit, Heftigkeit*. See 'violent'.

[3] In reference to a body of men German only has the term *Streitkräfte*. For air force, police force, etc. see section **D**.

[4] *Stärke* also means 'intensity'. See *stark* under 'severe'. Another sense is 'stark'. While *Stärke* is used less than 'strength', the opposite is true of the frequency of *stark* as compared with 'strong'. A further meaning of *Stärke* is 'starch'.

[5] *Gewicht* is weight as a measurement, also 'importance' of persons, and weight, e.g. of an argument, which appeals to reason.

POWER

B. Sense: 'a faculty[1] or active property' (*S.O.D.*).

1. Vermögen is applied now only to persons and denotes the inner structure or disposition which enables us to produce an effect. It suggests a latent state[2] rather than the actual expression or functioning of this disposition, and so approximates more to 'capacity' than to 'ability'. It is applied mainly, but not exclusively, to well-defined faculties of the mind (frequently in compounds) such as: *Empfindungsvermögen* (=sensibility), *Sehvermögen*, *Fassungsvermögen*. But its use with a following infinitive to denote less well-defined, but generally possessed, capacities is also possible, though it occurs mostly in generalizations about human beings and only when the idea of a capacity as such is stressed. Thus, while the term *Sprachvermögen* exists, it would be pedantic to use it to translate such a sentence as: he has lost the power of speech (*er hat die Sprache verloren*). Similarly it is possible to say: *sein Konzentrationsvermögen* (power of concentration) *nimmt ab*; but, unless special prominence is to be given to the idea of a capacity, the normal statement would be: *er kann sich nicht konzentrieren*.

Vermögen is applied only to conscious actions, i.e. not to purely physiological functions or reflex actions (e.g. the power to digest food, the power of blushing).

It has the further meaning of 'fortune' and 'estate'.

Sein Ausdrucksvermögen ist beschränkt.

Sein Vorstellungsvermögen ist sehr gut.

Sie besitzt ein starkes Ahnungsvermögen.

Der Mensch hat das Vermögen, das Zusammenleben der Völker friedlich zu gestalten, aber er macht oft keinen Gebrauch davon.

Das Vermögen, sich in jeder Lage zurechtzufinden, ist sehr nützlich.

Ich habe alles getan, was in meinem Vermögen stand.

2. Fähigkeit suggests a special ability or gift and its actual expression or functioning, whereas *Vermögen* is more general and tends to be latent. 'Ability' is therefore a closer equivalent than 'capacity'.[3] A high degree of consciousness and control in its exercise is implied. It is accordingly only applied to persons.[4]

Er hat die Fähigkeit, rasche Entschlüße zu fassen.

Nicht viele Menschen besitzen die Fähigkeit, den Wortlaut eines Gedichts nach der ersten Lektüre zu behalten.

3. Kraft means energy, and by extension can refer to the source of this, i.e. to the faculty or capacity from which flows the energy that produces an effect. Its meaning of 'energy, force, strength' (see **A, 3**) must be distinguished from that of 'source', i.e. faculty. In the latter sense it refers only to the well-defined faculties of the mind, and has in this use come to be practically synonymous with *Vermögen*.

---

[1] The terms discussed in this section also translate 'faculty' of the mind. Other terms sometimes found are: (*Unterhaltungs*)*talent*, (*Überredungs*)*gabe*.

[2] As is also *Anlage* which is a potentiality, a disposition, a capacity which requires development.

[3] 'Capacity' is, however, sometimes translated by *Fähigkeit*; e.g. in its sense of receptiveness as applied to persons. Examples: *Eindrucksfähigkeit*, *Aufnahmefähigkeit*. *Kapazität* refers to (*a*) the holding power of things, particularly as a chemical term; (*b*) occasionally to the mental power of persons, particularly in the phrase *er ist eine Kapazität*.

[4] It is sometimes applied in compounds to the holding power of things in the sense of 'capacity' (e.g. *Ladefähigkeit*—of ships). The adjective *fähig* is applied regularly to things (e.g. *diese Maschine ist fähig*, 1000 *Kilogramm zu heben*).

It can also denote an active property in a thing (e.g. *die Brennkraft der Kohle*). The property is normally expressed by compounding the term in question with *Kraft*.

A following infinitive to denote the activity of the property is impossible when 'power' is thought of as a capacity, a source of energy, i.e. after the combination in which *Kraft* is followed by the thing in the genitive case (*die Kraft der Hitze, Sonne*). In other words, the English 'the power of heat, of the sun, to burn' is untranslatable. On the other hand, when 'power' is thought of, not as a capacity, but as actual functioning, i.e. 'strength', a following infinitive is admissible; i.e. after such combinations as: *die Sonne hat die Kraft zu brennen*.

> *Einbildungskraft, Vorstellungskraft, Urteilskraft, Fassungskraft, Geisteskräfte.*
> *Die Heilkraft gewisser Kräuter, des Schlafes.*

4. Eigenschaft, quality, property, may be used for 'power' in the sense of 'active property' when applied to things.[1]

The explanation of the use of the infinitive after *Kraft* holds good for *Eigenschaft* too.

> *Diese Medizin hat die Eigenschaft, die Infektionsgefahr zu verringern.*

5. To denote an involuntary action (e.g. a reflex action) or a purely physiological function, none of the above terms is applicable. *Können* as a verb is often the only possible rendering.

> *Sie kann nicht mehr gehen, erröten* (has lost the power to walk, to blush).
> *Sein Magen kann solche Speisen nicht verdauen.*

C. Sense: delegated authority.[2]

1. Gewalt, in addition to its meaning of 'overwhelming force', can denote legal, constitutional power, authority, in which case it always refers to the organs of power through which the state functions or to the power exercised by an officer appointed to such organs.[3] In this sense it occurs mainly in fixed phrases.[4]

> *Die Staatsgewalt, die kaiserliche Gewalt.*
> *Die gesetzgebende, vollziehende, Gewalt.*
> *Unter einer Diktatur gibt es keine Trennung der Gewalten.*
> *Ich habe nicht die Gewalt, diesen Mann verhaften zu lassen.*

2. Befugnis is a formal, official term, and means the 'power to act' conferred legally, constitutionally on an individual or a body by virtue of his office, or special circumstances. It should only be used in a formal discussion or statement which seeks to define specific powers, i.e. not in an informal conversation.

The verb *befugt sein* is used in the same sense.[5]

> *Die Befugnisse des Vize-Kanzlers sind ganz empfindlich gekürzt worden.*

---

[1] *Wirkung* (effect) may be used as a close synonym.

[2] *Autorität* is only used in the sense of 'power, influence'. It cannot stand for persons themselves.

[3] *Walten* = to rule (now used only in fixed phrases or figuratively). *Verwalten* = to administer.

[4] *Gewalt* can mean 'control' in fixed phrases, mostly 'self-control'. *Er hat sich in der Gewalt. Er hat die Gewalt über sich verloren. Kontrolle* only means 'administrative supervision which acts as a check'. Similarly *kontrollieren*.

[5] *Fug* is now only used in fixed phrases (e.g. *mit Fug und Recht*). It is connected with *fügen*, and so has the fundamental sense of 'what is fitting, suitable'.

Er hat seine Befugnisse überschritten.
Der Vize-Kanzler sagte, er habe nicht die Befugnis, das zu tun.
Das gehört nicht zu meinen Befugnissen (a common expression).

3. **Berechtigt sein,** to be entitled, is a more general term which can denote human rights[1] as well as specially conferred power, and can be used informally as well as formally.

The noun *Berechtigung* is used, though less frequently, in the same sense.
Ist der Senat berechtigt, das zu tun?
Wir sind berechtigt, Anleihen vorzunehmen.
Sind Sie berechtigt, mich zu fragen?
Die Treuhänder sind berechtigt, ihn zum Vormund zu bestellen.

4. **Ermächtigung, ermächtigt sein,**[2] denote the exercise of power allowed by a higher authority. Power in a specific matter is implied, whereas *berechtigt sein* can refer in a more general way to the possession of power.

Sind Sie ermächtigt, mich zu fragen? (i.e. in this specific matter, whereas *berechtigt* would ask if this was amongst the powers of the interrogator).
Der Kanzler hat mich ermächtigt, nach Gutdünken zu handeln.

5. **Vollmacht** means exclusively 'power of attorney'. It is used also in the plural without distinction of meaning. *Ein Bevollmächtigter*: a plenipotentiary.
Vollmacht zu verhandeln ist ihm erteilt worden.
Er hat seine Vollmachten überschritten.

D. Some other senses of 'power' and 'force'.

Electric current: *Strom.* A body of men: *Luftwaffe* (air force); *Streitkräfte*: armed forces; *die Polizei* (police force). *Potenz* (in mathematical sense). German has no exact term for 'force' in the sense of 'real import of a word or document'.

PRACTISE, EXERCISE 1. **Üben:** (*a*) to practise in order to acquire proficiency, mastery; (*b*) do, perform, carry out.
Sie übt zehn Stunden täglich Klavier.
Er übt sich im Reden.
Ein geübtes Auge.
Er hat Gnade, Gerechtigkeit, geübt (exercised).

2. **Ausüben:** (*a*) to carry on, exercise something in which one is already proficient; (*b*) to put into practice, into action, to make use of something one already has.
Er übt seinen Beruf, sein Amt, seine Kunst aus.
Seine Worte übten einen starken Einfluß aus.
Er hat sein Stimmrecht nicht ausgeübt.

3. **Einüben:** to study thoroughly, particularly a role in a play.
Er hat seine Rolle gut eingeübt.

PRAISE, EXTOL 1. **Loben,** like praise, is the general term, the sense of which is 'to express a favourable judgment on' a person or thing.
Der Lehrer lobte ihn, seine Arbeit.
Das Stück wurde in den Zeitungen sehr gelobt.

---

[1] *Recht* = (i) a right; (ii) 'law' as a principle.
[2] *Sich ermächtigen* is now obsolete. It means 'to usurp power', 'to seize possession' of a thing (i.e. *sich bemächtigen*; see 'seize').

2. Beloben is 'to say so much in praise of a thing (not a person) that the result is practically a speech of praise'. A formal occasion is often suggested.

Er wurde wegen seines mutigen Verhaltens belobt.

'*Ich ließ mir herzlich dankbar alles und jedes wohl gefallen, belobte und pries; nur nahm es mich wunder, wozu er das Gartengerät gekauft*' (Mörike, *Mozart auf der Reise nach Prag*).

3. Preisen: to draw the attention of other people emphatically to the qualities of a person or thing so that he or it becomes known. Unlike *loben*, it does not mean to praise a person to himself.[1]

Er pries das Buch, den Wein, die Kochkunst der Frau.

Er hat den Redner sehr gepriesen.

4. Rühmen suggests even more strongly than *preisen* the spreading of the fame of a person or thing.[2]

Seine Taten wurden von der Presse gerühmt.

PREPARE[3] 1. With a noun object.

(a) **Bereiten** is only regularly used in present-day German[4] in reference to the mixing of substances. It is short for **zubereiten** which is used in the same way. Both the skilled process of preparation and the result are stressed.

Er hat das Essen, eine Medizin, die richtige Mischung von Farben bereitet, zubereitet.

Sie hat ein wunderbares Essen bereitet.

(b) **Vorbereiten** is used in all other senses of 'prepare'. It includes every action, however trivial, involved in any preparation.

Ich habe die Berichte für meinen Vorgesetzten schon vorbereitet.

Sie bereitet das Essen vor (the stages before the blending of the substances, e.g. getting the materials, cleaning, cutting them).

Er bereitet sich auf das Abitur vor.

Wir waren auf die schlechte Nachricht nicht vorbereitet.

2. With the following infinitive.

(a) **Sich vorbereiten** can only be used in reference to elaborate preparations.

Er bereitet sich auf sein Examen vor.

Ich bereite mich jetzt schon darauf vor, das nächste Jahr in China zu verbringen.

(b) **Sich anschicken** is used of small adjustments for immediate action of a limited character.

Ich schickte mich an zu gehen, seine Frage zu beantworten, als das Telephon klingelte.

3. 'To be prepared' followed by the infinitive can be translated by *vorbereitet sein* in the sense described in the preceding section. In the sense of 'to be willing'[5] (under conditions or with tacit reservations, or the like) its only equivalent is **bereit**, i.e. ready.[6]

---

[1] *Anpreisen* has a commercial sense, and means 'to recommend', 'to urge a person to take a thing'. The object is generally a thing (e.g. *Waren anpreisen*).

[2] *Sich rühmen* followed by the genitive means 'to boast of a thing'.

[3] *Präparieren* refers only to a technical process.

[4] The use of *bereiten* with such words as *Bad, Bett* is old-fashioned or rarefied.

[5] In synonymous use 'willing' is also translated by *bereit*. *Willig* suggests absence of compulsion, but not eagerness. *Bereitwillig* suggests a certain amount of the latter. *Gern* is 'gladly' or 'willingly' when this implies the former. *Willig* is only followed by an infinitive when inactivity or submission is stressed (e.g. *willig, den Tod zu erleiden*). Further, it is applied to persons only in more or less fixed phrases (e.g. *er ist nicht recht willig*). 'To

Ich bin bereit, Ihren Plan zu unterstützen.
Ich bin bereit, das Risiko auf mich zu nehmen.

PRESS, SQUEEZE, URGE, DEPRESS, OPPRESS 1. In the literal sense of 'press' and 'squeeze' **drücken** is the general term. **Pressen** denotes very strong pressure, sometimes 'to press both sides of a thing together', often by means of machines. The figurative sense of both verbs is 'to weigh heavily upon', 'to oppress', of feelings, conditions, or circumstances. Here too *pressen* is stronger than *drücken*.

Er drückte sie an seine Brust.
Er drückte ihm eine Mark in die Hand.
Er drückte auf den Knopf.
Er preßte sie an seine Brust.
Er preßte so viel in den Koffer hinein, daß er platzte.
Er preßte den Saft der Zitrone in ein Glas.[1] (*Drücken* cannot mean 'to squeeze out the contents'.)
Der Kummer, die Not, drückt, preßt, ihn sehr.
Drückende Hitze (the present participle of *pressen* is not used adjectivally).

2. In the sense of 'to urge', 'press for a thing', 'press a person to do a thing', both **dringen** and **drängen** are used. The distinction is that *dringen* means to insist in general, while *drängen* suggests a demand for immediate action. Both are followed by *auf* when the object is a thing, *dringen* by *in* when the object is a person. **Bedrängen** is sometimes, though infrequently, used in this sense. It stresses the emotional state into which one is thrown, the subject being a person close to one. See also next section.

Die Gläubiger drangen, drängten, auf Zahlung.
Er drang in mich, drängte mich, den Mann zu entlassen.
Sie bedrängen mich, meine Reise zu unterlassen.

3. Bedrängen: to press hard, to beset, i.e. from all sides. Used of emotions it means to cause concern, not 'to depress' (see *bedrücken*). The past participle is used adjectivally, particularly with reference to circumstances that press hard upon one.

Sie bedrängen mich mit ihren Ansprüchen.
Er befindet sich in einer bedrängten Lage.
Das Elend meiner Geschwister bedrängte mich.

4. Bedrücken means 'to depress' the spirits. It also means 'to oppress' in the sense of 'to pinch, to squeeze' taxes and the like out of a population. In the more general sense of 'to govern tyrannically', **unterdrücken** (which also means 'to suppress') is the normal term.

Daß es ihm schlecht geht, bedrückt mich sehr (depress).
Eroberte Länder werden von ihren Eroberern immer bedrückt.
Die militärische Besetzung wurde als bedrückend empfunden.
Die Nazis unterdrückten ihr eigenes Volk.

be willing' can sometimes be translated by *wollen*, but not, of course, when the latter means 'to insist'. See article on 'want'. Similarly, 'unwilling' is rendered by *nicht bereit, nicht wollen*. *Unwillig* means 'indignant'. *Widerwillig* means 'reluctant', but cannot be applied directly to persons in any combination.

[6] 'Ready' in the sense of 'having made all the necessary preparations' is *fertig*, which, however, cannot be followed by the infinitive. *Bereit* must be used in this case.

[1] To press grapes: *keltern*. 'To press' in reference to technical processes differs from case to case.

5. Quetschen is 'to squeeze' or 'to crush' a thing from both sides so that it becomes flattened, both literally and figuratively. It approaches the meaning of 'squash'.[1]

Die Früchte sind auf dem Transport gequetscht worden.
Ich habe meine Hand in der Tür gequetscht.
Ich quetschte mich noch in die übervolle Straßenbahn.

PREVENT 1. Hindern, verhindern[2] with the following infinitive.

Hindern concentrates attention on the act of preventing itself, and is therefore more dramatic and vivid than *verhindern*, which emphasizes not the act but the result. *Hindern* can suggest physical intervention on the part of a person by an act that is characteristically brief and sometimes sudden. With a personal subject *verhindern*, correctly used, suggests less an act of intervention than the mere existence or presence of the person or something about him that acts as a deterrent. The deterrent operates not in one brief act, but gradually, after the lapse of time, or permanently though weakly. It is thus appropriate in generalizations about the permanent or repeated operation of a deterrent, or when the deterrent functions indirectly.

(a) Examples with a personal subject:

Er trat ihr in den Weg und hinderte sie daran, in den Saal zu treten.
Er schloß ihre Kleider in den Schrank und verhinderte sie dadurch, den Ball zu besuchen.

(b) When the subject is not a person, but, for example, a motive, emotion, idea, and the like, the same distinction holds good. *Verhindern* is more usual, since *hindern* indicates a sudden and forceful assertion of the motive or emotion.

'*...so schien ein Etwas in seiner Haltung auszudrücken, daß nur Erziehung ihn hinderte, sich umzuwenden*' (Thomas Mann, *Der Tod in Venedig*).
Seine Erziehung verhinderte ihn, die Leute anzustarren.
Meine Grundsätze haben mich verhindert, auf seinen Vorschlag einzugehen.

(c) German regards the following forms of the verb as having something of the dramatic: the imperative, the interrogative form (but not a mere rhetorical question), often the infinitive in combination with modal verbs. *Hindern* is therefore more usual.

Hindern Sie ihn daran, das Zimmer zu verlassen.
Wer wird mich daran hindern, das Zimmer zu verlassen?
Was hindert Sie daran, das Zimmer zu verlassen (what is there to prevent...)?
Ich mußte ihn daran hindern, was sollte mich daran hindern, das Zimmer zu verlassen?
'*Ich mußte den Molch in der Hand halten und am Weglaufen verhindern*' (Ricarda Huch, *Teufeleien*).

(d) *Verhindern* is used with the effect of a mere report in unstressed, undramatic parts of a statement, even when the same idea, emphasized, would be expressed by *hindern*. In such cases some other word in the sentence (often the subject) bears the stress, particularly when it is already known that an action has been prevented and it is decided to draw attention to the cause.

Er sagte: 'Ich will ihn totschlagen und niemand wird (or: *wer kann*) *mich daran hindern.' Der Schutzmann hat ihn aber daran verhindert.*

---

[1] *Zerquetschen* is 'to squash completely'.
[2] *Abhalten*: deter from some act that the object, which must be a person, consciously means to carry out. In this sense it is used as commonly as 'stop'. *Lassen Sie sich dadurch nicht abhalten* (don't let it stop, deter, you).

Er trat vor mich, was mich verhinderte, weiterzugehen.

Ihr Mann war es, der sie verhinderte, in den Saal zu treten.

(e) The infinitive after these verbs is only possible if it denotes a conscious, deliberate act.

Daran is generally used to anticipate the following infinitive, though it is sometimes omitted for reasons of rhythm (see the above example under 1(b) from *Der Tod in Venedig*). It is obligatory when *verhindern* is used absolutely (e.g. *er hat mich daran verhindert*).

Further examples are:

Er hat sie daran gehindert, Selbstmord zu begehen.

Seine Überredungskraft hat sie verhindert, Selbstmord zu begehen.

Das Parlament hat den König daran gehindert, Krieg zu erklären (actively intervened).

Das Parlament hat den König verhindert, Krieg zu erklären (by its mere existence).

Die Wachen hinderten den Gefangenen daran, zu entkommen.

Die Wachen verhinderten den Gefangenen zu entkommen (with stress on *Wachen*, not *verhinderten*).

Der Lärm hinderte mich, seine Worte deutlich zu hören (die Musik zu genießen).

Der Lärm der Straßenbahnen verhindert mich, in diesem Zimmer geistige Arbeit zu leisten.

Wir haben den Feind daran gehindert, den Fluß zu überschreiten.

Kein Gesetz kann uns daran hindern, ein neues Haus zu bauen.

Die Schmerzen hinderten mich daran, fest zu schlafen.

Könnte seine Liebe zu ihr ihn verhindern wegzufahren?

Ich habe so lange mit ihr gesprochen, daß ich sie dadurch verhindert habe, den Zug zu erreichen.

Seine Eifersucht verhinderte ihn, sie in ihrem wahren Licht zu erkennen.

Seine Liebe zu ihr verhinderte ihn wegzufahren.

Der niedrige Stand meines Bankkontos hat mich verhindert, die Reise zu unternehmen.

Sie haben ihn doch hoffentlich nicht verhindert, den Garten zu verlassen (a mild rhetorical question, stressing the result rather than the action).

Es war der Regen, der uns verhinderte, die Reise anzutreten.

Ich war geschäftlich verhindert, das Büro früh zu verlassen.

2. *Verhindern* with a *daß* clause.

The preceding account of *verhindern* with the infinitive largely applies to its use with a *daß* clause. In general, the prevention is still less active and direct than with the infinitive construction.

(a) It is therefore more appropriate, though not obligatory, in the following cases:

(i) When the activity on the part of the subject (i.e. the author of the preventing) is absent or weak. A negative frequently has this effect.

Der Mißerfolg der anderen verhinderte nicht, daß er selbst den Versuch machte.

Die Unerreichbarkeit des Ziels verhinderte nicht, daß er Zeit und Geld dafür opferte.

Sein Wissen um die Absichten, die sie gegen ihn hegen, verhindert nicht, daß er noch mit ihnen verkehrt.

(ii) When the whole action (both the action of preventing and that prevented) is vast, complicated, and indirect, so that it cannot be seen as a single act; the subject or object or both being frequently not one person, but a group.

Bei all ihrer Tüchtigkeit konnten die deutschen Generale nicht verhindern, daß die Heere der vereinigten Nationen an allen Fronten siegreich durchbrachen.

Er konnte nicht verhindern, daß Spanien dazu überging, eine selbstständige Politik zu treiben.

Der Westen kann nicht verhindern, daß Rußland in Osteuropa nach Gutdünken waltet.

(b) The *daß* construction is normally obligatory in the following cases:

(i) When the whole action (both subject and object) belongs to the world of inanimate nature. *Hindern* with the infinitive would be unusual in so far as it would personify the action.

Die Gebirge verhinderten, daß die Gewässer weiterflossen.

Die Bäume verhindern, daß die Sonne zu den Pflanzen dringt.

(ii) When the action prevented is involuntary, i.e. in the sense of 'save'.

Der Felsvorsprung verhinderte, daß er tiefer abstürzte.

Das Betäubungsmittel verhinderte, daß ich Schmerzen empfand.

Further examples are:

Das Fehlen eines wohlhabenden Mittelstandes in gewissen Ländern hat verhindert, daß ein liberales Regierungssystem aufkam.

Seine Hilflosigkeit verhinderte nicht, daß sie ihn übel zurichteten.

Der starke Donner verhinderte, daß ich den Ruf meines Kameraden hörte.

Der Nebel verhinderte, daß er den Graben sah, und so stürzte er hinein.

3. A noun or verbal noun (or corresponding pronoun), that refers to the action prevented, as the object of (*ver*)*hindern*.

In this case 'prevent' is mostly translated by *verhindern*. *Hindern* fluctuates between the meanings of 'prevent' and 'hinder'[1] (impede, delay). If the verbal noun is accompanied by an adjective meaning 'quick', or the like, it tends to mean 'hinder'. In terse statements coloured by emotion it is the preferred term for 'prevent'.

Die Ausführung des Plans hat er verhindert, wurde verhindert.

Den Verrat müssen wir um jeden Preis verhindern.

Das werde ich zu verhindern wissen.

Der Fluß verhinderte das Heranführen von Verstärkungen (prevented).

Der Fluß hinderte das schnelle Heranführen von Verstärkungen (hindered, impeded).

Wenn du in dein Unglück rennen willst, ich kann's nicht hindern (prevent).

PROTECT **Beschützen** stresses the personal nature of the protection extended to one. **Schützen** is used in all other cases.

Fühlen Sie sich beschützt, wenn er in der Nähe ist?

Während der ersten Jahre seiner Kindheit wurde er geliebt und beschützt.

Diese warmen Kleider werden Sie vor der Kälte schützen.

---

[1] *Behindern*, which takes a personal object, means 'to hinder'. *Seine Gicht behindert ihn beim Gehen. Er kann die nötigen Bücher nicht bekommen und findet sich deswegen in seiner Arbeit behindert. Hindern* can mean 'hinder', generally with a personal, but sometimes with a non-personal object, and therefore admits ambiguity. *Behindern* is more common in the passive than in the active voice, while the reverse is true of *hindern* in the sense of 'hinder'.

PROTECT

Australien glaubte lange Zeit, es sei durch seine geographische Lage vor feindlichen Angriffen geschützt.

Sie müssen sich vor seinen Anschuldigungen schützen.

PROVIDE[1] **1. Versehen** can only be used in the sense of 'equip',[2] whether literal or figurative, i.e. when 'equip' could be substituted in English. It is always followed by a phrase with *mit* denoting the thing provided. With intangibles *versehen* is more common in the passive than the active voice.

In the sentence 'Can you provide us with beds?' the sense of equipment is present if the question is addressed to a house-agent. The German is therefore *können Sie uns mit Betten versehen?* If, however, it is a request for accommodation, this sense is absent, so that German would say: *können Sie uns für die Nacht unterbringen?*

Das Heer wurde mit den neuesten Waffen versehen.

Die Kandidaten wurden mit Papier versehen.

Das Haus ist mit Betten, Tischen, Stühlen wohl versehen.

Die Firma versah ihn mit einer Schreibmaschine.

Er versah uns mit dem nötigen Geld, mit warmen Kleidern.

Bevor er nach London fuhr, versah er sich mit ein paar guten Empfehlungsbriefen.

Er war mit einer guten Entschuldigung versehen.

2. Versorgen refers only to the necessities of life, food, clothing, etc. Used absolutely without a *mit* phrase, it translates 'to provide for'. In this use it is best preceded by some adverb such as *gut, reichlich* (see *sorgen für*).[3]

Der Staat muß die Arbeitslosen mit Nahrung und Kleidung versorgen.

Die Witwe ist gut versorgt.

3. Sorgen für: (*a*) to provide permanently for a person, i.e. to supply the necessities of life. Unlike *versorgen*, this expression requires no adverb such as *gut*. (*b*) To see that something is done or made available.

Für die Witwe ist gesorgt.

Der Staat wird für Arbeit sorgen.

Für Luftschutzkeller wurde in diesem Viertel nicht gesorgt.

Die Firma wird für Schadenersatz sorgen.

4. Liefern: (*a*) to make goods available, by placing them ready to hand, delivering them; (*b*) to provide something needed by producing it (as from the earth); (*c*) to furnish something intangible which is sought after.

(a) *Können Sie hundert Exemplare dieses Buches liefern?*

Amerika hat die neuesten Waffen geliefert.

(b) *Der russische Boden liefert fast alles, was die Wirtschaft braucht.*

(c) *Seine Taten liefern einen Beweis für seine Einstellung.*

Seine Saumseligkeit lieferte mir den Vorwand, den ich suchte.

---

[1] *Ausrüsten* is 'to equip for action', whether physical (e.g. *ein Kriegsschiff ausrüsten*), or mental (e.g. *mit guten Kenntnissen ausgerüstet*). *Ausstatten* means 'to endow' a person with natural gifts and 'to furnish' or 'fit out' a thing with features that enhance its appearance (e.g. *ein schön ausgestattetes Buch* = a beautifully got-up book). Compare 'well-appointed'.

[2] *Versehen* is often better translated by 'equip'. *Der Wagen ist mit einer neuen Bremse versehen.*

[3] Some such adverb as *gut* tends to be necessary with many other verbs compounded with *ver-* (e.g. *gut verpackt, gut verwahrt*).

5. Stellen is used to denote contributions made by two or more persons.

Ich stelle die Pferde, wenn Sie einen Wagen haben.

Er wird das Benzin stellen, aber Sie müssen für alles andere bezahlen.

Bei dem Aufmarsch wird dieses Regiment die Musik stellen.

6. Aufkommen für: accept the responsibility for financing a thing.

Der Staat wird für das Geld aufkommen.

Wenn Sie für die Nahrungsmittel sorgen, bin ich bereit, für den Wein aufzukommen.

7. In other cases a more specific term must be used as in the following:

Sein Besuch bietet uns die Gelegenheit, die Frage aufzuwerfen (approximates to 'liefern'; see 'offer').

Sie müssen ihm Arbeit verschaffen (procure).

Es hat uns viel Vergnügen bereitet.

Die Firma hat ihm einen Sekretär zur Verfügung gestellt.

Ich kann es mir nur leisten, meinen Gästen ein einfaches Essen vorzusetzen.

Wir müssen gegen solche Vorkommnisse Vorkehrungen treffen.

PUBLIC   Öffentlichkeit means 'the community at large',[1] but is used much less than 'public' as a political concept to refer to a body of opinion which addresses demands to its rulers. For this meaning German has no distinct term.[2] **Publikum** is generally a specific part of the community; particularly an audience or concourse of people or a section of the community that follows some particular activity, e.g. one that is interested in art, literature, racing.

Ich spreche im Namen der Öffentlichkeit.

Der Minister muß sich vor der Öffentlichkeit rechtfertigen.

Die Polizei richtete einen Appell an die Öffentlichkeit.

Das Publikum zeigte sich sehr ungeduldig über den späten Beginn des Konzerts.

Er hatte ein dankbares Publikum.

PULL, DRAW, DRAG, TUG, TEAR   German has no term as general as 'pull', and so uses the equivalents of 'draw', 'drag', 'tug', 'tear', etc.

1. Ziehen is 'to draw', i.e. either when the effort required is not stressed or when control is implied.

Er zog das Hemd aus der Schublade, den Kork aus der Flasche.

Ich muß mir einen Zahn ziehen lassen.

Das Pferd zieht den Karren.

Die Lokomotive zieht den Zug.

Ziehen Sie den Stuhl weg.

Er zog die Glocke.

Ziehen Sie das Seil fester.

2. Schleppen is 'to drag', i.e. behind one and when a heavy object is implied.[3]

Die Fischer schleppten den Haifisch, das Boot, ans Ufer.

---

[1] It also means the 'publicness' of a thing (e.g. *die Öffentlichkeit der Verhandlungen*).

[2] *Volk* (see 'people') is sometimes used. *Öffentliche Meinung* is common.

[3] *Verschleppen* has as one of its meanings 'to drag a person or thing away to an unknown destination' so that he, she, or it is to be regarded as lost. *Die Verschleppten*: displaced persons, i.e. dragged off into slavery in war.

3. Zerren suggests a violent or convulsive pulling or tugging by the subject and resistance on the part of the object pulled or tugged.[1]

Er zerrte die Kiste an die Oberfläche des Wassers.

Sie zerrten den Baumstamm in die Scheune hinein.

Sie zerrten ihn aus dem Schlamm.

4. Zupfen is 'to pluck' at a thing, mostly a part of the body, as an expression or sign of an attitude or meaning, but not in order to detach one thing from another.

Er zupfte ihn bei den Haaren, am Ärmel.

5. Reißen implies not only force on the part of the subject and resistance on that of the object, but, in certain cases, unlike *zerren*, also a tearing or wrenching of one thing from another.[2]

Er riß sie an sich, an seine Brust.

Er riß die Pflanzen mit allen Wurzeln heraus.

Er riß die Tapete von der Wand.

PUNISH   1. Bestrafen is the ordinary term. It means to make the penalty fit the offence.

Ein faules Kind muß bestraft werden.

Zuwiderhandelnde werden bestraft.

Jeder Mißbrauch wird bestraft.

2. Strafen is also 'to punish for an offence', but it suggests punishment by God or by Nemesis. It is therefore mostly used in elevated and emotional diction.

'Gott strafe England' (said by the Germans in the 1914–18 war).

Gott straft den Sünder.

Die ganze Familie ist gestraft worden.

PUT (literal sense)   **1. Tun** is the most general term[3] and translates 'put' in many of its literal senses when a thing is the object. It differs from 'put' in the following ways: (*a*) it does not suggest firmness of position, and therefore cannot normally be substituted for *setzen*; (*b*) it does not carry any implication of effort or difficulty, and accordingly should not be used when these are emphasized (e.g. when attention is focused on the act of putting, carrying, as opposed to the result); (*c*) it is more off-hand than 'put'; (*d*) it cannot normally govern a person or a part of the body as object; (*e*) it is not freely combined with prefixes (mostly only with *weg, hinein, hinaus*); (*f*) it is rarely used figuratively[4] in the sense of 'put'; (*g*) it is used less for *stellen* and *legen*, though this use is possible, than 'put' for such specific terms as 'lay', 'set', 'stand'.[5]

---

[1] *Verzerren* is 'to distort' or 'to contort', particularly the face.

[2] In the sense of 'to tear a thing into two or more parts' *zerreißen* is generally used. Example: *ich habe meine Schuhriemen zerrißen.* It does not necessarily suggest tearing to shreds. *Reißen* is rather 'to tear' one thing from another. Example: *er riß mir die Zeitung aus der Hand.* See also 'break'.

[3] In Austria *geben* is used instead of *tun. Geben Sie die Papiere dorthin.*

[4] Examples are: *hinzutun* (see 'add'); *Geld auf die Bank tun.* The explanations given of the literal uses of *legen, stellen, setzen, stecken* do not always hold good for the figurative uses (e.g. *er legte mir die Worte in den Mund*; not *steckte*). Further, the figurative uses of 'put' are most frequently not rendered by these terms at all. For example: *Das ist milde ausgedrückt* (putting it mildly); *seine Gedanken zu Papier bringen.*

[5] Certain compounds of *machen* are used colloquially in the sense of 'put'. *Wir könnten das Bild in diesen Rahmen hereinmachen.*

Tun Sie die Papiere auf den Stuhl, in die Schublade.
Er tat den Anzug in den Kleiderschrank.
Wir haben eine ganze Menge Möbel in dieses Zimmer getan.
Tun Sie etwas Butter auf das Brot.
Ich habe zwei Briefmarken drauf getan.

2. Legen means *liegen machen*, to make lie, to lay flat. It suggests care, solicitude and the like.

Er legte das Buch auf den Tisch.
Sie legte die Decken auf das Bett.
Er legte die Hand aufs Herz.
Der Kranke wurde aufs Bett gelegt.

3. Stellen means *stehen machen*, i.e. to make stand, to place upright on the narrowest base, to stand (used transitively).

Er stellte die Flasche auf den Tisch.
Er stellte das Buch in den Bücherschrank.
Sie stellte den Kessel auf den Herd.
Sie stellte den Regenschirm in die Ecke.
Wir haben das Klavier in dieses Zimmer gestellt.

4. Setzen is *sitzen machen*, to make sit, to set, to sit (used transitively). It suggests that one thing is made to fit into, onto another, and sometimes that it 'sits' firmly or permanently in position. It must also be used when 'put' means 'to sit' (transitive) or when the putting of one edge to another is strongly suggested (e.g. *er setzte den Becher an den Mund, ihm das Messer an die Kehle*). Because of its reference to fixed position it is used for all matters pertaining to writing.

Er setzte den Fuß auf den Stuhl.
Sie setzte das Kind auf den Stuhl (sat).
Setzen Sie Ihren Freund hinten in den Wagen.
Er setzte das Gebiß in ihren Mund (ein).
Er setzte die Pflanzen in weiten Abständen voneinander.
Er hat sich den Hut aufgesetzt.
Setzen Sie Ihre Unterschrift hierher.
Setzen Sie das Wort hier herein.
Muß ich ein Komma setzen?

5. Stecken: (*a*) to put one thing into another which covers or encloses it;[1] (*b*) to put a thing on another thing so that it encircles it; (*c*) it has the meaning of 'stick' (though not in the sense of make adhere with gum and the like),[2] but unlike 'stick' it is not colloquial.

Er steckte die Hand in die Tasche, die Papiere in die Schublade, das Schwert in die Scheide, eine Zigarette in den Mund, den Brief in den Briefkasten.
Er steckte den Ring an den Finger.

6. Hängen should be used when the idea of hanging is emphasized. Otherwise *tun* is possible.

Hängen wir die Bilder an diese Wand.

---

[1] *Stecken bleiben* = to get stuck (see 'catch'); *stecken* in intransitive use and as a weak verb means 'to be' in the sense of 'not visible, hidden' (e.g. *wo stecken Sie denn so lange?*) or 'in the inner being, at the core' (e.g. *es steckt sehr viel in ihm*).
[2] 'To stick' in this sense is *kleben*.

QUALITY

QUALITY 1. **Qualität** means (*a*) degree of excellence, relative nature; (*b*) general excellence. It is generally used in a material, particularly a commercial sense, though it is sometimes applied—loosely—to spiritual qualities. It means 'attribute' (e.g. *Eigenschaft*) only as a philosophical term.

Dieser Stoff ist von erstklassiger, schlechter, Qualität.

Wir haben Anzüge in allen Qualitäten.

Bei der Herstellung unserer Waren sind wir immer auf Qualität bedacht (general excellence).

2. In the sense of 'attribute, characteristic, property', **Eigenschaft** must be used. It does not in itself denote excellence.

Der Sinn für Humor ist eine besondere Eigenschaft der Engländer.

Intoleranz ist eine Eigenschaft aller Diktatoren.

Er hat gute, schlechte, Eigenschaften.

3. Vorzug is an excellence, merit, of any kind, whether material or spiritual.

Seine Vorzüge sind bekannt.

Dieses System hat den Vorzug, daß es schnell funktioniert.

4. In the sense of 'faculty', 'gift', and the like, the German equivalents of these terms must be used.

Er hat das Vermögen, Ungläubige zu bekehren (*Vermögen* can suggest an act of will, see 'power').

Er hat die Gabe, Vertrauen zu erwecken (*Gabe* is a more unconscious quality than *Vermögen*).

QUITE, ENTIRELY 1. **Ganz** has as its primary meaning 'entire', 'whole',[1] and is less used than 'quite' in other senses. Accompanied by a negative it invariably means 'entirely' (e.g. *es ist nicht ganz klar, es ist ganz unmöglich*). This is also the meaning when in positive use it modifies a verb (e.g. *ich verstehe es ganz*) or a prepositional phrase (e.g. *es ist ganz in Ordnung*).[2]

Another use it has—in common with 'quite'—with certain adjectives and adverbs is to indicate that one concedes to a thing the quality attributed to it by the adjectives, but not in the highest degree, i.e. not entirely. It thus expresses a reservation (e.g. *er ist ganz nett, ich finde Ihre Arbeit ganz schön*).

Used adjectively with the indefinite article it means 'whole' in all senses of this term. It is frequently an equivalent of 'quite' (e.g. *eine ganze Meile*, a whole mile, quite a mile;[3] *eine ganze Menge*, a whole lot, quite a lot; *ein ganzes Ende*, quite a way). Generally, however, when 'quite' is accompanied by the indefinite article it must be otherwise translated (e.g. he is quite an expert, a celebrity).

It cannot be used apart from these meanings, e.g. as an affirmation that a thing is as it is stated to be (e.g. it is quite possible, that is quite sufficient). Further: quite soon, quite recently.[4]

Das Tuch deckt den Tisch ganz zu.

Ich verstehe nicht ganz, worauf Sie hinaus wollen.

Er hat sich ganz unvernünftig benommen.

Er blieb ganz still.

Er ist ganz bereit, Ihnen zu helfen.

[1] See 'all'.
[2] More emphatically *ganz und gar*. For *gänzlich* see 'complete'.
[3] Or: *eine gute Meile*.
[4] *Recht bald, erst neulich.*

Ich bin ganz Ihrer Meinung.
Ich habe es ganz vergessen.
Die Stadt ist ganz zerstört.
Es liegt ganz außerhalb meiner Sphäre.
Es ist heute ganz warm.
Ich habe es ganz gern.

2. Durchaus is accented either on the first or on the second syllable. When accented on the first the meaning is 'in every respect, through and through'; when accented on the second it is an affirmation that a thing is as it is stated to be. In the latter sense it corresponds to 'quite', e.g. before a verb, an adjective or adverb, before a superlative adjective.

Durchaus is not normally used (*a*) with adjectives or adverbs combined with the prefix *un* or the suffix *los* (but can be used with *nicht*) (e.g. *ganz unzweifelhaft, ganz würdelos*); (*b*) with adjectives denoting qualities in persons or things considered in themselves (e.g. he is quite clever, bold). It is possible, however, if these adjectives have an impersonal subject (e.g. *es ist durchaus klug, das zu tun; das ist durchaus irreführend, widersinnig*).

Es ist durchaus möglich.
Was Sie getan haben, genügt durchaus.
Das ist durchaus der beste Bericht über den Vorgang.
Ich habe durchaus Lust, dahin zu gehen.
Ich sehe durchaus ein, warum Sie darauf bestehen.
Ich bin durchaus Ihrer Meinung (or *ganz*).

3. When 'quite' is followed by the indefinite article and has the sense of 'real', it can generally be translated by **richtig** (more objective) or **recht** (with subjective emphasis).[1]

Das Stück war ein richtiger Erfolg.
Es hat richtiges Aufsehen erregt (quite a stir).
Er ist ein richtiger, rechter, Narr.
Es war ein richtiges, rechtes, Vergnügen.

RAISE, LIFT, HEIGHTEN   A. Literal sense.

1. Heben[2] is the general term. It means 'to lift a thing higher than before', not 'to add to its height'.

Er hob das Glas zum Mund.
Er hob den Deckel seines Koffers.
Er hob sein Gepäck vom Wagen.
Das Schiff wurde vom Meeresgrund gehoben.
Der Kran hob die schweren Maschinen aus dem Schiff.
Er hob die Hand, das Bein, den Kopf, die Augen.

2. Erheben is a more dignified term and often suggests emotional or symbolical gestures. Similarly *sich erheben* (to arise).

Er erhebt die Hände (e.g. in prayer or supplication).
Er erhebt das Glas (e.g. solemnly).
Er erhob den Blick gen Himmel.

3. Erhöhen is sometimes used in the sense of adding to an object in order to make it higher.

---

[1] A synonym is *ziemlich* (e.g. *ein ziemlicher Erfolg, ein ziemliches Aufsehen*).
[2] *Aufheben* and, more colloquially, *hoch heben* are used in the sense of 'lift' and 'lift up'.

Die Mauer ist etwas erhöht worden.
Das Gebäude ist um ein Stockwerk erhöht worden.

4. Aufziehen should be used in the sense of 'draw up'.
Der Vorhang, die Zugbrücke, wurde aufgezogen.

B. Figurative senses.

1. Heben: to improve. It cannot be followed by any prepositional phrase meaning 'to a level, standard'.
Die Gesundheit, den Geschmack, die Leistungsfähigkeit, das Niveau der allgemeinen Bildung, den Mut der Truppen heben.

2. Erheben.
(a) To elevate a person to a higher rank.
Er wurde in den Adelsstand erhoben.
Die Gesandtschaft wurde zur Botschaft erhoben.
(b) To start[1] vigorously,[2] particularly with reference to sound.
Ein Geschrei, die Stimme erheben.
(c) To make known, particularly a point of view.
Zweifel, Einwände, Ansprüche erheben.
(d) To collect money.
Steuern erheben.

3. Erhöhen.[3]
(a) To raise a thing to a higher level, standard (not to raise a person to a higher rank). As in the literal use, the sense is 'to add to, to increase', i.e. not simply 'to lift' from a lower to a higher position. It cannot be followed by any prepositional phrase meaning 'to a level, standard'.
Die Produktion, die Wohlfahrt des Landes, das schulpflichtige Alter, Preise, die erlaubte Geschwindigkeit, erhöhen.
(b) To heighten, to intensify a thing so that it is more readily apprehended or felt.
Die Wirkung, seine Freude, wurde erhöht.

4. Bringen: to raise to a certain level. It is followed by such phrases as *auf ein Niveau.*
Das Volk muß auf ein höheres Bildungsniveau gebracht werden.

RANGE, REACH, SCOPE As compared here, 'range' denotes the area that can be covered by or the limits that can be reached by the powers of a person or thing. From this implication of possibilities develops that of the limits within which a person or thing exists or operates. According to *W.S.* 'when the reference is to something stretched out or stretching itself out as an arm, or in the manner of an arm, so as to grasp, to attain, to embrace, or the like "reach" (sometimes in the plural reaches) is the preferred term: usually it denotes that which lies within the limits or at the uttermost boundary of a thing's powers, influence or capacity'. 'Scope' denotes 'room, or space for free uncircumscribed activity, growth, expression, or the like (*W.S.*)'. But it can also denote 'the extent between established or predetermined limits which encompass one on all sides and which for one reason or another cannot be overpassed (*W.S.*)'.

---

[1] Compare *anheben* (to start).
[2] Reflexively: *ein Sturm, ein Streit erhebt sich.*
[3] See also *steigern* under 'increase'.

1. **Reichweite** is the German term that comes closest to 'range' and 'reach' in the sense of the possibilities of a person or thing. (Similarly in the area of vision and hearing *Sehweite* and *Hörweite*).

Die Reichweite des Geistes, seiner Einbildungskraft.

2. **Bereich, Gebiet:** the area or field actually covered, corresponding to both 'range' and 'scope' as used in this sense.

Das ist eine technische Frage, die etwas außerhalb meines Bereiches (Gebiets) liegt.

Gehört Politik in den Bereich, das Gebiet der Gewerkschaften? (A.L.).

3. **Umfang** suggests the limits within which a thing operates. **Ausmaß** suggests that these limits are so wide as to be almost absent. For both words see under 'extent'.

Der Umfang ihrer Stimme ist erstaunlich.

Seine Belesenheit hat einen großen Umfang.

Die mühseligste Frage im ganzen Ausmaß der Politik.

Das Ausmaß seiner Forderungen ist unglaublich.

4. **Spielraum** corresponds to 'scope' in the first sense of that term defined above. **Lauf** has the same sense in the phrase *jdm, einer Sache freien Lauf lassen.* **Wirkungskreis:** a field for effective activity. Similarly **Betätigungsfeld**.

Das gibt mir wenig Spielraum, um mich durchzusetzen.

Er ließ seiner Phantasie, seinen Gefühlen freien Lauf.

Spielraum für seine Talente.

Er sucht einen Wirkungskreis, ein Betätigungsfeld für seine Energien.

5. **Auswahl** (see under choice), **Vielfalt** (diversity) render 'range' when the meaning of this comes to be a multiplicity contained within an area or within certain limits.

Dieses Geschäft bietet eine große Auswahl von Schuhen.

Die Vielfalt der Erzeugnisse war geradezu verblüffend.

Die Engländer leiten ihren Stammbaum von einer großen Auswahl, Vielfalt von Völkern ab (S.O.D.).

RATE   The basic meaning of this term is an amount or degree of something measured in proportion to something else (*A.L.*), clearest in the common phrase 'at the rate of'. When extended to mean charge or tax it still retains something of this meaning. German has no such term and often uses terms corresponding to English terms which would be used in specific contexts to explain 'rate', or sometimes omits it. German **Rate** means 'instalment', but is now being used more and more in the English sense (e.g. *Wachstumsrate*).

1. The basic sense.

Der Zug fuhr mit einer Geschwindigkeit von 100 Kilometer in der Stunde.

Sie spült die Tassen in einem Tempo von 10 Stück in einer Minute.

Sie können sie zu einem Preis von 10 DM. pro Tausend haben.

Die Sterblichkeitsziffer war in diesen Wochen 30 pro Tausend.

Die Geburtenziffer nimmt in Indien ständig zu.

Das Tempo des Fortschritts im neunzehnten Jahrhundert.

2. A fixed relation (as of quantity, amount or degree) (*W.*). **Der Kurs** (or more fully: *der Wechselkurs*): rate of exchange of one currency for another.

Wie hoch ist der Kurs der DM. im Verhältnis zum Dollar?

3. A charge, payment, or price fixed according to a ratio, scale, or standards (*W.*).

> *Hotel-Preise.*
> *Der übliche Betrag, den der Verleger für Kurzgeschichten zahlt* (the p's usual rate for...) (*W.*).
> *Tuchstoffe, die zu einem Preis von einem Dollar per Meter gekauft wurden* (*W.*).
> *Zu Schleuderpreisen* (at cut-rates) (*W.*).
> *Was ist der Preis für das Porto, (wieviel kosten) Drucksachen per Luftpost?*
> *Eine Stromgebühr von 7 cents per Kilowatt-Stunde* (*W.*).

4. In English countries a sum of money which must be paid to local authorities for local purposes (*A.L.*), i.e. a tax in this case on property owned: German **Abgabe** (to the municipality for specific purposes), **Steuer**. The first of these terms is the more general (see Duden).

> *Eine Abgabe von zwei Mark für den Bau eines Sportplatzes.*
> *Gemeindesteuer, Armensteuer, Vergnügungssteuer, Steuerzahler.*

5. Sense: class. German **Klasse** and compounds with *klassig*, **Rang**.

> *Die Leistung war nur zweitklassig.*

RATIONAL, IRRATIONAL **1.** 'Rational' in the sense of possessing, endowed with, reason and of exhibiting reason.

(a) **Rational** exists but is less used than the English term. It has a philosophical flavour. Applied directly to mankind **vernunftbegabt** is more usual.

> *Der Mensch ist ein vernunftbegabtes (rationales) Wesen, ein Vernunftwesen.*
> *Wir sind rationale (mit Vernunft begabte), aber gleichzeitig auch materielle (körperliche) Lebewesen (S.O.D.).*
> *Er denkt immer streng rational.*
> *Eine rationale Erklärung des Universums.*
> *Er benimmt sich nicht immer rational.*

(b) *W.S.*, comparing our term with 'reasonable', says 'when the term is applied to policies, projects, systems, or to anything already conceived or formulated, rational is preferred when justification on grounds that are satisfactory to the reason is specifically implied'. The German term in this sense is: **rationell**, which is applied particularly to rational planning in a practical sphere.

> *Rationelle Planung.*
> *Rationelle Bewirtschaftung* (a control of the economy or part of it).
> *Die Vorteile einer rationellen Rechtschreibung.*
> *Eine rationelle Welthandelspolitik.*

(c) When English 'rational' used in every-day contexts means nothing more than 'sensible' German uses **vernünftig** (see under 'mind', particularly footnote to *Verstand*).

> *Männer tragen im Sommer nicht immer vernünftige Kleidung.*

2. Care should be exercised in using German **irrational** as an equivalent of the English term. The German term since the literary movement '*Sturm und Drang*' in the eighteenth century has repeatedly been used in a positive way and identified with the life force, with feeling and intuition, which have been seen as the spring of great deeds and works. The English term knows nothing of this glorification. Most often *Vernunft* or *Sinn* or some derivatives of them will be the German equivalent.

Die Tiere, die auf einer niederen Entwicklungsstufe stehen, werden allgemein als vernunftlos bezeichnet (W.).

Er war nicht bei Vernunft (was irrational) (or: *nicht normal*) *während einiger Tage nach dem Unfall (W.).*

Er hat sich unvernünftig benommen.

Er hat eine sinnlose Angst vor dem Verkehr in Großstädten.

Er hat gegen alle Vernunft gehandelt.

Das sind unvernünftige Ideen.

Sein reizbarer Trieb zu energischer praktischer Tätigkeit und das Gegenteil davon, die Passivität und die Absonderung, die die Kurzsichtigkeit mit sich brachte, erschienen ihm schlechthin unsinnig (W.S.).

REAL, TRUE, GENUINE 1. **Wirklich** means 'existing in actuality and effect' as opposed to something which exists in name or mere possibility. It lacks the other sense of 'real' defined by *P.O.D.* as: genuine, rightly so called, natural, sincere.

Das ist ein wirkliches Ereignis (not imaginary).

Ein wirklicher Professor, eine wirkliche Kultur.

2. **Real** has the same meaning as *wirklich*, **Reel** means 'material', *reelle Werke; das ist ein ganz reelles Geschäft.*

3. **Wahr** means 'corresponding to the prototype' and 'conforming with the real idea of the thing as it should be', opposed to the false and apparent. It can thus translate 'real' and 'genuine' as well as 'true'. For the rendering of the adverb 'truly' see *wahrhaft*.

Ein wahrer Professor, eine wahre Kultur.

4. **Echt** is 'genuine' only in the sense of 'unadulterated', 'not spurious'.[1] Thus while both *wahr* and *echt* can mean 'genuine', *echt* goes further than *wahr* in suggesting the idea of greater or more typical perfection.

Ein echter Professor, eine echte Kultur.

5. **Wahrhaft**, used adjectively, normally means 'truth-loving', 'sincere'. Its use in the sense of 'conforming to the real idea of a thing', 'not a sham', is rare. It must be used to translate all senses of 'truly'.[2]

Ein wahrhafter Mensch.

Er ist ein wahrhaft großer Mann.

REALLY 1. **Wirklich**: in reality, as opposed to illusion, a fiction of the mind. It is often used to persuade the listener that one's statement is a fact.

Er steht wirklich da.

Er ist wirklich krank.

Er wohnt wirklich in Berlin.

2. **Eigentlich**: in reality, at bottom, though this may not be apparent because of external or superficial departures from the fundamental reality. The departure is often expressed in a following *aber* clause.

---

[1] See also *ernstlich* under 'serious'.

[2] *Wahrhaftig* expresses in present-day German an affirmation of a statement, and sometimes corresponds to 'veritable'. *Wahrlich*, mostly an adverb, is used only in exalted style and often corresponds to 'verily'.

Er wohnt eigentlich in München, verbringt aber viel Zeit in Nürnberg.
Er ist eigentlich ganz zuverlässig, wenn er auch diesmal sein Versprechen
nicht erfüllte.

RECEIVE (See also 'get'.) **1. Erhalten** suggests, like *bekommen*, that the receiver is passive, but unlike the latter is used almost exclusively in writing. Apart from its use with persons, the subject may be a thing, the object some treatment it receives.

Einen Brief, ein Geschenk, eine Antwort, einen Befehl, eine Strafe, eine gute
Schulbildung erhalten.
Er hat einen Schlag, einen Hieb, einen Stich erhalten.
Die Maschinen haben eine gründliche Ausbesserung erhalten.

2. Empfangen draws attention to the act of receiving. This is mostly ceremonious (the conferring of distinctions, the welcoming of guests). If the implication of ceremony is absent, either the manner of reception must be stated or the context must suggest activity on the part of the receiver.

Aus den Händen des Kaisers empfing er das eiserne Kreuz.
Er hat einen hohen Orden empfangen.
Er hat ein Diplom empfangen.
Er empfing den Preis.
Er hat die Sterbesakramente, das Abendmahl empfangen.
Die Hausfrau empfing die Gäste.
Er hat den Befehl voll Mißtrauen empfangen.
Er hat einen Schlag, einen Hieb, empfangen.

3. In Empfang nehmen: to take delivery of goods. A formal term.
Wollen Sie die Kiste in Empfang nehmen?

4. Aufnehmen.

(a) To accept,[1] admit into an organization, a society, as a member.
Er wurde in unseren Verein aufgenommen.
(b) To receive with a mental attitude.
Das Stück wurde mit Begeisterung aufgenommen.

5. Finden: to meet with some specified kind of treatment or attitude of mind.
Der Plan fand seine Billigung, keine Beachtung.

RECENTLY **1.** Both **kürzlich** and **neulich** refer to a point of time in the past, the former being more precise.[2] *Neulich* translates 'the other day'.[3] It looks at the action from the point of view of the present moment of speaking or writing. *Kürzlich* must also be used in cases of historical narrative, i.e. in the meaning of a short time before the present denoted by the past narrative, e.g. with the pluperfect tense.

Er hat kürzlich promoviert.
Ich war neulich im Theater.
Er wurde kürzlich abgesetzt.

2. In letzter Zeit is used in cases where the action continues up to the present.[4]
Ich bin in letzter Zeit sehr beschäftigt gewesen.

---

[1] See 'accept'.
[3] *Den anderen Tag:* the next day.
[2] *Jüngst*, 'recently', is somewhat old-fashioned.
[4] Until recently: *bis vor kurzem.*

RECOGNIZE, ACKNOWLEDGE 1. Recognize: to know again with the senses, either through having seen, heard, etc. the person or object before, or through distinguishing features, of which one is aware, but without such previous experience.

Erkennen translates this sense. If it is desired to make clear that the recognition is due to one's having seen, heard, the person or object before and not merely to a knowledge of distinguishing features, *wieder* is normally added.

Ich habe ihn an seinem Mantel erkannt.
Ich habe ihn gleich wiedererkannt.
Ich erkenne Sie nicht wieder.

2. *Erkennen* also 'means to come to a mental understanding, realization', with regard both to trivial matters and to the pursuit of scientific truth.[1,2]

Ich habe meinen Irrtum erkannt.
Ich habe allmählich erkannt, daß ich mich gründlich in Ihnen getäuscht habe.
Er hat den Ernst der Lage erkannt.
Er hat diese Wahrheit noch nicht erkannt.

3. Anerkennen translates both 'recognize' in the sense of 'to acknowledge by special notice, approval or sanction; to treat as valid, as having existence or entitled to consideration; to take notice of (a thing or person) in some way' (*S.O.D.*); and 'acknowledge'[3] in the sense of 'to recognize or confess' (a person or thing, to be something); or, simply, 'to own the claims of' (*S.O.D.*).

When these terms come into comparison, 'recognize' denotes a more formal according of standing, validity, and the like, and its translation into practice, while 'acknowledge' may imply nothing more than a mental attitude of acceptance. *Erkennen* translates both, except in sentences where English uses both in deliberate contrast (e.g. 'The ladies never acted so well as when they were in the presence of a fact which they acknowledged but did not recognize', Meredith, quoted in Webster's *Dictionary of Synonyms*). In such cases 'acknowledge' must be rendered by *gelten lassen* (see 'accept') and the like.

Man muß seine hohe Begabung anerkennen.
Der Anschluß Oesterreichs an Deutschland wurde zur Zeit von den meisten
  Regierungen anerkannt.
Goethe wird allgemein als der größte deutsche Dichter anerkannt.
Seine Ansprüche wurden anerkannt.
Der Papst ist das anerkannte Haupt der römisch-katholischen Kirche.

RECORD (v. and s.) *W.S.* says of the s.: 'Record implies the intent to preserve as evidence of something: it therefore names something (either an item, or in a collective sense, all the items) written down so that exact knowledge of what has occurred will be perpetuated; as, 'to keep a record of a conversation'. The same applies to the corresponding uses of the verb, but the term has developed in some of its uses in a way which does not necessarily imply writing.

---

[1] Since *erkennen* means 'to come to know', it must be used to translate 'know' in this sense, e.g. in the imperative. *Erkenne dich selbst* (see 'knowledge').

[2] See also *erkennen* under 'see'.

[3] 'Acknowledge' in the sense of 'signify the receipt of' a thing is *bestätigen* (e.g. *den Empfang eines Briefes bestätigen*). In the sense of 'admit': *eingestehen*, etc.

RECORD

A. Verb. See also 'write down'.

1. To set down in writing, make a written account or note of (*W.*).

(a) **Aufzeichnen** suggests (i) making a written note of something.

In diesem Tagebuch finden Sie fast jede Einzelheit seiner Pariser Jahre aufgezeichnet.

Er zeichnete die Laute, die gehört wurden, in phonetischen Symbolen auf.

(ii) It can also mean to cause to be noted officially in or as if in writing (*W.*), in which sense it is equivalent to **registrieren**.

Die Wahlstimmen aufzeichnen und zusammenzählen (record and tally) (*W.*).

2. **Eintragen:** to enter as an item in a register, or the like.

Er trug alle Posten genau ein.

Bitte tragen Sie sich, Ihren Namen, hier ein.

3. **Verzeichnen:** to record an item in a list, a catalogue. But see also below for a different use.

Jeder Telephonanruf ist in diesem Buch verzeichnet.

Die eingesandten Bücher sind alle hier verzeichnet.

4. **Vermerken** is to put an official note on a document, something in the nature of 'stamp'. See also **Vermerk** under 'note'.

Am Rande des Schreibens war das Datum des Eingangs vermerkt.

5. To take minutes: **zu Protokoll nehmen**, particularly of proceedings as at a meeting or in a court of law.

Er nahm die Gerichtsverhandlungen zu Protokoll (*W.*).

Note also: *zu Protokoll geben*, to give, say, for recording as minutes.

6. To make an objective lasting indication of, in some mechanical or automatic way: register permanently by mechanical means (*W.*): **registrieren, verzeichnen**.

Er studierte die Stärke des Erdbebens, wie es von dem Erdbebenanzeiger registriert, verzeichnet worden war (*W.*).

Es fiel mir auf, daß in diesem Augenblick das Thermometer 90 Grad registrierte, verzeichnete (*W.*).

7. To make or have made an authentic official copy (as a deed, mortgage, lease) and deposit or have deposited especially as in an office designated by law (*W.*): **registrieren, beurkunden**.

Auf dem Standesamt sind alle Geburten, Ehen und Todesfälle registriert, beurkundet.

8. To cause sound to be transferred to and registered on something (as a phonograph, disc, magnetic tape) by mechanical, usually electronic means in such a way that the sound be subsequently reproduced: **auf Platten, ein Tonband aufnehmen**.

Die Salzburger Aufführung des Don Giovanni wurde auf Platten aufgenommen.

Eine Stimme, die auf Platten gut klingt (records well) (*W.*).

9. Visually: *aufnehmen, festhalten*.

Der Dokumentarfilm hat den Vorfall für die Ewigkeit festgehalten.

B. Substantive.

1. A piece of writing that recounts or attests to something; an official contemporaneous document recording the acts of some public officer (*W.*): **Dokument, Urkunde, Akte**, i.e. a document. *Urkunde* is generally something relating to the past. *Akte* is drawn up by an official (files).

Die Urkunden (Dokumente, die aus der Zeit Karls des Großen erhalten geblieben sind.

Bringen Sie mir die Akten (file).

Die Steuerakten (file).

Urkunden, Dokumente über die Frühgeschichte der Vereinigten Staaten.

2. An official contemporaneous memorandum stating the proceedings of a court of justice (*W*.): (**Gerichts)Akte, Protokoll.**

3. Something non-written but which serves as evidence: *Denkmal*, i.e. monument.

Die großen Kathedralen sind das beredtste Denkmal des inneren Lebens des Mittelalters.

4. From the sense of preserving the memory of something the sense of something worth preserving easily develops. Therefore an outstanding performance that has not been bettered: **Rekord** (the only use of this term in German), **Spitzenleistung, Höchstleistung.**

Zehn Sekunden dürften eine Spitzenleistung (Höchstleistung) für den Hundert-Meter-Lauf sein.

Er hat im Hochsprung seinen eigenen Rekord gebrochen.

Einen Produktionsrekord aufstellen.

Eine Rekordernte.

5. Performance, accomplishments, condition in a particular area over a period of time; cumulative data that indicate the quality of this. **Leistung, Zeugnis, Attest** (both the latter have the meaning of certificate issued to attest something; for the former see under 'performance'.

Seine Leistung im letzten Schuljahr war sehr befriedigend; läßt viel zu wünschen übrig.

Auf Grund seiner Leistungen in diesen zwei Jahren wurde er befördert.

Ein Kind, dem man ein gutes Schulzeugnis ausstellen kann (with a good school record) (*W*.).

Seine Gesundheitsatteste (-zeugnisse) lassen ihn als ungeeignet für solche Arbeit erscheinen.

6. A body of known, recorded, or available facts about someone or something, often in an unfavourable sense: no one term in German.

Er hat glänzende Leistungen als Leiter des Betriebs.

Ich möchte mehr über das Vorleben des Kandidaten erfahren.

Ein Mann mit einer solchen Vergangenheit dürfte ein so hohes Amt nicht bekleiden.

Er ist vielfach vorbestraft (has a long criminal record); (*vorbestraft sein*: have a police record).

REDUCE, LESSEN[1] 'Reduce' suggests much more strongly than 'lessen' the deliberate intervention of a personal agent.[2]

---

[1] See also *kürzen* (under 'shorten') and *einschränken* (under 'limit') which frequently translate 'to reduce' in the sense of a deliberate act on the part of a person. *Die Löhne, die Forderungen, sind gekürzt worden. Die Hausarbeiten wurden stark eingeschränkt.*

[2] Further synonyms are: 'diminish', which strongly suggests 'loss' and therefore corresponds more closely to *verringern* than to the other terms; 'lower', i.e. to a certain level; 'decrease', by a gradual process.

REDUCE

1. Vermindern and **verringern** (i.e. *geringer machen*[1]) are sometimes used interchangeably, but in discriminating use the following distinctions are observed. *Vermindern* is more serious, more accurate, and denotes a more drastic reduction than *verringern*, which means 'to take a little less of a substance', 'to relax', 'to lessen gradually'. Further, *vermindern* suggests more clearly a deliberate act, a decision. *Verringern* is therefore more common than *vermindern* when the subject is a thing (e.g. *das Auto verringerte seine Geschwindigkeit*; but, *der Fahrer verminderte die Geschwindigkeit des Autos*). Both verbs are used reflexively, but this use is more common with *verringern*, unless a drastic reduction is implied, since it does not strongly suggest deliberate intervention.

'Undiminished' as an adjective, is, however, *unvermindert* (*mit unverminderter Energie*); *un* cannot be combined with *verringert*.

It will be seen that these distinctions are only tendencies, which sometimes cut across each other.

Neither verb can be followed by a preposition to translate 'to reduce to', but *um*, meaning 'by' may follow.

Die Zahl der Unterrichtsstunden wurde vermindert, verringert.
Die Medizin hat die Schmerzen vermindert, verringert.
Wir haben die Zahl unserer Angestellten verringert.
Wir müssen unsere Ausgaben vermindern.
Wir müssen die Unkosten verringern.
Durch die Abwesenheit der Kinder haben sich unsere Ausgaben verringert.
Vermindern Sie die Zahl der Zigaretten, die Sie täglich rauchen.
Unsere Vorräte verringerten sich zusehends (not *verminderten*, because a gradual reduction is implied).
Durch die vielen verlorenen Schlachten verminderten sich die deutschen Reserven (not *verringerten*).
Sein Gewicht verringerte sich (not *verminderte*) (More commonly: *er verlor an Gewicht, er nahm ab.*)
Ich habe die Menge des Phosphats, das ich für den Garten gebrauche, verringert.
Verringere die Medizinmenge um zwei Tropfen pro Stunde.

2. Mindern is applied particularly to the weakening of a feeling or sentiment. It can also be used for *vermindern* in elevated prose and in poetry, which generally prefers the forms without the prefix, since they are more direct and vivid. Otherwise *mindern* is little used.

Das mindert nicht die Hochachtung, die ich vor ihm habe.
Das mindert meine Vaterlandsliebe nicht.

3. Verkleinern[2] (i.e. *klein machen*), is primarily applied to the reduction of size, but also to numbers where these imply size. It cannot be followed by a preposition to translate 'reduce to'.

Das Lehrpersonal wurde verkleinert.
Die Zahl der Banken hat sich verkleinert.
Der Ertrag des Grundstücks hat sich verkleinert.

4. Herabsetzen (i.e. to put down) generally implies the intervention of a

---

[1] *Gering* means 'slight, of little importance, negligible, trifling' (compare *geringfügig*), *klein* means 'small' without specific implications. *Das Bild hat nur einen geringen Wert* (in a bad sense). *Die Arbeit stellte nur geringe Anforderungen an ihn* (in a neutral sense).
[2] *Verkleinern* also means 'to disparage, belittle'.

personal agent. It is not used of size or intensity. It may be followed by *auf* to translate 'reduce to'.

Die Regierung hat die Steuern, die Löhne, herabgesetzt.
Er hat seine Forderungen herabgesetzt.
Wir müssen die Zahl der Sitzungen auf die Hälfte herabsetzen.
Die Preise[1] der Autos sind noch nicht herabgesetzt worden.

5. Herunterbringen means 'to get down', generally by an effort, but also more generally 'to bring down'.

Sie müssen versuchen, Ihre Temperatur, Ihren Blutdruck, herunterzubringen (or: *kriegen*).
Diese Politik hat den Lebensstandard heruntergebracht.

REFER **1. Sich beziehen** is used of words, statements, thoughts in the sense of 'to be related, directed to'. With a personal subject it can only mean to 'link up' something previously said or written with a present statement, e.g. in support of it; i.e. it cannot be generally used in the sense of 'allude to'.[2]

Seine Bemerkung bezog sich auf den schon erwähnten Plan, auf Sie.
Ich beziehe mich auf meinen Brief vom 5. Mai.
Zum Beweis bezog er sich auf zwei Dokumente, auf die schon zitierte Stelle.

2. In the general sense of 'allude to', **sprechen von** or some synonym such as *anspielen auf* must be used.

Ich spreche nicht von Ihnen.
Er spricht dauernd von seinen Kriegserlebnissen.

3. Verweisen means (*a*) to direct a person to someone as an authority; (*b*) to direct someone's attention to a thing. In the first case 'to' is translated by *an*, in the second by *auf*. See also under 'say'.

Ich verwies ihn an meinen Vorgesetzten.
Ich verwies ihn auf einige wichtige Stellen in der Rede.

4. Used intransitively in the sense of 'consult', 'refer' must be translated by equivalents of the latter.

Sie müssen das Lexikon zu Rate ziehen, zu Hilfe nehmen.

5. Weitergeben, übergeben, weiterleiten have the meaning of 'to pass on', 'to hand over', a matter to an authority.

Wir können die Angelegenheit nur an den Minister weitergeben (weiterleiten).

REFUSE, DECLINE **1. Sich weigern** is generally only followed by an infinitive and means 'to refuse'. *Weigern* is occasionally used transitively in the sense of *verweigern*, but unlike the latter stresses the force of the action, not the result.

Er weigerte sich, dem Befehl zu gehorchen.
Er weigerte ihm den Gehorsam.

---

[1] *Ermäßigen* means 'to reduce' prices, as a concession. *Dieses Theater hat auch Eintrittskarten zu ermäßigten Preisen.*
[2] *Beziehen* is also used non-reflexively in the sense of 'to relate one thing to another' or 'to make one statement apply to a further case'. '*Was ich in Nürnberg naturgemäß nur vom ersten Band sagen konnte, möchte ich hiermit auch auf den zweiten beziehen...*' (Gisevius, *Bis Zum Bitteren Ende*).

2. Verweigern means 'to refuse' only in the sense of 'withhold, not to grant'. It is commonly used of the withholding of what is rightly or lawfully demanded (e.g. *den Gehorsam, den Eid*). It is not normally followed by the infinitive. Used reflexively, it can have a sexual implication.

Er verweigerte den Dienst, ihnen seine Hilfe.

3. Abschlagen and **ausschlagen** translate 'refuse' only in the sense of 'to reject' a thing. Both are stronger terms than 'refuse' and suggest a flat, brusque refusal. *Abschlagen* is used more of a request, *ausschlagen* of an offer.[1] Neither term admits a person as direct object.

Er schlug mir meine Bitte, mein Gesuch, ab.
Sein Angebot wurde ausgeschlagen.

4. Ablehnen means 'to decline' and is therefore a less harsh expression than those treated under **1, 2, 3**. It should therefore be used to translate 'refuse' when this conveys no implication of brusqueness. It can refer to a request or to an offer, and can be followed by the infinitive.

Er lehnte die Bitte, das Angebot, die Einladung, ab.
Der Vorschlag wurde abgelehnt.
Er wurde als Lehrer abgelehnt.
Ich lehne es ab, die Verantwortung dafür zu übernehmen.

5. Abweisen: to reject firmly and definitely[2] a thing or a person who makes a request. With a thing as subject it frequently implies its rejection by an authority as inadmissible.

Sein Gesuch, seine Ansprüche, wurden abgewiesen.
Ich wurde abgewiesen.

6. When a thing is the subject of 'refuse', **wollen** (or some other term such as *sich sträuben*) may be used negatively. *Sich weigern* is here impossible.

Mein Haar will durchaus nicht flach liegen.
Die Tür will nicht offen bleiben.

RELATION(SHIP), CONNECTION, RATIO, PROPORTION 1. (a) **Verhältnis**[3] means primarily 'ratio' and 'proportion'. Applied to a 'relation' between things, it can only mean that they stand in a certain ratio to each other, i.e. that the relation is fixed in this way. It is not used in a general way to indicate a vague connection. It is the regular philosophical term (*das Leib-Seele-Verhältnis*). **Beziehung** is a relationship in which one thing influences the other, or where there is an interaction, therefore often in reference to two events. Further, in the phrase: *in dieser Beziehung*, i.e. in this connection, respect. The plural *Verhältnisse* is not used in this sense of the singular.[4]

Das Verhältnis zwischen Ursache und Wirkung.
Im Verhältnis zum Gewinn waren die Kosten zu hoch.
Die Sensationsnachrichten, die die Zeitungen bringen, stehen häufig in gar keinem Verhältnis zu der Wichtigkeit der Ereignisse.
Das Steigen des Yen stand in direkter Beziehung (not *Verhältnis*) *zur amerikanischen Präsidentenwahl im Jahre 1936.*

(b) In the sense of relations between people *Verhältnis* is much deeper and

---

[1] For *versagen* used synonymously, see 'deny'.
[2] *Einen kurz abweisen* = to send one about one's business.
[3] See also 'behave', 'attitude'.
[4] See 'state', 'condition'.

more intimate than *Beziehung*. Thus *ein freundschaftliches Verhältnis* means much more than *freundschaftliche Beziehungen*. *Beziehungen*, mostly plural in this sense, draws attention to externals, such as what people do, *Verhältnis* to the inner attitude. Though generally singular, the latter may be plural in this sense.[1] In reference to countries, however, *Beziehung* is stronger, since it denotes concrete realities, whereas *Verhältnis* is formal.

> *Es besteht ein freundschaftliches Verhältnis zwischen England und Frankreich.*
> *Es bestehen freundschaftliche Beziehungen zwischen England und Frankreich.*
> *Das Verhältnis zwischen ihnen war gespannt.*
> *Ich habe alle Beziehungen zu ihm abgebrochen.*
> *Er hat viele Beziehungen zur diplomatischen Welt.*

2. Zusammenhang indicates in a general way a close relationship between things or ideas, but not personal relations. In reference to ideas the relation is logical and necessary.[2]

> *Der Zusammenhang zwischen Ursache und Wirkung.*
> *Was damals geschah, steht in keinem Zusammenhang mit der gegenwärtigen Lage.*
> *Der dramatische Dichter muß bestrebt sein, den Zusammenhang zwischen den verschiedenen Vorgängen seines Werkes klar zu machen.*
> *Ihre Antwort steht in gar keinem Zusammenhang mit der gestellten Frage.*

3. Verbindung is a loose connection either between thoughts, things or persons.[3] In reference to thoughts it means no more than 'association', and applied to persons it denotes no more than the existence of channels of communication.

> *Die Verbindung zwischen diesen beiden Gedanken ist phantastisch.*
> *Er hat während des Krieges seine Verbindungen mit dem Feind aufrecht-erhalten.*

RELEVANT, IRRELEVANT   Sense: bearing upon or properly applying to the matter at hand: affording evidence tending to prove or disprove the matters at issue or under discussion: pertinent (*W.*).

German **relevant** exists, but as a learned word, and is not widely used. With the exception of **einschlägig**, which is applied to a word, a phrase, a passage of writing, a document, the terms used tend to mean significant in themselves.

> *Er begann an dem Problem zu arbeiten, indem er die einschlägige Literatur las.*
> *Der menschliche Begriff von einem Zoll Länge und einer Sekunde in der Zeitmessung...haben nur Bezug auf das menschliche Leben* (have reference to).
> *Eine Einzelheit, die für das Ganze belangvoll* (of importance) *ist.*
> *Sich an die wesentlichen Tatsachen halten* (essential).
> *Maßgebliche Einzelheiten* (authoritative).
> *Alle zweckdienlichen Angaben* (serving the matter in hand).
> *Rechtserhebliche Zeugenaussage* (a legal term).

---

[1] *Verhältnis* also means 'liaison'. Vulgarly: *sie ist sein Verhältnis*.

[2] *Im Zusammenhang*: in the context. Similarly: (*einen Gedanken*) *aus dem Zusammenhang reißen*. The plural is used idiomatically, and without an English equivalent. *Die großen Zusammenhänge erklären*, i.e. not details. *Das Buch läßt hinter die Kulissen schauen und deckt unbekannte Zusammenhänge auf.*

[3] See 'join'.

Similarly for 'irrelevant': **belanglos, unwesentlich, nicht zur Sache gehörig (gehören)**.

Das sind belanglose Bemerkungen, Einzelheiten.

Seine Angaben sind unwesentlich, gehören nicht zur Sache.

REPEAT   Wiederholen means 'to do or to say a thing again'. It cannot be used in the following senses: (*a*) to pass on information, which is **weitersagen**; (*b*) to say a thing over and over to oneself in order to memorize it, which is **aufsagen**; (*c*) to repeat after someone in order to learn, which is **nachsagen**.

Er wiederholte, daß er den Vorschlag ablehnen müsse.

Er wiederholte seine Frage.

Sie dürfen das Experiment nicht wiederholen.

Sagen Sie es nicht weiter.

Er sagte sich stundenlang die unregelmäßigen Verben auf.

Sagen Sie es mir nach.

RESPONSIBILITY   1. Verantwortung is the state of being responsible. The reference to the person who bears it is stressed. **Verantwortlichkeit**, a rarer term, draws attention to the nature of the objective obligation, the charge itself. Both *Verantwortung* and *Verantwortlichkeit* can mean 'sense of responsibility'.

Sie müssen die Verantwortung dafür übernehmen.

Er lehnt die Verantwortung dafür ab.

'*Auf Ihnen ruht eine große Verantwortlichkeit, und ich würde Sie um keine Gefälligkeit bitten, die Sie mit Ihrer Pflicht in Konflikt brächte*' (R. Huch, *Weiße Nächte*). (*Verantwortung* also possible, if it is thought of in close association with the person, and not as detached from him).

Das Prinzip der Verantwortlichkeit.

Ärzte müssen sich der Verantwortlichkeit bewußt sein, die ihr Beruf in sich schließt.

Das Wichtige ist, daß man dem Schüler die Verantwortung überträgt, um ihn zur Verantwortlichkeit zu erziehen (sense of responsibility).

2. The plural 'responsibilities' can only be translated by **Verpflichtungen**, i.e. obligations.

Er versucht dauernd, sich seinen Verpflichtungen zu entziehen.

REST (noun)   **1.** Followed by 'of' (which may be implied).

Rest is used in the same way as English 'rest',[1] and must be distinguished from **übrig**. The distinction is not concerned with size, except that with countries *Rest* mostly refers to the smaller, *übrig* to the larger area. In general, *übrig* suggests that which lacks or loses value[2] in our eyes, either absolutely or with regard to a specific matter.

---

[1] *Rest* can, unlike its English equivalent, be (*a*) preceded by the indefinite article, (*b*) pluralized. In these cases it means 'remainder' (also in a mathematical sense), 'bit', 'scrap' (e.g. *es bleibt nur ein kleiner Rest übrig; die Diener bekamen den Rest der Mahlzeit*). The plural *Rester* is often used (particularly in Saxony) for 'remnants', in a draper's shop, etc. *Überrest* (often pluralized) is a smaller and more insignificant part, often corresponding to 'remains' (e.g. *die Überreste der Mahlzeit frassen die Hunde*). *Überbleibsel* is what is worthless, unusable.

[2] Similarly: *was übrig bleibt* (e.g. *was...interessiert mich nicht*).

Übrig presents special difficulty when it qualifies a singular noun. It is only used with such nouns as can be conceived in terms of units, as consisting of items (e.g. a concert, which has numbers).

Essen Sie den Rest des Fleisches auf!

Wir behalten zehn Mark von Ihrem Gehalt, den Rest können Sie gleich haben.

Ich nehme ein Zimmer, der Rest des Hauses gehört Ihnen.[1]

Er ist in einem Fach durchgefallen, aber den Rest der Prüfung hat er gut bestanden.

Beethoven wurde entsetzlich gespielt, der Rest des Konzerts war prachtvoll.

Wir verbrachten den Rest des Abends zu Hause.

Westlich der Oder hat Deutschland keine Gebietsverluste erlitten, der Rest ist an Polen und Rußland gefallen.

Wenn die Ostgebiete endgültig verloren sind, wird das übrige Deutschland sich kaum ernähren können.

Beethoven wurde prachtvoll gespielt, das übrige Konzert war entsetzlich.

Zwei Gäste blieben im Wohnzimmer, die übrige Gesellschaft ging in den Garten (or, of course: *der Rest der Gesellschaft*).

Das übrige Programm bot nichts Besonderes.

Die übrige Saison war ein Fiasko.

Dezember war erträglich, aber der übrige Winter war schauderhaft.

Einige Bilder waren gut, aber die übrige Ausstellung war unter aller Kritik.

Er verbrachte die übrige Zeit im Gefängnis.

'*Den übrigen Abend zersplitterte ich wider Willen da und dort in Gesellschaft*' (Mörike, *Lucie Gelmeroth*).

2. Referring to a plural noun previously mentioned: **die anderen, die übrigen** (i.e. the remaining ones). For an explanation of *übrig* see the preceding section.

Um die anderen brauchen wir uns nicht zu kümmern, sie wissen sich im Notfall schon zu helfen.

Diese Möbel werden wir benutzen, die übrigen stelle ich unter.

REST (v.) 1. With reference to the physical resting of persons **ruhen** suggests sleep, while **sich ausruhen** means 'to relax', 'to refresh oneself by rest' whether through sleep or by lying down or merely by avoiding tiring activity. *Sich ausruhen* can apply to a part of, as well as to the whole, body. The reflexive pronoun can be omitted in exalted style, but also in ordinary prose to refer to 'rest' in general as distinct from a specific moment.

In a question designed to ascertain whether a person is resting or engaging in some activity *ruhen* is used (*sich ausruhen* referring to the result, i.e. recuperation, not the attempt to rest, unless accompanied by some verb such as *wollen*). If *ruhen* in such a question is felt to be ambiguous by referring to 'sleep', when it is desired only to indicate an attempt to rest, *ein bißchen* can be added.

Kinder, macht keinen Lärm, Vater ruht.

Haben Sie ein bißchen geruht oder Ihre Korrespondenz erledigt?

Ich wünsche, wohl geruht zu haben (said by a servant to his master in old-fashioned style).

Kinder, macht keinen Lärm, ich will mich ausruhen.

Haben Sie sich (gut, ein bißchen) ausgeruht?

---

[1] Colloquially *sonst* is often used in this sense. *Ich nehme ein Zimmer, sonst gehört das Haus Ihnen.*

Ruhen Sie sich in den Ferien aus.
Der Arzt sagte: 'Ruhen Sie erst mal aus'.
Man muß die Truppen ausruhen lassen.
Sie müssen die Augen ausruhen lassen.

2. Figurative senses.
(a) **Ruhen** denotes a state which is the opposite of activity or movement. Of a person it means 'to do nothing', of a thing (or a dead body) 'to remain in a certain position' or 'to lean on' anything that acts as a support. It is used also of a responsibility or a task. Applied to aspects of nature or inner states of being it means 'to be still, peaceful'.

Er ruht nie, er arbeitet wie besessen.
Er ruht auf seinen Lorbeeren.
Der Abend, der Wald, ruht.
Seine Hand ruhte auf dem Fensterbrett.
Mein Blick ruhte auf der Schönheit der Landschaft.
Das Dach ruht auf Säulen.
Napoleon ruht im Hôtel des Invalides.
Eine schwierige Aufgabe ruht auf Ihnen.

(b) **Rasten** suggests more definitely than *ruhen* a pause in the course of an activity.
Er kann nie rasten, er muß immer weiter.

(c) **Beruhen:** (i) to be based on; (ii) *etwas auf sich beruhen lassen* = to let a thing rest at that.
Die Klage gegen ihn beruht auf der Aussage zweier Zeugen.
Der Beweis beruht auf diesen Tatsachen.

REVEAL, DISCLOSE, DIVULGE 1. Offenbaren can only be used (*a*) of lofty truths that come to one as though by inspiration, and of matters so intimate as to be regarded as sacred or as concerned with one's deepest self; (*b*) of some deficiency about oneself.

Die (ge)offenbarte Religion.
Große Männer offenbaren der Menschheit neue Wege, neue Ideale.
In diesem Gedicht offenbart der Dichter seine innerste Seele.
Damit offenbart er nur seine Schwächen.

2. Enthüllen, i.e. to remove the covering,[1] is the most general term in the sense of 'to reveal what is hidden'.
Er hat das Geheimnis, seine Pläne, enthüllt.
Deine Bemerkung hat alles, deinen ganzen Charakter, enthüllt.

3. Entdecken means 'to discover' and, figuratively, 'to uncover', i.e. what is hidden. It may be used of what is bad as well as of what is good, but in both cases this is regarded as important.
Er hat ihr seine Liebe entdeckt.
Er hat uns den ganzen Betrug entdeckt.

4. Eröffnen, i.e. to open what is closed,[2] is used only of important matters, particularly intentions, plans and the like, and implies a trustworthy recipient of the disclosure.
Der Minister eröffnete seinen Kollegen seine Pläne.

---

[1] *Enthüllen* also means 'to unveil' a monument, statue and the like. *Entschleiern* means literally 'to unveil' a picture, figuratively 'to unveil' something mysterious. It is a less prosaic term than *enthüllen*. [2] See also 'open'.

RIVER, STREAM, BROOK, CREEK 1. In the literal sense of 'a natural surface stream of water of considerable volume and permanent or seasonal flow' (*W.*). Both the every-day and the scientific term in German is **Fluß**, no matter how deep, broad or long or swift-flowing it may be. Thus, in geography manuals the main as well as the minor rivers of a country are called *Flüsse*. The word **Strom** suggests, it is true, a broad and swift-flowing river, but it is in present-day German poetical or carries at least emotional connotations. In a few cases it retains its earlier meaning of *Strömung*, current, e.g. *der Golfstrom*, for which English also says 'stream'. But see under 'stream'.

Der Rhein, die Elbe, die Weser, der Main und die Donau sind die größten Flüsse Deutschlands.
Flußschiffahrt, Flußbett, unterirdischer Fluß, Flußgott, Flußmündung.
Der Rheinstrom—in emotional language.

2. In the sense of 'something resembling a river' (*W.*) **Strom** is used also in a purely metaphorical sense corresponding to English 'stream' (and **Strömung** for a strong current).

Lavaströme glühen gefährlich rot.
Der Regen, der während der Nacht in wahren Strömen fällt.
Kalte Luftströme.
Ströme von Blut wurden während der Schlacht vergossen.
Tränenströme; Lichtstrom.
Mit dem, gegen den, Strom schwimmen (stream).

3. *Fluß* is also used as a medical term of anything that flows, e.g. *Blutfluß* and *Bauchfluß*, and in some cases purely metaphorically, e.g. *der Redefluß*, which suggests continuous flow while *der Rede Strom* suggests a volume of words that threaten to engulf us.

4. 'Stream' in the literal sense of water flowing from a source: **Bach**, which, however, may also be used metaphorically.

Er fischt häufig in diesem Bach.
Hier fließen viele Bäche zu einem Fluß zusammen.
Bäche von Blut, von Tränen.

5. 'Brook': a small stream, is in German **Bach** or **Bächlein**.
Viele Bäche, Bächlein münden in diese Flüsse.
Ein Gebirgsbach.
Bachforelle (brook-trout).

6. 'Creek' in British use is a narrow inlet near the seashore or in the bank of a river (*A.L.*). In other English-speaking countries it need not be near the sea, it may contain little water, and may be a tributary of a river. German **Flüßchen, Bächlein**, or if a tributary, **Nebenfluß**.

ROLL Rollen (transitive and intransitive) is 'to roll smoothly, without impediment', of both light and heavy bodies. **Wälzen** (only transitive) is 'to roll with difficulty', or erratically, with contortions,[1] either forwards or about, and of bodies that are too heavy to roll or revolve easily.

Er rollte das Faß hinunter.
Der Ball, der Stein, rollte den Abhang hinunter.
Er rollte seine Augen.

---

[1] Hence also 'to writhe' (e.g. *sich vor Lachen wälzen*).

Der Donner rollt.
Der Fluß rollt dem Meere zu.
Der Sturzbach wälzte große Baumstämme über den Damm.
Er wälzte sich stundenlang im Bett, ohne schlafen zu können.

ROOM Sense: division of a house or building enclosed by walls or partitions.

1. **Zimmer** is now the usual term. It has lost its original meaning of *Bauholz* (cognate English term timber), so that it may now be of any material. It is not limited to rooms in a dwelling, though this is its commonest use.

> *Wohnzimmer, Badezimmer, Schlafzimmer, Speisezimmer, Sprechzimmer, Empfangszimmer, Musikzimmer.*
> *Wartezimmer* (e.g. in a doctor's apartments).
> *Zimmermädchen; Zimmertemperatur.*
> *Sie können mich jederzeit in meinem Zimmer finden* (may be office).
> *Eine Fünf-Zimmer-Wohnung.*

2. **Stube** was once as common for rooms in a dwelling as *Zimmer* now is. It is today small, simple and heated (cognate with English 'stove') and therefore comfortable, cosy. Thus one says *Dachstube*, but not *Dachzimmer*. It too is not limited to rooms in a dwelling, but, when not, appears mainly in compounds, often in military terminology.

> *Speisestube, Badestube, Weinstube, Gaststube.*

3. **Kammer** is in modern German still more humble and designates something very small, not one of the main rooms of a house.

> *Speisekammer* (pantry).
> *Dachkammer* (as well as *Dachstube*).

4. **Raum** in accordance with its original meaning of space is spacious, though **Nebenräume** exists, and is less used of rooms in dwellings than in public buildings and institutions.

> *Die Seminarräume der Universität.*
> *Die Empfangsräume, Büroräume, Gesellschaftsraum.*
> *Der Raum, in dem die Tagung stattfindet.*

5. **Gemach** is an elevated term and applied to rooms in a palace or the like, which are characterized by a degree of magnificence and comfort, which was the original meaning (now to be found only in the negative *Ungemach*, adversity).

> *Die Gemächer der Königin.*

6. **Saal** is a very large room, rather what English calls a hall, though it also appears in *Wartesaal*.

> *Vorlesungssaal, Konzertsaal.*

ROOM, SPACE Raum, like 'space', is the wider term. In the sense of 'available space', it also corresponds to 'space', while the equivalent of the more limited 'room' is **Platz**.[1] In reference to measurement *Raum* and 'space' are the more objective terms.

> *Ich habe hier nicht genug Platz zum Stehen, geschweige denn zum Liegen.*
> *Die Universität hat nicht genug Raum, um so viele Studenten aufzunehmen.*
> *Wieviel Schiffsraum wird für das Gepäck vorgesehen.*

---

[1] See also 'place'.

ROUGH, COARSE, RUDE, CRUDE, RAW, GROSS, UNCOUTH, RUGGED The range of application of these terms is so wide that it is not possible to show when each corresponds to each of the German terms treated. The main German terms here treated are: **grob, derb, rauh, roh, schroff, barsch.** But the more natural equivalent of the English term will sometimes be found among the following: **stürmisch** (stormy), **ungestüm** (impetuous), **uneben** (uneven), **primitiv** (primitive), **unsanft** (ungentle), **ungeschliffen** (unpolished, in the first place of a stone), **ungehobelt** (unplaned), **wild** (wild), **herb** (harsh to the taste), **heftig** (vehement, see under 'violent').

1. Grob The basic meaning according to Trübner is *massig*, i.e. in big lumps, a sense perceptible in many of its uses. Therefore big, gross as opposed to fine. It is thus often a close equivalent of English 'coarse'.

(a) Coarse in fibre of materials, large not fine.

> *Grobes Tuch, grobes Korn, grober Sand, grober Zucker, grobes Sieb* (with big holes).

(b) Big, not fine or subtle, acquiring a pejorative meaning. Often equivalent to English 'coarse' or 'crude'.

> *Grobe Hände, grobe Gesichtszüge* (coarse), *grobe Arbeit* (rough, crude), *ein grobgezimmerter Tisch, grob bearbeitet* (roughly, crudely wrought).

(c) Big in the sense of English 'gross'.

> *Eine grobe Lüge, ein grober Fehler, grobe Fahrlässigkeit* (gross negligence), *grobe Schmeicheleien* (gross flattery), *grober Unfug.*

(d) With things said it has the implication of aggressive, abusive, offensive. See also *barsch.*

> *Ein grober Scherz, Witz.*
> *Er hat ihn grob zurechtgewiesen* (contains a threat), *grob angefahren.*

(e) With actions directed against another person it means 'rough' in the sense of aggressive, otherwise it is rare with actions.

> *Er hat ihn grob behandelt.*
> *Er ist grob mit ihm umgegangen.*

(f) From meaning 'not fine' it easily passes to the sense of 'approximate'.

> *In groben Umrissen* (in rough outline).
> *Eine grobe Schätzung* (a rough estimate).

2. Derb The basic meaning is strong, sturdy, solid, tough in the way that nature is strong; it means the opposite of *fein*. In certain contexts, mainly with things said, it has sexual implications. It is often applied to the same things as *grob*, but with the distinction here indicated.

> *Derbe Kost* (e.g. peasant food), *ein derber Mensch, ein derbes Bauernmädchen, derbe Sitten, derbe Fäuste, ein derber Schlag, eine derbe Umarmung.*
> *Er hat ihn derb angefasst, derb zurechtgewiesen* (bluntly).
> *Derbe Schuhe, derbe Strümpfe, derber Stoff.*
> *Ein derber Witz, Spaß, derbe Ausdrücke, eine derbe Antwort, ein derber Brief.*
> *Er ist recht derb mit den Jungens (geht derb um)* (rough).

3. Rauh (a) Cognate with English 'rough'. In Middle High German the basic sense was hairy, shaggy, i.e. of a surface that is not smooth. From this developed the more general sense of not smooth, not even, particularly to the touch.

> *Rauhe Haut, rauhe Hände, rauhe Zunge, rauher Stein, rauhes Papier, rauhes Hemd.*

(b) When applied to land, countryside, it also suggests bleakness, unfriendliness. Although it is possible to say *ein rauher Weg*, both literally and figuratively, for 'a rough road' see example with *uneben*.

Eine rauhe Gegend.

(c) The agent that causes the sensation of roughness may also be termed *rauh* (*ein rauher Wind, rauhes Wetter, rauhes Klima*), but the agent in itself is often more accurately called *stürmisch* (see examples).

(d) From rough to the touch it is not a far step to the sense of hoarse.

Eine rauhe Stimme; ein rauher Hals.

(e) Applied to persons and to what they say or do it conveys the suggestions of not gentle, not sensitive towards others, though unlike *grob*, without any implication of aggressiveness. It is not necessarily pejorative (e.g. *rauh aber herzlich*) but often simply unrefined, unpolished on the exterior.

Ein rauher Soldat; rauhes Benehmen.
Eine rauhe Sprache gebrauchen.
Die rauhen Seiten des Kasernenlebens.

4. Roh (a) The cognate English term is 'raw', and basically *roh* means uncooked (*rohes Fleisch*). Therefore *Rohkost* does not mean coarse, crude, but vegetarian food (for other materials that are unprocessed, generally specific terms are used.

Ungegerbtes Leder.

(b) But *roh* is also applied to things made by man when they have hardly got beyond the raw-material stage. The suggestion of crude, rough, unrefined easily arises.

Ein rohes Bauwerk; ein roh gezimmerter Tisch; im Rohbau fertig; im Rohzustand, im Rohen.

(c) Extended to people, their actions and feelings, the meaning ranges from primitive and unpolished to brutal. In figurative use it is the most pejorative of the German terms treated.

Ein roher Volksstamm; rohe Sitten; rohe Scherze; rohe Späße; rohe Begierden; ein rohes Gemüt.
Ein Rohling = a brute.

5. Rüde Crude, rough in the sense of lacking in feeling for other people.

Er ließ rüde Attacken gegen den Kanzler los.
Ein rüder Volksstamm (uncivilized in its ways).
Hier herrscht ein rüder Ton.

6. Schroff means abrupt, without using many words or mincing matters.

Eine schroffe Antwort.

7. Barsch, harsh and unfriendly in voice suggesting: snapping at a person.

Eine barsche Antwort, Stimme.
Er hat eine barsche Antwort gegeben.

8. Examples of the other German terms listed are:

Ein stürmischer Wind; eine stürmische See (rough).
Die Straße ist sehr uneben (or *holperig*) (rough).
Sie wohnen in primitiven Häusern (crude).
Sie fassten ihn unsanft an (roughly).
Ein ungeschliffener Diamant (rough); *ein ungeschliffener Mensch.*
Ein ungehobelter Kerl.
Eine wilde Landschaft.

Ein herber Wein.
Ein heftiger Wind.

RUN (literal) **Rennen** is 'to run with great speed', whether in a race or otherwise.[1] **Laufen** is 'to run at a moderate speed', often implying little more than 'hurry', or intermittent running while moving about. It cannot therefore be applied to a race. In northern Germany *laufen* often means 'to walk'.[2,3]

Das Pferderennen.
Er rannte so schnell, daß niemand ihn einholen konnte.
Er rannte spornstreichs gegen den Feind.
Sie müssen rennen, wenn Sie nicht vom Regen überrascht werden wollen.
Als der Detektiv auf ihn zuging, lief er weg.
Laufen Sie, sonst werden Sie den Zug verpassen.
Trotz seines Gewichts läuft er sehr behende auf dem Tennisplatz herum.
Diese Kinder laufen in Lumpen herum.

SAFE, SECURE, SURE 1. **Sicher** corresponds closely to 'secure'[4,5] and 'sure', but means 'safe' almost only when this is practically interchangeable with 'secure' or 'sure'.

In the sense of 'free from doubt' it means 'sure'. From this it is a small step to the sense of 'free from anxiety, care, or danger', i.e. secure. In reference to a person and in combination with the verb *sein* it means 'sure', unless some phrase is added (e.g. *vor*, i.e. from), or a place which definitely gives it the meaning of 'secure' (or 'safe'). *Ich bin sicher* = I am sure. *Ich bin hier sicher vor einem Angriff* = secure, safe from...On the other hand, with many other verbs *sicher* tends to mean 'secure', 'safe'. *Mein Kapital steht sicher. Ich fühle mich sicher.*[6] *Ist der Wagen ganz sicher?*

In reference to things, places, courses of action, and the like, *sicher* means 'secure', 'not exposed to danger' in the sense given by the *P.O.D.*, 'impregnable, certain not to fail or give way or get loose or be lost'. To this could be added 'certain not to be stolen', a common sense of *sicher*. This is the primary meaning. The sense of 'affording protection' and 'not actively involving in or exposing to danger' is present only in a secondary way and not independently of the primary sense. Thus *die Brücke ist ganz sicher* means in the first place 'secure against collapse' because the foundations, etc. are solid. Only because of its own security is it able not to expose to danger

---

[1] *Rinnen* is 'to run or flow in drops', particularly from leaky vessels. *Der Sand rinnt ihm durch die Finger; das Bier rinnt aus dem Faß.*

[2] Examples: *ich laufe sehr gern; wie lange sind Sie gelaufen?*

[3] *Rennen* being applied exclusively to persons or in reference to racing also to animals, lacks the wide figurative application of *laufen*.

[4] *Sichern* = to secure (i.e. make secure, safe); to ensure, to assure, in the sense of 'to make a thing certain'. *Versichern* = to insure (life, property, etc.); to assure (i.e. remove doubt from the mind). In the latter sense it now governs the dative case, except in the combination 'to assure someone of something', where it is followed by the accusative and the genitive. *Ich versichere Ihnen, daß Sie sich irren. Ich versicherte ihn meiner Hilfe.*

[5] *Sicher* comes from Latin *securus*.

[6] Both 'I feel sure' and 'I am sure' must therefore be translated by *ich bin sicher*. 'Sure' followed by the infinitive in the sense of 'bound to' must be translated by the adverb *sicher* (e.g. *er wird sicher kommen* = he is sure to come). He is sure of coming = *er ist sicher, kommen zu können*. 'Surely', when it expresses a doubt and seeks confirmation, is *doch sicher* (e.g. *er wird doch sicher kommen*).

those who use it. For the sentence 'my car is safe' *sicher* could only be used in the sense of 'secure against theft', and the addition of *vor Dieben* would be necessary. *Dieser Strand ist sicher* could only mean 'secure against hostile attack' during a war, not 'safe (for swimming)', i.e. 'not presenting dangers through its own nature or structure'.

When 'safe' and 'sure' are practically interchangeable in the sense of 'reliable', both can be translated by *sicher*. *Sichere Methoden. Ich weiß es aus sicherer Quelle. Sicheres Geleit.* Similarly, 'secure of' = 'sure of' and may be rendered by *sicher*.

Sicher cannot be used in the sense of 'unscathed after passing through real or imagined danger', i.e. in the original meaning of 'safe': well, sound (e.g. to arrive safe and sound). Nor can it be used with *es ist* and a following infinitive (e.g. it is safe to walk there) or with an infinitive of the type: a gun safe to handle. It is possible, on the other hand, to say: *das Sicherste ist...zu...* (i.e. the surest thing, course, is to...).

Wir sind hier sicher vor einem Überfall, vor Verfolgung.

Das Geld ist in Ihren Händen ganz sicher.

Das Geld ist in sicheren Händen.

Eine sichere Anlage (secure, sure, reliable investment).

Eine sichere Straße (safe from thieves and the like; not 'so constructed as to eliminate accidents').

Ein sicherer Hafen.

Ein sicheres Türschloß.

Ist das Dokument sicher?

Er befindet sich in sicherer Entfernung.

2. In the sense of 'unscathed after passing through real or imagined dangers' **gut** is normally used to express the idea of safe arrival. In other combinations the sense of 'unscathed' requires a specific term.

Er ist gut angekommen.

Er hat sie gut nach Hause gebracht.

Eine gute Überfahrt.

Seine Ehre ist unbefleckt, gerettet.

3. When 'safe' is followed by an infinitive, use may be made of **Gefahr, ungefährlich**, etc. or the phrase may be recast.

Sie können dort ohne Gefahr gehen (it is safe to walk there).

Sie sind ganz sicher, wenn Sie dort gehen.

Es ist gefährlich, zu nahe an den Rand zu gehen.

4. In the sense of 'not exposing to danger', particularly with reference to a place, **ungefährlich**, etc. may be used, but often other terms are more appropriate.

Das ist ein Strand, der für Kinder ungefährlich ist.

Kann man sich auf Ihren Wagen verlassen? (is your car safe, trustworthy?).

5. In Sicherheit: in safety. **Mit Sicherheit:** with surety (certainty), safety, security (often interchangeable meanings).

Wir sind jetzt in Sicherheit (secure, safe).

Sie wurden in Sicherheit gebracht.

Man kann mit Sicherheit behaupten, daß der Preis nicht zu hoch war (it is safe to say...).

SATISFY In the sense of 'convince' only **überzeugen** is possible. **Befriedigen** is 'to satisfy' a wish, feeling, sensation, or demand.[1] **Genügen** is 'to comply with' a standard.

Ich habe mich überzeugt, daß er sein Bestes getan hat.
Er hat seine Wünsche, seine Neugier, seinen Hunger, seinen Ehrgeiz, befriedigt.
Seine Arbeit ist befriedigend.
Er hat allen Anforderungen genügt.

SAY 1. *Sagen* is often avoided in referring to what persons in authority say in their official capacity. Instead, terms such as **hinweisen auf, verweisen auf** (to point out, refer to the fact that) are common. *Sagen*, while not impossible, sounds in such contexts too casual.

Der Minister wies darauf hin, daß die Beziehungen zwischen den zwei deutschen Staaten besonderer Art sein müßten.

2. **Ausführen** replaces *sagen* in the case of a longish statement.

Der Minister führte aus, daß neue Kontakte mit der polnischen Regierung aufgenommen werden sollen.

3. **Heißen**, to be said, is used when a document is the subject and generally in the sense of 'it is said'. **Sagen** may be used in such contexts in the passive.

In seinem Bericht heißt es, daß Schritte schon unternommen worden seien, um eine Besserung der Beziehungen zu Polen herbeizuführen (the report says that...).
In dem Bericht wurde gesagt, daß die Hindernisse nur langsam überwunden werden könnten.

4. See also 'state'.

SAYING **Spruch** is a popular saying and has something of the character of the *Sprichwort*, naive, not concerned with fine distinctions or with exceptions, and anonymous. **Ausspruch** is the saying of an individual of note and bears the marks of reflection. It has something of the character of maxim.

Die Spruchweisheit des Volkes trifft oft den Kern einer Sache.
Goethes Aussprüche sind berühmt.

SEA The distinction between **Meer** and **See** (feminine) is far from clear. While *Meer* more readily suggests a vast expanse of water than *See*, we find on the other hand *Südsee* for the southern part of the Pacific Ocean. Again, there is a tendency in North Germany to name what is close to this part of the country *See* (e.g. *Nordsee, Ostsee*) and in South Germany to call what is close *Meer* (e.g. *das Mittelmeer, das Schwarze Meer*). The proximity of these seas to North Germany means that North German naturally says *an die See fahren* (to go to the sea-side) and South German *ans Meer fahren*. Both terms are used of inland lakes (*See* since the sixteenth century being masculine in this sense), but the same distinction does not hold good. In the South we find e.g. *Der Bodensee, der Chiemsee, der Wolfgangsee, der Wörthersee, der Genfersee*, whereas in the North there is the *Steinhuder Meer*. The only firm distinction is that *See* is used in practical contexts such as shipping, whether this be commercial or naval.

Seemannssprache, Seefahrt, Kapitän zur See, Seeschlacht, seekrank.

[1] *Befrieden,* to impose peace on, to pacify.

SEAL **Siegeln** is 'to stamp a seal on' a document. It is no longer in common use. **Versiegeln** means, literally and figuratively, 'to close a thing with a seal so as to keep secret its contents'. Since it includes the meaning of *siegeln*, it is mostly used for the latter. **Besiegeln** is only used figuratively, in the sense of 'to decide', 'to settle finally'.

Die Urkunde wurde gesiegelt.
Er hat den Brief versiegelt.
Alle Türen des Hauses wurden versiegelt (a police action).
Meine Lippen sind versiegelt.
Sein Schicksal ist besiegelt.

SECRET **Geheim** is applied to that which is deliberately kept secret, particularly to matters from which the State excludes the public. **Heimlich** can also imply deliberate exclusion, but never in relation to State matters, and not with the verb *halten*.[1] It is more frequently applied to that which happens to be hidden or is by its nature hidden. It evokes the atmosphere of secrecy or seclusion both in persons and in things, and in persons sometimes stealth. *Geheimnisvoll*: mysterious.

Geheimpolizei, ein Geheimbund.
Die Pläne müssen geheim gehalten werden.
Sie hat einen geheimen Kummer.
Er ist ein geheimer Säufer.
Er hegt den heimlichen Wunsch, Schauspieler zu werden.
Ein heimliches Laster, ein heimlicher Platz.
Er sagte es ihm heimlich ins Ohr.

SEE ('I see' used absolutely in conversation is treated in section 5).

1. Sehen denotes: (*a*) physical sight;[2] (*b*) perception with the mind. It expresses the latter only when understanding is immediate and implies no process of thought, i.e. not as an equivalent of 'realize'. A visual act may or may not accompany the mental perception. *Sehen* is used in fewer extended senses than 'see'. See also section 5.

Der Nebel ist so dicht, daß ich nicht sehen kann.
Ich sehe schon meinen Fehler (e.g. a visible error in a piece of writing, or purely in the mind).
Ich sehe, daß ich mich geirrt habe.
Er sah gleich, daß hier nichts zu erreichen war.
Ich seh' schon, worauf Sie hinaus wollen.
Ich sehe die Wahrheit (only as a vision in a biblical sense).

2. Einsehen: to come to an understanding of a thing after a process of thought, to realize. Insight into causal relationships, into the why and wherefore of things, is implied. (*Ich sehe nicht ein, warum...* is a very common phrase.) It can refer to every-day matters no less than to philosophic and scientific truths. It must be followed by an object (a noun or a clause).

Ich sehe jetzt meinen Fehler ein.
Ich sehe jetzt ein, daß ich mich geirrt habe.
Ich sehe nicht ein, warum Sie zögern.
Er sah ein, daß hier nichts zu erreichen war.

---

[1] 'To keep secret' is often *verheimlichen*.
[2] Also in memory and in imagination.

Ich sehe den Grund nicht ein, warum Sie so handeln mußten.
Ich sehe die Notwendigkeit dieser Maßnahmen nicht ein.

3. Verstehen: to understand.[1] A clear grasp of a thing as a whole in a general way, but no necessary reference to any preceding process of thought is implied. It translates 'see' in the above sense, particularly: (*a*) when the latter refers to the meaning of something said or written; (*b*) when it is used absolutely (see section 5).

Ich verstehe den Sinn dieser Stelle nicht (it is unintelligible; *einsehen* would imply insight into its why and wherefore).
Ich verstehe meinen Fehler.

4. Erkennen is a close synonym of *einsehen* in so far as it indicates a process of realization, a coming to know.[2]

Er erkennt seinen Fehler.
Er erkannte die Notwendigkeit dieser Maßnahmen.
Er erkannte, daß er sich geirrt hatte.

5. 'I see', used absolutely as an interjection or a comment. German uses *ich verstehe, ich seh' schon* (*schon* must be added) to indicate that one already sees. If a sudden realization accompanied by surprise is meant, German says: *So! Ach so!* (the second denoting a higher degree of surprise).

Ja, ich seh' schon (*ich verstehe*), *das ginge nicht.*
So (*Ach so*)! *Dann hat er das nicht ernst gemeint.*

6. Absehen: to form an estimate of some kind in relation to what is remote. It is used therefore with terms such as *Ende, Folgen.*

Ich kann das Ende, die Folgen, nicht absehen.
Es ist nicht abzusehen, was die Zukunft bringen wird.

7. Other compounds of *sehen* are **nachsehen** (to ascertain by inspection, to check); **zusehen** (to take care that...).[3]

Sehen Sie mal nach, ob das Buch in der Bibliothek steht.
Sehen Sie mal zu, daß Sie rechtzeitig ankommen.

8. Examples of terms that occur in less frequent senses are:
(a) *Dem leuchtet niemals ein Witz ein* (*einleuchten* means that the meaning or the rightness of a thing occurs to one in a flash).
Ihm leuchtete die Erklärung sofort ein.
(b) In the sense of 'to perceive' something good or bad about a thing *finden* is sometimes used.
Er findet viel an Paris, aber nichts an London.
Da finde ich nichts Schlimmes dabei (see no harm in it).
(c) *Kann ich Herrn Schmidt sprechen?* (interview). *Ich werde Sie zur Tür, nach Hause, begleiten* (see to the door, home).

SEIZE   A. Literal sense. In this sense it is synonymous with one of the uses of 'catch', which must be translated by the same German terms.

1. Ergreifen is restricted to such actions as can be performed by the hand and imply suddenness, impulsiveness, or violence, and, frequently, accompanying emotion. It stresses the act of seizing more than the retaining

---

[1] *Verstehen* is the most general term. *Begreifen* is 'to comprehend' a thing in all its aspects and in its causal relations with other things. See 'understand'.
[2] See 'recognize' and 'know'.
[3] See 'careful'.

of one's hold on the object, and cannot be used in contexts which emphasize the latter.

Sie ergriff den Eimer, um das Feuer zu löschen.
Er ergriff das Gewehr und schoß auf den Feind.
Er ergriff die Feder und unterzeichnete das Todesurteil.
Er ergriff meine Hand und dankte mir.
Die Polizei ergriff den Dieb.

2. Greifen with a direct object is only used in a few fixed phrases. *Die Polizei hat ihn gegriffen.*

3. Fassen: to seize, grasp firmly and retain one's hold.[1] It thus approximates more closely to 'catch' than does *ergreifen*.

Fassen Sie das Seil (e.g. said to a drowning person).
Er faßte das Fensterbrett und zog sich hinauf.

4. Packen suggests not only greater violence and effort in the act of seizing, but a firmer grip on retaining one's hold.[2] It is particularly appropriate where a struggle is implied.

Er packte den Ertrinkenden am Arm.
Er packte ihn bei der Kehle und schüttelte ihn tüchtig.

5. When 'seize' is followed by 'from' (i.e. snatch from), **entreißen** is used, with both small and big things.

Er hat mir das Messer entrissen.
Er entriß seinem Bruder den Thron.

6. Sich bemächtigen: to secure control of, power over, a person or thing by effort or violence.

Der Feind hat sich sofort aller Flottenstützpunkte bemächtigt.[3]
Die revolutionäre Partei hat sich des Staatsapparates bemächtigt.

7. Beschlagnahmen must be used in the sense of 'confiscate'.

Die Polizei hat seinen Briefwechsel, die gestohlenen Waren, beschlagnahmt.

8. Special senses of 'seize' must be translated by specific terms, e.g. *erbeuten*, to steal as booty.

Die Diebe haben große Mengen von Kleidern erbeutet.

B. Figurative uses.

1. Ergreifen.

(a) The idea of stretching out one's hand and grasping what one wants appears in such phrases as: *die Gelegenheit, die Initiative, ergreifen.*
(b) To grip suddenly and violently, with a strong or impulsive feeling as subject.[4,5]

Die Sehnsucht ergriff ihn, seine Heimat noch einmal zu sehen.
Die Furcht ergriff ihn, daß er die Gelegenheit schon versäumt habe.

---

[1] *Anfassen* means no more than 'to touch'. *Fassen Sie den Ofen nicht an. Den Hund können Sie ruhig anfassen.*

[2] *Anpacken* is only used figuratively. *Er hat die Sache richtig angepackt* (tackled).

[3] *Besetzen*, 'to occupy', is more common with reference to military or any other armed occupation, but does not in itself suggest force.

[4] *Ergreifen* with a personal object also means 'to move', i.e. emotionally. See 'move'.

[5] With weaker feelings *ergreifen* is inappropriate. *Der Wunsch, das Verlangen, überkam ihn.*

2. Packen is used of sudden, paralysing feelings such as terror, and of thoughts which suddenly and forcibly take possession of one.[1]

Eine plötzliche Angst hat ihn gepackt.

Der Gedanke packte ihn, daß sein Leben in Gefahr sei.

3. Erfassen: to comprehend, to lay hold of a matter.

Er hat den wesentlichen Unterschied sofort erfaßt.

SELF-CONSCIOUS, SELF-ASSURED 'Self-conscious' must be translated by such terms as **befangen** (embarrassed), **sich genieren** (to feel awkward). **Selbstbewußt** only means 'self-assured'.[2]

Er fühlt sich befangen, wenn er Fremde empfangen muß.

Er geniert sich zu fragen.

Er trat sehr selbstbewußt auf.

SELFISH *Selbstsüchtig* and *selbstisch,* which can also mean 'self-centred', 'absorbed with self', are little used in conversation, the common terms being *egoistisch* and *an sich selbst denken.*

Seien Sie nicht immer so egoistisch.

Er denkt immer nur an sich selbst.

SEND 1. Senden is a more dignified term than the more common **schicken**[3] and refers to the sending of persons and things of importance, particularly on a mission. *Schicken* is an almost exclusively human term, while *senden* is also applied to the world of nature (e.g. *die Sonne sendet ihre Strahlen zur Erde*) and to such utilizations of the forces of nature as radio, electricity, telegraph. Only *schicken* means 'to send away' in the sense of 'to get rid of'.[4]

Er wurde als Botschafter nach Paris gesandt.

Schicken Sie den Brief per Luftpost.

Ich habe ein Telegramm an ihn geschickt.

Schicken Sie die Kinder weg, sie machen zu viel Lärm.

Wir senden Ihnen einen Katalog der in diesem Jahr erschienenen Bücher.

2. Abschicken should be used when it is a question of whether a thing has been sent or not.

Ich habe den Brief schon abgeschickt.

3. Zuschicken, followed by the dative, suggests more definitely a personal interest in the receiver than *schicken,* often a good turn. It is, however, never obligatory.

Ich kann Ihnen das Buch zuschicken lassen.

4. Verschicken and **versenden** are commercial terms and are used particularly in reference to bulk. *Verschicken* is also used of sending people away, particularly for reasons of health.[5]

---

[1] *Packen* also means 'to grip' one's interest. *Das Stück hat mich sehr gepackt.*

[2] Similarly *selbstbesessen* means 'unduly occupied with oneself', not 'self-possessed', which is *selbstbeherrscht.*

[3] *Schicken* is the factitive verb to *(ge)schehen* and originally meant 'to make happen', then 'to arrange, to dispose one's affairs'.

[4] Neither *schicken* nor *senden* corresponds to 'send' used figuratively. I sent him word = *ich ließ ihm sagen.* To send regards = *grüßen lassen.*

[5] *Verschicken* can also mean to deport undesirable subjects.

Der Verlag schrieb mir, daß die Bücher baldigst versandt würden.

Die Kinder wurden schon vor den schweren Bombenangriffen aufs Land verschickt.

5. Entsenden is a dignified term used only in the sense of despatching someone on an important mission.

Ist es im gegenwärtigen Augenblick Amerika möglich, Truppen nach Europa zu entsenden?

SENSE **1.** As a synonym of 'meaning', 'point'.

Sinn differs from **Bedeutung**, as 'sense' does from 'meaning', in that *Bedeutung* is more objective and more exact, whereas *Sinn* is more subjective and often refers rather to one interpretation of a word or phrase amongst a number of possible others.

Sinn differs from 'sense' in one point. While it is possible to refer to the 'sense' of a word or its various senses as listed in a dictionary, *Sinn* only denotes the sense of a word either in a context or in reference to an idea as conceived by a person or a group of persons.

In certain fixed expressions *Sinn* means 'sense' in the meaning of 'point'. *Sinn* in this use cannot be pluralized.

Der Sinn einer Stelle, einer Bemerkung.

Im wahrsten Sinne des Wortes.

Schönheit in dem Sinne, wie die Griechen sie auffaßten.

In diesem Zusammenhang hat das Wort folgenden Sinn....

Dieses Wort hat fünf verschiedene Bedeutungen.

In der ersten Bedeutung des Wortes (as defined in a dictionary).

Was er sagt, hat keinen Sinn (point).

Es hat keinen Sinn, die Sache weiter zu verfolgen.

2. With reference to the five senses, seeing, hearing, etc., **Sinn** is used.

Die fünf Sinne.

Der Geruchssinn.

Die Vergnügungen der Sinne.

Seine Sinne waren wach.

3. Sinn in the sense of 'capacity for perception, appreciation of a thing', 'sensibility'. At times the thing for which one has sensibility must be defined more specifically than in English, e.g. by an adjective (e.g. *der Sinn für künstlerische, menschliche, Werte* = a sense of values).

Der Schönheitssinn.

Er hat Sinn für Schönheit.

Er hat Sinn für Humor.

Ihm fehlt der Sinn für die Kunst des Barock.

4. Gefühl translates 'sense' in a use allied to **3**, but, unlike *Sinn*, excludes subtle appreciation and sensibility. It should be used when feeling or mere awareness predominates. Most of the meanings of 'sense' given by *S.O.D.* under II are translated by *Gefühl*.

Ein Gefühl des Schmerzes, der Müdigkeit, der Sicherheit, der Dankbarkeit, der Leere, das Gefühl einer bevorstehenden Katastrophe, das Pflichtgefühl.

5. In the meaning of 'sanity', 'sense' occurs in a number of fixed phrases, translated by *Sinn, Verstand, vernünftig*. For examples see dictionaries.

SENSIBILITY The adjective corresponding to this noun can only be 'sensitive' (see under this term) since English 'sensible', unlike German *sensibel* and French *sensible*, has been given the meaning of having or showing good sense.

1. Sense: The power of feeling: **Empfindungsvermögen.**
Das Empfindungsvermögen der Haut.

2. Although it has often been used in exactly the same way as 'sensitiveness', i.e. capacity of emotion or feeling as distinguished from intellect and will, peculiar or excessive susceptibility to pleasurable or painful impression, acuteness of feeling (*W.*), it can differ from this term in stressing awareness, delicate appreciation, particularly of emotions of other people.
Unser Mitempfinden mit deinem Leid (our sensibility of your distress—*W.*).

3. **Feingefühl** = tact.
Ein Mann von großem Feingefühl.

4. In the late eighteenth century, especially as a result of the romantic movement in literature and art, sensibility was thought of as an essential part of the poet and artist and of the reader, and the observer, not only of works of art, but of nature. Consequently, the term acquired connotations of sentimentalism and of forced or affected emotionalism which still sometimes colour the word (*W.S.*). In this use German uses **Empfindsamkeit** (see under 'sensitive').

SENSITIVE 1. Empfindlich is mostly used in the sense of reacting with pain or simply receptive to external physical stimuli. 'To' following sensitive is mostly *gegen* in German, though *für* also occurs. Also: *gegenüber* and *in Bezug auf*: in regard to. In the sentences: *er ist empfindlich*; *er ist ein empfindlicher Mensch*, the meaning can only be 'touchy', easily hurt. It may also be applied to things, particularly instruments which record impressions.
Er ist empfindlich gegen Kälte (or: *kälteempfindlich*).
Das Auge ist empfindlich gegen Licht (or *lichtempfindlich*).
Er ist empfindlich den Leiden von Tieren gegenüber.
Er hat eine sehr empfindliche Haut.
Er reagiert empfindlich auf den leisesten Vorwurf.
Kinder sind empfindlich gegen, gegenüber Tadel.
Er ist gegen Kritik sehr empfindlich.
Die Zunge ist eines der empfindlichsten Sinnesorgane.
Die Börse ist empfindlich gegenüber allen Kriegsgerüchten.
Wir haben einen empfindlichen Rundfunkempfänger.
Eine empfindliche Waage.

2. In the sense of sensitive to values (the beautiful, the true, the good) the German equivalents of 'open', 'receptive', 'responsive' must be used: **offen, aufgeschlossen, empfänglich** (receptive); **Sinn, Gefühl haben für.**
Der Künstler ist für die Schönheit empfänglich.
Er ist sehr aufgeschlossen den idyllischen Seiten der Natur gegenüber.

3. Followed by 'of' 'sensitive' means appreciatively aware of, German can only say **bewußt sein, zu schätzen wissen** (see under 'appreciate').
Ich bin mir der Ehre, die Sie mir erwiesen haben, bewußt.

4. Empfindsam, which originally meant sensitive to values, came to mean sensitive in a tender way and enjoying this feeling and so came close to the meaning of sentimental. Common in the eighteenth and early nineteenth centuries, it has now fallen out of use. *Eine empfindsame Seele*: a sensitive soul, i.e. one easily moved to tender feeling. *Die empfindsame Reise*: the sentimental journey (title of the German translation of Sterne's novel).

SENSUAL, SENSUOUS *W.S.* says of 'sensual' that 'it implies an indulgence in bodily sensation for its own sake rather than for an aesthetic end'; also that 'very often in modern use, the word carries an implication of grossness and bestiality and not merely, as in the case of carnal, of an absence of higher qualities'. And of sensuous it points out that it 'was first used by Milton as a term descriptive of one thing which deals with sensations or has the power of evoking sensations as opposed to another thing which deals with ideas, and is intellectual in its character, as "(Poetry is) more simple, sensuous and passionate (than rhetoric)" (Milton)'. The former, apart from its use as a philosophical term, appears mostly in the context of sex, the latter is mainly applied to the arts (e.g. language, imagery, sound, colour).

German uses **sinnlich** in both cases, but if it is desired to be emphatic or in certain cases to avoid ambiguity, the terms *grob sinnlich*, *derb sinnlich* may be used for 'sensual', and *sinnenhaft*, *sinnenfreudig* for 'sensuous'.

> *Er hat immer kalte Füße und Hände und es gab ihm eine fast sinnliche* (sensual) *Befriedigung, ganz still zu liegen und die heiße Sonne in sich aufzunehmen* (*W.S.*).
>
> *Sinnliche Ausschweifungen, sinnliches Vergnügen.*
>
> *Ein grob sinnlicher Mensch.*
>
> *Sinnliche, sinnenfreudige Beschreibung.*
>
> *Ihre Religion war eine sinnenfreudige* (*S.O.D.*).

SEPARATE(LY) 1. **Einzeln** translates 'separate(ly)' in reference to the individual parts of a whole or a group. See article on 'single'.

> *Sie können die Gedichte dieses Zyklus einzeln lesen, da jedes in sich ein Ganzes darstellt.*
>
> *Die Zeugen kamen einzeln herein.*

2. **Verschieden.** For an explanation of this word see 'different'.

> *Wir brauchen verschiedene Gläser für den Wein und das Bier.*
>
> *Dieser Roman hat zwei verschiedene Handlungen.*
>
> *Das sind zwei verschiedene Probleme.*
>
> *Sie kamen durch verschiedene Türen herein.*
>
> *Die Zahlen wurden in verschiedene Spalten eingetragen.*

3. **Unabhängig** emphasizes that the two things in question have nothing to do with one another.

> *Ägypten war ein unabhängiges Mitglied des Völkerbundes.*
>
> *Das sind zwei unabhängige Probleme.*
>
> *Der Mensch, der leidet, und der Künstler, der schafft, scheinen oft zwei unabhängige Wesen zu sein.*

4. **Eigen:** of one's own, not shared. In this sense it must be clearly referable to the person who owns or enjoys the use of the article in question. Thus: *sie haben eigene Betten.* But it cannot translate: it is a room with separate beds. Unlike 'own' it can be preceded by the indefinite article.

> *Jedes der Kinder hatte sein eigenes Zimmer.*
>
> *Jedes Studienfach braucht eigene Räume.*
>
> *Ich habe einen eigenen Eingang zu meiner Wohnung.*

5. Für sich is often attached to nouns or referable to them in the sense of (*a*) for oneself; (*b*) in itself, i.e. not connected with other things of its kind. In the second sense it is linked only to nouns preceded by the verb *sein*.

Jeder braucht ein Zimmer für sich.
Das ist ein Problem für sich.

6. Getrennt, separated, is applied to things which are deliberately separated because separation is desired.[1]

Sie haben getrennte Interessensphären.
Sie handelten getrennt.
'Getrennt marschieren und gemeinsam schlagen.'

7. Gesondert is a term common among tradespeople and used of despatching or taking goods, letters, and the like, separately. It can, however, also be used in its more general sense, particularly in reference to the separate examination of problems.[2]

Schicken Sie mir bitte das Rindfleisch, und dann gesondert zwei Pfund Leber.
Der Brief wurde in gesondertem Umschlag abgeschickt.
Wir wollen die zwei Fragen gesondert betrachten.

8. Besonder(s) can mean both 'special' and 'separate', the former being by far the commonest meaning.

Ich habe die Bücher schon abgeschickt und werde Ihnen die Broschüren besonders zuschicken.

9. Sonder is used in a number of compounds, sometimes in the sense of 'separate', sometimes in that of 'special'. Thus: *ein Sondervertrag* (separate), but: *ein Sonderzug* (special).

10. Extra is used adverbially of the wrapping and taking of parcels separately.

Ich nehme das Kalbfleisch extra ('separately', not 'extra').

SERIES, SEQUENCE, SUCCESSION According to *W.S.*: 'series' applies to a number of things of similar or uniform character that stand in the same relation to each other or achieve the same end; often the term is indistinguishable from succession, but the separateness of the units is rather more stressed than the fact that they follow each other. 'Succession' always implies that the units (often things, sometimes persons) follow each other, especially but not invariably in order of time, or less often of place, and usually without break or interruption. 'Sequence' is more restricted than series for it implies either a closer connection between the things involved, such as causal or logical connection, a numerical or chronological order, or a settled recurrence in the same order.

1. The German terms **Reihe, Folge, Reihenfolge, Aufeinanderfolge** are not distinguished from each other in the same way. *Reihe*, which is cognate with English 'row' and often translates it, implies things of the same kind and also close succession. It is the most frequent of the terms used in this context. *Folge* in this sense now appears mainly in compounds, but singly

---

[1] *Der Einzelne* is the general term for 'the individual'. *Das Individuum* is used in more strictly philosophical contexts, and not like English 'individual' in the sense of 'person'.
[2] *Trennen* is 'to separate or cut off' a part from something to which the part is joined. *Scheiden* is 'to part or dissolve' things or parts of things inwardly united or fused. Hence *Scheidung* = divorce, *Trennung* = separation. *Sondern*: to sort out like things or parts in a medley.

in *neue Folge* referring to publications. *Reihenfolge* emphasizes the order in which things appear and is a closer equivalent of English 'order' thus used, more than of the above listed English terms.

Die Reihe von Plätzen, die Belgravia genannt werden (*S.O.D.*).

Dieses Land hatte eine Reihe von außergewöhnlichen Diplomaten während der letzten achtzig Jahre (*A.L.*).

Eine Reihe von Unglücksfällen (series or succession).

Sie müssen in dieser Reihenfolge behandelt werden (order, sequence).

Die Wirklichkeit ist eine Reihenfolge von konkreten und besonderen Situationen (*W.S.*).

Diese besondere Kompositionsmethode...war günstig für eine lebhafte Erzählungskunst und eine abwechselnde Folge von kriegerischen Schauplätzen (*W.S.*) (succession).

2. Right of succeeding to the throne, or any office or inheritance, set or order of persons having such rights (*C.O.D.*). **Nachfolge, Erbfolge.**

Er war von der Nachfolge ausgeschlossen (*C.O.D.*).

Gesetze, die die Erbfolge bestimmen (*C.O.D.*).

Er ist der zweite in der Nachfolge (*Erbfolge*) (*C.O.D.*).

SERIOUS, GRAVE, EARNEST None of the German words treated in this article corresponds exactly to the English. *Schwer* is the strongest and comes closest to 'grave', when this does not refer to appearance. *Ernst* is 'serious' or 'grave' according to the context and is stronger than *ernsthaft* and *ernstlich*. In some uses *schlimm* and *arg* (the latter when used adverbially) approach the sense of 'serious' (see 'bad').[1]

The idea of ardent conviction in and devotion to a cause expressed by 'earnest' is lacking in the German words. With nouns or verbs which in themselves suggest such moral fervour *ernst*, *ernsthaft* and *ernstlich* acquire by attraction something of the sense of 'earnest'. In most cases, however, this term can only be rendered approximately into German.[2]

Ernst and **schlimm** can be used adverbially only in a few of the senses corresponding to their adjectival use.

1. 'To be serious, in earnest about a thing' is translated by the impersonal phrase: *es ist einem ernst mit* (*um*)...

Ist es Ihnen ernst mit dem Vorschlag?

2. Ernst means 'serious' or 'grave' in reality, not only in appearance.

(a) Applied to persons it means 'serious in mind', 'having a serious content of mind', 'not gay'. It also corresponds to 'serious' when applied to any direct bodily expression of this temper of mind (mostly 'face', 'eye', 'look') or to thoughts, sayings, actions, works, and the like which proceed from and indicate it. It thus refers to inner content, not to external appearances.

Ein ernster Mann (serious, not gay by nature).

Ein ernster Wissenschaftler (takes science seriously).

Ein ernster Bewerber (serious in himself, not 'to be taken seriously').

Ein ernstes Gesicht.

---

[1] *Seriös* is used mainly in the sense of 'to be taken seriously' or 'wanting to be taken seriously'. *Dieser Student ist nicht ganz seriös. Nur seriöse Künstler sollten sich um den Preis bewerben. Seriöse Kunden.* It is often interchangeable with *ernsthaft*.

[2] Examples of renderings of 'earnest': *ein wahrhafter Christ, ein gewissenhafter Student* (*ein ernster Student* is one who is serious as a human being); *es muß unser ernstes Bestreben sein..., ich hege die ernstliche Hoffnung..., Ihr ernstliches Ansuchen....*

Ernste Gedanken.

Ernste Musik (not jazz and the like).

Ernste Worte.

Ein ernstes Buch.

Er hat ernste Absichten (normally refers to intentions of marriage and should not be used in any other way).

Trotz ernsten Nachdenkens habe ich die Lösung nicht finden können.

Ziehen Sie die Angelegenheit in ernste Erwägung.

Seit Monaten habe ich keine ernste Arbeit geleistet.

Ich habe in diesem Jahre nichts Ernstes gelesen.

Wir sind in eine ernste Auseinandersetzung verwickelt.

(b) Applied to an attitude of mind or a feeling (e.g. doubt, fear) arising from the awareness of an 'evil', actions taken, or warnings given because of an 'evil' and proceeding from this attitude of mind, *ernst* is very strong and comes closer to 'grave' than 'serious'.

Ich hege ernste Bedenken, ernsten Verdacht, gegen seine Ehrlichkeit.

Ich hege ernste Besorgnisse für seine Sicherheit.

Eine ernste Warnung, Ermahnung.

Das heißt einen ernsten Schritt tun.

(c) Applied to things which induce a serious or grave attitude of mind.

(i) With words denoting a situation, a condition, state,[1] *ernst* suggests that a recognition of the possibility of disaster induces a grave attitude of mind. It thus corresponds more closely to 'grave' than to 'serious'. As with 'grave', the probability of disaster is emphasized by the predicative position, which in this sense is used as freely as the attributive position. Words in this section denote an evil which is conceived as a situation or a condition and are to be distinguished from the evils treated under (ii).

Eine ernste Lage. Die Lage ist ernst.

Die Stunde ist für Europa ernst.

Ernste Symptome haben sich gezeigt.

Die Nachrichten von der Front lauten ernst.

Sein Leben schwebt in ernster Gefahr.

Wir haben ernste Verluste erlitten.

Der Verlust eines Gliedes ist ernst.

Seine Erkrankung ist ernst.

Er hat eine ernste Verletzung erhalten.

Die Niederlage hatte ernste Folgen.

(ii) *Ernst*, like 'grave', is applied attributively, but not predicatively, to a few evils not accounted for under (i). Since the predicative use emphasizes the probability of disaster, it is meaningless with a word which in itself indicates disaster as an accomplished fact, unless followed by some such phrases as *für jemanden*.

In the phrases *als ernst ansehen, betrachten, ernst* refers to the idea contained in the verb (i.e. *Ansicht*) and may refer to nouns which do not admit it predicatively after *sein*.

Ein ernster Schaden wurde ihm zugefügt.

Er leidet an einer ernsten Krankheit.

Das war ein ernster Unfall.

Er hat eine ernste Halsentzündung.

---

[1] Note the synonym *kritisch* (*eine kritische Lage*). It cannot be used adverbially.

Die Niederlage ist sehr ernst für ihn.

Die Wunde, die Niederlage, ist als ernst anzusehen.

(d) The use of *ernst* as an adverb is limited to its combination with verbs of saying and looking (compare (a) for the corresponding use of the adjective). A verb of saying, thus used, cannot be followed by a *mit* phrase (see *ernsthaft*). In a sentence such as *er ging ernst neben mir her, ernst* refers to *er*, not to 'going', i.e. it does not describe the manner of walking. It refers to the subject, too, when used with *meinen* and *nehmen*.

Er sprach ernst.

Er blickte sie ernst an.

Er sah ernst zur Decke empor, vor sich hin.

Er meint es ernst.

Er nimmt es, das Leben, seine Pflichten, ernst.

3. Ernsthaft: having the manner or the appearance of seriousness, serious-looking, while not necessarily excluding the inner reality. In emphasizing appearance it differs from *ernst*, which refers only to inner reality. Applied to facial expression, gestures, movements, bearing, tone of voice, and the like it covers not only 'serious' but 'grave', when this suggests appearance. Unlike *ernst*, it is not limited in the sphere of physical appearance to such expressions as proceed directly from an inner state of mind. It can even suggest appearance as opposed to reality (e.g. *trotz der Lächerlichkeit der Lage setzte er eine ernsthafte Miene auf*).

It differs from *ernst* in suggesting a judgment based on appearances (e.g. *wir hielten die Wunde nicht für ernsthaft*). It characteristically presupposes an observer who is asked to accept a thing as serious, not as a joke.

Its character as a judgment based on impressions normally precludes its use in the predicative position after *sein*, unless this is combined with a modal verb or *scheinen* (see 'appear'). It may be used predicatively after *werden*, since such a judgment is less categorical than in the case of *sein*, and occasionally after *sein* when followed by some phrase denoting the effect (e.g. *die Beweggründe, die er anführt, sind ernsthaft genug, um mich zum Nachdenken zu veranlassen*).

It cannot be used with the type of noun discussed in **2**(b) (i.e. words which exclude the idea of appearance), or the type described in **2**(c) (i.e. an objective situation, condition, evil, not a person).

Used adverbially, *ernsthaft* also refers to the manner and appearance of the subject and may include his attitude of mind. This restricts its range of application. It is closely connected with the manner or attitude of mind of the subject, not with the degree of vigour, the intensiveness with which the action of the verb is carried out (see: *ernstlich*). There is a tendency to limit its use as an adverb to cases where the verb excludes the idea of intensiveness. Conversely, *ernstlich* is the preferred term when this type of verb is used. This means that in translation from English into German *ernstlich* is sometimes obligatory, even though the idea to be expressed may refer to the manner, appearance or attitude of mind of the subject. It means also that, whereas *ernsthaft* is used with certain nouns, *ernstlich* is required with the corresponding verb. Thus: *er ist ein ernsthafter* (serious, earnest) *Bewerber für diesen Posten*; but: *er bewirbt sich ernstlich um diesen Posten*. *Ernstlich* here means 'intensively'.

The term 'tendency' was used above to describe this characteristic of *ernsthaft* and *ernstlich*. Germans exhibit, however, a measure of uncertainty in handling *ernsthaft*. Though no one would use *ernsthaft* in the sentence *ich ersuche Sie ernstlich*, one finds it combined with a word like *Warnung*, even though *ernstlich* is felt to be more correct. Similarly, though it is more natural to say *wir müssen uns ernstlich mit Latein beschäftigen* and *Sie müssen ernstlich darüber nachdenken*, *ernsthaft* would not be impossible. On the other hand, *ernsthaft* is sometimes used, not as in the preceding examples, where it can refer to the subject, but where there is no justification for it at all. Thus *Paris ist ernstlich gefährdet* (degree of danger) is the only correct way of expressing this idea. *Ernsthaft*, however, appeared in a number of German accounts of this phase of the 1939–45 war.[1]

> '*Da räusperte sich der ernsthafte Mann und sprach, indem er sich bemühte, in den Ton seiner Stimme recht viel Gewichtiges zu legen*' (E. T. A. Hoffmann, *Die Elixiere des Teufels*).
>
> *Ein ernsthafter Mann ist niemals auffällig angezogen* (an *ernster Mann* might or might not be *auffällig angezogen*).
>
> *Das ist ein ernsthafter Bewerber* (he appears not to be playing with the girl, but to intend marriage).
>
> *Mach' doch kein so ernsthaftes Gesicht* (said lightly to a child).
>
> *Der hat schon ernsthafte Absichten* (impression of observer).
>
> *Ziehen Sie die Angelegenheit in ernsthafte Erwägung* (in such a way as to convince others that you are seriously considering it).
>
> *Das war eine ernsthafte Frage und ich erwarte eine ernsthafte Antwort* (not a joke).
>
> *Seit Monaten habe ich keine ernsthafte Arbeit geleistet* (the results of which could be taken seriously).
>
> *Wir sind in eine ernsthafte Auseinandersetzung verwickelt* (in form, e.g. externally dramatic).
>
> *Ernsthafte Symptome haben sich gezeigt* (visible to anyone, e.g. inflammation; a doctor would say *ernst*).
>
> *Mir als Laien scheint das eine ernsthafte Krankheit zu sein* (but: *der Arzt hat dies für eine ernste Krankheit erklärt*).
>
> *Ihre Halsentzündung dürfte ernsthaft sein, wird ernsthaft.*
>
> *Er sprach ernsthaft mit ihr* (*ernst* impossible because of the addition of *mit ihr*).
>
> *Erst wagte er nicht, ihren Augen zu begegnen, dann blickte er sie ernsthaft an* (with verbs of seeing, looking, *ernst* is more usual as the adverb).
>
> *Er nickte ernsthaft.*
>
> *Er tat ernsthaft bemüht, uns zu helfen* (*ernsthaft* not *ernstlich* because *tat* suggests appearance).
>
> *Er ging ernsthaft an die Arbeit.*
>
> *Aber, ernsthaft gesprochen, wären Sie bereit, einen solchen Schritt zu unternehmen?*
>
> *Nur drei nahmen an der Besprechung ernsthaft teil* (refers to earnestness of purpose, not the vigour of discussion).
>
> *Er hat ganz ernsthaft geantwortet.*

4. Ernstlich differs from *ernsthaft* in that it does not refer to the manner or attitude of mind of the subject (the person), but to the object. It means 'serious' only in the sense that the noun, verb, or adjective to which it is

---

[1] In *Egmont* Goethe makes the character of this name say: '*Wenn ihr das Leben gar zu ernsthaft nehmt, was ist denn dran?*' Referring to *ihr*, not to *Leben*, *ernsthaft* expresses more clearly a reproach than *ernst* would. In present-day German, however, only *ernst* is normally used with *nehmen*.

attached is to be taken in its full, intensive sense. This reference to the object makes *ernstlich* a synonym of 'real', 'genuine'[1] (*ernstlich krank* is hardly more than 'genuinely ill'). Its meaning can thus be explained as 'sufficient', 'appreciable in amount', 'considerable' (e.g. *wir können uns keine ernstliche Herabsetzung der Steuern versprechen*).

For the preferment of *ernstlich* to *ernsthaft* with words which admit the idea of intensity, see *ernsthaft* in **3** above.

Ernstlich is much weaker than *ernst* (which can be applied to the object as well as to the subject) (contrast: *ernste und ernstliche Bedenken*). Consequently it can never mean 'grave'. From its exclusive application to the object it is obvious that it has nothing of the meaning of 'earnest'. It must, however, for lack of a closer equivalent be used to translate 'earnest' with words which in themselves can imply 'earnestness' (e.g. *Ermahnung*).

The meaning of *ernstlich* precludes its application to a person. It is, furthermore, too weak to be used as a predicative adjective.

> *Ziehen Sie die Angelegenheit in ernstliche Erwägung* (real, adequate consideration).
> *Ich hege ernstliche Bedenken, ernstlichen Verdacht, gegen seine Ehrlichkeit.*
> *Ich hege ernstliche Besorgnisse für seine Sicherheit.*
> *Eine ernstliche Warnung, Ermahnung.*
> *Er hat ernstliche Schritte unternommen, um den Verbrecher der Strafe zuzuführen.*
> *Sein Leben schwebt in ernstlicher Gefahr.*
> *Wir sind in einer ernstlichen Auseinandersetzung begriffen.*
> *Der Wind hat ernstlichen Schaden verursacht.*
> *Ich habe ernstliche Gründe, das zu bezweifeln.*
> *Sein Leben ist ernstlich gefährdet.*
> *Die Stadt ist ernstlich bedroht.*
> *Nur drei nahmen ernstlich an der Besprechung teil* (contrast example with *ernsthaft*).
> *Wenn Sie es ernstlich hätten sehen wollen, hätte ich es Ihnen gezeigt.*
> *Er hat ernstlich Lust, dorthin zu gehen.*
> *Ich habe ihn ernstlich dazu angehalten, die Stellung anzunehmen* (vigorously; 'earnestly' would be *ernsthaft*).

5. Schwer is a much used term and translates 'severe' (see article) as well as 'serious' and 'grave'. It is stronger than *ernst, ernstlich, ernsthaft, schlimm, arg* and is combined with the following types of words:

(a) With a word denoting wrong-doing, a mistake, or an accusation with regard to these. It is the only translation of 'serious' and 'grave' used in this combination.

> *Sie haben einen schweren Fehler, Verstoß, begangen.*
> *Er hat sich eines schweren Vertrauensbruches schuldig gemacht.*
> *Sie haben eine schwere Anklage gegen ihn erhoben.*
> *Er hat schwere Schuld auf sich geladen.*

(b) *Schwer* is used of other evils including those to which *ernst* is not applicable and indicates that they are highly oppressive. With regard to sickness it is a medical term (German does not distinguish in this case between 'serious' and 'grave').

> *Schaden, Verlust, Niederlage, Unglück, Unheil.*

---

[1] *Echt* corresponds to 'genuine' only in the sense of 'not spurious'. See 'real'.

(c) As an adverb it is used with verbs of wrong-doing and verbs denoting an objective evil.

Er hat schwer gesündigt.
Er ist schwer verwundet.
Sein Bein ist schwer beschädigt.
Die Schwerkranken.

SERVANT **Dienstbote** in the singular is not used in reference to any specific individual, but in general statements about servants. In the plural it can refer to females. **Dienstmädchen** is a servant girl. It is often abbreviated to *Mädchen*, as the English term is to 'girl', when referring to a specific individual. **Diener** is used only of a big private house; **Bediente(r)**[1] of the house of an important public figure. *Diener* is the only term used metaphorically. **Hausangestellte(r)** is the official term for a domestic, used as a classification. **Personal**: servants, i.e. as a staff.

Seit März haben wir keinen ständigen Dienstboten, kein ständiges Dienstmädchen, bekommen können.
Die Dienstboten haben heute Ausgang.
Der Diener hat gekündigt.
Er ist ein Diener seines Volkes.
Die Schloßbedienten sind augenblicklich mit den Vorbereitungen für das Fest beschäftigt.
Sie ist Hausangestellte.
Das Personal ist mit den Arbeitsbedingungen unzufrieden.

SERVE 1. **Dienen**: to carry out generally the will of a superior; to help a purpose or cause. It is used of persons and things.

Er hat seinem Herrn treu gedient.
Er hat jahrelang dem Staat gedient.
Er dient in der Armee.
Ihre Bemerkungen dienten dazu, viele Irrtümer zu berichtigen.

2. **Bedienen** is only used in the specific senses of attending to customers, acting as waiter at table.[2]

Er hat mich sehr schnell bedient.

SERVICE 1. **Dienst**: work, labour, effort.

Seine Dienste an der guten Sache.
Er bot der Regierung seine Dienste an.
Heeresdienst, Kriegsdienst, Staatsdienst.

2. **Verdienst** (neuter)[3] stresses the achievements that result from labour.
Seine Verdienste um das Vaterland.[4]

SETTLE 1. Sense: make one's home permanently in a place, whether a town, district or country: **sich niederlassen**.

Sie haben sich in Zürich, am Genfer See, in der Schweiz niedergelassen.

---

[1] The older form is: *Bedienstete(r)*.
[2] *Bedienen* also means 'to service' machinery. *Er bedient die Flugzeuge.*
[3] *Der Verdienst*: earnings, gain.
[4] *Sich ein großes Verdienst um etwas erwerben, sich verdient um etwas machen*: to deserve well of.

2. (a) To live in, to bring to a country as a colonist: **(sich) ansiedeln.**
Während des Krieges siedelten die Deutschen viele Holländer in Osteuropa an.
Viele Holländer siedelten sich in Südafrika an.
(b) To colonize a country (i.e. the country as object of the verb): **besiedeln.**
Die Holländer und die Engländer besiedelten Südafrika.
Welche Völker besiedelten Kanada?

3. Sense: decide, determine, agree upon so that further talk is unnecessary (*A.L.*): **entscheiden** (see 'decide'); **ausmachen** (see 'agree'), **erledigen** (deal with a matter so that a decision about it is reached); **in Ordnung bringen** (put in order). See also 'fix'.
Bis jetzt hat sich nichts entschieden.
Es ist bis jetzt noch nichts ausgemacht worden.
Damit ist die Sache erledigt (that settles the matter).
Er muß seine Angelegenheiten in Ordnung bringen.

4. Sense: to pay a bill and the like: **begleichen.**
Er hat die Rechnung, seine Schulden beglichen.

5. To settle with a person in the sense of to come to a financial arrangement: **sich vergleichen mit jdm.**
Er hat sich mit seinen Gläubigern verglichen.

6. Sense: make or become calm, composed, or regular: **beruhigen** (calm nerves, stomach), **sich legen** (abate), **zur Ruhe kommen** (come to rest).
Laß die Aufregung sich legen, zur Ruhe kommen.

7. Sense: unchanging (of weather and the like): **beständig** (see 'constant').
Das Wetter ist im Herbst oft beständiger als im Sommer.

SEVERE,[1] **STERN, STRICT** While 'stern' draws attention to a temper, an attitude of mind, which is characterized by inflexibility, 'severe', even when applied to persons, suggests their acts and the effects of these on a sufferer. It is also used of impersonal agencies which cause pain, distress, and the like. Thus 'stern discipline' makes one think of a temper of mind, while 'severe discipline' makes one think of the effect on those on whom it is imposed.

1. Streng denotes a temper of mind that manifests itself in the character, appearance, utterances, and acts for which a person is responsible. This attitude or temper of mind is, or believes itself to be, in accordance with strict standards. The closest English equivalent is therefore 'stern'. 'Severe' can only be rendered—approximately—by *streng* when it qualifies words which include a reference to a temper of mind as well as to the effects of an action. Since these words are, generally speaking, only those to which 'stern' can be applied, 'severe' does not really correspond to *streng*. Thus: *ein strenger Richter, ein strenger Vater, ein strenges Gesicht,*[2] *ein strenges Urteil, ein strenger Verweis, eine strenge Kritik,* all suggest the temper of mind described above and are more accurately rendered by 'stern' than by 'severe'.

---

[1] Study in conjunction with 'serious' and 'bad'.
[2] *Streng* also translates, as here, 'austere' as a term of praise denoting simplicity, self-denial, self-discipline and the like. This sense, as also that of 'strict' (see later in the article), widens the range of *streng* as compared with 'stern', and at the same time softens some of the implications conveyed forcibly by the latter.

The latter cannot be translated by *streng* in reference to impersonal agencies except those relating to the characteristics and phenomena of winter that are felt as severe or rigorous. The origin of this use is clearly metaphorical and can be seen in the English use of 'stern' as well as 'severe' to characterize winter. For this reason *streng*, unlike 'severe', is not applicable to summer and to heat.

Streng differs, however, from 'stern' in not suggesting the lack of sympathy[1] which can be implied by the latter. It can thus be applied in a good sense to art (e.g. *die Strenge des Georgeschen Stils*; *Bach komponierte in strengem Kontrapunkt*).

The last example could be rendered by 'strict', which is a regular meaning of *streng*. In this sense it implies the same attitude of rigid adherence to a standard.[2] *Ein strenger Lehrer* can thus mean 'a stern' or 'a strict teacher'. Extended to the products of the mind: *im strengen Sinne des Wortes*; *eine strenge Einteilung in Akte*.

Strenge Disziplin (stern, strict).

Eine strenge Strafe.

Ein strenger Befehl.

Eine strenge Regel.

Streng verboten (strictly).

Streng sein gegen, verfahren mit, jemand.

Ein strenger Winter.

Strenge Kälte.

Ein strenger Frost.

Ein strenges Klima.

Eine strenge Prüfung[3] (stern ordeal or strict examination).

Strenger Gehorsam.

Der Befehl wurde streng befolgt.

Das Dokument muß streng geheimgehalten werden.

2. **Hart**, like *streng*, refers to an attitude of mind, and only by inference to unpleasant effects. 'Hard' and even 'harsh'[4,5] are generally closer equivalents than 'severe'. Thus: *eine harte Kritik* (hard, harsh, severe

---

[1] It implies less of admonition, rebuke, and threat than 'stern'. Thus in diplomatic language 'a stern note, warning, answer to Franco' would be normally translated by *scharf*. In human relations, however, with stress on the moral aspect of the rebuke: *das sei dir eine strenge Warnung*.

[2] 'Strikt' can only be used with reference to the giving or carrying out of orders, instructions (e.g. *der Befehl wurde strikt befolgt*). It cannot be applied to persons to characterize their disposition.

[3] See also examples of *Prüfung* with *schwer* (section 3) and *genau* (section 6).

[4] *Harsch*, and *verharscht* are applied only to the outer surface, crust or covering of things, particularly to snow.

[5] The adverbial uses of *hart* rarely correspond to those of 'hard', and mostly mean 'harshly' (e.g. *er behandelte mich sehr hart*; *er spricht hart*). The following are common equivalents of 'hard' used adverbially. (*a*) *Fest*, which should be used when 'hard' means 'firm' (e.g. *etwas fest anfassen*; *jemand fest ansehen*; *fest bei der Arbeit sein*). (*b*) *Tüchtig*, which combines the meanings of 'capable', 'efficient', 'energetic', when applied to persons and their activities, can also, somewhat colloquially, combine the ideas of intensity and amount when applied to words which admit of this combination of meaning. *Er hat seinen Bruder tüchtig geschlagen. Er hat tüchtig gelogen.* It is used in this sense, both adjectivally and adverbially, more widely than 'hard' as the following examples show: *es ist tüchtig warm* (colloquial); *geben Sie mir tüchtig davon*; *essen Sie tüchtig*. (*c*) *Schwer* (see section 3) or *sauer* must be used in the sense of 'arduously' (e.g. *schwer, sauer, arbeiten*; *schwer, sauer, verdientes Geld*). (*d*) See also footnote to *stark* (section 5).

criticism). But it could not be used to translate 'severe damage'. On the other hand, it can, like 'hard', refer to effects which are arduous, painful and the like, provided its use with such nouns expresses one of its other senses, e.g. violence of impact (e.g. *ein harter Schlag*).

Ein harter Mann.
Eine harter Strafe.
Ein harte Urteil.
Harte Bedingungen.
Einen harten Fall tun.
Hartes Kämpfen.
Ein harter Marsch.
Er ist hart bestraft worden.

3. Schwer is a widely used term, which from its literal meaning of 'heavy'[1] develops those of 'difficult to do, to understand, to bear' (physically, mentally, emotionally, morally).[2] It always stresses the effect, which is injurious, onerous, not the attitude of mind of the agent, and corresponds most closely to 'grievous', which is, however, less commonly used than 'severe'. In this sense it is applied not to persons, but to actions and their effects as conditions and the like caused by persons or by impersonal agencies. In accordance with the fundamental meaning of *schwer*, the sufferer feels the effects as a crushing weight, which presses heavily on him, rather than a sharp, intense pain. It is not applied to words meaning 'acute pain' (as distinct from mental suffering). Most of the terms, however, to which it is applicable, are either evils in themselves or clearly imply evil effects.[3] It is therefore not used with words such as *Kälte, Kritik*.

Das sind schwere Bedingungen.
Er hat eine schwere Prüfung (ordeal, not examination), *Krankheit, überstanden.*
Er hat eine schwere Strafe erhalten.
Sie haben eine schwere Niederlage, schwere Verluste, erlitten.
Das war ein schwerer Schlag für ihn.
Der Sturm hat schweren Schaden verursacht.
Er ist schwer verwundet worden.
Die Stadt wurde schwer bombardiert.
Er hat schwer gelitten.

4. Scharf has a wider range of application than 'sharp'.[4] As an approximation to 'severe' it denotes primarily an effect that is felt as sharp or biting. It is applied mainly to the utterances of persons and, to a lesser extent, their actions. In so far as it suggests their attitude, this is subjective,[5] i.e. unlike

---

[1] 'Heavy', though it rather suggests bulk, can approximate in meaning to 'severe' (e.g. *eine schwere Geldstrafe*, heavy or severe). Other examples of *schwer* can also be translated by both terms (e.g. *schwere Verluste, schwer bombardiert*). When 'heavy' refers to clumsiness of the mind or of its expression it should be translated by *schwerfällig* (e.g. *ein schwerfälliger Stil*). For *stark* as a common equivalent see footnote to section **5**.

[2] See 'difficult' and 'serious'.

[3] See also *schlimm* and *arg* under 'bad' as approximate renderings.

[4] *Verschärfen* means 'to intensify' in the sense of 'to make more severe, aggravate' (e.g. *Maßnahmen verschärfen, das Übel verschärfen*). It must be distinguished from *schärfen*, which means: (*a*) to sharpen in the literal sense (e.g. *ein Messer*); (*b*) to sharpen the faculties of the mind.

[5] It is used, for example, with *Hohn, Spott*, but would be translated by 'sharp', 'acid', etc. rather than by 'severe'.

streng, without consciousness of an objective norm, and concerned only with the intensity of the effect on the sufferer. Impersonal agencies with which it may be used must suggest an effect that is biting in its intensity, and are not numerous, principally cold and pain.

Ein scharfer Tadel.
Ein scharfes Urteil abgeben.
Scharfe Kritik.
Eine scharfe Zunge.
Scharfe Maßnahmen.
Das Einfuhrverbot wirkt sich immer schärfer aus.
Scharfe Kälte.
Ein scharfer Schmerz.

5. Stark is a more widely used term than 'strong(ly)' and can express intensity.[1] With words which in themselves admit of this conception it can mean 'severe'. These are mainly (*a*) certain ills of the body, (*b*) natural phenomena such as heat and cold.

Starke Schmerzen.
Starkes Kopfweh.
Starke Kälte.
Eine starke Erkältung.
Starke Hitze.
Ein starker Frost.
Ein starker Hustenanfall.
Er hat stark gelitten.

6. The preceding articles will have shown that the suggested renderings of 'severe' are mere approximations and that in some cases closer English equivalents can be found for the German terms. Examples of the latter not yet noted are: *genau*,[2] *gründlich* in reference to an examination; *anstrengend* (i.e. strenuous) with reference to physical or mental effort (e.g. *ein anstrengender Marsch*); *gänzlich* to translate 'leave severely alone' (see Fowler's comment on this phrase in *Modern English Usage*); *empfindlich*, which means not only 'sensitive' (to stimuli or to pain), 'touchy'[3] with reference to persons, their mind and body (e.g. *eine empfindliche Stelle*, i.e. 'sore') but applies also to the evils which cause intense suffering or pain (e.g. with: *Schaden, Verluste, Kälte, Schmerzen, Schlag*).

With reference to style, aesthetic effect, whether this be pleasing or otherwise, 'severe' is untranslatable (e.g. a severe face, a severe style, severely plain). The dictionaries offer approximations.

SHAKE **1. Schütteln:** to shake about freely, without encountering much resistance. It is said frequently, though not exclusively, of things

---

[1] The idea of intensity is also present when *stark* translates 'heavy' and 'hard'. As an equivalent of 'hard' it suggests energy alone. When it renders 'heavy' it combines the idea of mass, quantity with the idea of energy, pressure. Examples: *es regnet, schneit, friert, stark*; *eine starke Forderung, Nachfrage*; *es bläst sehr stark*. *Stark* is so widely used in this sense that it must often be translated by other English terms (often 'badly', e.g. *er zitterte sehr stark*). Further: *stark geschwollen, erregt, bewegt, sinnlich*. 'Intense', referring to the inner life, is *innig* (e.g. *innige Freude, innig lieben*). 'Greatly' is often an equivalent.

[2] *Genau* means 'exact', but can also indicate the habit of mind called 'punctilious'.

[3] Applied to persons *empfindlich* generally has a bad sense, i.e. 'touchy', but rarely 'sensitive' to beauty, etc. *Empfindsam* is now rarely used, but was common in Goethe's day. It meant 'sentimental' (e.g. *der empfindsame Roman, Werther*, the novels of Richardson).

which can be moved, carried about, i.e. offering no resistance. Applied to emotions it means 'to give a shock, a scare'. It may be followed by prepositional phrases.

Er schüttelte die Erbsen im Topf (or: *aus dem Topf*).

Sie schüttelten den Teppich (or: *den Staub aus dem Teppich*).

Der Wind schüttelte die Bäume.

Der Wind schüttelte die Äpfel vom Baume.

Er schüttelte den Kopf.

Er ergriff den Dieb am Genick und schüttelte ihn heftig.

Der alte Wagen schüttelte uns tüchtig.

Sie schüttelten ihn aus dem Schlaf.

2. Rütteln: to shake something which stands firmly on its base and offers resistance, the sense being 'to try to shake loose, to move'. When the object is a thing of considerable size this verb is normally followed by *an* (i.e. to shake at). With a personal object it is followed by the accusative, often accompanied by a prepositional phrase with *aus* denoting the result of the action.

Er rüttelte an der Tür (to force it open).

Die Krise rüttelt an der bestehenden Ordnung.

Sie rüttelten ihn aus dem Schlaf (stresses the effort more than *schütteln*).

3. Erschüttern: to shake from within, to make the foundations totter, to undermine, with stress on the violence of the action. Its most common use is figurative. When applied to emotions, it means 'to move profoundly', 'to cause an emotional upheaval'.

Ein Erdbeben erschütterte die ganze Stadt.

Der Krieg hat die bestehende Gesellschaftsordnung in ihren Grundfesten erschüttert.

Mein Glaube an ihn ist erschüttert.

Die Nachricht von seinem Tode, der Anblick der Verwüstung, die Schönheit des Sonnenunterganges, hat ihn tief erschüttert.

SHAME (noun and verb), DISGRACE, ASHAMED, SHAMELESS, SHAMEFUL, DISGRACEFUL, BAREFACED

A. Nouns.

1. Scham, Schamgefühl refer to the feeling of humiliation which springs from a consciousness of having offended against standards of propriety, etc.; also to the restraint produced by fear of such humiliation. *Schamgefühl* is more common than *Scham*, except in prepositional phrases (e.g. *vor, aus, Scham*). Where 'sense of shame' is possible in English, *Schamgefühl* is generally used, *Scham* being more elevated in tone.

Scham in the sense of 'disgrace' is obsolete.

Sie errötete vor Scham.

Er hat kein Schamgefühl.

Er hat alles Schamgefühl verloren.

2. Schande is shame in the sense of 'disgrace' (which it also translates),[1] i.e. loss of reputation,[2] also, in predicative use, in the sense of 'a circum-

---

[1] 'Disgrace' in the weaker and older sense of 'disfavour' must be translated by *Ungnade*.

[2] *Schmach* is a synonymous term meaning 'ignominy', i.e. the state of being exposed to an extreme degree of contempt. *Schimpf* is 'insult to one's honour, self-esteem', etc.

stance which brings disgrace to a person', 'a matter for reproach' (it is a shame, disgrace, that...); also 'a person or thing that is a cause or source of disgrace' (*S.O.D.* 6).

Sie lebt in Schande.
Er hat seine ganze Familie in Schande gebracht.
Zu meiner Schande muß ich es gestehen.
Es ist eine Schande, daß er nicht freigesprochen wurde.
Er ist die Schande seiner Familie.

3. Schade, in predicative use, translates 'shame' in its weaker use, i.e. when it approximates to 'pity'[1] (which it also translates).

Wie schade!
Es ist schade, daß wir Sie zu spät verständigten.

B. Verbs.

1. Sich schämen: to be ashamed. 'Ashamed', used otherwise than predicatively after the verb 'to be', must be translated by *beschämt* (see next section).

Ich schäme mich, es gestehen zu müssen.

2. Beschämen: to make ashamed, i.e. to arouse a feeling of shame in a person. The past participle *beschämt* must be used to translate 'ashamed' when not preceded by the verb 'to be'.

Er sah tief beschämt aus.
Beschämt ließ er den Kopf hängen.
Sie beschämen mich (make me feel ashamed, or put me to shame).
Sie beschämen mich mit Ihren Kenntnissen (shame me, put me to shame).

C. Adjectives.

1. Schamlos means 'shameless', i.e. it suggests indifference to disgrace.

Ein schamloser Kerl.
Das ist eine schamlose Forderung.
Er hat ganz schamlos gehandelt.

2. Unverschämt[2] corresponds closely to 'barefaced' and 'brazen', i.e. effrontery in taking or demanding and absence of any attempt to disguise it. It draws attention more to the act, *schamlos* to the attitude of mind behind it.

Ein unverschämter Kerl.
Das ist eine unverschämte Forderung, Lüge.
Er benimmt sich ganz unverschämt.

3. 'Shameful' and 'disgraceful' in its stronger sense are close synonyms. They are translated by **schändlich**, i.e. meriting opprobrium.

Ein schändliches Leben führen.
Eine schändliche Tat.
Ein schändlicher Betrug.

SHAPE, FORM, FIGURE **A.** In visual sense.

'Form' suggests lines, outlines, structure while 'shape', though suggesting these too, also conjures up mass or bulk. However, the latter can emphasize the outlines rather than the bulk and is then practically synonymous with

---

[1] Also: *es ist ein Jammer, daß...*, i.e. something to be regretted.
[2] *Verschämt* means 'feeling shame unnecessarily' mostly in the sense of 'bashful'. *Verschämte Arme*, too proud to beg.

'form'. This is particularly so in the case of parts of the body (e.g. the shape of his nose). **Gestalt** at one time had this double possibility of meaning in German, even up to Goethe's time. In present-day German, however, it is limited to the first meaning, to the whole body whether human or animal and thought of as bulk. Hence it can be applied to a body which appears shadowy and indistinct (e.g. *drei Gestalten wurden allmählich im Nebel sichtbar*). When the outlines of part of a body or the shape of an object are referred to only **Form** is possible in German (e.g. *die Form seiner Nase, seines Gesichts, des Tisches, der Parkanlagen; Wolken in vielerlei Form*). Thus German *Form* often comes closer to *Figur* (figure) and is susceptible of qualification by adjectives (e.g. *eine runde, hagere, schöne, elegante, häßliche Form*). As a technical term in psychology English has borrowed *Gestalt*, sometimes, however, substituting 'configuration' for it. According to *W.S.* this is 'a form which derives its significance not from the various and varying parts or elements which comprise it, but from the pattern they assume when combined so as to be interrelated and integrated'. *W.S.* continues: 'The term is used chiefly, in psychology, in reference to physical, biological and psychological phenomena which affect or manifest the psychical life of the individual; thus a man's personality may be studied as a Gestalt.' In reference to the visual arts both terms are used in German but *Form* is the normal one, *Gestalt* being generally taken as the synthesis of *Form* and *Gehalt*. The same distinction applies to literature, with which we enter the sphere of non-visual application (e.g. *die klassische Form des Dramas; die Form des Sonetts*). A poem which is written or printed in lines of varying length which produce a shape on the page is called a *Bildgedicht* (e.g. some of Zesen's poems in the seventeenth century). The sense of 'mould' is a further development of *Form* (e.g. in *Hutform*).

B. In non-visual sense.

An example of the intermediary use between the visual and non-visual is: *die Form ihrer Bewegungen*. Here, and more so in the completely non-visual sense, the term tends to pass over into the meaning of 'way', 'kind' (e.g. *Staatsform, Regierungsform, Formen der Diktatur, Formen des Zusammenlebens, Religionsformen, Umgangsformen*; also in grammatical terminology: *Formen des Verbums, der Wortfolge, die verkürzte Form des Wortes*). In earlier German *Gestalt* also could be used in this way, with the meaning of *Beschaffenheit, Zustand, Art* (e.g. *die Gestalt des Wetters, nach Gestalt der Dinge*).

Today this use is found only in a few survivals, particularly in phrases meaning 'in such a way' (e.g. *dergestalt, solchergestalt daß...*, phrases much favoured by Kleist). The use of *Form* in connection with the condition of sportsmen is a development of this meaning (e.g. *heute ist er in guter, schlechter Form*). In uses such as: *der Hut hat seine Form verloren; er begrüßte den Präsidenten in aller Form*, the meaning has developed into 'proper', 'due'. *Gestalt* lacks this meaning.

Figur is used like the English 'figure' and is the normal term when referring to the proportions of the human body (e.g. *eine hübsche, wohlproportionierte Figur*).

Wuchs (only singular—see also 'growth') is used of height and 'build' of the human body (e.g. *ein Mann von hohem, kräftigem Wuchs*). Unlike *Figur* it cannot be used with *haben*. It is possible, however, to say: *sie ist schön gewachsen* (has a good figure).

SHARE A. Noun.

1. Both **Teil** and **Anteil**[1] are used in the sense of what is due from one as well as to one. *Anteil* is only possible where the division can be measured exactly or clearly discerned, i.e. with concrete objects and with some activities. *Teil* is vaguer and more general and can therefore refer to intangibles (e.g. qualities). In the sense of 'share' it is neuter.

(a) *Die Frau erhielt ihren Anteil aus dem Vermögen ihres Mannes.*
Er hat seinen Anteil aus der Erbschaft seines Vaters verpraßt.
Ich verlange meinen Anteil an der Beute, an der Geschäftsführung.
Haben Sie Ihren Anteil an dem Kuchen bekommen?
Haben Sie Ihren Anteil an der Entschädigung bekommen?
Er hat seinen Anteil an den Kosten getragen.
Sein Anteil an dem Verbrechen beschränkte sich auf Mitwisserschaft.
Ich habe nur geringen Anteil daran gehabt, ihn durch sein Examen zu bringen.

(b) *Du mußt dein Teil der Arbeit leisten.* (*Anteil* would be more precise.)
Sie haben ihr Teil zu dem Siege beigetragen. (*Anteil* is too precise to be used in such a context.)

2. Portion is common in reference to food.
Er hat seine Portion des Kuchens schon gegessen.

3. Entfallen (without a precise equivalent in English) is often used in the precise sense of *Anteil* in reference both to what one receives and to what is expected of one.
Dieses Stück Kuchen entfällt auf mich.
Die Hälfte der Kosten entfällt auf mich.

4. Note the idiom: *ich habe mein gerüttelt Maß an Leiden gehabt* (my share of suffering).

B. Verb.

Sich teilen in: to share equally. Otherwise **teilen** is used. **Repartieren** is a colloquialism for 'to share equally'.
Wir müssen uns in die Ausgaben teilen (die Ausgaben repartieren).
Wir teilten uns in das Zimmer.
Wir wollen uns in die Verantwortung teilen.
Ich mußte das Zimmer mit ihm teilen.
Wir teilen die Verantwortung für das, was geschehen ist.
Ich teile viele von Ihren Ansichten (sich teilen in is impossible).
Wir haben viele Erlebnisse miteinander geteilt (sich teilen in is impossible).

SHOOT It must be made clear in German whether 'shoot' means 'wound' or 'kill'.

1. Schießen means 'to shoot dead' only as a hunting term (see also *erschießen* in reference to animals, birds, etc.). A personal object must be accompanied by a phrase indicating where the person is shot. It is both transitive and intransitive. When transitive the object can be the missile as well as the person or thing shot at. In intransitive use it has most of the figurative senses of 'shoot'. The subject can also be the weapon. To shoot at =*schießen auf*.

[1] *Anteil* can also mean 'sympathy'.

Still, oder ich schieße!
Ich schoß den Vogel, das Kaninchen, den Löwen.
Er wurde in den Rücken, in den Arm, geschossen.
Er schoß die Pfeile durch die Luft.
Der Gedanke schoß mir durch den Kopf.
Ich schoß auf ihn.
Das Blut schießt ihm zu Kopf.

2. **Erschießen:** to shoot dead (*totschießen*), whether deliberately or by accident. It is applied to animals, birds, and the like in all circumstances other than the hunt.

Er wurde als Spion erschossen.
Ich habe ihn mit Absicht erschossen.
Wir mußten den Hund erschießen.

3. **Anschießen:** to wound on the surface by a bullet (for other uses see the dictionary). Intention is not necessarily implied.

Er ist angeschossen worden.

SHORTEN, ABBREVIATE, ABRIDGE, CURTAIL   1. **Kürzen** strongly suggests direct intervention, particularly, not exclusively, in an unfavourable sense, and generally with a personal subject. The implication is thus frequently: to reduce, to cut down, to curtail,[1] a thing in a way unwelcome to a person. But in reference to written material it can be used without these implications in the sense of 'to abridge'. Used of objects, e.g., it simply means 'to cut a piece off'.

Verkürzen often suggests that the reduction is the result of circumstances, habit, or the like, rather than of direct personal intervention.[2] In this case the subject is normally a thing. When the subject is a person, the reduction is more often favourable than the reverse, particularly with reference to time, i.e. to shorten a period of time for someone. Applied to objects *verkürzen* suggests an adjustment, not simply the cutting-off of a piece. In adjectival use, the distinction tends to be obliterated.

In reference to objects, in the sense of 'to cut off a piece', **kürzer machen** is more common, particularly in conversation.

Er hat das Tuch, den Mantel, gekürzt, kürzer gemacht.
'*...man verlängerte, man verkürzte die Steigbügel*' (Goethe, *Novelle*) (*kürzte* could only mean: cut off a piece).
Sie müssen Ihren Artikel kürzen (not *verkürzen*, because drastic intervention is implied).
Der Artikel erschien in gekürzter, verkürzter, Form.
Neue gekürzte Ausgabe (abridged).
Das Stück wurde in gekürzter Form gespielt (abridged).
Ich muß Ihnen leider Ihre Ferien, Ihren Urlaub, kürzen.
Wir haben Ihnen die Wartezeit, die Dienstzeit, verkürzt.
Durch den Erlaß des Königs wurde dem Gefangenen die Gefängnisstrafe verkürzt (*gekürzt* impossible).

[1] *Kürzen* is in this sense a common equivalent of 'to reduce', 'cut', i.e. in reference to an allowance or share of a thing. *Die Löhne, die Rationen, sind wieder gekürzt worden.* By transference it is also applied occasionally—somewhat loosely—to the person. *Wir sind wieder gekürzt worden.* See 'reduce'.
[2] *Verkürzen* also translates 'reduce' as a result of circumstances. *Scharfe Konkurrenz verkürzte das Einkommen aller Geschäftsleute* (here in an unfavourable sense).

Der Alkohol hat ihm das Leben verkürzt (gekürzt impossible).
Sein munteres Treiben verkürzte uns die Zeit.

2. Abkürzen is used in two ways. (*a*) To abbreviate, i.e. to represent the whole by a part, which becomes either a sign or the skeleton of the whole. (*b*) To cut a thing short in time so that it remains incomplete.[1]

Kürzen Sie dieses Wort ab.

Das ist ein abgekürztes Verfahren (e.g. legal procedure as shortened in a court martial).

Das Drama wurde in abgekürzter Form gespielt (only in skeleton outline, more drastic than 'abridge').

Ich mußte leider die Unterredung, meinen Aufenthalt, abkürzen.

3. Zusammenstreichen implies a radical cut in reference to written matter.

Sie müssen den Artikel, das Stück, stark zusammenstreichen.

SHOW: *Zeigen* and its compounds refer to the external act, while *weisen* and *erweisen* stress the content or attitude of mind from which an act proceeds.[2]

1. Zeigen is the most general term. It means primarily 'to bring a thing before a person's eye', or 'a quality, etc. before one's notice', and then 'to show how a thing is done', whether this be a physical or mental operation, 'to make a truth manifest'. The subject can be a person or a thing.

Ich zeigte ihm das Buch.

Er zeigte viel Begabung fürs Zeichnen.

Er hat sich sehr dankbar gezeigt.

Ich zeigte ihm, wie ich zu dem Ergebnis kam.

Die Folgen zeigen, daß er sehr unbedacht handelte.

2. Bezeigen only means 'to make an emotion or an attitude visible'. In drawing attention to the external act or token by which this is done it approximates to 'evince'. It sometimes suggests ceremony. *Zeigen* can also be used in this case, but does not emphasize the manner of the act.

Er bezeigte ein großes Verlangen, die Heimat wieder zu sehen.

Sie bezeigten ihm viel Ehre.

3. Erzeigen and **erweisen**, which are often interchanged, mean 'to show a person one's attitude' by doing something for him. In some cases 'do' is a more appropriate translation. In discriminating use the following distinction can be made: *erzeigen* concentrates attention rather on the external act, which is mostly ceremonial, *erweisen* on the attitude of mind. A noun which denotes one clear act is therefore preferable (though not obligatory) with *erzeigen*.[3]

---

[1] With other objects 'curtail' is often translated by *einschränken* (e.g. *Ausgaben, Rechte, einschränken*). See 'limit'.

[2] This distinction is evident also in *hinzeigen auf* and *hinweisen auf etwas*. Both mean 'to point out', 'to point to...', the first more in reference to a visible thing, the second to a fact, truth, etc.

[3] *Erweisen* also means 'to prove', and differs from *beweisen* in stressing the result (i.e. one of the senses of *er*). The meaning is thus 'to prove a thing so that it becomes absolutely clear, evident' (e.g. *seine Schuld ist einwandfrei, klar, erwiesen*). In this use it is commonest in the passive voice. *Sich erweisen als* = to prove, turn out, to be; particularly in reference to a quality. *Nachweisen* means 'to prove step by step', by tracing, tracking down evidence,

Sie haben ihm Barmherzigkeit, viel Gefälligkeit, erwiesen.
Sie haben ihm Ehre erwiesen, erzeigt.

4. Weisen is 'to impart instruction by showing', and is generally translated by 'direct', 'instruct.'[1] It is rendered by 'show' only in the sense of 'show out', i.e. expel.[2]

Er wurde zur Tür hinaus, aus dem Hause, gewiesen.

SIGN Zeichen is a 'clear sign' of any kind, the meaning of which is understood or established. **Anzeichen** is a 'symptom', an 'intimation' of something to come which may or may not be recognized and interpreted aright.

Das Licht gab das Zeichen zum Weiterfahren.
Was bedeuten die verschiedenen Zeichen auf diesem Blatt?
Wenn nicht alle Anzeichen trügen, wird es bald eine Lebensmittelknappheit geben.
Die Anzeichen einer politischen Krise häufen sich.
Das sind die Zeichen einer politischen Krise.

SILENCE Stillschweigen is used of deliberate silence, often enjoined on one, in order to exclude others from knowledge of a matter, and therefore only of human beings. **Schweigen** is a more general term, and can be applied to any kind of silence, deliberate (in which case it is unemphatic), of human beings, animals, or nature.[3]

Er hat Stillschweigen darüber bewahrt.
Stillschweigen wurde ihm auferlegt.
Ich kann mir sein Schweigen nicht erklären.
Er hat sich in Schweigen gehüllt.
Das Schweigen des Waldes ließ phantastische Bilder in seiner Seele aufsteigen.

SIMPLE Einfach has all the meanings of 'simple' except (*a*) that of guileless (with heart, soul, and the like), and (*b*) that of simple-minded. These meanings are both rendered by **einfältig**.[4] In reference to the heart and the mind *einfach* only means uncomplicated.

Er ist eine einfältige Seele.
Er ist ein einfältiger Mensch (simple-minded; *einfach* would mean 'uncomplicated' or 'unpretentious' or refer to class).

Schlicht means 'simple' with reference to the sensuous impression given off by a person or thing, while *einfach* is purely objective. *Schlicht* can therefore mean 'simple' in appearance but not necessarily in reality.

Er ist ein schlichter Mann.
Die Königin trug ein schlichtes Kleid (*einfach* would mean simple as an objective fact).

by demonstration, particularly by furnishing evidence in the form of documents (e.g. *seine Herkunft nachweisen*). Sometimes 'demonstrate' is a more appropriate equivalent than 'prove'.

[1] Hence *anweisen* (to instruct), *zurechtweisen, verweisen* (to reprimand).

[2] Hence *ausweisen, verweisen* (to expel).

[3] As a verb *stillschweigen* is both more emphatic and more familiar than *schweigen*, and like the noun most commonly suggests an order. *Schweig! still*, e.g. said to a child. *Stillschweigend* used adjectivally means 'tacit' (e.g. *ein stillschweigendes Abkommen*). *Schweigsam*, silent, refers to a trait of character.

[4] Distinguish from *albern*, which means 'silly in a drivelling way, fatuous'.

Er hat einen schlichten Glauben (einfach: uncomplicated, easy to understand).

SINGLE[1] **1. Einzig** means 'one only'.[2] In this sense it also translates 'only' (used adjectivally) and 'sole'.

Ein einziges Beispiel genügt.

Er ist von einem einzigen Gedanken beherrscht.

Er hat kein einziges Wort gesagt.

Nach dem Luftangriff blieb kein einziges Haus unversehrt.

2. Einzeln means 'individual', i.e. taken separately, by itself, in relation to the parts of a whole or to a number. See article on 'separate'.

Die Bände werden einzeln verkauft (singly or separately).

Die Zeugen wurden einzeln verhört.

3. Einzel is also used in a number of compound nouns in the sense: for or with one person or thing. *Einzelteile* means 'single parts' in the sense of *Ersatzteile*.

Einzelzimmer, Einzelkabine, Einzelbett, Einzelgänger.

4. In the sense of 'not double' or 'multiple' **einfach** is used.[3] *Ein einfaches Geleise, eine einfache Fahrkarte* (not return), *eine einfache Nelke*. **Ein** occurs in a number of compound adjectives. *Eingleisig* (e.g. *Strecke*), *einäugig*, *einbettig*.

5. In the sense of 'unmarried' **unverheiratet** (see article on 'marry') is the most general term. **Alleinstehend** is often used officially of a woman,[4] less commonly of a man.

SINK **1.** Intransitive.

(a) **Sinken** is used literally and figuratively in most senses of 'sink'.

Das Schiff, die Temperatur, die Sonne (poetically), *sinkt.*

Er ist in meiner Achtung gesunken.

Sein Mut ist gesunken.

(b) **Versinken** is used (*a*) literally in the sense of 'to disappear beneath the surface' of a thing, particularly by being sucked under; (*b*) figuratively in the sense of 'to be completely absorbed into a state and to lose consciousness of everything else'. When the preposition *in* follows in the literal sense, it governs the dative case.

Er ist im Schlamm, im Flugsand, versunken.

Er ist in Melancholie, in die Betrachtung der Landschaft, versunken.

2. Transitive.

(a) **Senken:** to lower a thing gradually, both literally and figuratively. It must frequently be rendered into English by 'lower'.[5]

Er senkte die Angel ins Wasser, den Kopf.

Der Baum senkt seine Wurzeln in die Erde.

(b) **Versenken:** to sink a thing so that it disappears completely and irrevocably.[6] It does not necessarily suggest gradualness of the process, but rather

---

[1] German has no close equivalent for the sense of 'sincere', e.g. single-hearted.

[2] *Einzigartig* means 'unique'.

[3] See article on 'simple'.

[4] *Ledig* is used in fixed combinations.

[5] Example: *er senkte den Eimer in den Brunnen.*

[6] As with *senken* 'lower' is a more frequent English equivalent. *Der Sarg wurde in die Erde versenkt.*

the result. In figurative use it is reflexive, and means 'to allow oneself to be absorbed' in a thing (compare *versinken* (*b*)).

Nach dem ersten Weltkrieg wurde die deutsche Flotte bei Scapa Flow versenkt.

Er versenkte sich in seine Arbeit.

SLIP (literal sense) **1.** To lose one's footing: **ausgleiten.**[1] More colloquially **(aus)rutschen** (also = skid).

Er glitt auf dem Eise aus.

2. To move easily, often unobserved, into or through a thing: **schlüpfen.**

Er schlüpfte in das Loch, in seine Kleider.

Der Gefangene schlüpfte an der Wache vorbei.

Der Aal schlüpfte ihm durch die Finger.

SOFT, GENTLE, TENDER, DELICATE, MILD **1. Weich** means in its literal sense 'yielding to pressure, soft as a tactile sensation', i.e. not hard. Applied to the impression of the other senses and to feelings it conveys the same suggestion. In reference to sound it thus means 'insinuating', 'not harsh'. It does not mean 'low, not loud' (e.g. he spoke softly).

Weiches Haar, weich wie Seide, ein weiches Bett, ein weiches Ei, weiche Wiesen, ein weicher Himmel, ein weiches Blau, weiche Linien, eine weiche Stimme, weiche Klänge, weich sprechen (see *leise*), *ein weiches Herz.*

2. Sanft suggests in both literal and figurative use (*a*) lightness of contact, and (*b*) pleasurable, often soothing,[2] sensations arising from such contact. Its closest English equivalent is 'gentle', i.e. not rough, violent.

Er berührte sie sanft.

Ein sanfter Druck, sanfte Gewalt.

Er klopfte sanft an die Tür.

Eine sanfte Stimme, ein sanftes Blau, ein sanfter Wind, ein sanfter Regen.

3. Sacht is the Low German form of *sanft* (both cognate with 'soft'), but is not always interchangeable with it. In reference to gentle contact it is a more popular and vigorous term than *sanft*, and, unlike the latter, can also be applied to movement or activity in the sense of 'steady', 'not precipitate'.

Er berührte sie sachte.

Sachte, sachte! Nicht übereilt!

4. Zart means in the literal sense 'fragile, easily cut or broken', and figuratively 'impressionable', particularly in the sense of 'vulnerable', 'sensitive to pain'. Its chief implication is passive receptivity, and in this sense it corresponds closely to 'tender' and 'delicate'.[3] It does not mean 'tender' in the active sense of 'loving, affectionate'.

Zartes Fleisch, zarte Haut, eine zarte Gesundheit,[4] *ein zartes Gewebe, ein*

---

[1] Glide: *gleiten*. 'Slide' has no exact equivalent in German and must be translated according to whether it approximates more closely to 'slip' or 'glide'.

[2] *Besänftigen*: to soothe.

[3] *Delikat* in figurative use means 'delicate' in the sense of 'tactful' (applied to persons) and 'requiring tact' (applied to things). Examples: *Sie müssen hier sehr delikat vorgehen*; *eine delikate Angelegenheit*. In literal use it is applied to food and drink.

[4] 'To be delicate', i.e. of frail constitution, is *schwächlich sein*. 'Tender' in the sense of 'sore' is *empfindlich*. Example: *Die Haut ist an dieser Stelle sehr empfindlich*. See 'severe'.

zartes Gemüt, eine zarte Stimmung, zarte Farben, eine zarte Stimme, ein zartes Gedicht.

Sie müssen ihn zart behandeln.

5. **Zärtlich** means 'tender' only in the sense of 'loving, affectionate'.
Zärtliche Gefühle, Liebe.
Sie flüsterten zärtlich miteinander.

6. **Leise** has the general sense of 'barely perceptible', faint. Applied to sound it means 'soft' in the sense of 'low, not loud'.
Ein leises Geräusch, eine leise Stimme, leise Musik.
Er sprach, klopfte, leise.

7. **Mild**, like English 'mild', means 'not severe or harsh'.[1] It is applied to an agent which because of its lack of intensity or severity affects us painlessly or even pleasurably.
Mildes Wetter, ein mildes Klima, milde Luft, eine milde Strafe.
Er urteilt sehr mild.

8. **Gelind(e)** means 'gentle or mild enough to cause no pain',[2] but not 'pleasurable' (contrast *sanft*). Attention is concentrated more on the effect, whereas *mild* suggests rather a property of the agent.
Ein gelinder Wind, Regen, Verweis, eine gelinde Strafe.

SOIL See also 'ground'.

1. Firm land, earth, ground (*W.*): **Boden, Erde**.
Zu unseren Füßen der heilige Boden, über uns die Sonne (W.).

2. The upper layer of earth that may be dug or ploughed; spec. the loose surface material of the earth in which plants grow usually consisting of disintegrated rock with an admixture of organic matter and soluble salts (*W.*): **Boden, Erde**. The second of these is the preferred term for loose portions and where there is no cultivation.
Der Boden war hart, weil wir Frost hatten.
Der Boden ist hier sehr sandig, lehmig, fruchtbar (also Erde).
Alluvialboden.
Lockere Erde.
Eine Handvoll Erde.
Blut-und-Boden-Mystik.

3. Cultivated or tilled ground (*W.*): **Boden, Erdboden, Acker**. For the latter see 'field' under 'meadow'.
Generationen haben hier den (Erd)boden, den Acker bearbeitet, gepflügt, bestellt.

4. **Scholle**, a clod of earth, is used in a more extended sense particularly in poetic contexts to denote the earth, soil or ground in so far as one cultivates it or is attached to it.
Er hängt an der Scholle.

5. Native soil, native land: **Heimat, heimatliche Scholle** (*Erde*).
Er verließ seine Heimat, heimatliche Scholle (Erde), um nie wieder zurückzukehren.

[1] *Mild*, unlike the English term, can in certain combinations mean 'kind, charitable'. Example: *milde Gaben*.
[2] *Lindern*: to assuage pain.

6. A medium in which something takes hold and develops, i.e. a figurative use: **Boden.**

Länder, in denen es so viel Elend gibt, sind fruchtbarer Boden für kommunistische Unterwanderung (W.).

SOME (adjective) **1.** With singular nouns.

Sense: a certain unspecified amount, part, degree, or extent of something, frequently implying 'not a little, considerable'. See *S.O.D.*

(a) **Etwas** suggests a quantity that is more or less measurable, while **einig** (declined) is much vaguer. The result of this distinction is that *etwas* is generally restrictive, meaning 'just a little', whereas *einig* means 'more than a little'. Hence, only *einig* is possible in such sentences as: *eine Stadt von einiger Bedeutung*; *er stand in einiger Entfernung*; *nach einiger Zeit*. The sense here approaches 'considerable'. On the other hand only *etwas* is correct in a sentence such as: *haben Sie doch etwas Mitleid mit ihm* (a plea for just a little pity).

Applied to substances, *etwas* is the normal term. *Einig* is sometimes used, but generally only of things that do not form one compact mass, but consist of separate parts (e.g. *einiges Geld, einiges Getreide*).

Er braucht noch etwas Übung (just a little).

Er braucht noch einige Übung (more than a little).

Geben Sie mir noch etwas Zeit, und ich werde alles erledigen (*einig* is impossible in a restrictive statement of this kind).

Es wird noch einige Zeit dauern, bis ich Ihre Angelegenheit erledigen kann.

Bei einigem Fleiß werden Sie es erreichen.

Mit etwas mehr Fleiß werden Sie es erreichen.

Ich habe die Sache mit etwas, einiger, Besorgnis beobachtet.

Ich brauche etwas Fleisch, Brot, Butter, für das Mittagessen.

In der Kanne ist noch etwas Tee.

(b) In some cases neither of the above terms is applicable. The sentence may be turned to use *etwas* as a pronoun or an adverb.

Es wäre gut, noch etwas über den Vorfall zu berichten (to give some account).

Sie müssen ihm das schon etwas auseinandersetzen, aber sagen Sie nicht zu viel (some explanation is necessary).

2. With plural nouns.

Sense: a certain number of; a few at least. See *S.O.D.*

Einige in the plural is more restrictive than in the singular. It corresponds to 'a few' and is used when 'some' is practically interchangeable with 'a few'. **Manche** means 'a considerable number', and is used when the intention is not to restrict the reference to a few.[1]

Die Regierung beklagte sich darüber, daß manche Mitglieder der Opposition aus jeder Angelegenheit eine Parteifrage machen wollen.

Manche müssen sterben, damit andere leben.

Ich weiß, daß manche Studenten mit dem Lehrplan unzufrieden sind.

Einige Worte über den Plan müssen genügen.

In jedem Jahrgang gibt es nur einige Studenten, die wirklich begabt sind.

Ich habe diese Woche einige Briefe aus Deutschland bekommen.

---

[1] *Manche* does not mean 'many'. *Manchmal* means 'sometimes', and can be modified by *nur*. It does not mean 'often', as is wrongly stated in some dictionaries and grammars. *Einigemal*: a few times.

SOPHISTICATED, UNSOPHISTICATED 1. German has no equivalent term and can only use approximations, which tend to render one or more aspects but not all. The English term expresses not only an intellectual superiority but a detachment which comes from an experience of and familiarity with a large number of things, particularly when it is applied directly to people. Applied to things it often acquires the sense of subtle and ingenious.

(a) **Weltklug:** possessing experience and knowledge of the world and of people. **Weltgewandt:** dexterous, because of experience of the world.
Sie benimmt sich immer sehr weltgewandt.

(b) **Artistisch:** possessing a clever and complicated technique. Applied to a work of art (and not to be confused with *künstlerisch*, artistic).
Thomas Manns 'Dr Faustus' ist ein sehr artistisches Buch.

(c) **Raffiniert** does not mean 'refined', but 'subtle', often in a cunning way, applied to both people and things. **Verfeinert**, refined, of things, a more dignified term. **Differenziert**, subtly differentiated.
Das war eine raffinierte Methode, ihn zu einem Geständnis zu bringen.
Verfeinerte (differenzierte) Methoden sind notwendig, um schwer sichtbare Objekte zu ermitteln (W.).
Immer mehr verfeinerte Instrumente werden erfunden.

(d) **Ausgetüftelt** is colloquial and means ingenious and at times far-fetched. It is the opposite of spontaneous.
Das war aber eine ausgetüftelte Antwort.

2. German also has no term for 'unsophisticated'. The most frequent approximation is **naiv** (naive). Care should be taken when using it since Schiller used the term positively to characterize a kind of poetry where the feeling and *Haltung* are natural in the sense of being in harmony with nature, partaking of the qualities of nature and the opposite of which he called *sentimentalisch* (often rendered into English by 'sentimental' or 'reflective').
Der Pfarrer ist sehr naiv.
Er gab eine sehr naive Antwort auf ihre Frage.

SOUND, NOISE 1. **Schall** denotes primarily any sound in so far as it is thought of as vibrations which impinge on the ear. It is therefore used in scientific statements on the nature of sound. Apart from this in contexts which deal with the audibility of sounds it can refer to a clear and strong sound, i.e. ringing or pealing, or to a sound which would have these qualities if it had an unimpeded passage, but which has become muffled (e.g. *ein dumpfer Schall*). In phonetic contexts it means 'a continuous stream of sound'. Finally, it is used figuratively in the sense of 'empty, meaningless sound'.
Die Geschwindigkeit des Schalles ist kleiner als die des Lichts.
Schallanalyse (i.e. a field of study).
Er entfernte sich, so daß der Schall seiner Stimme nicht mehr zu hören war.
Schallmasse.

2. **Laut** is the most general term for sound in so far as it is made by a living being, particularly the human voice. It refers exclusively to audibility, except in the science of phonetics, where qualities may be ascribed to it. In phonetic contexts it means 'individual sound'.
Ich hörte plötzlich einen Laut, und gleich darauf erschien ein Mann.
Er gab keinen Laut von sich.

SOUND

Sprechen Sie diese Laute nach!
Lauttafel (in phonetics).

3. Klang is a musical sound which is distinct and rings and whose vibrations are of equal duration. It is also used within this general sense of the total effect of a number of sounds, in so far as their sensuous quality is thought of as colouring (compare *Klangfarbe*). It is the normal term for the 'sound' of artistic prose and verse. **Ton**, as a musical term, refers to pitch, and corresponds to English 'tone'. When applied outside music to the human voice, it differs from *Klang* in suggesting an emotional attitude, often one felt as unpleasant,[1] whereas *Klang* evokes a sensuous impression that tends to be agreeable.

Der Klang der Geige hielt mich gebannt.
Seine Stimme hat einen warmen Klang.
Der Klang seiner Stimme gefällt mir.
Der Klang dieses Verses erinnert an das Plätschern eines Springbrunnens.
Er untersucht die Klangwerte von Hölderlins Dichtung.
Ich kann schrille Töne nicht ertragen.
Der Ton seiner Stimme geht mir auf die Nerven.
Der Ton der preußischen Stimme liegt dem Süddeutschen nicht.

4. Geräusch is indistinct and not loud. It is the most general term for both 'sound' and 'noise' when these terms have such properties.

Ich hörte ein Geräusch unter meinem Fenster.
Das Geräusch des Telephons weckte mich aus einem tiefen Schlaf. (*Geräusch* can only be applied to the telephone in so far as it is confused or indistinct, e.g. as heard in a semi-conscious state.)
Das Geräusch des Hagels auf dem Dach ist nicht unangenehm.

5. Lärm is 'noise' in so far as the latter is loud and continuous.

Der Lärm auf den Straßen läßt mich nachts nicht schlafen.
Es entstand ein ohrenbetäubender Lärm in dem Haus.

6. When the above terms are inapplicable, a specific term must be used. This will most often be a substantival infinitive, e.g. *Dröhnen, Klingeln, Läuten,*[2] *Rauschen, Brausen.*

Das Rauschen der Wellen am Strand regt immer meine Phantasie an.

SPARE Many former senses of 'spare' have now become obsolete. In a number of cases it has survived more in the negative than in the positive use (e.g. he does not spare himself, he spared no efforts). In certain negative uses, too, it only appears in fixed phrases.

A connection in meaning exists between *sparen* in the sense of 'save' and the practically obsolete sense of 'spare': 'not to use'.

A. To abstain from hurting, damaging, destroying, inflicting evils of any kind on people.

1. With one object.

(a) Schonen: to treat carefully (really *schön behandeln*). It suggests actual doing, using, and in such a way that one abstains from inflicting harm, etc. on the object (contrast the idea of abstention implied in *verschonen*).

---

[1] *Ton* can also refer to the manner of speaking, the actual sound not being given prominence. In this use it need not be unpleasant. *Er antwortete in ruhigem Tone.*

[2] *Klingeln*: 'ringing' in the sense of a series of sounds in quick succession, as the buzzing of a telephone. *Läuten*: 'ringing' as separate strokes, as of a church bell.

It translates 'spare' only with a personal object or a word meaning 'feelings' in the sense of 'to spare a person's feelings'. Used reflexively or with a thing as object it means 'to look after'.[1]

Sie müssen ihn, seine Gefühle, schonen.

(b) **Verschonen:** to abstain from inflicting physical harm, destruction which one is in a position to inflict. It can imply the sparing of a person's life.[2] Whereas *schonen* suggests treatment with care or consideration, *verschonen* emphasizes abstention from all action. It is not used reflexively.

Der Sieger verschonte die Besiegten.

Der Krieg verschonte diese schöne Stadt nicht.

Der Tod verschont niemanden.

2. With two objects (to spare someone something).

(a) **Verschonen:** to abstain from bothering, boring a person with a thing. It is used mainly in reference to trivial matters.

Verschonen Sie mich mit diesem Geschwätz (said impatiently).

(b) **Ersparen** is used in more serious matters and where deep feeling is involved. As a reflexive verb it cannot be used in the imperative (see *sparen*).

Ersparen Sie mir die Erzählung vom Tode Ihres Kindes (the story would affect me too deeply; *verschonen Sie mich mit*...: it would bore me).

Ersparen Sie mir den Verdruß, diesen Kummer.

Er hätte sich die Unannehmlichkeiten, die Mühe, die Kosten, ersparen können.

(c) **Sparen** is in this sense only used reflexively. It suggests something of a reproach or a rebuke, whereas *ersparen* makes a simple statement, which may be friendly in tone.[3] However, as a translation of the English reflexive imperative, only *sparen* is possible.

Er hätte sich die Mühe, die Kosten sparen können.

Sparen Sie sich den Verdruß.

B. To abstain from using.

'Spare' and *sparen mit* are sometimes used negatively in this sense, *sparen mit* also positively in contexts with a more emotional connotation (mostly with immaterial things). To translate the positive sense English uses 'to be sparing with', German *sparsam umgehen mit*.

Sparen Sie nicht mit der Butter.

Gehen Sie sparsam mit der Butter um.

C. To abstain from expending. *Sparen* is used negatively (with *kein*) with words such as *Kosten, Aufwand, Mühe, Fleiß*. In this sense *scheuen* is a synonymous term.

Er hat keine Mühe gespart (gescheut).

D. To abstain from demanding exhausting efforts from a person (mostly negative). German uses specific terms.

Er ist hart gegen sich selbst; mutet sich sehr viel zu (he doesn't spare himself).

Er stellt starke Ansprüche an seine Truppen (does not spare).

[1] *Er schont sich* (his health), *seine Gesundheit, ein Buch.*

[2] When the idea of 'sparing one's life' is to be made explicit German uses a specific term. *Schenken Sie mir das Leben* (spare me my life). *Wenn ihm noch einige Monate geschenkt sind* (if he is spared...).

[3] Both *sparen* and *ersparen* are also used in the sense of 'to save money', the former being an objective statement, the latter suggesting the attitude of mind or manner of living associated with the action of saving.

E. To give, to lend, out of a sufficiency or superabundance. German uses specific terms such as *übrig haben, entbehren.*
Haben Sie ein paar Minuten für mich übrig?
Können Sie das Buch bis morgen entbehren?

SPEND (time) **1. Verbringen** is the general term. It cannot, however, be used with *wie lange* as object.
Ich habe meine Ferien am Meer verbracht.
Er hat eine schlaflose Nacht verbracht.
Er hat drei Jahre im Gefängnis verbracht.
Ich verbringe jeden Sonntag bei ihnen.

2. Zubringen suggests that what one does or thinks absorbs one. It cannot, therefore, be used with phrases that suggest inactivity or idle pursuits. It is normal with *wie lange* as object.
Er hat 5 Jahre mit seiner Doktorarbeit zugebracht.
'*Die letzte Nacht, die ich in dem großen Spiegelsaale zubrachte, wo die Leiche des Prinzen aufgebahrt stand, lag mir eine liebliche, oder soll ich sagen traurige oder lächerliche Szene im Sinne, ich spreche von der Maiwiese*' (R. Huch, *Die Maiwiese*).
Wie lange haben Sie in Rom zugebracht?
Er hat den letzten Tag seiner Ferien in Gesellschaft seiner Freunde zugebracht.

SPIT Spucken is the normal term in the sense of 'to eject saliva or anything else from the mouth'. **Speien** means in its literal sense 'to vomit'. Figuratively, as applied to persons, mainly in fixed phrases it means 'to spit, emit' fire, sparks, and the like, as an expression of a feeling. It is used, further, of things which seem to do this.
Er spuckte auf den Fußboden, ohne sich um andere Leute zu kümmern.
Er spie Gift und Galle.
Die Geschütze spien Feuer und Flamme.

SPREAD With each of the following verbs it is necessary to determine whether the sense is (*a*) to extend over an area, without increasing the area, or (*b*) to increase the area concerned.

1. Breiten, ausbreiten: to spread one thing over another, the form with *aus*, like 'out' in English heightening the impression of extent. Only the context can decide whether an increase in area is meant. *Feuer*, e.g. admits only the idea of increase. Whether the increase is real or imaginary, it proceeds on all sides, i.e. not only in one direction, unless this is expressly stated. Both simple verb and compound suggest something poetical, ceremonious, or at least of considerable proportions, or that the action is performed with care and with attention to the various parts of the object (e.g. a map). Another sense of *sich ausbreiten* is 'to spread oneself' over a subject.
Der Baum breitet seine Zweige weit über die Rasenfläche.
Der Teppich wurde ausgebreitet.
Der Vogel breitet seine Flügel aus.
Das Feuer hat sich ausgebreitet.
Der Wald breitet sich bis zum Fluß aus.
Das Meer breitete sich vor uns aus.

Wir breiteten Karte aus.
Breiten Sie sich nicht zu sehr aus.

2. **Legen** or a similar verb must be used in reference to trivial things.
Wir legten den Teppich auf den Fußboden, die Decken auf das Bett, die Taschentücher auf das Gras.

3. **Streichen** and **schmieren**: to spread a substance over a thing, e.g. butter on bread, ointment on a wound.

4. **Übergreifen auf**: to spread from one thing to another, rather in one direction than in all, unless the latter is stated. It is used of such things as fire, disease, i.e. whose advance it is difficult to halt.
Das Feuer greift auf das Nebengebäude über.
Der Krebs greift auf andere Organe über.

5. **Verbreiten**: to diffuse,[1] to disseminate over a wide area, mostly with spaces between the points which diffusion reaches (unlike *ausbreiten*). It is applied to intangibles as well as to people and things. *Sich verbreiten über*...also has the meaning of 'to spread oneself at great length over' a subject.
Meine Freunde sind über das ganze Land verbreitet.
Die Angelsachsen haben sich fast über die ganze Erde verbreitet.
Er hat das Gerücht, die Nachricht, in weiten Kreisen verbreitet.
Diese Sitte hat sich überall verbreitet.
Der Geruch verbreitete sich sehr schnell.

6. **Verteilen**: to distribute at fixed intervals over space or time.[2] *Verbreiten* does not suggest deliberately fixed intervals, but the vague idea of diffusion.
Die Befestigungen waren über eine weite Fläche verteilt.
Sie können die Zahlungen über einige Jahre verteilen.

7. **Dehnen** means in its literal sense 'to stretch[3] a thing lengthwise so that it becomes longer' (e.g. elastic). In figurative use it does not mean 'to increase the length', but 'to be so extensive as to call for comment'. There may be spaces between the various parts.
Das britische Reich dehnt sich über die halbe Welt.

8. **Ausdehnen**: to increase the size of, to extend, to expand.[4] It is used particularly of land and of spheres of power, of operation.

9. **Streuen** must be used to translate 'spread' in the sense of 'strew', i.e. with masses of loose particles such as sand.
Er streute Sand über das Blut.

STAFF 1. **Personal** is the most general term and is usual with reference to any commercial undertaking or in any office.
Das Personal fordert bessere Arbeitsbedingungen.
Er hat eine Menge Personal abbauen müssen.

[1] *Breit* means in figurative use 'diffuse' (e.g. of a style).
[2] 'To spread out' in reference to small things is rarely *verteilen*. *Machen Sie die Abstände zwischen den Pflanzen größer* (spread the plants out more).
[3] *Sich erstrecken*: to extend or stretch lengthwise, without increase. It is used of large geographical features and of time. *Reichen*: to stretch or reach, of smaller things. *Der Garten reicht bis zum Fluß. Das Seil reicht nicht weit genug.*
[4] *Erweitern*: to extend, to expand, i.e. with increase. It is used mainly of intangibles (e.g. *Kenntnisse, Machtsphäre*).

2. Lehrkörper or **Lehrkräfte:** the teaching staff of a school or university. (A teacher in the context of the teaching strength of the staff may be referred to as a *Lehrkraft*. *Um mit der Studentenzahl fertig zu werden, brauchen wir mehr Lehrkräfte.*)

Der Lehrkörper ist pflichtbewußt und tüchtig.

3. Stab is used in military and industrial contexts, e.g. *der Generalstab.*

Er hat seinen Stab von Mitarbeitern.

STANDARD   1. In the sense of the standard reached: **Niveau;** in the sense of the standard demanded: **Anforderungen** (see 'demand').

Das Niveau der Klasse ist hoch; niedrig.

Er hat hohe Anforderungen gestellt, denen nur in seltenen Fällen entsprochen worden ist.

2. Something that is established by authority, custom, or general consent as a model or example to be followed: criterion, test (*W.*): **Norm.**

Wir kehren immer zu den Schriften der Alten als Norm des wahren Geschmacks zurück (S.O.D.).

3. A measuring rod: **Maßstab.**

Wir legen die üblichen Maßstäbe an.

4. Used adjectivally: **Standard.**

Ein Standardwerk, Standardpreise. But: *Hochdeutsch.*

5. Standard of living: **Lebensstandard.**

STATE (v.), **STATEMENT** According to *W.S.* 'state' 'stresses particularity, clearness and definiteness of detail and suggests the aim of presenting facts, ideas, feelings, etc. in their naked truth so that they will be distinctly understood and fixed in others' minds'. One might add that an assurance of truth is implied. German has no specific and, at the same time, wide term for these suggestions and must therefore use more or less close synonyms. At times one hears the English word 'statement' in German, but at the time of writing I have heard of no attempt to make a verb out of 'state'.

1. Angeben and **Angabe** suggest precision and detail. They also imply that the statement is made by or to an official. Care should be exercised in the use of the verb since it also means (*a*) to boast, show off, (*b*) to denounce.

Nach Angaben der Polizei soll der Täter einen braunen Anzug angehabt haben.

Er hat wissentlich falsche Angaben gemacht.

Der Detektiv hat alle Angaben sorgfältig aufgeschrieben.

Er hat das genaue Gewicht angeben müssen.

Keine genaue Zeit wurde angegeben.

Die Quittung muß die Bezugsquelle der Ware angeben. (Or, of course, *anzeigen*, i.e. indicate.)

Soll und Haben angeben.

Der Inhalt der Urkunde war falsch angegeben worden (S.O.D.).

Beide gaben an, sie seien während der Haft gut behandelt worden.

2. Feststellen and **Feststellung** have two meanings. In the first place the verb means to ascertain, to make sure, to establish something as a fact. Secondly, it means to state something which has been so established and is used, not exclusively, but frequently in reference to statements by someone in authority and says emphatically that a thing is so, even if it is in fact not the case. It often corresponds to the English verb 'note' used by someone in a position to know. See also under 'note'.

Nach Mitteilung der Zollfahndung konnte festgestellt werden (established), *daß das Rauschgift aus Afghanistan stammt.*

Seine Feststellung erwies sich als unbegründet (implies that he believed it was correct).

Die Polizei stellte fest, daß ein Pferd gestohlen worden war.

Zu der Deutschlandfrage stellte der Minister fest, daß alle Parteien sich darüber einig seien (stated or noted).

Vom ägyptischen Außenminister soll er die Feststellung verlangt haben, daß Kairo die Tätigkeit des U.N.O.-Vermittlers Jarring für beendet ansehe (a statement which is a confirmation of a fact).

Der Polizist stellte fest, daß er auf der falschen Seite gefahren war.

Ich habe schon damals festgestellt, daß die Tür nicht geschlossen war, aber erst jetzt habe ich es gesagt (a sentence which shows that this verb does not always imply 'to say').

Ich glaube, der Arzt hat es schon damals festgestellt, hat aber noch nichts darüber gesagt (same comment as on previous example).

Diese Feststellung genügt nicht, ich will Beweise haben.

Diese Feststellung reicht nicht sehr weit.

Ich sage es dir nur so, aber ich will nichts feststellen (do not want to state it as a fact).

3. **Behaupten, Behauptung:** assert, assertion, maintain. A forceful and definite but unproved statement.

Er behauptete, daß er um sieben Uhr fortgegangen sei.

Er hat behauptet, daß er an dem Unternehmen nicht interessiert sei.

Alle seine Behauptungen wurden widerlegt, angezweifelt.

4. **Darlegen, Darlegung:** to expound, exposition, i.e. with attention to the essentials and with a clear line of development of the whole.

Die Frage, das Problem, den Fall hat er sehr klar dargelegt.

Seine Darlegung des Sachverhalts war mustergültig.

5. **Erklärung:** declaration or explanation.

Der Premier Minister gab im Unterhaus eine Erklärung ab, wo die Regierung in der Einwanderungsfrage stehe.

6. **Darstellen, Darstellung:** (give) an account (of), suggesting narrative or description with details. The verb means to present or to represent, as in any of the arts.

Seine Darstellung der Lage hatte viele Lücken.

Seine Darstellung des Falles war nicht ganz unvoreingenommen.

7. A drawing up in words: **formulieren, Formulierung.**

Er hat das Thema sehr genau formuliert.

8. **Mitteilen, Mitteilung:** to communicate, communication. Commonly used of a statement made by an official.

Wie der Sprecher im Unterhaus mitteilte (*nach Mitteilung des Sprechers*) *würde der Premier-Minister um drei Uhr eine wichtige Erklärung abgeben* (*Erklärung*, declaration, also comes close to the sense of 'statement').

9. The enunciation of a theme in a musical composition: no specific term.

Die einleitenden Takte des ersten Satzes, in denen das Horn das erste Thema anschlägt (*ertönen läßt*).

STATE(MENT)

10. A financial record or accounting (*W.*).

Ein Rechnungsauszug: a summary of an account showing credits and debits and the balance at the end of the accounting period (*W.*).

11. Aussagen, Aussage: (*a*) statement of a witness in a court of law (see under 'evidence'); (*b*) expression of a theme in art or literature.

Die Aussage des Angeklagten war schriftlich verfaßt und er unterzeichnete sie.

Er hörte sich die Aussagen der Belastungszeugen genau an.

Der Zeuge hat den Sachverhalt sehr klar ausgesagt.

Dies war die letzte wichtige Aussage des Kubismus.

STATE, CONDITION 'State' is the general term. 'Condition' draws attention to the causes, the circumstances which bring about the condition. It is therefore the appropriate term where accurate measurement is involved (e.g. the patient's condition; the condition of the roads, in the eyes of a road-engineer; the state of the roads, in the eyes of the public). 'Condition' can, unlike 'state', stand for the external circumstances themselves, particularly in the plural.

1. Zustand is the general term, wider than both 'state' and 'condition', but cannot stand directly for external circumstances.[1] In the sense of 'conditions' it is thought of in relation to persons. It is casual and change-able. While it is applied to a person's physical or mental state or condition as controlled by medical intervention, it is not used of activities and opera-tions in so far as they are consciously planned and controlled and conceived of as moving from stage to stage towards a goal, or as it is measured according to an objective standard of fitness, perfection, or the like. In this sense **Stand** (see article on 'position') is the appropriate term. It refers to things and activities, not to persons themselves.

Stand is used in a number of fixed phrases which suggest an objective standard, a level. In reference to things or animals: *gut, schlecht, im Stande sein; in gutem, schlechtem, gehörigem* (and the like) *Stande sein; (gut) im Stande (er)halten; in den (alten) Stand setzen.* In reference to persons: *imstande sein, in den Stand setzen...zu. In der Lage sein...zu* refers rather to the nature of external circumstances.

Der Zustand seiner Gesundheit ist besorgniserregend.

Der Zustand der Straßen ist gefährlich.

Er befindet sich in einem Zustand der höchsten Aufregung.

Der Stand der Forschung ist befriedigend (the stage it has reached; but: *die Forschung befindet sich in einem beklagenswerten Zustand*).

Der Stand der Rüstungen läßt zu wünschen übrig (*Zustand* would indicate a less accurate assessment).

Das Pferd ist gut im Stand (in good condition).

Das Haus wird gut im Stand gehalten.

Obgleich das Haus seit 20 Jahren unbewohnt ist, ist es in gutem Zustand.

Die Zustände in manchen Gefängnissen sind haarsträubend.

2. Verhältnisse, plural (see article on 'relation'), refers to external cir-cumstances in the sense of 'a state of affairs', the nature of the elements or parts of these in relation to each other. It is used particularly of the important activities of life.

---

[1] 'Circumstances' are *Umstände*.

Wie sind die Verhältnisse in China?
Die Wohnverhältnisse sind heute überall besser als vor 50 Jahren.
Die kulturellen Verhältnisse in Deutschland sind als Folge der langen Nazi-
Herrschaft sehr verworren.
Unter den gegenwärtigen Verhältnissen bereitet einem das Reisen wenig Freude.
Er lebt über seine Verhältnisse.

STOP[1] **A.** To bring, come, to a motionless state, of a person, vehicle or any other object in motion.

1. Halten (intransitive only).

Applied to vehicles *halten* suggests a regular, prescribed stop. Applied to persons, it leaves open the question of whether the stop is prescribed or not and also that of its duration.
Die Straßenbahn hält hier.
Ich hielt auf meinem Spaziergang vor dem Schloß.
Halt!
Wir können hier für das Mittagessen halten.

2. Anhalten (transitive and intransitive).

Applied to persons *anhalten* definitely suggests a temporary stop (generally short). With vehicles it indicates in intransitive use a stop that is not prescribed, in transitive use one that is either prescribed or not.
Die Straßenbahn hielt zwischen zwei Haltestellen an.
Das Auto hat vor der Tür angehalten.
Ich hielt vor dem Schloß an und sah mich einen Augenblick um.
Der Lokomotivführer hielt den Zug an.
Ich wurde an der Ecke von einem Bekannten angehalten.

3. Aufhalten (transitive only): either 'to stop permanently', 'to check' or 'to delay', 'to hold up'. Only the context can indicate which sense is intended. The agency which causes the stopping can be an irresistible force or the intervention of authority.
Wir müssen den Feind mit allen Mitteln aufhalten.
Stürmisches Wetter hat das Schiff aufgehalten (held up; see *zurückhalten*).
Der Scheck, der Brief, wurde aufgehalten (held up in transit, e.g. by the censor; see *zurückhalten*).

4. Abhalten (transitive only): to intercept an object or something intangible (often moving through the air) and prevent it from reaching, hitting, or penetrating to its goal, to hold off.
Die Säcke hielten die Kugeln ab.
Die Mauern sind dick genug, um jeden Lärm abzuhalten.
Wir brauchen Vorhänge, die das Licht abhalten.

5. Halt machen suggests a more or less final stop, at any rate a lengthy one.
Die Soldaten mußten vor den Barrikaden haltmachen.
Wir machten beim Wirtshaus halt.

---

[1] 'Stop' comes from the popular Latin *stuppare* = 'to stuff' with oakum or tow (as does 'stuff', German *stopfen*). When it retains this original sense of 'stuff (up)', 'block', it must be translated by such verbs as (*ver*)*stopfen, füllen. Stoppen* tends to be colloquial in the sense of 'stop', but is becoming more and more prevalent. It is used intransitively of a person or thing in quick motion (e.g. of machinery), transitively of a vehicle and of some activities which involve motion.

6. Stehen bleiben, applied to persons and other animate beings, leaves open the question of whether the stop is momentary or not and intentional or not. It definitely implies standing, i.e. not sitting, lying. Applied to vehicles and other machinery, it implies a defect or breaking-down of the machinery (but see **B** for another use).

> *Ich blieb an der Ecke stehen und sah mich um.*
> *Er blieb stehen und legte sich nach einiger Zeit hin.*
> *Nach einer tollen Jagd blieben die Pferde stehen.*
> *Mein Auto ist plötzlich stehen geblieben.*
> *Die Uhr, die Maschine, ist stehen geblieben.*

7. Zum Stehen (Stillstand) bringen (kommen). The phrase with *stehen* means 'to stop a person or a thing in headlong motion' (see *bringen* under 'make'), the one formed with *Stillstand* is applied to objects such as machinery that revolve regularly.

> *Mit Müh' und Not brachte er das Auto zum Stehen.*
> *Er brachte die Maschine, das Mühlrad, zum Stillstand.*

B. 'Not to (be allowed to) begin moving, to leave' (a sense more correctly conveyed by 'stay' in the case of persons).[1]

1. Bleiben, stehen (sitzen, etc.) **bleiben.**

> *Bleiben Sie zum Mittagessen.*
> *Bleiben Sie sitzen.*
> *Dieser Wagen bleibt hier stehen* (will not leave).

2. Zurückhalten: not to allow a thing to start, to be sent.

> *Das Schiff wurde vom stürmischen Wetter im Hafen zurückgehalten.*
> *Der Scheck, der Brief, wurde zurückgehalten.*

C. To cease from an activity. Distinguish whether one stops (*a*) one's own activity, or (*b*) that of someone else. The subject may be animate or inanimate.

1. To stop one's own activity.

(a) **Aufhören** is the most general term and can mean 'to stop' finally or for a certain time. It is used with the infinitive and with *mit* followed by a noun. In combination with *mit* and a verbal noun it is more familiar than with the infinitive.[2]

> *Er hörte auf, zu fragen.*
> *Es hat zu regnen aufgehört.*
> *Hören Sie mit dem Nörgeln auf.*
> *Hören Sie mit dem Unsinn auf.*
> *Der Regen hat aufgehört.*

(b) As a familiar equivalent of 'prevent' in the imperative mood.

> *Tu' doch was, damit das Kind nicht mehr schreit* (*damit die Tür keinen Lärm mehr macht*).

(c) Each of the following compounds of *halten* has a specific sense.

(i) **Einhalten** is used only of something explosive or violent.

> *Er hielt mit dem Fluchen ein.*
> *Die Wilden hielten mit dem Gemetzel, Gebrüll, ein.*

---

[1] Used loosely in the sense of 'sojourn', 'stop' is *sich aufhalten*. To stop and spend some time at an inn = *einkehren*.

[2] *Schluß machen (mit)* indicates a sharp and final stopping. *Lassen* (only in the imperative) is familiar. *Lassen Sie das (das Heulen).*

(ii) **Innehalten** denotes an involuntary, often sudden, cessation. In other uses it has an old-fashioned flavour.

Als er Schüsse von der Straße hörte, hielt er in seiner Rede inne.

(iii) **Anhalten** denotes an act of will.

Er hielt in seiner Rede an, um sich an den Vorsitzenden zu wenden.

2. To stop the activity of someone or something else. German mostly uses specific terms, the only more general ones being *ein Ende machen* (put an end to), *Einhalt tun, gebieten* (stop someone's machinations, manœuvres, and the like in an authoritative way).

Wir müssen ihren Umtrieben ein Ende machen.

Man hätte Hitler gleich am Anfang Einhalt gebieten sollen.

Die Polizei löste die Versammlung auf (dissolved).

Die Polizei verbot die Versammlung (before it started).

Der Regen unterbrach das Spiel (finally or temporarily).

Das Spiel mußte abgebrochen werden (finally).

Das Feuer wurde rechtzeitig gelöscht.

Der Strom wurde abgeschnitten.

Die Zahlungen sind eingestellt worden (suspended).

Sein Gehalt ist suspendiert worden.

Sein Herz hörte zu schlagen auf (elliptical use of 'stopped' in English).

Sein Herz setzte aus (temporarily) (*aussetzen* also of breath and the like).

STRANGE[1] **1. Fremd:** unknown to one, not one's own, out of one's element. It does not necessarily mean 'foreign'.

Diese Handschrift ist mir fremd.

Ich schlief in einem fremden Haus.

Ich sah viele fremde Gesichter.

Er kann nicht auf einem fremden Klavier spielen.

Ich bin hier fremd (a stranger).

Es läuft ein fremder Hund im Garten herum.

2. Sonderbar is a stronger term than **seltsam** (which is connected with *selten*). The latter means little more than 'surprising, unexpected', sometimes with the suggestion that a thing is so because it is rare. No desire to fathom causes or reasons is implied. 'Odd' is sometimes an appropriate translation. *Sonderbar*, on the other hand, strongly suggests this desire, or, again unlike *seltsam*, evokes the sensuous impression of strangeness in the appearance of persons and things and in actions. Thus: *er ist heute etwas sonderbar gewesen* (*seltsam* impossible). *Sonderbar* can mean 'queer'.

The phrases 'it is strange that...', 'I find it strange that...' can be translated by either adjective, but both are strong in this context. *Sonderbar* often implies a reproach. *Ich finde es sonderbar, daß er das verschwieg*, suggests both a reproach and a search for an explanation. *Es ist seltsam, daß er sich zu dem Handel bereit gefunden hat*, means that I would not from my knowledge of him have expected this, but do not rack my brains for the reason. More commonly used terms, are: *merkwürdig* (as weak as 'peculiar'), *komisch* (see article on 'funny'). What is laughable, amusing in its strangeness

---

[1] Study together with 'funny'.

STRANGE

is expressed by *komisch,* not by *sonderbar* or *seltsam* (e.g. *sie trägt die komischsten Hüte,* the strangest hats).[1]

Er sieht sonderbar aus.
Sein Benehmen ist höchst sonderbar.
Ein seltsamer Fremder.
Das ist eine seltsame Beschäftigung.
Das ist ein seltsamer Befehl (sonderbar would engage one's thoughts much more intensively).
Es ist merkwürdig, daß er nicht geschrieben hat (the most commonly used term in conversation).

STREET, ROAD, PATH 1. Straße translates both 'street' and 'road', i.e. in the city and in the open country.[2]

Die Straßen dieser Stadt sind sehr eng.
In dieser Gegend gibt es schöne, breite Autostraßen.

2. Gasse: a small narrow street (often 'lane').

3. Weg translates only 'path', or 'way' in the sense of 'direction', i.e. not 'road'. It mostly denotes a made path.

Ein Gartenweg.
'Der Weg Zurück' (title of a novel by Remarque).
Den falschen Weg einschlagen.
Alle Wege führen nach Rom.

4. Pfad is a path worn by being trodden on, not one marked out and constructed with implements.

Ein Pfad durch den Wald, die Wiese.

STRENGTHEN 1. Stärken: to restore from weakness to normal strength. It is applied particularly to the strengthening of limbs. *Sich stärken* used absolutely means 'to strengthen oneself by liquor'.

Diese Übungen werden Ihr Bein stärken.
Stärken Sie sich ein bißchen, bevor Sie die Reise antreten.
Ich möchte, daß meine Ausführungen dazu beitragen, Ihren Entschluß zu stärken.

2. Verstärken: to strengthen further what is already strong, i.e. to reinforce, the commonest sense of 'strengthen'.

Die Regierung muß durch eine Umbildung des Kabinetts verstärkt werden.
Ein Regiment verstärken (Verstärkungstruppen = reinforcements).
Das wird Ihre Sache (= cause) *verstärken.*
Das verstärkt nur noch meine Entschlossenheit.

3. Bestärken: to strengthen, to confirm in an attitude of mind. It is generally followed by *in* when the object is a person. The object may also be a word meaning 'belief', 'view' and the like.

Das bestärkt ihn in seinem Glauben, Wahn, Entschluß.
Das bestärkt meine Auffassung.

---

[1] *Wunderlich* also means 'strange', 'queer'. Do not confuse with *wunderbar* (wonderful).
[2] In Vienna *Gasse* is often used in the sense of 'street'.

4. Kräftigen:[1] to increase physical energy.

Die Suppe wird Sie schon kräftigen.

Sie müssen sich etwas kräftigen, bevor Sie die Reise antreten.

STRIKE, HIT[2] (literal sense)[3] **1. Schlagen** with a direct object can mean 'to deal deliberately a blow to' a person, animal or thing with the intention of doing harm.[4] It also means 'to propel' a thing with a part of the body or an instrument.

Er schlug ihn so hart, wie er nur konnte.

Er schlug ihn (or: ihm) ins Gesicht.

Er schlug das arme Tier.

Er schlug den Ball gegen die Wand.

2. Schlagen with a prepositional phrase denoting the person or thing struck means (a) to strike deliberately, but without necessarily intending harm; (b) collision or contact[5, 6] which is not deliberate. It does not, however, refer to a collision of vehicles or ships.

Er schlug mit der Faust auf das Pult.

Er schlug mit der Rute auf die Erde.

Er schlug mit dem Kopf auf den Boden.

Er schlug mit dem Kopf gegen die Wand.

Die Bombe, der Blitz, schlug in das Gebäude ein.

Die Wellen schlagen ans Ufer.

3. Collide,[7] with reference to vehicles, etc. Here German uses a variety of terms.

(a) **Fassen** is used of two vehicles, one of which normally runs on rails. Its subject must be the bigger of the two, i.e. ordinarily the one on rails.

Der Zug faßte das Auto.

Das Auto wurde von der Eisenbahn gefaßt.

(b) **Fahren in** is used if the smaller strikes the side of the bigger vehicle on rails or if two vehicles not on rails collide.

Mein Auto fuhr in die Eisenbahn.

Sein Auto fuhr direkt in meines.

(c) **Anfahren** is used of a vehicle which strikes a person or another vehicle.

Er wurde von der Straßenbahn angefahren.

Ich habe das andere Auto leicht angefahren.

---

[1] *Bekräftigen* is now used only metaphorically in the sense of confirming an agreement by some gesture. *Sie haben ihre Versöhnung durch einen Handschlag bekräftigt.*

[2] 'Hit' is treated here as a more colloquial equivalent of 'strike'. If there is any other distinction, it is that 'strike' stresses more the dealing of the blow, 'hit' more the force of the impact. When 'hit' refers exclusively to the reaching of the mark aimed at, it must be translated by *treffen*. See footnote to 'affect'.

[3] Though both 'strike' and *schlagen* are much used figuratively, these uses rarely correspond.

[4] *Hauen* is a more colloquial term for 'hit', 'punch', etc. *Prügeln*: to beat, to give a thrashing. *Klopfen* indicates a more gentle contact, 'to rap', 'to tap', 'to knock at the door'. *Pochen*: to knock with insistence, to thump.

[5] Also in the less literal sense of 'impinge'. *Der Lärm schlug an mein Ohr.*

[6] *Stoßen*: to collide with a sharp jerk or knock. It therefore translates 'knock' thus used (e.g. *er stieß mit dem Kopf gegen die Wand*) and 'thrust' (e.g. *er stieß ihm den Dolch ins Herz*).

[7] To collide: *zusammenstoßen*. *Kollidieren* is used of two moving objects (ships, aircraft); also of a clash of lectures. 'To collide' with an iceberg is *zusammenstoßen* since the iceberg is not conceived as moving in the same way as the ship.

(d) **Auflaufen** followed by *auf* is used when a vehicle or a ship collides with a stationary object which juts up in its path.

Das Schiff lief auf einen Felsen auf.

SUCCESSFUL

Erfolgreich can only be applied to a thing. Of a person: **Erfolg haben**.

Das Unternehmen war erfolgreich.

In allen, was er tut, hat er Erfolg.

Klappen, somewhat colloquial, is used of a thing in the sense of 'to come off'. It is often used with the impersonal *es* as subject and a *mit* phrase.

Der Plan hat geklappt.

Es hat also mit Ihrem Versuch nicht geklappt.

Gelingen, to succeed, with a thing as subject.

Der Plan ist gelungen.

SUFFER 1. Leiden.

(a) To suffer pain (mental or physical), damage, or the like. In this sense it may be transitive or intransitive. *An* or *unter* may follow, the distinction being that with an ailment, whether physical or mental, *an* tends to suggest a permanent state, whereas *unter* suggests 'on one or more occasions'. The distinction is, however, not rigidly observed, *an* only being possible with *Kopfschmerzen*, both with *Halsschmerzen*. With physical ailments *an* tends to prevail. When mental distress is caused by an external agency, i.e. not an illness, only *unter* is used.

Er hat starke Schmerzen, Hunger und Durst, gelitten.

Die Gärten haben in den letzten Wochen gelitten.

Er leidet an Arterienverkalkung (unter impossible).

Er leidet an Größenwahn (unter impossible).

Er leidet an, unter, Größenwahnanfällen.

Er leidet an, unter, Wahnvorstellungen.

Sie leidet unter seinen Sticheleien.

(b) *Leiden*, like 'suffer', also has the sense of 'tolerate', 'allow', 'brook'. In this sense both *leiden* and 'suffer' are somewhat old-fashioned in flavour.[1]

Er leidet keinen Widerspruch.

Die Sache leidet keinen Aufschub.

2. Erleiden: to undergo, to be subjected to an external evil. Only transitive use is possible.

Sie haben eine Niederlage, Verluste, Schaden,[2] Schiffbruch, erlitten.

SUGGEST Most of the German terms are no more than approximations.

1. Sense: to propose for acceptance.

Vorschlagen corresponds to 'propose' rather than 'suggest', but for lack of any other German term must be used to translate the latter.

Er schlug einen Spaziergang, neue Bedingungen, diese Auslegung, vor.

Er schlug mir einen Ausweg aus dem Dilemma vor.

Er schlug vor, daß wir uns um 4 Uhr treffen sollten.

---

[1] *Dulden* is more commonly used in this sense. It means 'to tolerate' (*Er duldet keinen Widerspruch*), 'to endure patiently, with mildness of spirit'. See also 'bear'.

[2] With *Schaden*, *leiden* can also be used.

2. Sense: to cause an idea, which may initiate a train of thought, awaken a desire, lead to action, or the like, to present itself to the mind.[1]

(a) **Bringen** (*auf einen Gedanken, eine Idee*, or the like) is the most general term.

> *Was hat Sie auf diesen Gedanken, diesen Plan gebracht?*
>
> *Seine Geschichten brachten mich darauf, daß ich als Textilfabrikant viel Geld verdienen könnte.*
>
> *Der Rauch brachte uns auf den Gedanken, daß Menschen in der Nähe seien.*

(b) **Nahelegen:** to suggest something to someone as the obvious or natural thing to do.[2] The subject is normally, but not always, a person.

> *Ich legte ihm nahe, daß er sein Geschäft erweitern solle.*
>
> *Es wurde ihm nahegelegt, daß er sein Amt niederlegen solle.*
>
> *Dieses Ereignis legt ein Wort des Dankes nahe.*

(c) **Suggerieren** can only be used in the sense of insinuating a thing into a person's mind by, as it were, hypnotic methods, or by the use of tricks.

> *Sie hat ihm suggeriert, daß er sie hieraten solle.*

(d) **Eingeben** is 'to inspire', i.e. in reference to a suggestion which comes as an inspiration.

> *Ein Erlebnis als Feldarzt hat ihm den Grundgedanken des Gedichts eingegeben.*
>
> '*...seine Durchtriebenheit, die ihm eingab, jeweils nur die dunkelsten Schleichwege zu benutzen*' (Gisevius, *Bis Zum Bitteren Ende*).

(e) **Anregen** means primarily 'to stimulate' (see article on 'excite'). As a rendering of 'suggest' it can only mean 'to prompt the doing or the production of' a thing by stimulating suggestions, i.e. the suggestion must lead to production.

> *Er hat meinen Aufsatz über Rilke, diese Politik, angeregt.*

(f) **Andeuten** is a closer equivalent of 'to indicate' than of 'to suggest', i.e. it is more definite than the latter, and can even convey an order.

> *Er deutete die Form an, die der Artikel haben sollte.*
>
> *Er deutete mir an, daß ich das Geld sofort abholen sollte.*
>
> '*...denn man kann einem Menschen ohne Brutalität andeuten daß er nicht in die Zeit paßt, aber nicht, daß er nicht in die Welt paßt*' (F. Gundolf, *Heinrich von Kleist*).

(g) **Deuten auf:** to point to the existence of something not fully revealed or to something which is likely to become a reality, as knowledge, not as a sensuous experience (see **3**).[3] Often with *hin*.

> *Die letzte Entscheidung deutet auf Krieg (hin).*
>
> *Sein Gesichtsausdruck deutete darauf hin, daß er Angst hatte.*

(h) **Schließen lassen auf:** to allow an inference, which is presented as more definite than with *deuten auf*.

> *Sein Gesichtsausdruck läßt darauf schließen, daß er Angst hat.*
>
> *Schon der Preis läßt darauf schließen, daß Eier sehr knapp geworden sind.*

(i) When 'suggest' implies 'to suggest the desirability or advisability of' a thing **erscheinen lassen als** (see 'appear') with an appropriate adjective may be used.

---

[1] 'A solution suggested itself to me' (i.e. reflexive use): *eine Lösung fiel mir (ohne weiteres) ein.*

[2] *Naheliegen*: to be obvious, to be the natural thing to do. *Die Lösung liegt nahe. Es liegt nahe, ihn des Verbrechens zu beschuldigen.*

[3] *Deuten auf* also means 'to point to' a thing in the literal sense.

SUGGEST

Die Vorsicht läßt diese Maßnahme als ratsam erscheinen.

Die Schönheit des Ortes ließ einen längeren Aufenthalt als wünschenswert erscheinen.

3. Sense: to evoke as a sensuous experience.

(a) **Erinnern an** may be used in the sense that one thing because of its sensuous properties makes one think of another.

Seine Nase und seine Ohren erinnern an ein Kaninchen.

Der Wind erinnerte an einen schluchzenden Menschen.

(b) In reference to the suggestive power of art phrases involving **suggestiv** may be used.

Es ist das Wesen der Kunst, suggestiv zu wirken (to suggest).

Das Suggestiv-Machen einer Stimmung, nicht deren Ausdruck, ist der Lyrik eigen.

(c) **Ahnen lassen** may be used in the sense of 'to suggest as a sensuous experience, particularly in art, the existence of something not fully revealed'. For *ahnen* see footnote to 'suspect' (p. 337, n. 1).

Mörikes Nachtgedichte lassen das Geheimnisvolle der werdenden Natur ahnen.

Das Bild läßt mehr ahnen, als es deutlich darstellt

4. In reference to an accusation **unterstellen** is used in the sense of 'to impute', 'to insinuate'

Wollen Sie mir unterstellen, daß ich lüge?[1]

SUIT, FIT   A. Passen.

1. Used absolutely its general sense is: to be the right thing, either in respect to the requirements of a thing or of circumstances or to the wants of a person. Thus: *ich habe nichts, was passen würde*, which would do, i.e. meet your requirements or those of a thing. This meaning could also imply 'fit'. As an intransitive verb, mostly accompanied by an adverb such as *gut* or *schlecht*, it means 'fit' in a general way in reference to clothes (e.g. *der Anzug, der Hut, paßt gut, schlecht*). The meaning of 'fit' as applied to clothes is given more precisely by *sitzen* (e.g. *der Anzug sitz gut*). *Paßt dir der Anzug?* = is the suit what you want? (does it fit you?). See **A, 2**.

Passen is followed by the simple dative or by prepositions with the shades of meaning explained in the following sections.

2. Followed by the simple dative of the person without preposition *passen* means: to be convenient, either as an arrangement of circumstances or in reference to the structure and the like of a thing.

Die Zeit, die Sie vorschlagen, paßt mir schlecht.

Es paßt mir gar nicht, hier übernachten zu müssen.

Das Haus paßt mir nicht.

Eine solche Stellung würde mir ausgezeichnet passen.

3. Followed by *zu* it is used in two closely related ways:

(a) To match, to harmonize with, i.e. one person or thing with another. Do not confuse with **B**.

Diese Eheleute passen nicht zueinander.

Rot paßt nicht zu ihrer Gesichtsfarbe.

---

[1] More familiar: *soll das heißen, wollen Sie damit sagen, daß ich lüge?*

(b) To be suitable[1] in, for, a certain capacity, function. A close synonym is *sich eignen*. The distinction is that while *sich eignen* stresses inherent qualities, *passen* draws attention to these as they manifest themselves in practice.

Er paßt, eignet sich, nicht für die Rolle.
Er paßt, eignet sich, nicht zum Lehrer.

4. Followed by other prepositions *passen* means 'to fit', i.e. to be of the right size and shape.

Der Deckel paßt genau auf den Topf.
Die Schublade paßt nicht in den Schrank.
Seine Hand paßt nicht in den Handschuh.

B. In reference to clothes 'to suit' in the sense of 'to become' is normally **stehen**. It is generally accompanied by an adverb. A dative of the person follows.

Das Kleid steht ihr gut, schlecht.

C. To agree with, in reference to food: **bekommen**. A dative of the person follows.

Gewürzte Speisen bekommen mir nicht.

D. Transitively, in the sense of 'to adapt' one thing to another: **anpassen**.
Er paßte seine Worte dem Ernst der Lage an.

SUPPORT **Stützen, unterstützen.**

1. Sense: to prop up an object by another in order to keep it from falling. *Stützen* is much more common than *unterstützen*. It is also more active and more vivid. It occurs frequently in the phrase *sich stützen auf*, to support oneself, to be supported, on, by.

Die Brücke, der Stollen, mußte gestützt werden.
Der schwere Zweig wurde von einem Pfahl gestützt.
Ein Haus wird mit Balken gestützt.
Er stützte seine alte Mutter, damit sie leichter die Treppen steigen konnte.
Der Krüppel stützte sich auf seinen Sohn.

2. Figurative sense: to give strength to a plan, argument, and the like *Unterstützen* is used as well as the more active *stützen*. (*Sich*) *stützen auf* is, however, freely used in the sense of 'to base on', 'to be based on'.

Er hat den Plan tatkräftig unterstützt.
Ich unterstütze sein Gesuch.
Er hat seinen Standpunkt mit wohlfundierten Beweisen gestützt.
Er stützte seine Argumente auf zweifelhaftes Material.
Sein Standpunkt stützt sich auf folgende Tatsache.
'Ich war nicht unschuldig daran, seine Kandidatur gegen manche Bedenken im anderen Lager gestützt zu haben' (Schlange-Schöningen, *Am Tage Danach*).

---

[1] The adjectives 'suitable' and 'appropriate' are translated by *passend* and *geeignet*, which derive their meanings from their corresponding verbs. *Passend*, accompanied by an adverb such as *gut* or *schlecht*, can therefore mean 'fitting' in reference to clothes (e.g. *ein gut passendes Kleid*, or more commonly: *ein gut sitzendes Kleid*). 'Fitting' in the sense of 'befitting', 'meet' is *schicklich* (e.g. *eine schickliche Antwort*). *Angemessen*, which is much used, has rather the meaning of 'commensurate' (e.g. *ein angemessener Lohn*).

SUPPORT

3. Sense: to supply with the necessities of life. Only *unterstützen* is possible. But see also 'keep' and 'provide'.

Er muß seine Eltern unterstützen.

SUSPICION, SUSPICIOUS, SUSPECT (verb)   **A.** Suspicion. For 'to have a suspicion' see also 'suspect', **C.**

1. With reference to wrong-doing.

(a) **Verdacht** is a suspicion based on the observation of signs in the object suspected. It therefore tends towards objectivity. It cannot be pluralized.

Er begründete seinen Verdacht mit einer Reihe von Argumenten.

Sein Zögern erregte meinen Verdacht.

Mein Verdacht, daß er es getan hatte, erwies sich als begründet.

(b) **Argwohn,** i.e. *arger Wahn,* is a subjective state of mind due more to character, temperament, prejudice, and the like than to objective signs.

Er hat, hegt, einen unbestimmten Argwohn gegen mich.

2. With reference to a fact, which need not be wrong-doing.

Ahnung: inkling, presentiment. It suggests a glimpse, not a prolonged feeling.

Ich habe eine Ahnung, daß er ungern kommen wird.

Ich hatte keine Ahnung von dem, was geschehen war.

B. Suspicious.

1. Verdächtig is used only in the sense of the adjective 'suspect', i.e. arousing suspicion.

Ein verdächtiger Typ.

Er sieht verdächtig aus.

Seine Beteuerungen kommen mir sehr verdächtig vor.

2. Argwöhnisch:[1] inclined to suspicion, as a permanent characteristic of a person.

Er ist in seinem Alter argwöhnisch geworden.

Er ist so argwöhnisch, daß man ihn nicht belügen kann.

3. Mißtrauisch: suspicious, in the active sense of 'distrustful', with reference to the existence of a thing or to intentions.

Ich bin immer mißtrauisch, wenn er so redet.

Ich war vielleicht zu mißtrauisch gegen ihn.

Ich bin sehr mißtrauisch seinen vorgeblichen Sprachkenntnissen gegenüber.

4. Stutzig, mostly with *werden* or *machen* suggests that one is made or becomes suddenly distrustful. It is somewhat popular.

Die Bemerkung machte mich stutzig.

C. To suspect, to be suspicious of, to have a suspicion. See the meanings of 'suspect' given in *P.O.D.*

1. Im Verdacht haben:[2] to accuse mentally of wrong-doing. The passive 'to be suspected' is translated by *im Verdacht stehen, in Verdacht kommen.* It may be followed by the accusative of the person and the genitive of the thing, a *daß* clause, an infinitive.

---

[1] *Arglos,* 'unsuspecting', is old-fashioned except in a few expressions such as *ein argloses Geschöpf.*

[2] *Verdächtigen:* to throw suspicion on. *Er verdächtigt meine Absichten.* It is, however, used loosely, actively, and particularly passively, in the sense of 'suspect'.

Ich habe ihn, seine Motive, schwer im Verdacht.
Ich habe ihn im Verdacht des Diebstahls.
Er steht im Verdacht des Mordes.
Er wurde in der Nähe der Leiche gesehen und kam folglich in Verdacht des Mordes.
Ich habe ihn im Verdacht, ein Gewohnheitsverbrecher zu sein.
Ich habe ihn im Verdacht, das Geld gestohlen zu haben.

2. Argwöhnen, beargwöhnen. To be disposed, because of one's nature or condition, to see evil, to think evil of. *Beargwöhnen* requires a noun or pronoun object, even when followed by a *daß* clause. *Argwöhnen* can only be followed by a *daß* clause. Neither verb is in common use.

Er beargwöhnt mich des Diebstahls.
Sie beargwöhnen und bestehlen sich gegenseitig.
Er argwöhnt, daß sie böse Absichten haben.
'*Ich redete mit Lotte über die unglaubliche Verblendung des Menschensinns, das einer nicht argwöhnen soll, dahinter müsse was anders stecken, wenn...*'
(Goethe, *Werthers Leiden*).

3. Mißtrauen: 'doubt the innocence of, doubt the genuineness or truth of' (*P.O.D.*). This is a common meaning of suspect.

Ich mißtraue seinen Plänen, seinem Urteil, seinen Fähigkeiten, dem Text.

4. Vermuten: to regard it as probable that a thing is a fact or a truth.[1] It is frequently, but not exclusively, used of wrong-doing.

Ich vermutete eine neue Tücke seinerseits.
Er vermutet sofort böse Absichten unsererseits.
Es wird Mord vermutet.
Ich vermute, daß er nicht kommen wird.
Man würde nichts Ungewöhnliches dahinter vermuten.

SWALLOW 1. Schlucken is the normal verb meaning 'to swallow' in the literal sense, i.e. the action of letting something pass from the mouth to the stomach. It is also used figuratively in the sense of accepting something unpleasant aimed at one from without.

Ich habe beim Schwimmen viel Wasser geschluckt.
Er schluckte die Medizin, obwohl sie bitter war.
Beim Schlucken tun mir die Mandeln weh.
Schluck' mal endlich die Pille.
Er mußte die Vorwürfe schlucken.

2. Schlingen: to swallow ravenously or greedily, without chewing, in a manner suggesting an animal. Manner, not quantity is stressed.

Er schlingt alles, was man ihm vorsetzt, herunter.
Schling' doch nicht so schrecklich (to a child).

3. Verschlucken denotes the completed action, whereas *schlucken* emphasizes the action itself. In the literal sense *verschlucken* therefore means 'to get rid of' a thing, especially when it is unpleasant, or 'to swallow inadvertently'. Figuratively it is used in three main ways: (*a*) to make disappear by opening, metaphorically speaking, the jaws and closing them again (see *verschlingen*); (*b*) to repress feelings, from within; (*c*) to slur sounds.

---

[1] *Vermuten* requires to be distinguished from *ahnen*, which means to have an inkling and suggests that one regards the thing suspected as real or true, not, as with *vermuten*, only probably true. *Ich ahne so etwas wie eine Verschwörung.*

Sich verschlucken: to swallow the wrong way.
Verschluck' mal endlich die Pille.
Er hat den Kern verschluckt.
Die Wellen verschluckten ihn.
Die Dunkelheit verschluckte ihn.
Seine Spielsucht verschluckte sein ganzes Vermögen.
Er verschluckt Worte, wenn er schnell spricht.

4. Verschlingen suggests, like *schlingen*, great avidity, but stresses the completed action and therefore conveys the idea of making a thing disappear quickly. Both literally and figuratively it means 'to devour'. It differs from *verschlucken* in implying, figuratively, greater activity, a reaching forward to seize the object.

Er war so hungrig, daß er alles verschlang, was man ihm vorsetzte.
Ein großer Konzern verschlingt viele kleine Betriebe.
Das Feuer verschlang eine Reihe von Häusern.
Rauchwolken verschlangen ihn.
Die Wellen verschlangen ihn.
Er verschlingt Bücher haufenweise.
Seine Spielsucht verschlang sein ganzes Vermögen.

TAKE I. Nehmen.

A. Literal. The fundamental meaning of *nehmen* is 'to take' something or someone from a place or another person to oneself with one's hand or into one's hand. Some degree of activity, however slight, is generally implied, whether mere voluntary acceptance or, on the other hand, reaching for or going and getting. With the action (in the literal sense) 'to oneself' is associated the purpose 'for oneself'. In extended use the latter idea is more easily perceptible than the former.

The idea of 'to' and 'for' oneself can recede before that of removal from the original position, i.e. before the idea of 'away', which is to be conceived in its vaguest sense, i.e. with no implication whatsoever of destination (unlike 'take' in some important uses). German equivalents of 'from' are accordingly common after *nehmen*. The sense may be (i) that of removal in space, (ii) deprivation. The latter is translated by the simple dative without preposition. *Von* with a person indicates acceptance.

The addition of the dative reflexive pronoun emphasizes the idea of conscious purpose, i.e. for oneself, for one's own use, interest.

The taking of food and drink[1] are considered here as instances of the literal meaning, despite additional associations, because of the distinct action of taking a thing from a place to oneself.

Er nahm das Geld, das ihm gereicht wurde.
Er nahm den Teller vom Tisch.
Er nahm die Briefe aus der Schublade.
Er nahm den Korb auf den Rücken.
Er nahm die Hand aus der Tasche.
Sie nahm das Kind auf die Knie, in ihre Arme.
Das Klavier wurde aus dem Wohnzimmer genommen.
Nehmen Sie diese Stühle weg.
Der Polizist nahm dem Verhafteten die Pistole (weg).

[1] To ask whether one takes tea or coffee or the like, *trinken* is normally used.

Er nahm die Pistole von ihm.
Ich werde mir eine zweite Portion nehmen.
Ich habe Medizin genommen.

B. Some extended uses.

(i) The sense is 'deprive', the idea 'to oneself' being absent, since the subject is not personal.

Ihre schwer erkämpften Rechte wurden ihnen wieder genommen.
Wir dürfen uns unsere Freiheit nicht ein zweites Mal nehmen lassen.
Die Nachricht hat mir alle Freude an dem Ausflug genommen.

(ii) The sense: take for use or interest. 'Take' is, however, more widely employed in this sense.

(a) To hire, to engage, to buy, a person or thing; to occupy; to accept; to seize; to capture; to steal; to seize something non-tangible; to borrow words, ideas, and the like; to ascertain a measurement. The manner of taking is left vague.

Wir nahmen das Haus auf drei Wochen.
Ich habe einen neuen Sekretär genommen.
Er nahm einen Autobus zum Bahnhof.
Er nahm sie zur Frau.
Nehmen Sie Platz.
Die Stadt ist genommen worden (in military language).
Die Diebe nahmen alles, was sie nur finden konnten.
Er nahm eine Karte für die Oper, eine Fahrkarte nach Berlin.
Sie nahm den Schleier.
Er nimmt Stunden, Unterricht.
Diese Stelle wurde aus einem früheren Werk genommen.
Ich habe mir die Freiheit genommen, den Fehler zu verbessern.

(b) To perform an action denoted or suggested by the noun objects. The range of such expressions is less wide than in the case of 'take', partly because of the capacity of English to use verbs as nouns (e.g. to take a look,[1] a kick at...). Even where a suitable German noun exists, some verb other than *nehmen* is, however, often preferred (e.g. *Maßnahmen treffen,*[2] *Schritte tun*).

Ein Bad, eine Wendung, einen Anlauf, den Weg nach dem Fluß, neh-
men.

(c) A mental or emotional attitude. The sense is passive rather than active.

(i) To accept as (not to be confused with *halten für,* i.e. consider as).

Ich nehme ihn als vollgültig.
Ich nehme ihn so wie er ist.
Ich nehme es für ein günstiges Zeichen.

(ii) To react in an emotional way, in fixed phrases. This sense needs to be distinguished carefully from that of interpreting in a certain way (see *auffassen,* **IV**(a) below).

Etwas ernst, leicht, schwer, (sich) zu Herzen, nehmen.
Anstoß, Ärgernis nehmen.

---

[1] But Middle High German: *er nam im mange schouwe/an mislichen buochen* (*Der Arme Heinrich*).
[2] *Nehmen* is sometimes found with *Maßnahmen,* but is clumsy because of its relation to *nahme.*

(d) *Nehmen* is sometimes followed by a preposition and the reflexive pronoun where English can either add or omit the prepositional phrase. The following are common:[1]

(i) *An sich* in the sense of 'to arrogate to oneself'.

Er hat alle Macht an sich genommen.

(ii) *Auf sich* in the sense of 'to accept', 'to assume', something onerous.

Die Verantwortung, die Folgen, auf sich nehmen.

(iii) *Zu sich* in the meaning of 'to eat', and in a number of fixed expressions (e.g. *der Herr hat ihn zu sich genommen*).

II. Some compounds of *nehmen*.

In certain cases German uses only a specific term (here a compound) where English uses either the general term 'take' or a specific verb (e.g. to take, to accept a challenge). Thus while it is possible to say in English: 'he took, accepted, adopted, the suggestion' (with differing shades of meaning), German only says: *er nahm den Vorschlag an*. In other cases German, like English, uses both the simple verb and the compound (with differing shades of meaning). In the following list indications as to whether the simple verb can also be used are added.[2]

(a) **Annehmen:** to take on, to accept, to adopt, to assume, to absorb on to the outside of a thing. The addition of *an* often suggests beyond the act of taking that of keeping. See article on 'accept'.

Eine Herausforderung annehmen.

Einen anderen Namen annehmen.

Einen anderen Glauben annehmen.

Der Stoff nimmt die Farbe gut an.

(b) **Aufnehmen** implies the taking of someone or something into something else or something connected with the subject, whether this idea is made explicit in a prepositional phrase or not. See article on 'accept'.

Er nahm ihn in sein Geschäft auf (also *nahm*).

Das Protokoll aufnehmen (also *nehmen*).

Der Saal nimmt niemand mehr auf.

(c) **Benehmen:** to take away in the sense of depriving a person of the free use or enjoyment of something. The object cannot be a concrete object. *Nehmen* is used in the same sense, but expresses the idea less absolutely.

Jemandem die Aussicht, alle Gelegenheit, den Atem, die Sprache, den Appetit, den Schlaf, benehmen.

(d) **Einnehmen:** to capture, to take food or drink (on official instructions, e.g. on the label of a medicine bottle), to take a seat, to adopt an attitude (with *Haltung, Standpunkt*, and the like). The addition of *ein* expresses the idea of thoroughness and importance.

Die Festung wurde eingenommen (*genommen* also).

Diese Medizin muß dreimal täglich eingenommen werden (*nehmen* is the ordinary human term).

Der König nahm seinen Platz ein (but: *nahm Platz*).

Er hat eine unverständliche Haltung eingenommen.

[1] *Nehmen* is of course used to form numerous fixed phrases. Expressions involving the preposition *in* are common (e.g. *in Anspruch, Schutz, Miete nehmen*).

[2] *Abnehmen* is normally rendered into English by 'relieve', the sense being 'to take from'. *Kann ich Ihnen einige Pakete abnehmen?*

(e) **Entnehmen.** The only common uses[1] are figurative. (i) To infer, (ii) to take information and the like from a source, to borrow it.

Ich habe aus Ihren Worten entnommen, daß Sie jetzt anders denken.

Ich habe alle diese Tatsachen einem Nachschlagewerk entnommen.

(f) **Festnehmen**: to apprehend, to arrest formally.

Der Dieb wurde festgenommen.

(g) **Hinnehmen**: to take something unpleasant passively, to accept it. See article on 'accept'. It should be distinguished from a closely related use of 'take': to have something inflicted on one, to suffer, without adopting any attitude towards it (e.g. Berlin took terrible punishment from allied air-attacks).

Wir können eine solche Niederlage nicht ohne weiteres hinnehmen.

Er nahm das von uns hin (without demur).

(h) **Übernehmen**: to take over, primarily from someone else, but also in the more general sense of 'to assume'.

Können Sie jetzt die Aufsicht übernehmen?

Sie müssen die Verantwortung, Verpflichtungen, übernehmen (or: *auf sich nehmen*).

III. Convey to a destination.

The simple verb *nehmen* cannot be used in this sense.

(a) **Bringen**, the most general term, 'means to take to a destination and then leave'. It is accordingly not used in the sense of 'take' a person to a place of entertainment and remain there with him or her. It corresponds to this sense of 'take' because, unlike the English 'bring', it does not necessarily suggest that the destination is the place where the speaker is when he uses the word 'bring'.[2]

Ich werde ihn an den Bahnhof bringen.

Sie brachte die Kinder von England nach Amerika.

Das Schiff brachte die Flüchtlinge in ihre neue Heimat.

Ich brachte ihm die Bücher, um die er gebeten hatte.

Bringen Sie ihm bitte diesen Brief so schnell wie möglich.

(b) **Mitbringen**, to bring, to take, with one, in the literal sense can suggest a friendly attitude of mind, and is used typically of taking a gift to a person. *Bringen* does not imply a gift.

Sie brachten ihr ein Geschenk mit.

Willst du mir ein paar Flaschen Wein aus der Stadt mitbringen? (not necessarily a gift).

(c) **Mitnehmen**: take with one on foot or in a vehicle, suggests a friendly relationship and can mean: to give a person a 'lift' to his destination, to take out or with one for entertainment.

Kann ich Sie in meinem Wagen mitnehmen?

Wir haben ihn auf unseren Ausflug mitgenommen.

Er nahm sie ins Theater mit.

Sie nimmt die Kinder immer mit, wenn sie ausgeht.

(d) **Führen** suggests a leader in the sense that he knows more than those he leads about what he shows them or that he is officially acting as host or guide. In this sense it can refer to entertainment. It is also applied to the relation between author and reader.

---

[1] *Entnehmen* is sometimes used in the sense of 'to take' goods from a dealer.
[2] *Bringen* is a much wider term than 'bring'.

Er führte uns durch das Museum (*bringen* would suggest a destination, to reach which it was necessary to pass through the museum).

Der Botschafter führte den ausländischen Gast in eine Aufführung von 'Figaros Hochzeit'.

Die Handlung der 'Penthesilea' führt uns auf den Kampfplatz vor Troja.

Thomas Mann führt uns im 'Zauberberg' durch die ganze europäische Welt der Vorkriegszeit.

(e) **Tragen**, to carry, i.e. in the hand or on some other part of the body, is frequently used for carrying things a short distance, e.g. about the house when weight or manner is implied. English generally uses 'take' if no idea of weight or manner is conveyed (e.g. take this tray into the next room; carry...carefully...).[1] *Tragen* can refer to the weight a vehicle is capable of supporting, but unlike 'carry' is not used in the sense of transporting goods by vehicle. It can, however, be used of a ship or an aeroplane with reference to the carrying of people.

Wir müssen den Tisch in das andere Zimmer hinübertragen.

Tragen Sie bitte die Teller sorgfältig ins Eßzimmer hinüber.

Der Portier hat Ihr Gepäck in Ihr Zimmer getragen.

Er trug den Brief auf die Post, sein Geld auf die Bank.

Das Flugzeug trug ihn schnell nach Amerika.

(f) **Befördern:** to transport goods in an organized way, by a firm, the railways, and the like.[2]

Die Eisenbahn wird diese Güter befördern.

IV. Some extended meanings of 'take' not rendered by *nehmen* or its compounds. The aim of the following list is to point out these meanings rather than to discuss exhaustively their German equivalents. The German terms given are merely the commonest of a number of possible translations.

(a) To interpret in a certain way: *auffassen* (see 'sense'). *Nehmen* is used in a closely related sense, but means to take more passively, also emotionally.

Wie soll ich diese Bemerkung auffassen?

Er faßte die Bemerkung anders auf.

(b) Not to be able to take a thing with equanimity: *vertragen* (see 'bear').

Er verträgt keinen Spaß, wenig Wein.

(c) To derive an emotional experience from: *finden*.

Er findet Freude, Vergnügen, an Ihrem Hiersein.

(d) To conceive an emotional attitude towards: *fassen*.

Diese Familie hat eine Neigung zu ihm gefaßt.

(e) To require: *erfordern* (see 'demand') is the most general term with an impersonal subject. *In Anspruch nehmen* (see 'claim'), for which *nehmen* alone is occasionally used, means: to draw heavily on time or energy. *Dauern* (see 'last'), used impersonally, is applied to time. *Brauchen* is used with a personal subject.

Der Plan würde viel Zeit, Geld, Energie, erfordern (also *kosten*).

Die Reise hat viel Zeit, Energie, in Anspruch genommen.

Es dauerte nicht sehr lange, bis ich das Buch fand.

Ich brauchte nur zwei Stunden für die Fahrt.

---

[1] See also 'move'.

[2] *Befördern* also means 'to promote' a person to a higher position. In earlier German it was sometimes used in the sense of 'to further', 'to advance', i.e. of *fördern*.

TASTE **1. Schmecken** suggests sensitiveness to flavour. It can mean (*a*) to perceive the taste of a thing; (*b*) to test the taste of a thing. The first meaning is sometimes rendered by using *schmecken* intransitively.[1]

While *schmecken* in sense (*b*) suggests a connoisseur (compare *Feinschmecker*), **abschmecken** can be used of anyone and means 'to test during the process of cooking whether the ingredients and quantities are correct'. It does not suggest the testing of subtle flavours.

(a) *Ich schmeckte den Knoblauch im Salat (heraus).*

Man kann nichts schmecken, wenn man eine Erkältung hat.

(b) *Schmecken Sie diesen guten Wein.*

Eine gute Köchin muß abschmecken können.

Schmecken Sie jetzt die Suppe ab.

2. Kosten only means 'to test the taste of' a thing. In conversation it is apt to sound pretentious or genteel and is better replaced by *probieren* or *versuchen* (see 'try out', 'test').

Sie müssen diesen Käse kosten, probieren.

3. Both *schmecken* and *kosten* are used figuratively. *Schmecken* suggests greater sensitiveness, but *kosten* is more common, particularly in conversation. Both may be ironical.

Er hat das Glück, die Freude, gekostet.

'*Wer die anderen Tage geschmeckt hat, die bösen, die mit den Gichtanfällen . . .*'
    (H. Hesse, *Der Steppenwolf*).

4. In the sense of 'to eat or to drink a small quantity of' *essen* or *trinken* must be used.

Ich habe seit 3 Tagen nichts gegessen (tasted food).

TEACH **1. Lehren**[2] draws attention to the teacher and to the subject rather than to methods of instruction. It is used of imparting knowledge, skills, behaviour, and attitudes of mind, admitting with the latter both a personal and impersonal subject. With reference to knowledge it suggests an authority in the subject as teacher, and is accordingly used regularly of a university teacher, but rarely of a school teacher or private coach. In reference to skills (e.g. swimming, singing) it is applied to a superior (e.g. *mein Vater lehrte mich reiten*) when no question of systematic lessons arises. When ascribed to a teacher other than of the kinds mentioned, it sounds pretentious. Its use with the dative is gaining ground in popular speech.

It cannot be used in the passive with a personal subject.

Er lehrt an der technischen Hochschule.

Er lehrt Geschichte in Wien.

Er lehrte mich schwimmen.

Er, die Erfahrung, lehrte mich die Dinge anders sehen.

Die Geduld kann nicht gelehrt werden.

---

[1] Of the verbs treated in this article only *schmecken* can be used intransitively in the sense of 'taste'. *Der Wein schmeckt süß, sauer.* Followed by the dative of the person *schmecken* can be turned by 'like', 'enjoy'. *Der Wein, das Gemüse, hat mir geschmeckt. Lassen Sie es sich gut schmecken* (enjoy it).

[2] *Belehren* also concentrates attention on the teacher as a superior and means (*a*) to correct an error (with personal object); (*b*) to preach at, of someone given to correcting faults in others. *Er belehrte uns über die wahre Sachlage* (which we had mistaken). *Sie lassen sich nicht belehren. Er will immer belehren.* English has no exact equivalent.

TEACH

2. Unterrichten (and *Unterricht geben, nehmen*) refers to methods of instruction, with regard to both knowledge and skills, and therefore suggests a school teacher or a paid private coach.

Er unterrichtet Geschichte an einem Gymnasium.
Er unterrichtet mich in Geschichte.
Er hat mir Schwimmunterricht gegeben.
Sie nimmt Gesangunterricht (in a small way, *Gesangstunden* refers to something more ambitious).

3. Beibringen is the most modest of the three terms. It means: to get a thing into a person's head, to make him see; to train a person or an animal in a skill. It is therefore used of casual instruction or help.

Er hat mir Deutsch, Tanzen, beigebracht.
Hast du dem Hund diesen Trick beigebracht?

TEASE Necken is an intimate and affectionate term, and can easily suggest affectionate physical contact. For this reason it is not normally used in conversation. For the latter purpose **aufziehen** is the commonest term. **Hänseln** is not quite as strong. **Veräppeln** is a slang term for *aufziehen*.

Er neckt sie sehr gern.
      '*Uns aber neckten von fern und lockten*
         Freundliche Stimmen....'   (Mörike, *Peregrina*).
Seine Gutgläubigkeit gab uns manche Gelegenheit, ihn aufzuziehen.
Den haben wir heute schrecklich aufgezogen, veräppelt.

TEMPT,[1] ENTICE, ALLURE 1. Versuchen is strong and always serious, but not necessarily in a bad sense. Except in a few fixed phrases, it is used in the sense of 'tempt' only in the passive voice. It is not a common term.

Das Schicksal, die Vorsehung, versuchen.
Bei dem schönen Wetter fühlte ich mich stark versucht, meine Arbeit zu vernachlässigen und auszugehen.
Ich bin versucht, Ihr Angebot anzunehmen.

2. In Versuchung kommen, bringen are used more freely in conversation and ordinary prose than *versuchen*. They cannot be used with *Schicksal, Vorsehung* and the like.

Jedesmal, wenn ich hier bin, komme ich in Versuchung, nicht mehr wegzugehen.

3. Locken and **verlocken** both mean 'entice' and 'allure', and because of the restricted range of application of the above verbs are often used to translate 'tempt'. Both suggest a strong appeal, but *verlocken*, unlike *locken*, is applied to something conceived as bad. *Locken*, on the other hand, unlike *verlocken*, can mean 'to entice' a person to a place. *Verlocken* differs again from *locken* in that it can be followed by an infinitive. 'Tempting' used adjectivally is *verlockend*.

Die Speise, Ihr Angebot, lockt mich sehr.
Wir haben den Feind in eine Falle gelockt.
Das schöne Wetter lockte uns hinaus.
Das schöne Wetter verlockte uns auszugehen.
Ich war verlockt, seinen Ratschlägen zu folgen.
Die Qualität des Weines verlockte mich, zu viel davon zu trinken.
Der Posten ist sehr verlockend.

---

[1] See also *reizen* under 'charm'.

4. Große Lust haben may be used of trivial things, particularly with reference to oneself and in the present tense. The addition of *große* to *Lust haben* suggests hesitation, which may, however, be merely polite or deferential.[1]

> *Ich habe große Lust, ein zweites Stück Torte zu essen, aber ich muß darauf verzichten.*

TERM   1. (a) Sense: a word or expression that has a precisely limited meaning in some uses or is peculiar to a science, art, profession, trade or special subject, German has no exact equivalent but uses **Wort, Ausdruck, Begriff** (concept); for 'technical term' it says **Fachausdruck** or **terminus technicus**.

> *Das ist ein juristischer, philosophischer Fachausdruck.*
> *Wir haben keinen Ausdruck (kein Wort) dafür.*
> *Im englischen gibt es diesen Begriff nicht.*

(b) When 'term' means no more than 'word', *Wort* or **Bezeichnung** (designation) should be used.

> *Er lobte sie in überschwenglichen, begeisterten Worten.*
> *Das ist eine passende Bezeichnung für einen solchen Fall.*

2. Sense: a fixed period of time.

(a) At school, university: **Semester, Trimester**, according to whether the year falls into two or three terms.

(b) A term of imprisonment: **Gefängnisstrafe**.

> *Er hat eine Gefängnisstrafe von fünf Jahren bekommen.*

(c) A term in any office: **Amtszeit**.

> *Die zweite Regierungsamtszeit des Präsidenten.*

3. Sense: conditions: **Bedingungen**.

> *Solche Bedingungen sind unannehmbar.*
> *Nur unter solchen Bedingungen könnte ich zustimmen.*
> *Die Bedingungen des Waffenstillstands waren hart.*

4. Sense: relation, footing: see 'relation(ship)' for **Beziehung** and **Verhältnis**.

> *Sie haben freundschaftliche Beziehungen zueinander* (are on friendly terms...).

5. Sense: price, charge. **Preis, Tarif.**

> *Der Preis, der Tarif in diesem Hotel ist 50 DM. pro Tag.*

6. The phrase 'in terms of' is variously rendered into German: **im Sinne von, von...her, nach.**

> *Unschuldig im Sinne der Anklage.*
> *Er beurteilt die Situation von der Ethik her.*
> *Er sieht alles vom Gelde her.*
> *Den Anforderungen nach ist er ungeeignet für die Stelle.*

THANK   1. Danken is the general term in the sense of 'to express gratitude' to a person for something. **Sich bedanken** (*bei jdm.*) is a formal expression of thanks, either spoken or written. It is not used, however, in the first person of the present tense, i.e. in addressing the person to whom thanks are due.

> *Ich danke Ihnen sehr für Ihre Hilfe.*
> *Ich bedankte mich und ging weg.*
> *Ich möchte mich für das Paket bedanken.*

---

[1] *Ich habe keine Lust dazu*: it does not tempt me.

2. 'Have to thank' in the sense of 'owe'[1] is translated both by **danken** and **verdanken**. The distinction is that *danken* merely expresses a consequence, while *verdanken* denotes also the intention. Further, *danken* mostly indicates an unfavourable consequence, which is sometimes expressed ironically.

Meine Stellung habe ich ihm, seinen Bemühungen für mich, zu verdanken.

Dieses Buch verdankt seine Entstehung einer Anregung meines alten Lehrers.

Sein unstetes Leben dankt er den gespannten Verhältnissen des Elternhauses.

'...*wenn man merkt wie sehr Kleists Zeitgemäßheit seiner Abnormität selbst zu danken ist*' (F. Gundolf, *Heinrich von Kleist*).

THEN **1. Dann** has all the meanings of 'then' except 'at that time', i.e. in the past. The latter meaning can only be translated by **damals**.

Dann ging er weg.

Dann müssen Sie sich fragen, ob es viel Zweck hat.

Was soll ich dann tun?[2] (that being so, under those circumstances).

Wenn er mir die nötigen Versicherungen gibt, dann kann er es haben (on that condition).

Dann wollen Sie es mir verbieten (as is to be inferred).

Damals war er sehr arm (at that time).

Der damalige Sekretär schrieb den Brief.

2. Neither *dann* nor *damals* can be preceded by a preposition. In some cases other adverbs are possible.

Seither, seitdem (since then); *bis dahin* (till then).

THERE When the meaning is 'clearly away from the speaker' or when pointing *dort* is the strictly correct term. **Da** can mean close at hand, here. This distinction, however, is observed more scrupulously in Austria than in Germany. In the sense of in the matter, *da* is correct. *Da* can also mean 'then', i.e. following something.

Ich war dort, habe ihn aber nicht gesehen.

Er ging dorthin.

Dort steht er.

Ist er schon da? (here, present).

Ich war in letzter Zeit in Berlin und habe dort viel Theater gesehen.

Da ist Ihr Bleistift (close at hand).

Er war vorige Woche in Berlin und hat dort den regierenden Bürgermeister kennengelernt.

Ist Herr Petersen da? (e.g. in the next room).

Da haben Sie recht (in the matter).

THEREFORE, HENCE, ON THAT ACCOUNT, SO, THUS[3] **1. Daher**, i.e. from there, is the most objective of the German terms and introduces a statement of the effect of the cause given in the preceding clause. Its reference to cause and effect is seen clearly in the phrase *daher kommt es, daß...*, in which *daher* could not be replaced by any of the other terms. It should only be used in objective statements.

---

[1] 'To owe' money and the like is *schulden, schuldig sein*.

[2] *Denn* in a question in combination with *wer, was, wie*, corresponds to 'ever'. *Was soll ich denn tun?*

[3] 'So' is to 'this' as 'thus' is to 'that'.

Es hat vier Monate lang nicht geregnet, daher verdorrt das Gras, muß das Wasser rationiert werden.

Das Obst war schlecht, daher konnte man es nicht essen.

2. Darum is emphatic and less objective than *daher*. It introduces a statement of an action or an attitude and follows a statement of the motives for this. 'That is why' is a common English equivalent.

Er hat uns früher sehr schlecht behandelt, darum wollen wir heute nichts mit ihm zu tun haben (this is the reason and no other).

Er war sehr unzuverlässig, darum habe ich ihn entlassen.

3. Deshalb indicates only in a vague way that one thing is the result of another. It means no more than: in consideration of what precedes, on that account, that being so. Because of its vagueness it can be used instead of the above terms, but without their precise reference. It must, however, be preceded by a clause setting out the circumstances taken into account.

Er hat nicht die nötigen Kenntnisse, deshalb können wir ihn nicht anstellen.

Die Reise ist sehr anstrengend, ich möchte deshalb lieber zu Hause bleiben.

4. Also indicates nothing more than that there is a connection between two things. It concentrates attention more on the result than on the reason, and can even be used in reference to a reason that is implied and not stated. In this it corresponds to 'so'.[1]

Er kommt also nicht (so he's not coming).

Er hat nicht angerufen, also wissen wir nicht, ob er zurück ist.

THICK   1. Dick refers primarily to the third dimension, i.e. between opposite surfaces.[2] **Dicht** means 'close in texture, dense'.[3] The normal objective term for 'thick' as applied to words such as *Dunkel, Nebel* is *dicht*. *Dick*, applied to these words, has an emotional connotation (e.g. *er tappte im dicksten Dunkel*).

Ein dicker Baumstamm, ein dickes Buch, eine dicke Mauer, dicke Lippen, dicker Schlamm.

Ein dichter Wald, dichter Nebel, ein dichter Bart, dichte Augenbrauen.

Diese Gegend ist dicht bevölkert.

Dicke Wolken (refers to their shape); *dichte Wolken* (density).

Ein dichter Nebel zog herauf (subjectively felt as vast and impenetrable).

2. *Dick* is also applied (*a*) to liquids which tend to become solids; (*b*) in the sense of 'in large numbers'; (*c*) in the sense of 'intimate' (a slang use).

Dicke Suppe, Milch (sour milk).

Die Leichen lagen dick auf der Erde (contrast third example in **1**).

Sie sind dick befreundet, dick miteinander.

THIN, LEAN   1. Of living beings.

[1] German *so* renders other meanings of English 'so', but not that discussed here.

[2] (*a*) *Dick* is therefore the normal term for 'fat' in reference to the size of persons (e.g. *Sie sind in den letzten Monaten etwas dicker geworden*). *Fett* is applied to persons in reference to layers of fat, particularly when they are felt as repulsive (e.g. *ein fetter Mann*). It is the regular term when the substance 'fat' is meant (e.g. *fette Kost*). (*b*) *Dick* also means 'swollen' with reference to a part of the body (e.g. *eine dicke Backe*).

[3] *Dicht* also means 'tightly closed so that nothing can penetrate', particularly of containers (e.g. *wasserdicht*: waterproof).

THIN

Mager: having little fat, i.e. lean.[1] **Dünn:** having little thickness, i.e. between opposite surfaces. *Dünn* is therefore applied to the figure and to extremities.

Er ist sehr mager (lean, thin).

Seine Wangen sind sehr mager.

Er hat dünne Beine, Arme, eine dünne Haut.

2. Other uses of **dünn**.

(a) Having little thickness, of things (the opposite of *dick*).

Dünnes Papier, ein dünner Faden, eine dünne Scheibe Brot, ein dünner Baumstamm.

(b) Having little density, sparse (the opposite of *dicht*).

Ein dünner Wald, Bart, Nebel.

Diese Gegend ist sehr dünn bevölkert.

(c) Unsubstantial, weak, particularly of liquids, sounds, and mental products. Applied to the last of these it is somewhat popular.

Dünne Suppe, dünnes Bier, dünnes Blut, eine dünne Stimme.

Ein dünnes Argument, eine dünne Entschuldigung.

Ihr Aufsatz war sehr dünn.

3. **Dürftig** means 'lacking what is regarded as sufficient', either as a statement of fact or a judgment of value. It draws attention to the state or condition, i.e. thin, poor, paltry, shabby, needy. It does not emphasize the need for any specific thing.[2]

Der Aufsatz ist sehr dürftig.

Ein dürftiges Argument.

THING 1. (a) **Ding**[3] is applied to all concrete objects except those defined under *Sache*.

Ein Stuhl ist ein Ding.

Was ist das Ding da drüben?

Wie nennen Sie dieses Ding?

(b) In a figurative sense it is little used in the singular, mostly only in fixed phrases, in which, however, *Sache* could also be used.

Das ist ein ander Ding.

Das ist ein komisches Ding.

(c) It is used freely in the plural in a figurative application. Its serious, sober tone contrasts with that of *Sachen*.

Er hat manche Dinge getan (gesagt, gedacht, verlangt), die ich ihm nie zugetraut hätte.

Er hat mir wichtige Dinge mitzuteilen.

Das sind Dinge, die nur mich angehen.

Solche Dinge dürfen nicht wieder vorkommen.

---

[1] *Mager* corresponds to 'lean' in most uses (e.g. *die mageren Jahre*). *Feist* is 'obese', *hager* the opposite, 'gaunt'. *Schlank* means both 'slim' (suggesting little of a thing) and 'slender' (suggesting gracefulness and good proportions) in reference to the human body. 'Slim' has, particularly in figurative use, something of its German cognate *schlimm*, therefore 'meagre, insufficient' (e.g. his chances are slim).

[2] This latter sense is rendered by *bedürftig*, i.e. in need of (e.g. *ruhebedürftig*). See 'need'. *Notdürftig* means 'sufficient at a pinch, barely sufficient' (e.g. *das Zimmer war nur notdürftig möbliert*). *Kümmerlich* as a synonym of *dürftig* differs from it in suggesting a subjective attitude, therefore 'miserable' (e.g. *eine kümmerliche Predigt, ein kümmerliches Geschöpf*).

[3] *Dings*, neuter, is used colloquially like 'thingumajig'. Plural: *Dinger*.

Die Dinge wachsen ihm über den Kopf.

Wie die Dinge nun einmal liegen (things being what they are).

(d) It is applied to persons in an affectionate or derogatory sense.

Sie ist ein niedliches, kleines, ein dummes, Ding.[1]

2. (a) **Sache**[2] is applied to concrete objects which are things of immediate concern, personal belongings, particularly clothes, or small things (e.g. implements) used for a specific purpose. *Ding* is impossible in the sense of personal belongings.

Ich packte meine Sachen zusammen und ging fort.

Nehmen Sie bitte Ihre Sachen weg.

Wollen Sie Ihre Sachen ablegen?

Das sind die Sachen, die sie brauchen, um ihre Schuhe zu reparieren.

(b) In figurative use, singular and plural, *Sache* corresponds to 'affair', 'business', 'matter', as well as to 'thing'.[3] In the plural it is more off-hand than *Dinge*, and vaguer in the sense that the speaker has a less serious attitude to, and a less clear idea of, what he refers to. It translates 'thing' in the singular in a statement which makes a judgment about a thing.

Die Sache geht Sie, nicht mich an.

Um seine Sachen steht es nicht gut.

Die Sache ist schlimm.

Es ist eine gefährliche Sache, ihm zu widersprechen.

Es ist Ihre Sache, die Berichte zu überprüfen.

Er hat dumme Sachen gemacht.[4]

Verrat ist eine häßliche Sache (a judgment).

3. In the sense of 'something done, to be done, said, thought', 'an act, achievement, happening, fact', 'the proper thing' (see *S.O.D.* 'Thing', 1, 4, 5), German often uses (a) the neuter adjective or (b) an indefinite pronoun. When 'thing' is qualified numerically the forms in *lei* may be used and *Dinge* omitted (*zweierlei, dreierlei, mancherlei,* etc.). *Eins* = one thing.

Das Wichtigste ist auszuhalten, bis Hilfe kommt.

Das Beste wäre, ihm Ihre Pläne mitzuteilen.

Was Sie sagten, war sehr unfreundlich (that was not a kind thing to say).

Gut, daß Sie es mir sagten (a good thing).

Es ist gerade das, was ich brauche.

Es ist etwas Ernstes geschehen (a grave thing).

Er sagte gestern etwas sehr Ulkiges.

Wissen und Handeln sind zweierlei (two different things).

Eins möchte ich klar machen.

THINK **1.** To have an opinion, mostly with a following 'that' clause.

Denken is only used to indicate surprise that an opinion one has held has proved erroneous or when one seeks confirmation of an opinion about which one entertains doubts. In the sense of 'believe', whether the grounds for belief are sufficient or insufficient, **glauben** must be used.

---

[1] *Ein kleines Ding von Mädchen*: a slip of a girl.

[2] The primary meaning of *Sache* is *Streit*, particularly at law (e.g. *Sachwalter*). It also means 'cause', often with the addition of *gut* (e.g. *für die gute Sache kämpfen*). See under 'cause'. Also 'point' in such phrases as: *die Sache ist die, daß...*; *bei der Sache bleiben*; *zur Sache!*; *von der Sache abweichen.*

[3] *Angelegenheit* is the weightiest term for 'affair, matter', etc. It means a 'matter of concern'. See also under 'concern'.

[4] See 'do' for *Ding* and *Sache* combined with *tun* and *machen* respectively.

Ich glaubte, Sie hätten schon bezahlt.
Ich dachte, Sie hätten schon bezahlt.
Ich glaubte, Sie wollten gehen.
Ich dachte, Sie wollten gehen.
Wer hätte das gedacht?

2. 'To think of' in the sense of 'to direct one's thoughts towards', 'to call to mind',[1] must be distinguished from 'to think of, about' in the sense of 'reflect, ponder over'. The former is **denken an**, the latter **nachdenken über**.[2]

Ich habe garnicht daran gedacht.[3]
Ich habe garnicht darüber nachgedacht.
Sie müssen an Ihre Pflicht denken.
Sie müssen über den Begriff der Pflicht nachdenken.

3. 'To form or have an idea of (a thing, action, or circumstance, real or imaginary) in one's mind; to imagine, conceive, fancy, picture' (*S.O.D.*, I, 4). The sense is not 'to hold an opinion' (see **1**), but 'to represent a thing to one's mind'. **Sich denken** must be used.[4]

Ich kann mir nicht denken, was Sie meinen.
Ich kann mir nicht denken, wie ich ihn für den Plan gewinnen soll.
Ich kann mir nicht denken, daß Sie es ernst meinen.
Wenn ich mir denke, daß er mich belog, werde ich wütend.
Denken Sie sich bloß, er ist freigesprochen worden.

4. To have an opinion with regard to the value of a person or thing.

Halten must be used with the indefinite pronouns *was, viel, nichts, allerhand*, and the like. With words which have a more concrete content (e.g. well, badly) **denken** is used.

Was halten Sie von ihm, von dem Plan?
Ich denke nur Gutes von ihm.

5. 'To conceive or entertain the notion of doing something; to intend, mean' (*S.O.D.*, II, 4). **Denken** is the usual term in the present tense and with a following 'that' clause, **glauben** is used to indicate a firmer intention than is expressed by *denken* (compare **1**).

Ich denke, morgen wegzugehen (also *gedenke*).
Ich dachte, ich würde hier warten.
Ich denke, ich werde nach Hause gehen (said tentatively).
Ich glaube, ich werde nach Hause gehen.

6. *Denken* cannot be used impersonally in the passive voice to translate 'it is thought (that...)' (German = *man denkt*). On the other hand it can be used passively with a thing as subject. Example: *Das Ding wird als belebt gedacht* (thought of, conceived).

THOUGHT **1. Gedanke** is a mental image formed in the process of thinking, the content of thinking, a notion.[5]

---

[1] For the close synonym *bedenken* see 'consider'.
[2] *Nachdenken* suggests prolonged thought, which need not be the case with *sich überlegen* (see 'consider').
[3] *Einfallen*, to occur, is much used in the sense of 'to think involuntarily of something'.
[4] For the close synonym *sich vorstellen* see 'imagine'.
[5] *Gedanke* is, unlike 'thought', sometimes used in the sense of 'conception'. *Der Staatsgedanke* in Hebbels '*Agnes Bernauer*'.

Ein Gedanke fiel mir plötzlich ein.
Der Gedanke an deinen Abschied beschäftigt mich sehr.
Sein einziger Gedanke ist, Geld zu verdienen.
Er hat viele fruchtbare Gedanken im Kopf.
Es ist ein beruhigender Gedanke, daß so viel guter Wille in den Menschen steckt.

2. Denken must be used for 'thought' in the sense of the 'activity of thinking' or a 'way of thinking'.

Das Denken ist frei.
Im Denken und im Handeln ist er gleich unberechenbar (in thought and in action).
Hegels Denken hat Marx beeinflußt.
Das Denken des Mittelalters war teleologisch, das der Neuzeit ist kausal.

3. Nachdenken, i.e. reflection, must be used when the activity of thinking is meant as distinct from its content. See 'think'.

Angestrengtes Nachdenken tut not.
Er war in Nachdenken versunken.

4. Gedankengut refers to a body of thought of a specific age, movement, or the like.

Das romantische Gedankengut.
Das griechische Gedankengut des 5ten Jahrhunderts v. Ch.

5. To have no thought, i.e. intention, of....

Ich dachte nicht daran, Sie zu beleidigen.

THOUGHTFUL, LOST IN THOUGHT 1. Gedankenvoll means not 'thoughtful', but 'lost in thought', i.e. absorbed in thoughts, musings, which take one away from the present. It is mostly used to describe facial expression, hence as an adjective qualifying nouns such as *Blick* and as an adverb. Direct application to a person as in the following example from Hermann Hesse's *Der Steppenwolf* is rare. '*...vielleicht auch waren sie vereinsamte und entgleiste Burschen wie ich, stille gedankenvolle Säufer über bankrotten Idealen, Steppenwölfe und arme Teufel auch sie.*'

Er hatte einen gedankenvollen Blick.
Er saß gedankenvoll da.

2. In the sense of 'giving thought to a matter', i.e. as a contrast to 'rash, unthinking', the following terms, which are approximations to 'thoughtful', may be used.[1]

Überlegt suggests an examination of all sides of a matter with a view to action. **Nachdenklich** suggests caution and particularly the presence of doubts. **Besonnen** refers to a temper of mind, which is level-headed, balanced, but not necessarily on an exclusively practical or prosaic level.[2]

Das ist ein wohl überlegter Plan.
Er handelt überlegt.
Er ist ein nachdenklicher Mensch.
Er hat einen nachdenklichen Gesichtsausdruck.
Es stimmte mich nachdenklich.
Er ist ein besonnener Mensch, Künstler.

[1] See 'to consider'.
[2] Further: *bedächtig*, which adds to the idea of circumspection that of slowness. *Er sprach sehr bedächtig.*

3. For the sense of 'giving signs of original thought' (*P.O.D.*), as applied to persons and their writings, German has no exact term. 'A thoughtful student' could be paraphrased by *ein Student, der voller Gedanken (Ideen) steckt*. A thoughtful essay: *ein gedankenreicher Aufsatz* (an abundance of ideas with a touch of brilliance).

4. In the sense of 'considerate' **rücksichtsvoll** may be used, i.e. taking care not to hurt, inconvenience, people. In the more positive sense of 'going out of one's way to do things for people', i.e. when omission would not cause hurt, inconvenience, or the like, **aufmerksam**, i.e. attentive, can be used.

Er ist immer sehr rücksichtsvoll.
Ein aufmerksamer Freund, Gatte.
Es war sehr aufmerksam von ihm, mir diese Zeitungsnotiz zu schicken.

THOUGHTLESS, WITH ONE'S MIND A BLANK   1. Gedankenlos generally means 'with one's mind a blank' and is mostly used as an adverb. It can also mean 'unthinking', as a mild criticism of one's own behaviour towards others. It is not as strong as 'inconsiderate', the implication being: I did not mean it.

Ich saß stundenlang gedankenlos da.
Ich habe es gedankenlos hingesagt.
Es war gedankenlos von mir, das gesagt zu haben.

2. In the sense of 'not reflecting sufficiently' **unüberlegt** and **unbesonnen** (for explanation see 'thoughtful'), further, **unbedacht** may be used. The latter is as a stricture the weakest term and simply means 'without thinking'.[1]

Ich war unbedacht genug, ihm meine Pläne mitzuteilen.
Ich habe meinen Besuch unbedachterweise abgesagt.

3. German has no exact equivalent for the sense of 'inconsiderate'. **Rücksicht nehmen** in the negative may sometimes be used.[2] See also **1**.

Warum nimmst du so wenig Rücksicht auf die Eltern?

THREATEN   1. Bedrohen suggests the immediacy of violent action, not the uttering of a threat with regard to future action. It cannot therefore be followed by an infinitive or be used adjectivally in the present participle.

Der Feind bedroht die Stadt.
Er bedrohte mich mit einem Hammer.
Ich fühle mich bedroht.

2. Drohen suggests weaker or more remote action, often nothing more than an attitude. This action need not be physical violence, and can even take the form of a reprimand. An infinitive can follow or, in its place, a phrase with *mit* indicating what is threatened. The present participle is used regularly as an adjective.

Er drohte mir mit der Faust, dem Hammer.
Der Staat drohte ihnen mit Beschlagnahme ihrer Güter.
Er drohte, ihn anzuzeigen.

---

[1] *Leichtsinnig*, light-minded, means either 'not sufficiently serious', 'frivolous in thought', or 'exposing unthinkingly to danger'. In the latter use it approximates closely to 'thoughtless'. Examples: *eine leichtsinnige Haltung* (frivolous); *es ist sehr leichtsinnig von Ihnen, so lange in der Kälte zu sitzen. Leichtfertig* suggests irresponsibility (e.g. *ein leichtfertiger Schritt*).

[2] *Rücksichtslos* means 'ruthless', not 'inconsiderate'.

Ein Sturm droht.
Er gab uns einen drohenden Blick.

TIME **1. Zeit** is used in the sense of duration.
Zehn Jahre können eine lange Zeit im Leben eines Menschen bedeuten.
Er hat eine lange Zeit in Afrika verbracht.

2. Mal means 'occasion' in the sense of one of a number of occasions. It is often preceded by a numeral, in which case it is generally not pluralized and is written with a small letter.
Er war fünfmal hier.
Er war unzählige Male in Rom.
Das war das letzte Mal, daß ich ihn sah.

3. Frist is a period of time with a definite limit and to which conditions are attached. Its meaning is seen quite clearly in the derivative past participle, as: *ein befristetes Ultimatum*—with a time limit. From its basic meaning develops that of a limited breathing space, reprieve.
Die Versicherungsgesellschaft hat eine Frist von einem halben Jahr, um ihre
Finanzen in Ordnung zu bringen.
Die Operation wird ihm eine Frist von zwei bis drei Jahren geben.

TIN, CAN, JAR, JUG, POT The metal 'tin' is German *Blech*. The sense treated in this article is that of a container, i.e. a tin can. In Britain the latter is referred to simply as 'tin', in America as 'can' (e.g. tinned fruit, canned fruit). 'Jar', according to *W.*, is a rigid container having a wide mouth and often no neck, and made typically of earthenware or glass. **Kanne** is not necessarily made of tin, and is extended to cover even china, e.g. *Kaffeekanne*, *Teekanne*, coffeepot, teapot, which does not make clear of what material the vessel is made any more than English 'pot' does. Likewise *Milchkanne*, a jug of milk (see below, *Milchtopf*).

On the other hand *Gießkanne*, watering can. It will be seen that *Kanne* contains liquids whatever the substance of which it is made. *Kännchen* if the pot is small (*ein Kännchen Kaffee*). **Dose** and **Büchse** correspond to all the English terms, but are generally wide at the mouth and with no neck. They may hold anything, but often preserved food. The distinction between the two is that *Dose* is better made than *Büchse*, which may be crude (*Schnupf-tabaksdose*). Thus it is possible to say *Dosenfleisch*, as well as the more usual *Büchsenfleisch*, the distinction in every-day speech often being obliterated. Likewise *eine Dose* (or: *Büchse*) *Marmelade, Sardinen, Zigaretten*. Normally, however, only *Tabaksdose* (jar of *t.*), though it is possible to say *mein Tabak ist in dieser Büchse*. *Dose* is often a well-made tin or jar into which food is transferred from a *Büchse*.

Topf is mainly used in cooking as in *Kochtopf, Wassertopf, Eintopfgericht*, but also *Blumentopf*. It may be used for keeping the milk as against *Milch-kanne* (for receiving it).

TOTTER, SWAY, ROCK, STAGGER, REEL, LURCH, WOBBLE 1.
Schwanken suggests a wide swing from side to side and is mostly applied to tall and slender objects. [1]
Der Zweig, der Mast, schwankt heftig im Winde.

---

[1] In figurative use it means 'to vacillate'. *Er schwankt sehr in dieser Angelegenheit.*

Als er aufstand, schwankte er und schlug dann hin.
Der Boden schwankte unter uns (heaved violently in one direction and then
in another).

2. **Wanken** suggests an inner instability[1] rather than a wide range of move-
ment and is applied mostly to broad-based objects.
Das Gebäude, der Boden, wankt.
Die Knie wankten mir.
Das Reich wankt.

3. **Taumeln** suggests disorderly movement, inability to keep a regular
course, a headlong pitching in some direction. It approximates most closely
to 'lurch' and 'reel'.
Er taumelte ein paar Schritte und sackte dann zusammen.
Er taumelte in die offene Tür hinein.

4. **Torkeln** suggests an unsteady walk, without actual falling, and is commonly applied to a drunk, i.e. to stagger.
Der Betrunkene torkelte über die Straße.

5. **Wackeln** is mostly applied to objects which are loosely attached to
another object and so often rattle when in movement.
Das Schild mit der Nummer ist so locker am Wagen angebracht, daß es
wackelt (wobbles).
Das Bett wackelt.

6. **Schaukeln** always suggests a rhythmic movement from side to side,[2] i.e.
not irregularity. Only in this sense does it translate 'rock'.[3]
Der Kahn schaukelte auf den Wellen (but not of the rocking of a ship).

TOUCH 1. **Berühren** means in its literal sense 'to touch lightly'[4] with a
part of the body, mostly the fingers, or with an extension of these (e.g. a stick).
It cannot indicate forceful contact, pressure, or the laying hold of a thing
with the whole hand. It is used in the negative imperative only with such
objects as suggest danger to the person or to the object itself because it is
precious or fragile. In the same way it is applied to things which touch, either
while in movement or when lying alongside each other.

Figuratively, it is used of: (*a*) food and drink in the literal sense of contact
with the lips, the application to food growing out of the literal sense of
touching with the fingers; (*b*) touching a place on a journey; (*c*) brief reference
to a subject.[5]
Er berührte bloß den Hahn, und das Gewehr ging los.
Er berührt schon das Ufer (of a swimmer).
Er berührte ihn leicht mit dem Schwert.
In diesem Teich kann ich den Boden berühren.
Können Sie die Zehen mit den Händen berühren?
Sie berühren eine wunde Stelle.
Berühren Sie diese Blumen nicht.
Die zwei Häuser berühren sich.

---

[1] In figurative use it means 'to falter' in a decision. *Er wankt in seinem Entschluß.* The
addition of *in seinem Entschluß* is necessary.
[2] Therefore also 'to swing'.
[3] Also in transitive use. *Die Mutter schaukelt das Kind.*
[4] For lightness of contact *berühren* is comparable with the French *effleurer*.
[5] For another sense of *berühren* see 'affect'.

Seine Lippen berührten den vergifteten Wein.
Auf der Reise berührten wir Heidelberg.
Ich habe dieses Thema berührt.

2. Anrühren, which is mostly used negatively or with a virtual negative, expresses an attitude of mind, one of aversion, to the object. It may, but need not, imply contact in the literal sense.

Alkoholische Getränke, süße Speisen, rührt er nie an.
Er hat seine Suppe nicht angerührt.
Das Geld werde ich nicht anrühren, wenn es in dieser Weise verdient worden ist.

3. Anfassen: to make contact with a thing with the hand, particularly with reference to whether it is safe to do so or not. It is the normal term to render the negative imperative.[1]

Wenn Sie den Hund anfassen, wird er beißen.
Fassen Sie den Teller nicht an, er ist heiß.

4. Betasten: to touch in order to ascertain the feel, the nature, quality of a thing; to finger. See 'feel'.

Er betastete die Wunde, um ihre Empfindlichkeit festzustellen.

5. Rühren.
(a) With a direct object: to touch emotionally.[2]

Ihr Schicksal hat mich tief gerührt.
Eine rührende Geschichte.

(b) With *an* and the accusative case: to interfere with. Actual contact is implied.

Rühren Sie nicht an meine Papiere.

6. Examples of more specific terms used in the literal sense of 'touch'.

Ich klopfte ihm auf die Schulter.
Drücken Sie den Knopf (press).
Die Decke ist so niedrig, daß er daran stößt, wenn er aufrecht steht (knocks against it; *berührt* would suggest that he touches it with his fingers).

7. Examples of specific terms used in the figurative sense of 'touch'.

Er fängt an, das Geld, das er gespart hat, anzugreifen (make a hole in).
Es ist ein Werk, das die Phantasie nicht anspricht (does not appeal to the imagination).
Was Sie sagen, reicht nicht bis in den Kern des Problems.

TROUBLE (v.) As with the noun 'trouble' the closest German equivalents of the verb are mostly synonyms of 'trouble'.

1. Sense: to agitate mentally and spiritually; bring distress or uncertainty of mind, to worry, bother. German **Sorgen machen** (see under 'care'), **bedrücken** (to depress), **stören** (to disturb), **beunruhigen** (alarm).

Was mir Sorgen macht, ist, daß das Kind in der Schule nicht vorwärts kommt.
Daß sie sich nicht an die Adresse erinnern konnte, störte sie (W.).
Die unnatürliche Stille beunruhigte ihn (W.S.).

---

[1] See footnote to 'seize' (p. 292, n. 1).
[2] See footnote to *bewegen* under 'move' (p. 223, n. 1).

TROUBLE

2. (a) To put to exertion or inconvenience usually by asking for some service (*W*.). This sense often occurs in polite or ironical phrases. While German can use **bemühen** (see *Mühe* under 'trouble' s.) in this sense, it generally avoids it in polite requests.

Es tut mir leid, daß ich Sie bemühen muß, aber würden Sie...?
Wollen die Herrschaften sich ins andere Zimmer bemühen?
Bitte reichen Sie mir das Salz. (may I trouble you for the salt?)
Darf ich um Feuer bitten? (may I trouble you for a light?)
'*Ich muß schon bitten, daß Ihr ruhig seid,*' *sagte der Lehrer* (ironically: I must trouble you to be quiet) (*A.L.*).

(b) **Belästigen:** to pester; **jdm. zu schaffen machen** (cause bother to), but could also render the meaning of **1**; **jdm. zur Last fallen** (to be a burden to someone).

Ich möchte Sie nicht mit einer solchen Bitte belästigen.
Wir wollten ihr nicht mit der Sorge um die Kinder zur Last fallen.
Seine Vergesslichkeit macht mir viel zu schaffen.

3. Sense: to produce physical disorder in; cause physical distress or suffering to. German **plagen** and more strongly **quälen** (torture). Also: **leiden** (see under 'suffer').

Starke Schmerzen plagten, quälten sie weiter.
Sie litt unter zunehmender Taubheit (was troubled by...).

4. Sense: to put into confused motion (a sense closest to the late Latin *turbulare*, and French *troubler*). German **trüben**.

Wolken trübten den Himmel.

5. In transitive and (less commonly) reflexive use: German: **sich die Mühe geben** (see under 'trouble' s.) But often: **nicht brauchen** (particularly for negative imperative).

Er gibt sich nicht mal die Mühe, es einem zu sagen, wenn er nicht kommen kann.
Sie brauchen das Boot nicht wieder zurückzubringen (don't trouble to...).

TROUBLE (s.) There is no exact German equivalent of 'trouble' in any of its senses, the nearest being in that of pains, exertion, effort. It will be seen that the German term is generally the equivalent of synonyms of 'trouble'.

1. (a) Sense: effort, exertion, pains. As compared with these terms, 'trouble implies exertion that inconveniences or incommodes' (*W.S.*). The nearest German equivalent is: **Mühe**, which stresses the burden imposed by some activity. Often, like 'trouble', in fixed phrases: *sich die Mühe geben, machen*.

Er hat viel Zeit und Mühe darauf verwendet.
Es gelang ihm nur nach unglaublicher Mühe.
Er gibt sich nicht die Mühe, die Tatsachen festzustellen.
Ich möchte Ihnen keine Mühe machen, verursachen.
Ich kann Ihnen die Mühe sparen.
Es war nicht der Mühe wert.

(b) Often, however, 'trouble' is used indiscriminately for 'difficulty'. German uses **Schwierigkeit**.

Ich hatte viele Schwierigkeiten, mir einen Pass zu besorgen.
Er hat mir Schwierigkeiten gemacht, als ich um Mitgliedschaft im Verein bat.
Sie bringen mich in große Schwierigkeiten.

2. (a) Sense: distress, worry, vexation. German often: **Sorge, Kummer** (see under 'care'), but also such terms as *Unglück* (misfortune), *Not* (distress caused by want or other circumstances), *Beschwerden* (hardships), *Verdruß* (vexation).

Das Kind macht uns viele Sorgen, viel Kummer.
Das Leben besteht aus lauter kleinen Sorgen.
In Zeiten der Not können wir uns immer auf ihn verlassen.

(b) To be a trouble, i.e. nuisance to someone: **jdm. lästig fallen, zur Last fallen.**

Ich möchte Ihnen nicht zur Last fallen.

3. Sense: unpleasantness, mostly with people. German **Unannehmlichkeit.**
Er hat Unannehmlichkeiten mit der Polizei, seinem Nachbarn.

4. Sense: public disturbance, disorder, or confusion (*S.O.D.*). German **Unruhe.**
Die Unruhen in Nordirland nehmen kein Ende.
Die Arbeiterunruhen kosteten das Land riesige Summen.

5. Sense: ill-health, generally with mention of where the trouble is located. German: **Leiden**, which suggests that the trouble extends over a considerable period.
Er hat ein Beinleiden, ein Augenleiden, das ihn sehr mitgenommen hat.

TRUST (v.) **1. Trauen** expresses a generalization about the character of a person or a thing, i.e. an absolute judgment that he or it can be trusted without reference to any particular action. Since it indicates a judgment, not faith, its use with *Gott* as object would amount to blasphemy.

It must be used also in the sense of regarding a thing (but not a person) as reliable on a particular occasion.

Ich traue ihm (nicht) (a judgment about his (un-)trustworthiness in general).
Ich würde ihm nicht über den Weg trauen.
Ich weiß nicht, wieweit ich ihm überhaupt trauen kann.
Wenn Sie ihm nicht trauen, wäre es doch besser, alle Beziehungen zu ihm abzubrechen.
Ich traue deiner Freundschaft nicht.
Ich traue seinem Talent nicht.
Ich traue seinem Wort nicht.
Ich traue dem Wetter nicht.
Ich traue den Berichten, dem Frieden, nicht.
Dem können Sie ruhig mit dem Auto trauen.[1]

2. Vertrauen: to trust a person or some quality he has or some action he performs (but not a thing) with reference to what it is expected the object will or will not do in a specific matter. This specific reference gives it an emotional connotation.

(a) Followed by the dative it means that the subject has confidence that the object will refrain from any action that may harm him, i.e. it has a negative colouring.

Ich vertraue ihm, daß er mich nicht verraten wird.
Ich vertraue seinem gesunden Menschenverstand.
Ich vertraue der Rechtsprechung dieses Landes (*trauen* also is possible).

---

[1] *Dem können Sie das Auto ruhig anvertrauen* (entrust). The sense is wider than that of 'trust', i.e. he will look after it for you, not steal it, and the like.

TRUST

(b) Followed by *auf* with the accusative *vertrauen* means that the subject has confidence that the object will do something, i.e. it has a positive colouring.[1]

Ich vertraue auf ihn, daß er Schritte für mich bei der zuständigen Stelle unternehmen wird.

Ich vertraue auf seinen gesunden Menschenverstand.

Er vertraut auf Gott.

Ich vertraue auf deine Freundschaft.

Ich vertraue auf sein Talent, daß er sich aus dieser Schwierigkeit ziehen wird.

Ich vertraue auf sein Wort.

3. Zutrauen: to think capable of bad as well as good. It can thus be used ironically.

Sie können es ihm zutrauen, Sie im Stich zu lassen (or: *daß er Sie*...).

4. 'Trust' followed by the reflexive accusative and the infinitive: **sich getrauen.**

Er getraute sich nicht, das Thema zu berühren.

5. In the sense of 'hope', e.g. at the end of a letter: **hoffen.**

TRUST (noun), **CONFIDENCE, FAITH**[2] **1. Zutrauen** is more intimate and personal than **Vertrauen.**[3] Germans often use the latter, however, to express both shades of meaning. They are followed by *zu* and *in*, the former being more intimate than the second.

Ich hatte kein Vertrauen zu ihm (*in* impossible).

Wir haben unser Vertrauen zu unseren Führern (*in unsere Führer*) *verloren* (*Zutrauen* impossible).

Ich habe kein Vertrauen in deine diplomatischen Fähigkeiten (*Zutrauen* and *zu* impossible).

Ich habe kein Zutrauen mehr zu ihm.

2. Zuversicht[4] expresses a high degree of confidence that things will happen as one wants them. It denotes confidence in a person only as a secondary idea, and then only in the phrase *Zuversicht setzen auf.*

Meine Zuversicht, daß der Sieg unser sein würde, war unerschütterlich.

TRY (OUT), TEST, PROVE[5] 'Test' and 'try (out)' are at times practically synonymous, particularly with personal qualities (e.g. to test, try out, someone's courage), but in discriminating use, 'test' suggests an accurate, often a scientific, method, frequently preceding the use for which the thing is intended. It also suggests a more precise result. 'Try (out)' means 'to put a thing to the use for which it is intended and to observe it'. The process is stressed more than the result.

---

[1] Only *vertrauen auf* can be followed by a *daß* clause (i.e. not *vertrauen* alone or *trauen*). It translates 'trust' followed by a 'that' clause or by the accusative and the infinitive (but not the reflexive accusative). *Ich vertraue darauf, daß er die Erlaubnis für mich erlangen wird* (trust him to..., trust that he...).

[2] 'Faith' in the religious sense of 'belief' is *Glaube.*

[3] *Zutraulich* = confiding, trusting in an intimate way (e.g. *ein zutrauliches Kind*). *Vertraulich* = confidential. *Vertraut* = 'familiar' in the sense of 'well-known'.

[4] *Zuversichtlich* (confident) is only correctly applied to a person in an emphatic context (e.g. in the imperative, with *sehr*) (*Sei zuversichtlich; er ist sehr zuversichtlich*). But: *eine zuversichtliche Stimmung.* I am confident that... = *Ich glaube zuversichtlich, bin voller Zuversicht, erwarte mit Zuversicht, daß....* *Getrost* (used only as an adverb) = 'confidently' in the sense of 'with nothing to worry about', rather because of the absence of evils than because of the presence of positive good. It is cognate with *Trost.*

[5] For the sense 'to give a logical proof of' a thing see footnote to 'show' (p. 313, n. 3).

1. **Versuchen** and **probieren**, which are close synonyms, mean 'to put a thing to the use for which it is intended'. *Versuchen* emphasizes effort, and can, though it need not, suggest a systematic procedure, while *probieren* always denotes an empirical, non-expert, often casual approach. Both can be applied to food and drink.[1]

Wollen Sie nicht etwas von dieser Platte versuchen?

Probieren Sie diesen Wein!

Versuchen, probieren, Sie diesen Federhalter.

Nun werde ich noch diese Schraube probieren (e.g. a layman using it as a last resort).

Ich habe alle Mittel versucht, aber nichts hat geholfen.

2. **Prüfen** means 'to submit before use to a test which will yield exact knowledge'. It therefore corresponds closely to 'test'.[2]

Der Kandidat, die Tragfähigkeit des Flugzeugs, ist sorgfältig geprüft worden.

Der Arzt hat sein Herz geprüft.

Ich habe seine Zuverlässigkeit geprüft.

3. **Erproben:** to prove the value of a thing by experiment. This can mean (*a*) to put to the test, particularly with reference to the future; (*b*) but more often 'to prove' the mettle, the work, of a person or thing. The past participle used adjectivally has only the latter sense. Reflexive use is not possible. The object is not normally a person.

Diese Arznei muß erst mal erprobt werden.

Wir haben seinen Mut erprobt.

Ein erprobtes Mittel, ein erprobter Freund, ein erprobter Wein.

4. **Bewähren** is now used only reflexively or adjectivally in the past participle. It means that the worth of a thing has been proved through the lapse of time, often despite doubts. It does not mean 'to subject to a test', the results of which are unknown.

Dieses System, diese Methode, hat sich bewährt.

Ein bewährter Freund, ein (alt)bewährtes Mittel.

TURN 1. The verbs *wenden, kehren, drehen* translate 'turn' in its literal sense of bringing into another position, to which is sometimes added that of facing another direction. Only to a very limited extent does *wenden* render the numerous figurative uses of 'turn', while *kehren* and *drehen* do so still less.

(a) **Wenden** is a more dignified term than the others and normally implies consciousness of the action performed. It can mean 'to turn partly or completely (round)'. The distinction between the weak and the strong verb is in general that *wandte* emphasizes the result, the new direction, while *wendete* draws attention to the operation of turning in its various stages. From this dominant tendency follow others which are more or less clearly recognizable: (*a*) that *wandte* tends to be sudden, quick, *wendete* slow; (*b*) that while both can mean 'right round' *wandte* only has this meaning in certain contexts, a partial turn being expressed by *wendete*. In any given case one or all of these tendencies may be operative. Further distinctions are that only *wendete* can be used intransitively, and that *wandte* when used reflexively is normally

---

[1] See also 'taste'.

[2] *Überprüfen* means 'to check' in the sense of 'to run over a thing quickly' to make sure that it is in order. *Die Bremse überprüfen. Nachsehen* is used similarly. See 'control'.

followed by a phrase denoting or suggesting the new direction (e.g. *um*). In reflexive use the distinction is often obliterated, the form *wandte* being the commoner.[1]

Er wendete, wandte, den Kopf.

Er wandte das Gesicht von dem Richter (ab).

Er wandte den Blick nach oben.

Er wendete den Wagen, den Stuhl, den Schrank, das Bett, den Anzug (an operation in stages, *wandte* being impossible).

Er wandte die Matratze (um) (turned over).

Er wandte die Waffe gegen sich selbst.

Ich wandte mich um (suddenly).

Ich wendete mich um (more slowly).

Ich wandte mich nach ihm um (*wendete* impossible because the new direction is stressed by *nach ihm*).

Er wandte sich seinem Sohne zu.

Der Botschafter wandte sich zur Linken.

Er wandte sich zum Gehen.

Der Wagen, das Flugzeug, der Schwimmer, wendete.

Der Wagen, das Flugzeug, der Schwimmer, wandte sich in eine neue Richtung.

(b) **Kehren** generally means 'to make face the opposite direction', but sometimes denotes merely a partial turn. Often it suggests that the broad side is turned. It can also imply speed, force, or hostility.[2] It also has the meaning of 'to sweep'.

Sie kehrte ihm den Rücken.

Kehrt! (about turn!—a military command).

Er kehrte die Waffe gegen sich selbst (more forceful than *wandte*).

(c) **Drehen** means (*a*) to make turn, spin round an axis,[3] (*b*) to bring into any new position, except that of upside down. In the second sense it does not suggest any special care or skill, and is the most common rendering of 'turn' when the latter implies the dragging or pulling of a thing round. It is the normal colloquial term when reflexive or when a thing is the object. Sometimes *umdrehen* is required.

Er drehte den Schlüssel um.

Das Wasser dreht das Rad.

Sie drehte sich um, um ihn nicht ansehen zu müssen.

Er dreht sich viel im Schlaf (um).

Dreh' dich um.

Er glaubt, daß die Welt sich um ihn dreht.

2. Biegen: to turn in a new direction when the person or thing is in motion and then proceeds in the new direction, i.e. does not merely face it. It is followed characteristically by a preposition.

Wir bogen in die zweite Querstraße.

Biegen Sie rechts ab, ein.

---

[1] In compounds (e.g. *verwenden*) both forms are sometimes used, one being more common with one noun, the other with another (e.g. *er verwandte das Geld für sich; hier wird nur gutes Fett verwendet*). But in general the distinction is the same as in the literal use.

[2] In figurative use it sometimes suggests vigour or violence (e.g. *das Haus von unterst zu oberst kehren*). *Umkehren*: to retrace one's steps, e.g. because one has gone the wrong way: *sich umkehren*: to turn round and stay where one is.

[3] The idea of spinning, twisting is preserved in figurative use. *Es dreht sich mir alles im Kopf herum.* Note: *Er hat die Geschichte gedreht*: worked it by tricks. *Verdreht*: twisted.

3. For 'turn into' in the sense of 'change into' see 'change'. The verbs treated above are not used in this sense. Note: *etwas in sein Gegenteil verkehren.*

UNDERSTAND   1. **Verstehen** is the general term and refers to clear ideas or knowledge. **Begreifen**, in accordance with the literal meaning of *greifen*, suggests an effort to grasp, to encompass, to bring within one's powers of understanding. It raises the question whether the object is thinkable, conceivable for the mind of the subject, but says nothing about clarity of ideas. It thus corresponds more closely to 'comprehend' than 'understand', and like the former has a more limited range of application than *verstehen*. Kleist constantly uses it negatively to refer to what is unreasonable or monstrous. '*Das Unbegreifliche*' is a dominant motive in each of his works.

> *Kinder begreifen sehr gut, daß sie ihren Eltern gehorchen müssen.*
> *Ich kann nicht begreifen, warum er eine Frau heiratet, die so viel älter ist als er.*
> *Können Sie begreifen, warum er sich so seltsam benimmt?*
> '*Er begriff nicht, warum er dem Tode, den seine jammervolle Seele suchte,*
>   *entflohen sei*' (Kleist, *Das Erdbeben in Chili*).

Meanings of *verstehen* which correspond clearly to those of 'understand' are: to perceive the meaning of (words, person, or language, etc.); to perceive the significance or explanation or cause or nature of; to interpret as meaning; to express uncertainty or surprise or indignation; to introduce a warning or threat.[1,2] See *P.O.D.*

> *Ich verstehe nicht, was Sie sagen.*
> *Verstehen Sie mich?*
> *Er versteht Deutsch.*
> *Ich verstehe nicht, warum er kam.*
> *Ich verstehe seine Schwierigkeiten.*
> *Ich kann ihn, sein Benehmen, nicht verstehen.*
> *Darunter verstehe ich, daß Sie zu einem Kompromiß bereit sind.*
> *Soll ich verstehen, daß Sie sich weigern?*
> *Verstehen Sie mich, das muß aufhören!*

2. Sich verstehen auf combines the meaning of 'understand intellectually' and 'be expert in doing, in dealing with'. Similarly **verstehen** followed by the infinitive means 'to understand how to deal with a thing.'

> *Er versteht sich auf Pferde, die politische Taktik.*
> *Er versteht es, aus seinen Studenten das Beste herauszuholen.*

3. Sense: implied, not stated. This sense frequently approaches that of 'implicitly agreed'. **Sich verstehen** with an impersonal subject means: it is a matter of course.

> *Es versteht sich, daß wir die Beute teilen.*
> *Das versteht sich.*

4. Meanings of 'understand' which can be translated by *verstehen* only in special cases. The senses: to have knowledge of, to know or learn, by information received; to take or accept as a positive fact, without positive knowledge or certainty, to believe. See *S.O.D.* 4 (*b*) and (*c*). **Zu verstehen**

---

[1] *Verstehen*, not *hören*, is used in the sense of 'to catch' what a person says. *Was haben Sie gesagt? Ich habe nicht verstanden.*

[2] *Kapieren* is much used colloquially in the sense of 'to understand the meaning or significance of' a thing. *Ich kapierte nicht, worauf er hinaus wollte.*

UNDERSTAND

geben is used in the same way as 'to give to understand', often with an implied warning. Otherwise such expressions as *erfahren* (to learn), *sich sagen lassen* (after enquiry), *entnehmen aus* (to infer from), must be used.

> *Man hat mir zu verstehen gegeben, daß die Löhne in diesem Betrieb erhöht werden sollen.*
> *Ich habe mir sagen lassen, daß alle Bankkontos gesperrt werden sollen.*
> *Ich habe erfahren, daß Ihr Gesuch abgelehnt worden ist.*
> *Niemand hätte das aus meinen Worten entnehmen können.*

5. In the sense of 'supply mentally something not expressly stated' (mostly a grammatical term), German has to use such expressions as *hinzudenken*, *ergänzen* (see 'complete').

> *Das Fürwort muß man hinzudenken, muß ergänzt werden.*

UNDERSTANDING 1. **Verstand:** the faculty of, capacity for, understanding.

> *Der Verstand ist ein unschätzbares Gut.*
> *Er ist ein Mann von Verstand.*
> *Das geht über meinen Verstand.*

2. **Verständnis:** the act or process of understanding in a specific matter. It often approaches sympathy.

> *Ihr Verständnis der Lage geht nicht sehr weit.*
> *Er hörte meinen Vorschlag mit Verständnis an.*
> *Er hat wenig Verständnis für unsere Schwierigkeiten.*

3. **Einverständnis:** an agreement between people. It suggests a process of reflection followed by agreement. It is not interchangeable with *Verständigung*.

> *Er hat sein Einverständnis erklärt.*
> *Es besteht ein Einverständnis zwischen ihnen.*
> *Er hat im Einverständnis mit mir gehandelt.*

4. **Verständigung** suggests a formulated agreement, either written or spoken, after the clearing away of obstacles by discussion.

> *Sie haben endlich eine Verständigung erzielt.*
> *Es war keine Verständigung zwischen ihnen möglich.*

UNDO 1. Sense: unfasten, untie, loosen, generally a garment or part of it, or a knot. German mostly uses verbs compounded with *auf* (in the sense of open), but in some cases **lösen** and sometimes **öffnen** (see under 'open').

(a) *Er knöpfte die Jacke auf* (unbuttoned).
> *Er band den Schlips (die Krawatte) auf.*
> *Er knüpfte die Schnürsenkel auf.*
> *Sie trennte den Saum auf.*

(b) **lösen:** to loosen.
> *Er löste seinen Gürtel.*
> *Er löste die Fesseln des Gefangenen.*
> *Er löste den Knoten* (or *knüpfte...auf*).

(c) **auflösen**, which generally means to dissolve, can also be applied to things of which the parts come asunder.
> *Sie löste das Haar auf.*

(d) **öffnen, aufmachen:** to open.
> *Er machte das Paket auf.*

2. Sense: to reverse what has been done: German **ungeschehen machen.**
Was nun einmal getan ist, kann man nicht ungeschehen machen.

3. Sense: cancel. See under this term.

4. Sense: destroy the worldly means or standing of, ruin the reputation of.
German **ruinieren** (see also under destroy). *Ruinieren* can mean to ruin
financially, to ruin an object (e.g. clothes, motorcar), to ruin intangibles, to
ruin health.
Er hat seinen Ruf in der Gesellschaft ruiniert.
Die Trunksucht hat ihn ruiniert.

UNFORTUNATE, UNHAPPY 1. Applied directly to persons.
(a) **Unglücklich** thus used, whether attributively or predicatively, can only
mean 'unhappy', i.e. depressed in feeling.[1]
Er ist ein sehr unglücklicher Mensch.
Er ist sehr unglücklich.
(b) 'Unfortunate' (and 'unlucky'), applied directly to persons, can be
translated as follows. (*i*) Attributively, only by some such phrase as *vom
Unglück verfolgt*, i.e. dogged by misfortune. (ii) Predicatively, by **Unglück
haben** (i.e. ill-luck).
Ein vom Unglück verfolgter Mensch.
Er hat viel Unglück gehabt.

2. The impersonal phrase 'it is unfortunate that...' can only be translated
by **es ist ein Unglück, daß....**[2]
Es ist ein Unglück, daß Sie so lange gewartet haben.

3. In other uses 'unfortunate' and 'unhappy' approach each other more
closely in meaning, and both are translated by *unglücklich.*
Er hat eine unglückliche Tendenz, aus einem Extrem ins andere zu fallen.
Seine unglückliche Veranlagung.
Ein unglückliches Zusammentreffen.

4. Unselig approaches 'unfortunate' in meaning as under **3**, but is stronger,
i.e. as though the misfortune were the working out of a curse.
Ein unseliges Laster.
Eine unselige Begegnung.
Der unselige Krieg zwischen den europäischen Völkern.

5. Bedauerlich, regrettable, must be used in formal expressions of regret.
Ihr bedauerlicher Unfall.
Ich muß Ihnen die bedauerliche Mitteilung machen.

URGE, INCENTIVE, IMPULSE[3] **1. Trieb** is an innate disposition
towards a thing and is therefore thought of as permanent. It is therefore a
close synonym of *Instinkt*[4] (e.g. *der Selbsterhaltungstrieb*).

---

[1] *Unglückselig* means 'very unhappy', 'wretched'. *Ein unglückseliges Geschöpf.*
[2] The same difficulties and distinctions arise in the translation of 'fortunate' and 'happy'
in the predicative position. *Er hat Glück gehabt; es ist ein Glück, daß...* (fortunate; lucky).
Er ist sehr glücklich (happy). In the attributive position, however, *glücklich*, while it primarily
means 'happy', often suggests the meaning of 'fortunate'. *Er ist ein glücklicher Mensch.*
[3] The *Fremdwort* '*Impuls*' suggests suddenness and capriciousness more clearly than
any of the native German terms. When these aspects are not emphasized, *Regung* (a stirring
of feeling) and *Antrieb* may be used.
[4] *Trieb* is a wider term than *Instinkt*. As a psychological term it is translated and introduced into English by American psychologists as 'drive'.

Er kann seine Triebe nicht zügeln.

'*Selbst die scheinbar einzige Ausnahme, die Hermannsschlacht, ist keine Ausgeburt ursprünglichen Haßes...sondern ebenfalls jenes rasenden Ausdruckstriebs—nur traf hier allerdings dieser Trieb mit dem Affekt zusammen...*' (F. Gundolf, *Heinrich von Kleist*).

2. Antrieb denotes the stimulus, the inciting cause of an urge or impulse as well as the latter itself, and is therefore thought of as functioning at a particular moment. It is frequently, though not necessarily, followed by a phrase with *zu* denoting the action in which the impulse issues. Its closest English equivalent is 'incentive'.[1,2]

Die Habsucht ist ein sehr starker Antrieb zum Handeln.

Er fühlt keinen Antrieb, sein Geschäft zu erweitern.

'*Gewiß ist der Wille zum Ausdruck ein Grundantrieb jedes Künstlers, der etwas zu sagen hat*' (F. Gundolf, *Heinrich von Kleist*).

'*Bei allen echten Dichtern kommen die Versbewegungen und Versinhalte aus demselben Antrieb...sie verhalten sich zueinander wie die Lebenskraft und der Leib eines Menschen*' (F. Gundolf, *Heinrich von Kleist*).

3. Drang is a particularly strong, almost irresistible urge, which is not innate, but dominates one at the moment. The plural is rare.[3]

Er fühlte einen unwiderstehlichen Drang zu morden.

Der Drang, den er fühlte, alles stehen und liegen zu lassen, war außerordentlich heftig.

USE (v.) **1. Benutzen** (or: *benützen*) points to a definite, specific purpose for which a person or thing is used, these being regarded as nothing but means to this end. It should not be used in the sense of 'use up', even if a purpose is stated.

Er benutzte ein Beil, um ins Haus einzudringen.

Er benutzte ein unbewohntes Zimmer zum Aufbewahren seiner Bücher.

Das ist ein viel benutzter Weg.

Er benutzt Worte, nur um sich daran zu berauschen.

Er benutzt das Wörterbuch, um einen Artikel zu übersetzen.

Er benutzte mich zu seinen Zwecken.

Die Kinder dürfen dieses Zimmer zum Spielen benutzen (the purpose is known before the room is found).

2. Gebrauchen: to find, to see, some use for. When a purpose is present, it is not necessarily represented as a specific purpose. The treatment of, or the effect on, the person or thing used is rather emphasized. With substances the sense approaches that of *verbrauchen* (use up).

Können Sie diese alte Jacke gebrauchen?

Wieviel Butter würden Sie eventuell gebrauchen, wenn Sie Kuchen backen?

Die Kinder dürfen dieses Zimmer zum Spielen gebrauchen.

Ich gebrauche ein neues Heilmittel gegen Schnupfen (stresses the act of using rather than the purpose).

Sie könnten den Ausdruck hier gebrauchen.

---

[1] In the phrase *aus eigenem Antrieb* the meaning approximates closely to 'initiative', which in general can only be translated by the *Fremdwort* '*Initiative*'.

[2] Synonyms are: *Anreiz*, a sensuous stimulus or incentive to something pleasant (*Antrieb* is not limited to what is pleasant); *Ansporn*, a spur to action. For *anstiften* (=to incite) see footnote to 'found' (p. 138, n. 3).

[3] *Drang* also means 'pressure' in a figurative sense.

Ich gebrauche noch das Wörterbuch.
Rilke gebraucht ausgefallene Reime.
Das ist ein viel gebrauchter Weg.
Sie gebrauchen mich zu schlechten Zwecken.
Soviel Geld kann ich gar nicht gebrauchen.

3. **Verbrauchen:** to use up, consume. It must be used to translate 'use' when the idea of consumption is stressed.

Wieviel Butter verbrauchen Sie, wenn Sie Kuchen backen?
Ich werde wahrscheinlich 1000 Mark auf dieser Reise verbrauchen.

4. **Ausnützen**, to exploit, should only be used to translate 'use' when the idea of exploitation is stressed, or 'to make full use of' limited facilities, i.e. in a good sense.[1]

Er nützt mich nur aus (nur stresses the idea).
Wir müssen den Raum stärker ausnützen.

5. **Anwenden**[2] suggests care, skill, discrimination of means to an end. It is the normal equivalent of 'apply' in this sense. See under 'apply'.

Er wandte all seine Überzeugungskraft an, aber umsonst.

VAIN (IN) 1. **Umsonst** indicates merely that a result has not been achieved.[3]

Ich habe mich umsonst bemüht.
Ich habe ihn umsonst darauf aufmerksam gemacht.
Die Mühe war umsonst.

2. **Vergeblich** suggests in addition the effort expended. Of the three terms treated it alone can be used as an attributive adjective.

Ich habe mich vergeblich bemüht.
Ich habe ihn vergeblich darauf aufmerksam gemacht.
Vergebliche Mühe.

3. **Vergebens** adds to the idea of effort that of a lament that the effort has been fruitless. It is accordingly used in emotional and elevated style.

Ich habe mich vergebens bemüht.
Ich habe ihn vergebens darauf aufmerksam gemacht.
Die Mühe war vergebens.

VERY (adj.) Original meaning: true. God is a very spirit (1615): *Gott ist ein wahrer Geist.*

1. Mostly obsolete now in the sense defined by *S.O.D.* as 'emphatic use, denoting that the person or thing may be so named in the fullest sense of the term, or possesses all the essential qualities of the thing specified'. Only one example of those given by *S.O.D.* under this use can be regarded as modern:

---

[1] *Verwenden*: to turn to account, to utilize for some purpose. *Nur gutes Fett wird verwendet. Sie können dieses Eisen zur Herstellung von Betten verwenden. Er hat viel Zeit und Fleiß darauf verwendet.* It is often used in the sense of *gebrauchen*.

[2] *Nutzen* and *nützen*, used transitively, mean 'to turn to account in some way'. They are also common in the intransitive sense of 'to be of use', particularly with a following dative (e.g. *wenn Ihnen das Buch etwas nützt, behalten Sie es*). The forms without the *Umlaut* are more frequent in Northern, those with the *Umlaut* in Southern, German—contrary to what one would expect.

[3] The idea of 'for nothing' occurs also in the meaning of 'without payment'. *Sie können das Buch umsonst haben. Sie müssen umsonst arbeiten. Unentgeltlich* means that payment is not asked for, i.e. free of charge.

A region which is the very reverse of Paradise (Addison) (*S.O.D.*): *eine Gegend, die das gerade Gegenteil* (or: *gerade das Gegenteil*) *vom Paradiese ist.* His very defects make him likeable: *gerade* (*eben*) *seine Mängel machen ihn liebenswürdig.* For this very reason: *eben aus diesem Grunde.*

For *gerade* see 'just'.

2. Used as an intensive, either to denote the inclusion of something regarded as extreme or exceptional, or to emphasize the exceptional prominence of some ordinary thing or feature (*S.O.D.*). Generally in German: **selbst, sogar** (see 'even'), **schon** in the sense of 'not later than' or indicating that something in itself is sufficient to produce a certain result. **Schon am Anfang:** at the very beginning. The very possibility of a relapse disturbs me: *Schon die Möglichkeit eines Rückfalls beunruhigt mich.*

VIEW,[1] SIGHT 1. Blick means in the first place 'the act of seeing' (look, glance), and in this sense translates 'sight'. It also means 'thing seen', i.e. 'view' whether big or small. In this sense it cannot be followed by the genitive.

Auf den ersten Blick gefiel es mir garnicht (at first sight).
Von hier haben wir einen Blick auf das Meer, über den Hafen.
Der Blick von hier aus ist sehr schön.

2. Anblick: 'view', 'sight', only in the sense of 'thing seen'. It can be followed by the genitive. It suggests (*a*) the act of coming into view of a thing; (*b*) an emotional reaction on the part of the beholder.

Beim ersten Anblick des Meeres (at the first sight of...).
Der Anblick des Meeres erregt ihn sehr.
Der verstümmelte Körper bot einen schaurigen Anblick.
Der Anblick des Unfalls war grauenhaft.

3. Aussicht: a wide or distant view, a vista, prospect, panorama in which one thinks of all the individual objects seen.[2]

Die Aussicht aus dem Fenster ist überwältigend.
Das ist eine der schönsten Aussichten, die die Küste zu bieten hat.

4. Ansicht: a partial view of a thing from a side, an angle, as represented by a painting or a photograph. Apart from this use it occurs in this sense only in a few fixed expressions such as *zur Ansicht ausliegen* (to be on view).

Ansichtskarten.
Diese Ansicht von der Kirche ist sehr schön.
Dieses Buch bringt viele Alpenansichten.

5. Sicht: 'sight', 'view' in the sense of 'visibility'. It occurs mostly in fixed phrases (e.g. *in Sicht kommen, außer Sicht sein, auf lange Sicht*).

6. Sehkraft must be used in the sense of 'power of sight'. But: he has good sight = *er hat gute Augen.*

Seine Sehkraft ist geschwächt.

VIOLENT 1. Heftig is used of emotions which are eruptive, impulsive, uncontrolled or emphatically expressed.[3] It is applied in the same sense to physical phenomena. It excludes the idea of violent external actions.

---

[1] See also 'opinion'.
[2] *Ausblick* is a sudden vista seen when emerging from a narrow passage or defile. *Aussicht* suggests no such emergence.
[3] In this sense it also translates 'vehement'.

Sie schluchzte heftig.
Sie wechselten heftige Worte miteinander.
Er brach in heftigen Zorn aus.
Er stieß auf heftigen Widerstand.
Er hat heftige Kopfschmerzen.
Der Wind blies heftig.
Ein heftiger Ausbruch des Vesuvs.

2. Gewaltsam[1,2] is used of violent actions.
Ein gewaltsamer Tod (from without, not an illness).
Ein gewaltsamer Umsturz.
Eine gewaltsame Lösung des Problems.
Er wurde gewaltsam aus dem Saal entfernt.

3. Gewalttätig is applied to persons who are given to violence, and to their acts. It suggests crime.
Ein gewalttätiger Mensch.

4. A violent clash in an aesthetic sense: **schroff** (see also under 'rough').
Ein schroffer Gegensatz (e.g. of colours).

WAIT, AWAIT[3]   **Warten** is the general term.
Warten Sie! Ich komme gleich.
Ich habe stundenlang auf Sie gewartet.
Ich wartete eine Stunde auf seine Ankunft.

2. Abwarten: to wait in patience, to wait and see, to bide one's time.
Ich werde lieber abwarten (wait and see).
Warten Sie ruhig seine Ankunft ab, bevor Sie handeln.
Ich wartete seine Antwort ab, um mich danach zu richten.

3. Erwarten: to wait impatiently. In ordinary prose it only occurs in this sense in the negative or virtual negative, and mostly with *können*. In elevated diction it is used in other combinations. Its most common meaning is 'expect'.
Ich kann den Sommer, die Ferien, kaum erwarten.

WAKE (UP), WAKEN, AWAKE, AWAKEN[4]   **1.** Transitive.
(a) **Wecken** is the action of waking a person. It is the normal term for 'wake' or 'waken' unless the state of full wakefulness is emphasized, in which case **aufwecken**[5] is used. The distinction between these two verbs is observed more strictly than that between 'wake' and 'wake up'.
Wecken Sie mich bitte um 7 Uhr.
Der Lärm hat mich aufgeweckt.
(b) **Erwecken** is only used figuratively in the sense of 'call into life'.
Es gelang mir, ein reges Interesse für Musik bei ihm zu erwecken.

---

[1] *Gewaltig*: enormous, tremendous (not 'violent'). *Ein gewaltiger Saal, eine gewaltige Leidenschaft.*

[2] For *Gewalt* in the sense of (a) violence, (b) legitimate force, coercion, see under 'power'.

[3] *Auf etwas harren* is 'to wait persistently for something'. It is confined to literature. *Beharren* is 'to persist' in a state and represents the persistence as active, as an expression of will. *Er beharrt auf seiner Meinung. Verharren* means 'to remain' in a state, and stresses the persistence of the state, not the activity or will of the person. *Er verharrt im Amt, im Laster.*

[4] See Fowler's article on these verbs in *Modern English Usage*.

[5] *Aufgeweckt* as an adjective means 'wideawake, alert'. *Ein aufgeweckter Junge.*

WAKE (UP)

2. Intransitive.[1]

Erwachen, which in the literal sense is confined to literature, **wach werden** being a more common term, is the process of waking up, but does not necessarily indicate full wakefulness. In the latter case **aufwachen**, which does not exclude the process, is used (i.e. wake up). *Erwachen* is also used figuratively.[2]

Sie erwachte langsam (wurde langsam wach).
Ich wachte auf und sprang sofort aus dem Bett.
Hoffnungen erwachten in meiner Brust.

WALL **Mauer** is an outside wall which encloses a space such as a town or a prison, and therefore of strong brick, concrete, or the like. Its purpose is to prevent free entry or egress. **Wand** is the wall of a building. Both are used figuratively, *Mauer* as something that cannot be penetrated, *Wand* as something that separates. The two are often so close as to be interchangeable.

Die Stadt, das Gefängnis, hat dicke Mauern.
In vielen deutschen Städten standen nur noch die Wände der Häuser, das Innere war ausgebrannt.
Er schlug einen Nagel in die Wand (ein).
Die Wände dieser Hütte bestehen nur aus Stroh.
Es ist eine Mauer, eine Wand, zwischen uns.

WANT **A.** The sense of 'want' treated in this article is that defined by the *S.O.D.* as 'to desire, wish for', i.e. not 'lack' or 'need'. But 'want' in the sense of 'desire' can be weak or strong. When strong, it implies the power or authority, and sometimes the intention, to enforce one's will. Used positively, it then denotes a demand, a command, an intention, insistence, used negatively, a prohibition or a refusal. Examples of the weaker use are:

'I want this hat, please' (a request).
'Do you want sugar in your tea?'
'I really want you to stay here.'
'I did not want them to go out that day.'

Examples of the stronger use are:

'I want that money, give it to me.'
'I want that done immediately.'
'I don't want any nonsense.'

B. 1. Wollen has a still wider range of meaning than 'want'.[3] It translates 'want' in the sense of 'desire' in its strong, and in most of its weak uses. It also corresponds to 'will' as an auxiliary verb ('won't' as well as 'will not', in the negative), and to the verb 'to will'. The difficulty in considering *wollen* as a rendering of 'want' arises from the fact that *wollen* has the strong, peremptory sense more often than 'want'.[4] This applies particularly to the first person singular, present tense, less to the third person, hardly at all to the second person, more in the positive than in the negative, and not in the

---

[1] *Wachen* means 'to be, keep awake'; 'to watch'. *Ich wachte die ganze Nacht hindurch.*

[2] *Auferwecken* and *auferwachen* mean 'to awaken from the dead'. Compare *auferstehen*, 'to arise from the dead'.

[3] It does not mean 'lack', and means 'need', 'require' only when a thing is the subject. *Solche Dinge wollen* (=*müssen*) *geübt werden.*

[4] However, *durchaus* or *unbedingt* or a similar word is often added to *wollen* to give it the stronger sense (e.g. *wenn er durchaus will*, i.e. insists). *Wollen* in this sense must, on the other hand, often be translated into English by some term other than 'want'.

interrogative. Therefore, when 'I want' expresses a request, it should not be translated by *ich will*, which tends to mean 'I demand' or 'I insist' with reference to objects or the performing of actions which can be demanded or to actions which one insists on performing oneself. Thus *Ich will ein Zimmer für die Nacht haben* means 'I demand, I insist on...'. *Ich will hier bleiben* means 'I intend, mean to, insist on'. On the other hand, *Ich will deine Freundschaft* means 'I want' since friendship is not a thing that can be demanded. Similarly: *Das will ich mehr als alles andere in der Welt*; *ich will nur meine Ruhe.*

The negative *ich will nicht* is used more freely, in the sense of 'won't', 'forbid' (with a clause) and on the other hand 'do not want'. In the latter sense it implies a shorter rejection than *möchte nicht* (see **C**).

(a) Examples of the stronger use where *wollen* and 'want' correspond are:

Ich will den Revolver haben, gib ihn her.

Ich will keinen Unfug.

Ich will nicht, daß davon gesprochen wird (a prohibition).

Er will, daß die Arbeit schnell erledigt wird.

(b) Examples of the weaker use where *wollen* and 'want' correspond are:

Ich wollte diesen Hut haben.

Wir wollen den Frieden.

Wollen Sie Zucker in Ihrem Tee?

Wollen Sie Tee oder Kaffee?

Er wollte das Haus niederreißen lassen.

Wollen Sie, daß ich noch länger hier bleibe?

Ich wollte das Konzert hören, kam aber nicht dazu.

Ich wollte nicht bleiben, aber ich mußte.

2. The above examples show that sometimes *wollen* and sometimes *haben wollen* is used to translate 'want'. With a following dependent infinitive or clause *wollen* alone is used. The difficulty arises with a noun or pronoun object. Here it is necessary to distinguish the desire to possess (e.g. I want that hat) and the desire to see a thing exist or an action performed (e.g. Hitler wanted war).

(a) **Haben wollen** is normally used with reference to the desire to possess an object or a non-tangible thing; also to render 'want' used elliptically in the sense of 'want to have, to see' with reference to a thing or a person and accompanied by an adverb of place (e.g. I want you here).

Ich wollte eine Tasse Tee haben.

Er wollte ein Haus in der Nähe des Bahnhofs haben.

Wollen Sie das Auto für die Ferien haben?

Er will sein Portemonnaie haben.

Er will seine Ruhe haben.

Er wollte Anerkennung haben.

Ich wollte das Haus hier haben.

Sie will ihre Kinder immer um sich haben.

(b) **Wollen** is used in the sense of 'to desire to see' the existence of a thing, or the performance of an action; also with pronouns which do not refer to specific nouns denoting objects, in the sense of 'desire to possess' and 'desire to see exist'; furthermore, with persons in the sense of 'to possess sexually'.[1]

---

[1] 'Want' is also used with persons in two special senses: (*a*) to want to see, speak to (*wollen Sie ihn sprechen?*); (*b*) to seek (*von der Polizei gesucht*).

WANT

It is often used, furthermore, negatively and interrogatively for the desire to possess an object or a non-tangible thing, where, positively, *haben wollen* is normal.

Wir wollen nur dein Glück.
Er will den Frieden, den Krieg.
Sie wollen ein geeintes Europa.
Was wollen Sie?
Sie können alles haben, was Sie wollen.
Das haben wir nicht gewollt.
Sie wollen immer, was sie nicht bekommen können.
Er will alles umsonst.
Ich will kein Geld von Ihnen.
Ich will keine Anerkennung.
Wollen Sie Tee oder Kaffee?

C. Mögen, to like (see also under 'like'), is used in the imperfect subjunctive (*möchte*) for 'want' in the sense of 'should, would, like', in cases where *wollen* would be too peremptory or absolute, i.e. for the first person singular, present tense (and to a lesser extent the third person) of 'want'. *Haben* is added or omitted in the same way as with *wollen*.

Ich möchte diesen Hut haben.
Ich möchte Sie nicht beleidigen.
Ich möchte, daß er hier bleibt.
Er möchte nicht, daß wir kommen.

WARM **Wärmen** is the most general term and can be used of the warming of persons and things with the exception of food and drink. **Erwärmen** emphasizes that the object is cold before warmth is applied; and suggests a lesser degree of warmth than *wärmen*, i.e. to take the chill off. It is also used figuratively in reference to feelings. **Warm machen** is the common term in respect to anything which should be warm, e.g. food and drink. **Aufwärmen:** to warm up what has become cold.

Ich habe mich, meine Hände, das Zimmer, die Teller, gewärmt.
Der Ofen wärmt gut.
Die Sonne hat mich durch und durch gewärmt.
Die Sonne hat die Ziegelsteine gewärmt.
Er hat sich die Hände am Ofen erwärmt.
Die Sonne hat die Erde wieder erwärmt.
Ich kann mich für die Idee nicht erwärmen (warm to the idea).
'Ein Lächeln, das jedes Herz erwärmte...' (Heine, *Das Buch Le Grand*).
Er hat mir das Wasser warm gemacht.
Machen Sie das Essen warm.

WARN 1. **Warnen.**

Warnen can only be used in the sense of 'inform' when the information explicitly refers to a danger or a threat, i.e. when the latter are not left to be inferred.

When a negative order is given by an infinitive following *warnen*, *nicht* should be omitted, although it is sometimes inserted in popular speech. The absence of *nicht* does not, however, necessarily mean that 'not' is used in the English equivalent. Thus: *ich warne Sie, vorsichtig zu sein; den Mund zu halten*, means 'I warn you to be careful, to keep quiet', not 'not to be careful, not to keep quiet'. When the infinitive itself indicates an abstention from activity, the form is positive, but the sense negative, both in English and German.

Die Truppen wurden gewarnt, daß der Feind heranrücke.

Er warnte die Polizei, daß Diebe in der Nachbarschaft tätig seien.

Wir haben ihn vor der Möglichkeit eines Unfalls gewarnt.

Man hat uns davor gewarnt, daß dieser Weg gefährlich sei.

Er wurde gewarnt, daß er ausziehen müsse, wenn er die Miete nicht rechtzeitig bezahle.

Wir wurden gewarnt, unangenehme Änderungen zu erwarten.

Ich habe ihn oft genug (davor) gewarnt, das zu tun (not to do).

Ich habe ihn davor gewarnt zu zahlen.

2. Verwarnen is used only of a warning in the form of a threat given by a superior officer. *Er ist verwarnt worden.*

3. Other terms must be used when neither danger nor a threat is explicitly mentioned. Those in common use are:

(a) **Mahnen:** to remind someone emphatically of an obligation that he is bound to fulfil, particularly of a debt that he is expected to discharge.[1]

Er wurde gemahnt, daß er bis zum 5. März zahlen müsse.

(b) **Vorbereiten**, to prepare (see article on 'prepare'), i.e. to draw one's attention to something about to happen; **anweisen**, to instruct (see article on 'order'); **benachrichtigen**, to inform, must at times be used.

Wir wurden auf große Änderungen vorbereitet.

Die Truppen wurden angewiesen, sich bereit zu halten.

Ich benachrichtigte ihn, daß er bis zum 5. März ausziehen müsse.

WASTE[2] **1.** *Verschwenden, vergeuden* and *vertun*[3] all mean 'to use more of a thing than is necessary', often recklessly. They do not mean 'to leave a thing unused'. None of them is possible in official exhortations to be sparing, even with small amounts. The first two are used figuratively as well as literally.

(a) **Verschwenden**, i.e. *verschwinden machen*, a factitive verb, means 'to use lavishly, to squander'. Since 'lavish' implies no objective standard of measurement, the amount used in excess of what is necessary may, but need not, be great. In reference to small quantities, it should, however, only be used in emotional contexts, e.g. in the imperative or in exclamations.

Er hat sein Vermögen innerhalb von sechs Monaten verschwendet.

Verschwende keine Elektrizität.

Du verschwendest aber viel Mehl!

Er verschwendet seine Zeit mit unfruchtbaren Experimenten.

Er verschwendet seine Kräfte an unbegabte Studenten.

(b) **Vergeuden** (in M.H.G. in the simple form without *ver*, 'to be loud, to boast') is stronger than *verschwenden* in its implication of greater senseless-

---

[1] *Vermahnen*, like *verwarnen*, in present-day German implies a warning in the form of a threat. *Ermahnen* expresses an exhortation rather than a formal reminder. Its subject can only be personal, while that of *mahnen* can be a thing. *Sein Zustand mahnt zur Vorsicht. Gemahnen*: to put someone in mind of a thing.

[2] 'Waste' is cognate with G. *wüst*, L. *vastare*, F. *gâter*.

[3] There are numerous synonyms compounded with *ver*, which mostly indicate specific ways of squandering: *verprassen, verspielen, verschleudern* (to sell rashly at a ridiculously low price). *Verzetteln* means 'to fritter away' goods, time, energy, and the like. *Durchbringen* is 'to get through money in riotous living'.

ness and unprofitableness, though not necessarily with regard to the extent of the waste.

Er vergeudet sein ganzes Geld.

Vergeude kein Wasser bei der Trockenheit!

(c) **Vertun** refers only to money or goods and means 'to consume completely and without benefit'. It carries no secondary implications. Only the compound tenses are used.

Er hat sein ganzes Geld vertan.

2. In an official exhortation *sparsam sein, umgehen mit...* would be used.

Sei sparsam mit dem Kaffee! (geh'...um!).

3. German lacks a general term in the sense of 'not to use' with the implication of 'throw away' or 'allow to perish'. The following examples use specific terms which require no explanation.

Lassen Sie den Wein doch nicht stehen! (can also mean simply: don't take it away).

Es ist eine Sünde, Lebensmittel umkommen zu lassen, Brot wegzuwerfen.

WAY, MANNER, METHOD, MEANS The two main senses of 'way' treated here are those defined by the *S.O.D.* as follows: (*a*) 'Manner in which something is done or takes place; method of performing an action or operation; (*b*) 'a course of action; a device, expedient, method, or means by which some end may be attained'. Each of these senses can imply the other, one, however, normally being emphasized. Thus: 'I discussed with them the way I had got letters through to the occupied territories' (manner); 'I am looking for a way to get letters...' (means). German uses different words for these two senses. In a few cases, however, the words for 'manner' (*Art, Art und Weise*) tend to emphasize the sense of 'means'. These border-line cases are discussed in this article.

A few other clearly defined and less clearly defined uses of 'way', which present difficulty in translation, are dealt with briefly.

A. MANNER, METHOD.

1. Art and **Art und Weise** contrasted with *so, wie*.

Neither *Art* nor *Art und Weise* is normally used to refer to trivial every-day acts. When so used, they tend to be emphatic. While it is possible to say *das ist die beste Art, abzuwaschen*, the normal statement is *so wäscht man am besten ab* (thus, in this way). Similarly *zeigen Sie mir die richtige Art, den Baum zu stutzen* and *zeigen Sie mir, wie man den Baum am besten stutzt*. In both these examples *Art* is possible because it suggests a method. When the idea of method is not present, or only in a rudimentary way, *wie* is preferred. *Ich sagte ihm, wie ich seine Adresse entdeckte* (the way I..., 'way' being used so universally that it can refer to something accidental).

When 'way' is accompanied by an adjective, German uses an adverb with *so* or *wie*. *Am besten schneiden Sie Blumen so* (that's the best way...). *Ich erklärte ihm, wie man Blumen am besten schneidet*. Further examples:

Beachten Sie, wie er den Ball anschlägt (*Art* would indicate a style).

Man tötet eine Schlange so: man tritt beiseite und schlägt ihr mit einem Stock auf den Kopf (the way to kill a snake is to...).

Hören Sie, wie sein Herz pocht (listen to the way...).

Es herrscht Besorgnis darüber, wie Unruhen überall ausbrechen (there is alarm at the way...).

2. Weise refers strictly to action, i.e. to the manner of doing, or happening. Unlike *Art* it cannot refer to what a person or a thing is, i.e. to its nature. For further explanation of its meaning see *Art und Weise*, with which in present-day use its meaning is identical, but by which it has been supplanted in most formal combinations.

Weise is now practically restricted to its use with *auf* and *in* (see 8(a)).

It is followed by an infinitive only when the idea contained in the phrase thus formed can also be expressed as a compound noun (*seine Weise, die Dinge zu betrachten = seine Betrachtungsweise*).

It is sometimes found in combination with the possessive adjective, but with a rather old-fashioned flavour (see Grimm's Dictionary: *das ist doch sonst seine Weise nicht*).

It is not pluralized except in compounds. With words such as *viel, all, verschieden, zweierlei, vielerlei, mannigfach, mehrfach* it is used in the singular with a plural sense (*in verschiedener Weise =* in various ways).

3. Art.

(a) The primary meaning of *Art*[1] is 'kind', 'species', that of 'way' being a development from this meaning. The closeness of meaning in the English terms is seen in such phrases as 'a kind (style) of life', 'a way of life'.[2] Sometimes German prefers to follow *Art* by the genitive of the noun instead of the infinitive or a *wie* clause (the latter, however, not being impossible). Thus: *die Art des Möbelarrangements* (the way the furniture is arranged); *eine neue Art der Krebsbehandlung* (a new way of treating cancer); *einige Arten des bildlichen Sprachgebrauchs, die die Anschaulichkeit der Darstellung erhöhen* (a few ways in which the figurative use of language heightens the vividness of presentation).

To sum up: *Art* denotes a clearly recognizable type in its general characteristics.

> *Das ist eine bequeme Art zu reisen.*

> *Es gibt verschiedene Arten, Brühe für ein Schwein zu machen (S.O.D.).*

(b) *Art* refers to the result of an action, its effect, to a whole. The result of an action may be the production of a thing. *Die Art, wie das Schiff gebaut ist, macht es unbrauchbar für gewisse Manöver* refers to the nature of the ship, not to the process of building it (see *Art und Weise*).

> *Die Art, wie das Heer organisiert ist, trägt den neuesten Methoden der Kriegsführung Rechnung* (the finished product).

> *Die Art, wie er unterrichtet, zeigt ihn von Pestalozzi beeinflußt* (the type, character of his instruction).

(c) The effect of an action can be style, which is a common implication of *Art*. In the same way it denotes a person's manner of doing or being, his behaviour considered as an effect.

> *Die Art, wie Toscanini Beethovens fünfte Symphonie dirigiert, ist grundverschieden von der Furtwänglers.*

> *Die Art seines Klavierspiels (wie er Klavier spielt; seine Art, Klavier zu spielen) stempelt ihn zum Schüler Schnabels.*

> *Die ganze Art, wie der Staatsanwalt den Prozeß führte, war höchst eindrucksvoll.*

---

[1] Kluge (*Etymologisches Wörterbuch der deutschen Sprache*) connects *Art* with Latin *ars* (art), which is, however, not a universally accepted view.

[2] In older English 'kind' was sometimes used in the sense of 'way' (see *S.O.D.* and *A Shakespeare Glossary* by C. T. Onions). Note also 'manner' in the sense of 'kind' in the phrase 'what manner of man' (see *S.O.D.* under 'manner').

Die Art seines Benehmens zeugt von guter Herkunft.

Ich mag die Art nicht, wie er antwortete (lachte, seine Kollegen behandelte).

(d) From this reference to a whole follows a tendency of *Art* to denote a short act, i.e. one which is seen more or less in one moment of attention as a whole. This is clear in a movement of the body (*die Art, wie er den Arm hebt*). But it can also refer to other types of acts. *Die geschickte Art, wie er mit X fertig wurde...* implies a momentary device.

(e) In the plural *Arten* needs to be preceded by some defining adjective such as *verschieden, möglich, vorhanden* in cases where 'ways' is not preceded by any such defining word. *Zählen Sie die verschiedenen Arten der Krebsbehandlung auf.*

(f) Whereas 'way' can mean 'the right way', *richtig* must be added to *Art* (and *Art und Weise*) to render this sense. *Das ist die richtige Art, Wein zu trinken* (that's the way...).

4. (a) **Art und Weise** is used to refer to the sum of the details of an action, both those intimately and those loosely connected with it. It suggests the course of the action, a procedure, a technical process, and the like. Since it does not refer to the general characteristics of the whole, it cannot be qualified by adjectives which indicate only these (e.g. *neu, ungewöhnlich*).

Strictly speaking the phrase should mean the sum of the general plus the sum of the particular characteristics (details).[1] In present-day use it has lost the sense of *Art*, retaining only that of *Weise*, and is used in those formal combinations where *Weise* alone is impossible. It can denote an individual and even arbitrary and capricious way, while in reference to style or behaviour it is often derogatory.

Die Art und Weise, wie das Schiff gebaut wurde, spricht viel für die Organisation der Arbeit.

Die Art und Weise, wie das Heer organisiert wurde, war ein Wunder.

Die Art und Weise, wie er unterrichtet, ist mustergültig.

Die Art und Weise, wie der Staatsanwalt den Prozeß führte, war sehr geschickt.

Die Art und Weise seines Klavierspiels paßt ins Kino (derogatory).

Die Art und Weise seines Benehmens war hanebüchen.

Die Art und Weise, wie er sich an seine Aufgabe machte, war verkehrt.

Er tadelte scharf (lobte) die Art und Weise, wie wir die Verhandlungen führten.

Er sprach ein paar Worte über die Art und Weise, wie er Briefe nach den vom Feinde besetzten Gebieten durchgebracht hatte.

Er beschrieb die Art und Weise, wie die verbotenen Waren eingeschmuggelt wurden.

Die Art und Weise, wie das Auto dahinsaust, zeigt, daß es nicht mehr in fester Hand ist.

(b) It follows from the fundamental meaning of *Art und Weise* (the sum of the details) that the action to which it refers tends to be an extended one (contrast *Art*).

Die geschickte (gerechte) Art und Weise, wie er X behandelte....

(c) *Art und Weise* cannot be pluralized.

---

[1] See Sanders-Wülfing, *Handwörterbuch der Deutschen Sprache*: '...*Art und Weise, wo Weise die Art näher bestimmt, weil Weise genau genommen, sich auf die zufälligen, besonderen Eigenschaften bezieht, wie Art auf die wesentlichen, inneren, der Gesamtheit gleicherweise gemeinsamen....*'

5. Manier tends to be familiar in tone. It can be friendly, but is frequently derogatory or ironical. It is characteristically used with colloquialisms. As a synonym of *Stil* it can suggest a mannerism,[1] but compare the title of E. T. A. Hoffmann's work: *Fantasiestücke in Callots Manier.*

Das ist die richtige Manier, Wein zu trinken (said to a friend, whereas *Art* is more objective and distant).

Er hat eine tölpelhafte Manier, Brot zu schneiden.

Das ist eine nette Manier, Geschäftchen zu machen (but: *eine nette Art, Geschäfte...*).

Die einzige, beste, Manier, den Kerl loszuwerden, ist, ihm Grobheiten zu sagen.

Die unnatürliche Manier dieses Menschen geht einem auf die Nerven.

6. Methode translates 'method' and also 'way' when the latter clearly denotes a scientific process or strongly suggests a systematic procedure.

Es gibt eine neue Methode, Krebs zu behandeln (also: *eine neue Art der Krebsbehandlung,* i.e. kind of...).

Er hat eine neue Methode erfunden, alte Kleider zu entglänzen.

Er hat verschiedene Methoden ausprobiert, seine Studenten für lyrische Dichtung zu interessieren.

Ärzte haben jetzt schmerzlose Methoden, Zähne auszuziehen.

Wir haben uns eine Methode ausgedacht, Briefe nach den besetzten Gebieten durchzubringen.

Keine der Methoden, die sie angewandt haben, um die Moral der Truppen aufrechtzuerhalten, hat Erfolg gehabt.

7. Haltung (see 'attitude') is often used in the sense of a manner towards someone else.

Seine Haltung mir gegenüber wurde plötzlich anders.

8. IN A WAY, MANNER, FASHION[2]   (a) *Auf, in* before *Weise.*

(i) *Auf* concentrates attention on the manner in which the action expressed by the verb is performed or takes place. The manner of the action is apprehended with the senses in its concrete reality and is felt as vivid, direct, immediate, individual, unique, as though one were pointing to it. An appeal to the eye is frequently suggested. In addition to this objective vividness *auf* can indicate an emotional participation on the part of the speaker (commiseration is expressed by its use in the sentence: *er starb auf dieselbe Weise wie sein Bruder*).

The verb with which such a phrase is associated is normally, though not necessarily, a verb of external action. If it denotes an inner attitude of mind, this is by the use of *auf*, so to speak, externalized, made palpable to the senses. Such uses should be left to the accomplished writer (see example below from Thomas Mann's *Lotte in Weimar*).

Führen Sie den Prozeß auf diese Weise (followed by a detailed description).

Auf diese Weise brachte er die Gesellschaft wieder in heitere Laune (following a full description of the way).

[1] The plural *Manieren* means 'manners' and can be used in a good or bad sense.

[2] Where 'in this way' does not describe the manner of an action, but merely emphasizes the fact of its being performed, only *so* is possible in German. 'I cannot let you cut an old friend in this way' (*S.O.D.*)=*Ich kann es nicht zulassen, daß Sie einen alten Freund so schneiden.*

Er drohte ihm mit einem Revolver und hinderte ihn auf diese Weise, ins Haus zu treten.

Wir erfreuten uns auf diese Weise der neugewonnenen Freiheit (the way has been described in detail).

Dazu war er auf keine Weise zu bewegen (we think of the possible ways individually).

'*Madame Mozart konnte oder wollte von der Richtung, die sein leicht bewegliches Gefühl hier mehr und mehr nahm, auf keine Weise ablenken*' (Mörike, *Mozart auf der Reise nach Prag*).

'...*den entnervenden, sich täglich erneuernden Kampf zwischen seinem*... *Willen und dieser wachsenden Müdigkeit*...*die das Produkt auf keine Weise, durch kein Anzeichen des Versagens und der Laßheit verraten durfte*' (Thomas Mann, *Der Tod in Venedig*).

'*Und er*...*schürte und nährte sie (die Flamme seiner Liebe) auf alle Weise, weil er treu sein wollte*' (Thomas Mann, *Tonio Kröger*).

Ich habe es auf alle mögliche Weise versucht.

Das Abenteuer konnte nur auf zweierlei Weise enden: entweder würde er unerhörte Macht gewinnen, oder er würde das Land dem Untergang nahebringen.

Er hat sich auf seltsame Weise benommen (we visualize the way).

Er ist auf jämmerliche Weise umgekommen.

Die Gefangenen wurden auf barbarische Weise umgebracht.

'*Können Sie einen vernünftigen Gedanken fassen, Kröger,*...*wenn es Ihnen auf eine unanständige Weise im Blute kribbelt und eine Menge von unzugehörigen Sensationen Sie beunruhigt*' (Thomas Mann, *Tonio Kröger*).

'*Er spricht wirklich ganz so, wie Ingrid es nachgemacht hat: nasal und auf besondere Weise gedehnt, aber offenbar ohne jede Affektation...*' (Thomas Mann, *Unordnung und frühes Leid*).

'...*daß Kestner ihm (Goethe) auf eine Weise vertraute, die ihm nicht grade zur Ehre gereichte*' (Thomas Mann, *Lotte in Weimar*) (a daring use of *auf*, normal practice requiring *in*).

(ii) The use of *in* with *Weise* makes the reference to the manner of the action expressed by the verb less vivid, dynamic, and individual than *auf*, in other words, more remote. In place of the visualization and sensuous appeal suggested by *auf*, *in* indicates an intellectual awareness of the manner of the action. This may take the form of a mere report of or reference to the manner (*in solcher Weise verlor er sein Vermögen* gives a colourless reference to the manner, whereas *auf solche Weise* would evoke it). It may be a judgment (*er hat sich in gradezu schändlicher Weise benommen*, where not an image of a disgraceful act is suggested, but a moral judgment that the way is disgraceful). In contrast to the individual, unique way denoted by *auf*, *in* refers to the normal, well-established way (*in dieser Weise kam er nach England* gives a mere reference to some usual way such as ship, aeroplane, whereas *auf diese Weise* would conjure up a complete picture of some strange way in its individual features).

In combinations where attention is focused less on the manner in its sensuous reality than on some association gathered to it, *in* is normally used, *auf* being exceptional, emphatic and generally denoting emotional participation. Examples of such combinations where the association is stressed more than the manner of the action are *Weise* followed by a result clause (often in the form of a relative clause) or in comparison (*er sprack in solcher Weise, daß uns allen die Galle überlief; er sprach in einer Weise, die uns alle empörte; er spricht in derselben Weise wie sein Bruder).* Another association may be that of content, sense *(in dieser Weise läßt sich der Roman befriedigend auslegen,* where the reference is to content, *auf,* which would refer to the act of interpreting, being absurd; *er sprach in folgender Weise,* a sentence which would be followed by an account of the contents of what is said, while *auf* would look forward to a description of the manner; *Sie können das Wort nicht in dieser Weise gebrauchen,* i.e. sense).

Since *in* does not evoke an image of a particular way, its use in such phrases as *in keiner Weise, in solcher Weise, in jeder Weise* often gives *Weise* the meaning of 'respect' (see **D**). These phrases are practically equivalent to 'altogether', 'in no wise', 'not at all', 'thus'.

Nur wenn man das Radio in dieser Weise gebraucht (e.g. for educational purposes, where *Weise* refers not to the manner of handling it, but to an idea associated with its use).

Die Kunst des Dichters kommt hier in einer Weise zur Geltung wie sonst selten.

Handeln Sie in solcher Weise, daß Ihr Gewissen rein bleibt.

Hier tritt der Philosoph des Sozialismus hervor, aber in ganz anderer Weise als im 'Kapital'.

'Wir wagten es nicht, dem alten Mann in derselben Weise mitzuspielen wie den anderen... .bewegten wir uns mit solcher Geschwindigkeit und in so mannigfacher Weise, daß er sich durchaus keine deutliche Vorstellung von uns hätte bilden können' (Ricarda Huch, *Teufeleien*).

Er ist imstande, den Vorlesungen in jeder Weise zu folgen.

Dazu war er in keiner Weise zu bewegen (not at all, *keineswegs*).

Er äußerte sich in einer Weise, wie sie für eine solche Haltung typisch ist.

Er handelte in der ihm eigenen Weise (in his usual way).

'Aber andererseits kann er auch in der Weise die Contenance verlieren, daß er selbst in das unangenehmste Ausplaudern gerät und sein Intimstes nach außen kehrt' (Thomas Mann, *Buddenbrooks*).

Man hat ihm in der übelsten Weise mitgespielt (*auf* would make one see the manner).

Sein Zorn wuchs in unerträglicher Weise (from the point of view of the sufferer, *auf* from that of the onlooker).

Er redete in unzusammenhängender Weise.

'...indem er in etwas unerzogener Weise den Damen den Rücken zuwandte' (Thomas Mann, *Tristan*). (*Auf* would produce a purely visual effect and sacrifice the detachment at which Mann is here aiming).

'Er verbeugte sich und begann dann, offenbar ein wenig verlegen, zu essen, indem er Messer und Gabel mit seinen großen, weißen und schön geformten Händen, die aus sehr engen Ärmeln hervorsahen, in ziemlich affektierter Weise bewegte' (Thomas Mann, *Tristan*). (*Auf* would unduly emphasize the movements of the hands).

(b) *Art* preceded by *auf* and *in.*

(i) *Art* distinguished from *Weise.*

Sie ist schön auf südländische Art (she is a southern type of beauty; *Weise* being impossible, because it must refer to the manner of doing something, whereas only *Art* can express what one is).

Auf diese Art werden wir alles verlieren (a method mentioned as a type).

Auf diese Weise would be preceded or followed by a description of the details of the action.

(ii) *Auf* and *in* distinguished. *In seiner* (*ihrer*, etc.) *Art* means 'in his (her) species, class, category', while *auf seine* (*ihre*, etc.) *Art* means 'in his (her) individual way'. *Diese Katze ist in ihrer Art ganz nett* (nice for a cat, *auf* suggesting nice in an individual way, unlike other cats).

B. MEANS TO AN END.

As was pointed out in the general introduction to 'way' the senses of 'manner' and 'means' are often both present, though one or the other is the primary sense. With certain verbs such as 'find', 'invent', 'seek', 'apply', the idea of 'means' is stressed. In such cases *Art* and *Art und Weise*, which primarily refer to 'manner', are impossible. *Mittel, Weg, Mittel und Wege* must be used or another construction resorted to. With verbs such as 'have', 'know' either sense of 'way' may predominate. Contrast 'he has a way of making you feel uncomfortable' (manner), with 'he has a way to bring him to his senses' (means). Similarly 'I know the way his confidence was won' and 'I know a way to win his confidence'. German normally uses different words for these senses.

1. *Art* as 'means'. *Art* makes a statement about the manner in which an action has been performed or has taken place. If it suggests a plan or advice how to achieve a purpose, this is subordinate to the primary meaning. In the sentence *ich tadelte seine Art, ein Vermögen zu machen*, what is stressed is his manner or method in making money. In *das ist eine einfache Art, reich zu werden*, *Art* denotes manner, but combines with it a suggestion of a means to an end. The important point is that the sentence merely points out objectively this existing 'way', without regarding it first and foremost as an instrument to achieve a purpose. This combination (*Art* and the verb *sein*), which expresses purpose in a secondary sense, is not uncommon. Similarly: *das ist die beste Art, eine Stellung zu bekommen*; *die beste Art, Lebensmittel zu bekommen, wenn sie knapp sind, ist, morgens um 9 Uhr im Laden zu sein.*

In other combinations (e.g. with *kennen* or *wissen*) *Art* is found, but less commonly, other words being preferred. Thus, while it is possible to say *ich weiß eine sichere Art, das Geld, das Sie im Augenblick nicht brauchen, anzulegen*, it would be more common to turn the sentence as follows: *ich weiß, wie Sie Geld...sicher anlegen können.*

It will be observed that the infinitive or *wie* clause may be taken as indicating a result, intended or not intended, as much as a purpose. Thus *das ist die beste Art, sich unbeliebt zu machen* clearly expresses a result not intended. *Art*, thus used, is most common and natural when it refers to behaviour.

If the phrase which denotes the purpose or the result (the infinitive phrase or the *wie* clause) is omitted, *Art* is impossible. Thus, while the following is admissible: *die sicherste Art, das Buch zu bekommen, wäre, es in Amerika zu bestellen*, the omission of *das Buch zu bekommen* would make it necessary to substitute *der sicherste Weg* or *das Sicherste* (the safest thing to do) *wäre...*'.

2. Mittel, Mittel und Wege translate the English 'means' and 'ways and means' and also 'way' when the latter is considered primarily as an instrument to achieve an end.

Ich habe ein wirksames Mittel in der Hand, ihn zur Vernunft zu bringen.

Sie wandten ein bekanntes Mittel an, ihn zum Reden zu bringen.

Er hat ein neues Mittel erfunden, Malaria zu heilen (or: *Heilmittel gegen*).

Ich suchte Mittel und Wege, meine Ansichten in weiteren Kreisen bekannt zu machen.

3. **Weg** can be used in this sense provided that something of the physical image contained in its literal sense is preserved. The verb, adjective, preposition combined with *Weg* should therefore be compatible with this image. Hence it is found in such combinations as: *einen Weg finden, suchen, kennen, beschreiten*; *ein Weg, der...führt*; *der Weg zu...*, *auf einem Wege*. It should not, however, be used with verbs like *haben, verstehen*. Because of this condition the process indicated by *Weg* tends, though not necessarily, to be lengthy. A loose use, without retention of the image, sometimes occurs.

A following infinitive, but not a *wie* clause is possible.

Ich habe einen Weg ausfindig gemacht, Briefe nach den vom Feinde besetzten Gebieten durchzubringen.

Daß sie diesen Weg eingeschlagen haben, die Finanzen in Ordnung zu bringen, macht sie gradezu zu Revolutionären.

Ich sehe mich nach einem Weg um, der mir aus dieser Sackgasse heraushilft.

Ich sehe einen Weg, der uns vielleicht eine Stufe weiterbringt.

Er hat auf neue Wege zum Verständnis der Kunst hingewiesen.

Ich weiß (kenne) einen sicheren Weg, Geld zu verdienen.

Er ist auf indirektem Wege an die Schwierigkeit herangegangen.

C. Möglichkeit translates 'way' in the sense of 'possible way', i.e. in contexts which define the number of ways in which a thing can be done (or thought, conceived). It is thus common with numerals and words such as *kein, einzig, viel, verschieden*. The emphasis is on the fact of possibility rather than on the content of the way.

Gibt es denn keine Möglichkeit für ihn, seinen Lebensunterhalt hier zu verdienen?

Die einzige Möglichkeit, ihn für Ihre Pläne zu gewinnen, wäre, ihn zum Partner zu machen.

Ich sehe (wüßte) keine Möglichkeit, ihm weiter zu helfen.

Es bestehen unendlich viele Möglichkeiten, Waffen hier einzuschmuggeln.

Es gibt zwei Möglichkeiten, diese Stelle zu deuten.

D. RESPECT, ASPECT, FEATURE.

Weise (in the singular) can be used in such expressions as: *in jeder, keiner, mancher, keinerlei, vielerlei, zweifacher, dreifacher*, etc., *Weise. Hinsicht* is also used in the singular in this sense.

Er kann dem Vortrag in jeder Weise (Hinsicht) folgen.

Sie haben in zweifacher Weise (Hinsicht) recht.

E. EXTENT, RATE   (See also under 'rate').

When 'way' has these meanings, *Umfang, Ausmaß, Tempo* must be used. *Es besteht Besorgnis über den Umfang (das Ausmaß, das Tempo) des Geburtenrückganges* (the way the birthrate is falling). *Das Tempo, in dem der Baum in den letzten Monaten gewachsen ist, ist erstaunlich* (the way the tree has grown).

F. POSITION.

Die Stellung, in der (colloquially: *wie*) *er im Bett liegt, muß sehr unbequem sein* (or: *es muß sehr unbequem sein, wie...*) (the way he lies...).

G. 'Way' does not denote 'manner' or 'means' but emphasizes the fact itself. Here only a noun or verbal noun or *wie* is possible.

Das Wellige der Landschaft macht sie idyllisch (the way the landscape undulates...).

Das Flickern der Lichter verleiht dem Hafen einen Zauber (the way the lights twinkle . . .).
Ihr Lächeln gewinnt alle Herzen (the way she smiles . . .).
Der Haß gegen den Besiegten zeigt sich darin, wie die Soldaten nicht zögern, Vorübergehende vom Bürgersteig zu stoßen (in the way the soldiers . . .).

WEAKEN   Schwächen is 'to make weak', i.e. lacking sufficient strength.
Abschwächen is 'to make a thing (not a person) weaker than it was before', but not in such a way that it completely lacks strength. It is mostly used in the sense of 'to tone down' the intensity of an effect. Hence, it is the only possible term with *Wort*.
Die Strapazen haben mich sehr geschwächt.
Eine solche Politik muß die Regierung schwächen.
Der Gebrauch von 'gern' schwächt 'möchte' ab.
Diese Szene hat die Spannung, die Wirkung, des Stücks (ab)geschwächt (*abschwächen* could be deliberate).
Er muß manchmal seine impulsiven Äußerungen abschwächen.

WEIGH   1. Wiegen is used both transitively in the literal sense of 'to ascertain the weight of' a person or thing by any means, and intransitively in the literal sense of 'to be of a specified weight'. Figuratively, it means 'to have influence'.
Er wiegt das Gemüse sehr genau.
Wieviel wiegen Sie?
Das Buch wiegt 3 Pfund.
Solche Gründe wiegen nicht schwer bei mir.

2. Wägen is used in the literal sense only in poetry and in exalted prose. *Wog* and *gewogen* have replaced *wägte* and *gewägt* in ordinary prose. Figuratively, it is used in ordinary prose in the sense of 'to estimate the effect, values, of' a thing only with a few nouns (e.g. *seine Worte, Handlungen, wägen*; see Duden). **Abwägen** means 'to balance' one thing carefully against another. **Erwägen** means 'to consider all aspects of a matter' (see 'consider'), but does not emphasize the balancing of two things against each other.
Sie müssen das Für und das Wider, die Argumente, gegen einander abwägen.
Ich habe meine Chancen noch nicht erwogen.

WELL   The original meaning was according to one's wish or will (*W.*). In modern English the basic meaning underlying the main uses is: in such a manner as one would wish. Therefore:

1. (a) Excellently, satisfactorily, skilfully, expertly, in a proper manner; further: to a good, proper or suitable degree, suitably, abundantly, fully, adequately. The German adverb which corresponds to this meaning is normally **gut**.
Sie kocht, singt, strickt, schwimmt gut.
Das Haus ist gut gebaut.
Der Garten wurde gut bewässert.
Es ist ein gut durchdachter Plan.
Er ist gut imstande, sich zu verteidigen.
Er behandelt sie gut.

(b) When 'well' acquires the force of a substantive the German equivalent becomes **Gutes,** i.e. the neuter of the adjective, meaning 'good things'.

Er spricht nur Gutes von jedermann.

(c) Well done (an exclamation) =*gut! bravo!*

(d) In some cases German uses **wohl,** though not as extensively as in earlier German. Trübner gives a list of verbs with which *wohl* is usual, amongst these its use with verbs of knowing and of perception being particularly common. With these two classes **genau** is a close equivalent, and sometimes *gut* is also used.

Ich weiß wohl, worauf er hinaus wollte.

Er weiß wohl (genau), was sein muß.

Ich sehe wohl (genau), daß uns kein anderer Weg offensteht (intellectually; *ich sehe gut*: with the physical eye).

Ich bin mir wohl bewußt.

While *gut* stresses the workmanship, *wohl* draws attention to the aesthetic effect.

Wohl gebaut, wohl gebildet, wohl gestaltet, wohl geraten.

Wohlriechende Blumen.

(e) With reference to health **gut** is used with the impersonal verb *gehen,* **wohl** with *sich fühlen* and in the substantives *Wohlergehen, Wohlbefinden.*

Es geht ihm sehr gut.

Ich fühle mich wohl (unwohl).

But: *ich fühle mich besser (als gestern).*

(f) Implications often contained in the sense described under **1** are:

(i) Thoroughly, effectively, intimately, clearly. **Gut** can render the first three of these implications, but for the first two **tüchtig** and **ordentlich** are often used.

Schütteln Sie die Flasche gut (tüchtig, ordentlich).

Er wurde gut (tüchtig, ordentlich) durchgeprügelt.

Ich kenne ihn gut.

Er ist in diesem Fach gut bewandert.

Das Schloß hebt sich deutlich von den anderen Gebäuden auf dem Berg ab (stands out well from).

(ii) In a prosperous manner.

Er lebt in Hülle und Fülle (he lives well).

(iii) In accordance with the circumstances, the occasion, one's condition, or the like. With reason, propriety, or the like; properly (*W.*). The common expression 'may (might, could) well' contains this implication. German **wohl, mit gutem Grund** and, with the negative, **nicht leicht.**

Er könnte wohl den Sieg davontragen.

Das ist eine Verordnung, deren Rechtsgültigkeit sehr wohl in Frage gestellt werden könnte.

Du kannst mit gutem Grund erstaunt sein.

Er hielt sich in einigem Abstand von der anderen, und zwar mit gutem Grund (or: *er hatte auch guten, allen Grund dazu* =and well he might).

Sie können ihm Ihre Hilfe nicht leicht (or: *schwerlich*) *verweigern* (you can't very well refuse to help him).

An example of this meaning is also the phrase 'may as well' (=with equal reason, profit, without harm).

2. To the full degree or extent, fully, quite: **ganz, völlig; so recht, richtig.**

Er war ganz (völlig) ausser Sichtweite (well out of sight).

Er kam gerade an, bevor das Nachtmahl so recht (richtig) begonnen hatte (he arrived before dinner had well begun) (*W.*).

3. A sense close to **2** but not identical with it: to a considerable degree or extent. This sense must be variously rendered into German, but common approximations (not equivalents) are: **weit, ein gutes Stück.**

Er lehnte sich weit zurück.

Er ritt weit vor den anderen (well in advance of) (*W.*).

Er ist mit seiner Arbeit ein gutes Stück voran gekommen (is well ahead).

This meaning must not be confused with that in the sentence: he is well out of it, i.e. he did well, acted wisely, to keep out of it, or: he was lucky to be out of it. *Er tat gut daran, sich herauszuhalten; er kann froh sein, sich herausgehalten zu haben, nicht dabei gewesen zu sein.*

4. Fortunate, advantageous, suitable, proper—only in predicative use (*W.*) and mostly only in the following expressions:

It is well for him that he came: *Es war klug von ihm, daß er kam; er kann sich glücklich schätzen (froh sein*—see note to **3**), *daß er kam.*

All is well: *Es ist alles in Ordnung.*

5. As an intensive meaning very, very much (Ox. III, 3), but less common today than in earlier English. Mostly: **sehr,** sometimes **wohl, gut.**

Die lange Reise war sehr der Mühe wert (well worth the trouble).

In Studentenkreisen ist er sehr beliebt (well liked).

Sie hätten es wohl verdient, gepeitscht zu werden (well deserved).

Die Kürze seiner Ausdrucksweise gefällt mir gut (wohl).

6. As an exclamation, originally an ellipsis for 'it is well' (*W.*). While it may be used in isolation, demanding a statement or explanation from someone, it is generally used to introduce a remark or statement (*S.O.D.*). Basically it means that one notes a fact (i.e. that is so), but also adopts an attitude to it. Thus it carries a number of implications, in general that one accepts the fact or desires a further explanation of this. German uses both *nun* and *na*, followed by *gut* (sometimes *schön*) when acceptance is stressed. *Nun* implies more reflection than *na*, which implies a quick, often emotional explanation. Simply to resume a narrative, particularly after hesitation or a false start or a linguistic breakdown German uses *also.*

(a) Agreement, acquiescence.

Nun gut, nehmen Sie was Sie wollen (in Gottes Namen also possible in this sense).

(b) Resignation, dissociation of oneself from a thing.

Nun gut, da ist nichts zu machen.

Nun gut, tu was du willst.

(c) Concession.

Nun (or: nun gut), es kann stimmen.

(d) Relief.

Nun, danket aber Gott (thank God for that).

(e) Surprise, annoyance, indignation.

Na (or: zum Teufel), damit habe ich nicht gerechnet.

(f) Expectancy, a demand for further information.

Na, was machen Sie hier?

Na, was willst du eigentlich?

Na, hör mal!
Na, ich warte auf das, was du mir zu sagen hast.
Na, da hört sich alles auf.
Na, das ist ja unglaublich.

(g) A reservation, qualified recognition of what has been said, often preceded by 'very' or followed by 'but'.

Nun, das muß ich mir noch überlegen.
Nun gut, aber wie steht es mit den anderen?
Nun, tu' es nicht nochmal.
Nun gut, wir treffen uns heute abend.

(h) *'Also'* to resume a statement.

Er sagte mir...also er weigert sich, mitzumachen.

WHILE 'While' must always be translated in ordinary prose by **während**, except when it expresses a condition, i.e. when it is equivalent to 'as long as'. In the latter case it must be translated by **solange**.[1]

Während ich die Straße hinunterging, marschierten Soldaten vorbei.
Diese Politik wird Sie retten, während die andere bestimmt zum Untergang führen wird (whereas).
Sie können nicht herein, solange Sie keinen Paß haben.

WISH (v.) Case treated: 'wish' followed by a dependent clause.

1. Wollte and **wünschte** (both imperfect subjunctive) have a narrower range of application than 'wish'. The distinction between them is as follows. *Wollte* is strongly emotional, often expressing feelings that are near breaking point, and represents fulfilment as remote, if not altogether impossible. *Wünschte* is less emotional and more detached, sometimes, as in a rebuke, to the point of superiority. Fulfilment is conceived as less remote than with *wollte*.

Ich wollte bloß, er würde mit dem Geschwätz aufhören.
Ich wollte, ich hätte ihn frühzeitig genug gewarnt.
Ich wünschte, Sie würden das nicht tun (almost a request to desist).
Ich wünschte, ich hätte ein Auto.

2. In conversation, when it is not desired to express the above shades of meaning, 'wish' can best be rendered by an exclamation with *wenn*, etc.

Wenn das Feuer bloß brennen würde!
Hätte ich ihm das nur rechtzeitig gesagt!

WOMAN Weib emphasizes the sexual side of 'woman', and should be used where 'woman' is conceived or presented exclusively in this way (e.g. in Wedekind's plays). It is also used to denote an ugly old woman without special reference to sex, and when preceded by an appropriate adjective approximates to 'hag'. The plural is only used pejoratively. **Frau**, while it refers to sex, does so less emphatically and less exclusively. It can denote all the qualities of a woman and is thus the most general term. The adjectives

---

[1] In present-day German *indem* does not mean 'while'. It indicates manner, means, and can be translated by (a) 'by' as an approximate synonym of *dadurch, daß*, (b) 'in that' or (c) the present participle without preposition. *Indem er ins Zimmer trat, sagte er...* ('entering', not 'while entering', which would separate the two actions in all except time). *Indem* now rarely occurs where the subjects of the two clauses do not refer to the same person. It associates the two actions very closely.

which can be combined or not combined with the two words are the best illustration of their meaning. Thus *ein schönes Weib* refers only to a beautiful body, *eine schöne Frau* includes this, but can suggest other qualities as well. *Gebildet* can be applied to *Frau* only. In compounds *Frau* is the normal term to denote the social, intellectual activities, and the like, of woman (e.g. *Frauenverein*). *Weib* is sometimes used disparagingly (e.g. *Weiberklatsch*).

Frauenzimmer,[1] which has gone through several changes of meaning, is now pejorative, and refers particularly to stupidity or silliness (e.g. *ein blödes Frauenzimmer*).

WONDER 1. **Sich wundern**: to be astonished, not to be able to understand. It is followed by *über*, the infinitive, or a clause (e.g. *daß*). It is stronger, more emotional than the impersonal *es wundert mich*.[2]

Ich wundere mich, daß Sie sich so etwas gefallen lassen.
Ich wundere mich, Sie hier zu finden.
Ich wunderte mich über seine Kenntnisse.

2. **Verwundern** is used in the same sense as *wundern*, but normally only in the passive with *sein*, and in the phrase *es ist nicht zu verwundern*.[3]

Es ist nicht zu verwundern, daß er durchgefallen ist (not to be wondered at).
Darüber war ich äußerst verwundert.

3. **Wissen mögen** suggests curiosity, a desire to know; *gespannt sein, wie* (etc.) intense interest or curiosity; *sich fragen* deliberation or doubt.

Ich möchte wissen, wie er das fertig gebracht hat.
Ich bin gespannt, was er sagen wird.
Ich frage mich, ob es möglich ist.

4. 'I wonder' used alone to cast doubt on something said: *Wer weiß?*

5. **Vielleicht** is used in a polite request or question.

Könnten Sie mir vielleicht sagen, wie man am schnellsten zum Bahnhof kommt?

WORK (intr. v.) 1. Sense: to function or operate according to plan or design (*W.*). Of machinery, mechanism, plant; of arrangements, plans.
(a) **Funktionieren** (English function) may always be used and must be used when elaborate pieces of machinery, plant are referred to. The working together of all parts is implied. It may also be used of a method.

Bei einer Probe funktionierten die Atomwaffen in jeder Hinsicht einwandfrei.
Der Motor, die Waschmaschine, funktioniert nicht.
Das elektronische Gehirn, der Computer, funktioniert sehr schnell.
Diese Lehrmethode funktioniert nicht.

(b) **Gehen** in strict use is applied to smaller and simpler mechanisms, but in ordinary speech is said of most things.

Meine Uhr geht nicht mehr.
Geht der Motor noch?

---

[1] Both *Weibsbild* and *Mannsbild* refer to sex, but the former is more vulgar than the latter.
[2] *Es wundert mich* is the closest equivalent of 'to be surprised' (e.g. *es wundert mich, daß der Kerl noch nicht eingesperrt ist*). *Überraschen* suggests suddenness and unpreparedness much more forcibly than 'surprise' does.
[3] But note the reflexive use in the following passage from E. T. A. Hoffmann's *Klein Zaches*: '*Der Professor Mosch Terpin war sonst ein aufgeklärter, welterfahrener Mann, der dem weisen Spruch Nil admirari gemäß sich seit vielen, vielen Jahren über nichts in der Welt zu verwundern pflegte.*' This is a rare use and only appropriate in ironical style.

Die Waschmaschine, der Lift (Fahrstuhl, Aufzug; formerly *Lift* was used for big cases in which furniture was packed for removal), *der Rasierapparat geht jetzt wieder.*

Der Kühlschrank geht nicht.

(c) **Arbeiten** is used less extensively in this sense in German than 'work' in English. It is used of things that work without interruption such as the organs of the body, but is also extended to machinery which seems to work in this way.

Das Herz, der Magen, arbeitet normal.

Die Waschmaschine arbeitet sehr befriedigend.

In reference to the landing of the American space ship on the moon, the German press and T.V. translated the astronauts' statement 'all systems are working perfectly' by *'alle Systeme arbeiten einwandfrei'. Funktionieren* would also have been appropriate.

(d) **Laufen** in such contexts corresponds to English 'run', i.e. not to be turned off, and is, like 'run', also used in reference to the smoothness or otherwise of the performance.

Lassen Sie den Motor laufen!

Der Motor läuft reibungslos.

(e) **Ausser Betrieb** used as a sign on a piece of machinery corresponds to English 'not working', e.g. of a telephone, a lift.

2. Of a plan, method, arrangement, something used or attempted (*A.L.*). **Gelingen, erfolgreich sein,** colloq. **klappen.**

Ich wollte ihn mit dem Auto abholen, aber es klappte nicht.

Der Plan gelang, klappte, restlos.

Die Methode war in jeder Beziehung erfolgreich.

3. To be effective, either in the sense to influence or to impress: **wirken, wirksam sein.**

Die Medizin wirkte schnell.

Seine Rede wirkte (auf seine Zuhörer).

Der Zauber wirkt.

Das Stück (play) wirkte stark auf die Zuschauer.

WORK Arbeit is primarily 'labour, activity'; **Werk** primarily 'result of labour', 'finished product'. *Arbeit* can also be used in the sense of the finished product, but in reference to more humble things, particularly school-boys' and students' essays, a piece of work. *Werk* is used in the sense of 'activity' only in a few fixed phrases meaning 'to set to work' (e.g. *zu Werke, ans Werk, gehen*).

Die Arbeit war sehr anstrengend.

Er hat sein Arbeitspensum noch nicht erledigt.

'Faust' gehört zu den größten Werken der Weltliteratur.

Laut einem Bericht des früheren Botschafters U. von Hassel sagte Hitler einmal zu Frank, er möchte mit seinem Teufelswerk in Polen fortfahren.

WRITE DOWN See also 'record'.

1. Aufschreiben is the general term and may always be used. It means to put down in writing one's own thoughts or what is said by someone else. In the latter case it can suggest the taking of notes (see under 'note').

Ich habe meine ganzen Erinnerungen an diese Zeit aufgeschrieben.

Ich habe alles aufgeschrieben, was der Vortragende sagte.

2. Niederschreiben intensifies the meaning of *aufschreiben*: to perpetuate a thing in writing so as to leave no uncertainty about it.

Bestreite nicht, daß du das gesagt hast, ich habe es niedergeschrieben.

Ich habe den Vortrag gehört und alles genau niedergeschrieben.

Ich habe seine Aussage Wort für Wort niedergeschrieben.

YARD 1. Whether in the sense of 'piece of enclosed ground, especially one surrounded by or attached to building(s) or used for some manufacturing or other purpose' (*C.O.D.*), or in that of 'the grounds immediately surrounding a house and usually comprising lawn, shrubbery and other plantings, recreation and service areas' (a sense common in U.S.A. and Australia, but not in Britain), the German equivalent is generally **Hof** (see also under 'farm'), which often appears in compounds.

Unsere Nachbarn haben immer einen Wachhund im Hof.

Ihr Haus hat einen großen Hof, auf dem vier Autos stehen können.

Die Wäsche wird im Hinterhof zum Trocknen aufgehängt.

Hühnerhof, Schlachthof, Gefängnishof, Kirchhof, Viehhof (stockyard), *Rangierbahnhof* (railway yard).

2. In the second use of 'yard' listed above, it is possible also to say **Vorgarten, Vordergarten, Hintergarten**. In Britain these or simply *Garten* would be said of the grounds immediately surrounding a house.

3. Examples of special terms are: **Ziegelei** (brick yard), **Gerberei** (tanning yard or tannery), **Schiffswerft** (dockyard), **Weinberg** (vineyard), **Kohlendepot** (coalyard).

LIST OF WORDS TREATED

live (*v.*)
lively
lock
longer (no)
look (at)
look (after) *45
loose
lot (*n.*) *121
low
lower (*v.*) *315
lurch 353

maintain 171
make (construct, produce)
make (cause)
man
manner 372
mark (*v.*)
mark (*n.*)
marry
matter (*v.*)
may
meadow 125
meal *136
mean (*v.*)
meaning 294
means 372
measure (*n.*) 114
meet
memorandum *231
mend *158
merry
method 372
might (*v.*) 207
mild 316
mind (*n.*)
mingle 220
minute *231
miserable *348
miss
mistake (*n.*)
mix
morals *150
more (no) 193
mountain
move (*v.*)
much
murder

name (*v.*) 53
narrow
nasty *36
native
nature
necessary
necessity 229

need
negate 91
nevertheless 154
noise 319
nominate 23
note (*n.*)
note (*v.*) 231, *233
notice (*n.*)
notice (*v.*)
nourishment 136
now
number
nutrition 136

object (*v.*)
objection 235
obliterate *92
obtain 143, 144
obvious *333
occasion 62
occur
offer (*v.*)
only (*adv.*)
open (*v.*)
opinion
oppress 258
order (*v.*)
ordinary 72, 150
other
owe *346

paddock 125
painful
pale
pallid 241
paper
pardon 112
passage 242, 246
path 330
pattern
pay
people
perfect (*a.*) 73
performance *164, 245
permanent 79
persistent *79
person *203
pillar 251
place (*n.*)
point *294
poky *227
pole 251
pond 246
pool
popular
position (1, 2, 3)

possibly
post (*n.*)
power
practise
praise
precious 84
prepare
preserve 171
press
pretty 118
prevent
proclaim 16
proportion 278
propriety *150
prosecute *135
protect
protest 235
prove 358
provide
public (*n.*)
puddle 246
pull
punish
pursue 134
put

quality
quick *68
quite

raise
range (*n.*)
rate 369, 379
rather 118
ratio 278
rational
raw 285
reach 268
ready 128, 257
real
really
reason *62, 215
reasonable *215
receive
recently
reckon 53
recognize
record
reduce
reel 353
refer
refuse
regard (*v.*) *78
rejoin 17
relation(ship)
relevant

fehlgetroffen 205
Fehlgriff 220
fehlschlagen 116
Feingefühl 294
feist 348
fern 49
fertig 75, 129
fertigen 196
fest 305
festhalten 174f.
festigen 79
festnehmen 241
feststellen 231, 324
Feststellung 324
fett 348
Feuer 131
Figur 213, 310
finden 133, 341
finden (sich) 38
flach 133
Fläche 27
Fleck 204, 246
fliehen 108
fluchen 87
flüchten 108
flüchtig 59
Flur 243
Fluß 283
Flüßchen 283
Folge 297
folgen 134
fordern 91
Forderung 90
Form 310
formulieren 325
Formulierung 325
fortfahren 80
fortsetzen 80
Frage (in...kommen) 78
fragen 30
fragen (sich) 384
Frau 383f.
Frauenzimmer 384
freilich 116
fremd 329
Freude (machen) 104
freudig 145, 214
freuen (sich) 104, 145
Freund 139
freundlich 139, 177
freundschaftlich 139
frieren 138
Frist 231, 353
froh 145
fröhlich 145, 214
fügen 167
fühlen 123
fühlen (sich) 124
führen 164, 174, 341
Fülle (in Hülle und Fülle) 381
füllen 127
Furcht 139

fürchten 121, 122
für sich 297
Fürsorge 57
Fuß (zu...gehen) 145
füttern 122

Gang 243
ganz 15, 266, 382
gänzlich 75, 307
Garde 149, 231
Gasse 330
geben 144, 264 (es gibt) 39
Gebiet 28, 269
gebieten 239
Gebirge 221
Gebrauch 151
gebrauchen 264
gebräuchlich 71, 150
Gedanke 155, 350f.
Gedanken 216
Gedankengut 351
gedankenlos 352
gedankenvoll 351
geeignet 335
Gefahr 288
gefallen 104
Gefängnisstrafe 345
Gefühl 294
gegen (sein) 235
geheim 290
gehen 86, 105, 145, 146, 188
(vor sich) 38
Gehirn 47
gehören 42
Geist 215
geistig 215
geistreich 69
Gelegenheit 59
gelegentlich 59
gelind(e) 317
gelingen (nicht) 117, 332
gelten (lassen) 2, 22
Gemach 284
gemahnen 371
gemein 71, 195
Gemeinde 72
gemeinsam 72
Gemeinschaft 72
Gemut 217f.
gemütlich 70
genau 307 (nehmen) 59
genehmigen 146
genial 82
genieren (sich) 293
genießen 103f.
genügen 289
geraten 145
Geräusch 320
Gerberei 386
gering 276
gern (möchten) 19
Gesang 230
Geschäft 51

geschehen 38
Geschehnis 111
gescheit 68f.
Geschick 121
geschickt 68
gesondert 297
Gestalt 310
gespannt (sein) 19
gestatten 147
Geste 3
gestehen 76
Getränk 101
getrauen (sich) 358
getrennt 297
getrost 358
gewählt 67
gewähren 147
Gewalt 252f., 255, 367
gewaltig 367
gewaltsam 367
gewalttätig 367
gewandt 68
Gewicht 253
gewinnen 144
gewissermaßen 114
Gewohnheit 150
gewöhnlich 72, 150
glatt 37, 71
Glaube 41f., 373
glauben 358
gleichgültig 59
gleiten 316
gliedern (sich) 120
Glosse 231
Glück 363
glücklich 363
gönnen 147
Grad 114
grenzen 168
grob 285
Grund 46, 62, 381
gründen 138
gründlich 307
Grundton 230
grüßen 147
gültig 22
gut 71, 288, 380, 382
Gutachten 238
Gutes 381
gutheißen 146
gutherzig 177
gütig 177

haben 173, 174
haben (wollen) 369f.
hager 348
halten 172, 173, 174, 181, 327, 350
halten (an-, auf- etc.) 327
halten (für) 78
Haltung 30, 40, 248, 375
Handeln 6
handeln (sich um) 52

397

lernen 183
letzt 182
letzter Zeit (in) 272
leugnen 91
Leute 244
liebenswürdig 177
liefern 262
liegen (an) 19, 38, 249
listig 68
loben 256
locken 344
locker 194
los 194
löschen 115
lose 194
lösen 362
loslassen 187
Lust (haben) 345
lustig 214

machen 144, 195, 196, 206
Macht 252
mager 348
mahnen 371
Mal (*occasion*) 353
Mal (*mark*) 204
manche 318
Mangel 220
mangeln 180
Manier 375
Mann 203
markieren 204
Maß 114
Maßnahme 7
Maßstab 324
Mauer 368
Meer 289
mehr (nicht) 193
mehren 161
meiden 32
meinen 211
Meinung 42, 78, 237
melden 17
mengen 221
Mensch(en) 203, 244
merken 233 (sich etwas merken) 231
Merkmal 205, 230, 231
Methode 376
mild 317
mindern 276
mindestens 183
mischen 196, 220
Mißgriff 220
mißlingen 117
mißtrauen 337
mißtrauisch 336
mitbringen 341
Mitleidenschaft 12
mitmachen 167
mitnehmen 341
mitschreiben 231
Mittel 378

mitteilen 325
Mitteilung 325
Modell 243
mögen 19, 189, 208, 370
möglicherweise 251
Möglichkeit 379
morden 227
Mühe (sich die Mühe geben) 356
mühsam 241
mühselig 241
munter 214
Muster 243
Muttersprache 228

na 382
nach 340
nachaffen 84
nachahmen 84
nachbilden 84
Nachdenken 351
nachdenken 77, 350
nachdenklich 351
Nachfolge 298
nachfolgen 135
Nachfrage 90
nachkommen 136, 213
Nachlaß 163
nachmachen 84
Nachricht (bekommen) 152
nachsehen 291
nachsprechen 84
nachsuchen 23, 30
nahe gehen 12
nahe (kommen) 27
nahelegen 333
nahen 27
näher (kommen) 27
nähern (sich) 27
nähren 122
Nahrung 136
Nahrungsmittel 136
naiv 319
Narbe 204
Narr 137
Natur 228
natürlich 228
Nebenfluß 283
Nebenräume 284
necken 344
nehmen 1, 338, 342
neigen 43
nennen 54
Nerven 16
neugierig 19
neulich 272
nicht einmal 110
nieder 194
Niederlande 194
niederlassen (sich) 303
niederschreiben 386
niedrig 194
noch 10

noch ein 40
nochmal 13
nonchalant 59
Not 229
Note 205, 230, 231
notdürftig 348
notieren 231
nötig 229
Notiz 231
notwendig 229
Notwendigkeit 230
Nummer 235
nun 234, 382
(nun gut) 382
nunmehr 234
nur 236, 251

offenbaren 282
Öffentlichkeit 72, 263
öffnen 237, 362
ordentlich 381
ordinär 72
ordnen 28
Ordnung (in O. bringen) 304
original 82
originell 82
Ort 254

packen 292
Papier 241
Passage 242
passen 334
passend 334
peinlich 241
penibel 241
Person 203
Personal 303, 323
Pfad 330
Pfahl 251
Pflege 56
pflegen 151
Pflicht 52
Pfosten 251
Pfuhl 246
Pfutze 246
Phantasie 157
Plafond 65
plagen 356
Plakat 232
Plan 28
planen 29
planlos 59
platt 133
Platz 205, 246, 251, 284
platzen 48
pochen 331
populär 247
Porte-monnaie 47
Portion 311
Position 247, 249
Posten 149, 250
Poststempel 205
Preis 345

solange 383
sonder 297
sonderbar 329
sonst 281
Sorge 56, 140, (Sorgen machen) 355
sorgen 58, 262
Sorgfalt 56
sorgfältig 57
sorgsam 57
Sorte 177
spalten 87
sparen 321
sparsam 321, 372
speien 322
Speise 137
speisen 122
sperren 45
Spesen 85
sprechen 277, 291
springen 49, 96
Spruch 289
spucken 322
spüren 61, 123, 234
Stab 252, 324
stand 248
Standard 324
ständig 79
Standort 249
Stange 252
stark 307
Stärke 253
stärken 330
Stätte 246
stattfinden 38
Stecken 252
stecken 265
stecken (bleiben) 61, 265
Stegreif 59
stehen 38, 200, 249, 328, 335
Stehen (zum...bringen) 328
steigern 161f.
Stelldichein 25
Stelle 28, 246, 249, 250
stellen 263, 265
stellen (sich) 31
Stellung 25, 248, 250, 379
Stellungnahme 31
stet 80
stetig 80
Steuer 270
stiften 138
Stillschweigen 314
Stock 252
stoppen 327
stören 355
stornieren 56
stoßen 168, 331, 355
strafen 264
Straße 330
Strecke 28
streichen 55, 323
Streit 349

streiten 127
streng 304
streuen 323
Strom 283
Strömung 283
Struktur 243
Stück (ein gutes) 382
Stube 284
studieren 183
stürzen 120
stützen 335
stutzig 336
suggerieren 333
suggestiv 334

tadellos 73
tadeln 43
Tarif 345
Tasche 47
tasten 123
Tat 4 (in der Tat) 116
Tätigkeit 51
tauchen 96
taumeln 354
tauschen 64
täuschen 89
täuschen (sich) 220
Teich 246
Teil 311
teilen 311
Tempo 379
Termin 89
Terminus (technicus) 345
teuer 84
tief 194
Tiefland 195
Tod (finden) 176
Ton 320
Topf 353
Tor 137
torkeln 354
töten 175, 176
totschlagen 175
träge 183
tragen 39, 342
Trank 101
trauen 200, 357
treffen 10, 61, 196, 212, 331
treiben 134
trennen 297
treten (and cpds.) 105f.
Trieb 363
Trimester 345
trinken 101, 343
trotzdem 154
trüben 356
Truhe 47
trügen 89
Trunk 101
tüchtig 305
Tümpel 246
Tun 6, 206
tun 52, 96, 264

tunken 96
Typ(us) 177

übel 36
übelnehmen 44
üben 256
übereilen 155
übereinstimmen 14
übergeben 277
übergreifen 323
überlassen 186
überlegen (sich) 77
überlegt 351
übernehmen 1, 341
überqueren 86
überraschen 60, 384
überschreiten 86
überstürzen 155
übertragen 25
überwachen 81
überzeugen 289
Uberzeugung 42
üblich 71, 150
übrig 280f.
übriglassen 186f.
umbringen 175
Umfang 115, 269, 379
umknicken 48
umkommen 175
umsonst 365
umwandeln 65
unabhängig 296
Unannehmlichkeit 357
unbedeutend 59
unbekümmert 59
unbesonnen 352
unentgeltlich 365
unerzogen 102
Unfall 1f.
ungehalten 16
ungeniert 82
ungeschehen (machen) 363
ungezwungen 59
Unglück 1f.
unglücklich 363
Unheil 2
unkonventionell 82
Unkosten 85
Unruhe 357
unselig 363
unten 46
unterbrechen 329
unterhalten 172, 174
Unterlage 241
unterlassen 118
unternehmen 7
unterrichten 344
unterstellen 334
unterstreichen 204
unterstützen 335
unüberlegt 352
unverheiratet 315
unvermindert 276

GERMAN WORD LIST

unverschämt 309
unwesentlich 280
unwillig 16
Urkunde 274
Ursache 62
urteilen 168
urwüchsig 228

Vaterland 227
verabreden 14, 29
Verabredung 25
verängstigen 140
veranlassen 210
veranstalten 28
verantwortlich 44, 62
Verantwortlichkeit 280
Verantwortung 280
veräppeln 344
verärgern 16
verbannen 37
verbergen 153
verbessern 158f.
verbeugen 43
verbieten 37, 329
verbinden 167f.
Verbindung 279
verbitten (sich) 235
verbittern 102
verblenden 44
verbrauchen 129, 365
verbreiten 323
verbrennen 50
verbringen 322
Verdacht 336
verdächtig 336
verdächtigen 336
verdanken 346
Verdienst 303
verdrießen 15
vereinbaren 14
vereinigen 168
verfallen 120
verfälschen 120
verfangen 61
verfehlen 118, 219
verfeinert 319
verfertigen 196
verfluchen 87
verfolgen 219
vergebens 365
vergeblich 365
vergeuden 371
vergleichen (sich mit jdm.)
    240, 304
vergönnen 147
vergraben 51
Verhalten 30, 41, 250
verhalten (sich) 30, 41
Verhältnis 26, 278, 326, 345
Verhängnis 121
verharren 367
verhauen 126
verhehlen 153

verheiraten 206
verhindern 259f.
verkehren 221
verklagen 2
verkleiden 100
verkleinern 276
verknüpfen 168
verköstigen 122
verkünden 17
verkürzen 312
verlagern (sich) 225
verlangen 18, 30
verlassen 184
Verlauf 85
verlegen 224
verleihen 188
verleugnen 92
verlocken 344
Vermächtnis 163
vermählen (sich) 206
vermahnen 371
vermehren 161
vermeiden 32
Vermerk 231, 274
vermerken 274
vermengen 221
vermindern 276
vermischen 221
vermissen 218f.
vermitteln 29
Vermögen 254
vermuten 337
vernachlässigen 118
verneigen (sich) 43
verneinen 91
vernichten 92
Vernunft 215
vernunftbegabt 270
vernünftig 270
verordnen 244
verpassen 118, 219
verpflanzen 225
verpflegen 122
Verpflegung 137
Verpflichtungen 25, 280
verprügeln 40
verringern 276
verrücken 225
verrückt 137
versagen 116, 278
versammeln 142
versäumen 118, 219
verschaffen 143
verschärfen 306
verschieben 225
verschieden 93, 296
verschleppen 263
verschließen 193
verschlingen 338
verschlucken 337
verschollen 229
verschonen 321
verschwenden 371

verschwinden 95
Versehen 226
versehen 262
versenken 315
versetzen 18, 224
versichern 287
versiegeln 290
versinken 315
versorgen 262
versperren 45
Verstand 215, 294, 362
verständigen (sich) 14
Verständigung 362
Verständnis 26, 362
verstärken 330
verstatten 147
verstecken 153
verstehen 61, 291, 361
verstehen (sich) 361
verstellen 225
versuchen 344, 359
Versuchung 344
verteilen 323
vertilgen 92
vertragen 40, 342
vertragen (sich) 14
Vertrauen 358
vertrauen 357
vertun 372
verursachen 197
vervollständigen 131
verwahren 173
verwahren (sich) 235
verwandeln 65
verwarnen 371
verweigern 278
verweisen 37, 277
verwenden 22, 360, 365
verwickelt (sein) 221
verwundern 384
verwünschen 87
verzeichnen 234
verzeihen 112
viel 226
Vielfalt 269
Viertel 28
Volk 245, 263
volkstümlich 247
voll 128, 131, 141
vollenden 130
vollendet 73
vollends 75
völlig 74, 382
vollkommen 73
Vollmacht 256
vollständig 74
von...her 345
vorbei- 219
vorbereiten 257, 371
vorbereiten (sich) 257
vorbestraft 275
Vorbild 243
Vorfall 111

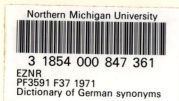
DATE DUE

Demco, Inc. 38-293